The Italian Language

THE ITALIAN LANGUAGE

by

BRUNO MIGLIORINI

Dott. Lett.,
Professor of the History of the Italian Language,
University of Florence; Emeritus President of the Accademia della Crusca

abridged and recast by
T. GWYNFOR GRIFFITH

B.Litt., M.A.,
Professor of Italian, University of Hull;
formerly Fellow of Trinity College, Dublin
and of St. Cross College, Oxford

BARNES & NOBLE INC
NEW YORK
1966

First published in U.S.A. 1966
by Barnes & Noble, Inc
New York, New York
Printed in Great Britain by
R. MacLehose and Company Limited
The University Press Glasgow
All rights reserved

Manufactured in Great Britain

Contents

Preface

A little over a quarter of a century ago, Bruno Migliorini, a scholar who was already well known for his contributions to the study of several aspects of the development of Italian, undertook to give Italy something she had hitherto lacked—a history of the Italian language. The task he then set himself was an arduous one, not simply because any major historical survey must involve difficult decisions of interpretation and emphasis, but also because much fundamental research remained to be carried out before certain stages in the growth of Italian could be properly understood. Nevertheless, when his *Storia della lingua italiana* was published in 1960, it was seen that Migliorini had produced an admirable account of the development of the language from its earliest stages to the twentieth century. This work has come to be recognized as one of the landmarks of Italian scholarship in our time.

When I was asked to prepare an abridged version of the *Storia* in English for publication in the Great Languages series, I realized that the task presented problems as well as opportunities. To have merely translated sections of the work while omitting the rest would have been to destroy its proportions and to risk making parts of it unintelligible. It seemed to me, therefore, that it was neccessary to try and digest this history and then produce an English version in which the material was, whenever possible, reorganized to occupy less space; whereas some paragraphs could indeed be omitted and others merely translated, most would have to be recast. But here again I feared that there might be a danger of upsetting the balance, of suggesting emphases that the author had not intended. My trepidation was increased, rather than diminished, when he declared himself ready to give me a free hand. A free hand with the results of someone else's research (and a lifetime's research at that) was more than I wanted. I was grateful and relieved, therefore, when he accepted my suggestion that I should submit each chapter to him, as it was written, for his approval. This procedure, I discovered, far from inhibiting alterations, facilitated them. Professor Migliorini has always emphasized his desire to see his work regarded as a starting-point for further research, and he himself certainly did not give up thinking about the Italian language in 1959. It became clear to me in discussion with him that, while reviewers were singing his praises in 1960-62, his interest was confined to the occasional writer who (like Professor Dionisotti) had an original contribution to make that could lead to revision of an opinion or correction of a detail. I am happy that this English edition is serving as a vehicle for a reconsidered view of a number of matters.

In preparing the English text I have kept in mind the sort of reader who normally uses books in this series. The fact that *The Latin Language* by L. R. Palmer and *The Romance Languages* by W. D. Elcock have already appeared in it has enabled me to cut more from the first two chapters of the *Storia* than I should otherwise have done. I have done so in the knowledge that the reader who requires more details of the Latin foundation and the early development of Romance will find in those volumes fuller information concerning them than he would expect to find in any book primarily concerned with the growth of Italian. That some space could thus be saved has meant that slighter reduction has been required in certain later chapters—chapters which contain the fruits of much original research by Professor Migliorini which I have been unwilling to sacrifice. Although my general aim has been to condense, I have felt obliged here and there to add a few words to explain matters which, I thought, would be self-evident only to native speakers of Italian. Here it has been difficult to draw the line; I can only hope that I have neither wasted space in explaining the obvious nor left unexplained anything that would baffle an intelligent reader. Here and there too, I have added to the text a few phonetic symbols in order to clarify the pronunciation; in these instances I have used IPA symbols in square brackets. I have not, of course, assumed that any person reading an English account of the history of Italian must necessarily be unable to make out the sense of even *La dolce vita* without an appended translation. Difficult phrases and unusual vocabulary (e.g. the more unfamiliar items among examples of Germanic elements in Chapter 2, dialect words, slang expressions, etc.) I have translated. But to have translated all of the thousands of words and scores of short passages quoted as examples (many of them significant for other reasons than their meaning) would have taken up so much space as to have occasioned much more fundamental cutting of the text. I can only trust that the reader will bear this in mind if he finds (as I hope he will not) that I have miscalculated in assessing his knowledge and that he has to reach for his dictionary to look for more than an occasional word.

In the *Storia* of 1960 Professor Migliorini was surveying many areas of Italian linguistic history for the first time. To indicate the basis of the statements he then made, he appended a large number of footnotes to his pages. Here the reader will find few footnotes. Where the Italian footnotes contained extremely interesting linguistic material, that material has been incorporated in the text. So have many references. In cases where a footnote referred to a work of considerable importance as a source of knowledge for students of the Italian language, the title has been added to the bibliography, which has thus become longer than the select list of books published in the bibliography of the *Storia*. No attempt has been made, however, to reprint in the bibliography the title of every book mentioned in the text. The student who wishes to know about the principal dictionaries and grammars written in a particular period, for instance, can easily find the particulars in the appropriate section of the appropriate chapter (which is clearly indicated in the table of contents); he will not find the information scattered about the bibliography.

The work that Professor Migliorini published in 1960 gave an account of Italian linguistic history up to 1915. Here a chapter has been added to bring the story up to 1965. To the study of the growth of Italian in this century Migliorini made important contributions in his *Lingua contemporanea* and *Saggi sulla lingua del Novecento*. He authorized me to make use, in the final chapter of *The Italian Language*, of any material I found useful in those works. I have taken a great deal from them, particularly from the first. Just after I had started to work on this chapter, I received from Professor Ignazio Baldelli a manuscript copy of a brief survey of the development of Italian in the years 1915-63 which he was then writing for *La Rassegna della letteratura italiana*. With characteristic generosity, he invited me to take advantage, too, of his labour in this field. My debt to him is great, and I wish to thank him. I must add that anyone who writes on twentieth-century Italian and who takes recent research into account must have a score of other debts also: he must bear in mind, for example, the work of Alfredo Schiaffini and Fredi Chiappelli on the language of poetry, of Alberto Menarini and Albert Junker on the growth of vocabulary, of Robert A. Hall and a number of other contributors to *Lingua nostra* on modern grammatical usage, etc. My principal debts I have tried to indicate either by footnotes or by additions to the bibliography. Other material I have ventured to supply from my own notes. It should be added, however, that this final chapter, like the others, has been submitted to Professor Migliorini and has gained from his observations and corrections.

In the final chapter, I have quoted from a number of books still protected by copyright law. For permission to do so, I am indebted to the following publishers: Arnoldo Mondadori for the brief quotations from poems by Eugenio Montale and Salvatore Quasimodo and for the prose extract from Gabriele d'Annunzio, Valentino Bompiani for the passage from *La noia* by Alberto Moravia, and Aldo Garzanti for the lines from *Le ceneri di Gramsci* by Pier Paolo Pasolini. Thanks for special cooperation are due Sansoni, who published, not only the original *Storia della lingua italiana*, but also Professor Migliorini's *Lingua contemporanea* and *Saggi sulla lingua del Novecento*. They have also recently issued a *Breve storia della lingua italiana* by B. Migliorini and I. Baldelli. This is an adaptation of the *Storia* for use in Italian schools. It contains a valuable additional chapter containing the material of the article by Professor Baldelli mentioned in the previous paragraph. To Professor Elizabeth Wiskemann and the Oxford University Press I am grateful for permission to quote a passage she wrote in 1946, and which appeared in the following year in her *Italy*. I also wish to thank Professor Piero Bigongiari for his kindness in allowing me to reproduce his poem *Giunchiglia*.

I have other debts nearer home. Mr. G. S. Nowell Smith read the first seven chapters of this book in manuscript and constructively criticized the sentences he found obscure. Mr. I. P. Foote read the remaining chapters, and made many valuable suggestions for improvement. Mr. J. R. Woodhouse read the whole work in galley-proof and detected errors and inconsistencies that had escaped me. To my wife I am indebted, not only for suggestions and corrections, but also for the transformation of a difficult manuscript into a readable typescript. Finally, it gives me pleasure to thank the publishers and the general editor of this series for their forbearance, and the printers for their efficiency.

T.G.G.

October, 1965

I

Aspects of Imperial Latinity in Italy

Many of the characteristics of Italian have their origin in features that already existed, or in changes that took place, in the Latin spoken in Italy between the time of Augustus and that of Odovacar, and in this chapter we shall use the reigns of these two men as rough chronological boundaries. We shall thus be dealing with a period of approximately five centuries, extending from the modifications in social structure that accompanied the personal rule of Augustus, through the rise of Christianity, to Italy's loss of imperial authority in 476. In view of the length of this span of time and the importance of factors introduced during it by the new religion, it might seem tempting to divide it into pagan and Christian eras, conventionally accepting the Edict of Milan (313) as a convenient line of demarcation. But, since some of the phenomena with which we shall have to deal cannot be exactly dated, such a division would not be really useful, particularly since our purpose is merely to indicate those things that had a bearing on the subsequent development of Italian, without reference to their precise chronological distribution within imperial times. The period will therefore be treated as a whole.

Linguistically, its most striking feature is a widening gap between the written and spoken languages. These had clearly been close to each other in the last two centuries of the Republic, when, indeed, the literary language was formed by a stylization of the spoken tongue. But, of course, even then the speech of the less cultured classes in Rome was not identical with that of highly literate persons, and in other places there existed other, and more abundant, variations. These differences grew in the time of the Emperors. Grammatical tradition and love of elegance made themselves strongly felt in the literary language even after the triumph of Christianity and the emergence of plebeian elements that characterized it; but on the spoken tongue the effect of these social changes was obviously much greater. While conditions still favoured the exchange of persons and things between various parts of the Empire, possibilities of linguistic penetration also existed. And while Rome retained her prestige, the innovations that had the greatest chance of acceptance were those that she had created or, at least, adopted. When that prestige failed, the linguistic situation, too, was affected.

In this field, of course, the student of language faces a grave difficulty: speech is most inadequately recorded, and nearly always stylized, in written records. His attempts at studying the spoken language in the period we are discussing must therefore rest on two kinds of evidence: what he can make of the testimony left in writing from that time and what he can reconstruct from the subsequent development of the Romance languages.

The written evidence varies in kind and in value. Sometimes in a literary work the tone will reveal to the reader that in some passages the author is writing in a language akin to the speech of his time; the *Satyricon* of Petronius is an example. Non-literary writings, like treatises on practical (e.g. agricultural or veterinary) subjects, may provide useful evidence because of the author's desire not to depart from popular vocabulary. Inscriptions, too, provide much information, for, although the more important are likely to be in literary language, the more humble frequently betray the linguistic habits of local stone-cutters. Even rude sentences that have survived on the walls of barracks and brothels may be valuable for plebeian elements which their authors have combined with literary elegance. And when we read at Pompeii

Quisquis ama valia, peria qui nosci ama(re)
bis (t)anti peria, quisquis amare vota

instead of what we should expect in the literary language:

Quisquis amat valeat, pereat qui nescit amare
bis tanti pereat, quisquis amare vetat

we can detect, in what has been written, evidence of certain tendencies in popular pronunciation (disappearance of *t*, semivocalic *i* for *e*, VOTARE instead of VETARE). Similarly, when we see ISCOLA, ISMYRNAE, ISPERABI, etc. in inscriptions, we have a reflection of the habit of pronouncing a prosthetic *i* before an *s* followed by a consonant. And when we find SPANIA for HISPANIA in the time of Trajan we really have further proof of the existence of the same tendency, seen this time through a hypercorrection. Direct testimony of linguistic peculiarities is rarer, though more precise. Such is the known fact that Augustus dismissed a consular legate for writing *ixi* for *ipsi*. And amongst the evidence supplied by writers and grammarians actually discussing linguistic matters the *Appendix Probi* is of exceptional importance. This work, written to help the reader achieve a better Latin, puts its 227 recommendations in the form VETULUS NON VECLUS, VIRIDIS NON VIRDIS, MILES NON MILEX, thus revealing what the commoner 'errors' in fact were.

Such evidence as we have, though much rarer than we would wish, is enough to show that notable variations existed in the Latin speech of various regions of the Empire, though these would not have been such as to cause mutual unintelligibility. Some of the innovations dating from this period died out, others persisted in the Romance languages or survived in the dialects of particular areas. Their vitality and the development of which they proved capable can only be studied from the Romance viewpoint: by an examination of the results they have given in the languages and dialects into which Latin developed.

The expansion of Latin led to the decline of other languages. Those that had shared the peninsula with it in the third and second centuries B.C. had already either disappeared or become of little importance by the time of Augustus. If we start with those that were pre-Indo-European, we should note that Ligurian had already suffered heavily from the spread of Celtic and that Latin merely completed its dissolution. As for Etruscan, it appears that none of the inscriptions known to us belongs to a period after the birth of Christ; but the Emperor Claudius must have been helped in his study of Etruscan by persons who knew it, and it probably survived until the fourth century A.D. as a ritual language for soothsayers. The Rhaeti, subjugated by Drusus and Tiberius, seem to have preserved the use of their own language at least until the time of Hadrian. The absorption of the Euganei, Picentes and Sicani was already in a very advanced stage at the beginning of our period. We have no palaeo-Sardinian inscriptions. The Punic language, however, held its ground for quite a time as a religious language in Sardinia; in it an inscription survives from the age of the Antonines. Among the Indo-European languages Celtic must have survived in parts of Gaul until the fifth century or later. There are no Venetic or Messapian inscriptions later than the first century B.C. Neither Umbrian nor Oscan was used as an

official language after the Social War (88 B.C.). And although the
date of the Iguvine Tables is disputed, it is estimated that the
Umbrian texts they bear range roughly from 400 to 90 B.C. Oscan
lived longer: the inscriptions at Pompeii are probably not much
earlier than the catastrophe of A.D. 79. The persistence of Greek
in imperial times in Calabria and Apulia is a question around
which controversy still rages. But even if it was territorially weak,
Greek derived great cultural and political strength from its prestige as a language of learning and as an official language in the
Eastern part of the Empire, and these were important factors in
its conservation.

The spread of Latin at the expense of other languages was due
to its prestige, not to conscious linguistic propaganda. In the
Augustan age Rome enjoyed such a privileged position that its
innovations had a very strong chance of being accepted wherever
Latin, not Greek, was the language of culture. But gradually the
situation changed. If the election of the Emperor Galba by the
legions of Spain is an isolated example, it is nonetheless true that
Trajan and Hadrian were Roman citizens from Spain and that
Antoninus Pius and Marcus Aurelius were of Gaulish origin. In
the time of the Antonines Rome slipped from its pedestal and the
provinces gained equality with Italy, while in the history of the
capital's prestige the nadir was reached during the crisis of the
third century. It is not surprising therefore that in the age of the
Antonines Italy accepted linguistic innovations that originated in
Gaul, and that during the third century we get neologisms
accepted in Lyons and Narbonne which did not get as far as
Umbria and Etruria, let alone Iberia or Dacia. When, after the
period of military anarchy, authority was established by Dioc-
letian, the checks imposed by the new regime limited linguistic
exchanges by restricting the movements of citizens. And tetrarchic
partition both reflected and favoured transverse rather than
longitudinal traffic and thus further diminished the effect of
innovations from Rome. Moreover, the foundation of Constantinople, instead of reducing differences in imperial administration,
consolidated them.

The absence of emperors from Rome enhanced the authority
of the popes. In the second half of the fourth century, while Milan
was the habitual seat of the Western Emperor, Rome was the
centre of Christendom and once again able to exercise a certain
linguistic influence for that reason. Indeed, half-way through the
fifth century Pope Leo I boasted that the seat of Peter had greater

influence than that of Caesar. The effect of Christianity on language was, in fact, great, not only on account of its direct impact
on syntax and vocabulary, but also because it acted as a social
leaven. In its first centuries of life it had appealed to the lower
strata of society, and its rise marked the triumph of recent and
popular tendencies at the expense of pagan traditions maintained
by more conservative sections of the population. Christian Latin
developed into a special language belonging to a particular social
and religious group. It must not be forgotten, however, that
Greek, not Latin, was the language of the earliest Christian communities in Rome and that their liturgy was originally in Greek:
only in the time of Pope Victor (at the end of the second century)
did Latin become their language. Moreover, the next phase, the
use of Latin as the official language of the Church, did not come
until the time of Pope Damasus, and the complete latinization of
the liturgy took place only in the fourth century.

But what caused Latin to develop so differently in various
regions as to give rise to the widely divergent languages and
dialects of the Romance group? Less importance is now attached
to the mere date of colonization than used to be the case; it is
hardly possible to maintain, for example, that the archaic features
of Sardinian are due simply to early conquest (238 B.C.), for, if
that were so, Sicily should have an even more archaic language or
traces of one. Several other factors have, in fact, also to be taken
into account.

The substratum is undoubtedly an important element, although
there has been controversy concerning its effect in particular
instances. When conquered peoples acquire a new language they
go through various stages in their relationship with it: usually
they first acquire a limited knowledge of the conqueror's language,
they then become bilingual, and gradually their own native
language becomes weakened and dies out. This process may take
a considerable time, and it would be strange if, in a period of prolonged bilingualism, they did not carry into their new language
certain habits of pronunciation proper to their native tongue, as
well as certain words connected with local things. Study of substrata in Italy sets various problems: why, for example, should
Etruscan have left less apparent traces than Celtic or Osco-
Umbrian? It has been suggested that it is because Etruscan was
so different from Latin that hybridism was hardly possible; in
other words, Etruscan speakers had really to learn a new language
and could not so readily corrupt it with adaptations of their own

as could Oscans and Umbrians. It may be for this reason that Tuscany preserved Latin better than Rome itself, for there spoken Latin was invaded by Osco-Umbrian tendencies (ND$>$$nn$, MB$>$$mm$, etc.). But even Etruscan was probably not without influence: it seems likely that Tuscan intervocalic aspiration and fricativization of k, t, p is of Etruscan origin. And in vocabulary Etruscans, Celts, Osco-Umbrians and others made contributions that are beyond controversy.

It is important to bear in mind, too, the methods of conquest or colonization adopted in various regions and the social structure of the peoples who acquired Latin. It has been maintained that the conservation of final s in Gaul, for instance, was due to the fact that Latin was first learned there by an aristocracy anxious to assimilate Roman culture. The rest of the population got Latin from above and therefore avoided some of the plebeian developments seen in the speech of the population of Italy. Students of Sardinian, on the other hand, have pointed out that this explanation will not fit the facts in Sardinia, where s is also kept.

Linguistic circulation is clearly a factor of outstanding importance. While intellectual and practical exchange went on freely all over Romania, innovations had a chance of acceptance in every part; but when the influence of Rome waned, when communication diminished and exchanges grew rarer, local peculiarities were able to develop in limited areas without being carried farther afield.

If one were to attempt a reconstruction of the linguistic condition of Romania, the result would naturally depend considerably on the weight one attached to some of the factors we have mentioned, and it is thus not surprising that opinions have been so divergent. Von Wartburg has prepared maps showing the differences between Eastern and Western Romance at the end of the third century; perhaps they give us the idea that there were more solid linguistic areas and more definite boundaries than existed in fact. Bartoli preferred to speak, according to circumstances, of Western (or Pyrenean-Alpine) and Eastern (or Balkan-Apennine) areas, or of continental, as opposed to Mediterranean, areas, or of intermediate and lateral areas. Merlo maintained that the classification of Italian dialects is primarily an ethnical problem. And while Muller (who bases himself entirely on documents) believes that all attempts to prove early division into dialects are doomed to failure, Lausberg has attempted a palaeogeography of the dialects of Italy at the end of the fourth century, dividing them into five groups.

It need hardly be said that in the period with which we are dealing the literary language never ceased to have *some* influence on the spoken tongue, for reasons both of prestige and religion; after all, the Bible in Latin dress was one of its texts. So it was that words which were originally of a literary or theological nature came into the spoken language. These included, not only those that retained religious significance, like DOMINICA or MISSA, but also others which developed a general meaning, like ANGUSTIARE (>*angosciare*) or PARABOLARE (>*parlare*). Nevertheless, generally the written and spoken languages grew further and further apart. It is time for us now to examine the main changes that took place in the spoken tongue.

Among these pride of place goes to the change in accent. The rhythm of spoken Classical Latin was based on the use of long and short vowels, and it was probably musical pitch that differentiated certain syllables. Both these things changed: distinction based on quantity disappeared, and stress replaced pitch. Generally the accent remained in the same position, except in words of the type MULĬĔREM, FILĬŎLUM (in which the *i* lost its accent and its vocalic character: *muljérem, filjólum*). In the type FECĔRUNT, DIX-ĔRUNT there is not really a change of accent: what we have is a survival in the spoken tongue of the ending -ĔRUNT (which in the classical age had given way to an -ĒRUNT resulting from a cross between -ĒRE and -ĔRUNT).

The new distinctions were not in quantity but in quality. The vowel-system that prevailed over most of Romania had one phoneme in place of ō and ŭ (so that *voce* from VŌCEM was pronounced like *croce* from CRŬCEM) and one in place of Ē and Ĭ (so that we have *rete* and *fede* with close *e*). While long E gave close *e* [e], short E gave open *e* [ɛ]; and while long O gave close *o* [o], short O gave open *o* [ɔ]. But Sardinia and a considerable part of southern Italy did not have this system; hence in Sardinia we have *ruke* < CRŬCEM. Italic tendencies prevailed in the reduction of the diphthong Æ to [ɛ] and of Œ to [e]. AU has a more complicated history. It already tended to become *o* in the Republican era (e.g. CAUDA >CŌDA, hence Italian *coda*, with close *o*) in a series of plebeian words, while it remained in others and in conservative circles (giving us eventually *oro* with open [ɔ] in Tuscan and literary Italian, while some dialects still keep *au* even in popular words).

Syncope of atonic vowels between various groups of consonants shows differences in time and region. Southern Italian is less inclined to syncope than Spanish, which is itself less so than

French. In Gallo-Italian dialects, ancient and modern, syncope is very extensive. When we examine examples like *fola, fiaba* and *favola* (<FABULA) it does not seem to us that the problems raised are explicable in terms of dates; it appears likely that a plebeian tendency to syncope co-existed for centuries with a conservative one which did not favour it.

Among the consonants the fate of final M, S, T had great import-ance because of their flectional functions. The M, which had already become so weak in classical times as to permit metrical elision, failed to survive, save in modified form in monosyllables: thus SUM>It. *son,* later *sono.* The fate of T was even more severe; the only trace of it in Italian is in the doubling of the initial con-sonant of words following *e* (<ET) and *o* (<AUT). Some dialects in Lucania and Calabria, however, keep T with flectional value: *mi piaciti,* etc. In northern Italy *s* must have survived for a very long period. Tuscany has traces of its survival in the -*i* to which it developed in words like *noi, voi,* etc. and in the doubling in phrases like *più fforte, tre llibri* and so on. The velar consonants *c, g,* palatalized before front vowels, giving [tʃe], [tʃi], [dʒe], [dʒi] for [ke], [ki], etc. This process, possibly Umbrian in origin, did not take place quickly or uniformly; it arrived late in Sicily and southern Italy, late and partially in Sardinia. Of the development of an affricate in the pronunciation of TI and DI there is direct testimony from the fourth and fifth centuries. The disappearance of H was in accordance with rustic tendencies. It had already been lost in words like OLUS and ANSER, and it was early weakened within a word (PREHENDO>PRENDO, NIHIL>NIL). The assimilation of PT, PS to *tt, ss,* and of CT, CS (x) to *tt, ss* has ancient origins (e.g. *issula* in Plautus, *isse* in Pompeian inscriptions). It seems to be Italic, and it serves to distinguish Italo-Romance from Gallo-Romance (which has -*it,* -*is;* thus French has *fait* where Ital. has *fatto*<FACTUM). Admonitions like CAMERA NON CAMMARA, AQUA NON ACQUA in the *Appendix Probi* reveal developments destined to be important in Italian: the strengthening of the post-tonic con-sonant of proparoxytones and the doubling due to semi-vocalic *u.* In the matter of the prosthetic vowel Italy occupies an intermedi-ate position between the western Romance languages, which always have it (Fr. *épée,* Sp. *espada*), and Rumanian, which never has it. Italian has (or did have) both forms (*la strada, in istrada*).

In the field of morphology and syntax, nominal and verbal flections were greatly simplified. The forms of the neuter dis-appeared (save for a few in -A and -ORA) and so did the category.

Construction with DE and AD gained ground at the expense of genitives and datives. Apart from a few that were frequently used and thus very familiar, synthetic comparatives gave way to forms with PLUS. BIS, TER, etc., were replaced by analytical constructions (e.g. *duas aut tres vecis* in the *Oribasius Latinus*). ILLE and IPSE weakened in meaning; their use to translate the Greek articles in the Scriptures undoubtedly contributed to this (e.g. *Dixit illis duodecim discipulis*). The deponent disappeared, while the passive found a new form (an analytical one with ESSE as an auxiliary, instead of the synthetic conjugation). HABERE also prospered as an auxiliary: constructions like COGNITUM HABEO ('I hold as a known thing') became used more frequently and faded in meaning until they became merely compound forms for past tenses. Alongside the normal forms of the future, some of which were now phonetically inadequate (the present DICIT and the future DICET, for example, would give an identical *dice*), there sprang up new, more vivid, ways of conveying what was to happen: 'Tempestas illa *tollere habet* totam paleam de area' (St. Augustine). There were some exchanges between the second and third conjugations, especially in the infinitive (e.g. from CADĔRE to CADĒRE). Parataxis prevailed over hypotaxis. QUIA gained ground (as in Petronius: 'dixit quia mustella comedit'), foreshadowing Italian *che*. Possibly on the model of Umbrian, SI was used in indirect questions. Spoken Latin had now, in fact, moved far from that of the classical era, and it contained many features that we associate with the new tongues.

There were considerable changes, too, in vocabulary, and we shall mention a few examples. But, before doing so, we should perhaps stress that, in a great many cases, there was no change; for very many concepts the same word has been used consistently from C.L. to modern Italian. Obvious instances are PATER, *padre*; MATER, *madre*; AQUA, *acqua*; CANIS, *cane*; BIBERE, *bere*. Those happen to be examples of words that survived all over Romania. Other words, however, survived only in Italy. Such are AEGYPTIUS (Tusc. *ghezzo*), CAMPSARE (*cansare*), CUNULAE (*culla*), SIDUS (Old Tusc. *sido*). Some such words, which survived only in Tuscany, were later once again given wider diffusion by becoming part of the national language of Italy. Others have remained restricted to dialects, like: BUCCELLATUM (Lucchese *buccellato*, Ven. *buzzolà*), HASTULA (Bol. *astla*) or ILLINC (Emil. *lenka*). And some Latin words live on only as place-names: AGELLUS gives *Agelli* (Ascoli Piceno), *Agello* (Perugia), *Gello* (Pistoia), *Aielli* (Aquila) and *Aiello*

(Cosenza, etc.), while FLUVIUS gives *Fiobbio* (Bergamo) and *Fiuggi* (Frosinone). At Rome we have REGIO -ONIS in *rione*, THERMAE in *Termini* and THEATRUM in *Satiri*.

So far we have limited ourselves to discussing words which we know to have existed in Latin. But, in the case of some words of which no written record remains, scholars have assumed their presence in Latin from the evidence of the Romance languages. Such reconstructions are marked by asterisks. *Bigoncio* and its variants (e.g. Tusc. *bigongio*) lead us to a presumed *BICONGIUS. Although this is not recorded, there was a TRICONGIUS, so called because he proved capable of drinking three CONGII. *Rozzo* should take us back to RUDIUS, neuter comparative of RUDIS. These could not have been medieval formations, for compounds of the BICONGIUS type were not formed in the Middle Ages and comparatives like RUDIUS were being replaced by analytical constructions. Some of the assumptions of scholars, like Gröber's ANXIA, have been confirmed by subsequent discovery in texts. On the other hand, there has doubtless been abuse of the asterisk, which has been allowed to produce a pseudo-certitude that has discouraged research into the real etymology of certain words. The following seem to be examples of reasonably safe reconstruction of words that have survived in Italian: *CASICARE (der. from CASUS) > *cascare*; *CINNUS > *cenno*; *COMPTIARE (der. from COMPTUS, p.p. of COMERE) > *conciare*; *RUBICULUS > Old Tusc. *rubecchio*; *PENDICULARE (der. of PENDERE) > *pencolare*.

The contributions to vocabulary that Latin drew from other languages in the peninsula (both pre-Indo-European and Indo-European) have been the object of careful study on the part of Latinists. But alongside the words to which they have given attention there must have existed other similar examples which left no trace in written Latin or in inscriptions; their presence in the language can be inferred from items in modern vocabulary. They are, for the most part, words connected with the land, its configuration and its flora and fauna. As is well known, Latin acquired from Etruscan some hundreds of words. Some of these were deeply rooted in the spoken language (e.g. POPULUS, PERSONA, CATENA, TABERNA, etc.); others did not have a continuous existence in the spoken tongue, being of a learned nature, and they were later introduced into Italian as latinisms (e.g. SPURIUS, ATRIUM, IDUS, HISTRIO, etc.). But, apart from words in these categories, there were probably others: it is likely that some Tuscan words for plants, for example, are of Etruscan origin (*brenti* 'heather', *gigaro* 'arum italicum', *napa* 'ulex europaeus'). A case apart is *chiana*, which has survived in Tuscany in connection with the well known stagnant water of *Chiana* (formerly Clanis), and which is probably a Tyrrhenian, that is Mediterranean, word. From the Ligurians, the Rhaeti and lesser Alpine peoples came words known to the Romans (GENISTA, LARIX, LIGUSTRUM; CAMOX, SEGUSIUS; PELTRUM) and others which have survived in place-names and in modern Alpine dialects (*balma* 'cave', *barga* 'hut', *grava* 'gravel', *malga* 'hut', *rugia* 'watercourse', etc.). But, since Celtic swallowed up Ligurian territory before the advent of Latin, it is difficult in some cases to distinguish between Ligurian (pre-Indo-European) and Celtic (Indo-European) words.

The close relations between Italy and Gaul meant that a large number of Celtic words entered Latin, some of them early, and became deeply rooted. Such were BETULLA, VERNA, ALAUDA, BECCUS, SALMO, LANCEA, CARRUS, BENNA, BRACA. Comparison of words in the Romance languages with the vocabulary of the Celtic languages enables us to reconstruct other Celtic words which presumably existed in Latin, e.g. *BRACUM (>It. *braco, brago* 'mud'), *PETTIA (>It. *pezzo, pezza*), *CAMMINUM (>*cammino*), *MULTO -ONIS (>*montone*), *GARRA (>*garretto* 'hock, leg'), *PARIOLUM (*paiolo* 'cauldron, kettle') and *COMBOROS (>*ingombro, sgombrare*, etc.). Whereas these words are assumed to have gained circulation in imperial Latin, others failed to spread beyond the areas where Celtic was spoken, or at least only survive in such areas. Some examples of this type are the bases of words still used in N. Italian dialects: CUMBA 'valley', CAVANNUS 'owl', BROGILUS 'garden', ATTEGIA, *TEGIA 'dwelling, hut', *CRODI- 'hard', etc. Other Celtic words entered Italian later, through French or Provençal; *veltro* 'greyhound', *vassallo*, *cervogia* 'beer', *lega* (in the sense of a unit of measurement equivalent to three miles) came to Italian through these channels.

Osco-Umbrian words in Latin have also been very thoroughly studied by Latinists. More interesting to us than those which were well established in C.L. (BOS, BUFALUS, LUPUS, SCROFA, URSUS, ANAS, TURDUS, CASA, LINGUA, LACRIMA, CONSILIUM, etc.) are those attested late or little (ĒLEX, which gave It. *elce*, instead of ĪLEX; PŌMEX, the source of It. *pomice*, for PŪMEX; TERRAE TUFER, whence *tartufo* 'truffle', for TUBER) and those that can be reconstructed from what we know of the phonological developments in Osco-Umbrian in relation to those of Latin: *STEVA for STIVA (It. *stegola*), *BUFULCUS for BUBULCUS (It. *bifolco*), *TAFANUS for

TABANUS (It. *tafano*), *METIUS for MITIUS (It. *mezzo* 'over-ripe'), *OCTUFER for OCTOBER (Lucanian *attrufu*), *GLEFA for GLEBA (Tarant. *gliefa*, *gliofa*).

Here we should also mention those Germanic elements that entered the vocabulary of Latin before the fall of the Empire. Since, however, there is difficulty in separating some of them from Germanic elements that entered later, when the barbarians invaded Italy, we shall discuss all the Germanic contributions together in the next chapter and seek to place them in their several categories then.

The influx of Greek words into Italy was huge. On the one hand, because of the cultural contribution of Greece, a host of learned words entered Latin from this source. At the same time, because of the symbiosis of the eastern and western parts of the empire and the colonies who came from the East to settle in Rome or southern Italy, Greek elements were also brought into spoken Latin at lower levels. The double development stemming from these circumstances can be seen in the treatment of words like Πύρρος which was imitated as BURRUS before it was transcribed in the literary form PYRRHUS.

Of the thousands of Greek words that were transplanted into Latin some hundreds became deeply rooted in the spoken tongue and survived as hereditary words into Italian. Of these we can give only a few examples. They included names of plants and fruits (*melo, ciliegio, olivo, dattero, giuggiolo, mandorlo, riso, fagiolo, sedano, prezzemolo, anice, garofano, pepe, bosso,* etc.) and of living creatures (*scoiattolo, balena, delfino, tonno, cefalo, grongo, acciuga, polpo, seppia, chiocciola, fagiano, ostrica, spugna*). There were among them, too, words referring to the configuration of the land (*poggio, grotta,* possibly *spelonca*) and words connected with life at sea (*governare* and *pelago*—which, although a learned word in Italian in the meaning 'sea', survived popularly in the sense of a 'dip in the land'). There were items connected with domestic objects and with arts and trades (*ampolla, borsa, bossolo, canestro, càntaro, cofano, lampada, lucignolo, madia, organo, tappeto, pietra, calce, malta, palanca, scheggia, doga, colla, inchiostro, gesso, carta, corda, porpora, olio, butirro— burro, massa*). And there were terms connected with the body (*braccio, stomaco, nervo, flemma,* and also *gamba* and *spalla,* which were first used for animals, then for humans) and with medicine (*cancrena, spasimo, empiastro, teriaca, cerusico*). *Cetra* and *zampogna* testify to Greek influence on music. Among the many general words were *aria, calare, colpo, orfano* and *gobbo*. The adoption of *cata*

(<Gr. κατα) as a distributive was also important (*catuno, caduno*);
its use can be seen in the vulgate: 'faciet sacrificium super eo cata
mane mane' (*Ezech.* xlvi, 14).

This brief list is enough to give some idea of the extent of Greek
penetration. In it is included *acciuga*, an example of a word which
survived in a limited territory (in this instance in Liguria), only to
attain wide diffusion again by becoming part of the national
language of Italy. Other words were not so fortunate and survive
only in dialects. Apart from the learned word *càttedra*, we have
from CATHEDRA (vulg. CATECRA) the N. Italian *cadrèga, carèga*
('seat, chair'), etc., while PESSULUS, PESSULUM (vulg. PESCULUM) >
Sienese *pèschio* and Calabr. *pièssulu*.

Alongside the actual borrowings from Greek we have examples
of 'calques': ARS and RATIO in the sense of τέχνη and λόγος,
LINGUA applied to 'language', following γλῶττα, and IPSIMUS
modelled on αὐτότατος. It is IPSIMUS which, reinforced by the
-MET of EGOMET, etc. will give us the Ital. *medesimo*, through French
(see p. 113).

We cannot leave the subject of grecisms in Latin without special
mention of the large number connected with the growth of
Christianity. A few examples of those which have survived into
Italian are: *chierico, monaco, prete, vescovo, basilica, chiesa, limòsina,
battesimo, cresima, befana, bestemmiare*. Some words which came from
this source did not remain restricted to the religious field. Such
are *parola* (originally 'parable' of Jesus, 'word' of God) and
parlare, ermo (Gr. ἔρημος whence also *eremo* and *eremita*), *geloso,
incignare* (*encaeniare*, from *encaenia*) and even *tartaruga* (from late
Greek ταρταροῦχος, name of an unclean spirit, for in Christian
symbolism the tortoise represented the evil spirit).

In some cases there was an attempt to use a Latin word for the
Greek (*tingere* for *baptizare, lavacrum* for *baptismus, testis* for *martyr*);
but in the religious, technical sense it was the latter that triumphed.
Some Christian Greek words were modelled on Hebrew. The
Italian *angelo* goes back to ἄγγελος which, from being merely a
'messenger' developed the meaning of 'messenger of God, angel'
on the analogy of the Hebrew *mal' âk*; *Cristo*, Gr. Χριστός, follows
the Hebrew *mashî'ah*, 'anointed of the Lord, Messiah'. And among
the imported words were some, of course, which had been
originally Hebrew: *pasqua, sabato, osanna* were among them.

Latin in the imperial age pullulated with new formations. Such
were numerous words denoting the agent ending in -ARIUS
(*clavarius*, etc.); feminine proper names in -ITTA (*Iulitta, Bonitta,*

etc.), in which we see the ancestor of the popular diminutive suffix -ITTUS (>-*etto*), which is probably of Celtic provenance; proper names (from Greek Christianity) in -ISSA (whence we get the suffix -*essa*, as in *contessa*); pseudo-anthroponymous creations like *RUFIANUS (>*ruffiano*); and numerous collectives (AERAMEN> *rame*, *CARONIA>*carogna*, *MONTANIA>*montagna*, SEMENTIA> *semenza*, VICTUALIA>*vettovaglia*). The many endings denoting endearment (MASCULUS, AURICULA, UNGULA, PORCELLUS, VITELLUS, ANELLUS, NOVELLUS, etc.) lost their diminutive value completely, and this process was followed in the case of many new formations (*GENUCULUM, *NUCEOLA, *FRATELLUS, *AVICELLUS). Adjectives frequently became nouns: HIBERNUM [TEMPUS]>*inverno*, DIURNUM >*giorno*, MATUTINUM>*mattino*, [DIES] NATALIS [CHRISTI]>*Natale*, etc. Abstract nouns were frequently formed from participles (COLLECTA, DEFENSA, *PERDITA, *VENDITA, etc.). Immediate derivation was responsible for substantives like LUCTA, PROBA, *MONSTRA and DOLUS (>It. *duolo*), while the locution PRODE EST, from PRODEST, gave rise to the noun *prode*, *pro'* and the adjective *prode*. Imperatival compounds (LABAMANOS, fourth cent.) began to appear. Verbs formed from nouns multiplied (MENSURARE, PECTINARE, RUINARE, *NEVICARE) and, alongside older formations ending in -ICARE, there sprang up in Christian times numerous verbs in -IZARE (of which the Italian -*eggiare* is the popular development). Just as ADIUTARE, CANTARE, IACTARE had for centuries existed alongside ADIUVARE, CANERE, IACERE, with intensive force and popular flavour, other such derivatives now appeared (PISTARE, TOSTARE, *TONSARE), etc. Simple verbs were sometimes replaced by compounds: INITIARE by *COM-INITIARE (It. *cominciare*), NOSCERE by COGNOSCERE and so on. Prepositions and adverbs were reinforced by the addition of other prepositions: ABANTE, DE ABANTE (whence *avanti*, *davanti*), INCONTRA, DE POST (whence *dipoi* and *dopo*) DE UBI (*dove*), DE UNDE (*donde*), etc. And there was an increase in Latin vocabulary at this period of onomatopoeic creations: TATA, PAPPA (which as PAPA flourished in Christian Latin), BABBUS, NONNUS, MAMMARE, etc.

Whereas the appearance of neologisms was sometimes occasioned by the need to find new words for new concepts (like the Christian examples SALVARE, DOMINICA), in a great number of cases new words replaced traditional vocabulary covering the same ground. In this period of social upheaval and linguistic change it was more difficult for isolated words to survive than for those belonging to families. BIS and TER, for instance, tended to be replaced by DUAE

VICES, TRES VICES, the analytic procedure being easier to the memory than the synthetic. Similarly, whereas HIRUDO suggested nothing, SANGUISUGA could be understood and remembered from the parts making up the compound. So PERA was beaten by BISACCIUM, NIHIL by NULLA, PROCUL by LONGE, etc. Simple verbs, which frequently were difficult to conjugate, were replaced by compounds or intensives or verbs formed from nouns: the forms ADIUTARE, CANTARE, which had existed alongside ADIUVARE, CANERE, replaced them; MENSURARE, PECTINARE, *NIVICARE push out METIRI, PECTERE, NINGUERE; and CONDUCERE, CONSUERE (It. *cucire*), OCCIDERE were preferred to the simple DUCERE, SUERE, CAEDERE, etc. It was not easy for monosyllables to survive; thus besides AES, AERIS arose AERAMEN (It. *rame*). In the triumph of OSSUM over OS another factor counted: the avoidance of homonymic clash. For, after the loss of the quantitative distinction between ōs and ŏs, confusion was possible. Similarly, it was not easy to distinguish between AVENA and *HABENA when the latter lost its H and began to suffer fricativization of its B, and this is probably why *RETINA (It. *redine*) was used instead. Words which had lost their force and colour yielded their places to more energetic and vivid rivals. Thus COMEDERE appeared alongside the more delicate EDERE (and survived in the Iberian peninsula as *comer*), only to be replaced in Italian territory by MANDUCARE; this new verb, derived from MANDERE through MANDUCUS, a character in farce, conveyed the idea of champing jaws, with which he was associated. FUR must have seemed weak, for it was replaced by LATRO ('brigand, highwayman'), which itself then faded to the meaning that *ladro* has today. Alongside CAPUT appeared TESTA, originally a 'pot'. CABALLUS 'gelding', often used with depreciatory meaning, eventually ousted EQUUS. Diminutive and affective forms and onomatopoeic words flourished; a word like UBER would disappear almost everywhere, giving way to MAMMA, MAMILLA, PUPPA and TITTA. In the case of ENCAUSTUM, which took the place of ATRA-MENTUM, we do not, of course, simply have one word substituted for another; ENCAUSTUM was first used because fire was used in the new process of manufacturing the ink, while ATRAMENTUM had simply been prepared from lamp-black or sepia.

In what we have written above no explanation has been offered for the varying fortunes of certain words in the different parts of Romania. Matteo Bartoli, with his 'areal linguistics', attempted to trace the development of Latin in the various regions of the Empire, to plot the expansion of linguistic phenomena and to account for the survival, in what he called 'lateral areas', of words and constructions that have disappeared elsewhere.[1] On the basis of his findings he was able to argue that certain words and phrases were current at particular times. In the period in which Iberia and Dacia were colonized, for example, the usual word for 'beautiful' was FORMOSUS (Port. *formoso*, Sp. *fermoso*, later *hermoso*, Rum. *frumos*). Later BELLUS, which had already existed in classical times, in the sense of 'nice', became the common word for 'beautiful'. Gaul, which was in close contact with Italy at this period (2nd-3rd centuries A.D.), accepted this innovation (hence It. *bello*, Fr. *beau*). But Iberia and Dacia were not affected by this linguistic wave. Hence we have two conservative lateral areas, and a central one in which innovation has been at work. (It will be noted that Bartoli's method takes into account, not only the date of colonization, but also material and cultural traffic in later times.) Not all the 'figures' he proposed are acceptable; often the distribution in them is such that considerable ingenuity is required to explain them. But the evidence and arguments used have produced a high degree of probability in many instances. We are sure that PATELLA (It. *padella*) is of more recent expansion than SARTAGO (which survives in the Iberian peninsula, Sardinia, and in dialects in northern and southern Italy). GRANARIUM (It. *granaio*) is more recent than HORREUM. CLUSUM (It. *chiuso*), derived from compounds like CONCLUSUM, INCLUSUM, caught on at a time when Gaul had already received CLAUSUM (Fr. *clos*). It is not surprising therefore that many Latin words persisted elsewhere when they had died in Italy: VERRERE lives on in Spain as *barrer*, while in Italy it has been swept away by *scopare*; FIMUS with its derivatives survives in Gaul (Fr. *fumier*, etc.), whereas LAETAMEN has taken its place in Italy, etc. Many Latin words, too, have no continuators in the Romance languages: such are AMNIS (replaced by FLUMEN), IGNIS (FOCUS), AMITTERE (PERDERE), LINQUERE (LAXARE) among others. Other words have gained ground. LOQUI left no trace. In its place came, first of all, FABULARE (Sp. *hablar*, Port. *fallar*) and FABELLARE (which survives in Sardinian and Ladin), then the Christian PARABOLARE, which prevailed in Gaul and Italy; early Italian texts, especially those of the centre and of the south, in which *favellare* is still lively, help us to understand the slow and progressive north-south expansion of PARABOLARE.

By the use of the areal method (which must, of course, be practised in conjunction with a study of all the testimony that texts can give us) we can see that in certain cases Italy had the same result as Gaul and Iberia, in others as Dacia; in a great many cases only Italy and Gaul coincided. This corresponds to what the historians tell us: that until the end of the third century circulation within the Empire was intense and that, while it diminished considerably later, relations between Italy and Gaul were never interrupted. Since it was difficult for innovations from Italy to get to the provinces in later imperial times, the Latinity of Iberia and Dacia (as also of Sardinia) displays a generally more archaic character than that of the Italian peninsula. Within Italy the south kept a greater number of archaic words and phenomena than the north, which often showed the same development as Gaul. Central Italy maintained a 'moderate' position, which helped it to play a mediating role in later centuries.

Numerous changes of meaning took place in the spoken Latin of this period. Thus ACER 'sharp' came to mean 'bitter', while BUCCA ('cheek') took the meaning 'mouth', since os was becoming unsuitable on account of a homonymic clash. Some of the changes that took place were indicative of material conditions and of ways of life and thought. That DISCUS (It. *desco*) should have become the word for the table on which the family took its meals shows that it was usually round. BUSTUM was the place where corpses were incinerated, hence the tomb; the custom of adorning these with sculpted effigies of the deceased gave rise to the Italian meaning of *busto*. The grecism ORGANUM meant 'instrument'; that it came to signify a specific musical one testifies to the vogue that that instrument enjoyed in imperial times.

It is symptomatic of the social upheavals amongst which spoken Latin developed in this age that when words had two meanings of which one was abstract and one concrete, it was almost invariably the case that only the latter survived: GRADUS survived as 'a step', and not as 'degree'; *grado* in the latter sense in Italian is a learned restoration from written Latin. PUTARE, which meant either 'to cut' or 'to think, believe' survived only in *potare* 'to prune'. STIRPS survived as *sterpo* ('stub, offshoot'); *stirpe* is a latinism. A rare exception, in which both the abstract and the concrete senses survived was INGENIUM (the concrete sense of which can be seen in such phrases as *l'ingegno della chiave* and in the derivative *ingegnere*). The predominance of plebeian influences in the linguistic innovations of this time shows itself, not only in this preference for the concrete, but also in the tendency to welcome the vivid and the highly coloured. EXEMPLUM lives on in *scempio*, originally 'a slaughter capable of serving as an example'; FUGA in *foga*; and FURIA in *foia*. Instead of PLORARE people used more picturesque verbs that suggested that they were lacerating their cheeks or beating their breasts; LANIARE SE and PLANGERE thus came to be used, only to mean in time nothing more than *lagnarsi* and *piangere*. The use of CASA ('hut, rustic dwelling') in the sense of DOMUS testifies to ruralization. And, since the machine *par excellence* was the miller's grindstone, Lat. MACHINA > It. *macina*. PULLUS was no longer the young of any animal, but specifically a chicken. And the importance of keeping chickens can be seen in the development of INDEX to *éndice* ('nest-egg' in the sense of an artificial egg placed in the nest as an inducement to the hen to lay there) and CUBARE to *covare*. In some areas, too, PONERE assumed the restricted meaning 'to set a hen on eggs' (Arezzo: *pónere*; Bologna: *pònder*), while in Friuli, as in France, it came to mean 'to lay eggs'. MINARI 'to threaten' became *menare* 'to lead', through the intermediate sense 'to lead animals, threatening or beating them'. The abstract meaning of the Italian *volta* (< *VOLVITA) can be explained as emanating from the turning of the oxen at the end of the furrow ('two turnings' = 'twice'). In fact, just as it could be said that Latin had a strong rustic flavour in pre-classical times, so it could be maintained that it again appeared predominantly rustic at the time when it was about to become Romance.

Some semantic changes took place in specialist circles. PAPILIO in the sense of 'tent' is a military metaphor inspired by the tent's likeness to a butterfly's wings; hence the meaning of the Ital. *padiglione*. ORDINARE in the meaning 'to command' also came from soldier's language. *Fegato* and *cervello* were words used in cooking before they were used more widely. FICATUM was originally IECUR FICATUM, 'the liver of an animal fed on figs'; the proparoxytonic accent is due to crossing with its equivalent, συκωτόν. It was in the kitchen too that CEREBELLUM prevailed over CEREBRUM; the term with the diminutive then came to be used generally for 'brain'.

If one word changed its meaning, of course, this had repercussions on others. If, owing to the ambiguity of os, the word BUCCA took on the meaning of 'mouth', then a new word would be required for 'cheek'. For this, GABĂTA ('bowl, cup') was, in fact, used metaphorically; from it we have the Italian *gota*. When MITTERE, from meaning 'to send', came to mean 'to put' ('et nemo *mittit* vinum novum in utres veteres' Luke v, 37), a new verb was needed for the first notion: *mandare*. The verb FERIRE came to mean, not 'to strike', but 'to wound': in its first meaning it was replaced by PERCUTERE. And in those areas where MULIER was restricted in meaning to 'wife' (*moglie*) another word had to be used to convey the concept 'woman'.

Christianity had, as one would expect, an immense influence on semantic development; to realize this one has only to consider the new significance of such words as FIDES, SPES, CARITAS, VIRTUS, PASSIO, MUNDUS, SAECULUM, PECCARE and COMMUNICARE. And an anecdote in a sermon of St. Augustine's reminds one of the difference between the pagan meaning of SALUS ('health') and its significance for the Christian ('salvation'). We shall limit ourselves here to a few examples of the semantic impact made by the new religion. The extension of MASSA from denoting 'a lump of dough' to meaning 'a group of persons' owes its origin to a passage in St. Paul (*Rom.* ix, 21) much quoted in the religious controversies of the fourth century. The passage of CAPTIVUS ('captive') to It. *cattivo* ('wicked') is due to its use in expressions like CAPTIVUS DIABOLI, though we must not forget that one already finds such expressions as IRAE CAPTIVUS in Seneca. Some general terms were through Christianity restricted to technical, religious use: VESPER came to refer in *i vespri* to 'evening prayers'; PLEBS developed into *pieve*, a rural 'parish church'; TUNICA became the ecclesiastical *tonaca*. Words associated with pagan worship were naturally affected. Some disappeared (as, for example, ARA, which was increasingly ousted by ALTARE, which eventually triumphed with its use by St. Jerome in the Vulgate). Others became laicized: such was the fate of LUSTRARE 'to expiate with sacrifices' which came to mean 'to clean, polish'. And a few assumed pejorative meanings: DIANA, from being the proper name of a goddess, has been degraded in some dialects to the status of a common noun meaning 'fairy', 'nymph' or 'witch', while ORCUS has become *orco*. Several of the semantic changes wrought by Christianity were due to 'calques'; PASSIO followed πάθος, SALVARE and SALVATOR took the meanings of σώζω and σωτήρ, and DOMINUS that of Κύριος. TESTAMENTUM became the equivalent of διαθήκη, which had itself taken the meaning of the Hebrew *berîth* 'covenant'.

In discussing, in the above paragraphs, the changes that took place in Latin vocabulary, we have limited ourselves to words that took root in the spoken language, and which thus appeared as hereditary words in Italian. We have not dealt with the much more numerous words which entered *written* Latin and which are

attested for the first time in texts of this period—words like
PARENTELA, INVENTARIUM, SECRETARIUS, PRIMICERIUS, LIMITROPHUS,
BREPHOTROPHIUM, NOSOCOMIUM, SCIENTIFICUS, MULTIPLICITAS,
VIVIFICARE, MORTIFICARE. We shall have to discuss words of that
kind in later chapters, when we shall be noting how, in every
century of its existence, Italian has had recourse to written Latin
in its search for additional means of expression.[1]

[1] Since the purpose of this chapter was the indication of those features which were of
particular importance for the subsequent development of Italian, no attempt was made
in it to cover all the ground normally traversed in those treatises on 'Vulgar Latin' that
deal with the whole of Romania. Nor was it intended to be primarily an essay of
interest to those studying Christian Latin. The reader who is specially interested in
these subjects is referred to chapters in two other books published in this series: the
sixth chapter, 'Vulgar Latin' (pp. 148-80), and the seventh chapter, 'Special
Languages. Christian Latin' (pp. 181-205), in *The Latin Language* by L. R. Palmer, and
the first chapter, 'The Latin Foundation' (pp. 17-169), in *The Romance Languages* by
W. D. Elcock.

2

From Latin to Italian
(476–960)

From 476 Italy was subject to foreign invaders, a fact of obvious linguistic importance. In this chapter we shall deal with the period between that year and 960, the date of the first document in which an author consciously writes the new language.

The dominion of the Heruli, Goths and Langobards followed for the most part a pattern of military colonization. The Goths had already been in contact with the Romans for a couple of centuries on the Danube and had undoubtedly been deeply influenced by them. Romanizing tendencies were evident, both among the Visigoths, who settled in the Iberian peninsula and southern Gaul, and among the Ostrogoths, who came down into Italy with Theodoric (489). Indeed, their leaders were anxious that their acquisition of Roman prudence should not be accompanied by loss of their barbaric valour ('Romanorum prudentiam caperent et virtutem gentium possiderent' Cassiodorus, *Variar.*, iii, 23). The epigram in the *Anthologia Latina* by the Latin poet who was bothered by the Gothic words he heard all around, probably belongs to a period shortly after the conquest.

> *Inter* eils *goticum*, scapia, matzia, ia, drincan,
> *non audit quisquam dignos edicere versus.*

But the art of writing in itself usually inclined people towards Latin. And the Gothic words that survive in Italy seem to testify to social decadence. 'How different', writes Gamillscheg, 'from the abundant series of notions through which Frankish culture manifests itself in Northern France. In the Gothic loan-words in Italian we see reflected all the wretchedness of the foreign population left in Italy, and living, until the arrival of new Germanic lords, the Langobards, the lives of pariahs'. The final capitulation of the

Goths in 555 marked the conquest or reconquest of Italy by Byzantium. To what extent this brought Greek influences to Italy it is difficult to say; what is important for us to bear in mind is the new political division of Italy which came about after the entry of the Langobards (568) and as a result of their victories.[1]

The Langobards were not very numerous; the most authoritative historians estimate their combatants at nor more than 15,000. They settled for the most part in the great *latifundia*, some of which became the seats of their duchies. The Langobardic settlements were thickest in northern Italy and Tuscia, being less heavy in the duchies of Spoleto and Benevento (though the Langobardic character of Benevento, both militarily and in its attachment to Arian religious beliefs, was marked). As a dominant military class, the Langobards seem to have both envied and despised their more cultured subjects, to whom they felt both superior and inferior. The extent to which the races had become fused by the time of the Frankish invasion of 773 is a matter of controversy, and it is difficult to judge the part of the problem which concerns us—that is, how far the Langobards had become latinized in speech (how quickly they became bilingual, how rapidly they then lost their native tongue and how this varied from area to area). A passage from the *Chronicon Salernitanum* composed about 978 speaks of 'lingua todesca quod olim Longobardi loquebantur' (*Mon. Germ. hist., Script.*, iii, p. 489), which indicates that in the tenth century Langobardic was no longer spoken in southern Italy, though the chronicler is able to explain the meanings of some words. While Bluhme believed that King Liutprand (d. 743) had only a limited knowledge of the language of his fathers, Bruckner held that groups of Langobardic speakers persisted in some areas beyond the year 1000. The arguments he used, however, were not all soundly based; the *ih* he sees in a document of 872, for example, turns out to be, not an *ich*, but a *hic*. Hartmann believes that there was a

---

[1] Elcock (*The Romance Languages*, p. 258) summarizes it thus: 'The Byzantines remained in control of the cities of central Italy. Their capital was at Ravenna, at that time more Greek than Roman, and while Alboin pressed southwards along the west coast to occupy Tuscany, they consolidated their hold on a belt of territory extending from Ravenna to Rome. Alboin himself remained in Tuscany, but certain of his nobles passed through the Byzantine lines and founded to the south and east the two large duchies of Benevento and Spoleto. The extreme south, including Apulia, Calabria and Sicily, remained Byzantine; so too did Naples, though almost cut off by Langobardic territory and linked at times to Rome, at times to Calabria. A further Byzantine area was left intact in the neighbourhood of Venice, forming a nucleus which was to develop into the prosperous state of later days. Throughout most of the two centuries of Langobardic occupation this patchwork division of Italy persisted'.

fairly rapid assimilation, and it seems likely that at the time of the Frankish conquest only a few nuclei of Langobardic speakers were left and that even those were bilingual. The coming of the Franks undoubtedly accelerated the process of romanization. They were already so latinized that they probably found it convenient, even in communicating with fellow-Germans, to use a sort of Latin mixed with Romance vulgarisms. The alternative was to use their own form of Germanic while the Langobards used theirs (a difficult matter since, after Langobardic had undergone its second consonantal change, the differences between Langobardic and Frankish were very considerable).

Whatever theories one accepts about life in Italy under the Langobards, it is clear that a certain culture, both lay and ecclesiastical, survived; this can be seen from the persistence of hagiographical and juridical traditions (the latter particularly in the unbroken vitality of the Pavia school), from the agricultural knowledge attested in the *Casae litterarum*, and from the metallurgical skills of which there is evidence in the *Compositiones Lucenses*. And, if the Langobards had begun by enjoying the fruits of the earth without cultivating it, the Edict of Rothari (643) shows us that they soon established closer links with the soil. It was this period that saw the development (only in the Langobardic, not in the Byzantine, areas of Italy) of the *curtis*, with its self-sufficient economy centred on a monastery or on the villa of a Langobard (later a Frankish) overlord. On the whole, political and economic evidence suggests that there was little circulation and increasing isolation in small, self-sufficient parochial or diocesan units. Yet there must have been a certain amount of intercommunication: this can be deduced from the existence of the *magistri com(m)acini* (mentioned in the Edict of Rothari, in the *Memoratorium de mercedibus magistrorum commacinorum* and elsewhere) and from the activities of the merchants. The *Transpadani* or *Transpadini* we find in Tuscany and Latium (Arezzo 715, Pistoia 742, Marta 765, Lucca 772) were presumably merchants or artisans. Liutprand's treaties with Comacchio and the fixing of tariffs testify to the regularity of river traffic.

The division of Italy occasioned by the Langobard conquest, and consolidated about 680 by a peace or truce that implied Byzantine renunciation of reconquest, had great political importance, for not until the *Risorgimento* were its boundaries cancelled. But this does not mean that linguistic circulation was entirely prevented. Rome was joined to the Exarchate by the Byzantine (later papal) corridor which followed the Via Cassia and the Via

Flaminia. Venice, Bari, Amalfi and Naples communicated with each other, as well as with the East, by sea. If we can still find traces of the corridor in dialect geography, we nevertheless do not find the divergencies that we should *a priori* expect between Bologna and Ravenna on the one side and Parma, Piacenza and Pavia on the other, though it is impossible to tell whether this was due to uninterrupted traffic or to a later smudging over of differences. In any case the connections of Lombardy with Tuscany and with the Langobards in the southern duchies were important factors in the cultural geography of the time. If the forces making for fragmentation at the end of imperial times (different substrata and lines of traffic which were more frequently horizontal than vertical) had been strengthened by divisions of dominion—if Tuscany had been left to Byzantium—then the differentiation between north and centre would have been much greater, and Tuscany would not later have been in a position to fulfil its historic role in mediating linguistically between North and South. It is fortunate, in short, that Italy was not divided in such a way as to jeopardize its later linguistic unity. On the other hand, the evidence does not allow us to go as far as believing that the Langobards were responsible for successfully reviving a failing linguistic circulation. Differences in phonetic development between the North and Tuscany (the sibilant development of CE, CI in the North and the palatal development in Tuscany) were neither eliminated nor attenuated. Moreover, Langobardic words themselves gave different results in various areas, as we shall see in due course, and this shows that circulation was not very intense.

Germanic elements could enter the Romance speech of Italy in two ways. The first was this: that the Italian population should hear certain words in the speech of their overlords and learn to repeat them in order to be understood by them. The second, which was probably commoner, was this: that certain Germanic words should remain in the speech of Goths and Lombards who acquired Romance speech and who became fused with the local population. Such words would be survivals. Only in the first case does prestige come into the matter, and only then can we speak of the working of a superstratum. In this matter, of course, it is difficult to strike a balance. But, although Langobardic influence was stronger than that of the Goths and exercised over a longer period, it was not even remotely comparable to that of the Franks in Northern France. The influence due to prestige, in fact, seems limited, but the later penetration of survivals copious.

The Frankish conquerors imposed their rule only on northern and central Italy, while the southern Langobardic duchies ended by becoming virtually independent. Because of the good relations they enjoyed with the papacy, the Franks had closer communications with Rome, as they had, too, with those duchies whose subjection to the Eastern Empire was becoming ever vaguer. Commercial connections became stronger, and the flow of pilgrims grew in volume. Unlike the Goths and the Langobards, the Franks did not move in search of new lands on which they could settle in force; after the battles, they merely sent a number of leaders to occupy positions of command. Thus, their prestige influence was great, while the number of survivals in vocabulary left by their settlements was very small. In any case, the Franks were by this time so romanized that the Germanic elements which entered Italian vocabulary through them must be put in a different category from Langobardic and Gothic words: for they are words which had already entered the Romance heritage of France, becoming Old French words, and they enter Italy, from the time of Charlemagne onwards, along with those Latin words whose phonetic and semantic development had taken place in France. Sometimes their phonetic form does not help us to distinguish them, while the geographical evidence can often tell us nothing more than that the word exists in France as well as in Italy. Occasionally, social indications are useful: a word that refers to the higher strata of society is more likely to be Frankish than Gothic or Langobardic. The great difficulty, of course, in the study of Frankish and Old French words is that of determining the date of their penetration. Since they came in before Italian was phonetically formed, it is frequently impossible to decide whether a particular word came in during the great expansion of the Carolingian period (eighth and ninth centuries), through the religious and commercial connections of the age of the Crusades, with the Norman conquest, or in the age of chivalric civilization (eleventh to thirteenth centuries). Only when the word appears in documents of the Carolingian period can we reach any degree of certainty; the fact that a word does not so appear allows no argument *ex silentio*. We must, finally, remember that, with the Franks, the feudal system came to Italy, and that its divisions presumably made for greater dialectal fragmentation.

When the Exarchate and the Pentapolis passed into papal hands, Byzantine dominion remained only in southern Italy. But, in the period between the Carolingian era and the age of the Ottos, there was a notable Byzantine cultural and political revival, and it was

at this time that various areas in the south were colonized or re-
colonized. Although Byzantine linguistic influence was decidedly
less important in Italy than Germanic influence, it is a curious fact
that Greek-speaking linguistic islands still remain in Calabria and
Terra d'Otranto, while we have no knowledge of Germanic
linguistic islands left over from the age of the invasions. Whether
the Greek linguistic islands derive ultimately from Byzantine
colonization or simply from Byzantine recolonization of areas that
were already Greek-speaking (having belonged to *Magna Graecia*)
has in recent years been a matter of controversy.

The Muslim conquest of Sicily in the ninth century brought
groups of Arabs to the island. But the separation of races due to
difference of religion, and the respect the invaders seem to have
had for the language and customs of their subjects, combined to
limit Arabic influence on the linguistic development of Sicily to
some contributions to vocabulary. The view that considerable
numbers of Sicilians became Arabic in speech and were later
relatinized is untenable.

That the spoken language of this period was developing steadily
away from Latin can be seen from the vulgarisms that crept into
the sentences of those writing in Latin. An example is a document
referring to the sale of some property drawn up by a notary called
Ansolf (Pisa 730):

'venondavi tivi Dondoni aliquanta terrula in locum qui dicitor
ad stabla Marcucci: uno capite tenente in terra Chisoni et alium
capite tenente in terra Ciulloni, de uno latere corre via publica . .'

Nor are the works of cultured men free from such features, particularly when they record dialogue. In the laws of Liutprand one
finds:

'Hoc autem rei veritas pervenit ad nos, quod quidam homo
diabolum instigantem dixissit ad servum alienum:"Veni et occide
dominum tuum, et ego tibi *facere habeo* bonitatem quam volueris".
Ille autem puer, suasus ab ipso, intravit in causam ipsam malam,
et hisdem qui eum suaserat in tantam malitiam perductus est, ut
aetiam praesentialiter dicerit eidem puero: "Feri ipsum dominum
tuum", et ipse ei pro peccatis feritam fecit, et iterum dixit ei: "Feri
eum adhuc, nam si non eum feriveris, ego te *ferire habeo*". Ipse
autem puer conversus fecit eidem domino suo alteram feritam, et
mortuos est'.[1]

---

[1] For a fuller treatment of this subject and different examples of medieval Latin, see
Chapter IV (*Medieval Latin and Romance Vernacular*) of *The Romance Languages* by W. D.
Elcock.

Of course, nobody spoke like that. These texts are all a mixture of the language that the scribe spoke and heard about him and the written Latin that he had learnt as well as he could in the place and time to which he belonged. One can imagine the difficulties of a man who had acquired the bare minimum necessary to his priestly or notarial office. In speech he did not use final s, M or T. But he knew that they were used in writing according to certain fixed schemes (e.g. M for the accusative). When he wrote he did the best he could with his limited knowledge. Moreover, from the time of Varro we have various references in Latin documents to forms used in popular speech and indicated by the formula *vulgo*. In 613 St. Columba (or Columbanus) pointed out in a letter to Boniface IV that his name existed, not only in Latin, but also in the vulgar speech of Italy: 'Columba latine, potius tamen vestrae idiomate linguae'.

A complete, methodical exploration of all the fragments of Romance embedded in medieval Latin documents has not yet been made. But useful results have been obtained from partial exploration (i.e. of particular collections or on a regional basis). Sometimes the value of the discoveries made is immediately obvious, e.g. in the case of the spelling *tz* in *uno petztzo, uno petztziolo* (Lucca 740, *Codice dipl. Long.*) At other times, careful interpretation is necessary. If we find *ligibus, heridibus, mercide*, this is not because these words were pronounced thus, but because they were written by a scribe who knew that the word he pronounced *prometto* had to be written *promitto* and proceeded from that to make hypercorrections of other words with *e* in them. (It is thus, too, that we get *u* in the medieval forms *curtis, octubris*, etc.)

It is well known that in France there was a great difference between the Merovingian and Carolingian eras, and that this was due largely to the cultural policies of Charlemagne. In Italy the break was less marked and took place a little later; the founding of the eight royal schools (Turin, Ivrea—entrusted to the Bishop—, Pavia, Cremona, Vicenza, Cividale, Florence and Fermo) in 825, and the resolutions of the Roman Council (ratified by Eugene II) on the need for diocesan and parochial schools in 826, provide us with convenient dates. The consequent improvement in the standard of written Latin led gradually to the clearer separation from it of the spoken tongue: pupils who had been taught to distinguish between the forms that existed in the language that they spoke and those of more 'correct' Latin were enabled to see the two languages as separate entities.

It is only in the tenth century that we have clear references to public use of the vulgar tongue; they bring us near to the date set as the limit of this chapter: 960. Novati enumerated these references thus: 'an allusion made by the panegyrist of Berengarius to the songs that the people of Rome in 915 mingled *voce nativa* with the learned Greek and Latin compositions performed during the coronation of their lord; the famous passage in the letter written in 965 in which Gonzone speaks of *usus nostrae vulgaris linguae quae latinitati vicina est*; the not less well-known reference which Widukind made to the ability of Otto I to speak in *lingua romana*; and, finally the praises which the author of Gregory V's epitaph heaped upon him because he had expounded the word of God to the people in three languages:

> *Usus francisca*, vulgari *et voce latina*
> *instituit populos eloquio triplici.*'

To these examples one can add that given in a Cassinese penitential of the tenth century (*cod. Cassin.*, 451): 'fiat confessio peccatorum *rusticis verbis*'.

As for the first written use of the vernacular, we could place that in the ninth century if we could only consider the *Indovinello veronese* as being really in the vulgar tongue. Since Schiaparelli discovered it at Verona in 1924, and especially since Rajna emphasized its Romance features, it has been given first place among the monuments of Italian language and literature. It is in a liturgical book written in the early years of the eighth century at Toledo, possibly before the Arabs occupied the city in 711. Various hands wrote in it after that date and so allowed Schiaparelli to trace its wanderings. It went to Cagliari and then probably to Pisa. At the end of the eighth century, or the beginning of the ninth, someone wrote in it in a hand that is probably Veronese, the following words: + *separeba boues alba pratalia araba & albo uersorio teneba & negro semen seminaba.*

Was the author deliberately attempting to write verse in the vulgar tongue, or was he extracting rhythmic Latin hexameters from his memory and unwittingly introducing vulgarisms into them as he did so? The answer is difficult and must depend on the interpretation of certain words. But it will be well to begin with the general sense of the text. It was at first believed to be a fragment from a ploughman's song; but it was then clearly explained as a riddle based on an ancient metaphor—writing as ploughing: the oxen are the fingers, the plough is the pen, the white meadows are the parchment, the black seed is ink. This riddle, still alive in many dialects ('Il campo bianco—nera la semente—tre buoi lavorano— e due non fanno niente') had wide diffusion in medieval Latin literature. Monteverdi, who quoted many examples, quoted one from Paul the Deacon which is particularly notable because it belongs to the same age and the same region as the Veronese riddle:

> *Candidolum bifido proscissum vomere campum*
> *visi et restrictas adii lustrante per occas.*

Although it has a popular flavour the Veronese riddle was undoubtedly composed by a cleric familiar with some such precedents.

The linguistic interpretation turns on the meaning of *se pareba*. At first sight it is tempting to see in it a form of *parare* in the sense of 'to drive (oxen, sheep)', especially since *parar i bò* is still used with this meaning in Venetia. If this were certain, one could see in the *indovinello* two characteristically vernacular features: an imperfect in *-eba* for verbs of the first conjugation (as in some dialects of the region) and *se* used as a dative of advantage. Rajna, in fact, made this *eba* the hub of his reconstruction, re-forming the other imperfects on the model of *pareba*:

> *Boves se pareba*
> *e albo versorio teneba*
> *alba pratalia areba*
> *e negro semen semineba.*

But there are serious difficulties in the way of such an interpretation: the discrepancy between the one *eba* form and the two *aba* forms in the manuscript, the precocity of *se* used as a dative of advantage, and, finally, the fact that one would have to assume that the subject of *pareba* was 'the ploughman' (understood), whereas it seems better to take *boves* as subject for all four lines. Although ingenious answers have been found to some of these objections, it seems better to take *pareba*, not as a part of *parare*, but as a part of *parere*, in the sense of 'to appear'. Many riddles have such beginnings (*c'è*, *ecco*, etc.). As for the *se*, this use of it would then be parallel with the use of *si* in early poetry (*qui si parrà la tua nobilitate*: Dante, *Inf.*, ii, 9; *sì, che l'effetto convien che si paia*: *Par.*, xxvi, 98; and indeed in prose by Boccaccio and others). Contini, in 1934, suggested that *pareba* meant 'seemed', 'was like', i.e. '(the thing to be guessed) was like. . . . ' But *se* is not used with *parere* thus. Nor is it likely to mean *if*, as suggested by Mastrelli (1953).

If *pareba* is not from *parare*, the remaining features in morphology and vocabulary are less remarkable: *pratalia* (not, be it noted, *pradalia*, although it seems probable that at Verona at the beginning of the ninth century, the consonant was voiced) and *versorio* could be used in Latin verse of a popular kind, and the treatment of *-lia* and *-rio* as monophthongs is normal in medieval rhythmic Latin poetry. The phonological features (the fall of the final *-nt* of the four verbs in the plural, the ending *-o* for *-um* in *albo*, *versorio*, *negro*, and—the most modern feature of all—the *e* for *ĭ* in *negro*) are such that they might well have belonged to the scribe rather than to the original author of the riddle. Moreover, certain features of the vulgar tongue are absent (although it could be argued that, so far as we know, it had not yet acquired regular use of them): articles and pronominal enclisis (as defined in Tobler and Mussafia's law; the text reads *se pareba boves*, not *boves se pareba*, which was to be the order in early Italian). And other characteristics of the riddle are clearly Latin: the final *s* of *boves* (possibly, it is true, in use in Verona in the time of Charlemagne, though we have no certainty of that), the *-t-* of *pratalia*, the final *-n* of *semen*, and the use of *albo*, *alba* (rather than **blanco*, **blanca*) for 'white'. In short, one feels that the new language is about to appear in this composition. But one cannot yet assert confidently that it was written by a person who was conscious of writing something that was different from the bad Latin that he usually wrote (whether we take the view that it was composed and written down by the same person or, as seems more probable, that the author was not our scribe). In the age of Charlemagne the difference between the spoken language (which had accepted the most notable innovations that were to be typical of the new tongue) and the written language (into which wretchedly ignorant clerics sporadically introduced vulgarisms redolent of their speech) was much more difficult to establish than it was to be after the Carolingian literary reforms had made themselves felt. For these reasons it seems wisest to keep to the most conservative reading of the *indovinello*, that given by Monteverdi, who has merely (for metrical reasons) taken out the two *&*'s:

> *Se pareba boves, alba pratalia araba,*
> *albo versorio teneba, negro semen seminaba.*

The influence of Germanic invaders on the development of the Romance languages is by no means a settled question. In Italy, the contribution they made to vocabulary can be more or less measured, and it is considerable. It is not so easy to deal with their effect on phonological and morphological evolution. Here less importance is to be attributed to the direct impact of the invaders' languages than to the indirect influence exercised through the social upheavals consequent upon their activities; the slaughter of sections of the upper classes, the long periods of anarchy and chaos, the reduced circulation of people, goods and ideas, all tended to widen the gap between the written and spoken languages. As the written language lost power, the spoken tongue lost much of its cohesion, and the only brake remaining on its development was the need for generation to communicate with generation. While we do not wish to deny that the barbarians might have had some specifically linguistic influence, we think that this other factor (the fact that the language was able to grow wild, and away from the language of culture, in various regions and minor centres) was incomparably more important. While we cannot know exactly what kind of language was spoken at Turin or at Florence, at Melegnano or at Milazzo, in 500 or 800, we must picture it as one gradually evolving from spoken Latin in the direction of what was to become the modern dialect of that place—but with the rather restricted vocabulary proper to a very modest culture.

In dealing with the period's phonological developments, we shall, though noting some of the most significant changes that took place elsewhere, give pride of place to what happened in Tuscany. The dropping of atonic vowels (the origin of which is to be connected with the use of the stress accent) is marked in north Italy, much less so in the south. That it was a feature of our period can be seen from the treatment of Germanic words in Italian: the Gothic *haribergo* was made to give *albergo*. Since one of the conditions for syncope is the kind of consonantal group that would result from it, Tuscany, which has always recoiled from having many consonantal groups, is sparing in syncope itself. Indeed, where the group *s*+cons. is found medially, it inclines to epenthesis: *cristianesimo*, *fantasima*. An interesting observation, which will have parallels in other fields, can be made about the evolution of *favola* and *tegola*. The modification in sound and meaning that these words have undergone oblige us to consider them as hereditary, not as learned, words. On the other hand, the forms *fiaba* and *tegghia* (and later *teglia*) show that popular syncopated versions also existed. The most probable explanation is that there were parallel traditions, one 'superior', nearer to Latin and averse to syncopation, the other 'inferior' and more inclined to accept innovations from France and northern Italy. While there are no certain traces of metaphony in Tuscany, the phenomenon is widespread in the rest of Italy and probably had a part in the origins of diphthongization. The diphthongizing of tonic ĕ to *ie* and ŏ to *uo* in free syllables appears in the eighth century: even if the *quocho* of a Lucchese document of 761 (*Cod. dipl. Long.*, ii, p. 75) is doubtful evidence, we have the placename *Quosa* in the same text. Moreover, it is quite clear that we have *aqua buona* in a Lucchese document in 983. Various and conflicting explanations have been offered for diphthongization and for the formation of the vowels [y] and [œ] in Piedmontese, Lombard and Emilian dialects. Phenomena which occurred so widely (in other Romance territories as well as in Italy) may be due to substratum or superstratum, but possibly less to their immediate effect than to the whole reordering of the vowel system which their influence set off. Among atonic vowels we should note the passage of pretonic *e* to *i*: there is a *nipote* in the Edict of Rothari. This is the origin of the preposition *di*: *di una parte . . . et di alia parte*, Chiusi 746-7 (*Cod. dipl. Long.*, i, p. 266). The modification of the velar [k] and [g] in CE, CI, GE, GI, probably well advanced at the beginning of our period, gave rise to sibilant affricates in northern Italy, but to palatal affricates in Tuscany and places further south. The voicing of voiceless intervocalic consonants also takes place in the period we are now concerned with: fully in northern Italy, partially in Tuscany. The idea that we can form of the process from surviving documents and from knowledge of today's geographical distribution, suggests that the phenomenon expanded rapidly over northern Italy, and that there was powerful infiltration of Tuscany, but that there was later partial reabsorption there. Political conditions (the Langobardic centre of Lucca having close ties with Pavia) and commercial relations (through the *Comacini* and *Transpadini*) explain this influence from above the Spezia-Rimini line exerted in Tuscany. And the survival of both voiced and voiceless series in Tuscany again suggests different traditions in different social strata. The development of the groups with L (PL, BL, TL, CL, GL, to [pj], etc.,) in central Italy probably goes back very far, and is certainly earlier than documentary evidence for it. (We find *Santa Maria inter piano* in 799 in the *Cod. dipl. cavensis.*) In groups with yod (*nj*, *rj*, etc.) the change is also very old. We have *vigna* in Lucca in 773. And the difference between the Tuscan *-aio* and the northern *-aro* < *-ariu* goes back at least as far as the eighth century.

We have already seen, in discussing those morphological changes that took place in imperial times, that the disappearance of the neuter from the spoken language belongs to that period. Analogy played a large part (in the speech and in the language of the chancelleries) in the use made of the old neuter endings. In the singular their repercussions were slight (since it did not matter whether *os* became *ossum* or *ossus*, as it did in the Edict of Rothari). In the plural the endings in -*a* and -*ora* (with the purely graphic -*oras*) multiplied. But, while the *le mura* type still lives in many words, the type represented by *domora, tectora, ortora*, is now nearly dead. For the plural of masculines and feminines, Tuscany moved towards -*i* and -*e* endings; but in the north words with -*s* plurals persisted for centuries. The influence of the Germanic weak declension can be detected in personal names: we have not only *Gudoloni, Gaidoni*, etc., but also *Ursoni, Loponi, Iustoni, Petroni(s)* and others. Outside the onomastic field its effect is slight and it is swallowed up by the Latin type represented by *glutto -onis*. Germanic and Latin influences also converge in the type -*a*, -*ane*, both in masculines (e.g. *scrivane(s)* in the Edict of Rothari, which gives us *scrivano*) and in feminines (e.g. *mammana*). The weakening of the demonstrative to a definite article and of the numeral *uno* to an indefinite article was a long process, starting with the Christian writers and continuing over centuries. For the definite article the north and centre used *ille* (*illa aeterna vita quod nobis Dominus preparare potest*, Gricciano di Lucca 755; *illu ortu ad illo ficu subtus casa mea*, Chiusi 774; and, with its modern form *rio qui dicitur la Cercle*, Lucca 779), while in the south, from the Marches to Sicily, there was an area which for a time preferred *ipse*, which, however, did not assume the full functions of the article and was pushed out by *ille*. In the eighth century the indefinite article is likewise fully formed (*presbiterum suum posuit unum infantulo*, Siena 715). *Lui, lei* and *loro* also make their appearance at this time, while the confusion of forms (*qui, quem, quod, que*) which we find used for the relative pronoun in documents shows that *che* was used in speech for all genders and numbers. Verbal flexion in these centuries also proceeds rapidly towards the modern type. We find forms like *somo* (Lucca 700), *essere* (Lucca 822), *offertum* (Lucca 685), *vinduta* (Lucca 754). The analogical extension of *dedi* in past definites can be seen in *battederit* (Liutprand, *Leg.*, § 123). The change of meaning in the past tenses (the pluperfect *fuissem* > imperfect *fosse*) is exemplified in: 'si aberet credentes homines, qui causa ipsa scirent, et *ausi fuisserunt* iurare a Dei evangelie, quod ita sic *fuisset* veritas, ad non?' (Lucca 892). It was not easy for the new forms of the future (formed from the infinitive +*habeo*) and conditional (infinitive + *habui*, *hebui in N. Italy, infinitive +*habebam* in S. Italy) to be used in writing; but what the situation was is clearly enough seen in the example we have already quoted (p. 40) from Liutprand's laws *si non eum feriveris ego te ferire habeo*. The formation of compound tenses by the use of *habere* as auxiliary was now normal: *a quo tempore ex quo auditum habetis*, 715 (*Cod. dipl. Long.*, i, p. 83); *si neglectum non habuisset* (Liutpr., law of 733); *si quis Langobardus habet comparatas terras in Liburia*, 780 (Bluhme, *Leges*, p. 181). So was the formation of the analytical passive with *esse*: *iram Dei incurrat et in Tartarum sit consumptus*, Pistoia 767 (*Cod. dipl. Long.*, ii, p. 211). The Italian preposition *da* goes back, in its principal meaning ('from') to *de ab*, and the first example known to us is in a Lucchese document of 700: 'neque subtragendum *da* vos hoc ipse *ecclesie*' (*Cod. dipl. Long.*, i, p. 31). As for syntactical features, we must here limit ourselves to noting that the accusative + infinitive construction, which had already in the Vulgate and in early Christian writers given way to constructions with *quia, quod, quomodo*, is now reduced still further (to the type *far fare* and to use with verbs of perception: *vedo fare, odo dire*).

In the field of word-formation certain suffixes flourished. For nouns which expressed feminine titles -*issa* was used (*abbatissa, comitissa, ducissa*, giving Italian *badessa*, etc.). New adjectives were formed through use of -*esco* and -*ingo* (-*engo*). The first of these goes back to a Germanic -*isk*, and we find it applied to common nouns, personal names, placenames and ethnical names: *warcinisca facere* ('to do shifts of obligatory work') Toscanella 736 (*Cod. dipl. Long.*, i, p. 180), *caballi Maurisci* in a letter of Leo III's, *utiles et optimos Mauriscos* in another by John VIII (Ducange), *fine Bulgarisca* in eighth century documents from Ravenna (Fantuzzi), *fontana Warcinisca* in Val di Susa in 814, *prehensa Gardonesca* at Verona in 844 (*Cod. dipl. Veron.*, p. 251), etc. The suffix -*ingo*, -*engo* has left many traces in northern Italian placenames and the documentation of it is early and extensive; in Tuscany, although documentation begins later, the type *terra Rolandinga* (Lucca 999, *Mem.*, V, ii, pp. 612-13) is frequent. *Wardingus, gardingus* ('commander of the garrison') used in various cities, probably had a Gothic origin, although the first documents in which it is attested belongs to 1133. The suffix -*ardo*, which appears later than -*engo*, is certainly French. Compounds based on the type *portabandiera* multiply: a vassal in Val Lagarina, in 845, bore the nickname *Suplainpunio*. Alongside words formed by these methods sprang up other words coined in ways already in use in imperial times: nouns from participles (e.g. *ferita* in the laws of Liutprand; *offerta*, Lucca 892), verbs from nouns, etc. Diminutives continued to be formed, and these not infrequently ousted the words from which they were derived; *avo, frate, suora, vetere* now live either in restricted areas or in restricted meanings, *avolo, fratello, sorella, vecchio* (from VETULUS, VECLUS) having taken over from them.

Among the innumerable semantic changes that belong to this period some are such that they might have occurred in any time or place, e.g. *testimonium* passing from meaning 'testimony' to meaning 'witness'. Others deserve closer attention because they are more closely bound to the conditions of the time. Connected with its religious life we had: *cella* ('room') coming to mean 'monastic cell, convent' and *caritas* taking the sense 'work (deed) of charity, alms', just as *elemosina, eleemosyne* had previously done. *Peregrinus*, from being just a 'stranger' came to be a 'pilgrim', a change that testifies to the number of strangers who appeared as pilgrims. *Cappella* goes back to Frankish Latinity: it is derived from the *cappa* of St. Martin kept in the oratory of the palace of the Frankish kings, and was spread by the influence of the chancelleries. The social, political, administrative and juridical aspects of life also became reflected in language. This we see in the title *dux* (in the hereditary form *doge* and in the grecizing *duca*), the development of which is bound to developments in social and military power. *Curtis* and *massa* became 'a great territorial possession' (hence *massarius, massaricia*). *Angaria* stood now for services due, not to the state, but to private lords. *Sclavus*, ethnically 'Slav', came also to mean 'slave' as a consequence of the Ottonian campaigns against the Slavs in the tenth century, when many were, in fact, enslaved. The Latin *classis* a 'division' of any kind, a 'section', became a 'lane': in a Lucchese document of 769 we have 'qui capu tene et lato in *classo*, alio capu in via' (*Cod. dipl. Long.*, ii, p. 276), and *chiasso* and *chiassuolo* are still living words in Tuscany. A custom which we know little about is revealed by the northern *toso, tosa* ('boy, girl') from *tonsus, tonsa*.

Naturally, in dealing with the history of vocabulary, we must always bear in mind the connections between the spoken language and medieval Latin. Just as words from common speech crept into the Latin writing of the scribes, so, too, did words from the written tradition enter spoken usage. The history of words like *papa*, used from the sixth century prevalently to designate the Roman pontiff, or of *cappella* or *forestis*, cannot be understood without assuming the existence, alongside the spoken tongue, of a written tradition, firmly based on notaries and chancelleries, and not without its influence on everyday speech.

The main problem presented by the study of Germanic elements in the vocabulary of Italian is that of determining to which stratum they belong: for such words may be due to the contacts the Romans had with Germanic peoples before the fall of the Empire (i.e. be palaeo-Germanic words), or they may be due to the invasions of the Goths, the Langobards or the Franks. The evidence for placing them in one of these four categories is only rarely direct (such as, for example, the testimony left by a writer in the case of a particular word). Recourse is therefore had to various criteria which help us to judge indirect evidence. Chronological criteria are obviously important, if one has enough evidence to apply them. So are areal criteria; to study the distribution of a word, in Italy and in other parts of Romania, may be helpful. Scholars have recently, for example, by applying such criteria, concluded that their predecessors attributed too many words to the palaeo-Germanic phase: whereas Brüch in 1913 put about a hundred words in this category, Bartoli thought that excessive, and Gamillscheg's estimate is about twenty. And the main argument for rejecting many of those words previously admitted is their non-appearance in Sardinian and Rumanian. However, there are obvious difficulties in the way of the areal method, such as the fact that the present distribution may be very different from that of a few centuries ago. Sometimes, of course, the type of Germanic to which a word belongs can be determined by consideration of its phonological or morphological features. The vowel *a*, rather than *e*, in *bara* and *strale* suggests that these words are Langobardic rather than Gothic. And words that have undergone the second consonantal change can only be Langobardic (or possibly High German words more recently imported); such are *panca* and *palla* (rather than *banca* and *balla*) or *zazzera* and *zolla* (as opposed to *tattera*, *tolla*). Semantic study also has its contribution to make. To give but one example: while *trescare* with the meaning 'to thresh' is probably of Gothic origin, in the sense of 'to dance' it is Frankish. But there is, of course, no reason why the presence of certain Germanic words in Italian should be considered to be due to only one Germanic tongue; it may well be that a word that penetrated first with one Germanic wave, continued its penetration aided by others. Such is probably the case with *ricco*, *spiedo*, *tregua*, for which successive waves of penetration have been distinguished.[1] Many Germanic words disappeared from the language when domination by Germanic peoples ceased. The nouns denoting their juridical institutions, for instance, have nearly all gone; the fact that *faida* and *guidrigildo* are still known to students of juridical history does not by any means make them a part of living usage. Some words have survived in dialects and some in placenames: the *sculdasci* and the territories they administered (*sculdasce*) have left traces in names like *Casale di Scodosia* (Padova) and, albeit rendered almost unrecognisable by popular etymology, *Scaldasole* (Pavia).

As we have already said, recent research has reduced the number of those Germanic elements in Italian that are believed to go back to imperial times. The Germanic words attested in classical and late Latin writers, like ALCES, URUS, TAXO, GANTA, GLESUM, FRAMEA, etc., are mostly nouns used to describe animals, objects and customs encountered in nordic countries. Very few took firm root. Such are *màrtora* ('marten'), *tasso* ('badger'), *vanga* ('spade') and *bragia* ('live coal'). Such, too, is *sapone*: for SAPO -ONIS was a word taken from Germanic through Gaul, and which, originally denoting a substance used for reddening the hair, came later to mean 'soap'. *Tufazzolo* ('bunch of curls, curler') is derived from TUFA, which Vegetius attests in the sense of 'tuft, an ornament for the helmet'. *Arpa*, too, is attested, the 'harp' being, according to Venantius Fortunatus, an instrument used by the Germans: 'Romanus lyra plaudat tibi, Barbarus harpa'. There are other words which less certainly belong to this period. These are *stalla* ('stable'), *roba*, *rubare*, *fresco*, *lésina* ('awl') and *smarrire* ('to get lost'). Even more doubtful is *borgo*, for the BURGUS ('castellum parvulum') of Vegetius is probably not Germanic at all, but the Greek πύργος. Moreover, we still do not know whether the word *werra* (*guerra*) entered at this period, or came in in Carolingian times. Its use suggests the disorderly warfare of the Germans prevailing over the more ordered *bellum* of the Romans, for *werra* is connected with the Old High Germ. (*fir-*)*wërran* ('confuse, mix') and therefore etymologically means 'brawl, tussle'.

Of the Gothic words, those that have survived, not only in Italy, but also in Gaul and in the Iberian peninsula, are probably due to the Visigoths (and had time to circulate in late Latinity before Romania broke up); but they may possibly, too, be words that the

[1]For a detailed treatment of the Germanic elements and the methods used in their attribution, the reader is referred to Gamillscheg's *Romania Germanica*, Berlin-Leipzig, 1934-36. See also Elcock, *The Romance Languages*, pp. 212-67.

Visigoths and Ostrogoths had in common. Those that are found in Italy only are presumably Ostrogothic. From the Visigoths come some military words like *bando* (or *banda*), *guardia* (and *guardiano*), *elmo* ('helmet'), *arredare, corredare* ('fit out, equip') and *albergo* (which, although it now means 'hotel', is from *hari-bergo*, 'refuge of armed men'). Some domestic words also belong to this category: *aspo* ('reel'), *rocca* ('distaff') and *spola* ('shuttle'). *Schiatta* ('stock, race') is also probably Visigothic. The presence of verbs and adjectives in this class argues close contact between Germans and Romans. Examples are *recare* ('to bring'), *smagare* ('to dismay'), *ranco* (from which comes *arrancare* 'to limp'), *guercio* ('squint-eyed') and *schietto* ('pure, genuine'). The joining of Latin prefixes to Germanic verbs, as in *smagare, arredare, corredare*, is also a proof of close linguistic symbiosis. From the Ostrogoths Italian acquired *bega* ('quarrel'), *arenga* ('meeting-place'), *lobbia* ('shed'), *stia* ('hencoop'), *fiasco* ('flask'), *nastro* ('ribbon'), *stanga* ('a bar', though this might be Langobardic), *stecca* ('stick'), *rebbio* ('prong'), *grinta* ('grim face'), *forra* ('gorge, ravine'), *greto* ('exposed river-bed'). Few verbs and adjectives came from this source, but among them were *astiare* ('to quarrel'), *smaltire* ('swallow, digest'), *sghembo* ('crooked').

Words of Langobardic origin constitute a more numerous and important series than the two we have already examined. It, too, has some items of a military character: *strale* ('dart'), *briccola* ('catapult') and *spalto* ('glacis') for example. Sometimes, however, the military sense has been lost: *spiedo* is no longer a weapon, but a kitchen implement ('spit'), while *guattero* or *sguattero*, instead of being a 'guard' (*wahtari*, Germ. *Wächter*), is now a 'dish-washer'. Another word, which originally indicated technical progress on the part of the Langobards, *stainberga* ('a stone house', or a stone-based house as opposed to a wooden one) degenerated to *stamberga* ('den'). Words connected with the structure of the house and its contents are *balco, palco* (originally a 'beam'), *banca* or *panca* ('bench'), *scranna* ('chair'), *scaffa* and its derivative *scaffale* ('shelf'). In the category of household objects we have *gruccia* 'crutch', *spranga* 'bar, bolt', *greppia* 'crib, rack, manger', *trogolo* 'trough', *zipolo* 'spigot', *zaffo* 'bung', *trappola* 'trap' and *palla* 'ball'. And *ranno* 'lye' is, of course, a primitive form of detergent used in washing clothes. Many Langobard terms are used for parts of the body: *guancia* 'cheek', *schiena* 'back', *nocca* 'knuckle', *milza* 'spleen, milt', *anca* 'hip, haunch' (and *sciancato* 'lame, with dislocated hip'), and *stinco* 'shin'. Others live on in the dialects: *magone* 'gizzard', *(l)uffo* 'hip', and *zinna* and *zizza* 'teat'. Some of them have a rather pejorative tone: *ciuffo* 'tuft', *zazzera* 'long, untidy hair', *nappa* 'nose', *sberleffo* (Genoese *lerfo*) 'scar', *grinza* 'wrinkle', *zanna* 'tusk, long tooth', *strozza* 'throat' and *grinfia* 'claw'. As animal names we have *stambecco* 'steinbock, ibex', *taccola* 'jackdaw' and *zecca* 'tick'. And the use of the horse gave *staffa* 'stirrup', *predella* 'ends of the reins' and *guidalesco* 'sore, gall'. Referring to the land and to agriculture we have *tónfano* 'pot-hole', *melma* 'mud', *grumereccio* 'late hay', *sterzo* 'plate (of plough)', *bica* 'stack' and *stóllo* 'pole (for hay-stack)', and there are others connected with woods and fire-wood: *gualdo* 'wood', *stecco* 'twig', *sprocco* 'shoot', *spaccare* 'to split'. From the art of building came *stucco*. Another word that casts light on the way of life of the Langobards is *schifo*, which meant 'ship' to other Germanic peoples, but 'river-craft' to them. For colouring material they had *biacca* 'white lead' and *guado* 'woad'; and *bianco* is probably a Langobard word. Of the many Langobardic words indicating occupations few have survived: apart from *sguattero*, we can record *castaldo* 'steward, land-agent', *scalco* 'steward, meat-carver', *sgherro* 'ruffian' and *manigoldo* 'executioner, scoundrel' (whether or not this is a degradation of *mundualdo*). Of the verbs many represent concrete technical activities: *(im)bastire* 'to baste', *gualcare* 'to full' and *gualcire* now 'to rumple', *riddare* 'to dance', *spaccare* 'to split', *strofinare* 'to rub' and *spruzzare* 'to sprinkle'. Others indicate, more or less effectively, everyday actions: *baruffare* 'to squabble', *guernire* 'trim, furnish', *graffiare* 'to scratch', *(ar)raffare* 'to snatch', *sbreccare* 'to chip', *scherzare* 'to joke', *tuffare* 'to plunge, dip'. Apart from *russare* 'to snore', Tuscany has its synonym *sornacare*. Abstract nouns and adjectives are few: *smacco* 'shame, disgrace', *tanfo* 'stench', *scherno* 'mockery, derision', *tonfo* 'splash', *gramo* 'wretched', *ricco* 'rich', *stracco* 'worn out'. This list could, of course, be much extended if one were to include words that survive only in dialects, or which, though once part of the language, are now no longer part of normal usage.

The identification of those Frankish words that entered Italy before the year 1000 is fraught with difficulties. First of all, phonetic features give us little help in distinguishing between Frankish words on the one hand and palaeo-Germanic or Gothic words on the other: it is thus probable, but it is not certain, that *guerra* is Frankish. Secondly, since the Franks that came to Italy in the Carolingian age were profoundly romanized (so that linguistically they were nearly always, not Germanic-speaking Franks, but palaeo-French), there is uncertainty as to whether certain items of vocabulary came in during the age of Charlemagne or during the age of chivalry. Finally, since Frankish or palaeo-French linguistic influence was due more to politico-cultural prestige than to immigration, one has frequently to bear in mind the role (as intermediary) of the written language, medieval Latin. Sometimes, however, medieval texts provide us with evidence going back to the ninth or tenth century: we are thus enabled to trace the expansion of *bosco* and *foresta* at the expense of *selva*, just as we can follow the fortunes of the Langobard *cafaggio* or *gaggio*. *Bosco* is probably Frankish. *Foresta* is doubtful: perhaps chancellery Latin *forestis* is a derivative of *foris*. It would be pleasant at this point to be able to give a list of the Old French words that came in before 1000, separating them from those we shall list in Chapter 4. But there would, in fact, be too many question-marks in such a list, and we shall therefore limit ourselves here to those words of Germanic origin whose importation was probably early. Among them there are a few military items: *baratta* 'quarrel', *battifredo* 'watch-tower', *dardo* 'dart', *galoppare* 'to gallop', *gonfalone* 'standard', *guaita* 'watch' and *guaitare* 'to do guard-duty', *guarnire* 'trim', *guardare*, *schiera* 'band' (and *scherano* 'ruffian'), *tregua* 'truce' (which probably came in chancellery form) and *usbergo* 'habergeon'. Referring to dress we have *cotta* 'surplice, coat' and *guanto* 'glove', also in latinized form. For *guanto* we have the testimony of Iona of Bobbio (*Vita Columbani*, 14): 'tegumenta manuum, quos Galli *wantos*, i.e. chirothecas, vocant, quos ad operis laborem solitus erat habere'; but the word became established as a juridical term, a glove being used as a symbol on the exchange of property. From the commercial field we have *bargagnare* 'to bargain', *sparagnare* 'to save', and also *guadagnare*, which originally meant 'to graze, pasture'. With the Franks, too, feudal terminology, of composite and partly uncertain provenance, entered Italy: *feudo*, *barone*, *ligio* ('liegeman') are three such terms whose origin is still controversial, while another, *vassallo*, was originally Celtic. Other political and social terms are: *marca* 'boundary', *scabino* 'judge', *guarento* and *guarentire* (much later, with phonetic changes due to later French influence, *garantire*), *guiderdone* 'retribution, reward' and also *abbandonare* (which means 'to leave *in bando*—to mercy'). There remain a few verbs and abstract nouns: *grattare* 'to scratch', *guarire* 'to cure', *trescare* 'to dance', *ardire* 'to dare', *schifare* and *schivare* 'to shun', *orgoglio* 'pride', *rigoglio* 'vigour' and *senno* 'sense'. Whereas it is possible that some of the above words came in later, in the age of chivalry, it is quite certain that the adverbs *troppo* and *guari* were very early importations.

In dealing with Byzantine words, the difficulty that confronts us is that of distinguishing between words that really came in at this period and words of Greek origin that entered later or had already become part of late Latin. Phonetic criteria are sometimes useful, e.g. the development of η to *i* seen in *bottiga, pontica* from ἀποθήκη, and the voicing of the plosive in the groups ντ, μπ, which became *nd, mb* e.g. in *gondola, indivia*, Sardinian *condaghe*, etc. Geographical evidence is also helpful: several words live on only in territories that were once Byzantine-dominated: the Exarchate and certain southern areas (the latter sometimes enjoying relations with areas colonized by Greek populations). The following grecisms probably go back to the earliest Byzantine times, though it is possible that some of them may have penetrated later. Connected with housing there were *androne* 'entrance-hall' and *lastrico* 'paving' (properly 'flooring made with crocks', τα (ὄ)στρακα). In the field of domestic objects this period acquired the words *mastra* or *màttera* 'kneading-trough' and *mastello* 'tub'. Nautical terms were very numerous. They included *galea* and *gondola* as well as many names of pieces of equipment and of operations: *àrgano* 'capstan', *sartie* 'shrouds', *calumare* 'to lay out (cable, chain)', *falò* 'bonfire', *molo* 'mole', *mandracchio* 'inner harbour', *squero* 'boathouse', *scala* 'unloading-place'. *Paragone* 'comparison' was probably originally a trade word pertaining to the goldsmith's craft, gold being tested on the *pietra di paragone* 'touchstone'. Another technical word was *smeriglio* 'emery'. The titles of military and civil authorities left some traces: *duca* is the grecised form of *dux*; *catapano* and *straticò* lived on for centuries. The Sardinian *condaghe* also belonged to the administrative sphere. Knowledge of certain plants spread at this period: such are *anguria* 'water-melon', *indivia* 'endive' and *basilico* 'basil'. To this time, too, belongs *ganascia* 'jaw' (*ganathos* in a tenth century gloss from γνάθος feminine). Strong Byzantine influence can be seen, too, in the fortune enjoyed by certain suffixes: *ia* with accented *i* (in formations like *abbatia*>It. *abbazia*), *-itano* and *-oto* (which later ran together with *-otto*).

In the case of Arabic words, it is so difficult to effect a separation between those that came in through the Arab domination of Sicily and those that penetrated later that we shall deal with them all in another chapter.

3

Early Stages
(960–1225)

I n this chapter we shall deal with the earliest documents in the
vernacular, beginning with the *placiti cassinesi*, in which we
first find a clear consciousness of the difference between Latin
and the vulgar tongue, and ending at the year 1225, which marks
approximately the beginning of a new phase in the history of the
language—its use in the *Laudes creaturarum* of St. Francis (written
in 1225 or 1226) and its use for obviously literary purposes in
the lyrics of the Sicilian school. It could be argued that to talk
of 'Italian' texts in this period (960-1225) is misleading. Italy
was not a political unit. And, if it is certain that Dante wrote with
all the literate inhabitants of the peninsula as his ideal audience,
it is far from clear that the Sicilian poets did so. Indeed, it is
obvious that the authors of some of the early texts wrote with
only people of their own region in view. If, therefore, we here
treat together texts from various parts of the peninsula, we do so
with its future linguistic unity (and their supra-dialectal features)
especially in mind, but without glossing over their regional
differences.

The appearance of the earliest texts is in itself a testimony of
the general awakening that seems to have taken place in Italy
around the year 1000. The maritime republics were then displaying great political and commercial energy: Genoa, Pisa and
Amalfi in the Tyrrhenian and on the shores of Africa; Venice
in the Adriatic. The religious reforms that we associate with the
name of Gregory VII, not only led to greater moral unity in the
west, but also lent a strong impetus to the crusades, which, of
course, also had conquest and economic gain as motive forces.
For Italy the most important crusade was the fourth, which
brought great political and commercial expansion to Venice
and established Italians in numerous fiefs of the Eastern empire.

The dichotomy between north and south, which has been an abiding characteristic of Italian history, and which was to give Tuscany its importance as a linguistic mediator, was accentuated between the eleventh and twelfth centuries. In the north and centre flourished that typically Italian institution, the *Comune*; numerous urban centres became city-states organized by the bourgeoisie and lesser nobility. In the south, conditions changed radically in the space of a century as a result of the Norman conquest. Around the year 1000 dominion was divided among Byzantines, Langobardic rulers and Muslim invaders fighting amongst themselves; in the following century Roger II, Duke of Apulia and King of Sicily (1130), had control over nearly all of southern Italy and Sicily. With him began a unitary tradition, which became firmer under the centralizing rule of Frederick II, and which was to last for centuries, contributing to the particular character of that part of the peninsula.

Culturally, France was pre-eminent at this time. Half-way through the century the chivalric ideal gained ground. Monastic reforms spread from Cluny, Cîteaux and the Chartreuse (and, in Italy, from Camaldoli). In the south, Cassino was an important cultural centre, a point at which Latin, Greek and Langobardic influences converged, and something of a linguistic regional capital. In architecture, the beginning of the twelfth century saw the florescence of Romanesque in the great cathedrals of Modena (1106), Cremona (1107), Piacenza (1122), etc., followed by that of Gothic. In mathematics, astronomy and in medicine Arabic influence was strong, and in philosophy, too, Averrhoistic ideas made themselves felt. Italian pre-eminence was evident in the field of law; Pavia and Ravenna prepared the way for Bologna. Monastic and diocesan schools enjoyed an uninterrupted scholastic tradition. The instruction in them, usually in the hands of ecclesiastics, was based on rhetorical and grammatical knowledge of Latin, the necessary foundation for possible further study of science, law or theology. Foreigners marvelled, in the eleventh century, at the fact that in Italy lay persons were among those who studied, and at the importance accorded to grammatical and rhetorical instruction. Wippo of Burgundy wrote in the *Tetralogus*:

> *Hoc servant Itali post prima crepundia cuncti,*
> *et sudare scholis mandatur tota iuventus:*
> *solis Teutonicis vacuum vel turpe videtur,*
> *ut doceant aliquem, nisi clericus accipiatur.*

The gateway to all knowledge, then, was *grammatica*, understood as knowledge of Latin. And it was in Latin that nearly everything, public and private, was written in this period. The local dialects were considered inferior, for they lacked the formality, regularity and dignity felt to be necessary in a written language. A long series of trials, as well as the triumphant examples of French and Provençal, would be needed before the vulgar tongue in Italy could overcome this conviction of its inferiority, especially in the literary field. Much ink has been spilt in attempts to explain why vernacular literature in Italy was so late in making its appearance, and usually spilt to very little purpose for the reason stated by Parodi: 'we should not ask ourselves why a literature is not born, but why it is'. The situation in Italy has been contrasted with that in France, where the *Chanson de Roland* and the lyrics of William IX of Aquitania had appeared before Italy had anything of note to boast of. The explanation usually given in Italy is that Latin enjoyed great prestige there and was looked upon as *the* correct, written language. But, in fact, Italy did not produce remarkable literature in those years in Latin either; there were no great poets to write in the ancient or the modern tongue. It may well be that the prestige of Latin, its wide diffusion and its comparative closeness to the spoken tongues of the peninsula, contributed to retard the appearance of vernacular literature. But the fact that there was so little of note even in Latin itself suggests that the main energy of Italy in these years went into practical pursuits: the creation of the *Comune*, the founding of overseas colonies and the pursuit of architecture, rhetoric, medicine and law.

That there was at least full awareness of the distinction between Latin and the vulgar tongue can be seen in the *placiti cassinesi*; only scribes of unusual ignorance could now confuse the two systems. And there is plenty of testimony to the fact (which would in any case be obvious) that everyday speech in the peninsula was in its various vernaculars. We have already quoted the epitaph from the tomb of Gregory V, who died in 999:

> *Usus francisca, vulgari et voce latina*
> *instituit populos eloquio triplici.*

We could add that Angerius, Bishop of Catania, in the twelfth century, decreed that the adult catechumen who was incapable of answering in Latin the questions put to him before baptism, should answer in the vulgar tongue: 'si nescit litteras, haec vulgariter dicat'. In 1133 King Roger caused a proclamation to be read to the inhabitants of Patti and then expounded in the vernacular: 'Audita tandem memoratorii continentia, et vulgariter exposita, Pactenses. . . .' Moreover, Boncompagno, in his *Rhetorica antiqua*, mentions the use that merchants make of the vulgar tongue: 'Mercatores in suis epistolis verborum ornatum non requirunt, quia fere omnes et singuli per idiomata propria seu vulgaria vel corruptum latinum ad invicem sibi scribunt et rescribunt. . . .' But with that we have reached 1215.

While Latin served as a common language for Western Europe, the dialect of each region served only a restricted area. But linguistic circulation gradually began to affect the new language, too. Although the clergy who moved from place to place could manage Latin more or less well, and could at least communicate with their own kind through it, the merchants could not; they had to adapt themselves to the speech of the places they were trading in. The appointment of a *podestà* ('mayor, chief magistrate') from outside the city in which he had to serve, also contributed to linguistic movement. The career of the Bolognese judge and poet Rambertino Buvalelli is an example: possibly *podestà* of Brescia in 1201, he was *podestà* of Milan in 1208, Consul of Justice at Bologna in 1209, ambassador at Modena in 1214, *podestà* of Mantua in 1215-16, *podestà* of Modena in 1217, *podestà* of Genoa in 1218-20 and *podestà* of Verona, where he died, in 1221. A career of that kind must have given the public servant concerned a very mixed kind of speech. Another group of persons who had every reason to modify their native dialects was formed by the minstrels; they, especially, depended on having their words immediately understood.

Practical and cultural contacts contributed to the diffusion of a certain knowledge of French and Provençal in Italy. Apart from the connections formed by pilgrims, by crusaders and by the representatives of monastic foundations, incentives to learn these languages were provided by the fact that, from about 1100, French and Provençal gave shining examples of successful literature in the vulgar tongue. On the other hand, the florescence of theological and philosophical studies, which won prestige for French schools in the eleventh and twelfth centuries, had little linguistic influence, since for their purposes medieval Latin sufficed.

In southern Italy Norman settlers and their court exercised great influence. The importance of French there can be seen in the attitude of Henry, Count of Montescaglioso, who turned down the chance to be regent during the minority of William II because of his ignorance of that, to him, indispensable language ('Francorum se linguam ignorare, quae maxime necessaria esset in curia'). By the routes prepared by the Normans, Carolingian and Arthurian legends travelled to Italy (and that is how the name of Arthur's sister, *la fata Morgana*, Morgan le Fay, came to Sicily). In northern Italy, at the end of the twelfth and the beginning of the thirteenth centuries, Provençal poetry attracted great interest, first in the courts (specially in Monferrato, Lunigiana and the Este court, the Trevisan March), then later in the cities. Numerous troubadours came into Italy, and there found imitators who succeeded in composing in the Provençal tongue. Of the oldest Italian troubadour, whose nickname was *Cossezen* ('fair'), no compositions remain to us; but there is still extant the poem in which Peire de la Cavarana, in 1196 or shortly afterwards, expressed the hatred of the Lombards for 'la gent d'Alemaigna'. We shall see presently how Raimbaut de Vaqueyras applied his talent to composition in an Italian dialect. Still later we shall come to the wider and more lasting influence which Provençal literature had in southern Italy.

The documents in which we have the first conscious use of the vernacular are the four *placiti cassinesi* (or, to be exact, three *placiti* and one *memoratorium*). These are legal documents, drawn up in Latin, but giving the sworn testimony of the witnesses in the vernacular. They are about the ownership of certain lands, and they all belong to the same period (960-63) and to the same region. They concern, in fact, three monasteries dependent on Montecassino; they record testimony given at Capua, Sessa and Teano, in the Langobardic principalities of Benevento and Capua (or, to be precise, in that of Benevento, for this was one of the periods when these territories were joined together), where Langobardic legal traditions determined the procedures adopted. Apart from the first of the documents from Teano (the *memoratorium*) the form is constant: the judge communicates the text of the formula to be employed to the parties involved; later, three witnesses, presenting themselves separately, repeat it. Thus, in each of the three documents, the formula appears four times. The passages in the vernacular are as follows:

Capua (March 960): Sao ko kelle terre, per kelle fini que ki contene, trenta anni le possette parte sancti Benedicti.

Sessa (March 963): Sao cco kelle terre, per kelle fini que tebe monstrai, Pergoaldi foro, que ki contene, et trenta anni le possette.

Teano (July 963): Kella terra, per kelle fini que bobe mostrai, sancte Marie è, et trenta anni la posset parte sancte Marie.

Teano (Oct. 963): Sao cco kelle terre, per kelle fini que tebe mostrai, trenta anni le possette parte sancte Marie.

The formulas are in line with others used for the same purpose elsewhere, except that they are in the vernacular, not in Latin. Examples are a formula from Lucca in 822, and, to come nearer to the area we are concerned with here, formulas from S. Vincenzo al Volturno in 936 and 954. Since the witnesses, who were clerics and notaries, could well have repeated the formula in Latin, the purpose of using the vulgar tongue must have been to impress the sense of the judgement on those present, and in this respect at least the documents have something in common with the Strasbourg oaths of 842, when Louis the German swore *romana lingua* in order to be understood by the French soldiers and Charles the Bald *teudisca lingua* in order to be intelligible to the Germans. The *placiti* seem designed, then, to give publicity to a judgement. And this judgement is probably occasioned, not by the claim of a genuine adversary of the monasteries, but by someone co-operating with them in order to have their right to certain lands confirmed by law, presumably in order to make it impossible for this to be contested by others later. (In fact, the 'adversary' who has brought the case, turns up at the hearing to announce that he has no document or witness to support him, and judgement is then given for the monastery.) The judge in each case prescribes the words which the witnesses must swear and which have probably been prepared by him, and the notary then underlines the perfect conformity (*toti tres quasi ex uno ore; quasi uno ore*) of the declarations made. It is quite clear, therefore, that these documents do not represent the reduction to writing of extempore phrases; they contain, rather, the earliest examples of Italian chancellery usage. This explains the rather complicated syntactic structure of the formulas (of which the most involved is that of Sessa). As for the use of genitives of proper names, *parte Sancti Benedicti* and *parte sancte Marie* are explicable as belonging to the same type that gave us the modern *Piazza San Giovanni* or *Via Garibaldi*. More difficult to explain in vernacular texts are the possessive genitives dependent on the verb 'to be': *Pergoaldi foro, sancte Marie è*. Since the vernacular is so clearly distinct from the Latin in the minds of the participants, the presence of these genitives in the formulas requires this explanation: that chancellery usage had transferred this kind of phrase from oral use of Latin to oral use of the vulgar tongue, and that the judges therefore felt they could be used even in formulas deliberately composed in the vernacular. On the other hand, *tebe* and *bobe* really represent derivatives of the Latin dative (TIBI and VOBIS) surviving in the speech of southern Italy (as we shall se in the *Ritmo cassinese*). A curious problem is presented by the form *sao*. In itself this is not at all surprising: it can easily be explained as an analogical form influenced on the one hand by the second and third person forms *sai* (<SAPIS) and *sae* (<SAPIT) and on the other by presents like *ao*, *dao*, *stao*, which we can suppose the Campanian dialects possessed about 1000, since we find them in texts not far removed from this: semi-Latin texts in the *Codice diplomatico Cavense* have *abo* ('I have') and *dabo* ('I give'). What raises doubts is the fact that the modern dialects of southern Italy present variants of the *saccio* type as the continuators of SAPIO. And a text from this region, the *Ritmo cassinese*, gives, a couple of centuries after the *placiti*, the form *sactio*. On the other hand, one cannot doubt the reading *sao*; it occurs twelve times in the formulas, and the originals are extant. There are two possible explanations. The first is that at Capua the phonetic continuator of SAPIO had dropped out and been replaced by the analogical *sao*, and that only later, under the influence of other centres, was the form *saccio* or *sazzo* accepted there. The second is that of Bartoli, who argued that *sao* came from the North and represented an attempt to get above dialect. He held that the formulas represented the language of jurists, and that it had, as well as regional features, inter-regional elements, some of them Latin and some Italian in character. This hypothesis is less likely than the first. Another interesting form in the formulas is *ko* (Capua), with the variant *cco* (*Sao cco*, Sessa, Teano II). This is certainly a survival of QUOD, which later coalesced with *ca* (<QUAM and possibly from QUIA) and with *che* or *ched* (<QUID) in the single form *che*. The earliest persons to try and convey Italian sounds by means of the traditional Latin alphabet had to contend with the difficulties of representing those sounds which Latin as pronounced in medieval fashion did not possess, especially the velar *c* [k] and *g* [g] before *i* and *e*. Where affinity with the Latin word was obvious, there was a strong tendency to adhere to the Latin spelling: *che* used as relative pronoun was written *que*. On the other hand, in *kelle* and *ki* the notaries had recourse to the symbol

k, rare in Latin (except in the crystallized *kal.*), but possessing the virtue of being free from ambiguity.

A century passes before the appearance of further texts in the vernacular. Although scraps appear in Latin works, there is no complete sentence in the vulgar tongue known to us before the last decades of the eleventh century. From that time there have survived two Sardinian and three central Italian texts. Those from Sardinia are of great interest for they show us that the vernacular was used there (in legal charters) for purposes which were long to remain the province of Latin on the mainland. But since those documents (like the *condaghi* of the following century) represent a separate linguistic tradition, they give rise to different problems from those we are dealing with here. And we therefore merely mention them before passing on to the texts from central Italy.

At the foot of a charter by which a certain Miciarello and his wife Gualdrada made over all their possessions in 1087 to the abbey of St. Salvator on Mount Amiata, the notary added these words (now known as the *postilla amiatina*):

> *Ista car*tula *est de caput coctu*
> *ille adiuvet de illu rebottu*
> *qui mal consiliu li mise in corpu.*

The assonance in *coctu*, *rebottu* and *corpu* suggests that the composition is to be read as verse: hendecasyllables if we read without elision, lines of nine syllables if we assume that the notary was giving Latin dress to vernacular words—which must have been more or less these:

> *Esta carta è de Capucottu*
> *e ll'aiuti dellu rebottu*
> *che mal consigliu i mise in corpu.*

The interpretation is not without difficulties, of which the main one is the meaning of *rebottu*. We should translate: 'This deed is Capocotto's [Capocotto, which probably meant 'tough nut', being the nickname of Miciarello]; may it help him against the Evil One, who has put bad counsel into him'. Whether this is the sense or no, this text shows the language in a less advanced stage of settlement than the *placiti cassinesi*. The notary Rainerio could write only Latin, and when he wrote a vernacular word he did so with Latin in mind. He pronounced *capucottu*, but wrote *caput coctu*. He said *è*; but in writing this became *est*. And perhaps behind his *adiuvet* (which he would certainly call *adiùvet* in the medieval fashion) was a vernacular *aiuti*. Nonetheless, behind the smoke-screen he has put up, some notable features are visible (*illu* used as an article and the endings in *-u*).

More important than Rainerio's *postilla* is an inscription on a wall in the church of St. Clement in Rome, which dates from the end of the eleventh century—more important because it was on view in a public place, and that a church. A fresco there represents an episode from the *Passio sancti Clementis*. The incensed pagan patrician Sisinnius alleges that the saint has exercised magic arts against him, momentarily depriving him of his sight and hearing in order to abuse his wife, Theodora, a convert to Christianity. He commands three servants to drag the bound St. Clement along the ground:

> *Fili de le pute, traite.*

He then names two whom he instructs to pull on the rope:

> *Gosmari, Albertel, traite.*

The third he orders to push with a pole from behind:

> *Fàlite dereto colo palo, Carvoncelle.*

But a miracle has taken place: the holy man that the patrician intended to drag to martyrdom, is free. In his place they are dragging a heavy column. From it comes a voice, which explains the miraculous event:

> *Duritia[m] cordis vestri[s]*
> *saxa traere meruistis.*

Numerous details here are worthy of note. In spelling, the scribe's only difficulty has been the representation of the sound *gli* [λ] (*fili*, and possibly *fàlite*). Gemination does not appear in spelling, even where there was doubling in pronunciation (*pute, Sisinium*, although we also have *Carvoncelle*). In final position Latin *-ŭ* gives *o*, never *u*. There is no diphthongization in *dereto* (dissimil. from *de-retro*). The passage of -RB- to -*rv*- (*Carvoncelle*) is characteristic of central dialects. There are two examples of articulated prepositions (*dele, colo*). The vocative has *e* in *Carvoncelle*, but is truncated in *Albertel*, this form being perhaps a harbinger of the southern truncation of vocatives. In the verb we have two imperatives: *traite* and *fa* (in *fàlite*). The order of pronouns (indirect before direct object) is the opposite of what it usually was in thirteenth- and fourteenth-century Italian, though there are rare exceptions.

The last of the three eleventh-century texts which have thus far come to light also belongs to central Italy. It occurs, along with Latin formulas for confession, in a manuscript from the abbey of S. Eutizio near Campli (now Campi), not far from Norcia, and it is consequently frequently referred to as "the Umbrian confessional formula". The first and longer part of it (that of the penitent) is an enumeration of sins:

'Domine mea culpa. Confessu so ad me senior Dominideu et ad mat donna sancta Maria [etc.] de omnia mea culpa et de omnia mea peccata, ket io feci [etc.], Me accuso de lu corpus Domini, k'io indignamente lu accepi [etc.]. Pregonde la sua sancta misericordia e la intercessione de li suoi sancti ke me nd' aia indulgentia [etc.].'

This is followed by the confessor's exhortation and absolution:

'De la parte de mme senior Dominideu et mat donna sancta Maria [etc.]. Et qual bene tu ai factu ui farai en quannanti, ui altri farai pro te, si sia computatu em pretiu de questa penitentia [etc.].'

The text probably belongs to the second half of the eleventh century (being certainly later than 1037 and earlier than 1089) and corresponds to Latin penitential formulas. Indeed, Latin influence is very strong throughout. One of its editors, Father Pirri, was reminded in reading it of the situation which frequently occurs today among illiterate persons using the prayers in Italian introduced by Pius X: they often stick to the Latin for such words and phrases as Confiteor; verbo et opere; mea culpa, mea culpa, mea maxima culpa; ad Dominum Deum nostrum. But, apart from such fragments in Latin, Latin influence is obvious in spelling, syntax and all else. In orthography we should note the use of k, limited to ke as conjunction or pronoun (and also the pronoun ked) and oscillation in syntactic doubling. One of the most characteristic phonological features is the distinction between final o (<Latin ŏ, ō) and final u (<Lat. ŭ): io, accuso, preso, como, but confessu, battismu, diabolu, Petru, Paulu, and so on. This difference seems also to distinguish (as in some central dialects today) the pronominal neuter ('come ipsu Dominideu lo sa') from the pronominal masculine ('lu corpus Domini, k'io indignamente lu accepi'). There are some traces of metaphony: puseru, dibbi. There is no diphthongization of ĕ and ŏ, but tonic E in hiatus gives i: mia, mie. In the treatment of atonic vowels one notes decema, iudecatu, but also, under Latin influence, genitore and genitrice, quadragessime, etc. There is a tendency to add a paragogic vowel or syllable: ene (and also farai for farà). There are some notable verb

forms (*abbi, dibbi*). And in the possessive pronouns there is distinction between the tonic series *meu, mia, mei, mie* and the atonic *me* (in *me senior*) and *ma* (if, as seems certain, *mat donna* is not an abbreviation of *mater donna* but a graphy for *maddonna*). As for the order, the words *Me accuso* are not in accordance with Tobler and Mussafia's law of pronominal enclisis; but that is due to the weight of the Latin model, for when there is an independent vernacular phrase we get *Pregonde*.

From the twelfth century and the beginning of the thirteenth we have some legal testimony and a series of private agreements, inventories and account-books. The inscription from the Duomo at Ferrara (1135) would be the only one of its kind, if it were authentic; we hold that it is not, and shall omit further mention of it. From the territory that stretches from Tuscany to Campania, through the Marches and Latium, come a number of minstrels' verse compositions on edifying subjects. Other poems, of historical and narrative inspiration, appear in Venetia and Tuscany. Twenty-two Piedmontese sermons are all that remain of preaching in the vernacular, though there must have been much of it throughout Italy. With the *Proverbi de femene* at the beginning of the thirteenth century begins the florescence of didactic poetry which Lombardy displayed in the Duecento. And some stanzas by Raimbaut de Vaqueyras attempt to cast into Genoese some of the material of the Provençal literary tradition. But there is no text from the Abruzzi in this period. Nor is there anything that is certainly Sicilian, in spite of the culture that flourished in Sicily at the time of the Normans and the imminence of the brilliant period which Sicilian literature was to enjoy under Frederick II. There is, on the other hand, no lack of Sardinian documents. We shall now review briefly these various types of text in order to find what they can teach us about the consolidation of the written language at this time.

A legal parchment of 1158 from Volterra tells of a dispute between Count Ranieri Pannocchieschi and his brother Galgano, bishop of Volterra. In it the judge records the testimony given by six men from Travale in support of Ranieri's ownership of certain farms. In the case of two of the witnesses the judge quotes some of their actual statements in the vernacular. This time the testimony consists, not of prepared formulas, but of their own words. Enrigolo says: *Io de presi pane e vino per li maccioni a Travale*. And Poghino says that he heard from Ghisolfolo that Malfredo, after doing guard duty at the *curtis* of Travale, complained of the way in which he had been treated, saying: *Guaita, guaita male, non mangiai ma' mezo pane*, after which he was excused further duty. This last sentence is the most important in the text, since, in spite of certain difficulties in interpretation, it is clear that it is some kind of witticism based on a popular saying or refrain, and that it is thus connected with a vernacular tradition. But even when he is reporting the testimony in Latin, the judge usefully leaves certain words in the vulgar tongue. The Travale testimony, like the *postilla amiatina*, belongs to western Tuscany. Some of its features are worthy of note. In spelling, the use of *ke, ki* to represent a voiceless velar has given the writer the idea of using *k* also for voiced velar: thus we have not only *Gerfalcki*, but also *Maccingki, Pogkino, Gkisolfolo*. A habit which was more widespread (being found also at Pistoia) is seen in the use of *th* to represent voiceless *z* [ts]: 'Ego *certetham* aliam non scio nisi per auditam', *Eldithelli, Benthuli*. As for phonology, we have early documentation here of the characteristically Tuscan development of -ARIU>-*aio*: 'Andreas Starna qui Napp*aio* vocabatur', contrasted with the plural 'li napp*ari*'. The atonic *e* in the preposition *de* (unarticulated) oscillates: 'la curte *de* Travale' and 'la curte *di* Travale'. Atonic INDE>*de*: 'io *de* presi pane e vino'. The singular *Starna* has the plural *Starni*. The construction *non ... ma* ('non mangiai ma' mezo pane') has parallels in old Italian: 'e nulla ci ho rimedio ma uno' in an *Ars dictandi* of the thirteenth century, though it is oftener found with *che*: 'non avea pianto ma' che di sospiri' (Dante, *Inf.*, iv, 26). Different scholars have, of course, translated differently, e.g. some as 'I ate only half a loaf', others as 'I have never had even so much as half a loaf'. In vocabulary, we should note *maccioni* 'masons' (from the Germanic *machio*) and also *mascia* for *massa*.

Among contracts, records, memoranda and similar documents of the period are some in which fragments of vernacular occur in Latin texts. In the *carta di Rossano*, for instance, there are fragments valuable to students of Old Calabrese, since there is a scarcity of texts in the dialects of Calabria. There are similar fragments of vernacular in a document from Monte Capraro (1171) concerning the consecration of a church in a hermitage there; the prior, Ruele, seems to find Latin too much for him at one point and proceeds in his own tongue. A more important document of this kind is the *carta fabrianese* of 1186. After starting in shaky Latin to note the methods the contracting parties are to observe in dividing the fruits of their common property, the notary breaks into the vulgar tongue and continues in it almost to the end of the document. Here are examples of his work:

'. . . de quale consortia nui advemo plu de vui, nui partimo et vui tollete; et o ('ove') advemo de paradegu, de paradegu parterimu . . . et set ce fosse impedementu varcante lu 'mpedementu sia complitu et pignu vet mecto per X livere de inforzati. . . .'

Again the distinction between final *u* and final *o* is kept in the majority of cases (*mecto, advemo, partimo*; but *paradegu, vostru, toltu, dictu, bonu, pignu,* etc.). Typical of the central zone of Italy is *arcoltu* for *raccolto* ('harvest'). The 1st plural present of *avere,* as of other *-ere* verbs, has *-emo* (*advemo, odstendemo, adtendemo*), while futures have *-imo* (*parterimu, adrenderimu, atverimo*). In its vocabulary this text has *sinaita, senaita* in the sense of 'boundary'; this is the Langobardic *snaida* 'a cut', properly 'a mark on a tree to indicate possession', which is documented in medieval Latin and is still alive in some dialects in the Abruzzi.

A document from Fiastra, in the Marches, belonging to the year 1193 has a private *scritta* in the vulgar tongue inserted into a notarial *carta*. (The *scritta* was a private agreement, without legal value, and was early written in the vernacular; the official, legal *carta* continued to require Latin for much longer.) In it, again, there is distinction between final *u* and *o*, though less scrupulously observed. And, whereas signs of metaphony were uncertain in the *carta fabrianese,* they were clearly present here: *Carvone,* but *Carvuni; quistu* beside *questo. Loro* is used as an oblique pronoun: *sia loro a proprietate.* In the meaning of 'or' we find *uo.* But this is not a continuation of AUT, which would not have diphthongized, but *vo* for *vuoi* (2nd pers. sing. of *volere*).

A Savonese *carta,* probably of 1182, gives us a text with notable Ligurian features. It is an inventory of the possessions of a widow, Paxia, as declared by her to the consuls of the city. In spelling, one notes in it the *x* in *prixon* and the *gu* in *brague* ('*brache*'). In phonology it is notable for the metathesis in *pairolo,* the treatment of Latin CL in *oreger* (Ital. *origliere*) and CT in *peiten* (Ital. *pettine*). The first pers. pron. is *ei.* The vocabulary is rich and interesting.

From the Pistoiese mountains we have (in the second half of the twelfth century) a list of the tithes due to a certain Arlotto:

'Alpicione dr XXVIIII et del due anni l'uno una spalla et una callina, et omni anno mezzo staio de orzeo, et ki fuori. . . .'

In it the velar is represented both by *k* (*Botaciatiki*) and by *ch* (*Finochio*), but *k* also stands for *qu* (*Kerardini*). The diphthongs *ie* and *uo* occur (*tiene, fuori*) and so does *i* <RJ (*dinaio*). The atonic suffix *oro* <*olo* is notable.

In a codicil to his will, written in Latin in 1195, another Pistoiese, Gradalone, promised to make restitution to those who had suffered from his practice of usury. In a note added to the will, in the vernacular, the notary who drew it up added an account of the restitution made:

'Gradalone si fue nanti Bonus, ke est aguale episcopus de Pistoria, et nanti l'arcipreite Buoso, sì si concioe con tuti questi omini. . . .'

One should note the lack of diphthongization in *omini* (*Buoso*, as a Germanic proper name, is in another category), the persistence of *i* in *arcipreite* (from ARCHIPRESBITER, -PREBITER) and the paragogic vowel in *fue* and *concioe*.

From the end of the twelfth century we have a partially preserved list of the possessions and income of the church of Fondi. It consists of a series of notes of this kind:

'Item vinale unu posto alla veterina a llatu Antoni de Trometa et a sancto Antoni a la via a longu la macera.'

'Item Pastena deve dare pro olo sanctu et pro crissima tomela de granum nove rase.'

Many expressions remain unintelligible. In the text *k* is widely used, as in *ke*. The distinction between -*u* and -*o* is usually observed. For the development of the vowels we should note *Valle maiure*, and for that of consonants *Vallecorza* and *cannele*. The measures used in the inventory (*cafise, tomela*) belong to southern vocabulary.

A much richer series of records is that provided by the well-known fragments from the account book of a Florentine bank (1211) which survived on two sheets of parchment used for binding. They are of this kind:

'MCCXI. Aldobrandino Petri e Buonessegnia Falkoni no diono dare katuno in tuto libre lii per livre diciotto d'imperiali mezani, a rrascione di trenta e cinque meno terza, ke demmo loro tredici dì anzi kalende luglio, e diono pagare tredici dì anzi kalende luglio: se più stanno, a iiii denari libra il mese, quanto fosse nostra volontade. Testi Alberto Baldovini e Quitieri Alberti di Porte del Duomo.'

The language of this text, in spite of some hesitations in spelling, has a clear-cut character of its own and is notable for its precision in the use of banking terms. In fact, it suggests the existence of written usage before this actual example, a suggestion supported by the text's mention of a *libro veckio*. In it *k* is predominant in all positions, but we also have *Rusticuci, Compagnino, Compangno, Ballacalza*. The writer is embarrassed in writing *ghi, ghe* [gi] [ge] (*Arrihi, Ugetti,* and, with doubling, *Teckiaio*) and *gui, gue* [gwi], [gwe] (*Bonaguida, Bonaquida,* etc.). The characteristics of Florentine, as they will be amply documented in following decades, are already in evidence. We have the typical anaphonesis, as also *er* for *ar* in atonic position (*Aquerelli, Kafferelli, quiderdone*) and paragogic *a* in *lia, prestoa* (found also in texts from San Gimignano). We have *ci* beside *no* (enclitically *ne*) as the first person plural atonic pronoun (*no promise, no die dare, ci diè, dene pagare*). We have *ponemo* and *avemo* (not yet *abbiamo*). The strange infinitive *avire* is explained by Parodi as being due to influence of the notarial type of which *placire* and *monastirium* are examples (and is thus to be distinguished from the *avire* found in Guittone, which is due to Sicilian influence). Latinisms are infrequent, except in formulas used for dates (*intrante, kalende aprilis*). However there are several examples of the construction *Arrisalito figlio Turpini, mamma Sinibaldi, per lo mercato San Brocoli, Borgo Sa Lorenzi* (though we also have *a konto Arnolfino*).

The statutes of the men of Montieri in the Tuscan *Maremma* are unique. Whereas other statutes in the vernacular are late in appearance and translations of statutes already existing in Latin, the document from Montieri consists of a draft made in the vulgar tongue, with emendations and additions evidently born of public discussion and intended to be of use in the eventual formulation of the statutes in Latin. Obviously, the writer had in mind the usual formulas of statutory legislation, and these stick out in his Italian ('non essare in consilio nè in facto nè in ordinamento con alcuna persona', 'observare ed adimpire a bona fede senza frode', 'se non fusse per se difendendo', etc.). The spelling is more modern than that of the Florentine bankers (*paghi, paghino, camarlenghi, rasgione,* etc.) but still displays considerable oscillation. Some features are clearly Sienese (*lettare, essare, rendare*). The syntax, which is rather involved, suggests that the writer was already composing rather hypotactically, with the eventual task of rendering the will of the meeting into Latin already in mind.

Of the poems of the minstrels the oldest is the *ritmo laurenziano*, which is the earliest composition in Italian that can fairly be described as literary. It consists of twenty double *ottonari* (octosyllabic lines) written on the last page of a manuscript in the Laurentian library in a hand that belongs to the end of the twelfth or the beginning of the thirteenth century. The minstrel addresses a bishop (Villano, archbishop of Pisa, according to the theory of Cesareo, adopted by Mazzoni) heaping fulsome praise upon him (and prophesying his eventual elevation to the papacy), in order to persuade him to give him a horse. If he is given one he will show it to the bishop of Volterra, Galgano. He has already, he says, received a similar gift from another generous bishop, Grimald(esc)o. It is difficult to establish the identity of these bishops, and, unfortunately, difficult to establish the part (possibly the west) of Tuscany to which the composition belongs. The allusions in it to *Fisolaco* (the *Physiologus*) and *Cato* (the *Disticha Catonis*), the metrical scheme akin to that of the Provençal *Sancta Fides*, the ordering of the composition according to the prescriptions of rhetorical tradition (*salutatio, captatio benevolentiae, petitio, exemplum*) point to a certain degree of culture in the poet.

But the *ritmo laurenziano* is on a lower level than the *ritmo di Sant'Alessio*, which comes from the Marches and the *ritmo cassinese*, which is preserved in the monastery of Montecassino, at which it was probably composed. Both these compositions, too, date from the end of the twelfth or the beginning of the thirteenth century.

The first of them relates the first half of the legend of St. Alexis (his birth, marriage, exhortation to his wife, flight to Laodicea and life as a beggar). The language confirms that the author, like the copy of the poem that has come down to us, was *marchigiano*. The distinction between final *u* and final *o* is very consistently observed. In pronouns and some demonstratives the masculine is distinguished from the neuter. ND gives *nn*, though with some oscillation and several regressions. The cons. +L group remains intact (*flore, slatta*, etc., except in *kinao*). In vocabulary we note *afflao* ('he found') <AFFLARE, which is still widely represented in southern dialects. The numerous oscillations in form which the text displays may be partly due to copying; but some of them are probably due to the mixed language of the minstrel himself, who introduces further variety by occasional gallicisms and latinisms (and by occasionally writing a word or a whole line in Latin).

The metrical scheme of the *ritmo di Sant'Alessio*, a series of stanzas consisting of a number of *ottonari* (or *novenari*) followed by a couplet in hendecasyllables, is found again, in slightly more complicated form, in the *ritmo cassinese*. In the latter poem the minstrel, after a kind of prologue and *captatio benevolentiae* followed by a declaration of the allegorical nature of the compositition, tells his hearers of a meeting and dialogue between two characters, one (the mystic) from the East, the other (a more worldly person) from the West. The language sets difficult problems, but is quite consistent with the poem's having been written in Campania, indeed in the environs of Montecassino. There is no diphthongization of ĕ and ŏ. In the treatment of atonic vowels *e* and *u* prevail. Final *u* is distinguished from *o* and produces metaphony. Almost throughout we have *b* for *v*. The group cons. +L remains intact. The survivals and analogical expansions of the dative personal pronouns are notable: *tebe, sebe, por vebe* (which recall the *bobe* of the Teano text on p. 61, but also *a tteve*, which occurs in the *ritmo di Sant'Alessio*). *Fora* and probably *boltiera* are pluperfects with conditional meaning ('would be' and 'I should like'). The appeal to the public, the possible use of an illustration of the narrated episodes, the nature of the dialogue (which suggests a recitation with mime) and the metrical structure connect this poem with the minstrel tradition. But the author is much more cultured than the authors of the two previous *ritmi* (the Laurentian and that on St. Alexis). This is shown by the use of unadapted Latin words (*ergo, vir,* etc.) and the numerous latinisms which argue acquaintance with the language of the law-courts and schools (*compello, interpello, albescente, sitiente,* etc.). There are also provençalisms and gallicisms (*deportare, fui trobata, destuttu,* etc.). And it would be appropriate, in describing the language of this composition, to speak of an ennobled Campanian.

Another poetic composition of a religious nature, this time a Judæo-Italian elegy, is preserved in Hebrew characters in two manuscripts. Written to be sung during the ceremonies connected with the fast of Ab, the elegy tells of the dispersion of the Jewish people, and dwells on the unhappy lot of two youngsters of noble stock, brother and sister, who are sold into captivity, and whose recognition and death are narrated. The lamentations of the Jews for these two young people are mingled with invocations to the Lord. The influence of minstrels' compositions of a religious character on this text is beyond doubt (in the dialogue of the prostitute and the inn-keeper, for example), and there is possibly direct reminiscence of the *ritmo di Sant'Alessio*. In the localization of the text we have no external assistance. Literary parallels (*S. Alessio, Pianto delle Marie*) suggest the Marches. The dialectal features tell us that it belongs to central Italy (Marches—

Umbria—Roman dialects) without enabling us to be more precise.

Two other texts show the vernacular put to a different use: the narration in facile and rousing verse, of battles in which certain cities have taken part. One, from Belluno, belongs to the year 1193, and consists of four lines only; the other, from Lucca, belongs to 1213 and is a little longer. Both are included in Latin chronicles; the chronicler, on reaching the event, which was versified soon after it occurred, quotes the versifier's effort. In the text from Belluno we pass from Latin, with no transition, to the following:

> De Casteldard avì li nostri bona part,
> i lo getà tutto intro lo flumo d'Ard;
> e sex cavaler de Tarvis li plui fer
> con se duse li nostri cavaler.

Here we should note the attempt to get above dialect, seen both in latinisms (*sex*, *intro*) and in the reintegration of the final vowel in *tutto* and *flumo* (especially obvious in the latter word, where the vowel concerned turns out to be an analogical reconstruction).

In the Lucchese text the chronicler begins to relate a battle between a group of his fellow-citizens and men from Massa, Pisa, Pistoia and other places. As he comes to record certain details, he recalls words and phrases from the vernacular versification of the events he is describing. Finally, he just repeats the versifier's information and political comments ('Di lui e li altri sia vendecta', etc.). Although so little remains to us, it is clear that we have here examples of an important use of the vulgar tongue.

Another use for vernacular verse is found in the lament of Mary, in three lines, rhymed and strongly southern in language, which closes a Latin liturgical passion play written at the end of the twelfth century:

> . . . te portai nillu meu ventre.
> Quando te beio, moro presente.
> Nillu teu regnu agime a mente.

This is an important testimony to the infiltration of the vulgar tongue into religious dramatic poetry. In the text one notes that, although *beio* is written with a *b*, the *v* is maintained in *ventre*; this is probably through reminiscence of *fructus ventris tui*.

Another aspect of the place of the vernacular in religious life is illuminated by twenty-two sermons from Piedmont; detailed

study of their language is still awaited. The preacher usually
begins by quoting a verse from scripture, which he then translates
and comments on. Thus we have in the second sermon:
'Dominus dicit in evangelio: Beati misericordes quoniam ipsi
misericordiam consequentur. Seignor frere, nostre Sire dit en
son evangeli que bonaurai sun cil qui an misericordia, quar il la
troveran plenerement. Perqué', etc.

Here we have Piedmontese written down by someone used to
French spelling. He nearly always uses *que, qui* for velar +*e* and
i; apart from the Latin *fratres karissimi* he has no *k*. The influence
of Latin, too, is notable; indeed, the author is able to distinguish
more clearly between Latin and vernacular than he can between
the vernaculars. The text shows that Piedmont was (as it was
long to remain) markedly detached from the rest of Italy
linguistically.

To the earliest years of the thirteenth century belongs a poem
of 189 four-line stanzas of double *settenari*, with the same rhyme
throughout each stanza. It is a series of misogynous statements
and counsels, the earliest extant example of that moral-didactic
literary tradition to which Uguccione, Patecchio and Bonvicino
belong. This composition, to which the title *Proverbi de femene* has
been given, is in Lombard dialect, but it is impossible to place it
more exactly. Here is a stanza from it:

> *E como son falsiseme*   *plene de felonia*
> *et unqa mai no dotano*   *far caosa qe rea sia.*
> *Or dirai qualqe caosa*   *de la lor malvasia,*
> *ond se varde li omini*   *de la soa triçaria.*

A single example suffices to show how, in the text, rough dialectal
forms are mingled with others representative of an archaizing
usage and still others conforming to Latin. If we examine the
words which had a -T- in Latin we find four developments:
disappearance (*spaa, mua*), dh (*redhi*), d (*mercadi, ramadi, resonadi*)
and retention (*muto, entenduto, recordato, dato* 'dado'). Sometimes
the reasons for the author's choice are only too obvious. The
examples of -*d*- given above are from stanza 55; in that stanza
the first line ended with the word *Barbacoradi*, which suggested
the form to be used in the following lines. In stanza 81 the poet
uses *scaltride* and *tride* to rhyme with *ride* and *aside*. But in stanza
56 to rhyme with *marito, partito* and *florito* he allows himself to
use *rito* for *rido*, a form which has certainly never belonged to the
spoken language. Other features worth noting in the text are: the

widespread use of *q* for velar *c* [k]: *riqe*; the tendency to apocopate words so that they end in a consonant or consonant group, except at the end of a line or hemistich ('Quel q'eu *digo* de femene, eu nol *dig* per entagna'); the form *lero* for *loro*, both as oblique plural pronoun and as possessive, although *loro* also occurs; the ending *-emo* for the pres. ind. of the first conjugation: *trovemo*; and oscillation between *-ave* and *-ia* in the conditional (*porave, devria*). In the vocabulary there is an abundance of gallicisms (*acolar* 'embrace', *cobiticia* 'cupidity'; *a lo men esciente* 'to the best of my knowledge', *esdito* 'saying', etc.) and of latinisms (*malicia, nequicia, sene*, etc.). In short, however ingenuous the author may seem in ideas and techniques, his language is composite.

Among the poems of the famous Provençal troubadour Raimbaut de Vaqueyras are a *contrasto* and a *discordo* containing lines deliberately composed in Italian. In the *contrasto*, which was written about 1186, a knight declares his love to a woman of the people, who disdainfully rejects him, treating him as a minstrel. The man speaks in Provençal, while the woman, a Genoese, speaks a version of her dialect modified by the poet. Raimbaut spent many years (as court poet and as warrior) in Italy; but he was not a modern dialectologist. The value of this text, therefore, is not that it gives us documentation of the Genoese dialect, but that it shows us the effort of a poet to adapt an unwritten dialect (with echoes of other dialects he had heard in Italy) to the literary patterns of Provençal culture. The result is naturally very mixed. Often one sees Provençal showing through the Genoese patina: Raimbaut, who had discovered that the Genoese equivalent of the Provençal *plus* is *chu*, applies the scheme of change that he sees in this to *chaidejai* and *deschasei* (but also gives us *plui* and *plait*). *Gauzo*, too, seems an attempt to give Genoese dress to the Provençal *gaug* (for, a century later, the *Rime genovesi* have *goyo* and *gozo*). It is interesting that we should find here the futures *scanerò* and *amerò*. These are found in the *Rime* also. Since there we have, too, the forms *Catarina, Margarita, masaritie* (not *Caterina*, etc.) it is probable that here this is due, not to phonetic change (*ar*>*er*), but to analogies with futures of the second and third conjugations.

In the *discordo*, which probably belongs to the last years of the twelfth century, Raimbaut indicates the unhinging effect his lady had on him by using five different languages, one for each stanza of the poem and all five in the *congedo* (or envoy). The languages can be described roughly as: Provençal, Italian, French,

Gascon and Ibero-Romance. The language of the fifth stanza is so mixed that it is impossible to tell whether the poet intended to write in Portuguese or in Galician (or, less probably, in Spanish). And this suggests that we should consider the second stanza to be an attempt to write, not in Genoese, but (to use the term in its old, comprehensive sense) in 'Lombard'. There are certainly features that are clearly Genoese; there is a *çhu* which reminds us of the *chu* of the *contrasto*. But the language is notably composite in these ten lines; we have *o* besides *aio* for instance. As futures we have *averò, partirò, farò*. We have, too, adaptations of Provençal words, e.g. *glaio*. But it should be emphasised that the manuscript tradition leaves us in doubt about many of the readings to be adopted in this poem.

As we have seen, Raimbaut's Italian shows strong Provençal influence. But, unlike the texts we have hitherto examined, it bears no trace of Latin influence. In other words, his own language was mature and noble enough, in the poet's eyes, to lend dignity to Italian when required to do so, and this made recourse to Latin unnecessary.

It is impossible to give a general survey of the language of the period on the basis of the texts we have examined in this chapter. We have, it is true, a rough picture of the development of dialects in Italy (and of the emerging influence of centres like Rome and Montecassino); but the details are missing. The influence of French and Provençal is apparent. As yet there is no work in Italian that can even remotely compete with the fruits of their literary traditions, no work that can act as a linguistic and literary model for writers in one of the vernaculars of Italy. What we have, in fact, is a series of modest, mainly practical and utilitarian, texts. There is some kind of poetic tradition to be seen in the work of the minstrels; but it is improbable that their rough efforts carried (as Torraca believed) Tuscan words or forms to the early poets of the Sicilian school. Yet there is evidence in some of the texts we examined of an ambition to avoid the crudest features of dialect; doublets are occasionally found, especially in verse. Undoubtedly, the study of vulgarisms in the Latin documents of the period has still much to contribute to the early history of Italian; unfortunately, thorough exploration of these documents has only just started.

In view of the scarcity and lack of uniformity of the texts at our disposal, therefore, we shall not attempt to compile a grammatical inventory for this period. Nor shall we try to give a survey of developments in vocabulary. One could certainly note certain new formations and new meanings, e.g. *podestà* used in the second half of the twelfth century for the Ghibelline *podestà*, and then at the beginning of the thirteenth century for those *podestà* appointed from outside the city. Recourse is often had to Latin (for words like *comune*, *console*, etc.), French influence is apparent (in the suffix *-iere*, in the word *mangiare* in the Travale testimony, etc.), and so also is that of Arabic. But it seems advisable to await the much fuller documentation of the Duecento before essaying a general picture of lexical phenomena. We shall not therefore attempt a balance-sheet of developments in grammar or vocabulary until the end of the next chapter.

4

The Duecento

(1225–1300)

In this chapter we shall deal with the main vicissitudes of the vernaculars of Italy from the third decade of the century (when works of serious artistic intention first appeared) to its end. In the course of it we shall witness the establishment, at least in verse, of a linguistic tradition destined to endure.

From the year of his coronation (1220) to that of his death (1250), the Italian political scene was dominated by the figure of Frederick II. Some of his policies had permanent effects; such were the administrative reorganization of the kingdom of Sicily (in which civil servants replaced feudal and ecclesiastical dignitaries) and the legislative work undertaken as a continuation of the *corpus iuris* of Justinian. But his attempts to join to the kingdom those parts of the peninsula not directly dependent on the pope failed, mainly because of the strength and taste for independence now enjoyed by the city-states, the communes and certain powerful families. The migration of (Franco-Provençal) Waldensian colonies to Calabria was due to Frederick's support. At Florence, which was in the forefront of the opposition to him, the names *Guelf* and *Ghibelline*, which had originated in Germany, took on new meanings in the context of Italian politics. In 1252 was minted the gold florin (*fiorino*), which soon won respect in the world's markets (and which was followed in 1289 by the Venetian ducat). The battle of Montaperti (1260) gave the Ghibellines the upper hand for a brief period, but the situation was reversed when Manfred was defeated and killed at Benevento (1266). Within Florence the *ordinamenti di giustizia* of 1293 marked the passing of political power to the popular sections of the community (though not to its lowest strata). In certain northern cities families like the Este, Visconti and Scaligers consolidated their authority. The Angevins, with papal support, had, after their victory over the Swabians, a platform from which to exercise authority in the peninsula. But, after little more than a decade, Sicily passed to the Aragonese. They attempted to gain control, too, of Sardinia, where the Pisans were still predominant.

At the court of Frederick, where cultured laymen filled places which in other courts were reserved for ecclesiastics and feudal lords, there was great intellectual activity. The emperor encouraged, not only philosophical, scientific and mathematical studies, but also that kind of poetry, based on Provençal troubadour models, which we associate with the Sicilian school. University studies, in which Bologna had primacy, now spread to other cities: Padua (1222), Naples (1224), Arezzo, Rome and Siena. In the universities the *ars notariae* and the *ars dictandi* both flourished: rhetoric and law joined together in public documents. And indeed notaries and judges had an eminent part in the cultural life of the period; one thinks of poets like Giacomo da Lentini (*il Notaro*, as Dante called him), Pier della Vigna, Brunetto Latini, Guido Guinizzelli and Cino da Pistoia, and of the founder of Paduan prehumanism, Lovato dei Lovati. Religious life, orthodox and unorthodox, was intense. The *'tempo dell'Alleluia'* (1233) and the devotion of the flagellants gave rise to religious songs and poems. The Dominican and Franciscan orders date from the early decades of the century. Greek writings, in the interpretations of Averrhoes and other Arab teachers, dominated the scientific field. Theological thought, which flourished mainly in Paris, was at first hostile to Aristotle; but, thanks especially to the labours of St. Thomas Aquinas, he became in due course one of the bases of the Christian thought of the period. In the artistic field, architecture was particularly notable; the cathedrals of Siena and Orvieto, and the churches of Santa Maria Novella and Santa Croce at Florence, were built, and Santa Maria del Fiore was begun in 1296.

The appearance of the adjective *Italiano* at this period may be a symptom of a growing feeling of relationship among the scattered members of the peninsula. In medieval Latin *Italia* was accompanied by the adjectives *Italus* and *Italicus*. North of the Alps, however, all Italians were frequently described as 'Lombards'; Salimbene remarks, in his chronicle, that the French 'inter Lombardos includunt omnes Italicos et cismontanos'. In his *Tresor* Brunetto Latini, between 1260 and 1266, used *Ytaile* and *Ytalien*. And an anonymous compiler of *exempla* (whose language suggests he was Sienese) wrote the following words in recasting Valerius Maximus: 'Et di ciò dice Valerio che avendo li romani preso uno grande *ytaliano* . . .'. The adjective is clearly formed from the noun, on the model of *Sicilia—siciliano, Venezia— veneziano*, etc.

Anyone who wishes to understand the nature of vernacular writing at this period must bear in mind that Latin was the language of the great majority of texts. It was the medium for theological and philosophical works, laws and legal commentaries, chronicles, treatises on medicine and astrology—for nearly everything, in fact. And the Latin of St. Thomas, St. Bonaventure, Albertano da Brescia, Iacopo da Voragine, Salimbene da Parma and their contemporaries offered a very wide variety of forms. In the letter of condolence that Pier della Vigna wrote to the professors of civil law at Bologna on the death of Giacomo Balduini we read:

'Iuris civilis professoribus universis magister Petrus, salutem . . . Amaritudo amarissima et materia concreta doloribus humanis noviter mentibus occurrerunt. Nam unicus et singularis in terris homo, in quo velut in suo proprio leges convenerant, et vivebat eloquentiae tuba, et consilii plenitudo sedebat, est revocatus ad patriam, de cuius revocationis amaritudine vox populi a fine usque in finem et terminos orbis terrae dolorosa multum exivit. Nec mirum, quia iam optimus persuasor bonorum operum, omnium excellentissimus Iacobus de Regio Iesu Christo vitalem spiritum resignavit.'

That text is full of rhetorical devices: etymological figures like *amaritudo amarissima*, rhythmical clauses like *mèntibus occurrèrunt, spìritum resignàvit* (cursus velox), *plenitùdo sedèbat* (cursus planus), etc. Let us now look at a passage from Salimbene:

'Nota quod Innocentius papa fuit audax homo et magni cordis. Nam aliquando mensuravit sibi tunicam Domini inconsutilem, et visum fuit sibi quod Dominus parve fuisset stature; quam cum induisset, apparuit grandior ipso. Et sic timuit et veneratus est illam, ut decens fuit. Item solitus erat aliquando librum tenere coram se, cum populo predicabat. Cumque quererent capellani, cur homo sapiens et litteratus talia faceret, respondebat dicens: 'Propter vos facio, ut exemplum dem vobis, quia vos nescitis et erubescitis discere'. Item homo fuit qui interponebat suis interdum gaudia curis; unde cum quadam die quidam ioculatur de marchia Anconitana salutasset eum dicens:

Papa Innocentium,
doctoris omnis gentium,
salutat te Scatutius
et habet te pro dominus,

respondit ei: 'Et unde est Scatutius?'. Cui dixit:

De Castro Recanato,
et ibi fui nato.

Cui papa:

Si veneris Romam,
habebis multam bonam,

id est 'bene faciam tibi'. Fecit papa quod gramaticus docet: *Per quemcumque casum fit interrogatio, per eumdem debet fieri responsio. Quia enim malam gramaticam fecit ioculator, malam gramaticam audivit a papa'* (pp. 42-43 Bernini).

Salimbene's periods (and, often, his vocabulary) allow the vernacular to show through, even though his grammar is reasonably correct, judged by the standards of his time.

But these are only two of the many varieties of Latin that existed. Some of them were well known to those who wrote in the vulgar tongue. Thus, alongside the influence of the vernacular on Latin, especially visible in those authors who had few literary pretensions, there was the very strong influence that Latin exercised on the writing of the vulgar tongue—both in structure and in vocabulary. It was natural that its prestige should be enormous. Translators into the vulgar tongue were conscious of its superiority. And to go to school meant, above all, to study *grammatica*, that is, Latin. This was considered necessary, not only for budding notaries and churchmen, but also for those who looked forward to a career in commerce; a Genoese notarial contract of 1266 speaks of 'grammatica communiter edocenda secundum mercatores Ianuae'.

Nevertheless, the authorities in civil spheres had henceforth to take account of those who knew no Latin. The statutes of Bologna in 1246 made it clear, in prescribing examinations for those who wished to be notaries, that the candidates should be able to read in the vulgar tongue the documents they had drawn up, for the sake of persons who had no Latin. And Pietro dei Boattieri, in the commentary to the *Summa artis notariae* of Rolandino, gave appropriate instruction. Moreover, statutes began to appear written in the vernacular only: those of Montagutolo del-

F

l'Ardinghesca (1280-97) are still extant. The *Commentationes* of Montecassino show us that even in that monastery daily lectures were given in the vulgar tongue. And, while the episcopal schools continued to provide education for future ecclesiastics, the bourgeoisie founded lay schools where a little Latin was learnt through the medium of, and on the foundation of knowledge of, the vernacular.

Connections with France, and with the great literatures that had sprung up in French and Provençal, were closer than ever in this period. The epic, particularly the Carolingian epic, enjoyed great popularity in northern Italy. The jurist Odofredo speaks of the 'orbi qui vadunt in curia comunis Bononie et cantant de domino Rolando et Oliverio', while at the end of the Duecento another writer describes the minstrel who, in barbarous French, purveys Charlemagne's deeds to the crowd:

> *celsa in sede theatri*
> *Karoleas acies et gallica gesta boantem*
> *cantorem aspicio; pendet plebecula circum*
> *auribus arrectis: illam suus allicit Orpheus.*
> *Ausculto tacitus: Francorum dedita lingue*
> *carmina barbarico passim deformat hiatu.*

This foreign poetry, welcomed by the lowest strata of society, was only partly intelligible. It is to be expected, therefore, that so-called Franco-Italian literature should show varying degrees of hybridism. Here, to give a single example, is a passage from the *Chanson de Roland* as it appears in a well-known Franco-Venetian text (*cod. Marciano V⁴*):

> *Rollant a messo l'olinfant a sa boçe*
> *inpinç il ben, per gran vertù lo toce;*
> *grand quindes leugue la vox contra responde,*
> *Çarlo l'olde et ses conpagnons stretute.*
> *Ço dist li roi:—'Batailla fa nostri home!'—*
> *Et Gainelon responde alo' inconter:*
> *'Se un altro lo disesse, el senblaria mençogne!'*
> *Li cont Rollant per poi e per achant*
> *et per dolor si sona l'ilifant;*
> *per me' la gole li sai for li sange,*
> *de soe cervelle se va lo tenpan ronpant.*

Lesser degrees of hybridism are to be found in the texts composed in prose by those Italians who, for various reason, wrote in

French: in the treatise on falconry translated for King Enzo by
Daniele Deloc of Cremona (ed. H. Tjerneld, Stockholm 1945),
the *Tresor* of Brunetto Latini (ed. F. Carmody, Berkeley—Los
Angeles 1948), the chronicle of Martino da Canale (ed. F. L.
Polidori, Florence 1845) and the *Milione* of Marco Polo, written
down by Rustichello da Pisa (ed. L. F. Benedetto, Florence
1928).

We must, too, bear in mind the contacts due to commercial
relations. St. Francis of Assisi's knowledge of French and indeed
his name (Francesco) stemmed from his father's connections
with France. Florentine account-books testify to the frequency of
dealings with the French, particularly with Champagne. And
when we read the *Fiore*, a compendium of the *Roman de la Rose*, or
the *Intelligenza*, we see that their authors had so close a familiarity
with French (and probably not only with literary French) that
they were induced to make their Italian all too receptive (mostly
in vocabulary, but sometimes in grammar as well). Here are some
examples of their borrowings:

> *sì non son troppo grossa nè* tro' *grella*
> (*Fiore*, son. 43)
> *ma 'l Die d'amor non fece* pà *semblante*
> (son. 104)
> *E s'ella non è bella di* visaggio
> *cortesemente lor* torni *la testa*
> *e sì lor mostri senza far* arresta,
> *le belle bionde trecce* davantaggio
> (son. 166)
> covriceffo o aguglier *di bella* taglia
> (son. 190)
> *la* grada *è di* cipresso inciamberlata
> (*Intell.*, st. 62)
> *e Cesar quand'uccise Artigiusso*
> *che non fu de'* musardi *sanza* faglia
> (st. 79)
> *Vergenteusso il fedì su la fronte*
> *sì forte che* ciancellò *tutto 'l ponte*
> (st. 126)

We should remember also the political and administrative
influence of the Angevins in southern Italy.

But if knowledge of French was aided by non-literary factors,
that of Provençal was almost entirely due to the prestige that its

poets had earned for it. The Albigensian war destroyed court life in Provence and with it the material basis of the troubadour's verse. The dispersal of these poets was a factor in the expansion of their language outside their country. As we have already seen, Provençal troubadours were welcomed in northern Italian courts and cities. The prestige enjoyed by them (and the lack of a national language in Italy) induced some poets in north Italy to compose, not only in their manner, but in their language. Thus, among the notable poets who wrote in Provençal are numbered Italians like Lanfranco Cigala and Sordello. In southern Italy, on the other hand, there was, not imitation in Provençal, but emulation in the vernacular (for the language of Provence was not so readily understood there as in northern Italy). Thus the Sicilian school was born. Percivalle Doria, a noble Genoese supporter of the Swabians, was one of those who belonged to both traditions: he composed in Provençal a *serventese* in praise of Manfred, but he also wrote *canzoni* in an ennobled Sicilian.

As a consequence of the influence exerted by French and Provençal models on the literature of the Duecento, gallicisms and provençalisms are numerous in certain authors—like Guittone d'Arezzo. Sometimes they are used for a particular literary effect: the abundance of French and Provençal expressions in the *contrasto* of Cielo d'Alcamo, for instance, constitutes a caricature of court language. Later in this chapter we shall give a summary list of the gallicisms that entered the Italian vocabulary at this time.

The lyric poets of the Sicilian school were the first group to produce a body of poetry of a serious artistic nature in the vulgar tongue and the first to succeed in forging a poetic language that could serve as a model for other Italian versifiers. It was transmitted, with modifications, not only to their pedestrian Siculo-Tuscan imitators, but to Guinizzelli and the poets of the *stil novo*, and to Petrarch and those who followed him. Certain features of this poetic language thus became permanent characteristics of the Italian poetic tradition. Moreover, a gap was created between the languages of poetry and prose that was to last for centuries. The poetic models proved satisfactory enough to provide a relatively uniform language that could be used in various regions—for verse; prose was to find it much more difficult to emerge from local pressures. It is true that an artistic kind of prose flourished at Bologna, with Guido Fava as master,

and that in Tuscany artistic prose was cultivated by Brunetto
and Guittone. But they never achieved anything as brilliant as
the work of the early poets. Nor is it so easy for prose, which is
used for practical purposes, to depart from regional characteristics, even if it is subjected by some authors to artistic elaboration.
The unification of the language of prose was, in fact, to be slower
than that of poetry. Nor must we forget that in the Duecento
Sicily and southern Italy had no Italian prose; theirs was still
in Latin. These factors explain the treatment we shall give to our
material in the remainder of this chapter. We shall be dealing
with the basis of the Italian poetic language. In prose, on the
other hand, we can only point to various currents; among them
artistic prose is only one, and it does not, in view of the subsequent history of the language, deserve exclusive attention.

The *Magna Curia* of Frederick II was the main workshop of
the Sicilian School, whose poetry may have originated under
the leadership of the notary Giacomo da Lentini, and with the
support (*heroico more*, as Dante puts it: *De vulg. el.*, I, xii, 4) of the
emperor. This court was based mainly on Sicily, particularly on
its cultural centres Messina and Palermo, though it also resided
for long periods at various places on the mainland. Although
poets who were not Sicilian belonged to it, therefore, its language
was based on a refined Sicilian, developed under the influence
of Latin and Provençal. Presumably, its poets adapted to their
own purposes the language of previous, more plebeian, Sicilian
verse, though here we are in the realm of conjecture. Its matter
followed, for the most part, the content of the Provençal lyric,
with its variations on the themes and conventions of courtly love;[1]
but the language, at least, was new. And when the school's
centre disappeared on the death of Frederick's son, Manfred,

[1] When Frederick writes

> *Dolze mea donna lo gire*
> *non è per mia volontate,*
> *che mi convene ubbidire*
> *quelli che m'a 'n potestate*

we are clearly in the realm of poetic fiction.

The *contrasto* by Cielo d'Alcamo beginning *Rosa fresca aulentissima* seems different
in tone from most of this poetry; Dante quoted (in the *De vulg. el.*, I, xii) its third line
(*Tragemi d'este focora, se t'este a bolontate*), which is full of plebeian features, and considered it to be written in ordinary Sicilian, 'quod prodit a terrigenis mediocribus',
unrefined by art. Recent scholarship presents the poet as a man not without culture
who deliberately sets out to portray two vulgar characters: hence the mixture of
aulic phrases (*rosa fresca de l'orto, donna col viso cleri*, i.e. 'dame au clair vis') with dialectal
elements (*bolontate, bolta, càrama*, etc.). These dialectal elements are used merely to
give plebeian flavour and are not attributable to a particular area.

bourgeois poets in Tuscany and Bologna were able to make use of the heritage it bequeathed to them.

What kind of language did these poets write in? Of the collections of poems written out at the end of the Duecento (or beginning of the Trecento) the most important is Vatican Codex 3793 (generally referred to as Cod. A). On its first page we find:

Notaro Giacomo

Madoña dire uiuolglio. come lamore mapreso. jnverlo grande orgolglio. cheuoi bella mostrate enōmaita. oilasso lome core. chentanta pena miso. cheuede chesimore. per benamare etenolosi jnuita.

If we separate the words from each other and introduce modern punctuation and the modern spelling for *u, v* and *gl*, we have:

> *Madonna, dire vi voglio*
> *come l'Amore m'à preso;*
> *inver lo grande orgoglio*
> *che voi, bella, mostrate, e' non m'aita.*
> *Oi lasso, lo me' core*
> *ch'è 'n tanta pena miso,*
> *che vede che si more*
> *per ben amare, e tenolosi in vita.*

This looks very much like what constituted Italian poetic language down to the nineteenth century. But if we examine it closely we shall find, not only the obvious slip *tenolosi* for *tenelosi* (=*se lo tiene*), but an imperfect rhyme *preso—miso*. The original rhyme here (*priso—miso*) is easy to reconstruct, not only from our knowledge of Sicilian, but because another early collection (Laurenziano—Rediano 9, generally known as Cod. B) has *como lamorprizo*. The Tuscan copyist of A, faced with a manuscript which had *priso*, clearly felt justified, in accordance with medieval practice, in changing it to fit his own linguistic habits, i.e. to *preso*. But he did not go so far as to put *messo* for *miso*. The change is revealed by the fact that *preso* is in rhyme position; modifications in the middle of lines are not so obvious.

The great majority of texts of the Sicilian school are in this condition. Nor is it possible now to believe, as some scholars (Caix, Gaspary, Monaci, Zingarelli, De Bartholomaeis) did in previous generations, that this confusion of forms goes back to the poets: that they, in attempting a koine, deliberately used forms belonging to the continental dialects of Italy. The theory that the original texts were tuscanized by scribes, accepted in the last century by Adolfo Bartoli, D'Ancona and D'Ovidio, was confirmed in an important, if controversial, book by G. A. Cesareo, *Le origini della poesia lirica in Italia* (Catania 1899, 2nd ed. Palermo 1924) and by I. Sanesi's study of the progressive tuscanization of the *canzonieri*. And the details of the process were further revealed by Tallgren and Parodi. But our knowledge of the original language of the poems is not entirely dependent on the reconstructions that philologists can effect from the tuscanized versions. A sixteenth-century scholar, Giovanni Maria Barbieri, copied, from a *Libro siciliano* now lost, a *canzone* by Stefano Protonotaro of Messina and two fragments by King Enzo. In Barbieri's transcription (modified here only by four slight and extremely probable corrections by Debenedetti) the first stanza of Stefano's canzone reads:

> *Pir meu cori alligrari,*
> *ki multu longiamenti*
> *senza alligranza e ioi d'amuri è statu,*
> *mi ritornu in cantari*
> *ca forsi levimenti*
> *da dimuranza turniria in usatu*
> *di lu troppu taciri.*
> *E quandu l'omu à rasuni di diri*
> *ben di' cantari e mustrari alligranza,*
> *ca, senza dimustranza,*
> *ioi siria sempri di pocu valuri.*
> *Dunca ben di' cantar onni amaduri.*

This then is the language in which the Sicilian poets wrote. In examining it we should bear in mind that it is not a complete language, but a stylization, based on Sicilian dialect, used for particular purposes. This dialect has been modified and ennobled by writers whose models in composition were Latin (an example constantly before the eyes of medieval writers) and Provençal (which was particularly closely followed in some features, since emulation of Provençal poets and development of their manner constituted the stylistic ideal of many Sicilian poets).

In their spelling *ch* had palatal value. The Bolognese notary who copied Giacomo da Lentini's *Madona, dir ve voio* kept this graphy in his text in *despiache: fache*. But *chi* also represented [kj], the result of Latin PL-. In the manuscripts this is sometimes kept, sometimes adapted, sometimes misinterpreted: the *chiacenza* that occurs (l. 113) in the *discordo* by Giacomo beginning

Dal cor mi vene is correctly tuscanized to *piagienza* in B, while A has *achia senza*.

Latin tonic short E and tonic short o do not diphthongize: *feri*, *bonu*. Latin short I and long E give, in tonic position, *i*: *vidi*, *taciri*. Short u and long o give *u*: *dundi*, *hunuri*. But the poet could also use an alternative latinizing form, which would still be different from continental Italian. Alongside *amuri*, the popular form, he could use *amori*, with the Latin vowel. But since Sicilian had (and has) only five vowels (lacking distinction between close and open *e* and close and open *o*) the pronunciation would be open: *amòri*. Words with *e* or *o*, for the spelling of which it was possible to have recourse to a latinism or provençalism, have two forms and two ways of rhyming: *amuri*, *doluri* or *amòri*, *còri*. Atonic *e* and *o*, especially in final position, give *i* and *u*: *timiri*, *placiri*; *mustrari*, *dintru*. The group cj gives *z*: *lanza*, *solazo*.

In morphology we note the alternation of *esti* with *è*, *avi* with *à*, *sapi* with *sa*, *fachi* with *fa*. The imperfect is of the type *avia*, *putia*. In the conditional we have generally the *diviria* type; but there is a small group of forms in -*ra*: *fora*; *gravara*, *sofondara*; *finera*; *partira*. On their provenance there has been disagreement: De Bartholomaeis held that they were 'continental', Debenedetti thought they were not Sicilian, Vitale considers them to be of Provençal origin. But the Latin pluperfect with conditional meaning is not found only in the continental dialects of Calabria and the Abruzzi; it is found also in Sicily. And there seems to be no good reason for doubting that these forms are indigenous. If they were an imitation of the Provençal, we should expect the ending -*era* even for the first conjugation.

In dealing with vocabulary we can take into account, not only what we find in the canzone by Stefano Protonotaro and the fragments by Re Enzo, but also the sicilianisms and the borrowings from French and Provençal presented by the other texts (though realizing that these other texts may have lost certain peculiarities in the process of tuscanization). Here are some Sicilian words: ABENTO ('peace, rest'); ADIVINIRI ('to happen'); AMMIRITATU ('rewarded'); *ghiora* ('glory'); (*i*)*ntrasatto* ('suddenly'); (*i*)*nvoglia* ('envelops'); *menna* ('breast'); *nutricari* ('feed'); *ricienta* ('rinses'); SANARI ('to cure'); *tando*, *intando* ('then'), etc.[1]

Even more important is the series of Gallo-Romance words.

[1] Those with strongest Sicilian colouring (taken from Stefano and Re Enzo) are given in capitals; the others are spelt in the way they are presented to us by the manuscripts in which they are to be found.

In the case of the French ones it is difficult to know whether they entered (more or less popular) usage in the time of the Normans or whether they are cultural or literary borrowings. In the case of the Provençal words we can be pretty certain that they are of literary origin. We should, however, bear in mind that it is often difficult to decide whether a borrowing is, in fact, French or Provençal.

The loan-words from French include *ciera* ('face'; O.F. *chière*), *cominzare*, (*i*)*ntamato* ('injured'; Fr. *entamé*; the word will be used again by Villani), *sagnare*. But there is a much fuller list of provençalisms, for they cover the whole gamut of ideas and feelings connected with courtly love: *amanza, intendanza, amistate* (and *amistanza*), *drudo, ascio, disascio, sollazzo, gioia* (and also *gio', gioi,* and *gaugio*), DULZURI, *alma, coraggio* and *corina* (both used for 'heart'), *simblanza, fazone* (Prov. *faisó*, Fr. *façon*), *speranza, dottanza, rimembranza, ballìa* ('power'), *argoglio, talento* ('desire'), *augello, pascore* ('spring'), *aigua* ('water'). Among the adjectives we have *avenente* (-*ante*), *gente* ('nice, gentle') and *genzore* ('nicer'), *corale*, LIALI, *sofretoso* ('scarce'). Among the verbs are: PLACIRI, *ciausire* ('choose, exalt'), BLASMARI, *dottare*, ALCIRI ('to kill'). Examples of adverbs are: *adesso, adessa* (at first in the sense of 'suddenly') and LONGIAMENTI.

Words from continental Italian dialects seem never to occur in the works of poets born in Sicily, only in poems by writers born on the mainland or by Siculo-Tuscans.

The poetry written by the Sicilians was admired and imitated in Tuscany. Thus the poetic language of the Sicilian poets contributed to the basis of a national poetic language. Although it lost certain of its specifically Sicilian features in the process, others influenced the habits of subsequent poets, especially in the use of rhyme. The new movement in poetry was not centred on a court, but was the work of a school of cultured bourgeois based on a number of centres: Arezzo (the home of its leader Guittone), Pisa, Lucca, Pistoia, Siena, Florence and Bologna. Linguistically, there is not much difference between the Siculo-Tuscans (Guittone, Bonagiunta and their associates) and the so-called 'poets of transition' (Chiaro Davanzati, etc.). But there is a break, a distinctly new kind of taste, in the language of the practitioners of the *stil novo*. We must remember, however, that Guinizzelli began as a Guittonian, and we shall, in fact, find Siculo-Tuscan linguistic features carried forward into the 'sweet new style'.

We have already seen how the works of the Sicilians were tuscanized by scribes; the collections of their poems that have come down to us bear, in varying degrees, the marks of this tuscanization. It is probable that those versifiers in Tuscany who set out to imitate the Sicilians in about 1250 had similar collections at their disposal, though it is possible that the degree of tuscanization may have been slighter. Now the Sicilians had, like their Provençal models, used perfect rhymes. But they had only five vowels. The Tuscans had seven vowels. When they read the works of their models in tuscanized manuscripts, they saw in them what was to them open *e* rhymed with close *e*, and open *o* rhymed with close *o*. What is more, they found examples of *u* rhymed with *o* and of *i* rhymed with *e*. They saw no reason to reject these examples, especially when they were using, in rhyme position, the same words as the poets they were imitating. In Tuscan poets we therefore find close *e* and *o* rhyming with open *e* and *o*, as in *core—maggiore*; *mostro—vostro*; *vene—pene*; *effetto—distretto*. Here, in spite of the discrepancy in sound in Tuscan pronunciation, there was no difference in spelling. And this kind of rhyme became a permanent feature of Italian poetry. Moreover, these Tuscans also used imperfect rhymes of the type *servire—avere—cherere—provedere* (Guittone, son. 17, cod. B) or *disire—piaciere—languire—miri* (Chiaro Davanzati, canz. *Molti lungo tempo anno*, cod. A), or *piaciere—servire* or *placire—servire* (Betto Mettefuoco, *Amore perché m'ai*, cod. A and B) or *fina—regina*: *s'ataupina*: *mischina*: *fina*: *camina*: *mena* (Pucciandone Martelli, canz. *Lo fermo intendimento*, cod. C), etc. Here they were following the Sicilians to the extent of 'rhyming' words which in Tuscan speech did not rhyme. Parodi maintained that, in doing so, they followed Sicilian spelling, e.g. *avire, piacire, mina*. Others believe (and Contini has recently given good reasons for this) that they wrote what amounted to imperfect rhymes. What is certain and important is the fact that they did not consider that they had licence to produce an unlimited number of rhymes of this kind (i.e. with close *e* rhyming with *i*); they considered that they could only do so in the case of those words where the Sicilians had provided precedent. Hypersicilianisms (e.g. *pena: affina* in Baldo da Pasignano in cod. A) are extremely rare.

There is a series of rhymes, which Caix held to be Bolognese-Aretine, where long -u- is treated as an -o-. Parodi pointed out that nearly all the examples belong to the *alcono, niono, ogni ono* family (for *alcuno, niuno, ognuno*), and it would seem wiser to speak of them as Guittonian rhymes. Forms like *altroi*, *coi* are probably due to copyists.

In the language of the Siculo-Tuscan lyric there is generally no diphthongization of open E and O. Thus Guittone writes *novo* in verse, but *nuovo* in prose (and in this he will be followed by Dante). The usage of contemporary documents confirms the prose version, which doubtless corresponded to Tuscan speech. The lack of diphthong in the verse tradition is due to the triple influence of Latin, Provençal and Sicilian, which continued to suggest that the undiphthongized form was nobler. We should note, however, that we also find in these poets traces of a reduction typical of the speech of southern Tuscany and Umbria: of *ie* to *i* and *uo* to *u*; Guittone has *rechire* for *rechiere*, *pui* for *puoi*. And we shall find *furi* for *fuori* even in the *Divina Commedia*.

The example of Sicilian leads to the use of the diphthong *au*, not only in those words where the *au* finds some support in Latin (*laudo*, *auso*) or Provençal (*augello*, *ciausire*), but also in *aucidere*, *aulire* and (though not consistently) *caunoscere*, *aunore*. The Tuscan poets frequently have -*r*- for -*l*- after a consonant: *prusore*, *sembrare*. Only the Pisan and Lucchese poets have -*ss*- for -*zz*-: *allegressa—messa* (Bonagiunta), *lasso—impasso* (Bacciarone).

The influence of the Sicilians is to be seen also in the verb forms (*aggio*, *saccio*, *veo*, *creo*, etc.), especially in the imperfects and conditionals in -*ia* (which, though existing in southern Tuscany, undoubtedly entered poetic usage through imitation of the Sicilians—and remained in literary usage in subsequent centuries). Conditionals in -*ra* (*fora*, -*ara*, -*era*, -*ira*) are also due to the influence of the poets of Sicily and Provence. The very rare conditional in -*era* for the first conjugation is a pure provençalism ('che morte mi *sembrera*—ogn'altra vita', Bondie Dietaiuti, A, n. 184). The composite character of this language can be judged from the fact that in a single *canzone* by Compagnetto da Prato ('L'amore fa', A, n. 88) we find three types of future: 'lassa, come *faragio*' l. 2; '*manderò* per l'amore mio' l. 23; 'gliele *dirabo* io l. 25. Alongside the usual Florentine form *manderò*, we have the sicilianizing (and southern Tuscan) form in -*aggio* and the western and southern Tuscan one in -*abbo*. We frequently find, in the Siculo-Tuscans, too, the *sono perdente* type (for *perdo*), this again through Provençal influence.

In vocabulary we note many of the provençalisms already adopted by the Sicilians, some sicilianisms, and some provençalisms of which we have no examples in the Sicilians themselves (*anta* 'shame', *barnagio* 'moral nobility', *amburo* 'ambedue', etc.). The suffixes -*anza*, -*enza*, -*ore*, -*ura*, -*aggio*, -*mento* continue to be prolific. Guittone is very fond, too, of the augmentative prefixes *sor*- (*sorbella*, etc.), *sovra*- (*sovrapiacente*, etc.) and *tra*- (*tradolze*, etc.), and his imitators follow him in this liking. There is much heavier use of latinisms than there was in the work of the Sicilians. The composite nature of the language of these poets is as obvious in their vocabulary as it was in their morphology. A single example will suffice: for 'looking-glass' they use at least five words: *miradore* (Guittone), *specchio*, *speglio* (Palamidesse di Bellendote), *spera*, *miraglio* (Bondie Dietaiuti).

Poets of this school were undoubtedly disturbed by the revolution brought about by the writers we associate with the *dolce stil novo*; Bonagiunta tells us in one of his poems that Guinizzelli 'muta la mainera' of writing poetry. Certainly, the new school's more rarefied atmosphere, mystic contemplation of woman, insistence on certain ideas of nobility, etc., was reflected in its vocabulary. But we must not forget the linguistic importance of the fact that Guinizzelli began as a Guittonian. Moreover, certain problems arise from his Bolognese birth and his formation in the cultural atmosphere of the University of Bologna. Did he write *assicura* or *asegura*, *ciò* or *ço*, *saggio* or *saço*? Did he write in the following way (as cod. A suggests)?

> *Omo chesagio nonchorre legiero*
> *ma passa egrada como vuole misura.*
> *poi ca pemsato ritene suo penzero*
> *jnfino a tanto che lo uero lasichura.*

Doubt is cast on this by the preservation of four complete versions and three incomplete versions of the same sonnet in Bolognese documents, the oldest of which was written in 1287, approximately a decade after the death of the poet. The text that Adriana Caboni has reconstructed from them reads:

> *Homo ch'è saço non corre liçero,*
> *ma pensa e grada sì con vol mesura;*
> *quand'à pensato reten so pensero*
> *de fin a tanto che 'l ver l' asegura.*

This is surely nearer to what Guinizzelli himself wrote. Yet it would be arbitrary now to try to re-emilianize the texts of his work that have come down to us. On the above extract we make only one observation. Two of the texts have *ligero*, and there seems no reason why the poet should not have written that.

But most of the *stilnovisti* were Tuscans. In their case we do not have the doubts that accompany the texts of Guinizzelli, especially after the textual and linguistic research carried out by Barbi when he was preparing his editions of Dante's *Vita Nuova* and *Rime*. In their work we can again find evidence of the persistence of Sicilian traditions; but with them sicilianisms and provençalisms play a much smaller part than with the Siculo-Tuscans. In the *stilnovisti* undiphthongized forms (*tene, pensero, core, mova*) still prevail over diphthongized forms, and *laudare* is more frequent than *lodare* (through the influence of poetic tradition and of Latin). There are still some examples of Sicilian rhymes: *vedite—sbigottite—ferite—partite* (Cavalcanti, son. *Deh spiriti ...*; here we should note that we have *vedete* in the Chig. ms. and in Vat. 3214). There are some Guittonian rhymes: *paurosi—chiosi* (Dante, son. *Degli occhi ...*); *come—lome* (Cavalcanti, canz. *Donna me prega*; this reappears in *Inf.*, X, 69, in the episode of Guido's father, and is found again in Cino, son. *Da poi che la natura ...*); *scritto—prometto—metto—intelletto* (Dante, double son., *Se Lippo amico ...*); *venta* [for *vinta*]*—penta—spenta—rappresenta* (Dante, son. *Voi donne ...*). There is possibly an echo of Guinizzelli in the Dantesque *conosciuda* (*-nuda—chiuda—druda*) in the same poem. There are, too, some Umbrian rhymes: *pui* in Dino Frescobaldi for *puoi* (as well as for *poi*), etc.

In vocabulary we note the frequent use of certain words with which the new school made great play: *nobiltà, onestà, gentilezza, pietà, piacere*, etc. Certain words which had already been used by the Provençal writers and by the Guittonians, like *mercede* (sometimes *merzede*) and *valore* are given new value. Prominence is given, too, to *angele, angiolette, angelico, angelicato, spiriti* and *spiritelli*, not to mention the *forosette, pasturelle, giovanette* and *giovanelle* whose *atterelli* and the aspect of whose *labbia* had, it seems, such importance for the poets. We still find a considerable number of words in *-anza, -enza* and *-aggio*, continuing the corresponding series so beloved of Sicilians and Siculo-Tuscans. (But there is considerable variety in the extent of their use by individual poets; Lapo Gianni is 'archaic' in this respect.) And there are scores of words belonging to the same tradition: *beltate, disio* (and *disiro*), *martiro*; *adastare, agenzare, gabbare, gecchire*; *manto*, etc. But *leggiadro*, which, for Guittone, had the pejorative sense of 'proud, frivolous' (in conformity with the Provençal *leujaria* 'frivolity'), assumes with the *stilnovisti* a favourable meaning.

The adherence of Dante to the *stil novo* and Petrarch's connections with its tradition, gave currency to its usage in the following centuries; this is what confers such importance on its distillation of the language of its predecessors and on the form it gave to literary Tuscan. There were other voices in Tuscan poetry at the time, those of the poets who, as Dante put it, 'differunt a magnis poetis, hoc est regularibus' (*De vulg. el.*, II, iv, 3). Some of them wrote important poems, some interest us for the evidence they supply of the development of the spoken language. But their example did not give notable linguistic results. In this matter at least we can lump together such diverse versifiers as the realistic and satirical poets of Florence and Siena, the writers of popular and amorous compositions and of political *canzoni*, and the authors of allegorical and didactic verse like the *Tesoretto*, the *Favolello*, the *Fiore* and the *Intelligenza*. The poets whose example counted for later poets were the lyric poets.

Umbria in the thirteenth century gave rise to religious movements which won wide support and spread to the rest of Italy: Franciscanism, the *Alleluia* of 1233 and the movement of the Flagellants (1260). We should therefore enquire whether these had any influence on the formation of the language and whether, through them, it acquired any particularly Umbrian features.

Of the writings of St. Francis in the vulgar tongue there remains but one: that referred to as the *Cantico di Frate Sole* or *Cantico delle creature* or *Laudes creaturarum*, and dictated by him in 1225 or 1226. The words were intended to be sung; unfortunately, we do not know to what tune. The text is in assonantal prose in an ennobled Umbrian to which very numerous Biblical reminiscences lend dignity. It begins:

> *Altissimo, onnipotente, bon Signore,*
> *tue so le laude, la gloria e l'onore e onne benedizione.*
> *A te solo, Altissimo, se confano*
> *e nullo omo ene digno te mentovare.*

Certain features in this work are clearly Umbrian, e.g. the third pers. plurals, *so, sostengo*. But other characteristics of Umbrian are missing (none of the manuscripts, for example, has *iocunno* or *iocunnu* in l. 19; they all have *iocundo*), presumably because they were felt to be evident deformations of Latin and too plebeian for so solemn a composition. Unfortunately, the very numerous manuscripts do not help us to decide exactly how Umbrian the original was. Final -*u* (*altissimu*), for instance, occurs only eight times in the most important codex, which in 19 cases gives *o* (having *altissimu* in the first line, *altissimo* in the third); one cannot therefore know whether it belonged to the language of St. Francis.

The most important of the Umbrian poets who wrote after St. Francis was Jacopone da Todi. In his language, as in his poetry, popular and learned currents flow together. Franca Ageno, using principally two manuscripts that originated in Todi itself, has given us an edition of his work that allows us to be reasonably clear about the language he used. It has several features that belong to the central dialects, which are analogous to those of Latium and not found in Florentine. Phonological examination reveals considerable evidence of metaphony, treatment of ND as *nn* (*spenne, monno, profonno*), GN as *nn* (*lenno* for *legno, penno* for *pegno, rennare*) and development of *a-* before R (*aracomanno, arfreddato*). Morphologically, we note enclitic possessives of the type *marìtota*, third pers. plurals like *vengo*, futures of the type *à penare* for *penerà* and pluperfects with conditional meaning. The paradigm of the verb *essere* in the pres. indic. is *so, ei* or *si, è* or *ene, semo* or *simo, sete* or *site, so*. The syntax reveals some clearly individual features: imperatives used as nouns ('bello me costa el tuo *ride*', XVI =*riso*) and infinitives with the value of gerunds ('abbrevio mia detta 'n questo luogo *finare*', XXXVI).

In Jacopone's vocabulary we note some words that are specifically Umbrian (*carace, cotozare*, etc.), others that are paralleled in some dialects of southern Tuscany (*encamato, entrasatto, finente, osolare*=*origliare*), and many that are used in large areas of central Italy (*cetto* 'soon', *oprire* 'to open', *peco* 'sheep'). He takes considerable liberties in adding suffixes to nouns (*amoranza, lascivanza; albergata, lamentata; assaiato, gloriato; grassìa*, etc.) and adjectives (li freddi *nevile*, LXI); indeed he has no scruples in adding the suffixes that are needed for his rhymes ('lo 'nferno se fa *celestìo*, prorompe l'amor *frenesìo*', XLVI, vv. 25-26; ''ngavinato al *catenone* . . ., pò tener lo mio *cestone* . . ., per empir mio *stomacone* . . ., estampiando el mio *bancone* . . ., a pagar lo mio *scottone* . . ., starian fissi al *magnadone* . . ., mentre ha a collo lo *scudone* . . ., gir *bizocone*', LV). We are not surprised thus to find, alongside many latinisms here attested for the first time (so far as is yet known) and destined to win a permanent place in the language (*angustiare, appetire*, *balsamo*, etc.), a number of individual adoptions (*decetto* 'deceived', *derenzione* 'separation' [from life], *morganato* 'condition of inferiority in a marriage', *è opporto* 'it is necessary', *preliare*, *prestolo* 'I wait', *puella*, etc.). The preceding love lyric, too, is not without influence: this is shown, not only by borrowings like *entennenza* 'love', but by the use of several rhymes of the Sicilian type.

Jacopone's language, like that of Umbrian religious poetry generally, is extremely interesting. But it did not affect the mainstream of Italian linguistic development, and it is not important in the history of the language in the following centuries.

When Jacopone's poems were transcribed in Tuscany they underwent the usual process of adaptation. This is how *lauda* XIX appears in the London manuscript (Brit. Mus., Addit. Ms. 16567) which is, in fact, the best:

Figli neputi frate rennete | lomal tollecto loqual uo lasai
Uui lo promecteste alo patrino | de rennerlo tucto e non uenir meno |
ancor non medeste | per lalma un ferlino
de tanta moneta | quanteo guadangnai.

Here are the same lines in a Tuscan manuscript (Ricc. 2841):

Figli et nipoti et frati | rendetel maltollecto
loquale io tapinello uilassciai |
Voi promectesti aluvostro patrino | di renderlo tucto e non uenir meno |
Ancora nonne desti pellanima unfrullino
di tanta moneta | che peruoi guadagniai.

The peculiarities of the Umbrian poets did not have the prestige once enjoyed by those of the Sicilians; to the Tuscans they probably seemed plebeian. Half a century had passed and Tuscan poetry was a good deal more mature.

The northern cities, too, had their share of religious movements (not all of them orthodox) and of poets who wrote with moral, didactic and religious ends in view.

The Cremonese notary Gherardo Patecchio, in the 606 alexandrines of his *Splanamento de li Proverbii de Salomone*, addresses his moral observations and advice, not to 'li savi', 'q'ig sa ben ço q'ig dé,—anz per comunal omini qe non san ogna lé' (14-15):

> *Quel qe de povertad mena çoi e legreça*
> *val des dig ric avari c'a tesor e riqeça*
>
> (434-35)

Pegr' om, voia o no voia, s'adovra de nient;
mai l'om qe ben s'adovra, serà ric e mainent

(457-58).

This *Splanamento* is preserved in the excellent Saibante codex, now
at Berlin. Unfortunately, the same author's *Noie* can be read only
in a fifteenth-century transcription that has reduced its linguistic
value almost to nothing.

The Saibante codex also preserves the *Libro* of another poet
who was probably likewise Cremonese: Uguccione da Lodi. The
Libro consists of two parts (in different metres) that Ezio Levi
entitled the *Libro* and the *Istoria*.[1] The poet's themes are the
typical ones of medieval ascetic literature: the wickedness of the
world, the imminence of death and damnation, etc.:

> *Avaricia en sto segolo   abunda e desmesura,*
> *tradhiment et engano   avolteri e soçura.*
> *Çamai no fo la çente   sì falsa ni sperçura,*
> *qe de l'ovra de Deu   unca no mete cura,*
> *del magno re de gloria   qe sta sopra l'altura,*
> *quel per cui se mantien   ognunca creatura.*

(130-15).

The *Sermone* of Pietro da Barsegapè (2440 lines in alexandrines
and *novenari*) was completed by the author in 1274 and is preserved in the Archinto manuscript in the Brera Library. The
language is an ennobled Milanese, very similar to that of Bonvicino. Lines 25-38, in which the poet tells us what subjects he will
deal with, are as follows:

> *E clamo marçé al me segniore*
> *Patre Deo creatore*
> *ke posa dir(e) sermon divin*
> *e començà a trar(e) a fin*
> *como Deo a fat(o) lo mondo*
> *e com(o) de terra fo l(o) hom(o) formo;*
> *cum el desces de cel in terra*
> *in la vergen regal polcella;*
> *e cum el sostene passion*
> *per nostra grand(e) salvation;*
> *e cum verà al dì de l' ira*
> *là o serà la gran(de) roina;*
> *al peccator(e) darà grameça*
> *lo iusto avrà grande alegreça. . . .*

---

[1] Its most recent editor, R. Broggini, attributes the *Istoria* to a pseudo-Uguccione.

In the last decades of the Duecento Bonvicino de la Riva wrote his *contrasti* and his expositional, narrative and didactic poems, using alexandrines grouped into quatrains. The poet's assurance in the use of an ennobled Milanese, the good manuscript tradition and the care with which the texts, versification and language have been studied by Mussafia, Salvioni and Contini, have made his works the best known of this kind. The spelling in the most satisfactory codex (that of S. Maria Incoronata, now in Berlin) is to some extent etymological, since metre and rhyme suggest that some of the sounds for which symbols are given must have disappeared. Here is a quatrain of the *contrasto* between a rose and a violet. The letters in brackets indicate sounds that had dropped out:

> *Anchora dis(e) la rosa:　　Eo pairo intro calor,*
> *in temp(o) convenievre,　　ke paren i oltre flor,*
> *il temp(o) ke (l)i lissinio(l)i　　cantan per grand amor;*
> *i olce(ll)i me fan versiti,　　k'en plen de grand dolzor*
> 　　　　　　　　　　　　　　　　　　(85-88).

From the pen of Giacomino da Verona we have 280 alexandrines on the subject of *Gerusalemme celeste* and 340 on *Babilonia infernale*; the codex in the Marciana that contains them also has other poems with a similar background. In the *Gerusalemme* and the *Babilonia* there are some clearly Veronese features. In the following lines, for example, we note an unetymological paragogic *o*, not only in *someiento*, but also in *diso*:

> *Lo re de questa terra　　si è quel angel re'*
> *de Lucifer ke diso:　　"En cel(o) metrò el me se';*
> *eo serò someiento　　a l'alto segnor De' ",*
> *dond'el caçì da cel　　cun quanti ge çè dre.*
> 　　　　　　　　　　　*(Babil., 25-28)*

The *Detto dei Villani* of Matazone da Calignano (Pavia) has no marked dialectal characteristics (possibly only *mazale* for *maiale* 'pig'). The *Bona çilosia* or *Fé lial*, long known to scholars as the *Lamento della sposa padovana*, seems to be a fragment of a poem dealing moralistically with aspects of love. Its language is an artistically elaborated Paduan. The Anonymous Genoese, who wrote at the end of the thirteenth or the beginning of the fourteenth century, alternated between enthusiasm for victories over the Venetians and moral and religious advice. This is how he counsels the man who is about to take a wife:

*Quatro cosse requer
en dever prender moier:
zo è saver de chi è naa,
e como el è acostuma;
e la persona dexeiver;
e dote conveneiver.
Se queste cosse ge comprendi
a nome de De la prendi.*

The efforts made by the authors of these poems to refine their dialects, and the fact that the northern dialects have certain characteristics in common, should not be allowed to persuade us that there was a Veneto-Lombard koine. Undoubtedly, there were linguistic exchanges and attempts at levelling certain features; one thinks of the epithetic *o* of Veronese (which was a reconstruction to replace a final vowel that had previously been lost) or of the co-existence of the conditional formed with the perfect and the conditional formed with the imperfect (e.g. *porave* and *devria* in Barsegapè). But these texts have widely different physiognomies, which vary in accordance with the dialects of the cities in which they originated: in the Lombard texts CT>*g* (*benedigi, condugio, confegi*), while only the Cremonese diphthongize ĕ to *ie*, and only the Milanese and Genoese have L>*r*: *gora, perigoro* (Bonvicino), *povoro* (Anon. Gen.). In short, these writers evince no strong tendency to move beyond their literarily elaborated vernaculars in the direction of a common language.[1] Political divisions were not conducive to such a process. Nor was any one of these texts brilliant enough to stand out as a model.

This lowly literature continued into the Trecento and the first half of the Quattrocento. It was not known to the Tuscans, and they were unaffected by it.

We turn now to prose. First we note that the vernacular was used more and more for practical purposes in this period. The collections made by Schiaffini and Castellani provide us with ample opportunity of examining this type of writing in various places in Tuscany; they include, among other things, account books, tax lists and letters containing commercial and political

[1] We must not, of course, be deceived by the levelling which is due, not to the author, but to the fact that the text has gone through several transcriptions which have well nigh obliterated its original features except in rhyme position. When Wiese edited the versified legend of St. Margaret, basing his edition on eight manuscripts, he thought it was Lombard. Later Salvioni maintained it was Veronese, only to change this to Placentine still later.

observations. There are, too, some inscriptions from this time. The teaching of Latin in lay schools made use of the vulgar tongue: *vendor* is explained by *fire vendù*, while as an example we find *Però fo despoià de le vestimenta dal maistro*. The chronicles of the period, brief and schematic, can be classed with utilitarian writing of this kind. Narrative prose, as we see it in the *Novellino*, is also simple and popular; but in it, we can see the lexical and stylistic influence of French and Provençal models. While the bestiaries echo the Latin of the *Physiologus*, Ristoro d'Arezzo provides us with the first example of original scientific prose.

In the formation of an artistically elaborated prose a notable part was played by Bologna and its University, where the *ars dictandi* flourished. That they were required to be able to read their documents in the vernacular as well as in Latin led notaries to pay attention to both languages. But a more important factor in the search for elegance was the practice, which grew up in the northern and central cities of Italy, of having the *podestà, capitani,* etc., harangue the public. While some of the famous professors at Bologna, like Boncompagno da Signa or Bene da Firenze, confined themselves to teaching the construction of ornate Latin prose, Guido Fava decided to apply their kind of skill to Italian. His *Gemma purpurea* and *Parlamenti ed Epistole* provide us with formulas for letters in the vulgar tongue and possibly represent the first real attempt to found literary prose in the vernacular. In spite of the difficulties that attend reconstruction of his text, we can see that his prose had certain northern features (the voicing of intervocalic consonants in *amigo, seguro, tenudo, fiada, savere,* the treatment of the palatal as in *çura*) and some characteristics of Old Bolognese (the behaviour of *s* before *i*: *sci, scia*) alongside Latin influences (correct and hypercorrect use of double consonants). Its possibly Tuscan elements (the treatment of atonic vowels in *signure, signoria,* the presents *diamo* and *sciamo,* the epithetic form *ene,* etc.) are the subject of controversy and doubt. Moreover, the Tuscan features in this kind of writing were probably due less to Tuscan literary prestige (which would be difficult to explain at this time) than to the large number of Tuscans studying and teaching at Bologna and to the conviction that Tuscan was nearer Latin than were other Italian dialects. Guido Fava's dependence on the Latin practitioners of the *ars dictandi* is obvious in his use of the *cursus,* of parallelisms, and of the other devices with which he teaches his pupils to 'favellare ornata mente e dire belleça de parole' (*Parlam.* 93, Gaudenzi

p. 159). Works of this kind continued to be produced in considerable number throughout the century and at the beginning of the next, mainly by Bolognese. Fra Guidotto, in his *Fiore di retorica* gives rules for 'favella giudiciale'. Matteo dei Libri writes '*dicerie*' in the vernacular. Giovanni da Viterbo, in his *Liber de regimine civitatum*, written probably in 1253, furnishes *podestà* and Captains of the People with outlines of speeches in Latin and Italian: 'In primis, sedato rumore populi, petat audiri, quod sic fieri consuevit: "Noi faimo pregu alla cavallaria et al popolo et a ttutta l'altra bona gente, la quale ene en quistu arengu . . .".' The language is an ennobled Umbrian, difficult to localize precisely.

A notable attempt at composing prose of elaborate elegance was made by Guittone d'Arezzo. His letters, even if addressed to private individuals, are 'open letters', moral dissertations in rhythmic language constructed with all the tricks that study of the *ars dictandi* suggested, the various kinds of *cursus* and etymological figures among them. He has been described as a clumsy, but tireless and courageous, innovator, both in his *canzoni* and his letters. Certainly he spared no effort to produce a solemn and learned form of writing; it must be admitted, however, that he was often prolix, not infrequently obscure, and sometimes vacuous. It could be argued, too, that the time and language were not ripe for such a venture. There was still much spadework to be done; people had to get used to reading the vernacular.

In this matter importance attaches to the vulgarizations and translations of Latin and French works, which were numerous in northern and central Italy, rare in southern Italy, and especially abundant in Tuscany. Apart from utilitarian translations, like those of statutes, they included rhetorical, moral, political and historical works, of which we shall mention a few. Brunetto Latini freely paraphrased, in his *Rettorica*, the first seventeen books of the *De Inventione* of Cicero. He kept close to the simplicity of narrative prose, and his writing is clear, if not firmly organic. Andrea da Grosseto and the Pistoiese Soffredi del Grazia turned the moral treatises of Albertano da Brescia into the vulgar tongue, the first with a surer stylistic touch, the second with a more marked dialectal colour (and Fantino da San Friano's version is still unpublished). Bono Giamboni translated Orosius, Vegetius and others from Latin and the *Tresor* of Brunetto Latini from French. Taddeo Alderotti translated (badly, in Dante's view) the *Nicomachean*

Ethics of Aristotle (working from Latin, of course). There were Lucchese or Pisan versions of the *Navigatio Sancti Brendani*, the *Thesaurus Pauperum* and of those passages from the *Speculum historiale* of Vincent de Beauvais that go under the title *Fiore e vita di filosofi*. Two Romans translated the *Liber Historiarum Romanorum*; a third version is markedly tuscanized. Many books of the Bible, too, were translated in this period for the use of merchants and artisans. There were also very numerous translations and (more or less free) adaptations from the French—tales from the cycles of antiquity (Troy, Thebes, Caesar) and Arthurian romances among them. Some Latin works were translated into Italian from French versions; an example is the *Disciplina clericalis* of Petrus Alphonsus.

In most of these texts local colouring was very strong. In style, of course, much depended, not only on the structure and degree of complication of the original, but also on the capacity of the author. But the general result of this considerable practice was that the language acquired a firmer periodic structure and a wider vocabulary. Sometimes modern terms were substituted, with curious effect, for concepts of the ancient world (*citharoedus=giullare, iurisconsulti=savi di ragione, respublica=comune*). In numerous other instances translation brought new items (which we shall list in the appropriate place) into Italian vocabulary.

We can now attempt a brief summary of the main linguistic features of this period.[1] In doing so we shall be almost exclusively concerned with developments in central Italy. It is of the utmost importance, too, that we should bear in mind, in making a survey of this kind, the differences between the usages of particular localities (as preserved, say, in texts of a utilitarian nature) and that of verse or artistic prose (where there is always some degree of deviation from ordinary language).

Spelling still shows great variety. In the case of sounds that medieval Latin did not possess (those we now represent with *cio, ciu, gio, giu, che, chi, ghe, ghi, gl*, and voiceless *z* in *za, zo, zu*) recourse is had to various expedients and usage is slow to settle. *K* is still frequent and alternates irregularly with *c*: in the *Capitoli* of the Compagnia d'Orsanmichele (1294) we get *chiesa* and *kiesa*;

---

[1] There is no work that gives a full treatment of them. But much help can be got from Bartoli's grammatical survey at the end of Savj-Lopez and Bartoli's *Altitalienische Chrestomathie*, from Wiese's *Altitalienisches Elementarbuch* and from the grammatical section of Monaci's *Crestomazia*. For Florentine we have the excellent introductions to Schiaffini's *Testi fiorentini* and Castellani's *Nuovi testi fiorentini*.

in the Laur.-Red. cod. of Guittone's letters *k* occurs only in
karissimo, and so on. (In northern Italy and Sicily, on the other
hand, *ch* occasionally still represents a palatal). *K* and *q* for
velar *g* (*Kerardi, quaddannio*, Pistoia 1259) lose ground, as does
the still rarer *c* for palatal *g* (*Ciunta, avantacio*, in the same text).
Some peculiarities can be precisely localized. *Th* with the sound
z [ts] belongs to western Tuscany (Pisa, Lucca, Pistoia) e.g.
vethosa for *vezzosa* (Schiaffini, *Testi*, x) while the Florentine *Conti
di banchieri* have *Matzingo*, etc., and the *Libro del Chiodo* (1268)
gives us *Veczosus*. (In northern Italy *th* is found at Brescia and
elsewhere, used probably for a voiced or voiceless interdental.
And in Lombardy in the second half of the Duecento *dh* is
frequent). There is, as one would expect, constant oscillation
between etymological spellings (preferred in learned texts) and
phonetic spellings (commoner in popular texts). Etymological *h*
is rather frequent (*homo*), but it disappears when the word is
preceded by a proclitic (*lomo*). Dante shows his preference for
etymological spellings in the *Convivio*: '[Epicuro] disse questo
nostro fine essere *voluptade* (non dico *voluntade*, ma scrivola per
p' (IV, vi, 11). There is so much oscillation, even in Tuscany,
in indicating consonantal doubling, particularly in certain
positions (e.g. after the prefix *a-*) that we are left in doubt as to
whether we are dealing with a question of spelling or of phonetics.

In Florentine we find diphthongs (*ie* and *uo*) from Latin ĕ
and ŏ in free syllables, even after the group consonant+*r* (*priego,
triema, pruova, truova*). In *figliolo* there is usually no diphthong,
and this is the case occasionally after other palatals. The reduction
of *uo* to *u* (as in *furi, figliulo, Ceriulo, Cavicciuli*) is Aretine—Cortonese—Umbrian, and in Florentine it occurs only in sporadic
examples which have their origin in that region. Reduction of
ie to *i* (cf. *priga, lita* in Jacopone) is even rarer. Numerous undiphthongized forms (of the type *novo, vene*) appear in poetry
under the triple influence of Latin, Provençal and Sicilian. Forms
without the typical Florentine anaphonesis (i.e. forms like *con-
seglio, someglio, ponto, onghia*) surround Florence on all sides. The
loss of *i* in descending diphthongs (*preite* becoming *prete*) takes
place about half-way through the century. The diphthongizing
of *o* and *u* to *au* in initial syllables (*aulire, aunore, ausignuolo,
rausignuolo*, etc.) is found only in the literary language and is due
to imitation of Sicilian and Provençal writers. We should note
that in atonic syllables the change *ar>er* (*loderò*) is typically
Florentine, while in Sienese we have its opposite (*er>ar: vivare*).

The syncope in *avrò, dovrò, potrò* took place towards the middle of the Duecento. The diphthong -*ia*- in atonic position becomes -*ie*- (*Bietrice, vie più; sie, sieno*; also *Die sa*). In the last decades of the century *ogni* overcomes *ogne*. Among consonantal phenomena we note that voicing of intervocalic voiceless consonants is commoner than it is to be later (i.e. at this period we have *imperadore, metade, segondo, savere*) and that it is found more frequently in artistic prose than in utilitarian documents. The reduction of -RJ- to -*i*- [j] led to the paradigm sing. *denaio* pl. *denari* (e.g. in the *Tavola di Riccomanno Iacopi*). But in numerous words we have semi-learned reduction to -*r*- (*contraro, memora, Grigoro, Melora*). Prosthetic *i*- before *s* impure (*e*- in Siena, etc.) is of almost constant occurrence.

We note that the great majority of nouns belongs to the three types that correspond to the first, second and third declensions of Latin. But there is also a number of survivals of the fifth in Tuscany (*merigge; adornezze, altezze, bellezze, face* in Guittone) with more in the northern and southern dialects. Apart from those survivals of the nominative case that are still with us (*uomo, sarto, orafo, moglie*, etc.) we note at this period *tràito* and *tràito* ('traitor'), *èdima* ('week') and the adjective *maggio* (for *maggiore* 'bigger'). There are also the semi-learned examples like *maiesta, poverta* and learned proper names like *Cato*, etc. Vocatives like *figliuole* (Dante) and *Criste* (Bonvicino) seem semi-learned. Learned, too, are the genitive singulars so frequent in notarial usage (*la figluola Guidi Tinaçi, lo kapitale Arriki*, etc.) and the genitive plurals in -*oro* crystallized in certain formulas and place-names (but also extended occasionally to nouns in -*a*, as in *regno femminoro*). There are some oscillations in the plural of words whose stems end in velars or palatals (*cuoci* 'cuochi', *cronice* 'cronache', etc.). There are still examples at this time in Tuscan texts of plurals in -*ora* (*bustora, campora, pratora, luogora*); but this type is more firmly rooted and more numerous in the south. The gender of *amore* and *fiore* in the old lyrics is often feminine (on account of Provençal influence). As for the article, *lo* is still the predominant form. But *il*, which was previously admissible only after a word ending with a vowel, becomes autonomous (*Il marito è morto*, Florence 1277, in Castellani, *Nuovi testi*, p. 368). Similarly in the plural we find *li* (more rarely, but also before a consonant, *gli*) and *i*, now autonomous. The singular *el* and plur. *e'* belong to the western dialects, but we find some examples in Florence. In southern Tuscan (and Umbrian) we have the type *in elle sale* (Guittone), *in ella croce*

(Jacopone), *en nella vigna* (Umbro-Tuscan Bestiary). Some organic comparatives in the early poets are due to Provençal: *genzore* (=*più gentile*), *forzore* ('stronger'). In *plusore* French and Provençal influences converge. The pronouns *meve* (*mevi*) and *nui* come into the language of the Siculo-Tuscans from Sicilian; the first disappears, but the second persists in the language of poetry down to the time of Manzoni. *Eglino* (*egliro*) and *elleno* (*ellono*) are due to analogy with verb forms. In pairs of atonic pronouns the *mi ne* gives way to the *me ne* type a little after 1250; the order *lo mi* begins to yield to *me lo* only towards the end of the century and persists for long after that time. In the present tense of the verb the poetic forms *aggio, deggio, saccio* are due to the Sicilians. *Abbo* (with variant *abo*) belongs to western Tuscan dialects, but there are examples of it in Florentine literary texts (Brunetto, Dante). In the future, apart from the normal forms in -*ò*, we have examples of -*aggio*, -*abbo*, -*abo*. In the imperfect the forms *savamo, savate* (for *eravamo, eravate*) will live on throughout the fifteenth century. The imperfect in -*ia* of -*ere* verbs is probably indigenous (being produced by closure of *e* in hiatus), but its expansion in the poetic language at Florence is due to Sicilian influence. In the past definite we often have weak forms where strong forms were later to prevail (*nascé*, Brunetto; *toglié*, Giamboni; *tacette*, Dante, etc.) and vice versa (*potti, cretti*). In the subjunctive *dea stea* are almost constant in Florence. The paradigm *che tu favelli* (I conj.), *che tu conduche* (other conjs.) is normal in Florence in the second half of the Duecento and is found in Dante, though, when he wrote, general usage had changed (see Ch. V). In the conditional, alongside the popular Tuscan paradigm formed with the perfect (-*ebbi*, -*ei*), we find in poetry the paradigm formed with the imperfect (-*ia*). We also have some conditionals (*fora*) from the Latin pluperfect. In the imperative in peripheric Tuscany the *crede* type is normal, and we find some examples of it in Florence.

The syntactic physiognomy of Italian is already clearly distinguished from its neo-Latin background and, save for a few features, it will remain stable. It should be stressed, however, that the periodic structure varies enormously from more or less popular narrative prose (of the kind we get in the *Novellino*) to learned prose based on Latin models (like that of Guittone). Here we shall limit ourselves to noting those constructions in Duecento Italian which are destined to disappear or be much weakened in the following century. *Dio* is used in some phrases with the meaning of 'to God, of God': *se Dio piace* (Sienese letter, 1260) *l'amistà del mondo è Dio nemica* (Guittone, letter XXXVI, p. 41 Meriano). And *la Dio mercé* will persist for centuries. The construction without preposition, limited to proper names, like *la gente Gieso Cristo* (*Fiore*), *il nodo Salamone* (Dante, sonnet to Forese) *il porco Sant'Antonio* (Dante, *Par.*, XXIX, 124), is to be connected with genitives of notarial type that have already been mentioned (*lo kapitale Arriki*, etc.) and will continue into the following centuries in the type *in casa i Frescobaldi, Piazza San Marco*. Other intensive words are admitted with superlatives: 'Gorgias Leontino, il più antichissimo rettorico' (Brunetto, *Rettorica*, c. 38); 'Cassandra cominciò a fare sì grandissimo pianto' (*Istor. troiana*, ed. Gorra). The indeterminate third pers. pron. is often indicated by *uomo, l'uomo*, but since *uomo* has always borne its full meaning 'man', there is at no stage in Italian a complete grammaticalization, as in the case of the Fr. *on*. The enclitic possessive, which in the following centuries will be restricted to southern and central areas, is still alive in Tuscany: examples from Florentine are *mógliama* ('my wife') and *càsasa* ('his house') (Castellani, *Nuovi Testi*, Gloss.). The indefinite *tutto* is frequently used without an article: 'a quella ch'ave *tuto* 'nsegnamento' (Rinaldo d'Aquino). The comparative may have its complement in a possessive: 'quand'omo è vinto da *un suo migliore*' (Guido delle Colonne); this is the type seen again in Dante's 'delli altri *miei miglior*' (*Purg.*, XXVI, 98). The verb *solere* is used in the present with the value of an imperfect: 'E la rica alegranza c'aver *soglio*' (Bondie Dietaiuti), probably on the model of Provençal. The passive can be formed, not only with parts of the verb *essere* and those of *fieri* added to the paradigm of *essere* (*fia, fiano*), but also with *venire* and *divenire*: 'e tal è che non mai *venta dovene*' (Guittone, 'Ai lasso', 41). In pairs of adverbs we frequently find the type *villana ed aspramente* (*Novellino*). We should note *fiore* used with adverbial meaning ('a trifle'; negatively 'nothing at all'): 'sé, ned amico, nè Dio guarda *fiore*' (Guittone). As is well known, several forms converge in the conjunction *che*; *ca* (<QUAM) still survives, not only in the poems of the Sicilians, but in those of the Genoese and the Tuscans. In Duecento and Trecento texts parahypotaxis is frequent: 'E cacciando in tale maniera dall'ora di prima infino all'ora di vespero, *e* allora pervenne a una fontana' (*Trist. Ricc.* Parodi, p. 3). Certain absolute constructions tend to become fixed formulas: 'lo Re d'onni rege . . .—fatto s'è sponso voi, *la grazia sua*' (Guittone, lett. X), 'e, *grazia di Dio*, non poté' (Schiaffini,

Testi, p. 104). There is almost complete observance of what has come to be called the Law of Tobler and Mussafia.[1]

We must now consider briefly the growth of vocabulary in the three centuries that follow the first appearance of Italian texts, that is approximately in the period 950-1300. It can be estimated that the 4,000 or 5,000 words used before A.D. 1000 had become ten to fifteen thousand three hundred years later; by that time the vernacular was learning to deal with philosophical, scientific and literary subjects. We shall, of course, have to take into account developments outside, as well as inside, Tuscany. Some words, born or adopted in various regions of Italy at this time, later became part of the national language: such are *molo* and *darsena* from Genoa, *arsenale* and *catast(ic)o* from Venice, *taccuino* from Salerno, *portolano* from Palermo. The most stable section of vocabulary is still, of course, that formed by hereditary words transmitted by previous generations. But, occasionally, some of them disappear or become semantically degraded. Thus Lat. CALIGARIUS, still alive, if not very flourishing, in some northern dialects (Ven. *caleghèr*, etc.), at Florence, in the form *galigaio*, first assumed the meaning 'tanner' and then disappeared. Words of Germanic origin lose some ground, especially on account of the renaissance of Roman law: *libero* gains on *franco*, etc.

Innumerable words are coined. Alongside hereditary suffixes (for nouns *-aio*, *-ore*, *-acchio*, *-oio*, *-ura*, *-ia*, *-mento*, *-zione*, etc.) some suffixes of foreign origin appear, notably *-iere* and *-aggio* from Provençal and French. For adjectives, alongside *-oso*, *-ano*, *-agno*, we have *-ale*, *-esco*, *-ingo*. And for verbs we note the multiplication of *-eggiare*. There is a proliferation of the prefixes *a-*, *in-*, *dis-*, *s-*, etc., which prove useful, moreover, in the formation of parasynthetic words (*allibrare*, *indenaiato*, *sbarbare*). Numerous nouns, both masculine and feminine, derive from verbs (*comincio*, *estimo*, *frodo*, *lascio*, etc., *dura*, *mena*, *monta* 'sum, total', etc.). Compounds of various kinds are not lacking (*fattibello*, *tecomeco*, etc.), and some lively examples are provided by nicknames (e.g. *Legalotre*, Lucca 1076, etc.). In the periods for which we have most information, and especially when we have literary texts, we can observe certain fashions and individual tastes; one thinks of the fortune enjoyed

---

[1] This states that in Old Italian, when a main clause begins with a verb, pronominal enclisis (e.g. *videmi*) is obligatory and proclisis (*mi vide*) impermissible. This applies even when the verb is preceded by *e* and *ma* (*E videmi*; *Ma videmi*). In coordinate clauses the rule is less rigorous. And enclisis is not obligatory when the main clause is preceded by a gerund or a subordinate clause: 'Vedendolo (Quando lo vidi), dissigli *or* gli dissi' (or, in Old Italian: 'Vedendolo, sì gli dissi').

by the *dolzore, riccore, calura, laidura* types and by the weak past
participle substantivized with abstract value (*turbato, perduta*)
in the late Duecento. Some of the new words are not without
humour: such is *scarsella* to denote what is always short of
money, 'a pocket, a purse'.

Of the many semantic changes of the period we can, of course,
quote only a few examples. We should record, first of all, the name
of that typical institution of medieval Italy, the *Comune*. And *popolo*
came to be used as synonymous with 'democratic regime'. The
symbol of the *Comune* was the *carroccio* (found at Milan in the
eleventh, and at Florence in the thirteenth, centuries). The
political centre of the city bears various names: the Milanese
Broletto was used in many northern centres. The name *podestà*
(which until the following century was feminine, *la podestà*) was,
like the institution it denoted, widespread. *Contado* 'land subject to
a count' came to mean the countryside subject to the *comune*,
and *contadino* a 'worker on the land'. The circulation of money
gave rise to a rich vocabulary: *ragione*, came to mean 'account,
book-keeping' and from it *ragioniere* 'accountant' was derived.
Other words adapted to accountancy were *saldare, scontare,
cambio secco*, etc. *Monte* (in Sienese letters of the thirteenth century)
refers to an accumulation of capital. *Tavola* in the Duecento in
Florence was the usual name for the money-lender's counter;
in the Trecento the word *banco* will prevail, and this, with its
derivative *banchiere*, will enjoy international currency. The
Church's attitude to usury led to the use of euphemisms. Such is
the use of the word *interesse* for 'interest' (used originally for the
length of the period between loan and restitution). *Dono* was
adopted in an attempt to make the transaction seem a gift;
merito is a metaphor from the spheres where labours lead to
reward. Coins presented a various nomenclature: *agostaro* (Lat.
augustalis), *aquilino* or *aguglino* (derived from *aquila*), *fiorino* (der.
from *fiore*), *ducato* (from the incription on Venetian coins), etc.
The application of *frate* and *suora* to members of religious orders
and their restriction to ecclesiastical usage had the semantic
consequence that *fratello* and *sorella* came to be the normal words
for 'brother' and 'sister'. *Pietanza*, apart from meaning 'pity'
('Villana morte che nonn a pietanza': Giacomino Pugliese)
means also 'food given to the friars on certain occasions' (as a
consequence of bequests, etc.). The word *grammatica* came to
refer to Latin; in contradistinction *lingua materna* was used for the
vernacular. The verb *compitare* may refer equally to arithmetical

calculations ('trentaquattro soldi ci kompitano' Schiaffini, *Testi*, p. 222) or to careful enunciation ('secundo ke aio compitatu et voi avete [uditu] kosì zurarete': *Volgarizzamento di Ranieri da Perugia* in Monaci—Arese, p. 65).

At a time when nearly everything that was written was written in Latin, numerous latinisms passed into vernacular usage. Aspects of the spiritual life of the time frequently found expression in Latin words which passed into Italian. Examples are to be found in the University terminology which came into being with the oldest Italian university, that at Bologna: there *universitas* came to mean, not only 'corporation, body', but 'body of students, University'. Other words that carried a particular University meaning were *facultas, rector, doctor, lectura, artista* ('student in the Faculty of Arts'), *legista* ('student in the Faculty of Law'), *canonista, decretista*. And Italian benefited from medieval Latin terminology in the vocabulary it used for philosophy, law, medicine, alchemy and other sciences and pseudo-sciences. We have already seen how certain words referring to religious matters found their way from ecclesiastical Latin into the vulgar tongue; words like *Cristo, spirito, profeta, apostolo, martire, diavolo* made this journey in very early times, but their popular forms were constantly subject to a certain degree of correction by reference to the forms heard in church. Late medieval contributions in this field were *edificare* (*adificare* in Guittone), *misericordia, divinitade*. From the mystics came words like *absorto, ratto* ('mystical transport'), *annichilare*. Philosophy contributed *scienza, coscienza, sapienza, dottrina, sostanza, accidente, causa, genere, specie, razionale, reale, attuale, formale, virtuale, corporale, naturale, eterno, eternale, sempiterno, equivoco,* etc. Indeed, many terms pertaining to the world of learning came from Latin: *studio, libro, capitolo, pagina, titolo, rubrica, dottore, grammatica, rettorica,* etc. Legal examples are: *legista, statuto, eredità, codicillo*. Some words, from being bookish, came to represent aspects of everyday life: those representing the offices of *console* and *senatore* (renewed at Rome), that of *assessore,* etc. The title *magnates* appears occasionally in medieval writers, who borrowed it from the Vulgate, but in Florence towards the end of the Duecento it acquires a precise meaning (expressing the viewpoint of the wealthy bourgeosie); in the 1281 reform of the *podestà*'s Statute there is a heading 'De securitatibus praestandis a *Magnatis* civibus'. And we can be sure that it came to be used in the vernacular at the same period. Other fields of knowledge represented by latinisms were arithmetic (*arismetica, arismetrica, numero, multiplicare*, etc.), geometry (*sfera, piramide*, etc.), music (*melodia, sinfonia*, etc.) and astronomy (Ristoro d'Arezzo, for instance, used *clima, declinazione, deferente, eccentrico, epiciclo, exaltatione, retrogrado, stationario, zodiaco*). And various general terms entered the vernacular in various ways: examples are *cibo, consolazione, fastidio, gaudio, timore*; *singulare, vago, verace*; *desiderare, esordire, vivificare*, etc. These examples, however, should not lead us to imagine that there was a boundless penetration to which no resistance was offered. Where popular words were already established it was not easy for latinisms to prevail. *Facile* did not exist in the Duecento; the concept was expressed by *agevole*. 'Army' was rendered by *oste* on nearly all occasions, and only Giamboni, in translating Vegetius uses *esercito* (or rather *exercito*), and that he does to support his etymological explanation: 'L'oste che di pedoni e cavalieri è mescolata per lettera [i.e. in Latin] si chiama *exercito*, cioè a dire operamento. . . .' And only at the end of the century does one find examples of *exercito* with the meaning of 'multitude, host'. Occasionally the exact source of a word can be traced: Virgil's 'Purpureus veluti cum flos *succisus* aratro' (*Aeneid*, IX, 435) is echoed by Bonagiunta in his 'che 'l core da lo petto—pare che mi sia diviso—com'albore *succiso*' in the canzone 'Novellamente amore' and again by Dante in his *Rime* ('come *succisa* rosa' in 'Tre donne', l. 21) and thus enters the literary tradition. Some semi-learned words bear the mark of difficult penetration in the changes to which they have been subjected: *alimenti* for *elementi*, *dificio* for *edificio*, *storlomia* for *astronomia*, etc. Sometimes erroneous notions of the etymology of words interfered with their form; an example is *rettorica*, which came to be spelt with -*tt*- (or -*ct*-) because rhetoric was imagined to be an art proper to a rector. (Brunetto Latini, curiously enough, writes *rector* though giving a definition that fits *rhetor*.) The sense borne by these latinisms in Italian is, of course, that which they bore in medieval Latin; a word like *storiare*, especially in the fixed expression *dipinto e storiato* (*Tavola Rit.*, etc.), has the meaning that *historiare* had in the Latin of the time (i.e. 'to represent in pictures'). 'Calques' on Latin are not always easy to trace; it is probable that *dirozzare* and *digrossare* were formed on the model of *erudire*.

The history of grecisms, classical and ecclesiastical, cannot be separated from that of latinisms. Knowledge of Greek was certainly not much advanced by works like the *Grecismus* of Eberard of Béthune (1124), which has such statements as:

Est universale cata *fitque* catholicus *inde*

. . . .

Et cata *sit fluxus, inde* catarrus *erit*

nor by the vocabularies of Uguccione and Giovanni da Genova, whose main source it was. Nonetheless, it is to the rules of grammarians that we must look for an explanation of the placing of the accent in the Duecento (and frequently later) in certain proper nouns and one or two common nouns: *Semelè, Calliopè, Iliòn, aloè,* etc. The rule which prescribed stressing the last syllable of all 'barbarian' names, especially Hebrew ones (*Iacob, Esau, Satanas*), was extended, principally through the influence of French scholastic tradition, to include Greek nouns that did not fit into normal Latin declension. We must bear in mind, too, political, commercial and cultural contacts with Byzantium. The title στρατηγός was kept in Byzantine territories that passed into Norman hands, taking the meaning 'criminal judge'. Frederick II kept the office at Messina and Salerno; hence *stradico, straticò* and their variants. Greek texts were read at Frederick's court and at the medical school at Salerno, and it is probably from there that we get the use of *ana* in medical prescriptions, which survives to this day. Venice, which always enjoyed more or less close relations with Constantinople, got from the Byzantines nouns like *liagò* ('balcony' <ἡλιακός), *dromo* and *squero* ('boat-house'). And it is she who begins, in the twelfth century, the listing of goods and chattels 'line by line', κατὰ στίχον —hence *catasticum* and later *catasto*. Of other words it is often difficult to say how they entered Italy and Europe: *andanico* 'steel', Med. Lat. *andanicum* is the Byz. ἰνδανικὸς σίδηρος, 'Indian iron', imported from India via Persia.

The main difficulty in dealing with gallicisms is that of deciding which belong to the period 1000-1300; in some cases it is difficult, as we said earlier, to distinguish Carolingian from later importations. Nor is it always possible to discover how a word came to Italy (brought by the Normans, acquired in the Levant from French crusaders, transmitted by pilgrims or merchants, culled from literary sources, etc.). Some of the fundamental terms of feudalism (*vassallo*, etc.) had already reached Italy in previous centuries. Among such titles were *conestabile* (Lat. *comes stabuli*; such an office was already in existence under the late empire), *siniscalco* and *camarlingo* (both of these in latinized form). *Assise* and *demanio* came in with the Normans. *Reame* is from the O.F. *reame* or *reialme* (in which the adjective *reial* 'royal' has intruded itself into the noun derived from REGIMINE). To feudal terminology, too, belong *omaggio* (declaring oneself the 'man', or vassal, of the feudal lord) and *ligio*. From the vocabulary of chivalry come *cavaliere, scudiere* ('squire'), *baccelliere, addobbare* (properly the act of conferring knighthood), *sire, sere, messere, dama, madama, damigello -a, donzello -a.* From the O.F. *lignage* (Eng. 'lineage') Italian got *lignaggio.* Many words pertaining to horses are gallicisms: *destriere, corsiere, palafreno* (Prov. *palafré*), and probably *ronzino* and *somiero.* In the military field we find *oste, schiera* (Prov. *esquiera*), *foraggio, foriere, berroviere* ('foot-soldier'), *mislea* (O.F. *meslee*), *ostaggio, arnese* ('armour', later 'baggage'), *usbergo* or *asbergo* ('hauberk'), *maglia* ('mail'), *camaglio* ('camail'), *cervelliera* and *targia.* Gonfalone (O.F. *gonfanon* < Frank. *gund-fano*) and probably *bandiera* also came from contact with the French, as did *stendardo,* which was used after the first crusade. With many variants due to para-etymological modification, the O.F. *berfrei* gave *battifredo* ('look-out tower, mobile siege-tower', etc.). In the domestic sphere we have *loggia, ciambra* or *zambra, sala* (in the sense of 'big room'; *sala* 'rustic habitation' already existed as a langobardism), *cuscino, origliere* ('pillow') and *doppiere* ('two-branched candlestick'). The world of dress and adornment yield *cotta* ('gown, surplice'), *sorcotta, corsetto, guardacuore* ('doublet'), *gioiello* and *fermaglio* ('clasp'). With the vocabulary of fashion came some words denoting colours: *giallo* (O.F. *jalne,* Lat. GALBĬNUS), *vermiglio, bloio,* etc. *Mangiare,* which came early to Italy, had to struggle for centuries against the native *man(d)ucare, manicare. Desinare* is a little less old; but we find *desinèa* in the *Novellino.* With them we should record *buglione* ('broth') and *cervogia* ('beer'). *Giardino* and *verziere* were also early arrivals. Falconry contributed *sparviere, astore* ('goshawk'), *artiglio* ('talon', from the Prov. *artelh* 'toe'), *zimbello* ('decoy'), etc. Hunting with dogs was also accompanied by the use of some French or Provençal words: *veltro, levriere,* etc. Music and poetry brought *caribo, liuto, ribeba* or *ribeca* ('rebeck'), *viola, cennamella* ('bagpipe'), *trovatore* (Prov. *trobador,* Prov. *trobar* meaning 'to write verse'), *giullare* and *ministriere* (whom the Romantics will prefer to call *mene-strello*). Referring to journeys and pilgrimages are *viaggio, passaggio, bolgia* ('bag'), probably *oste* (O.F. *oste,* Lat. HOSPITE[M]) and *ostello* (*ostero, stero* < O.F. *ostel*). Specifically religious borrowings include *palmiere, cordigliere,* Cert(r)*osa.* The entry into Italy of *grangia* (*grancia*) was due chiefly to Cistercian monks. And even *tovaglia*, when it first appeared, was restricted to liturgical usage. From commercial dealings came *derrata, detta* ('debt'), *civanza* ('livelihood'), *gaggio* ('pledge'), *improntare, dozzina, alla* ('ell'), some names of coins (*tornese, provisino, mergugliese*) and several names of cloths and material (*celone, mosteruolo, rensa, razzese, sargia*, etc.). Medicine, too, had its gallicisms: *sagnare, segnare* ('to bleed'), *signera* ('blood-letting'); and other arts and trades gave *ingegnere* and *copelli* ('shavings' in the *Novellino*). Literature, of course, was a very important source. Some French words came in with the epic (*paladino, prence*), others with the chivalric romances (*avventura*). But a much more numerous body of words was taken by Sicilian poets from their Provençal predecessors. With their development and the acceptance of many of them by the Siculo-Tuscans and the *stilnovisti* and their passage thus into literary tradition we have already dealt. We should note, however, that there are certain spiritual, abstract terms about which we are uncertain, not knowing whether they came via poetry or by other routes: *onta, damaggio, oltracotanza, mestiere, pensiero, preghiera, foggia, sorta, dibona(i)re, medes(i)mo, cominciare, corteare, donneare*, etc. Various tendencies converged to effect the penetration of the suffixes *-aggio, -ardo, -iere*, which proved productive after their introduction to Italy. The increase in the already indigenous suffixes *-enza, -anza, -ore* and *-ura*, which was marked while Provençal guidance was fashionable, fell off as that influence diminished.

Phonological and morphological features frequently allow us to distinguish between native words and borrowings from northern France and Provence: thus *cavaliere* is distinguishable from the native *cavallaio* or *cavallaro, somiere* from *somaio, ostaggio* from *statico, stadico*, etc. It is sometimes less easy to separate the Provençal from the French. Here it is useful to note, not only formal features, but also the geographical distribution of the earliest attested examples. There are some cases of double penetration: *damigello* (Fr.) and *donzello* (Prov.), *saggio* (Fr.) and *savio* (Prov.), etc. We must also bear in mind that some words arrived from France in Latin dress; such must have been the case with *marescalco* and *siniscalco, faldistoro* and others. We have recorded some words that subsequently fell into desuetude. We could have made the list much longer by including examples like *maccherella* ('go-between'), *agenzare* ('to please'), *(in)naverare* ('to wound', also fig.), *perzare* ('to pierce'), etc. But we should remember that, although many disappeared (as frequently happens after a massive in-

H

vasion of words), many are still enshrined in Italian literature, like *visaggio*, which we find not only in the *Fiore*, but also in our reading of Dante and Pulci. (Some scholars, of course, consider that there are strong reasons for believing that Dante *was* the author of the *Fiore*.)

Contact with the Islamic world in this period meant, for the most part, contact with the Arabs. For two and a half centuries Sicily was under their domination; they were pre-eminent for even longer in the Mediterranean Sea; and their scholars were influential in many fields of knowledge (astronomy, medicine, etc.). There are also some cases of Arabo-Persian contributions to vocabulary, but almost nothing from the Turks. It would obviously be helpful if we could establish the way in which each word entered (i.e. whether it came through Siculo-Arab symbiosis or in some other fashion). Unfortunately we are still unable to do this for many of them. There is no difficulty in the case of words restricted to Sicily, like *càmula* ('moth'), *giuggiolena* ('sesame'), *sciurta* ('sentinel'), or words which have only recently moved from the Sicilian into the national language, like *zàgara* ('flower of the orange'). It is possible to show the Sicilian origin, too, of numerous other words which enjoy wide diffusion: this is the case with *ammiraglio*, which first meant 'chief, commander', and only in the twelfth century in Sicily, and in the thirteenth elsewhere, became fixed in the sense of 'admiral'; and with *soda*, which is from the Arabic *suwwâd* and was used to indicate certain coastal plants of the genus *salsola* before coming to refer to a substance obtained from them. But others entered Italy by different routes. The Arabic *dâr-sinâ'a* ('workshop, factory,' later 'dockyard') gave *arzanà* (later *arsenale*) at Venice, *dàrsena* at Genoa, *tersanaia* at Pisa, *terzenale* at Ancona and *tarzanà* at Palermo (and in Spanish and Old Catalan *daraçana* and *teraçana*). Of these *arsenale* has won European currency, while *darsena* has become the Italian word for 'wet dock'. Genoa was the centre of diffusion of *cotone*. *Taccuino* must have spread from Salerno through the *Tacuinum sanitatis* (from *taqwîm* 'correct disposition').

In giving below a list of the main arabisms that entered Italian, we must mention that some may have entered after 1300. As we expect, many of them are commercial terms: *magazzino*, *fondaco* ('warehouse'), *dogana*, *gabella*, *tariffa*, *fardello*, *tara* ('tare'), *zecca* ('mint'), *cantàro* (a measure; 80 Kg. at Naples), *ròtolo*, *carato*, *risma* ('ream'), *sensale* ('broker'), *dragomanno*. Moreover, through commercial exchanges came *zucchero* ('sugar'), *zafferano* ('saffron'), the *azzurro* or *lapislazuli* and *balascio* ('balas'). There were, too, some maritime items: *libeccio*, *scirocco*, *gomena* ('hawser'), *sciàbica* ('trawl, drag-net') and *càssero* ('quarter-deck'). *Càssero* offers an example of a phenomenon frequently found among arabisms. It was transmitted to Italy by Arabs with, not only its naval sense, but also that of 'fortress'. The Arabs had, in fact, got the word κάστρον from the Byzantines, who had acquired it from the Romans (*castrum*). It also serves, when compared with the Span. *alcázar*, to exemplify another phenomenon: in Spain arabisms are often found with the article *al-* joined to the noun (It. *carciofo*, Sp. *alcachofa*; It. *cotone*, Sp. *algodón*, etc.). When we find in Italian an arabism beginning with *al-*, it probably means that it came in through Spanish. (It is not safe, however, to assume that those words without *al-* could not have done so.) Mathematical terms frequently have this *al-* (*algebra*, *algoritmo*, etc.), and it is known that Arabic numerals entered Europe through Moslem Spain. *Cifra* or *zifra* was originally the 'zero' or 'nought' which was the essential novelty of the new system. (Jacopone writes 'staraioce *per zifra* a la mascione', 43, l. 92, meaning 'counting for nothing'). Astronomical terms arrived via Latin translations from the Arabic made in Spain; such were *zenit*, *nadir*, *auge* ('apogee'). That *zenit* was a book word is seen from the fact that the original *m* (*zemt capitis* from *samt ar-ra's* 'direction of the head') was taken for *ni*. Arabic medical terms entered through Salerno. Alongside *taccuino*, which we have already mentioned, we had *nuca* ('nape of neck'), *racchetta* ('palm of the hand' before coming to mean 'bat'), *sciroppo*, *ribes*, etc. And *pomo d'Adamo* is a 'calque' on the Arabic. *Alchimia* has also left traces: *alambicco*, *alcali*, *borace*, *risagallo*. The Arabs were skilled cultivators, and various plants came to Europe through them; we therefore use their words in Italian for *arancia*, *limone*, *albicocca*, *carciofo* ('artichoke'), *spinacio*, *melanzana*, *zibibbo* ('raisin'). The names of certain musical instruments came from Arabic through Provençal: *leuto* or *liuto* and *ribeba* or *ribeca*. The games of *zara* and *scacchi* (chess) were brought in by the Arabs; hence some of their terminology is Arabic (*scaccomatto* 'checkmate', *rocco* 'rook', *alfino*, later *alfiere* 'bishop'). There are also, of course, some words referring to institutions of the Islamic world (*soldano*, later *sultano*, *califfo*). And *assassini*, before becoming a common noun, denoted the sect of Ismaelite fanatics gathered about the Old Man of the Mountain; they smoked Indian hemp, called *hashish* 'grass', whence our 'hashish'.

Influences from other sources in this period were slight. From

Germany came some political terms, the most important being *Guelfi* and *Ghibellini*, applied to an Italian context at Florence, and some military words like *saccomanno* and, judging by the proper noun taken from it, *riccomanno*. Commerce with England brought *stanforte* and *sterlini*.

In the exchanges between Italian regions, we note the expansion southward of certain words: *acciuga* ('anchovy'), *carena* ('keel'), *molo, scoglio* from Genoa; *arsenale* from Venice; *spada* probably from Lombard arms factories; and *cavezzo* ('remnant') from some unknown northern city. Of Sicilian and Bolognese influence on Tuscan poetry we have already spoken; it is unfortunate that documentation is still too scarce to permit us to draw up anything like a precise balance-sheet.

5

Dante

Petrarch referred to Dante (*Sen.*, V, 2) as *dux nostri eloquii vulgaris,* and he is commonly called the 'father of the Italian language'. Chronologically, he was neither the first poet nor the first prose-writer to use it. Yet the titles are not without justification: for Dante's work showed convincingly that Italian could be adapted to fulfil the most exacting requirements of literature and society. Before him in Italy, alongside the overwhelming preponderance of Latin and the occasional use of French and Provençal, we had merely a number of dialects in various degrees of refinement; in them minor writers had made sporadic attempts at great art. Dante's work was weighty enough to transform public opinion, not only in Tuscany, but beyond its boundaries. In his writings Italian could be seen to be a great literary language, capable of being the vehicle of a poetry that could bear comparison with any known to his readers, and capable besides of expressing adequately any aspect of the learning of his time.

Dante's thought was bound to that of his age, but he was the first layman in Christian Europe to master the whole culture of his time. The enthusiasm for vulgarization that had animated his master Brunetto and a handful of translators from the Latin became with him a conscious programme. He saw that *clerus vulgaria temnit,* and he saw that for too many men of letters their literacy in Latin was just a money-making business. He knew, too, as we see in the *Convivio,* that many worthy persons were deprived of knowledge through not knowing Latin. Dante wished to lead them to learning and virtue by means of the vulgar tongue: he wanted to create a body of cultured laymen. Luckily, he did not complicate the linguistic problem by seeking a solution in accordance with his views on universal monarchy; the area he had in view was Italy. His exile had acquainted him with many of her regions and had brought him to believe that enough linguistic conformity existed in them to allow him to picture her united by a single language. His audience then is sought in all those places that fall within Italy's natural boundaries, in all 'to which this language extends' (*Conv.*, I, iii, 4). At the beginning of the Trecento Italy's political and cultural condition was wretched. The Empire was vacant. The Papacy, after the humiliation of Anagni (1303) and the conclave of Perugia (1305), had migrated to France. The communes were torn by strife, and petty tyrants were finding suitable opportunities for establishing themselves. Italy as a nation did not exist, for she had no consciousness of cultural unity and no language more suitable than Latin to draw her people together. Dante gave her those things. For that the two unfinished treatises in which he expressed his views on the vernacular did not suffice. But he also wrote the *Commedia*; in it Italians found their language remoulded and ennobled.

Dante's opinions on the vernacular are set out in brief remarks in the *Vita nuova*, more fully in the *De vulgari eloquentia* and the *Convivio*, and incidentally again in the *Divina Commedia*. The *De vulgari eloquentia* and the *Convivio* are well-nigh contemporary. The chapters we have of the former were probably written in 1303; they have the appearance of a first draft. When Dante wrote the *Convivio*, probably in 1303-7, the poet still meant to complete the Latin treatise as well; but, when his time and energy came to be absorbed by his masterpiece, both theoretical treatises were left unfinished.

Whereas in the *Convivio* Dante speaks of the Italian language in general, the problem in the *De vulgari eloquentia* is both wider and narrower. In the first seven chapters of Book I he discusses human speech generally, dealing with some questions that now appear futile (did man or woman speak first?), but which were part of the culture of the time. In chapters VIII-X he treats of the tongues of Europe and particularly of Italy. Dante divides European languages into three branches: Greek, Slavo-Germanic and Romance. Romance is divided into French, Provençal-Catalan and Italian. He holds that the first threefold division goes back to the Tower of Babel, but thinks that the three varieties of Romance are due to later spontaneous differentiation, caused by the instability of human speech. As for Latin, that is an artificial fixing of threefold Romance regulated by common consent.

After commenting on the merits of French, Provençal and Italian, Dante moves on to a more detailed examination of the vernacular of Italy ('vulgare latium'). Here he makes his famous dialectal division of Italy into fourteen regions (not counting the innumerable sub-divisions).

Beginning with the eleventh chapter of the treatise, what Dante writes is (in spite of its close connection with what has already been said on the division into dialects) different in character. For up to this point (apart from the reference to their literatures in dealing with the virtues of French, Provençal and Italian) Dante has spoken only of language (*loquela, eloquium, ydioma*), and his attitude has been that of a student of language. Now he begins, as a student of literature, to treat a problem of style. It is at this point that the *De vulgari eloquentia* really becomes a treatise on composition in the vernacular. He now searches Italy for the most elegant vernacular, and he begins by eliminating the ugliest dialects (those of Rome, the March of Ancona and Spoleto; of Milan and Bergamo; of Friuli and Istria; of the Casentino and Fratta; and, finally, Sardinian). Chapter XII begins with the consideration of Sicilian. At the court of Frederick II and his son Manfred in Sicily there have been illustrious poets; indeed, because of the notable florescence of poetry there, the work of poets from other parts of Italy is dubbed Sicilian. Yet it is clear, says Dante, that the speech of the common people of Sicily is not in itself worthy of precedence. And to prove this he quotes a line from the famous *contrasto* by Cielo d'Alcamo. Similarly southern Italy (Dante speaks of *Apuli*) has had noble poets, but its plebeian dialects are barbarous. Next it is the turn of the Tuscans (ch. XIII), who are foolish enough to arrogate to themselves the title of possession of the illustrious vernacular; but Guittone d'Arezzo, Bonagiunta da Lucca, Brunetto and others wrote verses which were municipal, not curial. And here Dante quotes odd lines and phrases to demonstrate the markedly municipal features of some of the Tuscan dialects. From Florence, for instance, we have *Manichiamo introque, che noi non facciamo altro.* The claims of Genoese he dismisses more rapidly: if they were to lose their *z*, they would have to be dumb altogether or discover some new speech. East of the Appennines (ch. XIV) we find the excessively feminine dialects of Romagna and the excessively rough ones of Venetia. Bolognese is more pleasing, for it is tempered to a praiseworthy sweetness by a mixture of opposites (the smoothness of Imola and the sharpness of Ferrara); but we are again made to note that Bologna's famous poets (like Guido Guinizzelli) have had to look beyond their local dialect, which is not in itself courtly and illustrious. As for Trent, Turin and Alessandria, they are too near the frontiers of Italy to possess a pure language.

In no part of Italy then (ch. XVI) has he found the panther he was hunting: the *volgare illustre*. The vernacular, which is illustrious, cardinal, courtly and curial is that which belongs to all Italian cities and dwells in none of them. Dante calls it *illustrious* (ch. XVII) because it shines forth illuminating and illuminated (exalted by training and power, but also exalting its users with honour and glory); *cardinal* (XVIII) because, just as a door turns on its hinge, the municipal dialects turn on it; *courtly* because worthy of a court, if Italy had one; and *curial* because it would be suitable for a supreme tribunal of justice if one existed. The vernacular that belongs to all Italy is this illustrious vernacular (XIX); having got to know this, we can go on to study inferior forms (and this Dante proposed to do in one of the succeeding books).

In the fourteen chapters of Book II Dante deals with the kind of poem for which the illustrious vernacular is appropriate: the *canzone*. In chapter VII he deals with the selection, the process of sieving, by which the 'grandiosa vocabula' proper to it are obtained. Here only certain exclusions can be based on objective criteria; for most of the process we are dependent on good taste.

What the following books were to contain we know imperfectly from odd references: the third would perhaps have dealt with prose, while to the fourth Dante put off his treatment of the mediocre and humble vernaculars. (Nor is it certain that the fourth book was to be the last.) The fact that Dante never wrote these sections was probably the main cause of the misunderstandings to which the work gave rise in the sixteenth century.

Dante's search, even though it starts from the linguistic conditions of Italy in his own time, is not a search for a language (understood as a social instrument to serve Italians in general), but for a style (an artistic distillation). Given Dante's premises, it could not be otherwise: if 'the vernacular follows usage', if, that is, it is not tied to fixed rules like those artificially drawn up for Latin, it can only be elaborated in individual examples by writers who have as their goal an artistic ideal akin to that of the great poets of antiquity ('lo bello stile', as Dante puts it in the

Comedy). Nothing here depends on rules; what is all-important is the good taste, the *discretio* of the writer. The refinement to which the poet is to subject his raw materials is, above all, a process of elimination: in a *canzone* we must have only universal words, words taken from the stock that all Italians have in common, remote from petty reality and from all that is merely provincial or municipal. Those who cannot detach themselves from the reality of everyday life (and rise to this ideal sphere) cannot achieve this kind of art, whatever region they come from (even Tuscany). Since the illustrious artistic language has this ideal nature it cannot be said to dwell in any one place. A seat could be found for it only if (and here political hopes rise high above the wretched reality of the enslaved and divided peninsula) Italy had a sovereign and a supreme court of justice. The poets who, in Dante's view, have (since the time of the Provençal troubadours) achieved this ideal artistic language are: lyric poets of the Sicilian school; Guinizzelli and some other Bolognese; and the poets of the *dolce stil novo*: Guido Cavalcanti, Lapo Gianni, Cino da Pistoia and Dante himself. Since what he has in view is the art of writing elegantly, the refinement of a style, not a language for all, Dante pays no attention to his predecessors' dialectal differences. (In any case, he read the works of the Sicilians in versions already somewhat tuscanized by scribes). We have all too little concrete detail of the process of refinement as he visualised it. But it certainly consisted above all in the elimination of those features that jarred owing to their plebeian municipalism, not in a kind of mingling (for the concept of 'mixing' is only, in a certain sense, implicit in the *discretio* of the poet and adumbrated here and there in connection with the *vocabula curialiora* of the Apulians, I, XII, 8 and the *commixtio oppositorum* of Bolognese speech, I, XV, 5).

In the *Convivio* almost the whole of the first treatise is given over to justifying and exalting the vernacular, which has been chosen by the poet, in preference to Latin, for his commentary on his moral *canzoni*. But we are not given any notable statement of the criteria that govern the use of it. Dante tells us that he has chosen the vernacular for three reasons (I, V): the first is a scruple of artistic technique (that it would be inappropriate for a *canzone* in Italian to have a commentary in Latin); the second is the zeal of his liberality (his desire to benefit the many rather than the few); the third is his natural love of his own tongue. It is true that Latin is superior to the vernacular 'by reason of nobility,

virtue and beauty': it is stable and incorruptible, while the
vernacular is unstable and corruptible; it is capable of expressing
things that the vernacular is not in a position to express; and it
has greater harmony, for 'the vernacular follows usage and the
Latin art'. But a Latin commentary 'would not have been subject
to the *canzoni*, but their sovereign' (I, V, 15). Moreover Latin
would have conferred its benefit on few, whereas the vernacular
would indeed be of service to many (I, X, 4). A new warmth
inspires Dante's writing when he illustrates the third reason for
his choice of the vernacular: his love for his own language (I, X, 5).
He wishes to magnify it, to protect it from the risks which might
threaten it if some bad future translator were to turn his Latin
commentary into it, and to defend it against its detractors (I, X,
7-11). Through it he is going to express most lofty and original
concepts and thus demonstrate its excellence ('la gran bontade del
volgare di sì'): in prose the 'vertù' of the language itself can be
judged better than in poetry, where there are 'accidentali
adornezze' (I, X, 12). The evil men in Italy who prize the vernaculars of others and denigrate their own he will bring to
perpetual infamy (I, XI), exposing their motives: ignorance or
malice (attributing to the vernacular the incapacity that should
be attributed to themselves), or vainglory (born of a desire to win
admiration for mastery of a foreign language) or envy or pusil-
lanimity: all reasons for which men depreciate their proper
vernacular (I, XI, 21). His love for his own vernacular (I, XII, 2)
springs from its nearness to him and from its excellence. ('A
man's own vernacular is nearest to him . . . for it is singly and
alone in him before any other', I, XII, 5). From the vernacular
Dante has derived great benefits (I, XIII, 2), for it brought his
parents together, and it started him on the path of knowledge;
he came to Latin through it, and Latin opened the gate to further
progress (I, XIII, 5). It would help in the preservation of the
vernacular if it could achieve greater stability (I, XIII, 6), and
that it could accomplish by becoming a poetic language ('by
binding itself in numbers and rhymes'). 'And this study has been
mine, as is so clear as to need no witness'. The first treatise of the
Convivio ends with the famous words: 'This shall be the new light,
the new sun, which shall rise when the old sun will have set, and
shall give light to those who are in darkness and in shadow on
account of the old sun, which shines not for them' (I, XIII, 12).
In future, therefore, even those who have no Latin will be able
to approach the most serious kinds of thought. And Dante's own

work was to be an important contribution to making this prophecy come true.

There is always some risk involved in attempting to compare an author's theories on language and style with his own practice. In the case of Dante the most serious misunderstandings have occurred when scholars have sought in the *Commedia* those qualities which, in the theoretical treatises, are mentioned in connection with the sublime style. For we must not lose sight of the importance attached to grading styles to fit the various literary genres. Dante wrote apocalyptic letters and treatises of scholastic character in Latin, narrative and didactic prose in the vernacular, and in poetry he ranged from the tragic style to the humble. Here we shall omit consideration of his Latin works; even so, we shall still have a wide gamut of styles to deal with.

In his lyrics, he moved from early poems in which the influence of the Siculo-Tuscan tradition is felt to poetry written in what he himself called the *dolce stil novo*. In the *Vita Nuova* the passages of exposition which, rather in the manner of the Provençal *razôs*, accompany the poems, inevitably reflect the fashion for ornate prose, with etymological figures, built-in hendecasyllables and other formal refinements. Yet they succeed in combining with the music of the poems in praise of Beatrice to create an atmosphere of incomparable ethereality. (And as a stylistic model the *Vita Nuova* had no less effect than the *Divina Commedia* itself.) To this atmosphere the frequency of words like *miracolo* and *maraviglia* and of superlative expressions contributes. Dante's *Rime* include verse of great variety: allegorical poems which entitled him to refer to himself as a poet of righteousness; the realistic witticisms of his *tenzone* with Forese; the *rime petrose* and the *sestine* in which the poet vied with the difficult Arnaud Daniel; and the brief and vigorous *canzone* 'Tre donne'. The choice of diction in the lyrics of lofty style is fastidious and severe. In them we do not find those words that the *De vulgari eloquentia* condemns as 'puerilia' (*mamma, babbo*) or 'silvestria' (*cetera* or *cetra, greggia*) or 'urbana lubrica et reburra' (like *femmina* or *corpo*: *corpo* does, however, occur in the *canzone* on nobility, in which Dante tells us that he is abandoning his 'soave stile'). In the *Commedia*, on the other hand, all these words were used without scruple. Conversely, words are used in the *Rime* that are not to be found in the *Commedia*, e.g. *lagare, prenze, lastrare*. The poet recognises that he has acquired his 'bello stile' by assiduous study of the classics and especially of Virgil:

Tu se' lo mio maestro e 'l mio autore;
tu sei solo colui da cu' io tolsi
lo bello stilo che m'ha fatto onore.

(*Inf.*, I, 85-7)

In verse Dante adapted the vulgar tongue to the philosophical
lyric; in the *Convivio* he gives us the first notable treatment in
prose of the same kind of content. In it full periodic syntax, used
not for ornamental, but for ratiocinative purposes, testifies to
study of both classical and scholastic Latin:

'Volendo la 'nmensurabile bontà divina l'umana creatura a
se riconformare, che per lo peccato de la prevaricazione del primo
uomo da Dio era partita e disformata, eletto fu in quello altissimo
e congiuntissimo consistorio divino de la Trinitade, che 'l Figliuolo di Dio in terra discendesse a fare questa concordia. E però
che ne la sua venuta nel mondo, non solamente lo cielo, ma la
terra convenia essere in ottima disposizione; e la ottima disposizione de la terra sia quando ella è monarchia, cioè tutta ad
uno principe, come detto è di sopra; ordinato fu per lo divino
provedimento quello popolo e quella cittade che ciò dovea com-
piere, cioè la gloriosa Roma' (IV, v, 3-4).

In the *Divina Commedia* Dante uses the whole gamut of styles.
And, although his grammatical and lexical foundations are
undoubtedly Florentine, he makes free use of any linguistic forms
he needs that have received previous consecration in literature.
In some parts of the poem we find 'illustrious' lines in which no
local peculiarities are found. Lines like

Per te poeta fui, per te cristiano

. . . .

Oh Beatrice dolce guida e cara

could have been written, so far as their language is concerned, by
a non-Tuscan. The same could be said of certain lines of doctrinal
or philosophical content:

Ogni forma sustanzial, che setta
è da matera ed è con lei unita
specifica virtù ha in sé colletta,
la qual sanza operar non è sentita . . .

(*Purg.*, XVIII, 49-52).

At the other end of the scale we find lines in mediocre, or in
really plebeian, style. In them Dante uses words he would not

admit to the lyrics in lofty style, and which have a strong local flavour. Such is the last line of canto XX of *Inferno*:

> *Sì mi parlava ed andavamo* introcque

or some of the realistic lines elsewhere in the *Inferno*:

> *Già* veggia *per* mezzul *perdere o* lulla,
> *com'io vidi un, così non si pertugia*
> *rotto dal mento infin dove si* trulla
>
> (XXVIII, 22-24)
>
> *e non vidi già mai menare* stregghia
> *a ragazzo aspettato dal* segnorso
>
> (XXIX, 76-77)
>
> *e sì traevan giù l'unghie la scabbia*
> *come coltel di* scàrdova *le scaglie*
>
> (XXIX, 82-83).

There are two questions we must now put to ourselves: To what extent were Dante's grammar and vocabulary Florentine? Was his remoulding of his native dialect such as to transform its character beyond what we expect from the ennobling process to which poets subject their 'natural' language?

Dante's usage is, in comparison with the 'normal' Florentine usage of his time, rich in doublets.[1] In it we find *dicea* alongside *diceva* (as can be seen for certain in rhymes: *diceva* (*Purg.*, XXIV, 118) rhyming with *Eva*; *dicea* (*Purg.*, XXVII, 99) with *Citerea*); *vorrei* (*Inf.*, XXXIII, 97) alongside *vorria* (*Par.*, XXXIII, 15), *fero* and *feron* alongside *fenno*, etc. The strong perfect of *tacere* (*tacque*) is found ten times, the weak perfect (*tacette*) four. *Padre* alternates with *patre* and *madre* with *matre*; *lassare* occurs almost as many times as *lasciare*. *Manicare* and *manducare* are used as well as *mangiare*, and we have both *vendicare* (thrice) and *vengiare* (thrice): these examples gave Dante the choice of a three- or four-syllable word, as required, although that may not be the only reason. *Re* and *rege*, *imagine*, *imago* and *image* are freely used, and the reasons for the choice of a particular form are not always apparent. Alongside *specchio*, which is the 'normal' form and which is used 16 times, Dante has *speglio* (4 examples), *speculo* and *miraglio*; he uses *speme* (7 times) and *spene* (3 times).

---

[1] Still useful on this subject is the article by N. Zingarelli, *Parole e forme della Divina Commedia aliene dal dialetto fiorentino* in *St. di fil. rom.*, I, 1884, 1-202. A very important article for the study of Dante's language is that of E. G. Parodi, *La rima e i vocaboli in rima nella Divina Commedia* in *Bull. Soc. Dant.*, III, 1896, 81-156 (reprinted in *Lingua e lett.*, 203-84).

This shows that Dante, while based firmly on his native dialect, used, as well as contemporary Florentine, certain words and forms that were falling into disuse in his own day, some forms from western and southern Tuscany, occasional rare words from other Italian dialects, many Latin words and not a few from French. One principle governing his usage may, however, be clearly discerned. Whereas he is ready to use any Florentine word he needs, he uses from other sources only words already consecrated by use in literature. Latinisms naturally fall into this category. When he uses *vorria* he is following the usage of the Sicilians and the Siculo-Tuscans; *vonno* (3 pers. plur. pres. tense) belonged to literary Umbrian; *fenno, apparinno, terminonno* (3 pers. plur. perf. tense) had been used in western Tuscan literary texts; and the rhyme *lome* (or *lume*) with *nome* and *come* found precedents in Cavalcanti and the Bolognese. It is not, of course, surprising that Dante should have used forms common in his youth or in the preceding generation. Parodi, dealing with certain verb-forms of this kind, concluded that Dante had followed, not the usage of the lyric poets, but that of Florence a little more than a generation before his own time, and that he had in this moderate archaism sought nobility and solemnity of tone.[1] Castellani (*Nuovi testi*, p. 69) did not exclude the possibility of those forms being still alive in Dante's generation, but agreed that when the *Divina Commedia* was being composed they were on the way out. In the first *canto* of *Inferno*, in fact, we find Dante using both the form *vederai* (current in the generations that preceded his) and *vedrai* (the form prevalent among his contemporaries; ll. 116 and 118).

Dante has no scruples about using in the *Commedia* words from every social stratum in Florence, and some of them are markedly plebeian. Comparison with other texts or the testimony of other Tuscan dialects frequently allows us to interpret exactly words that were once only roughly understood; *bastare* in the sense 'to last' (*Purg.*, XXV, 136) is to be found in Pulci and in the proverb 'Tanto *bastasse* la mala vicina quanto *basta* la neve marzolina'; *burlare* for 'throw away, scatter' (*Inf.*, VII, 30) is used onomastically (*Burlafave* of Montepulciano, a soldier at Florence in 1290) and in Pucci; *piovorno* was heard by Giuliani in Val di Nievole (and *rubecchio* in the Pistoiese mountains);[2] *potere* meaning 'to be capable of carrying' (*Par.*, XVI, 96) is still alive in Tuscany (and elsewhere) in phrases like *lo puoi?*; of

---

[1] *Lingua e lett.*, p. 253.
[2] G. B. Giuliani, *Dante e il vivente linguaggio toscano*, Florence 1872.

punga for *pugna* (*Inf.*, IX, 7) there are many examples in the fourteenth and fifteenth centuries, though they frequently disappear from modern published versions of the texts to which they belong, owing to what Parodi referred to as the 'excessively loving attentions' of those responsible for the editions. It should be mentioned, of course, that Dante sometimes chooses dialect words for characterization, as when he attributes the Lucchese *issa* to Bonagiunta.

Dante's door is wide open to vocabulary from classical, late and medieval Latin. That even the strangest of them is considered theoretically admissible can be seen from the passage in the *De vulgari eloquentia* (II, vii, 6) where Dante quotes as usable in Italian a capricious coinage of medieval Latin '*honorificabilitudinitate*, quod duodena perficitur sillaba in vulgari, et in gramatica tredena perficitur in duobus obliquis'. Latinisms are especially abundant in the doctrinal cantos; hence we find an increase in their number as we move from *Inferno* to *Paradiso*. Many of them must have been adopted by scholastic Italian before Dante's time; but many are certainly his own. Sometimes latinisms are abundantly used to lend solemnity to a speech attributed to one of the protagonists. To give only one example, in Justinian's sketch of the history of the Empire (*Par.* VI) we find: *dal cirro negletto fu nomato . . . tu labi . . . triunfaro . . . si cuba . . . col baiulo seguente . . . dal colubro—la morte prese subitana ed atra . . . al lito rubro . . . e il suo delubro . . . era fatturo . . . nel commensurar di vostri gaggi . . . alcuna nequizia . . . la presente margarita . . . Cive* appears only in rhyme-position and then only in lofty discourses by Beatrice (*Purg.*, XXXII, 101), Charles Martel (*Par.*, VIII, 116) and St. Peter (*Par.*, XXIV, 43). At other times a latinism is suggested to Dante by his source: the *agricola* in St. Dominic's canto (*Par.*, XII, 71) derives from the parable of letting the vineyard to husbandmen; the *conservo* of Pope Hadrian (*Purg.*, XIX, 134) comes from the Apocalypse; the *iaculi* of Libya are a reminiscence of Lucan; the *libito* and *licito* confused by Semiramis occur already in what Orosius says of her; 'l'alte fosse che *vallan* quella terra sconsolata' (*Inf.*, VIII, 77) go back to the Book of Proverbs, already paraphrased in the *Convivio* ('quando [Iddio] con certa legge e giro *vallava* gli abissi'), etc. Zingarelli, in his article on the non-Florentine features of the *Divina Commedia*, listed some 500 latinisms; anyone who wishes to do further work in the field should try to distinguish those proper to Dante from those common in his time.

Owing to his ignorance of Greek, Dante used Greek words only when they had already appeared in Latin texts that he had read (e.g. *perizoma* in the Vulgate, *latria* and *tetragono* in St. Thomas). Only exceptionally does he venture to work out what he does not know: he takes the plural *entoma* (presumably found in Aristotle's *De historia animalium*) to be a singular and from it forms the false plural *entomata* (*Purg.*, X, 128).

Dante's gallicisms are numerous, but it is difficult to find among them any that are not found in other texts and which can thus be considered to be exclusively his. Even *flailli* (*Par.* XX, 14), from the O.F. *flavel*, *flajel*, not hitherto documented elsewhere, may have come to Dante from a Sicilian source. Its vowel development suggests that, as Schiaffini noted.[1]

It is also very difficult to draw a line between words coined by Dante and words which he may have got from sources of which no trace remains. Some immediate derivations are probably his: nouns from verbs, like *cunta* (*Purg.*, XXXI, 4) or verbs from nouns like *alleluiare*, *golare*, *mirrare*. Among words formed by addition of prefixes (*adimare*, *appulcrare; dismalare*, *divimare; indracare*, *ingigliare*, *impolare*, *inurbarsi*, *inventrare; rinfamare*, *ringavagnare; sgannare*, *spoltrire; transumanare*, etc.) several are certainly his own, especially those formed from possessives, pronouns, numerals and adverbs (*immiare*, *intuare*, *inleiarsi*, *inluiarsi*, *intrearsi*, *internarsi* [der. from *terno*], *incinquarsi*, *immillarsi*, *indovarsi*, *insemprarsi*, *insusarsi*). Of *imparadisare* Tommaseo wrote: 'It belongs to the living language, and Dante must have borrowed from it, not it from Dante'. But in the case of a coinage of this kind the opposite seems more likely. Certain words formed by addition of a suffix were probably also coined by Dante (*pennelleggiare*, *torreggiare*).

In subsequent centuries (as we shall note in due course) Dante's influence was constant, though varying in intensity at different periods. He influenced style (Boccaccio, for example, was affected by the *Vita Nuova* and writers of 'visions' by the *Commedia*), metre (as can be seen in the history of *terza rima*) and vocabulary (as we shall now note in a few examples). Since the *Comedy* has been treated, from the Trecento onwards, almost as holy writ, and much studied and commented on, it has furnished material for continual quotation, either of complete lines or of phrases that refer to episodes and figures from the poem and to Dantesque concepts: such are the *bramose canne* (of Cerberus), *fiero pasto* (of Ugolino), *disiato riso* (of Guinevere), *vendetta allegra*, *mala signoria*,

[1] *Italia dialettale*, IV, 1928, 229-30.

natio loco, morta gora, mondan romore, volgare schiera, velen dell'argomento, sapor di forte agrume, segnacolo in vessillo, femmine da conio, and *discender per li rami, raunar le fronde sparse, far tremar le vene e i polsi* and many more. Individual words used by him have also prospered: not only those that refer to the structure and moral order of the world he created, like *bolgia* and *contrappasso* (from St. Thomas's *contrapassum,*) but also many others: *lai, loico, macro, grifagno, tetragono* (in the abstract meaning 'unshakeable' as seen in *Par.,* XVII, 24), etc. Even so, Dante's influence on particular aspects of the language still counts for far less than his general impact: for, within a century of the birth of Italian literature, he proved what Italian was capable of: 'mostrò ciò che potea la lingua nostra'.

6

The Trecento

The fourteenth century is one of the most important periods in the history of the Italian language, not because the language and literature of Italy then reached their apogee, as Bembo, Salviati, Cesari and Giordani later thought, but because it was the age of the three writers (Dante, Petrarch, Boccaccio) who were to be the models for the linguistic unification of the nation. It was in Florence a period of prodigious vitality, expressed in activities as various as those of Giotto or Arnolfo and those of Florentine merchants who were playing so large a part in European commerce. And there is no doubt that the life of the commune at this time was favourable to the development of the vernacular; since Latin was the preserve of a professional class, its exclusive use could have closed the doors of culture, not only against women, but also against the merchants and against the nobles who had now entered the ranks of the citizenry. In our examination of this period we shall stop at the death of Boccaccio in 1375, for the triumph of humanism in the last quarter of the century makes it more appropriate to deal with that in conjunction with the Quattrocento.

The commune, which enjoyed longer and more vigorous life in Florence than elsewhere (though not without the predominance of families with oligarchic tendencies) yielded in northern and central Italy to the emergence of local *signori*. The tendency of certain cities to expand at the expense of their neighbours was exemplified in Tuscany, where Florence extended its dominion over Pistoia, Pisa and Arezzo (though without succeeding in doing so over Siena and Lucca), as well as in the cities where families like the Carrara, the Scaligers and the Visconti provided the impulse. Politically important courts tended to evolve their own koine. The influence of Rome was lessened by the absence of the popes. In the kingdom of Naples the capital (which was in close contact with the rest of Italy) was much more important than the rest of the state, which lacked focal points. Sicily, after Caltabellotta (1302) formed the closed, autonomous kingdom of Trinacria and became preoccupied almost exclusively with its own affairs. In Sardinia, where Pisan influence had been strong, Catalan penetration took place under the Aragonese. The Black Death cast its shadow over the life of the time in many ways, not only in 1348, but in later lesser outbreaks.

Certain aspects of the society of the period deserve special mention here for their contribution to linguistic unity. The long journeys of the merchants (in Italy and abroad) played their part in linguistic circulation. So did the travels within the peninsula of *podestà*, judges and teachers, and those of minstrels of various ranks who moved from court to court. Navigation brought together men of diverse origins; nautical texts (e.g. the *Compasso da navigare*) are linguistically very mixed. Soldiers of fortune, at first largely foreign, were later recruited from the poorer regions of Italy itself. Humanism radiated mainly from Florence to the rest of Europe. And we must not forget the contribution to Florentine influence made by the new styles in the figurative arts (Giotto, Arnolfo) and in music (for the *Ars nova* was accepted, and flourished, in Florence). To the universities already in existence those of Perugia, Florence and Siena were added. Through the efforts of two distinguished interpreters of the common law, Bartolo da Sassoferrato and his disciple Baldo, new juridical knowledge became the patrimony of Italy and of Europe. There are numerous testimonies to inter-regional cultural relations; an example is the knowledge of Florentine affairs and literature in Venice.

During the century the vernacular gained considerable ground at the expense of Latin. Yet we should not forget that the main contributions to the development of the vulgar tongue in the literary field were made by men like Dante, Petrarch and Boccaccio, who drew strength from their knowledge of the classics in their efforts to give artistic nobility to Italian.

Public correspondence continued to be in Latin. When we find public documents in the vernacular (as in the case of the peace treaty between Florence and Pisa in 1328) they are, in all likelihood, not the original documents, but translations made for the information of the public. But in statutory legislation the use of the vernacular was greatly extended. Numerous statutes, those of communes and those of corporations, were translated. The constitution of the city was translated in Siena in 1309-10, the city statutes of Perugia in 1342 and those of Ascoli in 1377. At Florence the statutes of the Guild of Physicians and Apothecaries, drawn up in Latin in 1314, were translated in 1349. In 1355 it was decided to translate the City Statutes, and in 1356 ser Andrea Lancia was entrusted with the task of producing a translation within a year of all the statutes and ordinances, which were then to be bound in a volume and made available to the public. Wills and petitions to authority were frequently in Italian, as were public bans, lists of goods subject to duty, and letters and instructions from the Florentine chancellery. There were, too, numerous translations and a few compilations in the domains of medicine, surgery and agriculture (e.g. those of Serapione, Pietro Spano, Guglielmo da Piacenza, and Pier Crescenzi).

In the literary sphere, too, the vulgar tongue made great progress. The *Convivio* was a conscious attempt to demonstrate its maturity in handling philosophical concepts. And what Dante had said in the *De vulgari eloquentia* on the lack of vernacular poetry on the subject of arms and military valour stimulated Boccaccio to write an epic, the *Teseida*:

> *Ma tu, o libro, primo a lor* [=le Muse] *cantare*
> *di Marte fai gli affanni sostenuti,*
> *nel volgar lazio più mai non veduti.*
> (Book XII, st. 84).

But, in spite of their contributions to the development of the vernacular, both Petrarch and Boccaccio were convinced that Latin had greater dignity. The fact that Petrarch annotated the autograph copy of the *Rime* in Latin (*hic non placet; dic aliter; hoc placet quia sonantior*, etc.) shows that for him Latin was the normal language for writing, while Italian was reserved for particular poetic experiments. His was by no means an isolated case. Francesco da Barberino provided a Latin commentary to his *Documenti d'amore*, the headings in Prodenzani's *Saporetto* are in Latin, and so are the headings, dates and occasionally the signatures on letters in the vernacular. Translations from Latin continued to appear; among the more important was Boccaccio's version of the third and fourth *Decads* of Livy. The prose evolved by translators from Latin tended to be remote from everyday speech and to seek elegance by leaning heavily on the devices of Latin syntax. Occasionally, writers wrote the same work in both languages; Bartolomeo da San Concordio wrote *De documentis antiquorum* and then translated it as *Ammaestramenti degli antichi*. Cristoforo Guidini produced a Latin version of St. Catherine's *Libro della divina dottrina*. Latin was the language of education; but teachers frequently used the vernacular as a medium, as we know from Dante ('con esso io entrai ne lo latino e con esso mi fu mostrato': *Convivio*, I, xiii, 5). Moreover, it was possible to obtain elementary education with a practical, vocational bias. At Florence in 1313 a master undertook to teach a boy 'ita et taliter quod . . . sciat . . . legere et scribere omnes licteras et rationes et quod . . . sit sufficiens ad standum in apotecis artificis'.

French language and literature were well known in Italy, especially in the first half of the century. Here the important factors were contacts with the numerous merchants who had settled in France, relations with the papal court at Avignon, and the influence of French fashions at the court of Robert of Anjou and again at the time of Jeanne I. French was used for literary purposes in northern Italy; Rustichello wrote down Marco Polo's story in it, and in 1379 Raffaele Marmora began the *Aquilon de Bavière*. Moreover, French influence is frequently discernible in Italian writers (e.g. Vannozzo and Prodenzani) of the period. Indeed, towards the end of the century Benvenuto da Imola, echoing certain passages in Dante's *Convivio*, protested against the gallicizers:

'Unde multum miror et indignor animo, quando video italicos et praecipue nobiles, qui conantur imitari vestigia eorum et discunt linguam gallicam, asserentes quod nulla est pulchrior lingua gallica; quod nescio videre; nam lingua gallica est bastarda linguae latinae, sicut experientia docet' (*Comentum*, II, p. 409).

But Petrarch, sent to the King of France by the Visconti in 1361, spoke Latin, not French: 'linguam gallicam nec scio nec facile possum scire'.

German was not much known. Catalan came to Sicily and Sardinia in the wake of the Aragonese. Frederick III of Aragon, who favoured use of the vernacular in Sicily, wrote political poems in a Provençal which had Catalan features. In Sardinia in 1337 the decrees of the governor to his officials were issued in Catalan. In 1372 the Sardinian population of Alghero was driven out to make way for a Catalan colony.

Calabria and Messina were notable centres of Greek culture. Elsewhere in Italy, prehumanism and humanism stimulated the study of Greek; as is well known, King Robert (and the translators favoured by him), Petrarch and Boccaccio had a large part in promoting Greek studies. The first Greek teaching at Florence, that of Leonzio Pilato (about 1360), was private and oral in character. Only at the end of the century (1397) was the chair for Chrysoloras established.

In Tuscany the use of the vernacular for practical purposes had, from the preceding century, been wider than elsewhere. From this fertile soil there now sprang three major writers, Dante, Petrarch and Boccaccio, who showed that Florentine could be used for the most exacting kinds of literature. It is with Dante's *Vita nuova*, in fact, that Florentine primacy in the literary field began. In the last decades of the century the development of literature in the vernacular was, however, to suffer somewhat from the predominance of latinizing humanism.

In discussing the literary use made of Italian at this time we should record the great importance, not only of Dante's *Commedia*, but also of the lyric poetry of his time, for that too, was imitated stylistically and linguistically. And if the poetry of the *stil novo* soon fell into the mechanical repetition of commonplaces, Petrarch, though deriving in part from it, produced new forms and motifs. The historical and chivalresque *cantari*, too, became lifeless, only to be exploited in new ways in the poetic works of Boccaccio. Realistic poetry, as it had already started to do in the Duecento, developed a vigorous and colourful language based on popular idiom, though naturally producing somewhat stylized patterns from it. In all parts of Tuscany, in fact, poetry was written: in Lucca (Pietro Faitinelli), in Siena (Folgore da S. Gimignano, Bindo Bonichi, Simone Serdini), and in Arezzo (Cenne della Chitarra, Giovanni de' Boni), as well as in Florence. In prose, doctrinal and didactic works (e.g. Dante's *Convivio* and Sacchetti's *Esposizioni*) showed scholastic influence in their form; so, to some extent, did those of the mystics (St. Catherine, San Giovanni delle Celle). Historians and those giving accounts of travels followed to some extent the manner of the chroniclers, to some extent that of bourgeois story-tellers. (Here we have in mind not only Sacchetti, but also the narrative parts of Passavanti; both continue the tradition of the *Novellino*.) The technical experiments of the last decades of the thirteenth and the first decades of the fourteenth centuries in periodic prose style (which owed more to the translators than to the theories of contemporary treatises) had by this time provided a supple instrument for the artist who sought one. And of the need that writers increasingly felt to master such an instrument we can judge from Filippo

Villani's statement that his father Matteo 'usò lo stile che a lui fu possibile, apparecchiando materia a più dilicati ingegni d'usare più felice e più alto stile' (Proemio).

Petrarch is important in Italian linguistic history on account of his lyric poetry alone. With the exception of a single letter to Leonardo Beccanugi, he left no Italian prose. His stylistic experiments started from the *dolce stil novo*. Dante influenced him mainly through the *rime petrose*. For, although the *Commedia* contributed to the *Trionfi*, the spirit of the two works (as indeed of the two poets generally) was profoundly different. The troubadours, too, had some part in his development. But most important was his reading of the classics, which was wider and carried out with a more mature critical attitude than that of his medieval predecessors. And his exquisite verbal music was achieved through long and patient revision and elaboration.

He described his work in composing the *De remediis* as 'doppio— tra lo stil de' moderni e 'l sermon prisco' (son. 40), possibly on account of his attempt to combine the scholastic and the Ciceronian styles. In his Italian poetry his task was even more delicate. Their basis is Tuscan, but of a composite kind; on it are superimposed reminiscences of previous poetic tradition, from the Sicilians to the *stilnovisti*, and the authority of Latin. Thus he considers himself free to use *propio* (even in rhyme-position) as well as *proprio*, *tesoro* and *tesauro*, *-me* and *-mi* and *-se* and *-si* enclitically; *proverai* but *lassarà* (28, 36). Above all, he considers himself free to use either a monophthong or a diphthong where spoken Florentine had *ie* and *uo*. In rhyme we frequently find the monophthong, but it is easy to see that his main consideration was euphony. For we have 'Nè per bei boschi allegre *fere* e snelle' (312) but 'Nè *fiere* han questi boschi sì selvagge' (288); indeed, we have nineteen examples of *fera* (or *fere*) against 5 of *fiera* (or *fiere*). And we have two forms in the same line in 'Che *bono* a *buono* à natural desio' (*Tr. Fama*, I 126). The changes *pie*' to *pe*', *dover* to *dever*, *begli occhi* to *belli occhi* show an attempt to depart from spoken usage and to achieve nobility of diction through slight archaizing. The latinizing forms *fenestra*, *curto*, *condutto* (where he had originally written *condotto*), *consecrare* have a similar aim, but occasionally go beyond the permissible: if we can admit *impio* within a line, we can hardly consider *impie* admissible in rhyme with *tempie*, *empie*, *scempie* (though it should be noted that this example exists only in a copyist's hand, not in Petrarch's). In morphology, Petrarch uses the two types of conditional in *-ia* and *-ei*, while of the third (that from the pluperfect) he has only *fora*. Past participles without suffix (*avria stanco*, 218) are very rare. What strikes one about the vocabulary is the deliberate restriction; Contini has described it as 'chiuso in un giro di inevitabili oggetti eterni, sottratti alla mutabilità della storia'. Unusual or strongly expressive words are avoided; the rare cases that exist are either in epistolary poems, where Petrarch has been unable to avoid difficult rhymes (*Etiopia, inopia, sfavillo, stillo* in reply to Stramazzo da Perugia, 24), or in binomial or polynomial series (*lappole e stecchi*, 166), in antitheses ('Oh poco mel, molto *aloè* con fele', 360) and in imprecations. Apart from the latinizing patina of the orthography, there are numerous latinisms (indeed an increasing number from the *Rime* to the *Trionfi*) in vocabulary (e.g. *ivernale, sorore*) and in syntax (e.g. *credere* in the sense of 'trust' or 'obey'; the Greek accusative; word-order). Petrarch's provençalisms are limited to words that Italian poetic tradition has already accepted (like *augello, despitto, dolzore, frale, savere, soglio* with the meaning of *solevo*, etc.); moreover, he avoids the words in *-anza* which previous poets had so abused. It might seem surprising to find in Petrarch a gallicism not previously used ('In su'l dì fanno *retentir* le valli', 219), were it not that this French word has obvious onomatopoeic value. There are very few words that can be presumed to have been coined by Petrarch: *disacerbare, inalbare*. But his work is rich in figurative expressions, not all taken from previous writers: *foco, fiamme, sole, tesoro, fenice* for the 'loved person', *liquido cristallo* for 'water', *rai* for 'eyes', *amorosi vermi, amorose vespe* for 'amorous passion', etc. And for the sake of harmony and elegance he is ready to use antithesis, parallelisms, polysyndetic or asyndetic enumerations ('Fior, frondi, erbe, ombre, antri, onde, aure soavi', 303; 'Non Tesin, Po, Varo, Arno, Adige e Tebro', 148), the adynata and other stylistic devices to which later imitators will be so strongly attracted.

In the codification of the Italian language which took place in the sixteenth century, little attention was paid to Boccaccio's minor writings (*Filocolo, Filostrato, Ameto, Teseida, Fiammetta, Ninfale*); usually, the main model was the *Decameron*. In his work two strains are, in fact, evident. One is love of ornament, of latinizing complication of style, of the rare and the luxurious, and this we can see indulged to excess in the *Filocolo*. The other is a frank realism, accompanied often in narration by a less aristocratic, simpler, more rapid style. And whereas the first tendency predominates at the beginning of his literary career, it is clear that in the mature years in which the *Decameron* is produced, his technique has become less ostentatious and a better balance achieved. The latinisms are less numerous, and so are the inversions. It is true that we still have very ample periods—in the Proem, or when, in the introduction to a story, Boccaccio is discoursing on the ways of Providence or Chance. But, when the story gets going, there is now a sparer and more popular style, and the loftier periods are allowed to appear only when some noble episode or character justifies them. We can see this if we compare the lively, popular speech of Cisti the baker (VI, 2), of the priest of Varlungo (VIII, 2), or of Maso talking to Calandrino (VIII, 3) with the words of Ricciardo to Catella (III, 6), the virile discourses of Ghismonda (IV, 1) and the noble orations of Zima (III, 5).

Substantially, Boccaccio conforms in the *Decameron* to the grammatical norms of the Florentine of his time, in accordance with his declared aim of writing it 'in fiorentin volgare' (Intro. Day IV). But the choices he makes reflect an aspiration to a noble style. Constructions like *mógliema* are found only in the mouths of his characters, not in the narration of the author, an indication that they were in his time restricted to plebeian usage. His vocabulary is rich, but no longer has the showy profusion of the earlier works. Sometimes the author uses unfamiliar words for local colour. Thus in the story of the Count of Antwerp (II, 8) we find many gallicisms in the speech of the characters (*donare* 'to give', *giuliva*, *biltà*, etc.); Tancredi (IV, 1) is called *principe* or *prenze*; the Venetians are twice (IV, 2; VI, 4) called *bèrgoli*, 'frivolous', 'chatter-boxes', a word then used with pejorative sense in Venetia. Anichino goes to the garden to strike Egano 'con un pezzo di *saligastro*'—a word that transports us to Bologna (VII, 7). *Jancofiore* (VIII, 10) not only addresses Salabaetto in dialectal words, but Boccaccio tells us that she used 'sapone moscoleato'. *Lucertola verminara* (II, 10, 6) 'gecko' is a term that Boccaccio must have acquired at Naples, and it is probable that his use of *menne* 'breasts' (*Filocolo*, pp. 361, 411, ed. Battaglia) is a reminiscence of his stay there rather than of his reading of the Sicilians. We should also note the *ciancioso* of the *Ameto*. But Boccaccio's tastes are less obvious in his choice of word than in his syntax, e.g. in his use of participles and gerunds or in his placing of the verb. Putting the verb at the end of the sentence (which in the sixteenth century will become one of the main ingredients of prose written in imitation of Boccaccio) is sometimes in his work merely a relic of rhetorical usage. But sometimes it is done by him, consciously or unconsciously, to obtain a synthetic effect: we are made to pass rapidly over the other parts of the sentence in our expectation of the final verb.

The diffusion of the *Divine Comedy* aroused widespread admiration. Most of Dante's imitators hardly deserve mention in literary histories. But his poem established *terza rima* firmly among Italian verse-forms and made a capital contribution to the formation of Italian. That the Venetian versifier Giovanni Quirini should have written what is substantially Tuscan with a dialectal patina shows how Dante's literary example led to an acceptance also of his language. Numerous copies were made of the *Comedy* and many commentaries written. Public readings were given of it in Tuscany and outside: at Siena it was read by a master from Spoleto, possibly even earlier than 1360; at Florence by Boccaccio; at Bologna, Ferrara, Verona and Milan by other interpreters.

Words and phrases used in the *Comedy* pullulated henceforth in the works of others. Petrarch was a reluctant imitator of Dante. Nevertheless he has 'il bel paese' (146); 'O Padre nostro che nei cieli stai' (*Purg.*, XI, 1) is echoed in his 'Signor che 'n cielo stassi' (*Trionfi della Morte*, I, 70); and 'l'ombra tutta in sé romita' of the Sordello episode reappears in 'con tutte sue virtuti in sé romito' (*Tr. della Morte*, I, 152), etc. Boccaccio was an enthusiastic apostle of the Dante cult, and in his works reminiscences abound. Moreover he was influenced not only by the *Comedy*; the *Vita nuova* had a part in the formation of his style. In Passavanti's *Specchio* we read of the '*donne della torma* che guidano l'altre' (319, Polidori) and Pucci uses 'dolenti note' and 'selva oscura' (*Merc. Vecchio*, 205; *Brito di Bretagna*, 49). Examples could be multiplied.

When Petrarch's Italian poems and Boccaccio's *Decameron* became known they were associated with Dante in what has come to be called the cult of the 'Tre Corone'. Henceforth writers in Italian had three models to whom they could turn in the same way as humanists turned to great writers of antiquity. In admiration for Petrarch and Boccaccio, as in that for Dante, Venetian men of letters were in the van; it is significant that humanism in the vernacular has its origin in the region in which Lovati, Ferreti and Mussato had made their pre-humanist contributions. Petrarch had passed the last years of his life at Padua, Venice and

Arquà, and in correspondence Francesco di Vannozzo had exchanged poems with him. In Francesco's sonnet XXVIII we find that although he uses the Venetian *fasse* for *fasce* and talks of *zoioso destino*, he ends with:

> *e la vermiglia gonna*
> *partia col bianco* (*in* megio *era oro fino*)
> *la palma letto e 'l bel* braccio colonna.

Imitation of Petrarch has caused him to write *braccio*, instead of *brazzo* and to hypertuscanize *mezzo* to *megio*. Boccaccio's influence can be exemplified in the chronicle of the Paduan Gatari; as early as 1372 it reveals knowledge of the *Decameron* and the *Corbaccio.*

Florence, and Tuscany generally, seem to have enjoyed some feelings of linguistic pre-eminence as early as the end of the Duecento and the beginning of the Trecento; Dante expressed his irritation at this pride, which he considered ill-founded, in the *De vulgari eloquentia.* As time progressed it grew stronger, and, as the works of Dante, Petrarch and Boccaccio became known, recognition of Tuscan primacy appeared elsewhere. A Tuscan contemporary of Dante's, Francesco da Barberino, in the Proem to his *Reggimento e costumi di donna*, writes:

> *E parlerai sol nel volgar toscano*
> *e porrai mescidare alcun volgari,*
> *consonanti con esso,*
> *di que' paesi dov'ai più usato,*
> *pigliando i belli, e' non belli lasciando . . .*

The Paduan Antonio da Tempo, in 1332, at the end of his *Summa artis rithimicae*, proclaimed the primacy of Tuscan: 'Lingua tusca magis apta est ad literam sive literaturam quam aliae linguae, et ideo magis est communis et intelligibilis' (174, Grion); but he added: 'non tamen propter hoc negatur quin et aliis linguis sive idiomatibus aut prolationibus uti possimus'. Later Benvenuto da Imola, in his commentary on Dante, affirmed unhesitatingly 'Nullum loqui est pulcrius aut proprius in Italia quam Florentinum' (*Comentum*, I, 336, Lacaita), while Monaldo di San Casciano reproached Simone Prodenzani for using too many Orvietan words, telling him:

> *che 'l vocabulo e 'l profazio*
> *del Patrimonio nel paese esperico*
> *non è accetto nel materno Lazio,*

which, according to Debenedetti's interpretation, means that, 'the words and pronunciation used to the west of the Patrimony are not good Italian'.

The development of the vernacular in various regions is a subject still requiring exploration. It would be interesting to know how and when, in each city, the vernacular replaced Latin and what kind of Italian was written.

It is clear that, in northern Italy, Piedmont and Liguria were somewhat isolated, while the Po plain (or Lombardy in the medieval sense), while not forming a single unit, yet enjoyed considerable circulation. It is also clear that prose and verse must be dealt with separately. In poetry the struggle between French and Provençal models on the one hand and Tuscan models on the other was still unresolved at the beginning of the century; but, after that, taste moved decisively towards the Tuscans. A verse composition written down in 1354, and of which we have a good text (probably in the hand of the author, Antonio Beccari) enables us to analyse the hybridism caused in verse by Tuscan imitation. (As Rajna stressed, it is most important to be able to distinguish in this period the few genuine texts we have from those transcribed in later years, when tuscanization was more advanced.) Beccari's first stanza reads:

> Prima che 'l ferro arossi i bianchi pili
> Et che uergogna et danno in uu se spiechi,
> Scopritiue i-orechi,
> Obtusi dal furore di uostri cori.
> Siti uu çoueneti, o siti uechi?
> Siti uu plebesciti, o uer çentili?
> Siti uu franchi, o uili?
> Siti uu in piçol grado, o uer sengnori?
> I credo pur che ça diuersi honori
> Ho receuuto in su i-uostri theatri:
> Però, miei maçori patri,
> Çaschun rafreni in si l'ardita mano
> Al son de mia tronbecta!
> Ch'a le parole d'una uedouecta
> Tardoe ça de ferire el bon Traiano.
> Et se mio dir fie uano,
> El no ue mancherrà finir questa opra,
> Che danno et desenor conuen che scopra.

The features which connect Beccari with the dialectal and inter-dialectal peculiarities of the Po Basin are: metaphony (not only in *pili*, which could be a latinism, but also in *accisi, arnisi, paisi*, although we have *honori, segnori* without umlaut), the tonic pronouns *mi, si, vu* (once *vui*), and, above all, the 2nd pers. in *-ati, -iti*, which can be considered a permanent characteristic of the ennobled vernacular of this region from Guido Fava to Boiardo. The influence of Latin appears especially in the spelling (*obtusi, honori, theatri*, legitimate and illegitimate *-ct-* for *-tt-*, etc.), but also in the vocabulary (*angue, audienza*, etc.). As for Tuscan influence, that appears, not only in the vocabulary, which is substantially that of Tuscan poets of the Trecento, but also in phonological and morphological features: palatal *-g-* (*già, giovenecto*) appears alongside the affricate *z* (*ça, çoveneti*); in the formation of the 1st conj. future and conditional we find (alongside a *bastarebe*) a *mancherrà*, where the *rr*, no less than the *e*, reveals tuscanizing intentions; and alongside the more frequent suffix *-ero -era* (*mestero, cavalero, altero*; *schera, bandera*) appears an example of *-iero* (pl. *destrieri*).

This *canzone* is, in fact, an excellent example of the influences at work in the language of poets of the Po valley halfway through the century. What can be said of it can be said of other writers of verse who flourished at this time in Milan, Verona, Padua, Treviso, Ferrara, Bologna and Ravenna. For in their works, too, the factors to be taken into account are: features coinciding with local speech; inter-regional ennobling features common to more or less vast zones; latinizing features; and, finally, Tuscan features, acquired from imitation of Tuscan poets. The texts show how this final feature increased in importance from generation to generation. Of course, Tuscan influence is less obvious when one passes from the lyric to other forms of verse (*laudi, cantari*, etc.); the capricious realism of many *frottole* is particularly suited to use of local, popular language. And there are, too, examples of serious poems in dialect (Marsilio da Carrara, Francesco di Vannozzo, Antonio Beccari).

Artistic prose still kept Latin as its language. There was precious little art in the moral, ascetic and didactic treatises, the epic romances and chronicles, written in the vernacular, not to speak of avowedly practical texts (letters, wills, statutes, etc.). If we go back to Beccari's poems, we shall find that the prose text that accompanies it belongs much more closely to the Po valley in language than the verse. An example is the treatment of intervocalic *-t-*: the prose has *inguadiada, fradello, armadi* (as well as *parentado* and *servidore*), while the verse has *recevuto, ardita, canuta, muta, togati, pentiti, date, prisato, coronato*. In morphology, too, we note that, whereas the prose has a gerund *siando*, of a type widespread in northern Italy (gerund and participle in *-ando* for all conjugations), the verse has *vincendo*, a form in which Tuscan and Latin influences converge. In short, prose lagged far behind verse in assimilating Tuscan features.

One notable feature in texts from the Po Basin in this period is this: that it is difficult to place them exactly, since their writers were anxious to eliminate purely local features in favour of linguistic usage of an area wider than their own locality. Within the area language became more uniform. We can consider as an example a phonetic feature covering many areas of northern Italy: the apocope of final *-o* and *-e*, not only after liquids and nasals, but also after other consonants (or groups of consonants): *dit, corp, mes*, etc. In writing there was a growing tendency to eliminate this feature. One can contrast, for example, the abundance of apocopation in Vivaldo Belcalzer, who wrote at Mantua before 1309 (*sot, element, serad* (=*serrato*), *did* (=*dito*), *old* (=*ode*), *lus* (=*luce*), *spess, log, soreg, negr*, etc.) with the abundance of final vowels found a couple of generations later in texts from the chancellery of Mantua (*fato, tuto, parte*, etc.) frequently with false regressions like *lialmento* (=*lealmente*), *cognossero* (=*conoscere*), *voliro* (=*volere*), *Esto* (=*Este*).

Similar aspirations to get above local features helped to modify the spoken dialects, too, especially in Venetia, contributing, along with other tendencies which became apparent in this century (diphthongization of *e, o*; breakdown of *pl, bl, cl, gl*), to making the Venetian dialects the nearest, in general appearance, to those of Tuscany.

In dealing with central Italy we must again distinguish between poetry and prose. Religious poetry, especially of a dramatic kind, still flourished in Umbria. Around 1350 Tuscan literary and linguistic influence made itself felt in Perugia: the poems of Nuccoli and Ceccoli are less Perugian in flavour than those of Moscoli, written a few years earlier. Francesco Stabili wrote his *Acerba* in a language which has many grammatical and lexical features linking it with Ascoli; but it also reveals study of Dante (the 'poeta che finge immaginando cose vane') and literary Tuscan. The *Giostra dei vizi e delle virtù* and the *Pianto delle Marie* display a koine with many latinisms, some provençalisms and some dialectal features (distinction between *-u* and *-o*; 1st pers. pl. pres.

ind. in *-ima*, etc.). But towards the end of the century Federico Frezzi of Foligno wrote a language in which very few Umbrian features survive.

Texts in prose from Umbria and the Marches are nearly all practical in character. They are markedly dialectal, though there is some attempt to avoid regional characteristics. (Hence regressions like *colonda*, perpetrated at Perugia in an attempt to get away from regionalism of the *quanno* type.) Latium provides the only prose text of the time outside Tuscany which can qualify as artistic: the *Historiae Romanae fragmenta*, noted for the chapters that constitute the *Vita di Cola*. Unfortunately, the lack of other texts suitable for comparison and the uncertainties of the manuscript tradition leave us in doubt as to the relationship of its language to the 'natural' speech of Rome.

Before leaving central Italy we should note that in the Abruzzi, too, prose showed less cultivation than poetry (the dramatic *laude*, the *Detto dell'Inferno*, Buccio di Ranallo); the final *-u* is frequently avoided in verse, for example, but still predominates in the prose. And in Buccio's poems we find symptomatic regressions: *vedembo* for *vedemmo*, *abembo* for *avemmo*, etc.

In the kingdom of Naples the situation at the beginning of the century recalls that in northern Italy: moral and didactic poems were written (like the *Libro di Catone* or the *Bagni di Pozzuoli*) in a koine which had numerous southern features. In the *Serventese del Maestro di tutte le arti*, composed near the end of the century (or the beginning of the next), there are numerous tuscanisms. As for prose, its most important monument, the so-called *Cronaca di Partenope*, is not only a conglomeration of four different sections, but has come down to us in a manuscript tradition which is anything but helpful to linguistic study. The *Tabula Amalfitana* is in even worse case. Moreover, various translations of treatises on practical subjects are still unpublished or have been badly edited. And lack of communal life in the kingdom prevented us from having copious local records to examine.

Sicily in the early decades of the century looked only to itself and showed signs of producing a stable chancellery Sicilian (the 'vulgari nostro siculo', as it was then called). In the second half of the century Tuscan began to gain authority as a literary language: Dante was read; and Tommaso Caloiro, a friend of Petrarch's, addressed him in a Tuscan sonnet. But there was little poetry: the *Quaedam profetia* or *Lamento di parte siciliana*, probably written in 1354, and not much else. The prose of the period con-

sists of documents and letters, religious constitutions and some
moral and historical texts (mainly translations or compilations):
the *Dialagu de Sanctu Gregoriu*, the *Sposizione del Vangelo della
Passione*, the *Istoria di Eneas*, the *Valerio Massimo*, etc. Folena has
shown, in his edition, that the *Istoria di Eneas* is based on a Tuscan
text (a translation by A. Lancia) which the Sicilian translator
quite often misunderstood (as when he made *sochira* of Lancia's
serocchia). Tuscanizing forms like *giornu* and *più* appear in the
translation of St. Mark's Gospel made in the second half of the
Trecento (and written in Greek letters).

Since there is obviously not enough space here to give a complete grammatical and lexical description of Trecento Italian, and
since many of its features are the same as those of modern Italian,
we shall concentrate in the next few paragraphs on those features
in it which differed from modern Italian usage or which underwent change in the fourteenth century.

Spelling was incomparably less stable than it now is. The sounds
causing greatest oscillation were velars and palatals: we have
cane and *chane* (the use of *k* diminished but did not disappear);
pace and *pacie*; *degno* and *dengno*; *figlio*, *figlo* and *filglio*. Nor was it
easy to decide to what extent the spelling of the vernacular should
be applied to learned words: we have *onore* and *honore*; generally
we find *atti honesti*, but also *lonesto* and *donesto* (in cases where we
now use the apostrophe), *rapto* and *ratto*, *letizia* and *letitia*, *teatro*
and *theatro*. Single and double consonants also give rise to uncertainties, especially after certain prefixes (*a-*, *pro-*). To represent
the doubling of *q* Petrarch writes *giaqque*, and then in the final
version *giacque* (in the son. 'Qual mi fec'io'). Punctuation is very
scarce; in the Trivulzian manuscript of the *Commedia*, for instance,
there is simply a dot at the end of each *terzina*. The use of capital
letters, at least in the better manuscripts, is close to ours today.
Acute accents are very occasionally found. There are some
regional peculiarities. In Tuscany only Lucca and Pisa distinguish voiced *s*, which they represent with a *z*. In the Po valley
ce, *ci* frequently stand for sounds for which modern Italian uses
ze, *zi*. At Genoa palatal *c* is expressed sometimes by *ih* (*sihavo*
for *sc'avo*). In southern Italy *cz* stands for voiceless *z* [ts] but also
for palatal *cc* [ttʃ] (*saczo* for *saccio*). In Sicily *ch* is constantly used
for palatal *c* [tʃ] (*chircari*), but also for [kj]: *choviri*, *chudiri*. When
use of *k* diminishes and continental Italy's custom of using *ch* for a
velar comes to Sicily (*chi* for *che*) uncertainties are caused; are we
to read *cantichi* with a palatal or with a velar? There was an

attempt to render velar *g* with *gk* (*longki* in the *Regula di S. Bene-dittu*, ch. 18, ed. Branciforti).

When we come to sounds, we note that the diphthongized forms still prevail in the series *priego* and *pruova* (after plosive +*r*). Resistance to the diphthong *au* (due to a reaction against the tendency to change *altro* to *autro*, etc.) is to be seen in the altera-tion undergone by latinisms containing it (*lalda, altore*), though these forms were, in fact, limited to plebeian strata. Syncopated forms like *rompre, lettre* (a western Tuscan type) are found even in poetry (Petrarch). It is probable that it was in the Trecento that the *c* of *aceto, dieci* changed from being an affricate to being a spirant, joining the -*c*- of *bacio, brucio* (Castellani, *Nuovi testi*, 29-31, 161-2). There was frequently oscillation in endings with palatal *c* and *z*: *tencione* for *tenzone*; *incalciare*; and, vice versa, *bonazza*; *trezze*. Before the pronoun *tu* one could omit the final vowel of verbs ending in -*si* and -*sti* and of the conjunction *se*: *fostù, postù, pregastù, stu*, etc. The final -*r* of apocopated infinitives could be assimilated to the following consonant: we find in rhyme-position *vedella* (=*vederla*, Petrarch), *emendallo* (Bocc.), *gittalla* (Pucci), *avella* (Canigiani), *guidàgli* (=*guidarli*, Folgore), *credégli* (Bocc.), etc. Outside Tuscany imitation of Tuscan features gave rise to hypertuscanisms, that is, regressions. In the north we find such forms as *gioglia, noglia*. Because of Tuscan pronunciation of -*aio* as a triphthong (i.e. as a single syllable), the author of the *Leandreide* makes *Nicolao* rhyme with *sezzao*. The Orvietan Pro-denzani extends the diphthong *uo* to *roco* (<*raucus*) making it *ruoco*.

Passing to morphology, we note certain variants in plurals of nouns: *cavallo* had the plurals *cavagli* and *cavai* as well as *cavalli*. These forms were originally conditioned by the initial consonant or vowel of the following word, but were later freely used as artistic effect required. Boccaccio, in the *novella* of Lisabetta, has 'il maggior de' *fratelli*', but 'i *fratei* domandandone' (*Dec.*, IV, 5). *Raggio* had as plurals *raggi* and *rai* (which long survived in verse). On the other hand, the phonetically regular paradigm *danaio*, pl. *danari*, began to seem strange and fall into disuse. Nouns and adjectives in -*co* frequently had plurals different from those that later prevailed: *fisichi* (F. Uberti), *grammatichi* (id.; Pucci), *salvatichi* (Bocc.), etc. Many words in -*a* still had plurals in -*i*: *le veni, le porti, far bocchi*. We have very many examples over wide areas of nouns in -*e* being regarded as invariable in the plural: *le parte, le chiave* (but Petrarch corrected *verde fronde* to *verdi fronde*

K M.I.L.

in the sonnet 'L'aura serena'). Plurals in *-a* were much more numerous than they are today: *le cannella, le letta, le merla*. So were those in *-ora*: *le borgora, le cambiora, le elmora, le palcora, le pegnora*. The plural of *malanno, maglianni* shows that the juxtaposition was in that case still not firmly established. Among the pronouns we already find occasional examples of *lui* and *lei* as subject-pronouns; and also constructions like *per lo colui consiglio* (Bocc.). The form *gliele* is used for any kind of accusative used with any third-person dative. The possessive adjectives show us *mie, tuo, suo* used for all genders and numbers (*al mie cor, e' mie desiri, la tuo veste, la suo camera, i suo atti*), even in tonic position: *da' lupi tuo* (Sacchetti). In the article, there is oscillation between *il* and *el*; *lo* is regularly used after a consonant, especially after *per* and *messer* (*per lo fresco, messer lo frate*). There is even greater freedom in the use of *i, li, gli* (*stracciò li vestimenti*). Among the numerals, *due* has still many variants (*due, dui, duo, dua*); syncopated forms of the *venzei, venzette* type are found in both prose and verse. As for the verb, we note first that there are numerous examples of differences between the tonic stem and the atonic: *lo aiuto*, but *aitare, atare*; *io manuco* with *manicare*, etc. In the present tense, *tu ami* is now normal, but *tu ame* persists as a poetic variant. The ending *-iamo* is now generalized to all conjugations (*noi amiamo, noi vediamo, noi finiamo*), but *-amo, -emo, -imo* persist at Pisa, Lucca and Arezzo. Indeed, some forms (especially *avemo*) are still usable, not only in verse (*avemo*, Bocc. *Tes.*, V, 52; *vedemo, sapemo*, and even *calchemo*, *Tes.*, XII, 7), but occasionally, too, in prose ('sì come già più volte detto *avemo*', *Dec.*, II, 7). In the imperfect the forms in *-avate* predominate in the 2nd conj.: Boccaccio has *avavate, ardavate, diciavate* in prose and verse. In the past definite tense the distribution of strong and weak forms sometimes differs from that of today (*crese* for *credette*, *vivette* for *visse*, etc.) and the forms, too, are sometimes different (*dolfe* for *dolse*). The short *perdé, salì* are now normal, but the epithetic *perdeo, salio* remain alongside them. In the 3rd plur. the struggle between various endings persists over a long period, both in the strong perfects (*scrissono, scrissoro, scrissero*) and in the weak (*andaro, andarono, andorno, andonno*). In the 1st conj. future and conditional Florentines use *-erò*, etc., though not without some exceptions (*gittarà*, Bocc., *Dec.*, II, 10). Syncopation is extensive: *lavorrò, lacerranno, dimorrò, rendrà, guarrò*, and even *dranno, srete*. The syncopation is optional: Pucci, for example, uses *menerò* and *menrò* according to the requirements of metre. Occasionally we have assimilation as well: *sarrò*

('salirò'). By analogy with the syncopated and metathetic forms
(*enterrà*) there arose numerous forms with non-etymological -*rr*-:
troverrò, *griderrete*. In the imp. subjunctive, the endings are slow to
settle; we have *io avesse* (Sacch.), *tu vedessi* (Petr.), (*voi*) *prendesti*
(Compagni), (*voi*) *credessi* (Boccaccio). The participles without suffixes are very numerous: *cerco, guasto, tocco, véndico, visso*, etc. The
startling superlative of the gerund found in Giordano da Rivalto
is purely individual and is not part of the usage of his time
('andronne in ninferno? Sì bene, ritto, ritto, correndissimo',
Pred., XXI, 119 Narducci). *Avere* has still several parallel forms:
aggio, found particularly in the poetic tradition, *abbo*, mainly at
Lucca. *Dea* and *stea* are still the prevalent forms for *dia* and *stia*.
Avere is frequently used as an auxiliary with reflexives of various
kinds: 'quando non *se l'avesse* messo' (Passavanti, *Specchio*, 62
Pol.), '*s'avea* posto in cuore di non lasciarla mai' (Boccaccio,
Dec., III, 6), '*avendosi* dato piacere' (Sercambi, *Nov.*, 226 Renier)
'ora *te l'hai* dimenticato' (*ibid.*, 300), etc. Coming to invariable
words we should note the frequency of the construction *incon-
trogli, dattornovi, addossoli, dentrovi*. *Mediante* can now be used with
plurals: '*mediante* molti avversi casi' (Bocc., *Filoc.*).

What we have said thus far refers to Tuscany. It would be
interesting to study as well the linguistic developments of other
regions—both in order to note abiding characteristics in those
areas and in order to study Tuscan penetration. Here we shall
limit ourselves to a couple of examples. We have already mentioned
that in the Po Basin the endings -*ati*, -*eti*, -*iti* are well established
in the 2nd pers. plur. Neapolitan texts show another peculiarity
that will remain for centuries—conjugation of infinitives and
gerunds: 'medici li quali sancza alchuna caritate domandano
essereno pagati' (*Cron. di Partenope*, c. XXVI). On the other hand,
the expansion of -*iamo* in the indicative (at the expense of -*amo*
-*emo* -*imo*) is well exemplified in Umbria, where prose texts (e.g.
the Perugian *Statuto* of 1342) have the phonetically regular forms,
while Umbrian *laude* and *sacre rappresentazioni* show the -*iamo* form
with some frequency.

In syntax, we note that the partitive *di* is still widely used:
'e domandar *del pane* (Dante, *Inf.*, 33), 'tra li uccelli à *di* valenti
medici' (*Esopo* Guadagni, XIII), '*di valentissimi vini* e confetti fecer
venire' (Bocc., *Dec.*, I, 10). An appositional construction with *di*
may follow a noun with definite article ('il cattivel *d'*Andreuccio',
Bocc., *Dec.*, II, 5; 'del cattivello *di* Calandrino', *Dec.*, VIII, 7;
'lo innamorato *di* Paolo', St. Catherine of Siena, the meaning here

being 'that soul full of love, St. Paul'). No preposition is needed
in the construction 'in casa i Frescobaldi', 'a casa il diavolo'. The
use of the article with *di* expressing complement of material is
still possible; indeed, if a definite article precedes, the articulated
preposition is preferred ('le colonne *del* porfido', Bocc.). Later,
however, *di* without article will become obligatory. The indefinite
article is used in the constructions 'una sua madre', 'una sua
donna' (Bocc., *Dec.*, II, 6, III, 9, IV, 3). The superlative in
-issimo is sometimes used as a relative superlative ('la Rettorica
è *soavissima* di tutte l'altre scienze', *Conv.*, II, XIII, 14). Other
intensive words can be used with it: 'di *sì* nobilissima virtù'
(Dante, *Vita nuova*, II, 9), '*assai* picciolissima cosa' (Sercambi,
Novelle, p. 200 Renier). Quantitative indefinites can agree with
the partitive nouns that follow them: 'Deh! com'ai *poca* di stabili-
tate' (Lapo Gianni, son. 'Amor nova ed antica vanitate') 'quivi
cresce con *tanta* di ferezza' (Dino Frescobaldi, canz. 'Un sol
penser'), 'l'altra (chiave) vuol *troppa*—d'arte e d'ingegno avanti
che disserri' (Dante, *Purg.*, IX, 124-5); 'in *poche* di volte che con
lui stato era' (Bocc., *Dec.*, VIII, 9). But we also find 'qui si con-
venne usare un *poco* d'arte' (*Purg.*, X, 10) cf. 'qui si vuole usare un
poco d'arte' (Bocc. *Dec.*, VIII). The second pluperfect (*trapassato
remoto*) can be used in main clauses: 'e questo detto, alzata
alquanto la laterna, *ebber veduto* il cattivel d'Andreuccio' (Bocc.,
Dec., II, 5); 'Non volendomi Amor perdere ancora—*ebbe* un altro
lacciuol fra l'erba *teso*' (Petr., 271). The impersonal verb is
frequently introduced by the subject *egli*: '*Egli* trapassavano poche
mattine che io, levata, non salissi' . . . (Bocc., *Fiammetta*, 50
Pernicone); '*el* mi restava molte cose a dire' (Bocc., *Filostrato*, II,
58, Pernicone). Participles and gerunds are put to more numerous
uses than in either the Duecento or the Cinquecento, and sometimes their stylistic function is worthy of note. The agent complement with *a*, now limited to the groups *far fare*, *lasciar fare*, is found
in the Duecento and Trecento with other infinitives joined to *fare*
and *lasciare*: 'non ti fare pregare ne' suoi bisogni *a colui*' (Paolo da
Certaldo, n. 335); 'elli (Sansone) si lasciò vincere *a* sua femina'
(Bencivenni, *Espositione del Patern.*, p. 55); 'la fa uccidere e mangiare *a* lupi' (*Dec.*, II. 9). The asyndetic sequence of two imperatives is frequent ('*va togli* quel canestro', Sacchetti, nov. 118) and
will remain alive, but only in popular usage. The same can be
said of the constructions *dar mangiare*, *dar bere*. The modal uses of
dovere, *venire*, *volere* are notable: 'Pirro adunque cominciò ad
aspettare quello che far *dovesse* la gentil donna' (Bocc., *Dec.*

VIII, 9), 'gli *venne* veduta una giovinetta assai bella' (ibid., I, 4);
'di così fatte femine non si *vorrebbe* aver misericordia' (ibid., V, 10).
Use of the accusative and infinitive, particularly with certain
verbs, indicates classicizing tendencies. Constructions with verbs
of fearing are also under Latin influence: 'sì ch'io temetti ch'ei
tenesser patto' (Dante, *Inf.*, XXI, 93); 'temendo no 'l mio dir
gli fosse grave' (*Inf.*, III, 80); 'li due fratelli, li quali dubitavan
forte non ser Ciapelletto gl' ingannasse' (Bocc., *Dec.*, I, 1); 'la
donna e 'l giovane . . . subito sospettano che non fosse quello che
era' (Sacchetti, nov. 84). One kind of concessive clause is governed
by *per che, perché*: 'Non andar mai a casa di niuna femina mondana
. . . *per ch*'ella mandi per te' (Paolo da Certaldo, n. 86); 'Tu,
per ch'io m'adiri—non sbigottir ch'io vincerò la prova' (Dante,
Inf., VIII, 121); 'da amare, perché io voglia, non mi posso partire'
(Bocc., *Fiamm.*, V). Some problems of word-order have already
received considerable attention from scholars. Such are the rules
governing pronominal enclisis—the 'law of Tobler and Mussafia'
to which we referred in Chapter IV, and the order of the atonic
pronouns in *li mi porta, mi si presenta*, etc.[1] Schiaffini has opened
the way to the study of others: the order of the noun-adjective
group, sometimes almost obligatory, sometimes free (*la lingua
latina, la tedesca rabbia, la cartaginese guerra*), and the order of words
in main and subordinate clauses, which has so much importance
in Boccaccio and his imitators.[2]

Again, many observations could be made on the language of
regions other than Tuscany. We limit ourselves to noting one
example: the use of *a* with personal object in Sicilian ('mandirà
ad Eneas a lu infernu' in the *Istoria di Eneas*, XII, § 4 Folena).

As one would expect, the many and varied activities pursued
in the Trecento led to a great expansion in vocabulary, both
generally and in specialisms. In some fields in which Latin had
been the medium of communication (philosophy, medicine, etc.),
Latin words passed into the vernacular when it came to be used
instead. In various arts and crafts certain words acquired a
technical meaning. We note a few examples from the artistic
field (stretching the period considered to the end of the century
in order to include Cennini). *A(c)querella* ('water-colour', now
acquerello) he speaks of thus: 'e poi aombrare le pieghe d'*aquerelle*
d'inchiostro; cioè aqua quanto un guscio di noce tenessi dentro

---

[1] A. Lombard, *Le groupement des pronoms personnels atones en italien* in *Studier i mod.
spr.*, XII, 1934, pp. 19-76.

[2] Schiaffini, *Tradizione e poesia*, pp. 194-9 and 229.

due gocce d'inchiostro' (Cennini, c. VII). For *aria* we have Petrarch's testimony ('umbra quaedam et quem pictores nostri *aerem* vocant, quo in vultu inque oculis maxime cernitur', *Famil.* XXIII, 19, 12). And it is used, not only by Cennini, but by Petrarch in his verse ('quell'*aria* dolce del bel viso adorno' 122; 'e mi contendi l'*aria* del bel volto', 300). *Fresco* Cennini also mentions: 'lavorare in fresco, cioè nella calcina fresca' (c. CLXXV). *Mensola* is in Dante (Purg., X, 132) and *sfumare* is another example from Cennini (c. XVII). That commerce made its contribution is seen in the example *milione*. Faitinelli uses it ('e gente paladina un *milione*' in the son. 'Se si combatte . . .' in 1315); but Iacopo d'Acqui still considers it necessary to explain it (about 1330): 'quod est idem quod divicie mille milia librarum'. So does Giovanni Villani: 'si trovò nel tesoro della Chiesa in Vignone in moneta d'oro coniata il valore di diciotto milioni di fiorini d'oro . . . ch'ogni milione è mille migliaia di fiorini la valuta' (*Cron.*, XI, 20). The way in which certain words were used in poetic vocabulary by the *stilnovisti* passed over into common usage (*angelo, stella, tesoro, occhi ladri*, etc.).

In word-formation we note that the *oltramirabile, oltrapiacente* type, common in the preceding century, went out of fashion. But *mis-* continued to be productive (*misavveduto, misavventura*, etc.). Suffixes that enjoyed increase were: *-esco, -evole, -ista* ('Messer Antonio piovano – eccellente *dantista*' writes Sacchetti in 1381). Sometimes there is uncertainty as to the suffix to be used; from *poeta* we find the adjectives *poetico* (from Latin: in Buti and others), *poetevole* (in the translation of Guido Giudice), *poetesco* (in Sacchetti) and *poetale* (in Zenone da Pistoia). Formations from verbs, without suffix, continue to be numerous: *bilancio, ploro, ruba*. But, even if we limit ourselves to Tuscany, the vocabulary of the period gives the impression of uncertainty. To express the concept 'sister', for example, we have, apart from *sorella*, the forms *suora* (Dante, Villani), *suore* (Cavalca), *sorore* (Petr.), *serocchia* (Villani), *sirocchia* (Dante), *sorocchia* (Sacchetti). Only one form, *suoro*, seems precisely localized (at Siena). Similarly, besides *lepre*, we have *levre, lievre*, and *lievore*. And we have, too, *altramente, altrimente, altramenti*, and (the eventual survivor) *altrimenti*. When a popular and a latinized form are in conflict the latter frequently triumphs.

Latinisms (and grecisms) had, in fact, a very large part in the expansion of Trecento vocabulary. The author of the *Fiore di virtù* tells us that 'le cose spirituali non si possono sì propriamente esprimere per paravole volgari come si esprimono per latino e per gramatica, per la penuria di vocaboli volgari'. But writers in less spiritual disciplines, like anatomy and medicine, also felt this penury; hence *congiuntiva, duodeno, ieiuno, poro, ulcerare*. And in astronomy we have the borrowings *Leo, Virgo, Scorpio, Tauro, Pisce*, etc. Sometimes, of course, a latinism was used, not out of necessity, but merely for elegance or to fit a metrical scheme: 'la traditrice *lepore* marina' says Faitinelli of Pisa (in the son. 'Poi rotti') when he needs a proparoxytone. But such words, for which there was no social need, usually died.

The forms given to latinisms varied. Sometimes they were taken as they were, sometimes they were adapted to Tuscan phonology. Writers had the possibility of using, not only *entrare, lottare, lecito* but also the latinizing *intrare, luttare, licito*, specially if useful for the rhyme. Alongside the popular *assempro* we have *essemplo* and *esempio*, by which *assempro* will eventually be ousted. Latin adjectives in *-undus* are given the ending *-ondo* in accordance with the development *profundus/profondo, secundus/secondo*; but we also have *-undo* (*vagabundo*, Bocc. *Tes.*, III, 76). Thus, too, we have *verecondia* and *verecundia, defonto* and *defunto* and oscillation between the endings *-anzia* and *-anza, -enzia* and *-enza*. Treatment of *J* also gives rise to hesitation; we have *Iove/Giove; iustizia/giustizia deiezione/degezione, addiettivo/aggettivo, plebeo/plebeio*, etc. And there is oscillation in the series *speciale/speziale, socio/sozio*, etc.

In morphology, it is usual to adapt the accusative form of the noun, without the final *-m*. But in 3rd. decl. nouns, and not only those in *-o* (*Apollo*, etc.), the adoption of the nominative is not at all rare: we have *aspe, ospe, satelle, vime*, etc., apart from the type *maiesta, podesta, mortalita, Trinita*, etc. At the end of the Duecento and beginning of the Trecento there is still great oscillation in classical proper names. For Venus (*Venere*) we find *Veno, Venusso, Venus*. But the French type of adaptation gradually yields to that now in use: Dante oscillates between *Cleopatràs* and *Cleopatra*; but Petrarch has only *Cleopatra*. The accent in some rare words, particularly proper names, tends to pass on to the penultimate: *Amazóne* (Bocc., *Tes.*), *baltèo* (Bocc.), *satìro* (Sercambi), etc.

Some locutions came from juridical or philosophical language into the vernacular: *de plano, di nottetempore* (or *di nottetempo*), *e converso*, etc. Naturally, borrowing was not confined to classical authors, but included ecclesiastical and medieval writers; hence *condegno < condignus* from St. Paul, *girovago < gyrovagus* in the *Regola* of St. Benedict, *duello, bravìo* from medieval writers.

Frequently, the writer introducing a latinism felt the need to explain it to his readers: 'quella *ostetrice,* cioè che leva i fanciulli' (*Pistola di S. Girol.*), 'Avvegna che per molte condizioni di grandezze le cose si possono *magnificare,* cioè fare grandi. . . .' (Dante, *Conv.,* I, X, 7). And sometimes, the introduction of latinisms led to the ousting of words previously in use. Thus *esercito, orazione, repubblica* replaced *oste, diceria,* and *comune* (in the senses 'army', 'oration', 'republic').

In many cases relatinization took place; the Latin forms were substituted for those words that had already developed Tuscan forms. In the doublets *cecero-cigno, diecimo-decimo, dificio-edificio, etterno-eterno, fedire-ferire, giogante-gigante, guagnelo/vangelo-evangel(i)o, ninferno-inferno, nicistà/necessità-necessità, orrato-onorato, orrevole-onorevole, sanatore-senatore, sinestro-sinistro,* the second form gradually triumphed at the expense of the first. Sometimes in this matter poetry preceded prose. Sometimes non-Tuscan influence tipped the scales in favour of the Latin form. In the Trecento the Tuscans used *Cicilia, ciciliano,* in prose (Boccaccio) and in verse (Dante, Petrarch). Villani (*Cron.,* I, 8) noted that 'per la varietà di volgari degli abitanti è oggi da loro chiamata *Sicilia,* e da noi Italiani *Cicilia.*' And it was *Sicilia,* with Latin backing, that prevailed. Relatinization did not always succeed, however; that Petrarch used *bibo* or *describo* in rhyme position or that Boccaccio used *limbo* for *lembo* did not prove adequate to shake popular use of *bevo, lembo* or the semi-learned *descrivo.*

To sum up, Italian in this period accepted hundreds of latinisms, not only in literary usage, but in everyday language (and, indeed, in official language, e.g. *censo, esattore*). Here is a brief list of examples (though it is possible that one or two may belong to the preceding century):

adunco, ambrosia, antropofago, atroce, austero, autentico, circonferenza, claudicare, compatriota, confabulare, consimile, discolo, energumeno, esistenza, eunuco, evaporare, faretra, frugale, girovago, ignavia, incolore (Cecco d'Ascoli), *indigente, industrioso, ingurgitare, invitto, mellificare, milizia, ostare, premeditare, prolisso, puerile, pusillanime* (-*o*), *qualificare, rubicondo, serico, settentrione, siccità, sofistico, spurio, stirpe, transitorio, truculento, venereo, venusto, verecondo, vigile, vigilare.*

On the other hand, many latinisms introduced by individual writers failed to take root; such were Sacchetti's *ablato* ('thing carried away', nov. 293), Canigiani's *ceno* 'mud' (*Ristorato,* cap. XL), etc. Sometimes there are obvious reasons for this, like homonymic clash. Thus *celare* 'carve, engrave' <CAELARE could

not live alongside *celare* 'to hide'. *Contento* 'contempt' <CONTEMPTUS and *contento* in the sense of 'content, thing contained' gave way to *contento* ('happy, content'). On the other hand the latinism *ostare* 'to obstruct' beat the gallicism *ostare* 'to take' (<*oster*, *ôter*). Certain Latin meanings and constructions also failed to catch on; such was *istituire* 'to educate', though *discorrere* 'to turn about, go round' lived for some time in the literary language.

With France there were, as we saw earlier, direct and literary contacts. The direct influence of French can be exemplified by reference to a letter written in 1330 by Balduccio Partini, a Pistoiese resident at Beaulieu, who wrote '. . . che io mi rappresenterei *dedens certana* giornata a Parigi . . . in questa *derniera* lettera ch'à mandata . . . no ci à *valletto* nè *ciamberiera* che possa durare con lui,' etc. In literature French and Provençal influences, which had been so great in the previous century, can still be perceived. Dino Compagni's *canzone del Pregio*, for example, has numerous gallicisms and provençalisms ('Ché pregio è un miro di clartà gioconda—ove valor *s'agenza* e si pulisce . . . en guerra franco a mostrar sua valenza—e *driturier*, quando *impronta*, al pagare. . . .'). Halfway through the century, many gallicisms still persisted, and those used in poetry only partly coincided with those used in prose (we have, for example, *dammaggio*, *plusori* in the *Teseida*; *civire*, *civanza*, *saramento*, *sugliardo* in the *Decameron*). But Petrarch made a rigid selection, and the gallicisms in verse that he avoided (e.g. *naverare*) disappeared for good. New gallicisms were, in fact, few in this century. Some words came in with the objects they represented, e.g. *dorè*, *tanè* in the Florentine dyers' tariff (1375); *bombarda*, first used with reference to the siege of Brescia in 1311 (and the suffix of which suggests it is French) and *petito* (a liquid measure in central Italy). Nor did gallicisms always maintain the elegant connotation they had when imported. *Ciambra*, *zambra* must have been adopted as superior synonyms for *camera*. But Pucci uses *camera* and *zambra* with indifference as to meaning, according to the exigencies of metre; at Siena *ciambra* comes to mean 'a hole for rubbish' (translation of the Constitution 1309-10) and the derivative *zambracca* (which is in the *Corbaccio*) is likewise a pejorative.

From the Iberian peninsula came few words: the name of the card game, *nàibi* (from Arabic), and *mugàveri* or *almogàveri*. At the end of the century came majolica vases (*maioliche*); but in Cennini the word has not yet got beyond being a proper noun ('belli vasi da Domasco o da *Maiolica*', c. CVII). It is difficult to tell whether certain arabisms, now documented, entered in this century or in the previous one; such are *cubebe*, *tazza* and *chermisì*. Few words came from German: *piffero* (in the *Pecorone*), and the game *zighinetta* (Lucca 1362). *Sciverta* (for 'sword' <*Schwert*) was used only by Prodenzani (*Sollazzo*, VI, 73) and did not take root. Some other terms, like *luffomastro* or *luvomastro* (Villani) and *dicco* ('I Fresoni ruppono i *dicchi*, ciò sono gli argini,' Villani) are used only in references to their places of origin. The same can be said of terms used by Italian merchants in England: *costuma* (the 'customs' =*dogana*), *cochetto* (receipt for payment of customs' dues), *feo* ('fee'), etc., and of the Greek and oriental words used in accounts of travels, e.g. Leonardo Frescobaldi's 'duecento *calòri*', that is *caloiri*, *calògeri*.

Words from other dialects entered Tuscan at this period. Here we do not mean to refer to words from other regions used by Tuscan writers for local colour or to those non-Tuscan words which persist as a substratum in the works of non-Tuscan authors (like *treppare* 'to jump' in a sonnet written in 'Italian' by Vannozzo), but rather to those that obtained a permanent position in the language. Among these, northern words predominate—words from Venice (*madrigale*) or from places in the Po Basin which it is difficult to specify (*cavezza*, *corazza*, *rugiada*, *filugello*). In words of this kind, too, there are oscillations in form: the Venetian *dóse* (*doxe*) gives *doge* in Giamboni and Boccaccio, *dugie* in Barberino, *dogio* in Villani, *dugio* in the 'Re Giannino', *dogio* or *dugio* in Sercambi. These variants are, of course, due to influence of Latin *dux* and vernacular *duca* and to the close semantic relationship. (Francesco da Barberino in his *Reggim.*, I, iv and I, v, speaks of the *duca di Storlich* in verse and the *dugie di Storlich* in prose.) Within Tuscany, too, exchanges were frequent; Florence gave and received. And if we still find frequent local characteristics in texts from Lucca, Pistoia, Siena and Arezzo, we find them mingled with forms from literary Florentine: *ponto*, *fameglia*, *merolla* alongside *punto*, *famiglia*, *midolla*.

7

The Quattrocento

Once again in this chapter our chronological limits will not correspond exactly to those of the century. We shall begin at 1375, the initial date of what has come to be known (with reference to Sacchetti's lament on the death of Boccaccio) as the *secolo senza poesia* (1375-1475). But we shall go on to the last decade of the fifteenth century. Within this period certain dates stand out: those of the *Certame coronario* (1441), the beginning of printing in the vulgar tongue (1470), the death of Lorenzo de' Medici (1492) and the invasion of Italy by Charles VIII of France (1494).

The days of the city-state were now over. The small *signorie*, too, tended to disappear, absorbed by regional states governed by a prince or an oligarchy. Venice extended its territory on the mainland by eliminating the Scaligers and the Carrara; Florence reconquered Pisa (1406) and acquired Leghorn (1421). In the first half of the century Filippo Maria Visconti, following in the footsteps of Gian Galeazzo, attempted expansion. The Aragonese added the state of Naples to their Sicilian domain. The papal state was seriously weakened by schism; only in the time of Nicholas V did it once again become a force in Italian politics. A certain equilibrium was established in the last decades of the Quattrocento, dominated by Lorenzo the Magnificent. But rivalry between the Italian states was strong enough to prevent them from taking concerted action when Italy was threatened from without by France and Spain. The fall of Constantinople (1453) had repercussions on Italian political and cultural life, and the expansion of the Turks caused the emigration of Albanian and Serbo-Croat colonies. The position of Savoy astride the Alps gave the French language an important place in Piedmont. Sardinia was in the hands of the Aragonese. Corsica depended politically on Genoa, Malta on the Kingdom of Naples, and coastal Dalmatia on Venice. Owing to the personal rule of the princes, their prestige and influence were enormous, not only on the life of the courts in their states, but on their chancelleries. In comparison, the work of the chancelleries in the oligarchies was very impersonal. There was considerable movement of population at this period, both within states (where there was much migration from the country to the towns) and from state to state (marriages, exiles, mercenaries, diplomatic activity, etc.), sometimes with notable linguistic effect. An example of this was the importation into Florence of dialectal peculiarities from western and southern Tuscany. There was much commerce, by land and sea, with other European countries. But Turkish expansion damaged certain colonial settlements and Italian commercial centres. Italian commercial life was to suffer more, however, from the opening of a new way to the East made possible by Portuguese circumnavigation of Africa.

Enthusiasm for humanism spread to all Italy; its main centre was Florence. The discovery of ancient manuscripts and the attempted reconquest of the ancient world were both causes and effects of a new confidence in human abilities and in the importance and dignity of man. Life on earth was no longer regarded mainly as a preparation for the next world, but was increasingly valued for its own sake. Whereas medieval culture had been almost exclusively ecclesiastical in character, humanist culture was mainly secular, both in its interests and in its participants. Alongside the Aristotelianism which was still predominant in the schools, there appeared Neoplatonic and mystical currents of thought, which were especially strong at Florence towards the end of the century. Whereas early humanism was a magnification of civil life and of the free construction by man of an earthly city, the end of the fifteenth century, as Garin has emphasized, witnessed a desire to escape from the world and the growth of contemplative tendencies.

In this period the professional man of letters became a common figure, and there are examples, too, of poets (like Serafino Aquilano) who earned their living by reciting their own work. The more rigorous examination of texts laid the foundations of modern textual philology. Problems of linguistic history began to be discussed; an example is the famous argument that took place in Florence in 1435 on the relationship between spoken and cultured Latin (i.e. whether there had existed in ancient Rome a difference between them analogous to the difference between Latin and the vernacular in Quattrocento Italy). Admiration of ancient writers led to imitation of them. Writers in Latin strove to purify their language of medieval characteristics and to forge a new style for themselves. Some attempted to skim the cream from a number of authors; others restricted the canon to Cicero. Their attitude found expression in Giannozzo Manetti's famous discourse *De dignitate et excellentia hominis*, where he asserted that language was not a gift of Nature, but a 'subtile quoddam et acutum artificium'. Coluccio Salutati did more than reform his own language; as chancellor of the Florentine Republic, he provided a new chancellery style. The humanists' search for a nobler language led them to inveigh against the traditional Latin of the schools and old manuals like the *Doctrinale* and *Grecismus*. The figurative arts also displayed a desire to throw off the medieval by means of a new realism and by assimilation of the teaching of the ancients. Plans for ideal cities were drawn up, and bold experiments in town planning were carried out. From them several cities acquired the physiognomy that they still have.

At Italian courts humanists enjoyed the favour of most of the princes, several of whom had either been the pupils of famous teachers or entrusted their sons to them. Some of the princes nevertheless openly and energetically promoted the use of the vernacular. At Milan, Filippo Maria Sforza, who was capable of improvizing a speech in Latin, took pleasure in reading Petrarch and Boccaccio. He got Guiniforte Barzizza to prepare a commentary on the *Inferno* (about 1440) and even got the reluctant Filelfo to comment on Petrarch. Whether he was the initiator of the use of Italian in the Milanese chancellery or no, he certainly supported it. Much later in the century, if we are to believe Francesco Tanzi, who published the poems of Bernardo Bellincioni (1493), Lodovico Maria Sforza called to his court 'il faceto poeta Belinzone, a ciò che per l'ornato fiorentino parlare di costui e per le argute, terse et prompte sue rime la città nostra venesse a limare et polire il suo alquanto rozo parlare' (I, p. 5, Fanfani). And Lodovico il Moro remarked to Giambattista Ridolfi (who reported it to Piero de' Medici) that 'la nazione fiorentina nel dire e nello scrivere volgare passa tutti gli altri'. At Ferrara, where the seeds of humanist education had been sown first by Donato degli Albanzani and then by Aurispa and Guarini, the Estensian court was also a seed-bed of vernacular culture. Ludovico Carbone tells us (*Facezie*, CVIII) that a certain *podestà*, having received a letter from the duke containing the words 'capias *accipitrem* et mitte nobis ligatum in sacculo ne aufugiat', sent him, not a falcon, but a priest (having taken *accipitrem* to mean *arciprete*). From that time letters were written, not in Latin, but in Italian. It is certainly true that Ferrara's rulers, beginning with Niccolò III (who had Pier Andrea Bassi comment on Boccaccio's *Teseida*) gave powerful support to vernacular culture. In the court and chancellery of Naples, after the cultural decadence of the Angevin period, there was a notable renaissance under the Aragonese. Latin and Catalan predominated in the chancellery, and comparatively few letters in ennobled Neapolitan date from the time of Alfonso I. In the reign of Ferdinand I, however, the vernacular came into its own, and Pontano gave a certain style to chancellery correspondence.

In a climate so favourable to study education prospered. It was based mainly on the Latin classics, but manuals frequently made use of the vernacular as a medium of instruction. Greek studies were encouraged, not only by the needs of a developing humanism, but also by external events (the council of Ferrara and Florence concerning the unity of the Greek and Latin churches, and the emigration of many scholars after the Turkish conquest of Byzantium). But translations from Greek were seldom direct: they were generally through Latin. Some scholars (Giannozzo Manetti, Giovanni Pico) took up the study of Hebrew. Nor was commercial instruction neglected, as we can see from treatises like Luca Pacioli's *Summa de Arithmetica, Geometria, Proportioni et Proportionalita* (Venice, 1494).

In churches preaching took place in Latin, in Italian and in a mixture of both. Among the preachers of the age were San Bernardino da Siena, Giovanni Dominici and Girolamo Savonarola. Moreover, some preachers addressed congregations, not only in churches, but also in the piazzas. And in their anxiety to make themselves understood they undoubtedly strove to adapt their speech to local habits. San Bernardino, in a sermon of 1429, stated: 'Quando io vo predicando di terra in terra, quando io giongo in un paese, io mi ingegno di parlare sempre sicondo i vocaboli loro; io aveva imparato e so parlare a modo loro molte cose. *El mattone* viene a dire il fanciullo, e *la mattona* la fanciulla' (pred. XXIII, p. 505 Bargellini). Nevertheless, the voices of preachers were less often heard in the piazzas than those of the *cantatori in panca*. We know that the Perugians, on several occasions, applied to Florence (or to Arezzo, Siena or Lucca) for good singers. Another form of entertainment much appreciated by the people was that afforded by the *sacre rappresentazioni*, or plays on religious subjects, which flourished particularly in central Italy, but also elsewhere. On the other hand, the performance of plays on classical themes was merely a court pastime. And that applied, not only to plays written in Latin, but also to those in Italian, like Poliziano's *Orfeo* (1480) and Niccolò da Correggio's *Cefalo* (1487), and to translations into Italian like Pandolfo Collenuccio's *Anfitrione* (1487).

Humanism had its effect on handwriting, the art of copying and the book trade. Latin books were so much more numerous than vernacular ones that those who wanted the latter had to pay more for them. But the greatest revolution in this sphere was, of course, occasioned by the invention of printing in Germany. In Italy, soon after the printing of certain Latin works, Vindelino da Spira published at Venice in 1470 the *Canzoniere* of Petrarch. Whether the Neapolitan edition of the *Decameron* known as the *Deo gratias* edition belongs to that year or to 1471 is uncertain. Certainly produced in 1471 were the Venetian *Decameron* of Valdarfer, the Roman Petrarch of Lauer, two Venetian editions of the Bible and probably the *Fiore di canzonette* of Giustinian. In 1472 there appeared three editions of the *Divine Comedy* (at Foligno, at Mantua, and at either Iesi or Venice), one of Petrarch's *Canzoniere* (at Padua), one of Boccaccio's *Decameron*, two of his *Filocolo* and one of his *Fiammetta*, as well as editions of Burchiello, Giusto de' Conti and Cavalca. Venice, Florence and Milan led the way in the printing of works in the Italian language; the more conservative university cities (Bologna, Rome) published few in comparison with the many they published in Latin. It is important to notice the priority, in time and quantity, enjoyed during the first ten years of printing by the three major Tuscan writers of the Trecento.

Printing radically affected the development of Italian. A manuscript is intended for one, or for few, readers. But printers wish to sell their books to large numbers of readers living in different areas; to them the elimination of odd features and the achievement of a certain degree of linguistic standardization are very important. Moreover, the printers of the period we are now dealing with soon came to employ persons to correct the works to be published. These did not share the main anxiety of the modern textual critic: that the author's final intentions should be respected. Their concern was to present the book in coherent, clear and widely intelligible language. This was bound to affect grammar and vocabulary. In the period between 1470 and 1550 printing made a decisive contribution to stability and uniformity of language in Italy.

In examining the condition of the vernacular in the fifteenth century we note a great difference between the first half of the century and the second. The humanists' exaltation of Latin lowered Italian in public esteem in the early Quattrocento, and it was mostly confined to humble purposes. It is true that some writers produced prose and verse in it; but there was nobody who cultivated it with both love and great artistic ability. In these circumstances linguistic standards in Tuscany became more indulgent and eclectic, not to say anarchical: Florentine speech accepted many new forms, some of them from western and southern Tuscan, and the written language also accepted these without scruple, using them alongside the traditional forms found in Trecento literature. Since those who sought elegance wrote in Latin, elegance was not a major concern of those who wrote in Italian.

Moreover, there was the problem posed by the use of latinisms. Whereas there were still some persons who wrote a plain, unpretentious language (Alessandra Strozzi, Bernardo Machiavelli), those who wrote with literary preoccupations opened the gates to a flood of words taken from Latin texts. Here is an example from Feo Belcari:

> *Prendi esercizio e non fatica* nimia
> . . . .
> *Tieni il cor lieto senza verun* nubilo,
> *se presto vuoi non si veggia il tuo* funere:
> *questo ti chieggo spero bramo e* cupio.
> *Con tutte le virtù sta in festa e giubilo;*
> *ché d'ogni grazia e d'ogni eccelso* munere
> *ti troverai alfin pieno il* marsupio.

As Salviati noted in the following century, 'Chi non era da tanto, che dettar potesse in latino, l'appressarsi quanto potea, e usar modi, che del Latino avessero, gloriosa opera riputava.' And Landino in the oration with which he inaugurated his Petrarchan readings, stated: 'È necessario essere Latino chi vuol essere buono Toscano . . .: volendo arricchire questa lingua bisogna ogni dì de' latini vocaboli non sforzando la natura derivare e condurre nel nostro idioma.' But 'non sforzando la natura' was a precept neglected by many semi-learned writers.

For the reasons we have noted (neglect, uncertainty as to grammatical standards and abuse of latinisms), scholars have rightly spoken of a crisis in the history of the Italian language in the early Quattrocento.[1] Yet if the vernacular was spurned in the literary field, it was increasingly used for utilitarian purposes. The humanists, by improving the Latin of their time and ridding it of medieval and Romance features, made it intelligible only to cultured persons. The new princes needed the favour of the people, and some of them openly favoured use of the vulgar tongue. Thus, humanism caused a depreciation of the vernacular by direct action, only to increase by indirect action its use in practical spheres. But in literary spheres, too, humanism was to make a direct contribution in the last decades of the Quattrocento. For then writers who had absorbed the humanist experience and learnt from the Latin classics turned to cultivation of Italian; and there triumphed what is known as vernacular humanism. Again it was Florence, with Lorenzo de' Medici and Poliziano, which achieved the new literary and linguistic synthesis. And whereas in other European nations (France, Spain, and also, *variatis variandis*, England and Germany) the impact of humanism came later and caused a profound break between the medieval and the Renaissance phases in linguistic history, in Italy there was merely a crisis of growth. The solid pre-humanist foundations of the language of the Trecento made adjustment easier than elsewhere.

As we have already said, the cultural life of the Quattrocento found expression in two languages, and the history of either of them cannot be understood without reference to its relationship to the other. All men of letters knew Latin more or less well. But while in the early stages of humanism some of the major writers wrote exclusively (or almost exclusively) in Latin (like Salutati), in the second half of the fifteenth century there were authors who were masters of both Latin and Italian (like Poliziano, Sannazzaro and Pontano). Yet, even in the period of its literary depression, Italian was firmly established in practical use. The Florentine *signoria* wrote to its representatives in Florentine, and they usually delivered their orations in the vernacular. Messer Nello di Giuliano da San Gimignano, ambassador to Martin V in 1425, spoke thus:

'Ancora sarebbe di bisogno innanzi a tanta Santità di parlare

---

[1] See especially G. Folena, *La crisi linguistica del Quattrocento e l'*Arcadia *di I. Sannazzaro*, Florence 1952.

per gramatica [=in Latin] con quello ornamento che si richie-
derebbe e di quella materia la quale a noi dalla nostra magnifica
Signoria è stata imposta. Ma perché e' non è di consuetudine
degli altri oratori e ambasciadori fiorentini, e etiandio per più
propiamente e più congruo al proposito di quegli che ce l'anno
commesso, per vulgare si poterà meglio soddisfare a ciascuna
parte con quella facultà e brevità. . . .'

Charles VIII's ambassadors, requesting free passage through the
territory of the Florentine Republic (1494), spoke in Latin and
received their reply in the same language. But Maximilian's asked
for Florence's alliance (1496) *aetrusca lingua* and got their answer
in Italian. From March 1414 all documents relating to commercial lawsuits in Florence had to be in the vernacular or be
considered invalid. And in 1451 it was resolved that the chancellery's notaries should keep an account of expenditure 'scrivendo
in volgare, acciò s'intenda pe' Ragionieri, che aranno a ris-
contrare coll'entrata del Proveditore di decta Camera et col Camar-
lingho della Cassetta del Monte'. In correspondence the reasons
for choice of Latin or Italian were sometimes stated. The Florentines, in reply to the Sienese, who had written in Latin, wrote:

'E perché noi crediam che sia utilissimo a voi e a noi dichiarare
bene e apertamente senza punto di simulazione ovvero dissimu-
lazione qual sia la vera intenzione e il puro e sincero proposito di
ciascuno di noi, abbiamo deliberato di farvi questa risposta più
tosto in volgare che in latino, sì e per soddisfar meglio e più
agli animi nostri, sì etiamdio perché la S. V. non abbia di bisogno
nell'intendere di questo nostro così sincero proposito d'altra
interpretazione che della nostra propria, nè in altro sentimento si
possa intendere che in quello che è il naturale e il vero intelletto
delle parole volgari.'

But of the 49 letters sent between 1435 and 1440 by the Cardinal
Legate Vitelleschi to the Priors of Viterbo some are in Latin and
some in Italian. The reasons for this are not clear; perhaps it
depended merely on the abilities of various secretaries. Among the
many letters written by Flavio Biondo da Forlì there are two in
the vernacular addressed to Francesco Sforza: one recommending
his son to him (1459) and one requesting a subsidy for the publication of the fourth Decad of his histories (1463). Here the reasons
are easier to guess. What is surprising is that, among non-literary
writings, there were some of a very practical nature written in
Latin: such are two treatises on cookery, probably from southern
Italy and belonging to the Angevin period.

Translations into Italian from Latin (and indeed from Greek, but usually through Latin) were numerous. The translators frequently declare that they labour to benefit the less learned or that they are acting on the request of a prince. A letter of Boiardo's tells us how he was required to translate in haste a part of Alberti's *De Architectura* for Duke Ercole I (letter of Sept. 17, 1488; II, p. 572 Zottoli), and we gather that the duke would not otherwise have derived much profit from it. Matteo Palmieri complained bitterly (*Vita civile*, Proemio) that many of the translations of his day were hopelessly inadequate. Sometimes, of course, the translators found genuine difficulty in finding Italian equivalents for Latin words. Landino, in his introduction to his version of Pliny, tells us: 'Non so come interpreti *seminario* et *arbusto*, item *ablaqueare* et *interlucare*, se non per circonlocutione o per il medesimo vocabolo'. Occasionally, however, the severe judgments of the critics were based merely on a conflict of linguistic standards. Giovanni Brancati of Matera, librarian to Ferdinand of Aragon, censured Landino's translation of Pliny, not just because he considered the translator a 'filosofastro', but also because he disliked Tuscan, which he found difficult to read and pronounce. Through some of the translations new words came into use. Landino's Pliny (the first edition about which we can speak with certainty is the Venice, Jenson, 1467) provided Pulci with words for the bestiary he inserted in Canto XXV of the *Morgante*; from it come *caprimulgo*, *ippotamo* (sic), *ibis*, *rinoceronte* (in Landino *rhinocerote*) and some ghost-words.

We must not forget that there were also some translations from Italian into Latin. Petrarch's version of the Griselda story from Boccaccio's *Decameron* was followed by others: those of Ciappelletto (A. Loschi), Tito and Gisippo (F. Beroaldo), Guiscardo and Gismonda (L. Bruni) and King Alfonso and Messer Ruggieri (B. Fazio). Piero della Francesca's *De Prospectiva pingendi* was written in Italian and translated by Maestro Matteo. Vespasiano da Bisticci said he had written 'a fine che se alcuno si volesse affaticare a far latine queste vite, egli abbia innanzi il mezzo col quale egli lo possa fare' (Discorso dell'autore).

Throughout the age of humanism Latin and Italian were in constant symbiosis. Works in Italian frequently bore Latin titles (*Amorum libri*, the love-poems of Boiardo; *De prospectiva pingendi*; *Hypnerotomachia Poliphili*, etc.). In letters written in Italian the headings, salutations and signature were often in Latin. The letter of dedication of Pacioli's *Summa* to Guidobaldo of Urbino was in Italian and Latin. Moreover, in the text of many letters the two languages were frequently mixed. A letter from Sixtus IV to Galeazzo Maria Sforza, written on 28 July 1474, begins:

'*Carissime fili salutem et apost. benedict.* Ve habiamo scripto molti brevi per li quali asai amplamente avete potuto intendere la iustitia nostra in li fati de Cita di Castello. E per questo si mara-vigemo assai e non possiam credere quillo n'e scripto da Fiorensa cio che voi non solo incitati Fiorentini contro di noi, ma anco prometete a loro ogni subsidio contra di noi. *A, fili carissime, quid tibi fecimus?* Non se ricordiamo averve offeso mai *nec verbo neque opere;* anco per lo singulare amore vi portiamo tuto quello abiamo potuto fare per voi habiamo fato e faremo sempre. *A a, numquid redditur pro bono malum? Quare foderunt foveam animę mee? A, fili carissime* consciderate la iustitia de le mie petitione. Con-siderate *contra quem agitur. . . .*'

The words of Don Atteone in Latin in Sabatino degli Arienti's letter-novella (p. 418 Gambarin) concerning the 'capellano don Baptista, il quale *laborabat in extremis*' were intended as a euphem-ism. When scriptural subjects were treated Biblical phrases were frequently quoted in Latin, and in the *sacre rappresentazioni* characters frequently spoke phrases or entire stanzas in Latin. In Pulci's *Morgante* (XXVII, st. 142) the Archangel Gabriel appears to the dying Orlando and reminds him of Job's words to his wife. He quotes Biblical phrases and then translates:

> *E perché pur la moglie si dolea*
> *E' disse: 'Donna mia, ora m'ascolta:*
> Dominus dedit, *lui data l'avea,*
> Dominus abstulit, *lui l'ha ritolta,*
> Sicut Dominus placuit, in ea
> Factum est, *così fatto è questa volta'.*
> *E poi* 'Sit nomen Domini' *ebbe detto*
> '*Il nome del Signor, sia benedetto*'.

Words and phrases (particularly adverbial phrases) which had belonged to chancellery Latin were embedded in sentences of chancellery Italian with even greater frequency than in the Trecento or late Cinquecento (*assiduo, autem,* etc.). But the most curious mixtures were found in sermons. Alongside sermons in Latin and sermons in Italian we find bilingual sermons. In the *Quaresimale* of Valeriano da Soncino we read:

'*Scis quod facit vulpes quando abstulit galinam illi pauperculae feminae?* La se ne va in lo boscheto e se mette in la herba fresca e volta le gambe al celo e sta a solazar cum le mosche. *Sic faciunt isti prophete*, questi gabadei, questi hypocritoni, sangioni dal collo torto, quando *habent plenum corpus* de galini, caponi, fasani, pernise, qualie e de boni lonzi de vitello e qualche fidegeti per aguzar lo apetito, e lo capo de malvasia, vernaza, vino greco, tribiani e moscatelli cum qualche prosuto, salziza, cerveladi, mortadelli, beroldi o vero cagasangui a la bresana per bevere melio. Non vedesti mai, madre mia, li meliori propheti.'

And in the sermons of Bernardino Tomitano da Feltre we find '*Quid est illa* ballarina *nisi una noctua que ludit* su l'archetto per farse remirar?' Similar examples are found in Gabriele Bareleta, Cherubino da Spoleto and Giovanni dell'Aquila. Indeed, the frequency of texts of this kind must lead us to the conclusion that the sermons were actually delivered in this mixture of two languages (a conclusion which will surprise nobody who has heard a Welsh preacher address an audience in which the younger listeners have an inadequate knowledge of the language habitually spoken by their elders).

At the end of the Quattrocento Padua witnessed the birth (in the *Macaronea* of Tifi Odasi and the *Tosontea* of Corrado) of an artistic stylization of this hybridism in the form of macaronic poetry. It differs from the language of the preachers, since, in it, Latin grammar and metrics are substantially respected, and the burlesque effect is gained simply by use of vernacular words mingled with Latin vocabulary. Born in university circles with forms dear to humanists (as we see from the almost constant use of the hexameter), macaronic poetry may have been inspired by the mixed language of preachers or by other examples of mingling. (The mutilations inflicted on Latin by 'cooks', i.e. by lay brothers in convents, were proverbial.)

The age which saw such close relations between Latin and Italian witnessed controversies between the supporters of the two languages.[1] In the *Paradiso degli Alberti* several speakers lend support to the vernacular. But we must take their statements as representing, not a number of witnesses, but the attitude of the author, Giovanni Gherardi. Generally, however, the argument turned, not on the vernacular itself, but on the use made of it by the three major writers. In Book I of Bruni's *Dialogi ad Petrum*

---

[1] A fuller analysis of the arguments used can be found in English in C. Grayson, *A Renaissance Controversy: Latin or Italian? An inaugural lecture delivered before the University of Oxford on 6 November*, 1959; and in Italian in V. Cian, *Contro il volgare* in *Studi . . . Rajna*, Florence 1911.

Histrum (that is, to Pier Vergerio of Capodistria) we find Salutati asserting that Dante would have been superior to the Greek and Latin classics if he had written in Latin, while Niccoli talks of Dante's errors, his bad Latin and the uncouthness that makes him a poet fit for bakers. And although he withdraws the insults and praises Dante, Petrarch and Boccaccio in the second book, some doubt remains as to his real opinions. Cino Rinuccini, in an *Invettiva*, condemned those who denigrated the three great poets. And Domenico da Prato, after defending Dante and Petrarch, praised the vernacular: 'O gloria e fama della italica lingua! Certo esso volgare, nel quale scrisse Dante, è più autentico e degno di laude che il latino e il greco che essi [i.e. the detractors] hanno'. The opinions of Leon Battista Alberti are of considerable importance, not only because he wrote with sense and moderation, but because he enjoyed authority as a man versed in several arts and sciences and as an able writer in both languages. In the *Proem* to the third book of *Della famiglia*, Alberti affirms that writers have always written in order to be understood: therefore, he proceeds,

'forse e prudenti mi loderanno s'io, scrivendo in modo che ciascuno m'intenda, prima cerco giovare a molti che piacere a pochi: ché sai quanto siano pochissimi a questi dì e litterati ...; ... chi fusse più di me docto o tale quale molti vogliono essere riputati, costui in questa oggi comune troverrebbe non meno ornamenti che in quella, quale essi tanto prepongono e tanto in altri desiderano. ... E sia quanto dicono quella antica apresso di tutte le genti piena d'auctorità, solo perché in essa molti docti scrissero, simile certo sarà la nostra, s'e docti la vorranno molto con suo studio et vigilie essere elimata et polita ...' (pp. 232-233 Pellegrini-Spongano).

From this conviction of Alberti's that the vernacular was capable of expressing the noblest concepts, provided that it was properly cultivated, came the idea of the *Certame coronario*. This was a poetic competition organized by Alberti, supported by Piero de' Medici and held on October 22, 1441, in the Church of S. Maria del Fiore. Its name, formed of two latinisms, may seem displeasing to us; but, in fact, it, too, reflects a determination to ennoble the vulgar tongue. The poems read by the eight competitors on the set subject (True Friendship) proved disappointing, and the judges decided to withhold the laurel crown worked in silver which had been intended for the victor. An anonymous protest against their decision, which has come down to us, and which purports to be by an uncultured person, was probably the work of Alberti himself. The failure of the competition shows that in 1441 Italian was not yet rehabilitated in the opinion of the learned. And the judges possibly erred in looking upon the competition as a challenge to Latin, rather than, as Alberti himself saw it, as a method of recognizing, and contributing to, the capabilities of Italian.

Contradictory opinions were expressed by the mutable and venal Filelfo. He commented on Dante and Petrarch and wrote a discourse in Italian (1451) 'contro i suoi emuli i quali dicevono esser Dante poeta da calzolai e da fornai', only to affirm of the vernacular later 'hoc scribendi more utimur iis in rebus quorum memoriam nolumus transferre ad posteros'. Vespasiano da Bisticci was convinced that 'nello idioma volgare non si può mostrare le cose con quello ornamento che si fa in latino' ('Vita di re Alfonso'). On the other hand, Lodovico Carbone, in his Exhortation to Duke Borso (1459) defended both Dante and Italian. And Landino, Professor of Rhetoric and Poetics at Florence and chancellor of the *signoria*, was a commentator of both Petrarch and Dante, as well as a translator of Pliny. In the inaugural oration we have already quoted (1460) he expressed a desire to see the vernacular better cultivated. Later, in his introduction to his translation of Cicco Simonetta's *Sforziade* (1490) he praised 'la Fiorentina lingua, la quale è comune non solo a tucte le genti Italiche, ma per la nobilità dalcuni scriptori è sparsa et per la Gallia et per la Hispagna' (c. 3a). But that was thirty years later, and by that time humanism in the vernacular had made great strides.

Leon Battista Alberti's efforts, in his own writings and in his promotion of the *Certame coronario*, to raise Italian to the level of the classical languages, was a major contribution to the development of humanism in the vernacular, which achieved maturity with Lorenzo, Poliziano, Boiardo and Sannazzaro. Alberti's merit in this matter was, in fact, recognized by Landino in the inaugural oration we have already quoted:

'Ma huomo che più industria abbia messo in ampliare questa lingua che Batista Alberti certo credo che nessuno si trovi. Leggete priego i libri suoi e molti e di varie cose composti. Attendete con quanta industria ogni eleganzia composizione e degnità che appresso ai Latini si trova si sia ingegnato a noi trasferire.'

To us today the spelling, syntax and vocabulary of Alberti's language seem excessively latinizing; but we should consider it as a stage it was necessary to go through before a new and more mature fusion of Tuscan and Latin elements could be achieved.

Lorenzo de' Medici and Poliziano were not only great artists; they were fully aware of the quality of the language they used. The collection of lyrics which Lorenzo sent in 1476 to Frederick, the son of Ferdinand of Aragon (in which a taste for the *stil novo* predominates), is preceded by a critical epistle, written probably by Poliziano, which sings the praises of Tuscan. Lorenzo himself gives praise to the 'materna lingua', 'commune a tutta Italia' in his *Comento sopra alcuni de' suoi sonetti*. There he considers the conditions that lend dignity and perfection to a language and reduces them to four. The greatest merit a language can possess is 'essere copiosa ed abbondante, ed atta ad esprimere bene il concetto della mente'. Next he lists 'la dolcezza e armonia'. Next comes the fact that in it are written 'cose sottili e gravi e necessarie alla vita umana', i.e. the possession of an important literature. Finally, he mentions 'l'essere prezzata per successo prospero della fortuna'—diffusion over a wide area. He is firmly convinced of the dignity of the language in which the great Tuscan writers have expressed 'all meanings'. And he expects even more from it in the future: for the language is hardly in its adolescence 'perché ognora più si fa elegante e gentile'. The three great authors had already constituted a major argument in favour of the vernacular in the writings of those who defended it in the first half of the Quattrocento. Lorenzo, too, adds a page of unqualified praise. And to their names he adds (and this is not surprising in one with a taste for the *stil novo*) that of Guido Cavalcanti.

This is not the place to trace the history of the fortunes of Dante, Petrarch and Boccaccio in this century. But a line from the inscription that Bernardo Bembo, Pietro Bembo's father, was responsible for having placed on Dante's tomb in 1483, is worth quoting:

Nimirum Bembus Musis incensus Ethruscis:

for in it the Venetian patrician defines, not only himself, but vernacular humanism. With its absorption of the humanist lesson added to its pride in the three great writers, the vernacular acquired new confidence in itself. That the fame of Dante, Petrarch and Boccaccio was continuing to grow can be seen from the fact that they were now adopted as scholastic models. It would be very useful to have at our disposal the results of research into their stylistic, lexical and occasionally grammatical influence on various writers and their contributions to common usage.

Closely connected with the growing fame of Dante, Petrarch and Boccaccio, was the growing linguistic prestige of Florence. A Sicilian, probably Aurispa, claimed in 1420 to have forgotten Sicilian and Greek because of the sweetness of Tuscan and Latin:

> *Inter tam dulcis quales fert Tuscia linguas*
> *dedidici Graecam, dedidici Siculam.*

Among the vernaculars of Italy Filelfo considered Florentine to be 'elegantissimus et optimus' and asserted that 'ex universa Italia ethrusca lingua maxime laudatur'. The controversies on the name of the language had not yet broken out, and the terms *volgare*, *fiorentino*, *toscano* and *italiano* were frequently regarded as interchangeable.

One of the concerns of vernacular humanism was the acquisition for the vulgar tongue of genres which the classical languages had possessed; to the second half of the Quattrocento belong the earliest examples in Italian of tragedy, eclogue and satire. Another concern was the establishment of rules for the language. We know that Augurello sought such rules in Petrarch. But of these early attempts to establish rules only one document has come down to us from the fifteenth century. This is the grammar which in 1495 belonged to the private Medicean library and was entitled *Regule lingue florentine* or *Regole della lingua fiorentina*. A copy made in 1508 is preserved in the Vatican library. The *Regole* bear no author's name; but they are the work of L. B. Alberti. The earliest lexicographical compilations also appeared in the fifteenth century. They were: little glossaries in which the Italian (Venetian) word is interpreted in German (Bavarian), preserved in manuscripts written in 1423 and 1424 (and in incunables of 1477 and 1479); the *Vocabulista* in which Luigi Pulci collected some hundreds of latinisms; a list of Milanese words made by Benedetto Dei; a little glossary of thieves' slang; and the first Italian-Latin dictionary, that of Nicodemo Tranchedino.

The grammatical changes that took place in the spoken language towards the end of the Trecento and the beginning of the Quattrocento are more obvious in prose than in verse. In vocabulary latinisms are evident in the writings of all who had literary pretensions.

In Tuscany, both in prose and in verse, Florentine writings outstripped in quality and quantity those from other areas. Tuscan prose at this period could boast, apart from private letters (Alessandra Strozzi) and political letters (Rinaldo degli Albizzi), moral treatises (Palmieri, Alberti), ascetic treatises (Belcari, S. Antonino), *novelle* and *facezie* (Giovanni Gherardi of Prato, Sercambi at Lucca, Sermini at Siena, the *Grasso legnaiolo* and the *Piovano Arlotto*), sermons (S. Bernardino da Siena), chronicles and memoirs (Giovanni Cavalcanti, Giovanni Morelli, Bindino da Travale, Benedetto Dei), biographies (Vespasiano da Bisticci), commentaries (Landino), etc. An almost new type of literature was the technical ('cosa non appartenente a' precetti di rettorica', Ghiberti, *Commentari*, p. 2 Morisani); in this sphere contributions were made by Alberti, Ghiberti, Piero della Francesca and Leonardo. Philosophical dissertations (like Ficino's) were also rather different in kind from previous literature.

In the first half of the century more or less popular versifiers continued to produce epic poetry (*cantari*), plays in verse (*sacre rappresentazioni*) and burlesque poetry (Stefano Finiguerri, called 'il Za'; Burchiello). In the lyric jejune petrarchizing verse was given some new life by exchanges with other regions, often with the aid of singing and music ('Sicilian', Calabrian, Neapolitan and Venetian songs, *strambotti*, etc.). Literature with a popular flavour continued into the second half of the century when it was raised to a high artistic level in Lorenzo the Magnificent's circle: *rispetti*, *ballate* and *canti carnascialeschi* were among the genres cultivated by him and his associates. Pulci's *Morgante*, too, has a popular tone. Moreover, Lorenzo's 'cultured' lyrics, with their Neoplatonic elements and return to certain *stil novo* themes, stand apart from the flamboyant Petrarchism of the Quattrocento. Calmeta, writing ten years after Lorenzo's death, spoke thus of the prestige that the vernacular had regained:

'la vulgare poesia e arte oratoria, dal Petrarca e Boccaccio in qua quasi adulterata, prima da Laurentio Medice e suoi coetanei, poi mediante la emulatione di questa [Beatrice d'Este] et altre singularissime donne di nostra etade, su la pristina dignitade essere ritornata se comprehende' (*Vita di Serafino*, p. 11 Menghini, p. 72 Grayson).

In the *canti carnascialeschi* popular language was not only imitated, but deliberately heightened. The *Nencia* inaugurated the genre of rustic poems which were typical of cultivated dialect literature. Curiosity concerning other dialects and a tendency to satirize them (which had already appeared in some Tuscan writers of the

Trecento) were strong in the Quattrocento: think of the sonnets of Burchiello (which make fun of Venetians, Sienese and Romans), those of Pulci (in which he takes off Milanese and Neapolitans) and those of Benedetto Dei (in which he piles up words typical of the Milanese). The *novelle* of the time also used dialect for realism and satire; an example is the host from the Marches in the *Piovano Arlotto* ('Messore, non dicere chiù, che se 'n ce vene', etc., n. 50 Folena). Some writers, too (Pulci, Pistoia, Arienti) began to use slang for comic purposes.

In northern Italy the vernacular continued to make progress in the Quattrocento.[1] It was more widely used than formerly. It also achieved greater inter-regional generalization (Tuscan and Latin elements being used in its adaptation). Prose texts of a non-literary character from cities which possessed a court and a chancellery show us local languages which had moved a considerable distance from the dialects upon which they were based and which had come to resemble each other more closely. We can see this by comparing a text from Brescia that belongs to 1412 ('O De omnipotent sempiterno, el qual revelast la tua gloria in Yhesu Christ a tuti li zeng, guarda per l'ovra de la tua misericordia che la tua giesia sparta per tut el munt debia perseverà cum fe stabella . . .'), with one that belongs to 1431 ('infrascripta si è la spesa fata per lo Comuno de Bressa per far la festa de Nostra Dona del messe de avosto de l'ano suprascripto fata per Antonio de Vachi e per mi Agostino de Mazii. El Comuno de Bressa de dare per comperar una vacheta per scrivere susso li rassò del comuno e de la fabbrica . . .'). Between these two texts occurred Brescia's annexation to the Venetian Republic (1430). A similar comparison could be made between Veronese texts of this period and texts from the age of the Scaligers. In places which were less affected by cultural relations we find texts which are nearer to the spoken language. From the Bergamasque valleys, towards the end of the century, we get: 'A y è quey da Nes che i ne voraf tor i nos grumey'.

Literary intentions, of course, cause an ennobling of language. In this respect it is interesting to compare Boiardo's letters with the prologue to his translations. In one of the former (21 March 1492) we get: 'Thomaso, vede de remosscolare tuto Rezo per trovarmi uno strassinazo, et guarda che sia strassinazo proprio e non degagna. . . et cossì dilo a mia molgiera che ancora lei *fazza*

---

[1] The phenomena discussed in the following paragraphs can be studied in B. Migliorini and G. Folena's *Testi non toscani del Quattrocento*, Modena 1953.

cercare. . . .' But in his prologue to his version of the *Cyropaedia* we have: 'Havrete dunque la vita e gesti del primo Cyrro scripta da Xenophonte greco, la quale è assai più utile che piacevole. . . . Quivi non si vede la incredibile grandezza di Porro. . . . Ma le leggie con le quali infino de fanciulli si *faccino* e populi virtuosi et obedienti ali principi. . . . Come si conservino li amici e *facciansi* da principio. . . .' We should bear in mind, however, the fact that, whereas we have autograph copies of his letters, we do not have autograph copies of his prologues.

In view of its peripheral position and the influence of French, tuscanization was rare and slight in Piedmont. The poem on the capture of Pancalieri (1410) is strongly dialectal and also has French elements. On the other hand, the author of the *Passione* of Revello (1490) wished to write in Tuscan, though he felt obliged to apologize for his lack of skill in it:

> *la* Passione *in tal lingua è fatta*
> *che da noi è poco usitata*
> *imperò che non è da maravigliare*
> *se non l'abbiamo bene saputa fare.*

The diffusion of Italian in the humbler strata of society is reflected in the religious poetry of this period—when public documents were in Latin and court documents in French. Galeotto Del Carretto was probably the only Piedmontese poet at the end of the fifteenth century who wrote in the manner of the court poets of the rest of Italy. In prose there remain only some chronicles in very rough language.

In Lombardy, as we have already mentioned, the vernacular was favoured by Filippo Maria Visconti and later by the Sforza. Among the court poets Gaspare Visconti stands out. He apologizes in his prefatory letter to the Milanese edition of 1493 'del nostro non molto polito naturale idioma milanese'. It is interesting to note that he glosses the word *fromba* which he used in a sonnet (and which he perhaps got from the *Fiammetta* or the *Morgante*) thus: '*Fromba* in lingua toschana è quello che in lingua latina dicitur *funda*'. As for prose, Vitale's book gives us a useful account of chancellery language. Corio's *Patria historia* (1503), which gives an account of Milanese history up to 1499, is linguistically interesting, but has not yet been analysed.

At Bergamo at the beginning of the fifteenth century Frate Stefano Tiraboschi copied (sometimes condensing the original) the old Veronese poem on *Santa Caterina*. Comparison of the versions is very instructive. Here are some lines in the original Veronese:

> *L'imperaor Maxenço clama gi credenderi,*
> *gi baron de la corto et altri cavaleri,*
> *e dis: 'Or m'entendii quel che voio dire;*
> *e' v'ò clamado çae e fatovi vegnire:*
> *vui savì de Katerina quel k'ela m' à fato,*
> *per lei non è romaso ked e' no sia mato,*
> *ell'ae desorado lo nostro De del templo . . .*

And here is the version in italianized Bergamasque:

> *Lo imperadore Masenzo sì giamà li soi credenderi,*
> *li baroni de la corte e li altri cavaleri,*
> *e disse: 'Voy sapeti quello che Katherina me ha fatto,*
> *per ley non è romaso che non sia parso matto.*
> *Ella ha despresiado lo dio nostro del templo . . .*

At Mantua the copious correspondence of the Gonzaga bears witness to the existence of an advanced koine.

At Venice in the first half of the century Leonardo Giustinian composed poems on popular themes, for which he frequently provided the music himself. Although we do not have an exact idea of his language, or indeed a safe attribution for all his poems, since many poets composed in a similar vein, we can see that he had certain clearly Venetian features (e.g. *golta* rhymed with *volta*). The expansion of his type of verse, aided by music, led to the acceptance outside northern Italy of apocopated words ending in a consonant before a pause ('Quel che in sogno tue me fai — fussel vero e poi mor*ir* . . .'). About 1450 was composed a rhymed version of the *Sette savi* by a versifier who attempted composition in the literary language, though he was not well versed in it. But a little later, when the Veronese Giorgio Sommariva translated Juvenal, and when the Paduan Cosmico and the Veronese Antonio Vinciguerra attempted moral satire in *terza rima*, they all wrote an illustrious Tuscan, albeit with occasional northern features. Here are some lines from the fourth satire of Juvenal in Sommariva's translation:

> *Ecco che 'l mi convien anchor chiamare*
> *Crispino in ogni parte per suo vici,*
> *monstro senza virtude da sprezzare,*
> *debile, infermo, ma forte in flagici,*
> *excetto in le delicie viduile,*
> *ma in l'altri fa mille execrandi exici.*

> *Che zova adunque haver le signorile*
> *case con boschi e possessione a lato*
> *al foro, che non son già cose vile,*
> *se alchun maligno esser non può beato ...*

It is interesting to compare that extract with some lines in which the same writer stylized rustic speech (and which were left unpublished until this century):

> *O consegieri, e ti nostro massaro,*
> *e tuti vu del borgo mazorenti,*
> *pianzì sta morte, con grandi sbraimenti,*
> *de Pier Zafeta, nostro pare caro ...*
> *El ne schivava da tuti i sodè* ('soldati'),
> *e dai sberoeri e d' aotra mala zente,*
> *che cerca tor le nostre povertè. ...*

In prose, too, there was great variety. Marin Sanudo in his *Diari* used a chancellery Venetian which had marked dialectal features. On the other hand, the Veronese antiquary Felice Feliciano wrote a notably ennobled language containing many latinisms and some tuscanisms. Here is the beginning of his letter to Giovanni Bellini:

'Le vixere de la profunda terra mi da gli preciosi metalli, e'l Tago e 'l Nyllo con le salse unde di Gangie le margherite, l'India l'avorio, e gli olenti ligni d'oriente li balsami, e gli arbori di Sabba mi manda l'incenso, Sydonia le porpore, e gli picoli vermi di Siria gli sirici drapi, gli cupi e profondi gorghi il pescie squamoso, e le frondose silve le timide lepori, et il tenace visco gli uccelli volanti. E quello amore che più mi è caro mi dà el tuo cuore ...' etc.

With the growth of printing, Venice became one of the centres of diffusion of literary Tuscan; the importance of the Aldine editions of the early Cinquecento hardly needs stressing. It is not without interest to note, too, that the early printing of vernacular books in Venice was financed by Florentine merchants.

In Friuli (under the domination of Venice from 1419-20 onwards) it was felt that the local language was too uncouth for literature, and writers followed Venetian, and later Italian models. Pietro dal Zoccolo of Pordenone, in three *rappresentazioni sacre* and in his poem *Amore e Fortuna*, wrote in Tuscan with few Venetian features. The same author, when publishing his translation of *Costituzioni della Patria del Friuli* (Udine 1484), sought to explain the linguistic criteria he had followed. He had rejected Tuscan because it was 'troppo oscura a li populi furlani'. On the other hand the 'la furlana' also had its disadvantages ('non è universale in tutto il Friule' and 'mal se pò scribere e pezo lezendo pronunciare'). He had therefore chosen the language of Treviso: 'Imaginai in tal translatione dovermi acostar piutosto a la lengua Trivisana che ad altra, per esser assai expedita e chiara et intelligibile da tutti, come quilla che segondo il mio giudicio partecipa in molti vocabuli con tutte lingue italiane'. But, as these lines show, he in fact wrote a very tuscanized Venetian.

In Emilia the most important literary and linguistic centre was Ferrara. Among its poets Boiardo was the dominant figure. In his *Orlando innamorato* his ennobled Emilian moves decisively towards Tuscan: alongside regional words and forms (*gionto*, *panza*, *ziglio*, *cacciasone*, *fasso* 'fascio', *ve adunati*, *beccaro*, *pioppa*, etc.) we have Tuscan words and forms (*veniamo*, *rubesto*, *stordigione*, etc.), hypertuscanisms (*fraccasso*, *diffesa*, *gaglio* 'gaio', *piaccia* 'piazza', *struccio* 'struzzo', *avancia* 'avanza', *batteggian* 'battezzan', etc.) and latinisms (*strata*, *spata*, etc.). In rhyme-position the poet took advantage of the possibilities such variety offered: he used *scudo* to rhyme with *nudo*, but *scuto* to rhyme with *arguto*, etc. The mixture was not destined to please the fastidious critics of the Cinquecento. But Boiardo's path was that which Ariosto, too, was to take, only Ariosto proceeded much further. Of the literary prose of Ferrara we can form some idea from the *Facezie* of Carbone, while Sabadino degli Arienti gives us in his *Porretane* a stylized ennobled Bolognese (but with the Boccaccian echoes to be expected in a writer of *novelle*). Bolognese chronicles and documents of a practical nature were much rougher in language.

In central Italy the court of Urbino produced some literature. Giovanni Santi (Raphael's father) wished, in his pedestrian rhymed *Cronaca*, to echo Petrarch's *Trionfi*, and only rarely used regionalisms (*agionto*, *vinti*, *Vinesa*) or hyper-tuscanisms (*chiuodo*). Angelo Galli closely followed the usage of the great Tuscans of the Trecento. And the prose and verse of Collenuccio only rarely display linguistic features peculiar to his native Pesaro. From Umbria came texts in verse which was no longer very dialectal: the *Sollazzo* and *Saporetto* of Prodenzani, the 37 *sacre rappresentazioni* put together in 1405 by Tramo di Leonardo in Orvieto, numerous collections of *laudi* and, in the second half of the century, the poetry of the Perugian Lorenzo Spirito. Non-literary prose displayed the usual time-lag between that of cities that were important cultural centres (where the language was rapidly italianized) and that of less important localities (where regional characteristics were more persistent): at Perugia final -*e* for -*i* still appeared occasionally in the early decades of the century, although later the -*i* became general; at Spoleto the *Annali* of Zambolini still distinguished between final -*u* and -*o*, in the manner of the local dialect. The chronicle of Todi (by I. F. degli Atti), written at the end of this century and the beginning of the sixteenth, bears witness to a struggle between tuscanizing and romanizing tendencies.

At Rome the language used for poetry was now Italian. We find it, not only in petrarchists like Giusto de' Conti, but also in the lament of Paolo Petrone, imprisoned at Viterbo in 1420:

> *Roma, dov'è llo tuo nobil senato?*
> *dov'è 'l tuo Cesari che fo ssì altero?*

But when the same Paolo Petrone wrote his *Mesticanza* in prose his language was markedly Roman (*tierra, muorto, aitro, monno, menao,* etc.). So was that of other chronicles (Paolo di Benedetto dello Mastro, Stefano Infessura) and the author of the *Visioni di Santa Francesca,* Giovanni Mattiotti. On the other hand, Gaspare Pontani and Antonio da Vasco, the diarists, used a considerably tuscanized language. In the Abruzzi Serafino Cimminelli, a leading petrarchist, wrote with hardly a trace of his regional origin. (It is only fair to add that he had spent part of his life in Rome and in northern courts.) But the *Cantari di Braccio* were very dialectal. More tuscanization is visible in the chronicle of Aquila written in verse by Cola di Borbona. Dialectal and learned features mingled in dramatic poetry (especially in the Dominican dramatic *laude* from Aquila). There were few examples of literary prose from this area, and its utilitarian texts had a strong dialectal flavour.

At Naples the vernacular was very little used, for literary or practical purposes, in the Angevin age, and not much used in that of Alfonso I. But in the time of Ferdinand I the situation changed radically. Some Neapolitan gentlemen, with intentions analogous to those of the Medicean circle, though with less notable results, attempted to produce lyrics in a popular vein, which meant, linguistically, with numerous dialectalisms. Petrarchan influence also made itself felt. This can be seen in the *Canzoniere* of Pier Iacopo De Iennaro. In his *Sei etate de la vita umana* Dante is the model. He made an effort to avoid dialectal forms and showed a progressive tendency to tuscanize. Petrarchism and classicism coloured the verse of Benedetto Gareth (Il Cariteo). In the vigorous sonnets of the unfortunate Count of Policastro, Giannantonio de Petruciis, plebeian elements appear alongside cultured elements. Thus he freely used the article *lo* and the article *el* before a consonant:

> lo *sole con la luna e con li venti*
> lo *celo con le stelle è sucto al Fato*
> (son. I)
> el *corpo degli affanni ora riposa*
> (son. XLVI)
> *non saccio se* lo *cor de me te premi*
> . . . .
> el *crudo fato credo che blastemi*
> (son. LII).

The *gliòmmeri* (as the Neapolitans called their *frottole*) and the *farse* were also deliberately dialectal. Here, as an example, is a witches' scene from Pietro Antonio Caracciolo's farce *Lo Magico* (which was performed before Ferdinand I):

> *Una, la più valente, — in su la forca*
> *nde* saglie *et là se corca — a la* bucune
> *et taglia poi la fune, — et fa cascare*
> *l'*inpisi *a le* yanare; *— et prestamente*
> *chi lloro stirpa un dente, — et chi le lingue,*
> *et chi a llor toglie il* pingue, *— et chi i* denochii,
> *et chi llor cava l'occhii, — et chi i* capilli . . .

Iacopo Sannazzaro's *Arcadia* marks a decisive stage in southern acceptance of Tuscan standards in the writing of both prose and verse. While its first version, which belonged to the 1480's, had a strong Neapolitan flavour, the definitive edition, prepared by the author in about 1500, and published by Summonte in 1504, was very close to literary Tuscan. Folena's examination of the two versions has cast light, not only on the author's revision, but on tendencies common to others in his time. The main linguistic ingredients of his work (dialectal elements; Tuscan elements, acquired mainly from his reading, and mostly from Petrarch and Boccaccio; and Latin elements) are present in both versions, but in different proportions. The elimination of dialectal forms in the definitive version went so far that Varchi (*Hercolano*, Venice, 1570, p. 151) felt able to praise Sannazzaro for having written the work without ever have been in Florence, and yet with only a few features of which he could complain.

Since the Kingdom of Naples was so strongly centralized, both

M

culturally and bureaucratically, poetic activity in the peripheral areas was very scarce.

As for prose, we have already mentioned the importance of chancellery language and hence of the influence of Pontano, who, though Umbrian, entered the service of the Aragonese when he was little more than twenty years old. One of the literary fashions of the time was the publication of letters: De Tummulillis included some in his *Notabilia temporum*, while love letters were written by Ceccarella Minutolo, who imitated the style of Boccaccio's early works. In the memoirs of Diomede Carafa, in Giuniano Maio's treatise *De maiestate*, in Francesco Del Tuppo's *Esopo*, and in the *Novellino* of Masuccio Salernitano (the only work of literary importance in this list) dialectal colouring remains, in varying degrees, though they have many Latin and Tuscan (mainly Boccaccian) features. The same can be said of the few literary texts from other parts of the Kingdom: the Salentine *Libro di Sidrac*, Roberto da Lecce's *Quadragesimale* and the *Esposizione del Pater noster* by Antonio De Ferrariis, who was also from Terra d'Otranto. The rare statutes in the vernacular show the same marked hybridism.

In Sicily, religious verse had notably Sicilian grammatical characteristics, but both syntax and vocabulary showed strong influences from the mainland. Here is an extract from the *Istoria di la traslacioni di Sant' Agata* written in *ottava rima* by an author who was probably from Catania:

> dormendu Gislibertu et repusandu
> Agatha santa virginella et pura
> li apparsi in sompnu, bella si mustrandu
> quali esti in chelu avanti a Cui ipsa adura,
> cun li capilli xolti chi parìanu
> di oru perfectu, tantu straluchìanu. . . .

The familiar and jocular tone explains the strong Sicilian flavour of the comedy left to us by Caio Ponzio Calogero (or Calorio or Caloria), a Messinese who studied at Padua, of which the final lines are:

> La condannemu per questu in effectu
> che amar lu debia quantu amar si po,
> e per lu cor robatu, o volgia o no,
> li daga lu cor so che staga in pegnu.

But even here Tuscan influence is notable (not to mention Venetian features like *volgia*, possibly due to the copyist). Such

(Tuscan) influence is even stronger in the same author's strambotto:

> *Per la continua guerra chi a gran torto*
> *sustegno, piglio tanto di rispetto*
> *ch'il stanco corpo a poco a poco porto*
> *a morti, chi con gran piaciri aspetto,*

That is true, too, of the fifteenth-century lyrical fragments preserved in the quotations of Mario d'Arezzo. In Sicily in the Quattrocento, in fact, the three major Tuscan authors, as well as Tuscan and Umbrian religious literature, were well known.

Literary prose displayed more tuscanization than poetry. The *Leggenda della beata Eustochia*, composed in 1487-90, was meant to be in literary Tuscan, even if it is not by any means without sicilianisms. Of eight incunables printed at Messina at the end of the century, seven were in very tuscanized prose, although dealing with local subjects. (The eighth was the verse *S. Agata*.) The progress of tuscanization can be seen in the notarial records of Messina; from 1492 *Bando et comandamento* replaces *Bandu et comandamentu* as a heading.

As a postscript to this rapid survey of the fortunes of the vernacular in the various regions of Italy we can add that Italians abroad, who were in contact with compatriots of various origins, tended to the use of a koine. The *Libro mastro* of the Borromei Bank in London is much more italianized than contemporary Milanese documents.

In the Quattrocento there was much oscillation and variety in linguistic usage. The standardizing effect of printing was not felt until the end of the century. In the first half, the literary language was not in a position to impose standards. Later, the growth of vernacular humanism saw the transplanting into Italian of habits that the humanists had acquired in their dealings with Latin: each one tended to form his style individually from his selection of authors. In the absence of universally fixed schemes, writers in Italian had recourse mainly either to the guidance of Latin or to that of the three Tuscan models. Boiardo, as we have noted, wrote both *scudo* (following Lombard and Tuscan usage) and *scuto* (following Latin), and he oscillated between *piazza* and *piaccia*, *gaio* and *gaglio*, and so on. Similarly, southern writers, instead of keeping the indigenous use of *lo* in all positions, made wide use, alongside it, of the Tuscan forms *el* or *il*. Towards the end of the century there was a greater readiness to accept collective taste. And in this process importance attaches to the work of the most readable of the leaders of tuscanization: Boiardo in the north and Sannazzaro in the south.

In spite of the freedom enjoyed by writers of this period in grammar, style and vocabulary, certain tendencies or rules can be observed which were valid for certain cultural circles. We can find some guidance here in studies which deal with an individual author and his milieu, such as (speaking only of Tuscany) Folena's *Appunti sulla lingua* and *Glossario* in his edition of the *Piovano Arlotto* (Milan-Naples 1953), Grayson's notes on Alberti's language (*Lingua nostra*, XVI, 1955), Roncaglia's on Tanaglia (ed. Roncaglia, Bologna 1953) and Ghinassi's volume *Il volgare letterario del Quattrocento e le Stanze del Poliziano* (Florence 1957). Other such studies tell us of the development of the language in areas of northern and southern Italy.

In the manuscripts and early printed books spelling was most unstable: *cane, chane* and, sporadically, *hane*; *degno, degnio, dengno* and *dengnio*, etc. Humanist influence led to a predominance of etymologizing spellings: *maximo, apto, epso*, etc. These were particularly common in northern and southern Italy, but even in Tuscany they were much more widely used than in the thirteenth and fourteenth centuries. The group *ci*+vowel alternated with *ti*+ vowel (*ocio* — *otio*; *gracia* — *gratia*, etc.) as in contemporary Latin spelling. *Ch, th, ph, y* appeared in Greek words, not always in the right places. Certain regional spelling habits persisted: in northern Italy *c* was used for voiceless *z* [ts] (*anci, solacevole, discalci* plural of *discalzo*, etc.), *x* for voiced *s* [z]; in southern Italy we find *cz* and sometimes *tz* used for voiceless *z* [ts]. In Sicily *ch* was still written for palatal *c* [tʃ], *x* for *sc* [ʃ]. The groups *lh* for *gl, ny* for *gn* appeared sporadically in the South (for example in the Otrantine *Sidrac*). The spelling *sg* for [ʒ] sometimes encountered in Tuscany (*indusgiare, collesgi, Luisgi* in Bernardo Accolti) did not take root. Leon Battista Alberti wished to avoid the uncertainties that arose from the use of the symbol *u* for both vowel and consonants. But the distinction that he proposed between *u* and *v* finally became accepted usage only at the end of the Seicento. There was much oscillation in the spelling of medial double consonants, specially in compounds with *ad-, ob-, sub-* and in words of the *abbiamo, fuggire* types. In Tuscany, pronunciation served as a guide, but in northern Italy, whose dialects generally have no medial double consonants, spelling of them was very shaky. Even more uncertain was the representation in writing of phenomena due to syntactic phonetics: initial doublings like *a nnoi*, assimilations like *gram bene* and *illei* (<*in lei*), and phenomena due to enclisis and proclisis. Here the uniformity promoted by printing led to energetic simplification. In the matter of double consonants, the functional tendency which favoured a single form for each word (hence preferring *a lui, di lui, con lui* to *a llui, di lui, co llui*) was reinforced by a geographical factor: that important centre of printing, Venice, was situated in a region whose dialects have no gemination due to syntactic phonetics. In the representation of proclisis and enclisis there was great oscillation before stabilization eventually took place. In the manuscripts and early printed books proclitics are joined to the following word: *ilbene, lacarne*, etc. In some incunables they are joined or separated according to the space available in the line. There was still no apostrophe; hence *lanima, lerrore, longegno* (=*lo 'ngegno*). The practice of writing *huomo* but *luomo* was no longer followed, as it had been in the thirteenth and fourteenth centuries; Landino wrote *dHecuba*, Tanaglia *lhuomo*, etc. Usually there was nothing to indicate the accent in oxytonic words, let alone in others. But occasionally (as in the *Commedia* accompanied by Landino's commentary, 1481) we find *e/, volonta/, mitigo/*. And when G. Ridolfi copied a list of Milanese words collected by Benedetto Dei, he added accents (using acute accents within a word, grave accents on the last syllable, as in Greek: *zighéra, pinchieruò*). As for punctuation, humanist grammar had three signs (*virgula sine puncto, virgula cum puncto, punctus planus*), and occasionally four or more. But in the manuscripts and early printed books punctuation was scarce and oscillating: some writers used none at all, some used the full stop, some had both full stop and colon, and some had full stop, comma and colon. Not infrequently we find an oblique line used as we should use a comma (but it was also used for accents, as we have just seen, and sometimes it merely separated words on a closely printed page). Sporadic use was made, too, of stops at different levels: a high dot, a middle-level dot, and the oblique bar with a low-level dot. It was only in the following century that punctuation became fuller and more regular.

In Tuscan writers diphthongs were still prevalent in the series *triema; pruova, truova; ceraiuolo; puose, rispuose*. Forms like *venardì, iarsera*, documented at Florence, seem to be importations from southern Tuscany. Instead of the *domane, stamane* of Trecento usage, *domani, stamani* became prevalent. Pretonic -*i* abounded in the series *filice, piggiore, mimoria, sicondo, timore*. Poetic tradition

influenced the forms found in verse: B. Giambullari used *core*
(*chore*) in his more noble compositions, *cuore* (*quore*) in his popular
ones. Boiardo used *suave* in his *canzoniere*, *soave* in his eclogues and
oscillated in the *Orlando innamorato*. The normal phonetic development -*aio*, -*ari* (*danaio* — *danari*, *scolaio* — *scolari*) still frequently
appeared, but analogical forms grew at its expense. But the most
interesting phonological feature in this period was, perhaps, the
popular reaction against the widespread acceptance of latinisms,
especially those Latin phonetic features which did not exist in
Tuscan. The diphthong *au* was difficult to swallow; hence the
substitution of *al* (*altore*, Leonardo) or simplification to *a* (*arora*,
Agazzari). The group consonant +*l* provided similar difficulty;
hence *cripeato* (=*clipeato*, Gherardi), *compressione* (for *complessione*,
Alberti), *Prinio*, *exempri* (in a letter of Bisticci's), *frutto* (for *flutto*),
pepro (for *peplo* in the *Vocabulista* of Pulci), *fragello*, *obrivione* (Leonardo). This also explains *sopperire* (for *sopplire*, *supplire*, in Morelli,
etc.). The prosthetic vowel before groups beginning with *s* (and *sc*)
was used, not only after a consonant (*per escriptura*, Palmieri, *per
iscienza*, Piov. Arlotto; *per ispelonche*, Pulci), but also optionally after
a vowel (*una sua ischiava*, S. Bernardino; *fresco isposo*, Alberti). *Gn*
could also have a prosthetic *i-* (*un tale ignocco*, Pulci; *ignuno*,
passim). In Tuscany popular forms of the type *stiena* (for *schiena*)
and *diaccio* (for *ghiaccio*) multiplied. Before proclitic -*lo* and -*la* the
r of the infinitive and the *m* of the 1st pers. pl. could be assimilated:
coprilla (Bisticci), *pensalle* (Pulci; but also *trovarlo* rhyming with
Carlo), *perdonalli* (Piov. Arlotto), *trovalle* (Poliziano); *vogliallo*
(Bruni), *finirella* (Poliziano). There were still frequent examples
of syncope of the type *s'tu* (Pulci), *vorres'tu* (Alberti), *cades'tu*
(Piov. Arlotto), *vedes'tu* (Pulci) and of the type *guarti* ('guardati',
Pulci, Lorenzo Med.). Shortened forms of the articles and
demonstrative adjectives were less frequent than the full forms:
uno giorno (Piov. Arlotto), *alcuno riscaldamento*, *quello dono*, *quello
bello vecchio*. On the other hand shortened forms like *buon padri*,
maggior bellezze (Alberti) were admissible. We have already
mentioned the possibility, introduced by northern poets, of using,
in verse, shortened forms of words ending in a consonant before a
pause. We find some examples also in southern prose-writers
(*vanno ad arrobar*, Carafa): this is probably to be explained as a
hyper-tuscan extension of the Tuscan shortening of infinitives in
connected speech (*voler bene*, etc.), though possibly aided by
Spanish influence.

Although we cannot give an account here of the phonological

features of non-Tuscan writers, it is interesting to note some tendencies. One is the extension of the diphthongs -*ie*, -*uo* to words which in Tuscan would not have had them: *spiero* in a Venetian letter (Migliorini — Folena, no. 10), *infidieli* in Carbone, *crudiele* in Boiardo, *tieco* in the Bolognese Malpighi, *duono* in Sannazzaro, etc. There was a clear decline in metaphony (a dialect feature without equivalent in Tuscan) in both northern and southern writers: we find *ambasiaduri* but *depentori* in a letter by Francesco da Carrara, 'armata de' *genoisi*', but 'scolari *bolognesi*' in Arienti (p. 123 and 265 Gamb.), '*amorusi* sospiri' but '*religiosi*' (ibid. 208 and 362), *io motteggio, tu mottiggi* in Masuccio (p. 145 Mauro). When metaphonic forms coincided with Latin forms of the same word they had greater resistance to change (*profundi* in Sannazzaro). Voiced intervocalic consonants in the north gave way when the Tuscan form had voiceless medial consonants: in a letter (1440) from the Paduan Antonio de Rido to the Florentines we have, alongside *deliberado, zurado, cognosudo*, the forms *deliberato* and *potuto*. Arienti hypertuscanizes *dado* in 'toccare il *dato*' (p. 227).

We should mention, too, that, in adopting classical words, learned and unlearned alike frequently neglected Latin quantities and generally preferred paroxytonic to proparoxytonic rhythm: *arterìa, aurèo, funerèo, giubìllo, ostìco* (and even *metonymìce* in rhyme with *allegorìce* and *tropìce*: Mombrizio, S. Caterina, 730-5); *Amazzóne, Antiòco, Borèa, Caucàso, Demostène, Driàde, Ecùba, Eschìne, Euridìce, Gorgóne, Iapèto, Leonìda, Origène, Palàde, Persèo, Prometèo, Proserpìna, Sermàti* ('Sarmati'), *Sisìfo, Sosìa, Tesifóne*, etc.

Passing to morphology, we note that many nouns ending in -*a* had plurals in -*i*: *vaghe piumi* (Palmieri), *le porti* (Pulci), *le bianche areni* (Luca Pulci). Among nouns and adjs. in -*ca* there were many examples of latinizing plurals in -*ce*: *domestice, pubblice* (Alberti), *catolice* (Boiardo), *mendice* (Serafino Aq.). In those ending in -*co* and -*go* there was oscillation between velars and palatals in the plural: *sindachi, traffichi* (Cavalcanti), *tisichi* (Landino), *pratichi* (Poliziano), *fongi* (Cammelli), *Licurgi* (Ficino). Nouns in -*ello* often found a plural in -*egli*: *f32gli* (Macinghi, S. Bernardino, Piov. Arlotto, Pulci), *stornegli* (Pulci), *agnegli* (Piov. Arlotto). Nouns in -*e* frequently kept it for the plural (this form existing alongside plurals in -*i*): *coteste febbre* (Macinghi Strozzi), *le gente, le mente* (Pulci), *ardente fiamme* (Poliziano), etc. Singulars of the type *amistà, nimistà* often had untruncated plurals (*amistadi, nimistadi*). *Opinione, parete, tigre* were usually masculine. An attempt at using

Latin comparatives was made by Ghiberti (*densiore, suttiliore*), while Alberti had Latin-type superlatives (*difficillimo*, but also *difficilissimo*). For the article the forms *el*, pl. *e* were very common, while *il*, pl. *i* were a little less so. *Lo*, pl. *li* and *gli*, lost ground. Before *z* Macinghi Strozzi used *del* (*zucchero*) and Palmieri *el* (*zelo*). *Lui* and *lei* were increasingly used as subject pronouns, in spite of puristic scruples based on comparison with Latin: 'comprendiamo che *lui* desidera sommamente l'accordo' (Letter 1434 from the *Signoria* of Florence in Capponi, *Storia*, II, p. 506), 'ma *lui* mi rispondea e dicea' (Alberti, *Famiglia*, p. 226 Spong.), 'Dominus dedit, *lui* data l'avea' (Pulci, *Morg.*, XXVII, st. 142), '*lei* si percuote il petto e in vista piagne' (Poliziano, *Giostra*, I, 113). It was in the Quattrocento that the third pers. pron. began to be used to stand for *Vostra Signoria*. At first the pronouns used were *ella, essa, questa, quella*. Later *lei* was added, and in the following century it became the most frequently used: 'pregando essa V. Illma S. se degna fare tal demostrazione verso el dicto Iacopo che lo predicto Matheo et soi comprendano per mio amore *lei* lo ha trattato bene et clementemente' (letter of G. Pontano on behalf of the Aragonese chancellery, July 9, 1476); 'l'opera qual habia facto. . . . M. Augustino la riferirà pienamente a bocha alla S.V. R^ma, et *lei* dipoi la potrà significare ad Nostro Signore' (letter of Galeazzo Sforza Sanseverino, 1494). Among the numerals 'two' enjoyed great variety: *duo* (Macinghi Strozzi, Lorenzo Med.), *duoi* (Michele del Giogante), *due* (usually with a fem. or before a pause, *uno anno o due*, Lor. Med.), *dua*. *Venti*, *trenta*, etc., could be contracted when combined with other numerals: *venzei, cinquanzei* (Palmieri). In the verb we note that the forms that existed in the 1st pers. plur. before the expansion of *-iamo* had still not entirely disappeared: *avemo* (Alberti), *cognoscemo* (P. Arlotto), *avemo, conoscemo* (Lor. Med.). Metaplasms like *vedimo, corrite* we find in verse only. *Siàno, facciàno, andiàno* (1st. pers. pl.) were popular variants. In the imperfect the ending in *-o* for the 1st. pers. was an innovation (compared with the four-teenth-century *-a*), but at Florence it was easily the predominant form (and the only one recorded in the Laurentian *Regole*). *Potiva, sapia* for the 1st pers. were Palmieri's own. In the 1st pers. pl. *essere* had *eravamo* and *savamo* (also *savano*: Palmieri), in the 2nd *eravate* and *savate*. In the other verbs the 2nd pers. pl. also had *-avi*: *voi cantavi, voi dicevi* (Alberti). In the future the 1st pers. pl. of the *daréno* type reflected popular usage. Various phonetic combina-tions with the verbal stem produced forms like *uccidrò* (Pulci), *misurrai* (Palmieri), *giosterrò* (Pulci), *proverrò* (for *proverò*, Pulci), *troverrete* (Piov. Arl.), etc. In the past definite there were some strong forms which did not survive (*bebbi*, S. Bernardino; *missi*, Pulci; *tretti*, Laurentian *Regole*). In the 1st pers. pl. of the weak form the consonant was frequently single (*ragionamo* for 'ragionammo' in Pulci). In the 3rd pers. pl. of strong and weak forms there was considerable oscillation: *andaro*, *andarono*, *andorono*, *andorno*; *dissero*, *disserono*, *dissono*, *disseno*. In the 3rd conj. pres. subj. the persons with weak forms could have *-i*: 1st pers. sing. *ricognoschi* (Pulci), 3rd pers. sing. *possi*, *piacci*, *conoschi*, 3rd pers. pl. *conoschino* (S. Bernardino). The imp. sub. 3rd pers. sing. had *lavorasse* and *lavorassi*, and the 3rd pl. *andassero*, *andasseno*, *andassino*, *andassono*. In the verb *essere*, *fussi* was predominant. In the conditional the forms in *-ei* (1st pers.) *-ebbe* (3rd pers.) prevailed in Tuscany over those in *-ia*. There were some participles other than those which eventually triumphed (*dolto* Poliziano). Participles without suffix were frequent in popular usage ('voi mi avete *guasto*': Piov. Arl., etc.). As for auxiliaries, it was not yet necessary to use *essere* with reflexives: *aversi affannato* (Alberti), *s'ha sgretolato* (Pulci), *coperto m'ho* (Lor. Med.), etc.

On the morphology of regional Italian we shall make only a few observations. In central and southern Italy there were survivals of the Latin fifth declension (*fermecze* 'fermezza' at Rome, *faze* 'faccia'). In northern Italy *il* (*el*) was normal before *s* impure (*il scudo*, Boiardo, *il sdegno*, Tebaldeo). In southern Italy *il* (*el*) spread rapidly at the expense of *lo*. Among the pronouns some tonic dialectal forms persisted tenaciously: we find *mi* not only in poets of the Po valley: 'Misera *mi* che ho sedeci anni' in the lament of a Ferrarese girl (Fatini, *Le Rime dell'Ariosto*, p. 23), 'O fa l'altri morire o *mi* campare' (Boiardo, *Orl. Inn.*, II, v, st. 23); but also in the chorus of the Bacchantes in the Mantuan version of Poliziano's *Orfeo*:

> *Chi vuol bever, chi vuol bevere,*
> *vegna a bever, vegna qui.*
> *Voi imbottate come pevere.*
> *I' vo' bever ancor* mi.
> *Gli è del vin ancor per* ti.
> *Lassa bever prima a* me.
> *Ognun segua*, Bacco, te.

In the verbs we note the frequency in the 2nd pers. prs. indic. of *-ati*, *-eti*, *-iti* (*pensati*, *haveti*, *risponditi*, *finiti*) in Lombard and

Emilian authors, both of prose and poetry. In the imperfect, the 1st pers. in -a, on the way out in Florence, persisted in northern and southern Italy (*io ragionava*, Boiardo; *me maravigliava*, Arienti; *era*, Masuccio). In the past definite, the Lombard — Ven. — Emilian 1st pers. pl. ended in *-assimo, -essimo, -issimo* (or *-assemo*, etc.): 'venissemo a questa conclusione' (lett. of G. F. della Torre to Lorenzo Med., 1476); 'A caval *rimontassimo* in gran fretta' (Bello, *Mambriano*, VII, st. 57). A notable feature of illustrious Neapolitan was the conjugation of infinitives, present participles and gerunds by the addition of *-no* for the 3rd pers.: 'pensa de quisto fragele mundo li beni non *esserono* se non ombra e fummo' (Del Tuppo. *Esopo*); 'cose *spectanteno* ad uso del bene commune' (G. Maio, *De Maiestate*); *farnosi, starnosi, fermarnosi* for 'farsi, starsi, fermarsi' (Sannazzaro, *Arcadia*, ecl. VIII).

Among syntactic phenomena of the period Latin influence is frequently discernible.

The appositional construction with *di* was very much alive: '*il* traditor *di* Gano' (Pulci), 'l'ottimo cittadino *di* Giovanni' (Cavalcanti). In the complement of material the construction without article (*la palla d'oro*) prevailed, whereas in previous centuries the form with definite article had been preferred after a noun which had a definite article (*la palla dell'oro*). The superlative could be reinforced by intensives: '*la più ottima* parte de' mortali' (Palmieri, *Vita civile*, Proemio); '[costumi] *molto lodatissimi*' (Alberti, *Fam.*, p. 123, Spongano), '*assai dolcissime* parole' (Masuccio, p. 225 Mauro), etc. The possessive *suo* was used for resumption in writing of a popular kind: 'Della mia sopravvesta il *suo* colore' (Pulci). *Quale* was frequently used with the value of a relative *che:* 'Ganimede — *qual* di cipresso ha il biondo capo avvinto' (Poliziano, *Giostra*). One of the most conspicuous features of Quattrocento syntax was the omission of *che*, both as non-accessory relative pronoun and as declarative conjunction. It probably spread from the chancelleries, but it is found in both prose and verse, in Tuscany and outside: 'aveva uno povero giovane istava con lui' (Piov. Arl., *motto* 141, l. 4); 'per quel vedevo e udivo' (Lorenzo Med., *Beoni*, II); 'voglio questa mattina facciate' (Piov. Arl., *motto* 2, l. 26); 'Par di letizia ognun di loro osanni' (Palmieri, *Città di vita*, III, xxxii, v. 79). Construction with the infinitive multiplied under the influence of Latin, particularly in literary texts (Alberti, Lorenzo Med.), but also in humbler writing (and Latin constructions also influenced the prepositions governed by the verb): 'vietono li ragi del sole entrare nel delectoso boschetto' (Sannazzaro, *Arc.*, I, 34). Under Latin influence, too, the subjunctive was introduced into dependent clauses of various kinds: 'La natura dello ingegno nostro è tanto universale ... che ... in un medesimo tempo alle volte varie operazioni *eserciti.* ...' (Palmieri, *Vita civile*); 'vedesi ... che l'amicitia *sia* utilissima a' poveri' (Alberti, *Famiglia*, p. 145 Spongano); 'E disse: Chiarion, dimmi chi *sia*' (Pulci, *Morg.*, XX, st. 82); 'Colui che par di tanti pensier cinto — diss'io al duca mio, dimmi chi *sia*' (Lor. Med., *Beoni*, VI); 'a me pare che sien quattro, delle quali una o al più due, *sieno* proprie e vere lodi della lingua, l'altre piuttosto *dipendano.* ...' (Lor. Med., *Comento*). Latin influence is to be seen, too, in Alberti's use of imperfect subjunctive for conditional ('Quale austero uomo non *fuggisse* questi sollazzi?' *Famiglia*, p. 127 Spongano) and in his avoidance of the double negative ('che in tale casa porti seco nè scandolo nè vergogna'. ibid., p. 50; '[i filosofi] della materia lasciano adrieto nulla', ibid., p. 120). As for the order of words, the placing of atonic particles in enclitic position was no longer universally felt to be necessary (as it had been earlier, when the position was as defined in the law of Tobler and Mussafia): '*Vi priego* che con attenzione mi ascoltiate. ...' (Landino, *Orazione Petr.*); '*Ci fu* qui nuove. ...' (lett. of Piero de' Medici, 2 Jan., 1467); '*Si conveniva* che nel venire gli andasse incontro. ...' (Vespasiano da Bisticci, 'Donato Acciaiuoli'); '*Vi comandamo* che. ...' (letter of King Alfonso, 1454, in Migliorini-Folena, n. 56). But more literary texts were more traditional and generally still observed the Tobler-Mussafia law. A sporadic, but symptomatic, effect of Latin on word-order was Alberti's placing of *adunque* and *anche* as if they were *autem* or *quoque*: 'Le prime *adunque* parti del dipingere. ...' (*Pittura*, p. 59, Papini); 'per le antiche istorie e per ricordanze de' nostri vecchi *anche*' (*Famiglia*, Proemio).

We have already stressed the variety, the lack of linguistic uniformity, which characterized the fifteenth century. This is especially visible in the field of vocabulary. The Tuscans could follow their own living speech, having recourse in addition to Latin and to the three great Tuscans of the Trecento. But writers from other regions could not do this. They had to avoid the peculiarities of their own vernaculars. And while the vocabulary of Latin offered them a wide range, that of the great Tuscans often offered no guidance on subjects with which they wished to deal. (Moreover, even if they did, there were no works of reference which made their words easily available.) In the dictionaries of Barzizza and Cantalicio the explanations are very dialectal; their aim was to make Latin words intelligible to readers who knew only their own dialect. In Italian mutual intelligibility was easier in the case of abstract concepts than in the case of common objects; for certain domestic articles or plants, for example, each region had its own names. The names of fish tended to enjoy more circulation than certain other categories of names, owing to the necessities of trade; even so, 'anchovies' were *acciughe* to Sacchetti and Burchiello, but *anchiovi* to Boiardo.

Nevertheless, the names of certain new objects and new concepts, of certain institutions that were either born or gained widespread diffusion in this century, spread over the peninsula. *Catasto* ('register of possessions'), a Venetian institution which had spread to other centres in the fourteenth century, came to Florence in 1427, and its name with it. *Posta*, through the meanings 'place assigned to a horse' and 'place for changing horses', came to mean 'carrying of correspondence'. This period saw the establishment of *monti di pietà* (which were publicly financed and intended to make private usury unnecessary), especially at Perugia in 1462 as a result of the preaching of Barnaba da Terni. (*Monte* was already in common use to mean 'an accumulation of profitable debts'.) The *cerretani*, originally people from Cerreto, near Spoleto, who collected money for the alms-houses of St. Anthony, gave their name to all kinds of importunate mendicants and vagabonds. In political terminology *repubblica*, assumed, alongside the meaning 'state', that of 'republic' (as distinct from 'monarchy' or 'principate'). A precise diplomatic terminology developed: *autorità* gained a concrete meaning; *potenz(i)a* took the meaning of 'state' as well; and the term *credenzial lettera* was used (Giov. Cavalcanti). In military life *colonnello*, indicating what today we call a 'regiment', was used at Milan in 1472. *Partigiane* ('halberds') were introduced. The word *facchino* also made its appearance in this century. *Accademia* at the beginning of the century still meant the grove near Athens in which Plato and his disciples met. Its modern meaning began with the group of young men gathered about Argyropulos; in the sense we give to 'academy' today it was used in a letter from Donato Acciaioli written in 1455. Italians began to cultivate the *carciofo* ('artichoke') and imported *caviale* ('caviare'), *morona* ('sturgeon pickled in brine') and the *giulebbo* ('julep'). Words were coined or gained a technical sense in connection with the development of the fine arts. *Medaglia*, which at first meant a 'coin', assumed its modern

meaning with the development of the new art. *Torso* was transferred from the world of plants to that of statues and human
bodies. L. B. Alberti made a major contribution to architectural
terminology. He was very ready to adopt classical terms in this
field: 'Il capitello . . . partirassi per terzo: l'una parte sarà il
plinto; l'altra lo *echino* con l'*annulo*, il quale annulo sarà la sesta
parte; l'altro terzo serà lo *hipotrachelio*. Lo *astragalo*. . . .' (Alberti,
I cinque ordini). Others were less willing to accept them: 'El
capitello è capo della colonna. Vetruvio il chiama *epistilio* [an
error, for Vitruvius uses that word for 'architrave']. Questi
vocaboli antichi lui li usa: io non ve li voglio dire, perché sono
scabrosi e non s'usano oggi dì. . . .' (Filarete, *Architettura*, c. 56,
cod. Magliab.). Alongside *lume e ombra, bianco e nero* appeared the
asyndetic pair *chiaro oscuro*. Not all new terms were accepted, of
course. Among the rejects were two geometrical terms used by
Alberti: *ghirlanda* and *linea centrica* for *circonferenza* and *diametro*
(*Pittura*, p. 17 Papini). Technical inventions introduced new
terminologies; one example was printing, with which the following were connected: *stampare, imprimere, informare, libri da stampo,
libri in forma, componitura, compositore*, etc. The natural sciences,
through the example of the ancients and the work of some
modern pioneers, made some progress. We have already mentioned Landino's translation of Pliny. It brought into Italian,
not only the names of particular animals and plants, but also
terms corresponding to scientific categories, like *insetto*. Pulci, in
his *Morgante*, displayed great interest in technical vocabularies
of the most varied kind (military, maritime, musical, pharma-
ceutical, etc.). He also had great curiosity about rare and dialectal
words. And this was true, not only of him, but of a whole circle
of friends, one of whom was that Benedetto Dei, to whom Pulci
wrote a letter in 1481 beginning 'al mio caro Benedetto Dei
salamalec'. Thanks to such curiosity Italy got from the Levant
such words as *tafferuglio* ('fray, brawl'), *ciriffo* ('sheriff, descendant
of Mahomet'), (*a*) *bizzeffe* ('abundantly'). In the Levant travellers
got to know the kind of shutters made with slats which acquired
(from the sentiment thought to have inspired them) the name
gelosie, and for which the English language uses the French
'jalousie'. Barbaro spoke of 'una porta di rame alta tre passi,
lavorata a *gelosie*' (Ramusio, *Navig. e viaggi*, II, p. 105). They were
introduced into Italy (Vitale, *Cancelleria*, Gloss.), and the word was
extended to cover a kind of multiplication of one large number
by another in which the figures make a sort of grating on the

paper: *per gelosia* or *per graticola* (Pacioli, 1494). From travellers, too, came names proper to the northern seas, like *stoccafisso* ('stockfish'). Slang terms occasionally enriched jocular speech: *parlare in gramuffa* for 'parlare in grammatica', 'to latinize'.

Some of the most notable examples of semantic change were due to a revival of the classical meanings of certain words. *Virtù*, for example, was not only used in the Christian sense of 'virtue', but also increasingly with the meaning 'valour, heroism'. And *piacere* no longer meant 'sin', but a feeling, the condition and mainspring of existence. This correspondence to the ideas of the time explains the vogue enjoyed by certain words. *Unico*, which Petrarch applied to the Virgin, became used as a common compliment by later petrarchists ('Unico Bernardin, l'opra è sincera' in a sonnet of Serafino Aquilano's to a painter; *l'Unico Aretino*, honorific epithet of Bernardo Accolti). The use of *divino* was extended and reached its apogee in the sixteenth century (il *Divino Aretino*, etc.). The vogue enjoyed by *pellegrino* in the meaning 'elegant' also began in the fifteenth century. The metaphors of the period, of course, reflect eternal human tendencies and individual flashes of wit no less than fashions of the time: *cicala* was used for a talkative and slanderous woman, *perla* with reference to a more desirable lady, *arpie overo aringe* to denote skinny horses, etc. But in the case of many phrases which our documentation places in the Quattrocento (*aver l'assillo, far la civetta, far castelli in aria*, etc.) it is impossible to be sure that they did not exist earlier (and that we simply do not have written testimony before this century).

The fundamental component in the vocabulary of Tuscan writers was their 'natural' usage. We find many Sienese words, for example, in San Bernardino and Sermini. When Tuscan writers borrowed words from other regions, it was usually to describe non-Tuscan things or to produce a particular stylistic effect (e.g. 'E non dura la festa mademane — crai e poscrai e poscrilla e posquacchera — come spesso alla vigna le Romane' (*Morg.*, XXVII, st. 55). It is more difficult to assess the traditional, dialectal elements in writers from other regions. But it is clear that even those who strove hardest to use Latin or Tuscan words, kept dialectal or regional words for domestic objects. Here are a few examples from more or less literary texts: in Cornazzano we find *caravaggia* ('washerwoman'), *gradizza* ('gridiron'), etc., in Gaspare Visconti *capigliara* ('wig'), *pristinaro* ('baker'), etc., in Carbone *caleffare* ('to deceive'), *scarana* ('seat'), etc.; in Boiardo *gallone* ('flank'), *moglio* ('wet'), *strep(p)one* ('bastard, scoundrel'), *zambello* ('quarrel') and many other dialect words. Boiardo even has local words for spiritual conditions: in the lyrics (LXVIII, LXXI, CI) *rissor* is used for 'relief, comfort' (this apparently being formed from the Emilian word *arsurèr*, Lat. *RE-EX-AURARE). Arienti wrote *barbano* for 'uncle', *calcedro* for a 'copper receptacle', *lambrecchia* for 'trap'. In Masuccio we read *iopparello* 'jerkin', *làzaro* 'leprous', *zabbattera* 'shoemaker's wife', etc. Sannazzaro has *àlvano, elcina* ('holm oak'), *lùg(g)iola* ('wild sorrel'), *mantarro* ('cloak'), etc. Sometimes a writer, aware of the fact that different words were used in different regions to denote the same object, helped the reader by using synonyms. Leonardo, speaking of the concretions in the veins of old people, wrote: 'eran grosse come castagne, di colore e forma di tartufi, ovver di *loppa* o *marogna* di ferro' (*De anat.*, ff. B, c 10b).

The influence of the Trecento writers is obvious. Generally it is that of the three major authors; but the Medicean circle paid attention also to the lesser writers of the *stil novo*. Dante's influence is easy to pick out when certain characteristic unusual words are used: *cagnazzo, bolgia o caina d'inferno* (Pulci); *bobolce, incappellarsi, punga, sorpriso* (Poliziano); *lurchi, rubesto* (Boiardo), etc. Petrarchan vocabulary is less conspicuous and more difficult to recognize (*disacerbare, testore*, Poliziano; *ritentire*, Boiardo); but the whole terminology of love is based on his work. Boccaccio's influence is exercised, not only through the *Decameron*, but also through his minor works. It is unnecessary to add that influence in vocabulary cannot be separated from general stylistic influence.

In the formation of new words, the Quattrocento made use of the usual procedures. These were direct derivations from adjectives and participles: *furibondare* (Burchiello), *scultare* (Pulci), *sportare* ('to jut out', G. Rucellai, etc.). Among prefixes *cata* was not yet dead ('Se mi ci cogli, non mi ci catacogli': S. Bernardino, sermon XLII). Alberti liked *dis-*, coining, for example, *disgruzzolare, dislodare*. Fertile suffixes were *-ale* (*baccale*, Lorenzo Med., *conale*, Ghiberti, *nazionale*, first example 1488 in Rezasco, *vampale*, Bernardo Giambullari, not to mention Poggio's *bugiale* 'mendaciorum veluti officina'), *-ardo* (*rossardo*, S. Bernardino), *-ecchio* (*grossecchio*, Nencia), *-esco* (*burchiellesco*, Bellincioni), *-eggiare* (*setteggiare* 'to split up into sects', Bruni), *-ile* (*verginile*, Palmieri). It is not difficult to see that individual authors had personal preferences: Giovanni Cavalcanti was fond of *-esco* (*cerbiesco,* *cosimesco*, *volpinesco*, etc.). Palmieri, in the *Città di vita*, which abounds in quotations from Dante, returned to parasynthetic formation of the *induare* type (*imbernarsi*, *incrunare*, *inlotare*). Alberti attempted formations of Latin stamp ('Piladee e *Lelie* amicitie', *Fam.*, p. 142 Spong.). Pulci's capricious inventions include *dragata* for a 'blow with a dragon' inflicted by a giant (XIX, st. 38) and a title for a Muslim prince '*l'arcifanfan* di Baldacco (XXV, st. 294). Words with -*ozzo* were frequently used by San Bernardino. Pulci again had a liking for diminutives, augmentatives and pejoratives: 'un'altra *malizietta* trovò strana,' 'Orlando è *corbacchion* di campanile', 'Volle menargli d'un suo *bastonaccio*'. The Medicean circle was particularly fond of diminutives: apart from the felicitous use made of them by Poliziano, they were widely used by Lorenzo and Matteo Franco.

The words which disappeared from Tuscan speech, although living in preceding centuries, would be a useful (though difficult) subject for research. The use of *avale* ('now') in the *Nencia* suggests that it was restricted to the country. Sannazzaro's use of *otta* does not permit a similar conclusion (he found it in Dante and Petrarch). Some writers consciously revived poetic words that had fallen into desuetude, e.g. Poliziano's *desianza*.

In the degree of latinization there was, too, great variety from author to author. Indeed, in the work of a single author we can note variations according to stylistic intention; the Proem and the Fourth Book of Alberti's *Famiglia* are more latinized than the rest. In some texts we have the impression of an Italian grammatical framework carrying an almost entirely Latin vocabulary. Here is an extract from a letter by Domenico da Prato:

'molti ferocissimi *apri* et *onagri* et *linci* dintorno alle foltissime selve veggio, et poi *prospicio* li nuovi *bubi* et *milvi* et *vespertilii* et *noctoraci*, che per l'aree volano. Quici non *filomene* in dilettevoli gabbie sento cantare, ma gracidare assaissime *monedole* s'ode'.

A stimulus to the use of latinisms in verse came from the vogue enjoyed by *versi sdruccioli* (lines ending in proparoxytones), which were favoured by certain genres like the eclogue, though they were not limited to such. (One thinks of the *Pìstole* of Luca Pulci, or certain metric schemes involving *sdruccioli* used by Serafino Aquilano). Some writers kept a list of rare words (mainly of Greek or Latin origin) suitable for use in Italian; such is Pulci's *Vocabulista*. Leonardo, who took material from it for his own collection, registered the word *vocabulizare*, employed to describe this activity. The spelling of latinisms varied greatly. There was a general tendency to spell in Latin fashion those words whose Latin origin was recognizable: hence *apto* for *atto*, etc. But whereas a Tuscan used to saying *Affrica, piggiore, cicala*, usually wrote those words thus, non-Tuscans frequently wrote *Africa, peggiore* and even *cicada*. While Macinghi Strozzi and Poliziano preferred the forms *Cicilia, ciciliano* (as the Trecentisti had done), Leonardo preferred those with initial *s-*. There were some rare nominatives in *-o* from the third declension (*ingratitudo*, Pulci; *Rectitudo*, Del Tuppo) as well as those that were traditional (*Apollo, Cupido*, etc.). In some names the consonantal ending of the nominative was preserved (*Venus, Saturnus*, Burchiello; *Socrates, Demostenes*, but also *Socrate* in the *Libro de la vita de filosofi*, 1480). Lorenzo de' Medici used *nume* and *numine*. Words in the liturgical tradition were often given a paragogic vowel: *chirieleisonne* (Burchiello), *Tetragrammatonne* (Pulci). Latin adverbs and conjunctions were used with only occasional slight phonetic adaptation (*ipso facto, isso fatto, esso fatto*, Macinghi Strozzi). The following entered the language through chancellery usage: *assiduo, autem, breviter, demum, etiam, ex tempore, immediate, immo, improviso, in futurum, ipso facto, maxime, nuper, praesertim, praeterea, pro viribus, quidem, quodammodo, quominus, quoniam, raro, solum, sponte, taliter qualiter, tanto minus, tantum vero*, etc. Latinisms usually kept in Italian the meanings they had borne in Latin. But occasionally they were given instead the meaning they were wrongly assumed to have borne. A typical example is *tradurre*, which owes its present meaning to Leonardo Bruni. It gained ground with this meaning ('to translate') during the fifteenth century. Its other meanings disappeared from view, as did the words *traslatare, tralatare* which, with its new meaning, it replaced. There were also some attempts at imitating Latin through 'calques'. Alberti, in his *Pittura*, gives the Italian *scimmio* the meaning of Latin *simus*: 'altri aranno le narici *scimmie* et arrovesciate aperte' (p. 88 Papini). Lorenzo used *selva* (*Selve d'amore*) in the way in which Poliziano had used *silvae, sylvae*.

To give some idea of the enormous contribution made by latinisms to Quattrocento Italian, we give here a list of examples believed to have entered during that century: *aggetto, amaranto, amatorio, ameno, amminicolo* (*adminicolo*: Alberti, *Fam.*), *anelante, applaudire, arboreo, arbusto, armigero, bisonte, bonificazione, cataratta* (of a river), *certame, cèrulo, clava, concinnità, connubio, edicola* (eccl. term), *emolumento, epidemia* (*epidimia*: Alberti, Luca Pulci), *esangue, esilarare* (*exh-*), *esonerare* (in a concrete sense, euphemistically used: 'exonerare il ventre': Arienti), ilare, incile, insetto, lenocinio, lepido, madido, marittimo, missiva, mutilo, obliterare, onomatopea (-pia: Landino), opulento, ottemperare, pagina, paraninfo, plettro, prodigioso, quintessenza (alch. Latin), reboare, satellite ('body-guard'), sodalità, specioso, stria, tragelafo, tragicommedia, trofeo, veemente, vitreo, etc. That list, of course, does not claim to be complete! Moreover, it contains only words which succeeded in becoming part of the language. There were innumerable others which, though used in the Quattrocento, failed to keep their places. Such were alimonia (Cornazzano, Prov., I), arbuscolo (Sannazzaro), aure ('ears', G. Cavalcanti), cèntrico (Alberti, Pittura, passim), cistula (Sannazzaro), ecciso ('extirpated', G. Maio), exprobrare (Collenuccio), fulgetro ('thunder-bolt': 'lì fabbrica Vulcan le sue fulgetra': Lorenzo Med., Selve), etc. When so many latinisms were used, it is not surprising, of course, that some were abused in the process; Luca Pulci (Pist., XIV, v. 92) uses 'opera coturna' for 'opera tragica'. Nor is it strange that in popular use forms and meanings should be subject to transformation (lo Papa mundi 'mappamondo': Giovanni da Uzzano).

Contacts with other European countries and with the Levant brought a certain number of foreign words into Italian vocabulary. Of these the most numerous group was French. It included some military terms. Pulci used franco arciere (anachronistically, with reference to the age of Charlemagne), while a report of the Florentine ambassador to France in 1461 contains forriere. Some such terms became known through the expedition of Charles VIII: 'polvereri (così li chiamano loro) cinquanta' (letter from Boiardo, Aug. 26, 1494), 'le gentedarme regie' (letter from Card. F. Sanseverino, Dec. 19, 1494). That expedition also carried with it what became known in Italy as the mal francese. There entered at this time, too, names of objects (pattìni, Pulci), of various pastimes (farsa, Luca Pulci; scangè <escourgée, Piovano Arlotto), designations of persons (ceraldo 'charlatan' <charalt; mignotta), names of trades (mazzoneria, Antonio Manetti) and some general terms like dibatto. French chivalresque poems were not forgotten, and gallicisms abounded in Italian chivalresque epics: far carnaggio, franco combattante, pitetto, etc. Because of Savoy's close connections with France, French influence was particularly strong in Piedmont: the Passione of Revello has very numerous French words: contrea, fassone, regname (-o), etc. It is symptomatic that it even has the conjunction car.

Spanish influence is notable above all in Neapolitan territory and in Sicily, where it was due to the presence of the Aragonese (*verdatero*, Giun. Maio). But some Spanish words spread to other parts of Italy (Boiardo, for example, has *algalia* 'musquash', *giannetta* 'lance' and *giannetto* 'horse', and Pulci has *marrano*). The few words that came from German were due to military contacts: the *lanzi* were heard to say *goden dacche* ('good day'). *Fàlago* ('a shade of black') may have come in by the same route; it was used by Pulci. English contributions were very few; Arienti used *aldrimani* ('aldermen') for local colour in one of his stories (*Porretane*, XXII). From the Levant came words denoting perfumes and sweets (*belgiuì*, *bongiuì*, Piov. Arlotto, Lorenzo Med.; *giulebbo*), strange fashions in clothes (*albernuccio*, *bernuccio*; *ghelèr*), religious and civil customs (*moschea*, in place of the older *meschita*; *ciriffo*, *falquiero* from *faqîr*, Oddi: *tafferuglio* 'a noisy festivity', later 'brawl'). The Tartar *urdu* was modified to *lordò* ('unenclosed military camp'). These borrowings were due to the close relations which the maritime cities had with the Levant. But they also testify to the existence of curiosity concerning distant countries, that curiosity which had no small part in the discovery of a new continent.

8

The Cinquecento

The dates which are often symbolically used to mark the end of the Middle Ages (1492, 1494) can serve as a beginning to the period to be dealt with here. It is difficult to find a date to end it that does not seem arbitrary: for 1600 divides generations that were extremely alike. A more obvious division could be found a little over half-way through the century, at 1559, the date of the Treaty of Cateau-Cambrésis, or at 1563, the end of the Council of Trent, for both the political chess-board and the cultural atmosphere were very different in the second half of the century from what they had been in the first. From a linguistic viewpoint the fundamental dates, however, are 1501, the date of publication of the Aldine Petrarch, edited by Bembo with special regard for its orthography, 1525, the date of publication of Bembo's own *Prose della volgar lingua*, 1582, the traditional date of the foundation of the Crusca (or 1583, when Salviati gave its activities a new direction) and 1612, which saw the publication of the first edition of the *Vocabolario degli Accademici della Crusca*.

Charles VIII's invasion in 1494 had shown up Italy's military weakness, and the country now became the scene of a struggle for power between France on the one hand and Spain and the Empire on the other. Spanish supremacy, recognized in the Peace of Cambrai (1529) and the Congress of Bologna (1529-30), was confirmed and strengthened, after further battles, by the Treaty of Cateau-Cambrésis (1559). Milan, ruled by viceroys, lost all political importance. But in Piedmont, Emanuele Filiberto managed to keep his state free from foreigners and transform it from being feudal to being absolute. Genoa, which remained an oligarchic republic through the efforts of Andrea Doria, recovered Corsica. Venice was the only Italian state in a position to be prudently anti-Spanish; but her power was dwindling, owing to the pressure of the Turks and a decay in trade occasioned by the discovery of America. The Medici, who had been frequently cast out and had as frequently returned, extinguished republicanism in Florence. Sienese independence, too, was suppressed. Cosimo, nominated Grand Duke in 1569, subjected his state to firm reorganization. The port of Leghorn grew notably in importance under Ferdinand I. The papal states, which during the first half of the century, had seen warlike and nepotist popes (Borgia, Medici and Farnese) enter the lists with other Italian potentates, were during the second half reorganized under Sixtus V; the re-acquisition of Ferrara followed that of Perugia and Bologna. In Naples and Sicily, which were governed by viceroys, the interests of Spain prevailed over those of the local populations, and what resistance existed was on behalf of sectional interests rather than of the public good. But they continued to have relations with the rest of Italy. Sardinia, however, which was directly under Spain, had few contacts with the peninsula. The Jews, who had already been excluded from Sicily, were expelled in 1539 from the Kingdom of Naples. In 1516 at Venice, in 1555 at Rome and later in other cities they were compelled to live in ghettos; but in Leghorn and some north Italian states they were protected by the rulers. There was a tendency, in those states that retained something of their independence after the turmoil of the century, for power to become more concentrated in the hands of the rulers and for bureaucracy to gain in strength.

The art of war was transformed by the use of firearms. Infantry became more important than cavalry. Some states came to accept a principle on which Machiavelli had laid great stress: that of recruiting their soldiers from among their own citizens rather than depending on foreign mercenaries.

Although Italy did not achieve the political unity which other great European nations already enjoyed, a consciousness of belonging to a common civilization became general among her inhabitants. The very controversies on the nature of the language she should adopt show that those taking part thought of such a language as the vehicle for a single national culture. It is true, though, that the protagonists in these disputes nearly all belonged to the literate classes. Our knowledge of the life, opinions and speech of the lower orders is very limited; even the speeches attributed to them in the comedies of a Ruzzante are not authentic reproductions but the stylization of a cultured writer.

Circulation of persons within Italy was intense, and that for various reasons: some moved for military reasons, others were political exiles (to limit ourselves to Florentines, we can recall here members of the Strozzi family, Iacopo Nardi, Donato Giannotti, Bartolomeo Cavalcanti, Luigi Alamanni) and many were engaged in commerce. The Reformation, too, caused many to leave home, but they went abroad; Lucchese exiles were particularly numerous.

Although the Reformation and Counter-Reformation brought less national disturbance to Italy than to other countries, they had a great effect on public and private life. The doctrinal definitions and disciplinary prescriptions of the Council of Trent (1545-63) were applied with rigour and zeal, particularly in the papal states and the Spanish territories. That the new attitudes were accompanied in many cases by sincere religious fervour can be seen from the birth of new religious orders and the beginnings of missionary preaching outside Europe. But in many other cases there was readiness to drift with the current, either with an inert conformism or with the hypocrisy of the 'intus ut libet, foris ut moris est'. The Council of Trent was responsible for the institution of parish registers; these undoubtedly contributed to the stabilization of surnames. The Council also regulated the reading of the Bible, virtually restricting it to those who knew Latin. The establishment of the *Index librorum prohibitorum* led to the publication of expurgated editions. It also had the effect of leading authors to avoid words and phrases that were, or might seem, unorthodox.

Social life was very active. Castiglione's *Cortegiano* gives us a vivid (if idealized) picture of court conversation in the first quarter of the century. Academies, too, sprang up in many cities, and in them the most varied subjects were discussed, nearly always in Italian. The culture of the universities of the period was predominantly Aristotelian and scholastic. Many foreigners came to study at them and acquired a knowledge of Italian. Mainly from the teachings of Francesco Robortello at Padua arose the pseudo-Aristotelian doctrines which had such influence on the literary standards of the time. Princes and republics needed, for their correspondence and for administrative tasks, to employ people who could write well. Many of the most notable authors of the age spent years in such activities: Ariosto, Guicciardini and Guidiccioni with gubernatorial functions, Machiavelli, Bembo, Berni, Tolomei, Bernardo Tasso, Caro, Muzio, Contile and many others as secretaries. Another practical activity that absorbed many men of letters was publishing, which flourished in many cities, but particularly in Venice; it is possible that half the books published in Italy in the first third of the century were published in that city, and even after that period it remained the leading centre. Sometimes men of letters collaborated with publishers in carrying out particular tasks (as did Bembo with Manuzio). Sometimes they worked for them on a more permanent basis: Doni, Dolce, Domenichi, Ruscelli, Sansovino and several others were for years professional readers and compilers. Satirical manifestoes (at Rome called *pasquinate*) and public announcements began to circulate in manuscript. Letters and opuscules on the events of the time were precursors of modern journalism (with Aretino, Doni and others occasionally behaving like pre-journalists). While political and religious polemics were limited by the repressive attitudes of the authorities, literary and linguistic controversies, which did not seem to threaten their interests, were not. Literature and the arts which in the early decades of the century had been inspired by a joyful individualism, aspiring to an ideal perfection (Ariosto, Castiglione, Raphael), were later affected by the stifling intellectual and moral atmosphere, becoming more solemn, showy and gloomy, with creative talent escaping into the exuberance of form and structure that we associate with mannerism and with the birth of the *melodramma*. The *commedia dell'arte* (i.e. comedy of the professional players), intent only on amusing, schematized its characters by the use of masks.

After the progress of the thirteenth and fourteenth centuries, the Italian language had suffered a setback in status in the fifteenth, when humanist supporters of Latin had succeeded in having it largely confined to comparatively humble functions. In the sixteenth, however, their prejudices were sufficiently overcome for it to become firmly established. Although in bulk what was written in Italian still amounted to less than what was written in Latin, the vernacular made progress in all fields. But we must bear in mind, of course, that more was written and printed in the sixteenth century than in the fifteenth; thus, although Italian made gains in the proportion of its share, at the expense of Latin, much more was produced in each than in the Quattrocento. In the writing of Latin the victory of Bembian Ciceronianism over the eclecticism which had had such notable representatives in the fifteenth century as Politian and Pontanus, made the language more rigid, and removed it further from sources of renewal in the vernacular. Not all, however, were able to achieve the dead language of the humanists; a large number of documents of a practical nature survives in the Latin of authors who had less literary training.

The language of instruction was Latin, with very few exceptions: Italian was used in practical schools for future businessmen and in elementary classes for children who had not yet acquired Latin. University teaching was entirely in Latin; the proposal made in 1518 by the Rector of the Jurists at Padua that afternoon lectures (i.e. the less important ones) should be in Italian, came to nothing. Gelli cited as noteworthy the behaviour of Francesco Verino who 'leggendo filosofia e veggendo talvolta venire a udirlo il capitano Pepe, il quale non intendeva la lingua latina, sùbito cominciava a leggere in vulgare' and 'poco innanzi che egli si morisse, per dimostrare la inestimabile bontà sua, leggendo publicamente ne lo Studio Fiorentino il duodecimo libro de la divina Filosofia d'Aristotile, volse esporlo in vulgare, acciocché ogni qualità d'uomo lo potesse intendere' (*Capricci del bottaio*, p. 194 Gotti). As for the teaching of Italian language and literature, the Universities at the beginning of the century did nothing. Trissino wrote: 'hoggidi, quasi a niuno se insegna Italiano, ma a tutti se insegna Latino, e poi lo Italiano se impara da sé' (*Dubbii grammaticali*, Vicenza 1529, c. 3a). It was only in 1589 that the University of Siena appointed a 'lettore di toscana favella', who was Diomede Borghesi. Foreign students, however, took lessons in Italian language at other Universities, particularly from Tuscan teachers.

But if the Universities were fortresses of Latin, the Academies were centres for the diffusion of Italian. Not only in Tuscany, but also generally in northern cities, Dante and Petrarch were read, and rhetoric and poetics discussed in the vulgar tongue. Academies where Latin predominated were a minority; such a one was the Accademia Papinianea of Turin, founded in 1573, whose members were subject to the rule: 'Si quis in Academia temere aliter quam latine sermonem habuerit, iure statim reiicito'.

The Church, in opposition to the requests of the Reformers, prohibited the use of Italian in the liturgy. Translations of the Bible still circulated in the Quattrocento and early Cinquecento. But the Church became increasingly opposed to laymen reading and interpreting the Bible for themselves; finally, at the Council of Trent, it prohibited such practices. Paul IV's Index (1559) forbade the printing, reading or possessing of Bibles in Italian without the consent of the Holy Office. The rules approved by

Pius V in 1564 fixed the prohibition on the reading of translations of the New Testament made by heretics, while allowing bishops to give permission to read translations of the Old Testament; but even for reading approved translations laymen needed written permission. Still more severe were the prescriptions in the Indexes of Sixtus V (1590) and Clement VIII (1596).

In administration and law the vernacular gained ground. The majority of city statutes were still in Latin, even those of Tuscan cities like Arezzo and Pistoia. But many were now written in Italian: those of Molfetta in 1474 and 1519 (published by Volpicella, 1875); of the merchants of Bologna in 1550 (pub. 1550); of the Court of merchants of Lucca in 1555 (pub. 1557 and 1610); of Castiglion del Lago and Chiugi (=Chiusi) in 1571 (pub. 1750); of Corsica in 1571 (published in 1843, in an edition in which the language had undergone revision). An interesting example is provided by the statutes of Lucca, published in 1539 in two volumes, one containing the official Latin text and the other a translation into the vernacular intended to help the people understand the laws by which they were governed.

Correspondence with foreign princes was always in Latin, but that with Italian rulers was occasionally in Italian. And while Pope Leo X wrote to Cardinal Farnese in Latin (July 20, 1513), he wrote in Italian to Bembo (Jan. 1, 1515) to inform him solemnly that he had now been adopted by the Medici family and could henceforth style himself Pietro Bembo de Medici. The progress made by the vernacular was noted halfway through the century by Gelli. In his *Dialogo sopra la difficoltà dello ordinare detta lingua* (i.e. Florentine) he conjectures 'che ella abbia ancora a farsi più ricca e molto più bella', and one of the reasons he gives for this is 'il cominciare i Principi, e gli huomini grandi e qualificati, a scrivere in questa lingua, le importantissime cose de' Governi de gli stati, i maneggi delle Guerre, e gli altri negozij gravi delle facende, che da non molto in dietro si scrivevano tutti in lingua Latina'.

In trials, the interrogation of defendants and witnesses was conducted in Italian. In the records the questions were sometimes summarized in Latin, sometimes given in Italian, while the replies were nearly always reported in the vernacular. Sometimes the compilers of such records mixed summaries in Latin and verbatim passages in the vulgar tongue. Thus in the account of the trial of Tommaso Campanella (1599) before the Bishop of Squillace we find:

'Mauritius Rinaldus dixit de auditu à Campanella de mense Julii 1599, non recordatur de contestibus, che voleva far brugiare tutti li libri latini perche era un imbrogliar le genti che non intendono, et che voleva far esso libri volgari, subdens non recordari an dixerit de libris latinis de fide tractantibus che imbrogliassero le genti.'

If Italian was used in reports of trials out of concern for giving exact replies, in other instances it was used to avoid difficulties of nomenclature. When the treasurer of the church of Treviso went to the house of G. Augurello in order to make an inventory of his possessions (1524), he drew up the document in Latin, but gave the actual list in the vernacular.

In philosophy, Latin was almost exclusively used. When Alessandro Piccolomini dedicated his *Filosofia naturale* to Pope Julius III in 1550, he boasted that he was the first to have treated all natural and moral philosophy in Italian. Bruno, a rebel against the Aristotelianism of the Universities and against humanist teaching, wrote his *Dialoghi* in the vernacular during his residence in England, convinced that new thought required new language and probably influenced (as Aquilecchia has suggested) by developments in English prose. Anti-conformist motives can be discerned, too, in Campanella's use of Italian. As for the version prepared by Sertorio Quattromani (under the name of Montano Accademico Cosentino) of the *Filosofia di B. Telesio ristretta in brevità e scritta in lingua toscana* (Naples 1589; repr. Troilo, Bari 1914), it should be borne in mind that Quattromani was a student of Bembo and cultivated the vernacular.

In the vast domain of mathematics, the vulgar tongue was widely used for works of practical importance. Frate Luca Pacioli published a *Summa de Arithmetica, Geometria, Proportioni et Proportionalita* (Venice 1494, 2nd ed. Toscolano 1533) 'in materna e vernacula lingua' (though with passages in Latin here and there) and a *Divina Proportione* (Venice 1509, repr. Vienna 1889) also in an ill-composed Italian. Astronomy was a University subject, based mainly on Sacrobosco's *Tractatus de sphaera*. But there were translations and commentaries in Italian: examples are the explanation of Ptolemaic cosmography which Alessandro Piccolomini wrote for a Madonna Laudomia (Venice 1540) and the *Dialogo . . . de la Sfera, e de gli orti et occasi de le Stelle* (Venice 1545) by Giacomo Gabriele. On receiving this treatise as a gift Bembo praised Gabriele for being 'non solamente eccellente astrologo divenuto, ma insieme ancora maestro della Toscana lingua' (letter from Rome, Sept. 25, 1545). Perspective and architecture were by this time mainly written about in Italian. As for music, Pietro Aron, who had already published *Il Toscanello in musica* in Italian in 1526, still felt it necessary, in publishing *Il Lucidario* (Venice 1545), to excuse himself for not having chosen the 'more noble and worthy' language. In medicine the major authorities (Fabrizi d'Acquapendente, Falloppio, Eustachio, Cesalpino) wrote in Latin, and only the occasional practical manual was in the vernacular. Pharmacopoeias were usually in Latin, but a very full collection of prescriptions appeared in Florentine in 1499: *Nuovo Receptario composto dal famossisimo* [sic] *Chollegio degli eximii doctori della arte et medicina della inclita cipta di Firenze*, of which a later, revised, version was compiled by order of Cosimo I (*El Ricettario dell'arte et Università de medici et spetiali della città di Firenze*, Florence 1550). Metallurgy, an eminently practical discipline, was treated by Vannoccio Biringuccio (*De la Pirotechnia*, Venice 1540, 2nd ed. 1550; repr. of first book, Bari 1914). Accounts of journeys and discoveries were often still in Latin at the beginning of the century; but G. B. Ramusio's *Delle navigationi et viaggi* (Venice 1550-59) gave the public an imposing collection of original accounts in, and translations into, Italian.

In fact, the position of Italian in relation to Latin depended on a number of factors: on one hand the strength of humanist tradition and Aristotelian scholasticism, on the other practical exigencies and the influence of vernacular humanism. In 1589, in the Accademia della Crusca, Pierfrancesco Cambi proposed for discussion the question 'Se la lingua toscana sia capace di ricevere in sé le scienze' and on Dec. 21 Francesco Marinozzi read a paper on the subject; it is significant that it was still an arguable question.

The sixteenth century is probably the century that saw the greatest number of translations of works of learning originally written in Latin and Greek. (This category included many by modern authors, of course.) Aristotle, who had been known at second hand during the Middle Ages (through Arabo-Latin works) and again translated from Greek into Latin (by Argyropulos) in the fifteenth century, was now translated directly into Italian. Bernardo Segni dedicated his version of the *Ethics* (1550) to Cosimo I, beseeching him not to disdain it because it was written in Italian, a language which would make it accessible to more people than before. Euclid was translated more than once (E. Danti, N. Tartaglia); Cosimo Bartoli made a version from Latin of the *Protomathesis* of Oronce Finé which showed a certain academic elegance (*Opere di Orontio Fineo*, Venice 1587). The importance attributed to Vitruvius in Renaissance architecture was reflected in a succession of translations: C. Cesariano (Como 1521), G. B. Caporali (Perugia 1536), D. Barbaro (Venice 1556), G. A. Rusconi (Venice 1590), not to mention those that remained unpublished. A similar status in its own field was enjoyed by the pharmacology or 'materia medica' of Dioscorides: apart from the versions by Fausto da Longiano (1542) and M. Montigiano (1547), there was one accompanied by a very full commentary by P. A. Mattioli (Latin version, Venice 1544; Ital. vers., Brescia 1544). The *Mechanicorum libri* of Guido Ubaldo del Monte (Pesaro 1577) found a translator in F. Pigafetta (*Le mechaniche*, Venice 1581). The learned mineralogical and metallurgical works of the German Georgius Agricola were translated into Italian and published a few years after the original Latin editions (*De la generatione delle cose* ecc., Venice 1550; *De l'arte de' metalli*, tr. Michelangelo Florio, Basel 1563).

In historiography, Italian was incomparably more important than Latin. At Florence, where there were many historians, nearly all wrote in the vernacular. The anti-Medicean Gian Michele Bruto, who wrote in Latin, was a Venetian; his *Historiae Florentinae* were published at Lyons in 1562. Outside Tuscany both languages were used. Equicola defended his decision to write his *Cronica de Mantua* (Mantua 1521) in Italian, but hoped at the same time that it would be translated into Latin. Camillo Porzio, who had started to compose in Latin his account of the *Congiura dei Baroni*, wrote it in Italian on the advice of Cardinal Seripando. Antiquarian writings were mostly in Latin; not so, however, the elegant essays of Vincenzio Borghini. There were, too, numerous translations of historical works (e.g. of Livy, Suetonius, Plutarch). Bernardo Davanzati consciously vied with Latin and French in his version of Tacitus, paying special attention to conciseness.

In sacred oratory, Italian was predominantly, indeed almost exclusively, used. In civil oratory, which was less and less used for persuasion and more and more for elegant ceremony, both languages were used according to circumstances: Piero Angeli of Barga delivered the funeral oration for Henry II of France in Italian in the Duomo at Florence (1559), but that for Grand Duke Cosimo in Latin in the Duomo at Pisa (1574). But the vernacular predominated. The same was true of letter-writing. Luca Contile corresponded with Federigo Orlandini in Latin, but then changed to Italian, having become convinced that one could deal adequately with all kinds of ideas in it, sometimes better than in Latin (letter of Oct. 12, 1541). Francastoro and Aldrovandi published only Latin works, but in their private correspondence wrote a simple, realistic Italian. Latin continued to be mainly used in dealing with philosophical and philological concepts and in correspondence with foreigners. Letters were not always used for private communication, of course; they served, too, for publicly expressing one's opinions in elegant style. This was the century which saw the most abundant harvest of collections of letters—a field in which Aretino had sensational success.

In literature, humanist activity continued in Latin, producing eclogues, elegies, sacred, didactic and epic poems, comedies and tragedies; some of these works are still remembered for their intrinsic value. Moreover, a strong classical substratum was visible in writers of Italian. But by this time a triumphant spirit of emulation animated writers in the vernacular. The *Rosmunda* of Rucellai and the *Sofonisba* of Trissino were written in about 1516 to give the Italian language classical tragedy. In *L'Italia liberata dai Goti* Trissino intended to write the modern heroic poem. Tolomei wrote his *Orazione della Pace* (April 1529) 'per mostrare al mondo come questa nostra lingua Toscana era atta ad esprimere altamente e in orazioni tutti i grandi concetti, la qual cosa in quei tempi da certi letterati di debile stomaco non era creduta' (*Lett.*, c. 61a). Translations from the classical languages were numerous. The translators were inspired sometimes by a desire to bring the classics within the reach of those who could not read the originals, sometimes by the idea of breaking new ground in Italian and sometimes by the pleasure of comparing the capabilities of the new language with those of the ancient languages. Caro wrote that he began his translation of the *Aeneid* 'per ischerzo' and continued it 'fra l'esortazioni degli altri e un certo diletto che ho trovato in far pruova di questa lingua con la latina' (letter of Sept. 14, 1565).

The symbiosis of Latin and Italian gave rise to curious mixtures and combinations. On Italian letters that he received from Maria Savorgnan Bembo wrote notes that were mostly in Latin, concerning the date of receipt and other such details. Headings, addresses and dates on letters were for long written in Latin. And sometimes Latin passages were used in vernacular contexts.

Here, as an example, is a postscript from a letter by Scipione Forteguerri to Aldo Manuzio:

'Io sono ito dal Cardinale Hadriano, et mostroli quella parte della lettera vostra, il che li fu assai grato. Ragionammo molto di lettere, *ac multa etiam de te*. Aspetto lo esemplare corretto per darglielo, *nec alia occurrunt. Vale iterum*, et scrivete spesso, *si potes*, et dirizzate le lettere al Secretario dell'Ambasciatore veneto. *Romae die* 19 *decembris* 1505. *Tuus S. Cart.*'

Latin adverbs and particles like *solum, tamen*, etc. were widely used, embedded in Italian prose.

The mingling of Latin and vernacular in the literature and life of the period inspired two kinds of stylization for artistic purposes: the macaronic and the Fidenzian. Whereas in the macaronic the comic element was provided by the intrusion of vernacular and dialectal words into a correct Latin context, in the Fidenzian superabundant latinisms were used to mar an Italian context. The macaronic, which had its origin in the fifteenth century, reached its zenith with Folengo. Born in University circles, it continued to satirize the barbarous latinity of University philosophers:

> *Dum Pomponazzus legit ergo Perettus, et omnes*
> *voltat Aristotelis magnos sottosora librazzos,*
> *carmina Merlinus secum macaronica pensat*
> *et giurat nihil hac festivius arte trovari*
>
> (*Baldus*, l. XXII, 129-32).

The Fidenzian and pedantic styles satirized those who, not content with Italian, either spoke Latin or packed their speech with Latin words and phrases. Castiglione, an opponent of all affectation, condemned those who 'scrivendo o parlando a donne usano sempre parole di Polifilo' (*Cortegiano*, III, lxx). The pedant, in fact, became a notable character in Renaissance comedy (in Francesco Belo, *Il Pedante*, 1529; Pietro Aretino, *Il Marescalco*, 1533; Giordano Bruno, *Il Candelaio*, 1583, and many others). He spoke like this:

'*Omnia vincit Amor, et nos cedamus Amori*. Certamente pare al giuditio de i periti, che *totiens quotiens* un uomo esce dalli anni adolescentuli, *verbi gratia* un par nostro, non *deceat sibi* l'amare queste puellule tenere' (Belo, *Il pedante*, I, sc. 4).

In comedies which satirized the pedant there was frequently another character whose function it was to underline the pedant's ludicrous features by defending intelligible speech or pretending not to understand difficult words (confusing *copule* with *scrofule*, turning *ipocrita* into *pòrchita*, *ambiguo* into *anghibuo*, and so on). The Fidenzian variety of pedantic language was so called after Pietro Giunteo Fidenzio, a pedant of Montagnana, who really existed and to whom Camillo Scroffa attributed a series of sonnets composed about 1550 and published in 1562 (if not earlier). Here is one of them:

> Le tumidule genule, i nigerrimi
> occhi, il viso peramplo e candidissimo,
> l'exigua bocca, il naso decentissimo,
> il mento che mi dà dolori acerrimi;
>
> Il lacteo collo, i crinuli, i dexterrimi
> membri, il bel corpo symmetriatissimo
> del mio Camillo, il lepor venustissimo,
> i costumi modesti ed integerrimi;
>
> D'hora in hora mi fan sì Camilliphilo,
> ch'io non ho altro ben, altre letitie,
> che la soave lor reminiscentia.
>
> Non fu nel nostro lepido Poliphilo
> di Polia sua tanta concupiscentia,
> quanta in me di sì rare alte divitie.

There was, of course, controversy over the respective merits of Latin and Italian.[1] In Book I of Bembo's *Prose della volgar lingua* Ercole Strozzi defends Latin, which he describes as 'degna e onorata', against the vernacular, which is 'vile e povera'. But the other three speakers (Carlo Bembo, Giuliano de' Medici and Federigo Fregoso) do not agree with him, and he is worsted in argument. A bellicose combatant whose work provoked strong feelings was Romolo Amaseo, a humanist from Udine. In November 1529 he inaugurated the academic year in the Archiginnasio at Bologna with two orations *De Linguae Latinae usu retinendo* (published in *Orationum volumen*, Bologna 1563-64). In the first he maintained that the vernacular was only a corruption of Latin. What point was there, therefore, in striving to learn two languages, when one was good and the other corrupt? In the second he attacked the opinion that the vulgar tongue was useful and pointed to the immense store of practical knowledge to be found in the ancient languages. Moreover, the labour involved in learning Latin was repaid by its universal diffusion; but those who learnt

[1] C. Grayson, *A Renaissance Controversy*, Oxford 1960; V. Cian, *Contro il volgare* in *Miscellanea Rajna*, Milan 1911.

Italian found that there was dispute as to whether the language should be Tuscan or that of the courts. To Amaseo's arguments Muzio replied with the three books *Per la diffesa della volgar lingua* (written about 1533 and included in the posthumous *Battaglie*). But there were Latinists prepared to support Amaseo ardently. Francesco Bellafini, in a letter to Marcantonio Michiel, spoke slightingly both of the vernacular and of those who wasted time interpreting Dante's incomprehensible *Pape Satan Aleppe* (*Inf.*, vii, 1), when they might have been reading the classics. And Francesco Florido in his *in L. Accii Plauti aliorumque Latinae linguae scriptorum calumniatores Apologia* (*c.* 1537) was very hard on all those who had written in Italian, showing some indulgence only for Petrarch, who had at least written all his serious works in Latin and kept the frivolous ones for the vernacular. In his *Dialogo delle lingue* Sperone Speroni (who placed his dialogue in 1530, although in fact it was composed some years later) referred to the sensational Amaseo episode. In Speroni's work Lazzaro Bonamico defends Latin and opposes the vernacular, while a courtier speaks in favour of the spoken language, and Bembo in favour of four-teenth-century Italian. There is a dialogue within the dialogue; this gives an account of a discussion between Lascaris and Pom-ponazzi, which had taken place some years earlier, in which the linguistic problem is debated in relation to the needs of philosophy. In it Pomponazzi maintains that the important thing is to reason well, even if one reasons in dialect. A well-argued reply to the supporters of Latin was written by Alessandro Citolini of Serra-valle (Treviso) in his *Lettera in difesa della lingua volgare* (Venice 1540). Latin found a fanatical defender in Celio Calcagnini, who wrote to G. B. Giraldi (*Aliquot opuscola*, 1544) expressing the hope that Italian and all that was written in it would be forgotten, as an expression of 'foedissima barbaries'. Carlo Sigonio, on the other hand, in his *De latinae linguae usu retinendo* (1566) praised Latin without abusing Italian ('detur utrique quod utrique debetur'). And others, too, managed to write of the merits of Italian and the classical languages praising all three. A work which is interesting for its wealth of arguments and use of concrete examples was written by Uberto Foglietta of Genoa (*De linguae Latinae usu et praestantia libri tres*, Rome 1547): the second book deals with the problem of the suitability of Latin as a vehicle for modern concepts and of adding to classical Latin vocabulary.

But deeds were more important than words. And as the century advanced the growing ascendancy of Italian in contemporary life and literature made discussion on polemical lines increasingly futile.

The presence of foreign soldiers in Italy brought Italians into contact with Spanish, French and German. Italians abroad, too, came under the influence of foreign languages, though this made a less important contribution to Italian linguistic history than the many foreigners in the occupied parts of Italy. The dominant foreign tongue in sixteenth-century Italy was, of course, Spanish. Bembo, Castiglione and Valdés refer to the knowledge that Italians had, or pretended to have, of Spanish. And Tansillo wrote that

> *il viver con spagnuoli, il gir in volta*
> *con spagnuoli, m' han fatto uom quasi novo*
> *e m' hanno quasi la mia lingua tolta.*

Whereas other ambassadors had recourse usually to interpreters, those of Spain spoke in their own language before the Venetian senate. Numerous Spanish works were translated into Italian and contributed to the introduction of hispanisms. And characters who spoke in Spanish appeared quite frequently in comedies (e.g. in A. Ricchi's *I tre tiranni*, 1533). French was almost as well known, and was also considered necessary for a gentleman. French influence was particularly strong in Piedmont, and especially at Asti, where the French held sway for many years. The court of Ferrara felt the influence of Renée, the daughter of Louis XII, who gave hospitality to Calvin and to whom Marot acted as secretary. Emanuele Filiberto favoured the use of Italian, but some revealing observations on his linguistic capabilities were made by the Venetian orator F. Morosini (1570): 'a me ha detto più volte, che se gli occorresse dover fare un lungo ragionamento di cose serie, non lo sapria far meglio in alcuna lingua, che nella spagnola. Parla anco eccellentemente il francese, essendo si può dir quella la sua lingua naturale, poiché tutti li duchi passati parlavano sempre francese, così come parla ora sua eccellenza quasi di continuo italiano'. German was much less known, possibly because it was structurally much more different from Italian. In diplomatic relations with the Empire, Latin was used. But the words of German and Swiss soldiers made an impression because of their coarseness, and occasional words or phrases in German figured in carnival songs attributed to soldiers of fortune: 'Noi *trincare* un *flasche* plene—per le sante anime *fostre*', '*Trinche gote* malvasie—mi non biver oter vin', etc. On Italy's frontiers German linguistic pressure was strong, particularly in that part of Lombardy which fell into Swiss hands and in the north-eastern territories dependent on the Empire. Venetians, in the Levant and in Venice itself, heard various kinds of exotic speech on the lips of Slavs, Greeks, Turks, Arabs and Gypsies, and in some comedies attempts were made at imitation of some of them. But satire of foreigners soon lost its freshness, and Grazzini felt impelled to assure his audience in the prologue to his *Spiritata* (1561) that in it they would hear 'nè Tedeschi, nè Spagnoli, nè Franciosi, cinguettare in lingua pappagallesca, odiosa, e da voi non intesa'.

If we read a page of Italian prose written in the late Quattrocento or early Cinquecento, it is usually easy for us to tell from it (even in the case of literary prose) to which region of Italy the writer belonged. This is not the case with literary prose written at the end of the Cinquecento. In the interval, certain grammatical standards had been widely accepted. On the other hand, what was true of the written language of cultivated people was not true of the spoken language. Moreover, texts of a practical nature (inventories, documents from chancelleries in northern and southern Italy, etc.) were nearer than works of art to the spoken language, and bore a large number of regional features. Technical and scientific writings (on art, architecture, pharmacy, metallurgy, etc.) similarly contained regional terms. Dialectal, as well as foreign, speech was also used in comedy, for obvious reasons. Genuine letters were frequently close to the spoken language, but as the large number of published collections shows, letters were frequently written with publication in mind, that is, as works of literature.

Authors of literary works in this period cultivated an illustrious style. The search for elegance, the 'bello stile' cult, can be regarded as perennial features of the Italian literary scene, but they were never more evident that at this time. Some, like Bembo, sought to achieve harmony through attention to purity of diction and word order. Others, like Castiglione, concentrated on the balance of various clauses in the sentence. In Machiavelli and Guicciardini the exigencies of art were tempered by those of logic. Their contemporaries did not find enough elegance either in the prose of the former, who tended to use popular forms that were already on the way out in his own time and who was very dependent on chancellery vocabulary, or that of the latter, who made excessive use of latinisms.

In lyric poetry the Platonizing Petrarchism to which Bembo had opened the door held sway almost uncontested except by the anti-academic reaction of Berni and Grazzini. Alamanni sought to achieve a noble style in another way, through his Pindaric poems. The genius of Ariosto gave a fresh life to the octaves of the chivalresque epic; but when he revised his work, he went as far as his temperament permitted to conform to the new grammatical prescriptions. Tasso, in certain features of his epic poetry, was a harbinger of the baroque, and in the musicality of the *Aminta* a forerunner of the opera.

The differing stylistic ambitions of Italian writers at this time naturally led to varying grammatical and lexical usage. This was far more noticeable in the early decades of the century than later, for at the beginning of the century greater oscillation was felt to be admissible and different sources usable. The principle of imitation later led writers to pay particular attention to those authors who were held to have attained the greatest eminence in art. It was agreed that authors could borrow from Latin models; this had consequences that were slight for Italian morphology, important for Italian syntax and very important for Italian vocabulary. The three great Italian authors of the fourteenth century were read and admired, but the extent to which each should be followed was the subject of discussion. Bembo, the most important influence, imitated Petrarch and Boccaccio and held that the vernacular had achieved perfection in the Trecento; but, although he had published an edition of the *Commedia* in 1502, his insistence on abstraction and decorum prevented him from feeling great enthusiasm for Dante, who was so concrete and used 'rough and dishonoured words'. He also knew and appreciated the work of other fourteenth-century writers; the Gualteruzzi edition of the *Novellino* that appeared in 1525 was, in fact, his. How widely Petrarch was imitated is well known. Not only were aspects of his rhythm and style copied, but much of his choice vocabulary was accepted, not only in lyric poetry, but also in other kinds of verse (e.g. by Ariosto) and in prose. It may not be surprising that Maria Savorgnan should petrarchize when writing to Bembo ('Aspetto vostre letere, per hora *conforto di mia stancha vita*', lett. 34; 'seria troncato *il filo dil mio stame*', lett. 40, etc.); but that Aonio Paleario should write to his wife on the eve of his death (July 3, 1570): 'attendete alla *famigliola sbigottita* che resterà' shows that Petrarch's words had gone beyond the repertory of literary trainees and become accepted expression for life's most solemn moments. Yet from the earliest decades of the century there were those who protested against excessive imitation of Petrarch. They were mainly Tuscans like Firenzuola, Aretino (in the *Marescalco* and the *Ragionamenti*, though he himself petrarchized in verse), Berni, Doni and Grazzini; but there were among them some non-Tuscans, too, like Cornelio Castaldi and, later, Giordano Bruno. There were protests, too, against the tiresome imitation of Boccaccio's prose (from Firenzuola, Castiglione, Lenzoni, Nelli and others). Salviati, a strenuous supporter of the 'buon secolo', a collector of fourteenth-century texts, and, above all, an admirer and student of Boccaccio, was of the opinion that only one contemporary writer had completely succeeded in acquiring perfect Trecento language and style: Della Casa, in his *Galateo*. But the main touchstone was the writers' attitude to the spoken language. For Bembo good language was something to be acquired from a study of good authors of the Trecento; in his *Prose* (Book I) he makes his brother Carlo express the opinion 'l'essere a questi tempi nato fiorentino, a ben volere fiorentino scrivere, non sia di grande vantaggio'. Nor did he approve of a mixture. When, in the *Prose*, Ercole Strozzi suggests a mingling of ancient and modern Tuscan, Carlo replies that 'il pane del grano non si fa miglior pane per mescolarvi la saggina' (Book I). Some Tuscan authors agreed with his archaizing attitude. Many Tuscans, however, saw that they had at their disposal in their own speech a language which largely conformed to the accepted norm and which they could use with some sprinkling of Trecento features added. Moreover, they could also glean expressive words and phrases from the speech of nobles, bourgeois and ordinary people in their own time which would enliven their writings. In fact, Firenzuola, Aretino, Doni, Varchi, Cecchi, Davanzati and many others did this. To what extent they practised a manneristic exaggeration of popular speech of their time, it is difficult to judge. Few non-Tuscans strove to master spoken Florentine. The most important was Caro, who came from the Marches. In his *Commento di Ser Agresto* he asserted that he wished to use 'nè la boccaccevole, nè la petrarchevole, ma solamente la pura e pretta toscana d'oggidì, e della comune quella parte, che ancora da essi Toscani è ricevuta'. And while writing his *Straccioni* he appealed to his Florentine friends for a collection of proverbs they had made, which would be linguistically useful to him.

Some who were willing to recognize the importance of the living language were not ready to ascribe any more weight to

Florentine than that derived from the possession of the great writers of the fourteenth century, and paid attention to the speech of other parts of Italy, especially the courts (that of Rome, the centre of Roman Catholicism, and also those of Mantua, Ferrara and Urbino). But although these 'court languages' possessed some common elements (features due to the acceptance of Trecento models, a notable number of latinisms of the type *populo, commune, anatomia,* as contrasted with Tuscan *popolo, comune, notomia,* etc.), they did not make up a consistent language. The common elements were enough, however, to furnish some combatants in the *questione della lingua* with ammunition, as we shall see when we deal with it later in this chapter. Freedom of choice was championed by those who spoke of a common, universal Italian; some, like the Milanese Don Anselmo Tanzi, translator of Boethius, maintained that the language should be mixed. There were some ('Zoan' Gonzaga, G. Filoteo Achillini, Baldassare Olimpo from Sassoferrato, Antonino Venuti from Sicily) who declared their intention of writing in the language of their own parts of Italy; but, in fact, they did not depart as much as their declaration would lead us to believe from the literary language which was then becoming generally accepted. On the other hand, Mario d'Arezzo did write an ennobled Sicilian which departed markedly from it, as we can see in this extract from his *Osservantii dila Lingua siciliana et Canzoni in lo proprio idioma* (Messina 1543):

'disputando si la lingua siciliana, la quali hogi noi tenimo, per havir tutti soi vocabuli distisi, & interi, non mezi & mutilati, et per potirsi schietta scriviri, et per tutta Italia intendiri, appari tanto bona, como di tutti altri contrati chiusi di l'Appi, & di l'uno, & l'altro mari' (c. 10a, as printed in the edition of Grassi, Palermo 1912). But this did not have great historical importance; nor did Girolamo Araolla's attempt to forge a literary Sardinian based on northern Logudorese. And in the second half of the century, when many verse and prose works by contemporaries had been widely read, when the linguistic disputes were dying down, and when the grammatical and lexical standards laid down in treatises had become established, it was rare to find declarations of independence. Yet there were still a few, like Bruno, who went their own way, and there was still an occasional protest against archaizing tuscanism, e.g. from the Milanese Lomazzi (*Grotteschi,* Milan 1587, p. 290) or the Perugian Caporali (*Viaggio di Parnaso,* part II, *Il pedante*).

The realization in the first half of the Cinquecento that there was now a valid literary language for all Italy gave an impetus to literature deliberately written in dialect. Previously, dialect writers, with very few exceptions (like Francesco Vannozzo and Antonio Beccari in the Trecento), had sought to refine their language, to move towards a koine. But now there were attempts to remain faithful to particular dialects and to present stylizations of them purposely in contrast with the literary language generally accepted. The genre that most readily lent itself to this kind of writing was comedy. We find a rustic who speaks dialect in a *Commedia nuova* by Picr Francesco da Faenza (undated, but probably belonging to the early years of the sixteenth century). In the farces of Alione, alongside the interlocutors from Asti, appear Frenchmen, a Milanese and a 'Lombard'. In the *Venexiana* the rather affected Italian of the young man and the Bergamasque of a porter are contrasted with the fluent Venetian of the two ladies. In Ruzzante's *Pastorale* we have two Paduan countrymen and a Bergamasque doctor and his servant. Indeed, the dialect character became a common feature in comedies of the late Cinquecento and the Seicento. The characterization of the conventional protagonists of the *commedia dell'arte*, too, had dialect as one of its ingredients. The version of a dialect given in a comedy certainly cannot be guaranteed accurate; but the information provided by Ruzzante for Paduan is valuable, and for the study of Roman the speech attributed to the servant Perna in Castelletti's *Stravaganze d'amore* (1585) is useful. Nor was the use of dialect limited to comedy: there are poems and letters by A. Calmo in Venetian, Venetian lyrics by Maffeo Venier, a heroic poem with Ariostean reminiscences, the anonymous *Pulon matt* from Cesena, and some lyrics, too, by others, of whom we mention, as examples, G. B. Maganza (Padua), B. Cavassico (Belluno) and Paolo Foglietta (Genoa). A different attitude prevailed in Sicily: there an attempt was made at writing a dialect containing many local features, but culturally refined. There were also some attempts at literary stylizations of thieves' slang in the Cinquecento; these have been studied by Renier (*Svaghi critici*, Bari 1910, pp. 1-30) and, more recently, by Franca Ageno (*Studi di filol. ital.*, XVII-XVIII).

Many of the literary controversies of the sixteenth century contained elements of linguistic importance (the polemics on Petrarch and petrarchism, on Boccaccio, on Dante, etc.). But the most important was undoubtedly the *questione della lingua*. This controversy on the nature of the Italian language sprang from the uncertainty that existed in the first half of the century as to the standards to be adopted. To decide on linguistic standards had become, as we saw in the last chapter, an urgent question after printing in Italian had got under way.

There were three main currents in the *questione* in the first half of the century:[1] that of those in favour of archaizing, led by Bembo; that of the supporters of an eclectic solution, more or less based on the language of the courts of Italy; and the Tuscan current, that of those who held that modern Florentine (or, more generically, Tuscan) should be accepted as the standard.

Bembo transferred into the context of vernacular humanism the theories on imitation of the classics that he professed as a Latin writer; but this time imitation was to be, not of Cicero and Virgil, but of fourteenth-century Florentine writers. His *Prose della volgar lingua*, published in 1525, purport to record a dialogue that took place in Venice in December 1502. The speakers are Giuliano de' Medici, Federigo Fregoso, Ercole Strozzi and Carlo Bembo (acting as the mouthpiece of the author). In Book I (after a discussion of the relative merits of Latin and Italian, to which we referred earlier) the speakers talk about the origins of vernacular literature and the opinions expressed by Calmeta on the *lingua cortigiana* in his book (now lost) on vernacular poetry. But, we are told, there is no such language: it is true that it is spoken at the papal court, 'ma questo favellare tuttavia non è lingua', says Giuliano de' Medici, 'perciò che non si può dire che sia veramente lingua alcuna favella che non ha scrittore' (a remark that shows the eminently literary approach of the author, and which was to be typical of the treatment of the linguistic question in Italy). To show that Florentine is the best regulated language (here we see the rhetorician's faith in rules) Giuliano cites his 'due Toschi', that is, Boccaccio and Petrarch. It is the Florentine of these Trecento writers that is, in fact, exalted; to be born and brought up Florentine is not considered much of an advantage for a writer. When Giuliano suggests that literature should approach modern usage, Carlo Bembo tells us: 'la lingua delle scritture non

---

[1] On the *questione della lingua* there is considerable literature. For an account and a bibliography, see B. Migliorini, 'La Questione della Lingua' in *Questioni e correnti di storia letteraria*, ed. A. Momigliano, Milan 1949. In English there is an analysis by R. A. Hall, Jr., *The Italian Questione della Lingua*, Chapel Hill 1942. The social aspects of the *questione* are examined by B. T. Sozzi, *Aspetti e momenti della questione linguistica*, Padua 1955, and a historical survey followed by an anthology of the works of the participants is to be found in Maurizio Vitale, *La questione della lingua*, Palermo 1960.

deve a quella del popolo accostarsi, se non in quanto, accostandovisi, non perde gravità, non perde grandezza'. And when Strozzi suggests tempering the old with the modern, Bembo rejects the idea. Book II deals with the choice and disposition of words. We are told that it is necessary to choose 'le più pure, le più monde, le più chiare ... le più belle e grate voci'. Therefore, it would be better to leave Dante out of it, for he used words that were 'rozze e disonorate'. Practical advice for writing prose and verse follows. In Book III Giuliano expounds Italian grammar. The abundant examples are taken mainly from the *Decameron* and from Petrarch; but there are also quotations from Dante, from the minor works of Boccaccio and from thirteenth-century poets. Bembo's attitude is, then, that of the humanist-rhetorician: he is addressing writers, and he shows them how to achieve elegant language and style through imitation of fourteenth-century Tuscans. He uses the terms *fiorentino, toscano, volgare* indifferently: the quarrels about the use of such words, which were to occupy such a disproportionate place in the *questione,* had not yet broken out, and Bembo did not later allow himself to be drawn into them. Bembo is one of the speakers in the *Dialogo delle lingue,* written shortly after 1530, by Sperone Speroni of Padua. His opponent in the dialogue, il Cortigiano, asks him: 'Dunque se io vorrò bene scrivere volgarmente, converrammi tornare a nascer toscano?' And Bembo is made to reply: 'Nascer no, ma studiar Toscano; ch'egli è meglio per avventura nascer Lombardo, che Fiorentino; perocchè l'uso del parlar Tosco oggidì è tanto contrario alle regole della buona lingua Toscana, che più nuoce altrui esser nato di quella provincia che non gli giova'.

We turn now to the theses of supporters of eclectic solutions (*lingua cortigiana, lingua comune italiana*). The first name we come across is that of Vincenzo Colli, called il Calmeta. Born in 1460 in the isle of Chios, he died in 1508. Among his writings was a treatise *Della vulgar poesia* (in nine books) which was lost and which we know only by what others say of it (Bembo in his *Prose* and Castelvetro in his *Correttione d'alcune cose nel Dialogo delle lingue di B. Varchi, et una Giunta al primo libro delle Prose di M. Pietro Bembo,* Basel, 1572). To those who wished to write verse Calmeta recommended Florentine above 'all the other tongues of Italy' and counselled study of Petrarch and Boccaccio. But he also suggested that the language they had thus acquired could be enriched and refined by following the model provided by the court of Rome (hence his use of the term *lingua cortigiana*). Other supporters of such a court language were Mario Equicola, Angelo Colocci and Giovanni Filoteo Achillino, whose names we find, alongside that of Calmeta, in the *Collettanee Grece Latine e Vulgari* published in 1504 to honour the memory of Serafino Aquilano.

Equicola, who was born at Alvito in 1470, wrote in his youth a Latin treatise *De natura de amore*, which he later translated into Italian. The preface contains a defence of the *lingua cortigiana* and an attack on Tuscan. In many passages in the book Equicola deals with the choice between Florentine and the court language and inclines towards the latter. He praises Giovanni Iacovo Calandra of Mantua because, in the latter's *Aura* 'non con vocaboli dal latino fastidiosamente tratti ha sua inventione vestita ma di parole con indefessa diligentia dalla corte elette' (c. 38b, 1531 ed.). Later he gives advice to those who frequent courts on how to talk: they should avoid plebeian words from their own dialects, follow Florentine only if they are sure of being able to pronounce it well (a very difficult matter) and take pleasure in words that are not far removed from common usage (cc. 161-2).

Angelo Colocci of Iesi, who from 1497 lived at Rome and held important posts in the papal Curia, defended Serafino Aquilano (in his *Apologia* for him in the *Collettanee* we have already mentioned) for not having mastered Tuscan. We can learn more about Colocci's attitude to language from notes he left which are preserved in Vatican manuscript 4817. These show him to have differed from both Trissino and Calmeta: 'La lingua è comune. Ma quando ben in Italia non sia una lingua comune, certo quella che Petrarca di tante lingue ha facto per imitazione, è comune' (c. 1a). He saw a disadvantage in the abundance of idioms possessed by Tuscan; this made it difficult for foreigners. And he connected his 'lingua comune' with the pre-Roman languages of Italy (c. 115a).

Another contributor to the *Collettanee* (indeed the editor) was Giovanni Filoteo Achillino. Later expression of his ideas can be found in dialogue form in his *Annotazioni della volgar lingua* (Bologna 1536). Here Tuscan is satirized and the 'common' language defended. He is in favour of writing *cognosco* not *conosco*, *Gieronimo* not *Girolamo*, *Olempo* not *Olimpo*, *epistola* not *pistola*, and so forth. Some words used by Dante, Petrarch and Boccaccio which the author found strange are condemned.

Baldassarre Castiglione also treated the linguistic question in his *Cortegiano* (Book I, cc. 28-39). Although, because of the title of his book, he is always treated as a supporter of the *lingua cortigiana* (Tolomei put him into his dialogue *Il Cesano* as such), he himself did not use the term. In the *Cortegiano* Ludovico di Canossa represents Castiglione in the matter of language, while Federigo Fregoso puts forward views akin to Bembo's. The essential criterion here is that of social good taste: the avoidance of affectation. For this reason Canossa would avoid archaisms. Fregoso, however, maintains that they are permissible in writing. But, although Canossa agrees that greater care should be exercised in the choice of diction in the written language, he does not agree that the words should be different from those used in speech, only that the writer should choose the most beautiful of those words used in the spoken language. Fregoso, on the other hand, approves of the use in literature of words 'non dirò di difficultà, ma d'acutezza recondita'. He maintains, too, that, in order to avoid the difficulties that arise from regional differences, it is best to follow the usage of Petrarch and Boccaccio. Canossa's ideal is more eclectic; he is not against Tuscan, but does not wish choice to be restricted to it. He would avoid archaisms, but not those hispanisms and gallicisms that have already been accepted in Italian usage. In fine, his ideal is a language which 'se ella non fosse pura toscana antica, sarebbe italiana, commune, copiosa e varia.' In the dedicatory letter which preceded the 1527 edition Castiglione confirmed that he himself had not tried to follow modern Tuscan speech, still less the language of early Tuscan writers. And he asked why, if certain Latin words had become corrupted in Tuscany, but had remained intact and unchanged in Lombardy, he should follow the Tuscan forms. Instead, he insisted on the point of view he had adopted in the dialogue in relation to doublets like *popolo - populo, orrevole - onorevole*, failing to realize that the forms he referred to as 'rimaste integre' were, in fact, latinisms.

It is clear that discussions on the language were frequent in northern courts (especially Urbino and Mantua) and at the papal court at the beginning of the century, and that the solution favoured was that of a *lingua cortigiana*.

To the support of this solution Giangiorgio Trissino of Vicenza sought to bring the authority of Dante. He came into possession of a copy of the *De vulgari eloquentia*. During one of his visits to Florence, probably in 1514, he made its contents known to a group of men of letters who met in the Orti Oricellari, and he continued to speak of it during his sojourns at Rome (1514-18, 1524, 1526).

From the conversations at Florence sprang Machiavelli's dialogue on the language, to which we shall presently return. In November 1524 Trissino published his *Epistola de le lettere nuovamente aggiunte ne la lingua italiana*, in which he defended the new spelling he had introduced in his tragedy *Sophonisba* (with ε for open *e* and ω for open *o*) which had been published in September of the same year. In that letter Trissino spoke of an 'Italian' language, and he distinguished clearly between usage that he called *toscano, tosco* and *fiorentino* on the one hand and usage that he called *cortigiano* and *commune* on the other. He also said that in the *Sophonisba* he had followed Tuscan whenever he thought that in doing so he could easily be understood in the rest of Italy; but, when Tuscan had seemed to him to present difficulty, he had had recourse to the 'courtly and common'. The *Epistola* provoked a chorus of protest. Most of the objectors were Tuscans: Lodovico Martelli, Angelo Firenzuola, Claudio Tolomei (under the name of Adriano Franci) attacked the spelling reforms. But so did the Venetian Nicolò Liburnio. The name 'italiana' that Trissino had given the language was also attacked: Martelli in particular maintained that it should be 'Florentine'. Trissino replied in his dialogue *Il Castellano*. The two principal speakers in it are Giovanni Rucellai (commander of the castle of Sant'Angelo, who is here made to represent Trissino's views) and Filippo Strozzi (who frequently quotes passages from Martelli). Both, be it noted, were Florentines. When his opponents allege that he has 'spogliato la Toscana del nome della sua lingua', Trissino (through Rucellai) denies this; he has spoken of an 'Italian' language because he considers that Tuscan is Italian, one of the most noble of Italian languages. But he then goes on to claim that the early poets did not write Tuscan: the earliest poets were Sicilian, and the language of Dante and Petrarch was closer to theirs than to that of those who wrote in pure Florentine, like Burchiello, Alberti, Matteo Franco, Luigi Pulci and others. Strozzi objects (using the words of Martelli): the writings of Dante, Petrarch, Boccaccio, indeed Trissino's too, are more readily understood by those living in the country around Florence than in Ferrara, Vicenza or Genoa. Rucellai makes a curious reply: Petrarch is better understood in Lombardy than in Florence. And that this is so can be seen, not only in the case of men, but in the case of women, who better preserve the purity of their regional speech. Those of Lombardy understand Petrarch because of his adherence to what was common to all, rather than to what was peculiar to Florence. Trissino interprets

Dante's *De vulgari eloquentia* in his own way, identifying the 'illustrious' vernacular sought by Dante with his own 'Italian language'. Moreover, he takes the *Commedia* to be an example of what he claims; it is full of words from all parts of Italy which cannot by any means be called Florentine. The Dantesque *discretio* he understands, not as 'elimination', but as 'mingling': 'per meglio conoscere poi la lingua di Dante e del Petrarca, pigliamo i loro scritti in mano, e veggiamo se i vocaboli di quelli sono tutti fiorentini, o no; e chiaramente vedremo, che non saranno tutti fiorentini: perciò che ed *aggio* e *faraggio*, e *dissero* e *scrissero*, e molti simili, che sono formazioni siciliane; e *poria*, e *diria*, e molti simili, che sono lombarde, e *guidardone, alma, salma, despitto, respitto, strale, coraggio, menzonare, scempiare, dolzore, folia, cria, scaltro, quadrella, mo, adesso, sovente,* e moltissimi altri vi si leggono, che non sono fiorentini. Adunque non essendo i loro vocaboli tutti fiorentini, nè toscani, non si può la loro lingua con verità nominare fiorentina, nè toscana...' (pp. 45-6). Trissino used the *De vulgari eloquentia* without allowing for the difference in conditions between Dante's time and his own or for the difference in Dante's objectives.

G. P. Valeriano gave support to Trissino's views in his *Dialogo della volgar lingua* (probably written in 1524, shortly after *Il Castellano*), but he was fair enough to put in the mouths of Tolomei and Pazzi an effective version of the Tuscan thesis. His work is again an example (like the quotation from Trissino above) of the way in which the supporters of a 'court' or 'common' language tended to place emphasis on vocabulary, while the supporters of Florentine (as we shall see especially with Machiavelli) were able to rely on pointing out that the morphological and phonological features of the literary language showed that it had been based on the dialect of Florence.

As the century progressed, mention of the 'lingua cortigiana' became rarer and rarer. The name and concept 'Italian language' were defended by Girolamo Muzio (or, as he would have it, Hieronimo Mutio). His *Battaglie in diffesa dell'italica lingua* (Venice 1582) contain several works, ranging in time from 1530 to 1573, and in matter from his answer to the two orations of Amaseo to his *Varchina*, an attack on the *Hercolano* of Varchi. He will not admit that Florentine has any primacy. Foreigners who come to Italy will be able to learn Italian easily; but not Florentine, which is so full of idioms. Although he wanted an eclectic solution like the supporters of the 'lingua cortigiana', Muzio did not appeal to a social model, as they did, but cherished an ideal that was literary and more archaizing: 'Da' libri bisogna imparare a scrivere, ributtando la opinione di coloro, che hanno per sofficienti maestri di buona lingua le balie, & il popolo' (c. 116b). The supporters of a 'common', 'court' or 'Italian' language often objected to the idiomatic elements of Florentine or Tuscan; their aim was what was noble and universal. In phonetic and lexical features they preferred to follow Latin rather than Tuscan (*febre, obedire, patrone, populo, Capitolio, dicere, facere, honorevole* not *horrevole, palazzo* not *palagio*), they accepted analogically regular forms (like *leggei, leggiuto*), and they rejected tuscanisms which differed from forms already established in literary tradition (*messi, detti* for *misi, diedi*). To this the Tuscans rightly objected that these things did not add up to a language, but only to a few isolated features, and that not all non-Tuscans were in agreement about them. This language, said Martelli, had about as much right to be called 'cortigiano' as had the smelly smoke from sacrificial victims to be called sacrificial flesh (*Riposta alla Epistola del Trissino,* c. 5a).

Eclectic solutions were opposed by the Tuscans and particularly by the Florentines. Trissino's discovery of the *De vulgari eloquentia* served as a great stimulus to linguistic discussion among them. The conversations in the Orti Oricellari were remembered for decades at Florence. They stirred Machiavelli to write (probably in the autumn of 1515) a *Discorso ovvero dialogo in cui si esamina se la lingua in cui scrissero Dante, il Boccaccio e il Petrarca si debba chiamare italiana o fiorentina.* He sets out to show that the language of Dante, Petrarch and Boccaccio was Florentine, not Tuscan, as his 'least dishonest' opponents maintained, nor Italian, as his 'very dishonest' ones alleged. He resurrects Dante and argues with him, forcing the poet to admit that his *Comedy* is really written in Florentine. Machiavelli makes the point that no language is not mixed; what counts is its capacity to absorb foreign words and mould them to its own patterns: 'quella lingua si chiama d'una patria, la quale convertisce i vocaboli ch'ella ha accattati da altri, nell'uso suo, ed è sì potente, che i vocaboli accattati non la disordinano, ma ella disordina loro; perché quello ch'ella reca da altri, lo tira a sé in modo che par suo.' The nub of his argument is that if the literary language has kept the phonetic and morphological features of Florentine, there is no need to call it something other than Florentine simply because it has absorbed a few non-Florentine words from various sources.

He asks Dante: 'tu, che hai messo ne' tuoi scritti venti legioni di vocaboli fiorentini, ed usi i casi, i tempi e i modi e le desinenze fiorentine, vuoi che li vocaboli avventizii facciano mutar la lingua?' Machiavelli maintains that the speech of the courts is various and unstable. He points out, too, that if cultivated Italians have to some degree a common language, this is due to the diffusion of the writings of Dante, Petrarch and Boccaccio: many Florentine words have become common property. The outstanding feature of Machiavelli's treatise, of course, is the importance attributed to phonetic and morphological features.

Another energetic defence of Florentine came from Ludovico Martelli: to it is dedicated the first part (cc. 2a-8b) of his *Riposta alla Epistola del Trissino delle lettere nuovamente aggionte alla lingua volgar fiorentina* (published at Florence at the end of 1525). He objects to Trissino's speaking of 'tre delle Italiane lingue . . . cio è Toscana, Fiorentina et Cortigiana'. He holds that 'ogni lingua nasce dall'uso di chi parla'. And he invites Trissino to see if the writings of Dante and Petrarch are understood as well in other regions as they are in Tuscany. As for the *De vulgari eloquentia*, he doubts whether it is by Dante. Martelli, as we have already mentioned, was quoted and answered by Trissino in *Il Castellano*.

A notable participant in the dispute was Claudio Tolomei, a Sienese who is remarkable as a precursor of some of the discoveries of modern linguistics (notably in his understanding of phonological development, differences between hereditary and learned words, etc.). In *Il Polito*, published in 1525 under the name Adriano Franci, Tolomei criticized Trissino's spelling reforms. In *Il Cesano*, written in 1527 or 1528, but published only in 1555, he dealt with the question of the language. In it he combats the idea of a 'court language or Italian language' and also the archaizing solution. He is in favour of 'Tuscan', rather than 'Florentine', as a name. He wants other Tuscans to share in the glory of the language with the Florentines, because he sees that they have most of it in common. Dealing with Boccaccio's language, he writes: 'se fuora d'una sola città distender non la vogliamo, fiorentina era certamente; se conoscere quanto ella con pari forme si distenda, toscana senza dubbio; perché le differenze che sono tra le terre di Toscana nel parlar loro non son tali, che debbiano fare in guisa alcuna lingua nuova' (p. 101 Daelli). He is against making too much of little differences, as in *aggiunto* and *aggionto*, *bramarei* and *bramerei*; otherwise we shall also have to complain of certain popular Florentine forms like *i versi*

mia, dargnene, sta sera, etc. He condemns those who would im-
poverish the language by trying to restrict writers to the usage of
Petrarch and Boccaccio. His work is important, in fact, because he
sees that a language exists apart from the literature written in it
('Prima certo sono le parole, poscia li scrittori, che s'ingegnano
quelle con destrezza ed eleganza comporre insieme', p. 104
Daelli), though he is prepared to recognize that 'e' non fia mai,
ch'una lingua abbia splendore, se ella illuminata non è da questo
chiaro e quasi eterno sole delle scritture' (pp. 62-3 Daelli).

The 'Florentine' thesis was upheld by a group of scholars:
Giovan Battista Gelli, Pier Francesco Giambullari, Carlo Lenzoni
and Benedetto Varchi. Giambullari and his friends believed that
it was not true that only what famous writers had written, counted;
the usage of 'qualified persons' in speech and writing in one's own
day had to be taken into account. His treatise *De la lingua che si
parla e scrive in Firenze* (1552) was the first grammar by a Tuscan
author since the fifteenth-century *Regole*. This treatise was accompanied by a *Ragionamento sopra le difficoltà di mettere in regole la
nostra lingua* by the learned artisan G. B. Gelli. He rejects the idea
that Italian achieved its perfection in the fourteenth century; it
must not be restricted to what was written then since it is better
now and still on the way up ('e la è viva e va all'insù'). Carlo
Lenzoni expressed ideas similar to Gelli's in his *Difesa della lingua
fiorentina*, posthumously published in 1556. He criticized Bembo
for neglecting Dante while favouring Petrarch and Boccaccio.
Echoes of the mid-century Florentine discussions and of the
ideas of Gelli and his friends are to be found, too, in Doni's
Marmi (1553).

The *Hercolano* of Varchi, finished in 1564 and posthumously
published in 1570, is notable because, although Varchi is a
supporter of the 'Florentine' thesis, it shows the shift in opinion
towards acceptance of Bembo. In fact, by this time Florentine
men of letters had largely accepted Bembo's codification (and the
necessity for keeping an eye on the *trecentisti* when writing). In the
Hercolano Bembo is treated with great reverence. Varchi, however,
has enough respect for Florentine spoken usage to state that
one cannot write a language perfectly without having learnt it
from those who naturally speak it—at least not until all subjects
have been written about in it. On the other hand, he considers
the opinion of those who hold that one should write as one
speaks to be 'manifestly most false'. Varchi's work, like parts
of Trissino's *Castellano*, which it is intended to contradict, is

marred by arguments of an abstract and pseudo-philosophical nature.

Italian political, religious and cultural life had now entered a conformist period. At Florence, under Cosimo I, Francesco I and Ferdinando I, there were plenty of historians, scholars and grammarians, but no first-rate writer. This doubtless helps to explain the acceptance of Bembo's codification. The words *fiorentino* and *toscano* came increasingly to mean the language of the great fourteenth-century writers. A notable contribution to the growth of archaizing tendencies was made by Leonardo Salviati and the Accademia della Crusca. Already in 1564 Salviati had written an *Orazione in lode della fiorentina lingua* in which he had given great praise to Boccaccio's language. He gave further deep study to this subject in connection with the notorious 'rassettatura' of the *Decameron*. In 1573 the 'Deputati' had prepared an expurgated edition of Boccaccio's work in line with the demands of ecclesiastical censorship. The mutilation was considerable. Since the work was very badly received, the Grand Duke, with the agreement of Sixtus V, thought to improve matters by getting Salviati to reduce the damage. The new edition came out in 1582. Salviati's two volumes *Degli Avvertimenti della lingua sopra 'l Decamerone* appeared in 1584 (at Venice) and 1586 (at Florence); the third volume, which was to complete the work, was never written. Salviati's ideal is the language of the fourteenth century, 'il buon secolo'. Since then there has been a decline, due particularly to excessive latinizing. In the written language there has been an improvement following the attention paid by Bembo and Della Casa to the Florentine classics, but little progress has been made in speech. Those who wish to write for posterity should imitate the beautiful language of the Trecento and avoid current usage. Salviati mentioned in the *Avvertimenti* (I, p. 129) his intention of compiling a dictionary. He died in 1589 before doing so; but the work was taken up by the Accademia della Crusca, which he had transformed in 1583 from a mainly social to a predominantly literary and linguistic society.

Not everyone accepted the Bembo-Salviati line. Bernardo Davanzati conceded that many writers had written well in an Italian learnt like a dead language from the three Florentine writers, but thought they would have written better if they had used living Florentine, as those three authors themselves had done (letter to B. Valori, May 20, 1599). Sienese philologists like Diomede Borghesi and Celso Cittadini (who successively held

the lectureship in Tuscan at Siena), followed Tolomei in supporting a Tuscan language. Orazio Lombardelli tried to mediate
between Florence and Siena by claiming that perfect Tuscan, in
the words of the proverb, was 'Lingua Fiorentina in bocca Sanese'.
Local patriotism went further in Scipione Bargagli (*Il Turamino,*
Siena 1602), Adriano Politi and Belisario Bulgarini; but we shall
deal with them in the next chapter.

With the flourishing of vernacular humanism, Italians felt the
need for precise rules for the vulgar tongue. The *Regole della lingua
fiorentina* remained in manuscript until the twentieth century; their
influence was thus negligible. The first Cinquecento grammarians were Venetians: while Pietro Bembo hesitated for long
before presenting his *Prose della volgar lingua* to the public, Gian
Francesco Fortunio (a man of Dalmatian origin, who lived for a
long period at Pordenone) published his *Regole grammaticali della
volgar lingua* at Ancona in 1516. The work, which was frequently
reprinted in the following years, consisted of two books only. These
dealt with morphology and orthography. The other three books
promised by the author were not written. Fortunio follows
Latin grammarians, particularly Priscian, in method and terminology, but takes his examples from the three great fourteenth-
century writers. In the section on orthography he gives special
attention to the problem of double consonants, a subject particularly difficult for northerners.

In Bembo's *Prose* (1525) the strictly grammatical part is in
Book III. It is the handmaiden of a kind of rhetoric (and poetics)
based on imitation. Just as those who wish to write elegantly in
Latin imitate Virgil in verse and Cicero in prose, so in Italian
we should follow Boccaccio for prose and Petrarch for verse. But
the examples are not limited to these two: Dante is often quoted,
though not always with approval, and so are Guittone and some
thirteenth-century writers. The *Prose*, as we have already said,
had great influence. Many writers sought to follow Bembo's
counsels. Lesser grammarians also strove to compile manuals in
accordance with his principles. Such a work is Nicolò Liburnio's
Le Tre Fontane (1526), containing lists of words taken from the
great Florentine writers mingled with grammatical and rhetorical
observations.

In 1529 appeared Trissino's *Grammatichetta* (which, apart from
the author's new principles for spelling, is substantially descriptive
and based on paradigms) and also his *Dubbi grammaticali*, a
work mainly devoted to questions of orthography. Along with all

the early treatises from Venetia there appeared in 1533 one from southern Italy: the *Grammatica volgar dell'Atheneo* (Marco Antonio Ateneo Carlino). But it got no further than the first section ('Del Nome'). Ateneo's canon is based on Petrarch, Sannazzaro and Bembo's *Asolani*. By mid-century there was a spate of grammars (Jacomo Gabriele, *Regole grammaticali*, Venice 1545; Rinaldo Corso, *Fondamenti del parlar toscano*, Venice 1549; Lodovico Dolce, *Osservationi della volgar lingua*, Venice 1550). Only then appeared the first by a Tuscan since the fifteenth-century *Regole*: Giambullari's *De la lingua che si parla e scrive in Firenze* (1551-52). Among the numerous works published in the second half of the century mention should be made of the rhetorico-grammatical rag-bag of G. Ruscelli, *De' commentarii della lingua italiana libri sette* (Venice 1581). These grammarians had to face the difficulty of trying to reduce to clear, short rules an Italian usage that oscillated. In many instances no single form was recognized. In many cases where there were several possibilities, grammarians chose one of them, thus restricting the range of options. And when they did that, their choice usually fell upon an archaizing form.

In some scholars study of grammar was part of a wider philological interest. Claudio Tolomei, as we have seen, was an example of this. Acumen and a wide range of interest, as well as quibbling and cavilling, also characterized the work of Castelvetro (*Giunta fatta al ragionamento degli articoli et de verbi di M. Pietro Bembo*, Modena 1563; *Correttione d'alcune cose nel Dialogo di B. Varchi, et una giunta*, etc., Basel 1572). On the occasion of the ecclesiastical revision of Boccaccio several Florentine scholars studied fourteenth-century usage. Important observations are to be found in the *Annotationi et discorsi sopra alcuni luoghi del Decameron fatte dalli. . . . Deputati sopra la correttione* (Florence 1574) of Vincenzio Borghini. Not less important were the *Avvertimenti* of L. Salviati (1584-86), which we have already quoted and which were to give an archaizing attitude to the nascent Accademia della Crusca. At Siena, Tolomei's works found some echoes in those of D. Borghesi (*Lettere familiari*, 1578-1603), O. Lombardelli (among whose many works the most important is his *Arte del puntar gli scritti*, Siena 1585) and Celso Cittadini. With these philological interests, as well as with the development of similar interests in France, we can connect the first attempts at etymological research. Even if we neglect the extravagant contributions to etymology by an unknown Carafulla and the aberrations of Giambullari's *Gello*, there remain notable efforts by Varchi and also by Ascanio Persio (in his *Discorso intorno alla conformità della lingua Italiana con le più nobili antiche lingue, e principalmente con la Greca*, Venice 1592).

If we omit Latin-Italian word-lists, we find that the first real dictionaries of Italian came after Bembo's *Prose*. They were the fruits, in fact, of the same interests that produced grammars. First there were glossaries of limited scope, like Liburnio's *Le tre fontane* (1526) and a *Vocabulario* which Lucillo (or Lucio) Minerbi prefixed to his edition of the *Decameron* (1535). The first comprehensive work was Fabricio Luna's *Vocabulario di cinque mila vocabuli Toschi* (Naples 1536), which contains several curious errors (like confusing *estro* and *ostro*). But it was followed by works which, though containing odd defects, had considerable merits: those by A. Acarisio (*Vocabolario, grammatica, et orthographia della lingua volgare*, Cento 1543), F. Alunno (*Le osservazioni sopra il Petrarca*, Venice 1538, *Le ricchezze della lingua volgare sopra il Boccaccio*, Venice 1543, *La Fabbrica del mondo*, Venice 1546-48), A. Citolini (*La Tipocosmia*, Venice 1561), G. Marinello (*La copia delle parole*, in two parts, Venice 1562), G. S. Montemerlo (*Delle Phrasi Toscane*, Venice 1566), and, most popular of all, G. Pergamini (whose *Memoriale della lingua volgare*, Venice 1601, continued to be reprinted even after the Crusca had published its dictionary). The third decade of the century also saw the appearance of dictionaries of rhymes. That by Pellegrino Moreto (or Morato) of Mantua (*Rimario di tutte le cadentie di Dante e Petrarca* (Venice 1528) was followed by those of Giovanni Maria Lanfranco (Brescia 1531) and Benedetto Di Falco (Naples 1535) and, after an interval, by that of Girolamo Ruscelli, which fills a large part of his *Del modo di comporre in versi nella lingua italiana* (Venice 1559) and was reprinted many times during the sixteenth century and subsequently.

The *Ordonnance de Villers-Cotteret* (1539), which was so important in promoting the use of French instead of Latin in France, applied for some years to Savoy and the parts of Piedmont occupied by the French. In 1560 Emanuele Filiberto had a similar edict promulgated, prescribing official use of the vernacular. (This was to be French or Italian, according to the region. A further edict in 1561 made it clear that in the duchy of Aosta this meant French). But there was no central authority in Italy which could make provision for national action on the problems raised by the *questione della lingua*. The hope entertained by Firenzuola and Tolomei of organizing a linguistic council at Rome in 1525 came

to nothing. So did Tolomei's plan for holding one at Bologna in
1529 during Bembo's stay in the city. At Florence Cosimo I
strove to promote study of the language. Davanzati, in his
oration on the death of the Grand Duke, summarized his contribution thus: 'creò l'Accademia fiorentina, ottenne da Roma il
Boccaccio, chiedeva il Machiavello; voleva regolar la volgar
lingua fiorentina' (II, p. 469 Bindi). Here the reference to
Boccaccio concerns Cosimo's obtaining consent for the new
revision of the *Decameron*, and that to Machiavelli to the Grand
Duke's request that his works should be taken off the Index. But,
although academies played an important part in the diffusion of
knowledge of the vernacular literature in Italy, Cosimo's requests
to the Florentine Academy (on which he had conferred in 1541
'autorità onore e privilegi, gradi salario ed emolumenti') for an
official compilation of the 'rules of the Tuscan language' bore no
such fruit.

The Accademia della Crusca was to have far greater importance
linguistically. It began as an easy-going society whose members
called themselves *Crusconi* and their meetings *cruscate* (by which
they understood lectures without head or tail). It was probably
founded in 1582. But more important than its foundation was
its transformation when Salviati (admitted in 1583) said: 'Non
più crusconi ci facciamo chiamare, ma *Accademici della Crusca*'.
His interpretation of *crusca* involved the academy in separating
the chaff from the wheat, i.e. good usage from bad; its emblem
is a boulting-sieve. Not only did he transmit to the academy his
own linguistic opinions (the primacy of fourteenth-century
Florentine), but also the idea (which his death in 1589 prevented him from carrying out) of compiling a dictionary containing 'tutti i vocaboli, e modi di favellare, i quali abbiam
trovati nelle buone scritture, che fatte furono innanzi all'anno del
1400'. In March 1591 the Academy began to discuss methods
and to share out the work among its members. The dictionary
appeared in 1612, and we shall deal with it in the next chapter.

The sixteenth century witnessed the birth of spelling reform in
Italy. The first to present a system of radical reform to the public
was Giangiorgio Trissino. At first he was concerned with three
matters: distinguishing between open *e* and *o* and close *e* and *o*;
distinguishing between consonantal and vocalic *i* and *u*; distinguishing between voiced and voiceless *z*. In the case of the
second of these, it should be borne in mind that L. B. Alberti
had proposed the distinction between *u* and *v* in his *De cifra*.

Trissino thought he could achieve the distinction between open and close *e* and *o* by introducing the Greek letters ε and ω. For the other distinctions use could be made of symbols previously employed in writing Italian (*j, v, ç*). For the moment he did not propose to distinguish between voiced and voiceless *s*. He put his principles into effect in May-June 1524 in the printing of his *canzone* to Clement VII and his *Sophonisba*. In November followed the justification, his *Epistola de le lettere nuωvamente aggiunte ne la lingua italiana*. Apart from the points mentioned, Trissino's spelling was rather conservative. He kept etymological *h*, though convinced it had no function. He kept *x* and various consonantal groups in latinisms that were still recognizable as such, and also *y, th* and *ph* in grecisms. He also kept etymological *ti*, writing *pronuntia, innovatione*, etc. With the two sounds each, velar and palatal, represented by *c* and *g* he was not concerned, continuing to write *cia ce ci cio ciu, ca che chi co cu*, and likewise for *g*. He proposed no innovation in connection with *gl, gn, sc*. Trissino's proposals immediately provoked discussion. After the appearance of his *Epistola* the storm broke with the publication of Firenzuola's *Discacciamento delle nuove lettere* (1524), Martelli's *Risposta alla Epistola del Trissino* (1524) and Tolomei's *Polito* (1525), which came out under the name of Adriano Franci. Nicolò Liburnio joined the objectors with a brief dialogue at the end of *Le tre fontane* (1526). Trissino's sole supporter (and not a very strong one at that) was Vincenzo Oreadini (in a Latin letter to his fellow Perugian Tommaso Severo degli Alfani, Perugia 1525). Nothing daunted, Trissino, supervising the publication of his works at the press of Tolomeo Gianicolo at Vicenza in 1528-29, introduced further innovations. The *Epistola* was reprinted as before (except for a small difference: use of *zi* instead of *ti*: *pronunzia, innovazione*, etc.). But in the *Castellano*, printed before January 1529 and in the translation of the *De vulgari eloquentia*, the *Dubii grammaticali*, the *Poetica*, the *Sofonisba*, the *Grammatichetta* and the very rare *Alfabeto*, which followed in the following months, Trissino's second system was followed. In it: ε continued to represent open *e*; ω, instead of representing open *o* as in the first system, stood for close *o*; ʃ indicated voiced intervocalic *s*; ç stood for voiced *z*; *j* and *v* were consonants; *lj* indicated a lingual palatal (*dolja, lji*); *ki* represented the sound of modern Italian *chi*, whether followed by a vowel or not (*ki, kiamo, kiodo, genocki*). For capitals, too, new letters were used. The use of *x, y, h, th*, and *ph* in Latin and Greek words was confirmed. There was no innovation in connection with *ch, gh, sc*, *gn.* In spite of Trissino's pertinacity, nobody accepted his innovations for *e* and *o*; moreover, though *j* and *v* entered Italian usage, this took place only much later, and only the *v* was to remain incontestably. Some modern dictionaries have used ʃ as an aid to pronunciation, but along with ȝ, which shows that this derives from Tolomei or Giambullari rather than from Trissino.

The most notable work provoked by Trissino's *Epistola* was Tolomei's *Polito*, which is the most convenient starting-point for a survey of the Sienese scholar's views on orthography. Tolomei was as firmly convinced as Trissino that the Latin alphabet was not altogether suitable for Italian. Indeed, he claimed that he and his colleagues in the Sienese Academy had given attention to the matter twelve years previously. They had drawn up a complete alphabet, which had been used by some people and which Trissino could have known about. But an individual could not introduce major innovations; the consensus of scholars and the authority of rulers needed to be obtained. Tolomei criticized Trissino for certain errors (not perceiving that atonic vowels are closed, revealing by his transcription that he had an imperfect knowledge of the pronunciation of certain words) and did not like the use of Greek letters. From letters written by Tolomei after the publication of the *Polito*, it appeared that he had compiled two alphabets: 'l'uno per tenerlo segreto e godermelo solamente con qualche caro amico, l'altro per allargarlo e lassarli correr la sua fortuna' (letter to F. Figliucci, in *Lettere*, c. 224b). The first used new symbols which allowed one to see immediately whether a letter represented a vowel or a consonant, a mute or a liquid, etc. (letter of F. Benvoglienti to M. Celsi, 15 Sept. 1547, *ibid.*, c. 234a); it found no practical application. The second had no new symbols, but merely graphic variants that allowed the reader to distinguish the two types of *o, e, s* and *z*, and certain other peculiarities. This alphabet was used by Benvoglienti in the Gioliti edition of the *Lettere* (Venice 1547), and to it he (Benvoglienti) supplied a key.

In 1544 there was published at Florence Marsilio Ficino's translation from the Latin of his own treatise on platonic love, with the title *Marsilio Ficino sopra lo Amore o ver' Convito di Platone*. This, too, had various aids to pronunciation in it. The publisher, under the name of Neri Dortelata, introduces this system in a long letter. But it is probable that no individual called Neri Dortelata existed, and that the spelling is the work of Pierfrancesco Giambullari and Cosimo Bartoli. Special attention is paid to indicating stress: in polysyllabic words it is marked with an acute accent, on oxytones and monosyllables with a circumflex. Open *e* is indicated by the use of a hook above it to the right, open *o* by heavier type. The vowel *u* is distinguished from the consonant *v*. An *i* without a dot is used to mark an *i* which is asyllabic (*bianco*, *piace*). Short *s* indicates voiceless *s*, a long *s* voiced *s*. Similarly, short *z* marks a voiceless *z*, and a *z* with a tail a voiced *z*. The method, in fact, is intermediate between Trissino's and Tolomei's. Indeed, the latter's may have become known to Bartoli. And Tolomei, in thanking Bartoli for having sent him the volume, could not resist an insinuation: 'basta ch'io non so s'egli è stato furto o imitazione, o simiglianza di spirito. Queste sono cose state trattate, disputate, e risolute in una nostra Academia, e comunicate con molti' (*Lettere*, cit., c. 80b). However that may be, the new method, though discussed by many, was used by few, and died out.

The orthophonic devices used by Citolini in his still largely unpublished grammar, dedicated in 1565 to Lord Hatton, derive from Tolomei's system, as do those used by John Florio in his works for English students of Italian (though Florio's use of the symbol denoting open *e* and *o* in atonic positions shows ignorance of what Tolomei wrote in *Il Polito*). When Ruscelli prepared the manuscript of his *Commentarii* he used devices of the Tolomei type, but the work was published without them after his death. G. A. Gilio, in his *Due Dialogi* (Camerino 1564, cc. 32-3) suggested the use of capitals to indicate open *e* and *o* (*huOmo*, *pOrto*, *lascerEbbe*, *farEbbe*). V. Buonanni, probably developing a point made by 'Dortelata' ('alcuni dei nostri antichi . . . posero un *t* davanti al zeta & scrissero *belletza*, *patzo*, *matza*. . . .' p. 25) published a *Discorso sopra la prima cantica del divinissimo theologo Dante d'Alighieri* (Florence 1572), in which he used *tz* for *z* (*gratzia*, *accortetza*, and even *metzo*), thus arousing the ire of Salviati.

For a variety of reasons, the most important of which was the conservatism of literary circles, those attempts at spelling reform came to nought. What did come about, however, was a notable degree of standardization and of acceptance of the usage of certain models. In this connection, the collaboration of Bembo with Manuzio at the beginning of the century (for the editions of Petrarch's poems in 1501 and the *Commedia* in 1502) was clearly an important factor. So was the later employment by publishers of men of letters (Dolce, Domenichi, Ruscelli, Porcacchi, Sansovino) to correct works (by dead and living authors) and prepare them for the press. When, therefore, we speak of the influence of the fourteenth-century classics on the development of Italian, we must remember that in spelling they appeared in somewhat humanistic dress. Petrarch, for instance, wrote, in the manuscript of his first sonnet, the line:

Quadera ĩ parte altruom da q̄l chi sono

In the Aldine edition of 1501, edited by Bembo, and in the 1521 edition, edited by Vellutello, this became:

Quand'era in parte altr'huom da quel, ch'i sono.

Editors in that period, who so often found themselves confronted with archaisms, dialectalisms, etc., often took liberties in changing the text which would seem to us excessive. Petrarch's sonnet no. 219, 'Il cantar novo e 'l pianger de li augelli — in su'l dì fanno *retentir* le valli . . .' has in the Aldine and later editions *risentir* instead of *retentir*. But the changes were not always due to revisers. Authors themselves, as they acquired a better knowledge of the literary conventions of their time, or as they decided to conform to some stylistic development, took to revising early versions of their work. Sannazzaro and B. Gareth (Il Cariteo) are notable examples from southern Italy, Castiglione and Ariosto from the north.

Ariosto's revision of his *Orlando furioso* is one of the best examples for study, for here we can follow the changes in the 1516, 1521 and 1532 editions. (The 1532 text with the 1516 and 1521 variants can be easily consulted in the edition by Debenedetti and Segre, 1960). In the 1516 edition there is much that belongs to the ennobled vernacular of the Po plain (although even this version is a good deal more Tuscan than Boiardo's *Orlando innamorato* and the *Mambriano* of Francesco Bello). There is hesitation in the use of double consonants, in the use of *sc*, and in the use of *c* and *z* before *e* and *i* (*roncino* is more frequent than *ronzino*). We often find the type *gianda, giotto* (for *ghianda, ghiotto*) and the spelling *iusto, Iove*. In vocabulary latinisms abound: *cicada, crebro, dicare, difensione, mal dolato*, etc. Of some things Ariosto had repented by the time he wrote the *errata-corrige*: he corrected two passages in which he had used *mano* as a plural (but missed a third, which he corrected in the next edition). The changes in the 1521 edition were, in fact, few: *volgo* became *vulgo, ciucca* changed to *zucca, perse* to *perdette*, etc. They are less interesting than the opinions expressed by the author in the *errata-corrige*: he wished he had written, not *summo* but *sommo*, not *reverire* but *riverire*, not *devere* but *dovere*, not *volontieri* but *volentieri*, not *parangone* but *paragone*, not *de* and *dil* but *di* and *del*, etc. This is the direction he followed in the 1532 edition. In the meantime Bembo's *Prose* (1525) had been published, and Ariosto was thus helped to be much more thorough in his changes. Nonetheless, although the work of correction was dominated by a desire to conform to Bembo's taste and grammar, not all the changes were consistent or consistently carried out. He often introduced the diphthongs *uo* and *ie* (*ruota*, *scuola*, *figliuolo*, *truova* and *viene*, *priego*, *tiepide*). He changed *dreto* to *dietro*. But he corrected *schiena* to *schena*. The corrections he made to his double consonants generally brought his practice much nearer Tuscan usage; but he also changed *uccellator* to *ucellator*, *verone* to *verrone*, etc. *X* was usually abandoned (*esperimento*, *esempio*; in the autograph fragments he wrote *exempio* or *essempio*). The series *gianda*, *giotto* persisted even in the 1532 edition. On the other hand, the type *giumenta*, *giusto*, *Giove* now predominated (except in some Christian names: *Iocondo*, *Iulio*). The use of the article was almost entirely brought into line with Bembo's: *el* was abandoned for *il*, and in the plural *e* for *i*; before impure *s lo* was used; the groups *in lo*, *in la*, *in l'* were replaced by *nel*, *ne lo*, *ne la* (if the verse permitted). The pronominal particles, too, were made to fit modern usage. In the present indicative *-amo -emo -imo* gave way to *-iamo*. Imperfects in *-o* (*ero*, *andavo*, *potevo*) were corrected to *-a*, contrary to the usage of Florentine speech, but in accordance with Bembo's recommendations. To them is due, too, the change of *presto* to *tosto*. Of Ariosto's deference to Bembo there is, of course, direct evidence as well: the letter (23 Feb. 1531) in which Ariosto informed Bembo that he was nearing the end of his revision of his great poem and announced his intention of coming to Padua to consult him, and also, of course, the handsome tribute to Bembo in the *Orlando furioso* (XLVI, st. 15). Although some features of the language of the Po plain and some latinisms remain in the poem, it conforms substantially in its final version to literary Tuscan.

Many examples could be given of editors' revision, some of it discreet, some of it arbitrary and violent. Girolamo Chiaruzzi's edition (1521) of Boccaccio's *Amorosa visione* may be based on a Boccaccian version unknown to us, or it may have been substantially rewritten by Chiaruzzi (humanistically, Claricio); it is certain, in either case, that the editor made numerous grammatical, metrical and stylistic changes. Many modifications were made, too, by Ruscelli (1552) in his edition of P. Collenuccio's *Istorie del Regno di Napoli*: *exprobrare, eversioni, instrutti,* become *rimproverare, rovine, informati,* etc. Grazzini's *Spiritata* can serve as an instance of the liberties which printers took with the works of contemporary authors. This comedy was published by Giunta at Florence in 1561; when Rampazetto printed another edition at Venice almost immediately afterwards he changed *uffizio* and *benefizio* to *ufficio* and *beneficio, qualunche* to *qualunque, doppo* to *dopo, sopperire* to *sopplire,* etc. These are only a few examples of a widespread practice. The most famous revision, of course, went far beyond the correction of a few linguistic details: Berni's re-writing of Boiardo, generally known as his *rifacimento,* gave the work a new flavour and adapted it to the taste of an age very different from that in which it was written. It was finished in 1531 and published in 1541, and it enjoyed three centuries of popularity. Boiardo was also revised by Domenichi (1545).

The desire to adapt their works to the new linguistic standards induced some writers to submit their writings to persons competent to advise them: Cellini requested Varchi to revise his autobiography, while Vasari sought help from Caro. Guarini asked Salviati for his observations on the *Pastor fido,* and while he paid little attention to those concerning the action of the play, he accepted nearly all Salviati's suggestions for improving its language. But not all were ready to accept the situation, and rebellious remarks came particularly from Tuscan writers. Aretino protested against 'le notomie che ogni pedante fa su la favella toscana' (letter, I, 31, Nicolini), while Grazzini complained that 'la poesia italiana, toscana, volgare, o fiorentina che ella si sia, è venuta nelle mani di pedanti' (*Teatro,* p. 186, Grazzini).

In the second half of the Quattrocento and the first half of the Cinquecento, while French, Spanish, Swiss and Imperial troops trampled Italy underfoot, Italian culture enjoyed enormous influence all over Europe. War and commerce were far from being the only reasons for the circulation of knowledge. Italians left their native land to offer their services to foreign rulers (Columbus, Vespucci, Cabot; Leonardo, Cellini). Italian princesses married and went abroad (Caterina de' Medici to France, Bona Sforza to Poland). Ecclesiastics and laymen who had renounced Roman Catholicism went into exile (Ochino, Vergerio, the Socini, Alberico Gentile, Citolini, Michelangelo Florio, Pietro Martire Vermigli). Foreign students went to Italian universities. Other individuals travelled in Italy for study or for pleasure. In London, in Lyons and elsewhere Italian books were printed. Italian literature was treated as a third classical literature, on a level with Latin and Greek. Its influence was evident in the work of the Lyons school and Margaret of Navarre in France, in Boscán and Herrera in Spain, and in Wyatt, Sidney and Spenser in England. Petrarchism spread. So did Italian metrical forms (the sonnet, *terza rima*). Contemporary Italian authors (Castiglione, Bandello, Machiavelli) were translated and read abroad. To know Italian became an accomplishment prized in the highest circles (Charles V, Francis I, Elizabeth I).

In these circumstances the first grammars of Italian written in other European languages found a ready market. Jean Pierre de Mesmes modelled his *Grammaire italienne composée en français* (Paris 1548) on Bembo. William Thomas in his *Principal Rules of the Jtalian Grammer, with a Dictionarie for the better understandyng of Boccace, Petrarcha and Dante* (London 1550) was indebted to Acarisio for part of his grammar (Acarisio himself being indebted to Bembo for much of his); Thomas made use of works by Acarisio and Alunno for his Italian-English dictionary. G. M. Alessandri published a *Paragone della lingua toscana e castigliana* (Naples 1560). Since many foreign visitors to Italy knew Latin, the Neapolitan Scipione Lentulo (1567) and the Florentine Eufrosino Lapini (1574) wrote grammars in that language for them. A Welshman, Siôn Dafydd (or John David) Rhys (or Rhoesus), wrote in Latin an important treatise on Italian pronunciation (*De Italica Pronunciatione et Orthographia libellus* (Padua 1569). John Florio (the son of the Italian Protestant exile Michelangelo Florio) not only helped the English to learn Italian by writing works like his *First Fruites* (1578) and his *Second Fruites* (1591), but compiled an Italian-English dictionary for them entitled *A Worlde of Wordes* (1598), which was much fuller than that published by William Thomas. The *Vocabulario de las dos Lenguas toscana y castellana* by Cristobal de las Casas appeared at Seville in 1570. The *Dictionnaire françois et italien* by Giovanni Antonio Fenice (Phénice, Félis) appeared in 1584 (Morges and Paris); the Genevan edition of 1598 and subsequent editions bear the name of the reviser, P. Canal.

Nor was Italian known only in European countries. It enjoyed prestige also in non-European countries on the shores of the Mediterranean and the Levant. This period consequently saw Italian words penetrate a number of foreign languages.

We shall now survey the main developments of the century in grammar and vocabulary, beginning with spelling (and punctuation). At the beginning of the century, thirty years after the printing of the earliest incunables, the situation here was still chaotic. Spelling was prevalently humanistic, that is etymological: *h* was kept where Latin had it; *ti* was used for the present *zi*, as were digraphs (*ch*, *th*, *ph*) in Greek words; Latin consonantal groups (*ct*, *pt*, *x*, *ps*) were written without regard for the assimilation that had taken place in Italian; and there were sporadic examples of *ae*, *oe*. But mainly due to the efforts of a great publisher (Aldo Manuzio) and a great philologist (Pietro Bembo), conditions were soon to change. In 1501 appeared *Le cose volgari di Messer Francesco Petrarca*. This Aldine edition was partly more, partly less, latinizing than Petrarch's autograph manuscript (Vat. 3195). Bembo accepted from humanist spelling the *h* (*ho*; autograph *o*), the *ti* (*spatio*, *gratia* as in the autograph, but also *topati*, autogr. *topaçi*) and the Greek digraphs (*cethera*, autogr. *cetera*). But his spelling showed the assimilation of consonant groups (*tt* not *ct*, *pt*): this was a return to what was prevalent in Petrarch, but decidedly different from what was usual in Bembo's time. Bembo used the method again in his *Asolani* (1505); it gradually gained ground and by mid-century was dominant. The *x*, too, was almost entirely abandoned, being replaced by *ss*: the only point that gave rise to notable divergencies was a series of words which had *ex-* in Latin, which were first transscribed with *-ss-* (*essempio*), later, after oscillations which lasted throughout the century, with *-s-*. The *h*, the group *ti*, the Greek digraphs (especially in proper nouns) remained in the first half of the century, except in the writings of the more radical reformers. (Trissino and Tolomei tended to eliminate them, though in different ways, and with some concessions to usage. Neri Dortelata's publications were consistently phonetic: the *h* and the digraphs were abolished and *zi* was used). In the second half of the century, the Tuscans generally abandoned these latinizing features; in north and south Italy, however, writers were much more reluctant to do so, for the traditional spelling allowed them to lean on their knowledge of Latin. As for *h*, Ariosto, according to Giraldi, said that 'chi leva la H all'*huomo* non si conosce uomo e chi la leva all'*honore* non è degno di onore. E s'*Hercole* la si vedesse levata dal suo nome, ne farebbe vendetta contro chi levata gliela avesse, col pestargli la testa colla mazza . . .' *Z*, both in words which had *ti* in Latin (like *gratia*=*grazia*) and in those which had *ti* preceded by a consonant (*actione* = *azzione* = *azione*) gave rise to bitter disputes in the final years of the century between Tuscan supporters of *z* and anti-Tuscans (who were generally against it).

The new spelling made obvious certain examples of homonymic clash which latinizing spelling had concealed in writing (i.e. *atto* now appeared in writing, as well as in speech, for both *acto* and *apto*). The inconvenience of homonymy led to the elimination in certain cases of the less used of the words concerned: *orto* from *ortus*, *esterno* from *hesternus*, *correzione*, *direzione* from *correptio*, *direptio* all disappeared, while *orto* from *hortus*, *esterno* from *externus* and *correzione*, *direzione* from *correctio*, *directio* survived.

Fluctuation was very frequent in the use of double consonants, especially in those instances in which Tuscan differed from Latin. It should be borne in mind that in the dialects of northern Italy double consonants are almost unknown, and for this reason grammarians from Fortunio onwards gave the matter considerable attention. No distinction was made throughout the century between *u* and *v* or between the different functions of *i*, in spite of the various efforts of Trissino, Tolomei and Dortelata. At the beginning of the century the separation of words was very uncertain when proclitics were used (*i libri* or *ilibri*). A notable contribution to clarity was made by Bembo and Manuzio when they introduced the apostrophe. This, which was taken from Greek, was first used in Italian to indicate elision in the Aldine Petrarch of 1501; it very slowly entered usage. By mid-century it was generally accepted, and oscillations remained only between the sphere of elision and that of apocope and for certain minor features (*su 'l*, etc.). Accents, too, were modelled on Greek, as can be seen from the preference for an acute accent internally in a word (in the rare cases when an accent was used) and the grave accent on the final syllable. After sporadic appearances in the Quattrocento, they were used by Bembo and Manuzio in the *Asolani* (1505), which sometimes had the grave on the final vowel (*menò, altresì*; but also *amista, castita*, etc.) and very rarely an accent within the word (*restìo*).

Punctuation, which was very scarce in the manuscripts, and scarce and chaotic in printed works at the beginning of the century, became gradually fuller and more regular, until, at the end of the century, it was much like that of today. In handwriting, punctuation long remained scarce and confused. Ariosto knew of the full stop (used also for a comma and a semi-colon), the comma and the colon (used as equivalents), the interrogative, parenthesis, accent and apostrophe; but, as Debenedetti showed, he hardly ever used them in writing. Guicciardini knew the use of the comma (in the form /), the colon (used also for a semi-colon and for a stop at the end of a clause), the full-stop (used only at the end of a period) and the question mark, but he used them very sparingly. It was the printers who encouraged greater regularity and uniformity. Alongside texts with summary punctuation (with just stops and commas, or with stops, colons and commas) we find others elaborately punctuated. In the Aldine Petrarch there appeared (for the first time, it seems) the semi-colon, used to indicate a pause intermediate between a comma and a colon. Bembo used it (then and in later works) in many instances where we should now use a comma, particularly before relative clauses. In the Aldine edition of the Latin poems of Augurello (1505) the semi-colon had a different function: it was used at the end of each poem as an absolute stop. It should be noted, in fact, that the stop (a dot) was used for two kinds of pause: that at the end of a clause followed immediately by another (in which case it was called 'punto minore' or 'punto mobile' and was followed by a small letter) and that at the end of a period (in which case it was called 'punto fermo'). It took a long time for the exclamation mark ('punto affettuoso') to be distinguished from the question mark and accepted in practice. Aldo Manuzio described it clearly, but did not use it in his own editions. Giambullari, Dolce, Ruscelli and Salviati all dedicated some pages to the problems of punctuation. It was discussed at length and somewhat pedantically by Orazio Lombardelli (in his volume *L'arte del puntar gli scritti*, Siena 1585, and in other writings).

An examination of phonological development, too, shows that there was greater variety at the beginning of the century than at its end. Tuscans differed from northern and southern writers, and prose-writers differed from poets; but even if we compare the autograph manuscripts of two Florentine prose-writers, Cellini and Guicciardini, we find notable differences. The diphthong still predominated in the *truova*, *pruova* type; indeed Guicciardini corrected *trova* to *truova*. *Brieve* is in Machiavelli and Cellini, but in Guicciardini *breve* predominates. The alternation between forms with a diphthong in the tonic syllable and a monophthong in the atonic was mostly respected by Tuscans, though Cellini wrote *huomaccio*. Varchi (*Hercolano*, p. 143) and Salviati (*Avvert.*, I, III, III, 3) both recorded the rule and kept it. Outside Tuscany, analogy frequently upset this alternation: Bembo wrote *inhispagnuolita*, Sansovino *truovare*, etc. The development *-er-* < atonic *-ar-* was normal in Florence and its environs, but *-ar-* persisted at Siena and Arezzo. In the series of futures and conditionals the forms in *-erò*, *-erei*, prescribed by grammarians, prevailed. Some northern and southern writers still stuck to forms in *-arò*, *-arei* (e.g. Giovio in his letters). But when Vergerio wrote *invocarò*, *pendarò*, the anti-Florentine Muzio rebuked him for his transgression (*Battaglie*, c. 51a), apparently unaware that futures in *-erò* were Florentine in origin. But if these forms won their place in the verb-forms on account of their morphological value, in other cases (e.g. nouns in *-eria*, *-erello*, etc.) the forms in *-er-* did not prevail so easily. Salviati (*Avvertimenti*, III, c. II, part 11) noted *Barberia* and *Barbaria* in Boccaccio; he preferred the first since it seemed to him that the second sounded foreign. But Castiglione wrote *vecchiarella* and Valeriano *giovanotti dottarelli*, while Ariosto in the 1532 edition used *pescarecci* and *vecchiarel*, but *Bulgheria*. The Sienese Piccolomini wrote *vestarella* and Pietro Aretino *petrarchescaria*, while Muzio coined *fiorentinaria*. There was great oscillation in the treatment of latinisms containing short *u*: *vulgo/volgo*, *traduzione/tradozzione* (Contile), *suggetto/soggetto*, *facultà/facoltà*, etc. In latinisms containing *au* the pronunciation of this as *al* was widespread (*laldare*, *aldace*); Castiglione, Valeriano, Muzio, Lombardelli considered this a florentinism that should not be copied. Oscillation in the use of the sibilant palatals (*bacio/bascio*) was now rare. But there were frequent hesitations between voiced and voiceless palatals (*brugiare* in Caro, *straginare* in Vasari). Outside Tuscany the single palatal *g* [dʒ] was often replaced by a double (*malvaggio*, *raggione* in Raphael's letter to Castiglione on the antiquities of Rome, *caggionare* in G. Bruno, etc.). There was oscillation between the *cingere* type and the *cignere* type (*aggiugnere*, *dipigne*: Guicciardini; *istignere*: Cellini; *cignerò*: Cecchi, etc.), which was beyond the grammarians. In this century the forms *mugliare*, *ragliare*, *Figline* overcame *mugghiare*, *ragghiare*, *Figghine*; this was a reaction against peasant pronunciation of the *migghia* (for *miglia*) type. A struggle between plebeian and cultivated pronunciation took place in Tuscany in the series *schiavo/stiavo*, *ghiaccio/diaccio* (*stiavo*: Mach.; *stiaccia*, *mastio*: Cellini; *diacere*, *diacitura*: passim; *diaccido*: Soderini, etc.); and some survivals of this remain today (*mastio*, *diaccio*). On the other hand a change which developed at Florence in the groups of *l* + cons. (*aitro*) left no traces. Some phenomena of syntactic phonetics were obliterated by the stabilization of spelling due to printing (*a loro, il re*, even though Tuscan pronunciation was *alloro, irré*). In apocopated forms, when an *m* occurred before the final vowel, it was changed to *n* (unless a labial followed): *possian dire*, etc. In the case of enclitics assimilation was still widely practised: e.g. for *r +l*: *vedella, cascallo, fermallo* (Ariosto, *Orl. fur.* in rhyme); *pensallo, lasciallo, ristorallo* (Machiavelli); *vedelle* (Tasso, *Ger. lib.*, in rhyme). Where and when the final vowel could be knocked off was the subject of controversy. Whereas in prose of a familiar kind the spontaneous usage of Tuscan writers was reflected, in non-Tuscan writers the influence of Boccaccio was occasionally visible: 'quella *perfezion*, qual ch'ella si sia' in the dedicatory letter of the *Cortegiano*. There was argument about the legitimacy in verse of apocopation in lines like Ariosto's 'Il signor, o 'l *tiran* di quel castello' and Tasso's (in the *Ger. lib.*) 'Amico, hai vinto: io ti *perdon*..., perdona' (unhappily changed in the *Conquistata* to 'Amico, hai vinto; e perdono io, perdona').

In morphology, the century saw a considerable reduction in variants; this was largely due to the influence of the grammarians. Surveying the noun we note the late stabilization of the paradigm *la mano/le mani*. The etymological form *le mano*, used by Ariosto in his first version, was subsequently eliminated. The analogical form *la mana/le mane* was used by Cellini. In the plurals of nouns in *-ca* and *-ga* (and corresponding adjectives) there was great oscillation on account of Latin influence, and there were many other forms apart from those that eventually prevailed: *pratice* (Ariosto), *famelice* (Ariosto), *diabolice, filosofice* (Doni), etc. There was a good deal of oscillation, too, in nouns and adjectives in *-co* and *-go*: *equivochi* (Tolomei), *sindachi* (Nardi), *distichi* (Baldi), *dittongi, trittongi* (passim), *dialogi* (Contile); *pratichi* (Salviati), etc. For the article in the first half of the century there were examples of *el*: Cosimo often signed his name as *el duca di Fiorenza*. But the use of *il*, the form recommended by the grammarians, prevailed. The distribution of *il* and *lo* as codified by Bembo (*Prose*, p. 91) included also the types *da 'l* and *lo 'nganno*. Before *s +*cons. the grammarians recommended *lo*, but there were numerous exceptions. Before *z*, *il* was used. Bembo prescribed *lo* after *per* and *messer*; but the rule was by no means universally accepted (*per il passato, per il futuro*, Gelli; *per il fango* alongside *per lo suo buon verso* in the *Annotazioni* of the Deputati, etc.; in another post-consonantal group *far lo satrapo*, Caro). To Ruscelli *per lo papa* seemed provincial ('abruzzese', *Comm.*, p. 516), and Montemerlo praised

Aretino for having escaped from the 'superstition' of using *lo* after *per*. *In la*, opposed by Bembo (*Prose*, p. 155), lost much ground, and Ariosto frequently eliminated it in his revision. The distribution in the plural corresponded to that in the singular: *e* (for *i*) declined rapidly, Salviati denied that Bembo was right in preferring *per li* to *per gli* (*Avvert.*, II, II, xxii). Ruscelli recommended avoiding *gli* in proximity to another *gli* (*Comm.*, pp. 511-512). Among the numerals there were several forms for 2: *duo, dui, doi, duoi, due, du', dua*. Authors generally used two or three forms; these varied sometimes according to the gender of the noun following, sometimes according to the position of the numeral (before or after the noun), and occasionally according to the initial sound of the following word (*du'* before a vowel). There was a tendency among poets to distinguish between *duo* for masculine and *due* for feminine, according to the Latin rule and the frequent example of Petrarch (*duo amanti*, 115, 1; *due rose fresche*, 245, 1). This rule was followed by Ariosto (though not always without exception, and with the additional proviso that nouns in *-a* required *dua*: *dua dita*) and by Tasso. In prose *dua* abounded in the work of Florentines (Machiavelli, Gelli, Guicciardini); for this Salviati reproached them (*Avvert.*, I, II, 19); *duoi*, too, came from Florentine speech. The Crusca, abandoning distinctions of gender, recommended *due* for prose and *duo* for verse. The grammarians did not succeed in getting *lui* and *lei* ostracized as subject-pronouns. Nor did the hostility with which many of them looked upon the new allocutive function of *Ella* and *Lei* stop people addressing each other with these third-person pronouns. Three phases can be distinguished in their development. In the first (which took place mainly in the Quattrocento) the use of the pronouns *quella, ella, essa, lei*, referring to abstract allocutions like *Vostra Signoria, Vostra Magnificenza*, etc., became generalized. (The abstract allocutions referred to triumphed in the usage of the courts, while men of letters strove to keep *voi* alive alongside them). In the second phase (early sixteenth century), when *signore*, through Spanish influence, had come to be used of all manner of men and *Signoria* had thus become generalized, the other pronominal forms (*Quella, Essa*) disappeared, leaving only *Ella - Lei* (generally with *Ella* being used as subject and *Lei* for complements with preposition; but with *Lei* also sometimes used as subject). In the third phase (mid-sixteenth century) this allocution took on a status of its own, intermediate between *Voi* and the full *Vostra Signoria*. *Gli* for 'a lei', frequent in usage, was condemned by Ruscelli, Strozzi and Salviati, *gli* for 'a loro', also frequent, was condemned by Varchi. *Gliele* as a form for all genders and numbers was recommended by Bembo (*Prose*, p. 110 Dionisotti) and often thus used (as also in the more popular forms *gliene* or *gnene*), but at the end of the century Strozzi recommended its avoidance (*Osservazioni*, published as an appendix to Buonmattei). *Lo che*, which came into use in this century, particularly in southern Italy (e.g. in G. Bruno), was a hispanism. The demonstrative *cotesto* was sometimes badly used by non-Tuscans (Bandello speaking of his own writings as '*cotesta* sorte di novelle'), sometimes avoided (see Ruscelli's testimony in his *Commentarii*, p. 132). The enclitic possessives (*fratelmo*, *màtrema*) were limited to a few examples and to the lowest strata of the population. They appeared only in texts with a deliberately popular tone (e.g. comedies by Machiavelli and Cecchi). The grammarians, finding them in Dante and Boccaccio, explained them, but discouraged their use ('bassissima voce': Bembo), and they were soon to disappear even from plebeian Tuscan speech. In the verb, certain forms which had come to be used in the Quattrocento and still enjoyed a certain amount of favour at the beginning of the Cinquecento, were gradually eliminated. Such were 3rd pers. plur. pres. indic. first conj. forms in -*ono* (*pensono*, *s'ingannono*, Mach., *prestono*, *somigliono*, Gelli, etc.). Imperfects in -*o* (-*avo*, -*evo*, -*ivo*, *ero*) were used by the most spontaneous Florentine writers (e.g. Cellini). Other writers oscillated between -*o* and -*a*, and the non-Tuscans willingly obeyed the grammarians (Bembo, Trissino), who admitted only -*a*. Ariosto introduced -*a* forms in his final revision. In the 2nd pers. plur. imp. the forms -*avi*, -*evi*, -*ivi* widely attested as being part of living usage (*voi davi*, Cellini; *voi potevi*, Gelli), were condemned by Salviati; 3rd pers. imp. subj. forms in -*assi*, -*essi*, -*issi* (*mancassi*, *volessi*, Machiavelli) were abhorred by grammarians (and Tizzone Gaetano made war upon them in his edition of Politian). In the conditional, -*ia* forms were now limited to poetry, except for a few examples in prose (Cellini and — possibly through Aretinism — Vasari). Strong perfect forms in -*ono* (*scrissono*) gave way in the second half of the century to those in -*ero*, which Bembo and other grammarians had approved. Paradigms were much less stable than those of today, and aberrant forms abounded (weak perfects like *vivette*, Varchi; *morette*, Davanzati; participles like *fonduto*, Cellini, etc.). Oscillation was specially marked in non-Tuscans: in northern writers, for instance, in spite of Bembo's efforts, forms like *-assimo, -essimo, -issimo* cropped up in past definites and conditionals (*noi andassimo* for 'andammo', *noi potressimo* for 'potremmo'); in southern writers infinitives, participles and gerunds still occurred with plural suffixes ('*per esser*NO essi usciti in campo a spasso', '*avendo*NO quelli a sue male spese imparato', both in Bruno). The construction *tranquilla e pacificamente*, which Old Italian had possessed, but which had not been accepted by the great writers of the Trecento, now reappeared, particularly in chancellery language. Varchi, in his *Storia fiorentina*, wrote: 'molto *lunga e particolarmente* (per usare una volta ancor noi questo nuovo modo di favellare)'. And this new introduction of it makes it certain that it was this time a hispanism.

In syntax, we note that, in apposition with *di*, alongside the construction with the demonstrative ('*quella* cicala della Brigida': Gelli), the construction with the simple article ('*il* semplice dello istrice': Firenzuola; '*il* beccone del marito': Bandello) was still widely used in the sixteenth century. The use of the article with ellipsis of the noun, of which there is an example in Aretino's dedication of the *Orazia* to Paul III ('la vita di Gesù Cristo e *la* di Maria Vergine, e *la* di Tommaso d'Aquino') and another in a letter of Parabosco's ('Questa mattina ho avuto *la* di V. S.': *Lettere*, Venice 1546, c. 19a) was certainly a hispanism. *Tutti* could be followed by the noun without an article: *tutti mali, tutti corpi* (Tasso). Comparatives and superlatives were still occasionally accompanied by intensive adverbs: 'quella che *più* è *migliore*' (Bembo, *Prose*, p. 42 Dionisotti), 'beono sempre i *più pessimi* vini' (Aretino, *Cortig.*, III, 6). Pronominal enclisis at the beginning of a main clause was still predominant, especially in archaizing writers like Bembo, but by this time negative examples alternated with the positive (*si può, ti ringrazio*, but *dirotti* in the same scene in Grazzini's *Pinzochera*, I, 6). In pronominal groups the *se gli* (*se li*), *se le* type was more frequent than the *gli si, le si*. The *lo mi, la mi* type was rarer than *me lo, me la*, etc., but there were examples of it, e.g. in Bembo and in Ariosto ('perché *la le* diè Astolfo', *Orl.*, XXXII, st. 48). In absolute participial constructions the participle often remained in the masculine singular: 'fatto Pasqua' (Bembo, letter of 1503), 'stracciato la scritta e licenziato Nicodemo' (Grazzini, *Spiritata*, I, 3), 'restato la femina contenta', Doni, nov. XIII), 'gli operai, vistosi in vergogna' (Vasari), etc. There was, as is well known, a tendency to sustained periods with complicated use of subordinate clauses. The accusative and infinitive construction gained a lot of ground. The efforts of the grammarians and the care for clarity they introduced, brought about a decline in ellipsis of relative and declarative *che*, though there were still examples of it ('di quello vi sia di buono': Machiavelli; 'il tradimento aveva fatto al suo signore': Vettori). In concessive clauses *sebbene* was nearly always used with the indicative, *benché* with the subjunctive: 'le qual cose *se bene piacevano* allo universale' (Guicciardini, *Ricordi*, C 21 Spongano), 'non poteva, *sebbene gli dispiaceva*, tenere le risa' (Vasari, *Vita di Buffalmacco*).

Tuscans had the advantage over writers from other areas that they were able to draw freely on the vocabulary of their own region. Some of them, indeed, deliberately searched for colourful words and phrases in it, and found material that was not very intelligible to people from other parts of Italy and only partially accepted by them. Northern and southern writers made increasingly less use of their dialectalisms. For them the safe policy was to follow written tradition, and they were readier than Tuscans to adopt latinisms. Authors' declarations of policy were not altogether consistent with their practice: the 'Lombard' Castiglione had comparatively few lombardisms, and the archaizing Bembo, as Caro noted, used many words not to be found in Boccaccio. In the Cinquecento many words which today are obsolete were still in use; such were *stufa* in the sense of 'public bath' and *fornire* with the meaning 'to finish'.

There was lively circulation of literature, which helped to reduce regional differences; but men of letters tended to be divorced from life and to form a class apart. The literary atmosphere became steadily heavier, and even more conformist and closed: taste moved towards the heroic and the rhetorical. Latinisms and hispanisms abounded. The importance accorded to Trecento models established a large number of doublets, to which grammarians frequently attributed different functions. The distinction which great writers of the past had made between popular and literary forms became a matter for prescription. Not only were certain words considered suitable for prose and others for poetry; but various words were considered as appropriate for particular literary genres.

New concepts brought in new words and changed the meanings of others. Here we shall limit ourselves to a few examples of the effect on vocabulary of changes in thought and life in the Cinquecento. The title *signore*, once reserved for a person exercising power (*signoria*), was widely extended through Spanish influence.

Ariosto, in a satire addressed to his brother Galasso (1519), complained that the title by that time was being used even in addressing grooms and prostitutes:

> 'Signor', dirò — non s'usa più 'fratello'
> poiché la vile adulazion spagnuola
> messe la signoria fin in bordello ! —
> 'Signor' (se fosse ben mozzo di spuola)
> dirò. . . .   (ll. 76-80).

Indeed *signora* could mean 'courtesan' in the Cinquecento. And *cortigiana* itself was a word which, through euphemism, had come to have that meaning during this century. In the refined society of the time a man's accomplishments came to be called his *virtù*; hence the new meaning of *virtuoso*, born in court society and applied to artists, musicians and others. *Peripezia* was a word introduced into Italian by Speroni and others with reference to Aristotle; used first to discuss the vicissitudes of plot in drama, it was then applied to those of life (Sassetti). It is probable that *catastrofe*, too, came to Italian from Aristotle's *Poetics*. The noun *umanista*, later to cover so many meanings, was introduced (in Latin at the end of the Quattrocento, in Italian at the beginning of the Cinquecento) to cover the meaning of a teacher of *humanae litterae*. Since the Goths were considered the main destroyers of Roman civilization, the humanists applied the adjective *gotico* to architecture that they considered barbarous. The term *gusto*, which had been transferred in Spain from the physical sphere to the aesthetic, was adopted in Italy in that context ('l'aver avuto in poesia buon *gusto*', wrote Ariosto, *Orl. fur.*, XXXV, st. 26). The Reformation brought words like *luterano* (at first *luteriano*), *ugonotto*, *protestante*. The Counter-Reformation led Italians to *espurgare* many books. They eliminated *destino*, *fato*, *fortuna* in many instances, substituting *Provvidenza*. *Divino*, which had been very freely employed at the end of the fifteenth century and the beginning of the sixteenth, was more carefully used. Phrases like *per Dio*, *per la tua fede*, even *vatti con Dio*, were avoided in order to keep the writer out of trouble. Certain names were avoided by periphrases: Machiavelli was referred to as the *Segretario Fiorentino*. At the time of the *rassettatura* of the *Decameron* the Roman revisers wished to removed *bellezze eterne* and *non potere* (which was felt to suggest denial of free will). But there were some linguistic fruits of a reaction against prevailing hypocrisy in such coinages as *collotorto* (for 'a hypocrite') and in the pejorative meaning given to *chietino* ('Theatine', then 'hypocrite'). New names were given to new dances; *moresca* and *pavana* are examples. The word *pasquinate* was coined to denote satires affixed to a celebrated statue (*Pasquino*) in Rome.

A notable development of the time was the growth, in fields as far apart as painting and bureaucracy, or music and artillery, of technical terminologies. Chiappelli, in his *Studi sul linguaggio del Machiavelli* (Florence 1952) sought to show how Machiavelli gave a precise technical (political) meaning to certain words when using them to discuss the biology of the state. In other spheres, too, words were adapted to carry technical meaning. One of the fields which can serve to give us examples of various sources of technical vocabulary is that of grammar. Obviously, much terminology for use in Italian grammars was taken straight from Latin grammarians. Thus we find in Bembo *vocale, sillaba, nome, verbo, genere, condizionale, passato* and *passivo*. But he avoided in the *Prose* many other such terms which were used by contemporary grammarians (*apocope, sincope, transitivo, avverbio*, etc.). In fact, he substituted words which were common in ordinary language for terms that appeared too technical, using *genere del maschio* for *maschile*; *participante voce* for *participio*; *pendente tempo* for *imperfetto*; *proponimento* or *segno di caso* for *preposizione*, etc. Giambullari, too, accepted a number of traditional terms (*nome, verbo, pronome, soggiuntivo, participio*, etc.) but was reluctant to use others. He did not use *indicativo* when speaking of the indicative mood, but *dimostrativo* or *pronunciativo*. And he coined a whole series of words: *aggiugninmezo, aggiugninnanzi, aggiugninfine*, for *prostesi, epentesi, paragoge*; *rompiparole* for *tmesi*, etc. In those grammatical fields for which no established Latin terminology existed there was considerable uncertainty: while Dolce and Salviati used *coma* (and Toscanella *comma*) for 'a comma', Giambullari and Lombardelli used *coma* to mean 'a colon'. Salviati used *mezzo punto* for 'colon', but Lombardelli used *mezzo punto* for 'semi-colon', etc. Those terms which had the support of corresponding words in Latin or Greek eventually gained ground 'perciocché il dir *pronome, participio, congiunzione* meglio s'intende dalla più parte, che se tu dica *vicenome, partefice, giuntura*, e sì fatti' (Salviati, *Avvertimenti*, Part I, Proem to third book).

In the coining of new words onomatopoeia gave *tric trac*, the game mentioned by Machiavelli, and also 'un *tric trac* di pianellette' (Piccolomini), as well as *bronfiare* (Aretino), *barbandrocco* (Caro), etc. The still fertile suffixes were: *-ezza* (*rarezza*, Caro),

-ità (*medesimità*, Borghini; *petrarcalità*, Caro; *sororità*, Corbinelli), *-mento* (Muzio, *Battaglie*, c. 54a, complains of the excessive number of abstract nouns in *-mento* in Castelvetro), *-eria* (*bemberie*, Grazzini), *-ale* (*invernale*), *-ario* (*bancario*), *-esco* (*concubinesco*, Davanzati), *-ile* (*fratile*, Nelli), etc. In imitation of Boccaccio, Bembo had formed many adjectives in *-evole* (*difendevole*, *diportevole*, etc.). This suffix was also very frequent in Giovio (*cartellevole*, *salamandrevole*). Such imitation of Boccaccio was satirized by the invention of *boccaccevole* (Tasso, Cecchi, Salviati). Fertile prefixes were *in-* (*indifeso*), *anti-* (*antisatira*), etc. *Pseudo-* already tended to the status of a prefix: *pseudogazza, pseudolaude* (Giovio). Some new formations were of the parasynthetic kind (*attoscaneggiare*, Tolomei; *imparnasare, spoetarsi*, Caro; *svescovato*, Muzio) and some of the direct type (*complimentare, statuare*, Cellini; *ghiribizzare*, Vasari; *concerto*, taken from *concertare*, etc.). Among compounds, alongside many new formations of the imperatival type ('quei *minuzzapetrarchi*, *lambiccaboccacci* e altri *straccalettori*', Firenzuola), there were several latinizing formations (*piovifero*, Alamanni; *moltifronte*, Caro; *metallificare*, Biringuccio; *univalve*, Citolini, etc.). Greek elements were also used, sometimes alone, sometimes in combinations with Latin elements, to form neologisms, especially those referring to new fields of knowledge and to scientific instruments (*filografia*, Leone Ebreo; *ornitologia*, Ulisse Aldrovandi; *grafometro, olometro, planisferio*, etc.). The learned nature of these words facilitated their international circulation; some of them were coined outside Italy. There were also very many lexical innovations due to semantic changes: *scapolo* passed from the meaning of 'free' to that of 'unmarried, single'; *cotto* came to mean 'drunk'; *balaustro* was used to mean 'baluster' because this resembled the pomegranate blossom in shape. Specialist terminologies also provided metaphors: *contrattempo* from riding and fencing, *dar nelle scartate* from card-playing, etc. Metaphors are sometimes difficult to explain. We know that the locution *parere il secento* ('to show off') derives from the nickname of a horse for which the Benci family paid 600 florins; but we no longer know who the Buraffa was who is mentioned in *più dotto che il can di Buraffa* (if, indeed, he ever existed).

In the Quattrocento the flood-gates of Italian vocabulary had been opened wide to latinisms and grecisms. In the Cinquecento the flow was regulated by a greater respect for the vernacular. Nevertheless, it was natural that when Italian had to deal with certain fields for which its resources were inadequate, recourse should be had to terms already in existence in the classical languages. Translations of Euclid contributed *lemma*, those of Vitruvius brought *scenografia* (in the sense of 'perspective'), *stria*, *vestibolo*, *voluta*, *euritmia*, *simmetria*, while versions of Dioscorides added to Italian botanical vocabulary (to mention only a few of the spheres in which translators enriched the language). Legal Latin provided words like *collaudare*, *erogare*, *firmare*, *omologare* for the use of Italian bureaucracy. But need for technical vocabulary was not, of course, the only motive in the borrowing of Latin words. The desire for elegance and solemnity in writing also had its part, as we can see in Tasso. That many of his latinisms survived shows that they accorded with the taste of his time. An example is *precoce*, the use of which he himself thought of as stylistic licence: 'con frutti di cortesia (se è lecito d'usare una parola latina) *precoci*' (*Lettere*, II, p. 87 Guasti). In their use of single latinisms authors were frequently referring, of course, to particular passages. When Bembo wrote *offa* in the *Asolani* ('al corpo quello che è bastevole si dà, quasi un'offa a Cerbero, perché non latri') he was consciously alluding to a line in the *Aeneid* (VI, 420), while Giordano Bruno, in writing *vitello saginato* in the dedication to his *Candelaio*, had in mind the parable of the prodigal son (Luke, XV, 23). Adverbs, adverbial phrases, conjunctions, etc., in their Latin form were still scattered in Italian prose (*autem*, *continuo*, *etcetera*, *solum*), though abuse of them was now considered a form of pedantry. Nouns, adjectives and verbs, on the other hand, were adapted to suit Italian (with the exception of the odd quotation or allusion). The ways in which this was done varied. We have already seen that there was a hesitation in spelling on certain points, particularly in the treatment of consonantal groups (*absente/assente*), *h*, *ti* and Greek letters. Moreover, in certain cases hereditary forms of words existed alongside corresponding Latin forms. In other instances (*singolare/singulare*, *volgo/vulgo*, etc.) radical adaptations of Latin words existed alongside less radical ones. Here are just a few examples of the doublets that resulted (of which only one usually survived): *adunco/adonco*, *ancella/ancilla*, *aumento/augumento*; *Campidoglio/Capitolio*; *celabro/ cerebro*; *cicala/cicada*; *Chimenti/Clemente*; *ingegnoso/ingenioso*; *lio(n)-fante/elefante*; *loico/logico*; *oriuolo/orologio*, *particolare/particulare*; *quaresima/quadragesima*; *seno/sino*; *squitinio/scrutinio*, etc. Disputes between the supporters of the *lingua cortigiana* or *italiana* and those of Florentine or Tuscan often turned on such words; the former preferred the latinizing forms, while the second opted for those that came from Tuscan usage. The extent to which one should use latinisms was also, of course, a matter for argument. At the beginning of the century grammarians and lexicographers were usually in favour of a good deal of latinization: De Falco praised Ariosto's latinisms, and Acarisio approved of Boccaccio's. But later the tide turned. Not only were Tuscans like Borghini, Salviati and Lombardelli ready to protest against over-latinization; they were joined by non-Tuscans like Castelvetro and Muzio. This change in attitude was reflected in the revision of literary works. Ariosto removed latinisms in his correction of the *Orlando furioso*, Berni changed some of Boiardo's, Ruscelli took out some of Collenuccio's (*compilare, eversione, vilipendio*) when he published his *Historie*, and Tasso, after some oscillation, declared himself willing to eliminate some from the *Gerusalemme liberata*. Greek words were occasionally used in an unadapted form, either in Greek or Latin script. Cinquecento pronunciation of Greek was reflected in some of the borrowings: η was pronounced like Italian *i*, for instance (hence *rittorici*, Liburnio; *ritorico*, Castelvetro; *tecmirio* or *temmirio* from τεκμήριον, Caro; *sisamo*, Serdonati, etc.), as was οι (*sinalife*, Tolomei), and so on. Of the many latinisms and grecisms absorbed in the sixteenth century we can only give here, of course, a small selection. (In doing so we must again mention the possibility that some may have entered earlier than we at the moment know from our documentation). Here are some examples that probably came in during the Cinquecento: *abolire* (Guicciardini), *arguzia* (Castiglione), *assioma* (Varchi), *canoro* (Ariosto), *circonflesso* (Firenzuola), *congenito* (Gelli), *congerie* (Zuccolo), *continente* (Giacomini), *crisalide* (Domenichi), *entusiasmo* (G. Camilla, *Enthosiasmo de misterii*, Venice 1564), *esagerare* (in the modern sense, Davanzati), *omonimo* (Caro), *parafrasi* (Firenzuola), *parossismo* (Sanudo), *penisola* (Giambullari), *peripezia* (Speroni), *rapsodia* (Giraldi), *utero* (Ariosto). Other words, which had appeared sporadically before this century, now became part of current usage: *educare, elegante, frivolo, peculiare* are instances. It should be noted, too, that words were sometimes used with their Latin meanings, e.g. *numero* in the sense of 'rhythm'. *Interpellare* still meant 'to interrupt' in Calmeta; in its legal sense it was used by Varchi. *Seminarium* came to be used in the sense of 'school for future ecclesiastics' as a result of the Council of Trent; at Genoa (from 1576) *seminario* indicated the 120 citizens from amongst whom the magistrates were chosen by lot. *Eccentrico*, *eteroclito* were already used figuratively to indicate 'strange' people or things. There were numerous calques on Greek and Latin, but they did not always succeed in gaining a foothold; among those that failed were *aia* in the sense in which the Latin *area* was preferred, and *errante* for *pianeta* (πλανήτης). Many of the latinisms and grecisms used during the century also died out, of course; such, to name very few of them, were *aligero* (Ariosto), *allicere* (Bembo, Tasso), *àtavo* (Firenzuola, Speroni), *clade* (Ariosto), *contennendo* (Machiavelli), *cultro* (Caro), *direptione* (Machiavelli, Guicciardini), *erugine* (Giovio), etc.

In an anthology of literary texts from the Cinquecento we should find few dialect words. But with practical texts it would be a different story, particularly in the first half of the century. Moreover, in literature the dialectal content would vary with genre: there would generally be none in lyrical poetry or philosophical prose, but there might well be some in satirical poetry, and the more practical the prose (e.g. in diaries, letters, etc.) the more likely it would be to have dialectal vocabulary. Within Tuscany itself there were some lexical variations in the Sienese writers (e.g. Tolomei, Biringucci, Mattioli), whereas some Tuscans, particularly Florentines (Berni, Doni, Varchi, Cecchi, Davanzati) were particularly keen on local idiom and the colourful locutions and metaphors they could extract from it. As for non-Tuscan writers, here are a few examples of regional words used by them in the first half of the century. Castiglione had many which were either specifically Mantuan or belonged to the Po Basin generally: *angonia, cerasa, fodra, sentare, varola*. Trissino had *acciale, cappa* ('stack'), *faglia* ('sheaf'), etc. Bembo used some Venetian words, especially in his letters: *calmo* ('graft'), *cóppo* ('tile'), *frezzoloso, frisetto, zenzala*, etc. Ariosto had some Ferrarese words in his comedies, like *bigonzoni* in the *Suppositi* (of which Machiavelli complained), but used few dialectalisms in the *Orlando furioso*. In the second half of the century there were less. Nonetheless, there were lombardisms in Lomazzo (*anta, civiera, scosso*), umbrisms in Caporali (*biocca, cerqua*), neapolitanisms in Bruno (*balice, iùiuma, verzaglio*) and so on, though mostly in texts of a practical or technical nature. In fact, whereas there was now strong linguistic circulation in the higher, intellectual reaches of Italian vocabulary, people had recourse to local words for practical purposes and, of course, for local objects and customs. Let us take two extreme examples of developments in this field. How could Bembo, in mentioning Venetian institutions in his letters, have avoided using *daìa, pieggerìa, podestaressa, pregadi*, *procuratìe*? This necessity was to remain for centuries. On the other hand, there was not the same need for people to stick to different terms in speaking of the days of the week. In northern Italy at the beginning of the century forms without *dì* were prevalent (Bembo, Pigafetta, Castiglione used *luni, marti, mèrcore, giove* or *giobia, vènere*). That these terms corresponded exactly to the Tuscan ones with *-dì* was obvious, however, and those forms in *-dì* became general. However, even to this day unification has not taken place in the representation of certain concepts, and Italian has two or more words (used in different areas and thus 'geosynonyms') to denote them: *cacio/formaggio; filugello/baco da seta; merletto/trina/pizzo*, etc. Such cases were more numerous in the sixteenth century. Thus we find that alongside *arancio (-a)* existed *narancio -a* (Ariosto, Tasso) and alongside *zanzara* there was still *zenzara* (Tasso), *zenzala* (Equicola, Nelli) and *zampana* (in the *Viaggi in Moscovia* of the Viterbese R. Barberino, 1565). Sometimes authors, from a desire to be widely understood (or from a desire to show off), used several words for a single object. Makers of dictionaries, too, used regional words freely, since they were more concerned to explain meanings than to indicate choice in writing. Thus, to quote but one example, Sansovino, in his *Ortografia . . . o vero Dittionario volgare et latino* (1568) translates *Ritorte* as *vincula* and then adds synonyms: '*legami, vincigli*, disse il Bocc., *stroppe* a Padova'). Those who wrote manuals for foreigners often followed similar criteria. John Florio included regional words in his *First Fruites* (*àmeda, nezza*, etc.), and in his *Worlde of Wordes* he made it clear that he was deliberately including dialectal and technical items. Some regional words were fortunate enough to gain wider currency through circulation in this century. From Venice came *regata*, and to Venetian printing-houses was due the diffusion of terms like *proto*. And the *corridore* that at Rome connected Castel Sant'Angelo with St. Peter's was so well known that Vasari used the same term for the one he built at Florence to connect the Palazzo degli Uffizi with the Palazzo Vecchio.

The Dante-Petrarch-Boccaccio cult has made Italian apt to resurrect words which have died. By the sixteenth century many fourteenth-century words had disappeared from Tuscany (like *agenzare, baratta, caleffare, croio*, etc.). Gelli noted that there were in Boccaccio 'una infinità di parole, che sono oggi aborrite e fuggite da gli scrittori, come verbigrazia *buona pezza, la bisogna, gravenza, abitanza, niquitoso, avaccio, autorevole, contezza, deliberanza, sezzaia*' (*Ragionamento* prefixed to Giambullari's grammar, p. 35).

Other words, as we can learn from the testimony of writers or from contexts in which they occurred, had become relegated to plebeian or rustic usage: such were *atanto* (Cellini, Giambullari, Sassetti), *avale* (Cecchi), *calla, dónora* (Firenzuola, Cecchi), *gina* (Lasca), *maisì, mainò, otta* (especially in the phrases *otta catotta, otta per vicenda*, etc.). And some were preserved only in literary (particularly poetic) usage: *aita, alma, feruta, u'*, etc. With the imitation of fourteenth-century writers, attempts were made to give new life to some of these (as Bembo had tried to do in using *prossimano* in his *Asolani*). This provoked protests: Citolini, for instance, in his *Lettera in difesa della lingua volgare* (Venice 1540) objected to those 'i quali non si stimano poteressere tenuti buoni scrittori, se le lor carte non puzzano di *uopo, testé, hotta, altresì, guari, costinci, sezzai*, e se non ficcano *unquanco* in un sonettuzzo'. Satire of the abuse of archaic Tuscan gave rise to the expression *favellare per quinci e quindi*. The total result of the attempts to re-introduce archaic words was not great. But they succeeded in some instances (*altresì, guari, autorevole, sovente, soverchio, testé, uopo* etc.) in winning a place for such words in the literary language, and a few of them even regained a firm place in everyday usage. (Davanzati's efforts were directed to a rather different end: he concentrated on saving colourful and popular idioms and words which were on the point of dying out — *atanto, finare, gina*, etc.).

Since literary Italian gained vocabulary from the various sources we have noted, writers were often faced with a choice of words or forms for one concept. This wealth might be due to geosynonyms (*ciliegia, ciriegia, ciregia; legnaiuolo, falegname, marangone*), to the existence of latinisms alongside hereditary forms *cèrebro, cèlabro; officio, ufficio*), or to the authority lent by the classical authors to forms different from those in use (*diede* as opposed to *dette; renduto* to *reso; feruta* to *ferita*, etc.). In some cases writers turned for guidance to some recognized authority, as Ariosto did to Bembo. But the counsels given in the books of grammarians and rhetoricians sometimes conflicted. Often, too, they gave no useful advice on particular examples (the author being admonished to stick to words that were 'belle', 'gentili', 'oneste', 'vaghe', 'illustri' and to avoid those that were 'brutte', 'vili' and 'disoneste'). The difficulty of deciding between words often caused lexicographers to set up a sort of class-system, considering (often rather arbitrarily) some words suitable for prose and some for verse, e.g. *anche* (prose), *anco* (verse); *gastigare* (p.), *castigare* (v.); *fraude* (p.), *frode* (v.); *maraviglia* (p.), *meraviglia* (v.);

menomo (p.), *minimo* (v.); *spirito* (p.), *spirto* (v.); *veduto* (p.), *visto* (v.). Just as the age, in its myopic interpretation of Aristotle, produced rigid rules on the unities in the theatre, so also did it tend to make the free choice of writers in past ages an excuse for hard-and-fast rules on the use of words. Certain items of vocabulary and certain morphological forms came to be considered 'poetic', others not. This served to separate writers even more from everyday life, and to accentuate the restricted nature of the literary culture produced by a comparatively small and isolated class. It was to have dire effects on the poetic diction of Italy for over three centuries.

The modern languages that contributed most to Italian vocabulary in the sixteenth century were Spanish and French; but, owing to the new horizons opened by geographical exploration, they were far from being the only ones.

In assessing borrowings from French we must not allow ourselves to believe that all the words used by Italian writers discussing French matters had become part of Italian usage. Machiavelli, in his *Ritratto delle cose di Francia*, for instance, spoke of *'fauta d'argento'*, of the *'preposto dell'ostello'* and of *'lingi cioè tovaglie e tovaglioli'*. Here the context clearly influenced the choice of word. Nevertheless, the French contribution to Italian was quite considerable. In military terminology France provided *batteria*, *convoio* or *convoglio*, *foriere* or *furiere* (already used in the previous century by Florentine ambassadors in France), *petardo*, *picca*, *trincea* or *trincera*, etc. Machiavelli, in his *Discorsi*, noted that the term *fatti d'arme* was being replaced by the 'vocabolo francioso *giornate*' (Mazzoni - Casella, p. 162). In *rollo* (later *ruolo*) and *tropa* (later *truppa*) Spanish and French influences converged and contended. To nautical terminology French gave *equipaggio*. To that of dress it contributed the name of a cloth, *grograno*. Cellini, in his *Vita*, spoke of 'gioie e *dorure* franzese'; *dorura* was not peculiar to him, but common in Florence in the late Cinquecento. In the sphere of food and drink there were *potaggio* and *gigotto* (*zigotto* in Scappi) and *claretto* and *birra* (*bira* in Sanudo). In the field of communications there was *pacchetto*. And there appeared, too, one or two general terms like *regretto*, *risorsa*. The list would get much longer if one were to include borrowings in regional Italian, like the Piedmontese *desbauciarsi*.

Iberisms were even more numerous than gallicisms. Many referred to social life: *baciamano*, *complimento* (with the attendant *complire* 'to compliment'), *creanza*, *creare* (in the sense 'to bring up, educate'), *privanza* ('familiarity'), *impegno* and *disimpegno*, *sforzo* ('daring'), *sforzato* ('hard-working'), *disinvoltura, sussiego, sfarzo*. The new meaning of *flemma* ('calm', 'phlegm') was also Spanish. Spaniards' keen attention to points of honour was reflected in *disdoro* and *puntiglio* (originally, a 'little point'). There were general terms of abuse: *marrano, fanfarone, vigliacco*; the Spanish, on account of their frequent swearing, were called *Juradios*. Spanish example caused the title *signore* to be much more widely used, as we have already observed. So also *don*: 'quel *don* sì caro allo Spagnuol ventoso', Caporali. Through Spanish influence, too, *marchese* got a feminine *marchesa*. Connected with the household were *appartamento*, names of material (*laniglia*), clothes (*faldiglia, zammarra, montiera*, a sort of cap), ornaments (*maniglia*), perfumes (*ambracane*, etc.) and foods (*bianco mangiare, mirausto* or *miragusto, sopressata* < Sp. *sobreasada, torrone*, made with toasted almonds, *marmellata* < Port. *marmelada*, 'quince jam'). Military life gave: *continuo* ('viceroy's guard'), *bisogno, guerriglia, casco, morione, zaino, parata, quadriglia* ('unit of four men'), etc. There were many terms, too, relating to horses: *alazano* ('bay, roan'), *rabicano* ('black or bay flecked with white hairs'), *rovano* ('roan') *ubèro* ('roan, black roan'), *pariglia* ('pair of horses'), etc. There were numerous nautical items, too: *almirante, flotta, rotta, baia, cala, tolda, babordo, arpone*, etc. Even the points of the compass, although ultimately of Anglo-Saxon provenance, came to Italy through Spain (*nord, est*, etc., first appearing as *norte, oeste*, etc., and then acquiring their present form through the influence of the French equivalents). But the full extent of Spanish penetration can best be realized by noting how many general words came into Italian from Spain at that time: *accudire, buscare, render la pariglia, grandioso, lindo*, etc. Sometimes Italian syntax was affected, as in the use of *lo che*, which we mentioned earlier, and which became common in southern writers. Many more hispanisms could be found, of course, in passages from authors describing Spanish affairs (e.g. Guicciardini's 'la regina *duenna* Elisabel'); but these do not have much significance. It should be added, too, that many Spanish words which had gained a temporary place in Italian lost it when Spanish influence waned: such were *cagliare* 'to be silent', *nada* 'nothing', *a pesare di* 'in spite of', to give but three examples.

Contact with German-speaking countries led to the importation of a number of military terms: *raitro* ('Reiter'), *alabarda* ('halberd') and *lanzi*, which resulted from the convergence of two German words, as can be seen from the attested forms *lanzimanni* (*Lamzmann*) and *lanz(i)chinech* (*Landsknecht*). Religious struggles were carried on in Latin and left almost no German importation. *Ugonotto* came from Switzerland; but it passed from Geneva to France before coming to Italy (where it was used with reference to the Calvinists). Commercial relations brought the names of coins: *talleri*, *bezzi* and *craice* (which were called *crazie* when coined in Tuscany). The word *postemastro* (Franzesi) did not take root. From Germanic countries came the custom of the *brindisi*; at first there was oscillation, *brindis*, *brindes* and *brinzi* being used. The drinking habits of the *lanzi* gave rise to the phrase *alla trinchesvaina*. Metallurgy flourished in certain centres in Germanic countries and contributed *bis(e)muto*, *confrustagno* (*Kupferstein*), *mergola* and possibly *copparosa*. Other Germanic words were used by individual authors when describing Germanic countries, e.g. 'le terre hanno i loro *borgomastri*' (Machiavelli). Close commercial connections with the Low Countries led to the importation of *droga* (a term which was to be much used in overseas trade) and to knowledge of *caramessa* ('*kermesse*') and *stapula* ('store, depot'). Also known about were the *turba* (or *torba*), the *dune* and the *dicchi* ('dykes': 'dentro i dicchi della bassa Olanda', Chiabrera).

Anglicisms were few and hardly existed outside the writings of those who described England (such as ambassadors and exiles like Florio and Bruno). Examples were *ala* ('ale') and *smalto* (in the sense of 'malt'). Adaptation of English words gave rise to some vacillation. An example was the Order of the Garter. Alongside the form used today ('della *Giarrettiera* . . . una cinta delle gambe': Giacomo Soranzo, ap. Alberi, VIII, p. 56), there were 'del *Gartier*' (Castiglione, *Cortegiano*, III, 11), 'della *Gartiera*' (Sansovino, *Della origine de Cavalieri*, Venice 1570), and 'il Nobil Ordine de la Garatjèra' (Florio, dedication of the *First Fruites*, 1578), while Davanzati spoke of 'Niccolò Careo, cavalier *gerrettiero*' (*Scisma*, in *Opere*, II, p. 378 Bindi).

Slav and Hungarian words came through German (*cocchio*, *pistola*, *trabanti*, *usseri*). But some Croat words came directly: *sciabola*, *stravizzo* ('invitation to drink') and possibly *tacchino*. From the Greeks came *mustacchi*. Close contact with the Near East brought in Arabic, Turkish and Persian words: *sofà*, *divano*, *chiosco*, *serraglio*, *dolimano* and *turbante*. *Sorbetto* resulted from crossing *tzerbet* or *scerbet* with the verb *sorbire*. Coffee came to be known, both under the Arabic name *buna* (P. A. Michiel) and the Turkish *cavè* (*caveè* in G. F. Morosini, 1585). Arabic influence was also felt in the sciences. An example is the word *alcool*. This originally was a fine powder, antimony trisulphide, used to blacken the eyebrows. It then came to mean any 'impalpable powder'. Its present meaning dates from the sixteenth century: from its use by Paracelsus (*alcohol vini*, the essential part of wine).

The great geographical discoveries brought the names of hitherto unknown animals and plants, frequently from the languages of the indigenous peoples of America, usually through Spanish and Portuguese, more rarely through French. Among the animals and birds were: *caimano, condor, iguana, vigogna* (indigenous words) and *cocciniglia* (a Spanish word). Plants and fruits were represented by *ananas, batata* and *patata, cacao, mais, tomate, coca, guaiaco*. Sometimes, instead of (or alongside) an exotic word, a new word was coined: alongside *mais* sprang up *granturco* (i.e. 'grain of exotic origin'), alongside *tomate* appeared *pomodoro*, alongside *guaiaco* came *legno santo*, and in Tuscany *tabacco* became also known as *erba tornabuona* (since Monsignor Niccolò Tornabuoni had imported the plant in the time of Francesco I dei Medici). Other objects from beyond the seas were *canoa* and the *piragua* (later *piroga*), *amaca* ('hammock') and the *cicchera*, later *chicchera* ('receptacle made from the husk of a fruit', later 'cup'). Navigation brought contact with *salgazo* or *sargazo*, which was later, through French influence, to be *sargasso* ('seaweed'). Certain geographical features attracted attention, notably the *zavane*, later *savane*, as did atmospheric phenomena like the *uragano* (which was typical of the Gulf of Mexico, whose natives applied to it the name of the god of tempests, Hurakan, 'the one-legged'). Columbus's cosmographical error gave the terms *India* and *indiano* extension to territories to which they did not properly refer. The ethnical name of the Caribes was diffused in the form *cannibali* ('earum terrarum incolae *Canibales* esse affirmant, *sive Caribes*, humanorum carnium edaces': Pietro Martire d'Anghiera, dec. VIII, cap. 6). Journeys to India proper and the Far East also brought new knowledge and new words. Occasionally these were native words (*bonzo, monsoni, tifone*, etc.), sometimes badly mangled (the word for 'tea' became *qua* in Sassetti and *chia* in Serdonati's translation of G. P. Maffei). Occasionally they were Portuguese words which had acquired new meanings (*casta, cocco*). *Zebra*, too, used by the Portuguese for an animal they discovered in the Congo, was not an indigenous word, but Ibero-Romance (probably EQUIFERUM, *ECIFERUM). *Banana* came from equatorial Africa.

In previous centuries Italian had contributed words (notably in commercial and maritime spheres) to the vocabulary of other European languages. In the Cinquecento, when Italy provided literary, artistic and social models which other nations admired, the flow was much greater. To follow the fortunes of Italian words abroad would clearly take us very far afield, and this is not the place to embark on a subject on which a useful book could be written. It is interesting to note a few examples, however. In the social sphere *cortigiano* spread (into Spanish in 1490, French in 1539 and English in 1587), while its feminine, with the pejorative meaning it had acquired, gained even wider diffusion (entering German in 1566). In the military field there were a few items, e.g. *soldato* (Fr. *soldat*, 1548; Sp. *soldado*; Germ. *Soldat*, 1522, etc.), *colonnello* (Fr. *coronel*, 1542, later *colonel*; Sp. *coronel*, 1511; Eng. *colonel*, 1548) and *sentinella* (Fr. *sentinelle*, 1546; Sp. *centinela*, 1525), and in the naval sphere *portolano* and *bussola* ('compass') spread. But by far the most interesting group of italianisms that entered other European languages at this time concerned literature and the arts. Such were *sonetto* (Sp. *soneto*, fifteenth century; Fr. *sonnet*, 1525; Eng. *sonnet*, 1589); *madrigale* (Fr. *madrigal*, 1542; Eng. 1588; Germ. 1596; Span. 1615), and the adjective *maccheronico* (Fr. *macaronique*, 1546, Sp. *macarrónico*, 1600; Eng. *macaronic*, 1611). Some musical terms, too, were exported, e.g. *fuga*. The *commedia dell'arte* contributed the names of its conventional characters, e.g. *zanni* (Fr. *zani*, 1500; Eng. *zany*, 1588) and *pantalone* (Fr. *pantalonnade*, 1597; Eng. *pantaloon*, 1590), while in the visual arts *facciata*, *piedestallo*, *balcone* and *cartone* gained currency abroad. On the other hand, the italianisms that were accepted by Greek and Turkish at this period mainly concerned material objects (foods, clothes, furniture). As for the Scandinavian languages, their italianisms resembled those of other European nations, but they received them later, and usually through German or French.

9

The Seicento

In discussing chronological limits at the beginning of the last chapter, we noted that in the Cinquecento certain dates (1563, end of the Council of Trent; 1582-83, foundation and reform of the Accademia della Crusca) could be considered as more significant than the arbitrarily chosen 1600, but that it was difficult to choose between them. In this chapter we shall carry on the story to the end of the seventeenth century, though noting again that in some senses the period ends in 1670, which saw important changes in literature, philosophy and fashions. The date of the founding of Arcadia (1690) is also significant.

The century saw little change in the political map of Italy, which remained substantially as it had been after Cateau-Cambrésis. The only modifications of note were in north Italy and consequent on the two wars of succession over Mantua and Monferrato. Urbino (1631) followed Ferrara (1598) in becoming an integral part of the Papal States. The struggle between France and Spain only sporadically touched Italy (Piedmont being the state most involved). But the repercussions of that struggle were constantly felt: territories subject to Spain had to furnish men and money for it, while the independent states were faced in their diplomacy with the constant dilemma of supporting one or other of the contestants. The Peace of the Pyrenees (1659) marked the end of Spain as a great European power. After it, the influence of Louis XIV became increasingly obvious. Venice was engaged in wars in the Levant, lost Candia, but won the Peloponnese. The division of Italy into small states provided obstacles, but not insuperable ones, to the circulation of men and books. There was a widespread feeling among Italians that they belonged to a common nation, though this was not always the case in peripheral regions; Alessandro Segni at the court in Turin in 1665 kept hearing people speak of 'Loro altri Italiani', and was 'nauseato di tanta franzeseria'. There was serious economic decline, particularly in the provinces subject to Spain.

The self-confident age of humanist discovery and that of the mature and serene equilibrium of the Renaissance were followed by one of stagnation. Social life was dominated by formal questions; great attention was paid to precedence, titles and ceremonial. Political and religious pressures were answered by dissimulation and hypocrisy. Ecclesiastical censorship was strict, but ecclesiastical life itself was much affected by the wordly tastes of contemporary society: examples abound in the sensuality of religious pictures and statues, as well as in sermons. The existence of numerous states with their own capitals contributed to standardization within regions rather than between one region and another. At Milan, Naples and Palermo, Spanish domination crushed autonomy in local life. Venice and Genoa defended their independence firmly (as, for instance, in the Venetian attitude to the interdict), though not always successfully (as we see in the example of Genoese resistance to Louis XIV). Florence no longer enjoyed literary and artistic primacy, but her tradition of sobriety and restraint served as a dyke against the baroque flood from Naples and Rome. Galileo and his disciples made Florence an important scientific centre. Rome, as the political and diplomatic centre of Roman Catholicism and its new missions (1622 saw the setting up of the congregation *De propaganda fide*) was a linguistic centre of great importance; there courtiers got rid of their dialectal peculiarities, attempting a form of speech nearer Tuscan, while Tuscans themselves dropped some of their regional characteristics. In the visual arts (Bernini, Borromini, Caravaggio) there were developments comparable with those in literature; indeed, it is from their world that the word *baroque* was taken for description of the literary features of the period. The predominance of sound over sense in baroque taste gave rise to a new kind of spectacle, musical drama: in the librettos of O. Rinuccini (*Dafne*, 1597; *Euridice*, 1600; *Arianna*, 1608) and in numberless others that followed them, the words were subservient to the music. Opera took such firm root that appropriate theatres were founded for it; in them spectacular stage decoration added to the audience's pleasure. Observation and deduction were now applied, not only to cataloguing facts, but to explaining natural phenomena. Consciousness of a need for objectively verifiable laws led to a kind of scientific thinking far removed from that of the peripatetic philosophers, and here Galileo played an important part. Mechanics and optics, which were to be so rich in practical as well as theoretical consequences, began to flourish, while pseudo-sciences like astrology and alchemy became discredited. The increased importance ascribed to exact observation led to new progress, too, in the biological field. Old and new learning met in the academies, which multiplied enormously in this century and provided places where educated persons could discuss and debate. Some of them (Crusca, Lincei, Cimento) made contributions of lasting importance. After the foundation of the Arcadia (1690), its 'colonies' spread all over Italy. Whether its pseudo-pastoral tastes did more harm than good is a question that here concerns us less than the fact that it was a levelling influence, linguistically and stylistically. Scholars took to accumulating books; some of the great Italian collections (Angelica, Casanatense in Rome, Magliabechiana in Florence) date from this period. In this century there was much greater correspondence between scholars. It saw the birth of learned periodicals, like the *Giornale dei Letterati* (Rome 1688) and the *Galleria di Minerva* (Venice 1695).

Latin still enjoyed a privileged position in many fields. University lectures were entirely in Latin; only private lessons and compendiums of lecture-notes were in Italian. Lower down the educational ladder, the *Ratio studiorum* of the Jesuits in 1661 likewise made no concessions to the vernacular. Philosophical and scientific treatises were in Latin; Fioretti was condemned by 'persone di gran letteratura' for having written his *Proginnasmi* in Tuscan. In this field Galileo's example was to be of capital importance. In 1610 he had published his *Sidereus nuncius* in Latin in order to establish his priority in the world of scholarship. A few months later he moved to Florence. Thereafter, he wrote all his major works in Italian, in spite of protests from foreign scholars (Kepler accused him of *crimen laesae humanitatis*) and the allegation of the peripatetics that he was making use of the vernacular in order to impress the ignorant. He wished, in fact, to break away from the language of the schools and to adopt that of practical men. His attitude and that of his disciples (like Castelli, Torricelli, Viviani) had considerable effect. While the publications of the Accademia dei Lincei, at the beginning of the century, were in Latin, the *Saggi di naturali esperienze* of the Accademia del Cimento were in Italian. The great mass of medical literature was in Latin, though there were some items in Italian. The works of Marcello Malpighi and Lorenzo Bellini were in Latin; Bellini's work of vulgarization in Italian, the *Discorsi anatomici*, was not published until the following century. But there were some practical manuals in Italian dealing with medicine and obstetrics (S. Mercuri's *La commare o raccoglitrice* was frequently reprinted), veterinary medicine, pharmacopoeias, etc. In legislation and in the courts the vernacular made progress in several Italian states: Tuscany was in the van, while the Papal States showed most reluctance to abandon Latin. In public life the two languages were constantly juxtaposed. When Leonardo Donà became *doge* of Venice in 1606, various orators at the ceremony spoke in Italian, but the one sent by the Duke of Mantua in Latin. When Pietro Durazzo became *doge* of Genoa in 1620, the volume produced in his honour contained both Italian and Latin poems. Preaching was generally in Italian, but there were preachers who preferred Latin. There were even occasional performances of plays in Latin, mainly scholastic exercises.

If we consider how people wrote in the Seicento, we immediately come up against the baroque in literature and the resistance it provoked. Baroque writing did not last very long: its innovations, which were calculated to produce a sense of wonder and needed a constant supply of novelties (bold metaphors, ingenious conceits, kaleidoscopic series of images, juxtapositions, etc.), had an occasional character. When the taste for its gimmicks had died, little trace was left in linguistic usage. Just as baroque architects showed little respect for the styles of the predecessors to whose works they made modifications and additions, so too baroque writers failed to appreciate or understand the achievements of earlier Italian authors, to whom they felt superior. Poetic theory continued to assert that there was a noble style to be distinguished from others. But, whereas lyric and epic poets in the previous century had chosen only the universal and the decorous in diction, baroque versifiers, in their search for the astonishing, had no scruples in using the concrete or, for that matter, the technical and scientific. Marino's *Adone*, which has sections of encyclopaedic character, includes long lists of objects (lightened by an occasional epithet or compliment) and uses philosophical terms. Some lyric poets used words like *atomo, epiciclo, genealogia, iperbole,* while Lubrano in a sonnet on the silk-worm, stirred latinisms, periphrastic locutions and technical terms into his pudding:

Trasforma il cibo in stame; e torce e spreme
da le viscere sue globo lucente;

fatto subbio del sen, spola del dente
ordisce in trame le salive estreme.

No place escaped the baroque, and writers from various regions (Stigliani, Rosa, Schettini) objected to it. But resistance was particularly strong in Tuscany. Florentine men of letters were full of respect for their fourteenth-century authors and their more substantial diet. Moreover, the sober and rational attitude which favoured the development of Galilean method there could have little sympathy with the turgid and the extravagant. At the same time, the traditional lyric offered little of artistic or linguistic interest. Greater importance attaches to melic poetry, which sprang up in the voluptuous musical atmosphere of the late Cinquecento. Another kind of poetry which enjoyed great favour in the Seicento was the mock heroic; Tassoni's *Secchia rapita*, Bracciolini's *Scherno degli Dei*, Lalli's *Eneide travestita*, Dottori's *Asino*, Lippi's *Malmantile*, Neri's *Presa di Saminiato* and Corsini's *Torracchione desolato* have more stylistic and linguistic interest than the dozens of epics written in the same century. The element of surprise in these mock heroic poems was provided by the juxtaposition of incongruous elements, ancient and modern, solemn and trivial, Italian and dialectal. The door was opened wide, therefore, to variety in vocabulary. The Tuscans (particularly Lippi) took advantage of this fact to make liberal use of popular words and phrases which, not having appeared in the works of classical Italian writers, had found no place in the dictionaries. This extraneous preoccupation with collecting data for a kind of ideal museum of the Tuscan language does not give the reader an impression of spontaneity or sincerity. But, even where the intrinsic value of their works is slight, the documentation they provide is at least interesting. They influenced the development of the language: for through the reading of these texts and the commentaries that were written on them, and through the registering of examples from them in the Crusca and other dictionaries, many Tuscan locutions became part of general usage. The connections of this catch-phrase literature with the Crusca are evident in the activities of Michelangelo Buonarroti the younger, who worked on the first and second editions of the *Vocabolario* and was the author, besides, of a comic poem, the *Aione*, and two comedies, the *Fiera* and the *Tancia*. Whereas the allegorical scenes in the *Fiera* (1618) are stiff and lifeless, the fairground scenes are very lively. The *Tancia* is a comedy of country life. The 'rustic' was to Tuscany what the 'dialectal' was to other regions: an exploitation of native idiom. And, as we shall note frequently, writers who deliberately chose dialect had a large part in Seicento literature. Fidenzian poetry also continued to be cultivated, though now as an exercise in humour rather than as a satire on excessive latinism. Another highly expressive form of verse which had a wide following was the dithyrambic. The earliest authors of dithyrambs in Italian were Chiabrera and Fioretti (*Polifemo briaco*, 1627). Perhaps Redi's *Bacco in Toscana* is the only example of the genre that deserves to be remembered for its artistic value. But from the linguistic point of view even the minor authors in this sphere are interesting because they helped to spread a new kind of compound (*ebrifestoso*, etc.)—a point to which we shall return in due course. Satirical poetry enjoyed notable vitality. Satirical poets, in their realistic passages, frequently used plebeian and dialectal words.

Prose, as well as poetry, suffered from the fashion for the baroque. In sacred oratory, for example, the 'concetti predicabili', which had come from Spain through Naples, were all the rage. (The whole sermon developed a single metaphor in all its possible ramifications). At the same time preachers like Sègneri managed to preserve intrinsic seriousness by composing sermons of a different kind. Daniello Bartoli excelled in descriptive prose; he is interesting, not only for his style and because neo-classical writers took him as a model (Giordani considering him 'terribile, stupendo, unico, singolare'), but also because he is terminologically so rich. Scientific prose had not yet suffered from the divorce which in the following centuries was to separate science from literature. Its finest representatives, like Galileo, could expound their scientific proofs in a style that was clear and sober without being either arid or impersonal. Galileo's aim of writing in a manner that would be intelligible to non-specialist cultured persons had as a corollary his treatment of technical terms: rather than have recourse to new words built on Latin and Greek roots, he would adopt everyday words, but consistently use them for specific notions. His choice is still substantially that favoured by physicists; his influence here seems indubitable. Other sciences chose the other method; the enormous preponderance of Latin and Greek elements in medical terminology is an instance. Those who looked upon Galileo as a master of method were also influenced by his style: the 'chiarezza' and 'evidenza' which Redi sought, were Galilean, rather than Cartesian, aspirations.

Magalotti united a liking for clarity with a delight in the savour of words; the severity against foreign words of which there is evidence in his early writings gave way later to a moderate cosmopolitanism. Although the Accademia della Crusca would have no scientific or technical terms in its *Vocabolario*, it attempted (with modest results) to promote a scientific literature of traditional tone. Orazio Rucellai stated in a letter written in 1665 that the Crusca 'perché in nostra lingua non ci abbiamo scrittori di materie scientifiche, ha dato la cura al Sig. Carlo Dati, al Sig. March. Vincenzio Capponi, al Sig. Lorenzo Magalotti, e a mc, che c'induchiamo di provarci'. Legal writings in the vernacular drew freely for technical terms on the Latin of the law-courts. Learned words abounded, too, in compilations (like Fioretti's *Proginnasmi* or Menochio's *Stuore*) which displayed antiquarian knowledge. Historians and political writers found that in order to describe certain facts and institutions they needed to use many words which had hitherto not figured in the literary language. There were many such terms, also, in writings on practical subjects, as, for example, in administrative documents drawn up by secretaries. Such secretaries were not simply coiners of new words; they also frequently betrayed a liking for 'illustrious' diction and occasionally archaisms. Moreover, when bureaucrats had to draw up statements that the populace could understand, they very frequently proved capable of using dialectal terms. Here is an example from Naples which belongs to the beginning of the century:

'. . . tutte le taverne che faranno *cocina* e teneranno tavola de comodità da *mangniare*, pagaranno un tanto per ciascheduna taverna, accausa che per li soverchi forestieri . . . faranno soverchio guadangnio; tutti li *potecari* de l'arte lorda, come sono quelli che vendeno lardo, *cascio, presotta, salcicioni*, ovvero altra *robba* salata che si conviene a lo loro mistiero, pagaranno un tanto per ciascheduna *poteca* . . .'

Dialectalisms abounded, too, in treatises on trades and skills connected with particular areas. The Venetian translator of the *Arte di tagliar gli alberi* of Monsù della Quintinyè (i.e. Jean de la Quintinie), for example, in distinguishing the uses of various kinds of grafting, wrote: 'l'*Incalmo* a *Subiotto* serve per i Maroni, Castagne e *Figheri*'.

Everyone makes use of figurative language. With baroque writers such use became grotesquely forced; metaphors were ingeniously accumulated and tiresomely prolonged. Their principal theorist, Tesauro, divided metaphor into eight categories in his *Cannocchiale* and then proceeded to illustrate their practical uses with a wealth of examples:

'Se tu chiami l'Amore un *fuoco*: volendolo tu esagerare, puoi tu per *semplice hiperbole* chiamarlo una *Fornace portatile*, una *Face di Megera*, e non d'Amore, un *Fulmine di Cupidine . . .*, una *Bomba animata*, un *Mongibello del petto*, una *Zona torrida . . .*'

Metaphors used by Petrarch (like *fiamma* for 'love' or 'loved one') and others invented by baroque writers became used almost as a series of fixed equivalents: an 'eye' being called *stella* or *sole*, 'hair' *ruscelli* or *pioggia* or *selva*, 'tears' *perle*, 'water' *cristallo* and so on. Constant repetition, of course, deprived these words of all force of expression, as, for example, when Marino refers to a man as 'del destro *sole* orbo rimaso' (*Adone*, XIV, st. 123). This led to a constant search for new (and occasionally far-fetched) metaphors. It also led to accumulation where one was felt to be insufficient:

'Questa picciola dimostrazione della mia devota osservanza . . . è scintilla della fornace, stilla dell'oceano, scarsissima ricognizione degl'infiniti obblighi miei' (Marino, *Epistolario*, I, p. 176).

Another possibility was to prolong a metaphor by developing the subsidiary metaphors that could be derived from the main one. Tesauro (*Cannocchiale*, p. 321) tells us that, if we call the Rose the 'Queen of Flowers', then we can, by cultivating this fertile root, cause a thousand shoots to spring from it in each category of metaphor, e.g.

Rosa	Reina	
Pianta eminente	Dignità sublime	(Substantia)
Rossor delle foglie	Porpora del manto	(Quantitas)
Odori	Profumi	(Qualitas)

etc.

On the same system preachers constructed the 'concetti predicabili' to which we referred earlier. Father Emmanuele Orchi's famous sermon on penitence used washing as a metaphor for repenting, but followed the stages with detailed references to the washerwoman's every action. Another fashionable trick was to reverse the roles of noun and adjective: thus a 'singing bird' could become a 'flying song' or a 'winged violin'. A 'thick forest' for Marino (*Adone*, VIII, st. 23) became a *horror frondoso*, while Father Lubrano in a sonnet turned 'hares' into *animati tremori*. Of course, this process could make the train of thought a little difficult to follow, as when Artale used *nevi addensate* for 'spectacles', and the readers' pleasure became that of solving a riddle. In fact, riddles were also a fashion of the period. Another method of producing wonder in the reader was, of course, to describe something by use of phrases that provided contrasts; three octaves in which Marino gives a definition of love consist mainly of antitheses:

> *lupo vorace in abito d'agnello ...*
> *lince privo di lume, Argo bendato,*
> *vecchio lattante e pargoletto antico ...*

Contrast was often between concrete and abstract. In the mock-heroic poems it was between solemn and trivial; Tassoni in his *Secchia rapita* often used a comic couplet to give a burlesque ending to an octave that promised to be entirely solemn. Marino, too, was fond of the unexpected ending. In one of his poems we have a long list of vegetables enumerated with the joy of a painter of still-life studies; but it turns out to be a device for satirizing Mùrtola, for whom they are invited in the last couplet to form a laurel wreath (*Murtoleide*, fischiata 36). Difficult rhymes were used to provoke wonder, not only by Marino and his followers, but also by anti-Marinists like Salvator Rosa (*Annassimandri*: *Alessandri*: *Licandri*, sat. II, v. 905 ss.; *iride*: *Busiride*: *Osiride*, sat. III). But the Seicento poets were particularly fond of paronomasia, playing on words which sounded alike and which were used in close proximity:

> *I pria sì grati e poi sì gravi affanni*
> > (Marino, *Adone*, I, st. 4)
> *De la bella rubella in voce amara*
> > (IV, st. 34)
> *Fa de le proprie infamie oscena scena*
> > (VII, st. 184)
> *O mia dorata, et adorata Dea*
> > (XV, st. 99)
> *Corsi a le labra, e, quant'ardente ardito*
> *con grata allor non grave*
> *violenza soave*
> > (*Poesie varie*, ed. Croce, 47)

Sometimes the two words came from the same family, thus giving an 'etymological figure': 'al lor re *sconosciuto* — si mostrar *sconoscenti* (*La Sampogna*, 'Atteone', 199-200). Occasionally, a word of Latin origin was given its etymological meaning:

Di smeraldi cader vezzo serpente
si lascia al sen con negligenza accorta
(*Adone*, VIII, st. 33).

Another artifice, which was not rare in previous centuries, but which was now used with great frequency, was antonomasia: 'gli Homeri moderni non havranno fra le tenebre dell'antichità a mendicar gli *Achilli*' (Achillini, letter to Louis XIII, 1639); 'Un *Caucaso* di nevi ho su le chiome' (G. Battista, in Croce, *Lirici marinisti*, p. 432); etc. Titles of books were, of course, a good field for metaphor. A learned compilation could be called a *Giardino*, *Tesoro*, *Teatro*, *Galleria*, *Cornucopia*, *Officina*, *Miniera*, or *Scena* (like D. Calvi's *Scena letteraria degli scrittori bergamaschi*, Bergamo 1614). Moreover, the initial metaphor could be continued in the rest of the title, as in G. B. Racani's *Navicella grammaticale, nella quale chiunque s'imbarcherà con corso felice, e breve, arriverà al bramato Porto di quest'Arte* (Venice — Macerata 1686). Or the divisions of the work itself might follow the metaphor of the title, as in F. Frugoni's *Cane di Diogene* (Venice 1687) which is divided into seven *latrati* or 'fits of barking' (i.e. volumes). Members of academies assumed metaphorical names which were in line with the title of the academy itself; thus the members of the Crusca chose (from 1590 onwards) names that had to do with grain, bread and so on: *l'Inferigno, il Lievitato, il Macinato*, etc. Love of novelty inclined such people to look favourably on coining new words. To that we shall refer later, when dealing with vocabulary. Here we should mention another result of novelty-seeking: the vogue enjoyed by what was called the *lingua ionadattica*. In this 'language' words were replaced by others beginning with the same letters, e.g. *fagiani* might be substituted for *fagioli*, or *gomita rotte* for *gote rosse*, and instead of saying *vi riverisco di tutto cuore* one might say *vi rivesto di tutto cuoio*. This is only a development, of course, of the camouflaging of words which previous writers had adopted as a comic expedient, e.g. Palamidesse's *venire al Batastero* for 'venire a battaglia' in the Duecento, Dante's *cortonese* for 'corto', etc. Proper names were an obvious target for its practitioners, e.g. Marino's 'Signora, io son sì fattamente nel labirinto d'Amore che mi veggio *Persio* (*perso*=lost), né per uscire so ritrovare il *Varchi* (*varco*=passage), se la vostra cortesia non mi fa il *Guidoni* (*guida*=guide)' (*Epistol.*, II, pp. 93-6), etc. From all this it will be seen that none of the artifices exploited by Seicento writers were unknown in previous centuries; they are distinguished by their lack of discretion in using them. But their playing with words left few lasting traces in the language.

Dialect continued to thrive. We must assume that outside Tuscany and Rome regional varieties of speech were the usual means of communication, and that literary Tuscan was regarded as a model for speakers only by very few persons of elevated social position. But Italian was used in writing, even if it occasionally bore traces of dialect. Salvator Rosa wrote his verse and prose in Italian (though conscious of the occasional lapses in his 'tosco mio guasto idioma'), but he continued to speak his own dialect even when at Rome and Florence and used Neapolitan phrases for commenting on his satires to his friends ('*Siente chisso vè, auza gli uocci*'). With the exception of some *sacre rappresentazioni* and the Sicilian poem entitled *Historia siciliana supra lu riccu Epuloni cu Lazzaru* by Vito di Renda (Messina 1668), practically none of the considerable amount of dialect literature produced in the Seicento can be regarded as for popular consumption; it was the work of cultured persons turning to dialect in order to achieve a new literary flavour or in search of a kind of popular costume for their literary fancy-dress balls. There were many comic poems, often depicting scenes from local life (like Peresio's *Maggio romanesco*), translations into dialects of ancient and modern poems (including many of the whole or of parts of the *Gerusalemme liberata*), dialogues and stories in prose (of which the Neapolitan G. B. Basile's *Cunto de li cunti* is justly famous) and comedies with dialect-speaking characters. Jocose poems in Italian, too, not infrequently contained passages in dialect spoken by particular characters. In Tuscany the situation was rather different from that in other regions: there the poet stylized 'rustic' speech. (Here again there was no lack of precursors, from the *Nencia da Barberino* down; but now there were more numerous examples — Buonarroti's *Tancia*, Baldovini's *Cecco da Varlungo*, etc.) While these Tuscan 'rustic' compositions accentuated the caricature of the country bumpkin, putting a fair number of garbled words into his mouth, dialect writings generally toned down the dialect colouring by drawing the language towards Italian. A typical example is Peresi's *Maggio romanesco*, which in the printed edition (Ferrara 1688) is markedly less dialectal than a preceding version (which, after remaining unpublished for centuries was edited by F. Ugolini, Rome 1939, and which bore the title *Il Jacaccio overo il Palio conquistato*). In some cases, of course, the use of dialect was dictated, not by a search for local colour, but by genuine attachment to the life of the region. Boschini in his *Carta del navegar pittoresco* (Venice 1660) asks: 'Mi che son venezian in Venezia, e che parlo de pitori veneziani, ho da andarme a stravestir?'

On January 20, 1612 appeared the *Vocabolario degli Accademici della Crusca*. It was published by G. Alberti at Venice, where Bastiano de' Rossi had gone to supervise the printing of it. The preface made it clear that the academicians' intention was to 'preserve the language' by following the principles favoured by Bembo and Salviati: 'Nel compilare il presente Vocabolario (col parere dell'Illustrissimo Cardinal Bembo, de' Deputati alla correzion del Boccaccio dell'anno 1573 e ultimamente del Cavalier Lionardo Salviati) abbiamo stimato necessario ricorrere all'autorità di quegli scrittori, che vissero, quando questo idioma principalmente fiorì', i.e. in the fourteenth century. The authors mainly quoted were Dante, Petrarch, Boccaccio and Villani, followed by other Florentines or authors who had written in Florentine. From non-Florentines the lexicographers took only words that they considered 'belle, significative, e dell'uso nostro'. The less authoritative words (those taken from sixteenth-century authors or from the spoken language) were made to follow those supported by greater authority: *calappio* or *galappio* were put under *accalappiare*; *carota* and *carotaio* under *cacciare*, where the phrase *cacciar carote* was quoted; *cifera* and *gergo* under *enigma*, etc. Numerous variants were recorded (*avolterio-adulterio*, *notomia-anatomia*, *cecero-cigno*, *spelda-spelta*, etc.); this is understandable in view of the criteria of culling words from texts, but it gave little help to those who wanted to know which of the forms to use. For each meaning examples from prose and verse were cited wherever possible. Sayings and proverbs were freely recorded, even when not documented. The *Vocabolario* was notably better than previous dictionaries: it had more words, and it made a good attempt at defining, rather than explaining by means of synonyms. The influence of Salviati's approach to the problem of making a dictionary made it rather archaizing, and those who hoped for a codification of contemporary language were disappointed. But the fame of the Accademia della Crusca and its intrinsic merits gave it a position of pre-eminence; it soon won loyal supporters and fierce adversaries. Few modifications were introduced in the second edition (1623), which was also published at Venice, this time by Iacopo Sarzina (again under the supervision of Bastiano de' Rossi): a few forgotten words were added, either from literary tradition (like *eroe*) or from usage. There was then a slackening off in the Academy's work on the dictionary, punctuated by spurts following on the election of energetic secretaries (Benedetto Buonmattei in 1640, Carlo Dati in 1663 and Alessandro Segni in 1677). Prince Leopold, a protector of the Academy, had scientific and nautical words and terms relating to trades and professions collected, but the opinion of those who wanted to exclude professional and technical vocabulary prevailed. In 1677 one of the most learned members of the Academy, Magalotti, made a suggestion which would have made the dictionary much more useful if it had been acted upon: that archaic, poetic or plebeian words should be marked as such by the use of symbols set against them in the dictionary. But the work was too far advanced to allow this to be done without great trouble, and it was in any case too early for such a proposal to have much hope of overcoming the force of tradition. The third edition came out in 1691, this time from the 'Stamperia dell'Accademia della Crusca'. Apart from those represented in the previous edition, about fifty early and fifty modern authors had been gone through in the collection of items. The compilers at last included words from Tasso and also Pallavicino (but that appeared too daring to the compilers of the fourth edition, who expunged the examples taken from the latter). To add to the number of entries, verbal abstracts were collected, and many diminutives, augmentatives and superlatives were included as words in their own right. The desire to add notably to the stock of items proved too much of a temptation for one of the compilers, Francesco Redi, who invented a few words he alleged existed in manuscripts in his possession. Nevertheless, no other modern language possessed at the end of the seventeenth century a dictionary that could worthily compete with the Crusca's.

In 1629 Scipione Herrico wrote from Messina to Gaspare Trissino, lamenting the number of conflicting opinions held on questions of Italian spelling and grammar and alleging that it was easier to learn the rules of foreign languages than it was to learn those of the language they habitually spoke. In fact, progress had been made towards unity in the literary language; but areas of disagreement persisted. It was natural that controversy should centre on the Crusca, which had come out clearly in favour of a Tuscan and archaizing attitude. Even before its dictionary appeared, G. B. Pinelli, one of its members, made it clear, in his translation of the psalms of St. Bonaventura (1606), that he accepted the Accademia della Crusca's authority in linguistic matters. When the dictionary had appeared, many of the Crusca's supporters felt obliged to write in archaizing fashion. Not everyone was impressed. Paolo Beni, a Paduan professor, who was opposed to the Crusca's archaizing attitude as well as offended by Bastiano de' Rossi's lack of respect for Venetian men of letters, published in the very year of its appearance, *L'Anticrusca overo il Paragone dell'italiana lingua: nel qual si mostra chiaramente che l'antica sia inculta e rozza: e la moderna regolata e gentile* (Padua 1612). Beni held that sixteenth-century authors were superior to those of the fourteenth, defended Tasso strenuously, and attacked Boccaccio on morphological and syntactic grounds. He rejected the idea of Florentine supremacy ('o perche fia meglio dir *mandorlo* e *mandorla*, che *mandolo* e *mandola*, o pur, *amandolo* e *amandola* come costuma quasi il restante d'Italia?' p. 13) and above all complained that the Crusca 'intanto che lo stile e de' Cari e de' Tassi lor pute' had exhumed 'le *Tavole ritonde*, i Giacoponi, i *Morganti*' and even account-books. The Crusca was uncertain as to whether it should defend itself; finally, it decided not to do so. Not only was the answer it had drafted under the title *Antiminosse* not published, but Bastiano de' Rossi also persuaded Fioretti to suppress the *Frullone dell'Anticrusca* that he had drawn up. There was, however, a personal intervention from Orlando Pescetti, of Marradi, whose *Risposta all'Anticrusca* (Verona 1613) defended Boccaccio and the name 'Florentine language'. This provoked another little volume by Beni, *Il Cavalcanti overo la Difesa dell'Anticrusca*, which was published under the name of Michelangelo Fonte and dedicated to Grand Duke Cosimo (Padua 1614). In arguing in favour of modern authors, Beni cited Tassoni's recently published *Pensieri*. Alessandro Tassoni was himself a member of the Accademia della Crusca and had dedicated the first part of his *Pensieri diversi* to it in 1608. But he was bitterly disappointed in the dictionary, which contained, in his view, too much worthless old stuff, while omitting too many modern words. A few years after the 1612 edition appeared, he sent to the Crusca a document entitled *Incognito da Modena contro alcune voci del vocabolario della Crusca*, and he was greatly angered to find, when the second edition appeared, that no notice had been taken of it. That document was lost, but we know what Tassoni's attitude was: Tiraboschi had seen a draft of the manuscript and quoted it, Tassoni himself left three versions of notes he made on the second edition, and he also (under the name of Gaspare Salviani) added revealing notes to his own *Secchia rapita*. He objected to the inclusion of florentinisms like *abituro, agghiadare, contradio, guari, testé,* and asked why the dictionary should register *moccichino* and *popone* when all Italy said *fazzoletto* and *melone*. He also condemned archaic and pedantic items like *abbaglione, abbassagione, abitaggio, accalappiare,* etc., and after *Vocabolario* in the title added the words 'delle voci arcaiche'. He noted the omission of *accanto, amaranto, anemone, azzardare, circospezione, cumulo, davvero, decoro, delitto, equestre, lusso, nazionale, orrendo, plurale, regolare, scena, vigliacco* and many other words. He found fault, too, with some of the definitions. And in commenting on the word *pitale* in the *Secchia* he wrote of himself: 'egli ebbe opinione che la favella della corte romana fosse così buona, come la fiorentina, e meglio intesa per tutto'. Another series of *Annotazioni* to the first and second editions of the dictionary, although attributed to Tassoni (and published by Fontanini at Venice in 1698) was in reality the work of G. Ottonelli. Opposition to the Florentine norm came, too, from Siena. In the Cinquecento, Tolomei, Borghesi, Cittadini and Lombardelli had striven to keep Siena on a level with Florence, but without insisting on the differences between their dialects. Scipione Bargagli, however, in *Il Turamino, ovvero del parlare e dello scriver sanese* (Siena 1602) emphasized divergencies, even those which were dying out. He listed some Sienese equivalents (*povaro, dipegnare, longo, lassare, bacoca, citta, rantacare, stare a gallo,* etc.) of Florentine words and insisted that his fellow-citizens should not only speak, but write, as 'Nature taught' them. After the publication of the Crusca dictionary another Sienese, Adriano Politi (1542-1625), who did not think much of it, nevertheless exploited it for a work of his own, summarizing its definitions and adding Sienese equivalents to words that were markedly Florentine. His work appeared with the title *Dittionario toscano, Compendio del Vocabolario della Crusca* (Rome 1614), but the Academy protested vigorously, and in subsequent editions (which extended from 1615 to 1691) the title was reduced to *Dittionario toscano*. The use of Tuscan archaisms was, of course, satirized by some writers (e.g. Tassoni, *Secchia rapita*, X, st. 6; Boccalini, *Ragguagli*, III, 82; Salvator Rosa, *Satire*, II, 487-95, etc.). Other authors indicated their disagreement with the Crusca simply by briefly mentioning the criteria they followed in their writing (as when Pietro della Valle, publishing his letters on his travels, informed the reader that he did not presume to write them in pure Tuscan, but in his 'maternal Roman dialect'). With the grammarians as such we shall deal in a moment. Here we should note that on the whole they accepted the Tuscan canon and took their examples from the approved fourteenth-century writers. Father Daniello Bartoli did so and used the term 'buon secolo'; but he condemned those who affected archaisms and defended the right to use words and phrases not found in Trecento Italian (*Il Torto e il Diritto del Non si può*, Rome 1655). And, as we have already seen, some of the more broad-minded academicians (like Magalotti) realized that the Crusca's *Vocabolario* was doing two separate things: registering words (including archaic and plebeian items) and setting the seal of authenticity on the cream of the classical authors' vocabulary; much controversy might have been avoided if his plan for indicating distinctions had been accepted. In Naples around 1680 Lionardo di Capua, doctor, naturalist, anti-Aristotelian and anti-Marinist, established a pro-Tuscan, archaizing school of writers which came to be called the Capuists. Vico was among his followers. From all this it will be seen that throughout the century discussions on linguistic standards hinged on acceptance or rejection of the Crusca's criteria. As for the name given to the language, although 'Florentine', 'Tuscan' and 'Italian' were all used, the second was easily in the lead, being used occasionally even by those who rejected the Crusca's authority. Loreto Mattei was apparently the first to the speak of 'nostra national favella' in his *Teorica del verso volgare e prattica di retta pronunzia* (Venice 1695).

Among the grammars of the period[1] the *Trattato della lingua* of Giacomo Pergamini of Fossombrone (1st ed. Venice 1613) was clearly set out and useful for teaching. But more perception in the analysis of grammatical phenomena was shown by B. Buonmattei in his *Della lingua toscana* (Florence 1643, partial editions having been previously published with the title *Delle cagioni della lingua italiana*, Venice 1623 and *Introduzione alla lingua italiana*, Venice 1626). Buonmattei did not accept reduction of the parts of speech to 7, as Father Sanchez had done, but put them up to 12, including interjections. Another meritorious work was the *Osservazioni della lingua italiana* of Marcantonio Mambelli, called il Cinonio; these *Osservazioni* dealt with article, pronoun, adverb, preposition, conjunction and interjection (Ferrara 1644) and with the verb (Forlì 1685). Benedetto Menzini ably discussed the connections between grammar and style in the treatise *Della*

---

[1] A fuller account of the work of Italian grammarians can be found in Ciro Trabalza's *Storia della grammatica italiana*, Milan 1908, chapters X and XI. Here only the main trends are discussed.

costruzione irregolare della lingua toscana (Florence 1679). Daniello Bartoli in *Il Torto e il Diritto del Non si può* opposed those who were too ready to censure writers on the basis of the Crusca's principles: for him no exclusive criterion could be based on the decision of grammarians, the usage of a people or élite, or the prerogatives of time; one could only depend on good taste deriving from sound judgement. A series of *Avvertimenti grammaticali per chi scrive in lingua italiana* was published by Cardinal Sforza Pallavicino under the name of Francesco Rainaldi (Rome 1661). There was also a number of smaller treatises on particular areas of grammar (orthography, punctuation, pronunciation). The success that these works enjoyed showed that there was a lively interest in language and that the need for guidance was felt.

In the lexicographical field we should mention the *Memoriale della lingua volgare* of G. Pergamini (Venice 1601), which was frequently reprinted even after the appearance of the Crusca's *Vocabolario*; it is notable that Pergamini added to his words notes like 'nob.', 'pop.', 'di verso' and 'di prosa'. The Crusca's own work and Politi's *Dittionario toscano* have already been mentioned. A. Monosini, in his *Floris Linguae Italicae libri IX* (Venice 1604) provided a large collection of proverbs and sayings. The material collected by G. B. Doni for his Onomasticon, whose twenty books were to contain all the terms of sciences, arts, trades, etc., has been lost. However, one important dictionary of specialist vocabulary has come down to us: the *Vocabolario toscano dell'arte del disegno* by Baldinucci (Florence 1681). Etymological dictionaries, too, began to appear. Carlo Dati, in collaboration with other members of the Crusca, had started an *Etimologico toscano*, but Egidio Menagio (Gilles Ménage) got in before them with his *Origini della lingua italiana* (Paris 1669; 2nd ed. Geneva 1685). It contained several absurd etymologies, but also many that were right. And it was far superior to O. Ferrari's *Origines linguae Italicae* (Padua 1676).

The foreign language best known in Italy in the first half of the century was Spanish. There were Italian authors who wrote in Spanish (e.g. Pier Salvetti) and theatrical companies that performed in Spanish at Naples. French at first was little known. Writers of comedy who introduced a representative Frenchman (called *Claudio* or *Claudione*, *Raguetto* or *Raguetta*) into their works only very gradually dared to put French words into his mouth. But in the time of *le Roi soleil* the position changed. France had cultural prestige, and knowledge of her language increased.

Salvator Rosa closed a letter to a friend in 1654 with the formula 'con queste e con molte belle *sciose*' (ed. De Rinaldi, p. 70), while Redi makes Bacchus, in his *Bacco in Toscana*, tell the secretary of the Crusca to make a copy of its transactions 'e spediscane *courier* — *A monsieur l'abbé Regnier*'. Indeed, the diffusion of French made enough progress for Menzini to complain of it in his *Satire*. When dealing with vocabulary we shall give examples of the hispanisms and gallicisms that came into Italian at this time.

Outside Italy, Italian was still well known. Many foreigners studied at Italian universities and learned the language there. For learned correspondence foreigners usually used Latin, but they occasionally employed Italian (e.g. Welser of Augsburg writing to Galileo). In the France of Louis XIII many people knew Italian, and appreciated the comedies performed by Italians at Paris and the operas of Italian composers. (It will be remembered that Lulli settled there). Ménage, Chapelain and Régnier and various ladies knew Italian well. A. Oudin and N. Duez of Geneva compiled useful dictionaries (Paris 1639-40; Leyden 1641), and the learned fathers of Port-Royal, Lancelot and Arnauld, drew up a *Nouvelle Méthode pour apprendre facilement et en peu de temps la langue italienne* (Paris 1660). In German-speaking countries there was considerable knowledge of Italian among the upper classes. Of Welser Guarini remarked that his letters seemed 'dettate da huomo nato, & allevato in Firenze'. In Vienna, wrote Magalotti in 1675, there was nobody with the face and clothes of a gentleman who did not speak Italian fluently and perfectly. The Emperor Ferdinand III praised Antonio Abati, the author of the *Frascherie* in an acrostic madrigal, and his son the Archduke Leopold founded an Italian academy. Italian was studied from manuals written in Latin and German. In England the interest awakened in Italian during the Renaissance still persisted. Shakespeare used the manuals and dictionaries of Florio, and Milton wrote sonnets in Italian. Florio's dictionary, first published in 1598, was enlarged by the author for the 1611 edition and revised by G. Torriano for those of 1659 and 1687-8.

The controversies that raged over linguistic criteria reflected lack of uniformity in usage. Some idea of the oscillations in grammar can be gathered from the discussions of some of the disputed points in Bartoli's *Il Torto e il Diritto del Non si più*. But they were even greater than this would suggest, for they included dialectal variations which a grammarian would not feel obliged to record, regarding them as manifestly wrong.

In vocabulary, too, there were many variants, and the Crusca's efforts in registering the forms found in early writers served only to increase them. Writers still oscillated between *dopo*, *dopò* and *doppo* and argued as to whether *truppa* should have a double *p*. Alongside the Tuscan form *crogiuolo* there appeared *crocciuolo* (Marino) and *cruciolo* (Vannozzi). *Prencipe* was used as well as *principe*. Some wrote *butirro* (Buonarroti), some *butiro* (Redi) and some *biturro* (Tassoni). The Sienese still preferred *fadiga* to *fatica*. At Rome they frequently wrote *abbrugiare*, *defonto*, *lograre*, *sagro*. And these are but a few examples. Sometimes a word was characterized as belonging to a particular category — plebeian or poetic, for instance. A large number of words and forms were qualified as 'poetic'; if found in Petrarch or other accepted poets they were considered admissible, even though they no longer had a place in the spoken language. Marino still used *havièno* for 'avevano', and M. Zito defended Tasso, who had used *uscieno* (*La bilancia critica*, Naples 1685). Anyone who wishes to make a full study of these phenomena will need to examine the texts, printed and manuscript, of the period; its normative grammarians naturally presented a language less varied than it was in reality.

In spelling, the important cases of oscillation were four: in three of them (use of *h*; use of *ti* or *zi*; single or double *s* from *ex-*) resistance on the periphery gradually gave way to the Crusca's spelling, while in the fourth (distinction between the vowel *u* and consonant *v*) Trissino's suggestion was adopted by a few, but triumphed only after its general adoption by printers outside Italy. In the second and third editions of the *Vocabolario della Crusca* etymological *h* occurred only in *ho, hai, ha, huomo* and its derivatives; in the case of *huopo, huosa, huovo, huovolo* the reader was referred to the form without *h*. In the third edition only *ho, hai, ha, hanno* survived; those who looked up *huomo* were referred to *uomo*. Tuscan grammarians and printers mostly followed the Crusca. Magalotti wished to go beyond it: he wanted *ò, à* instead of *ho, ha*, which had nothing but habit in its favour. The Bolognese Lampugnani, too, was 'disdevoto dell'H', while the Roman Pallavicino kept it only in *huomo* and the whole conjugation of *havere*. But D. Franzoni and Domenico d'Aquino defended it. Bartoli, while not discussing it, continued to use it. And generally non-Tuscan writers preferred to keep it. The use of *h* in Greek digraphs had almost disappeared, but Marino still wrote *theatro*, *thesoro*, *christallo*, and sometimes *h* unexpectedly appeared elsewhere (as in Mattei's *etherogeneo*, etc.). In the case of *z* (as in *grazia*) the example of Salviati and the Crusca was followed by Tuscans and only gradually by others. With the problem of the substitution of *zi* for *ti* another was connected: whether the *z* should be single or double. The conservative generally wrote *ti* where Latin had *ti*, but *tti* where it had *cti* or *pti*. The innovators were divided: some distinguished between *zi* and *zzi*, others followed the Crusca in always using *zi*. In the polemic between Beni and Pescetti, the anti-Cruscan Beni wrote *ti* and *tti* (*gratia, construttione*), while Pescetti used *zi* throughout (*locuzione, dizionario*). Galileo in 1606 had his *Operazioni del compasso* published; in re-reading a letter of his to Nozzolini, he put in *zz* where his amanuensis has written *ti* in *affetione*. In his autograph work we generally find *zz* where we should expect *z* (*confutazzioni, dimostrazzioni*, etc.). De Luca accepted *z*, but distinguished between single *z* in words like *alterazione* and double *z* in *erezzione, adozzione*, etc. It is not known whether he carried this distinction into pronunciation. Tuscan grammarians, but few others, supported *z*: Buonmattei recommended single *z* (*grazia*), shutting the door against both *gratia* and *grazzia*. Lampugnani was rebuked for his abuse of *z*. Franzoni, on the other hand, defended *ti*, and Bartoli, although allowing freedom of choice (in accordance with his general attitude in his *Torto e diritto*), was himself in favour of *ti* and used it in his writings (*osservatione*, but *scorettione*). Menagio, too, favoured *ti* and, in answering the Crusca's criticisms of his observations on the *Aminta*, defended himself by quoting the example of Muzio. Using single and double *z* as a device for distinguishing between voiced and voiceless *z* (*gaza, rozo*, as opposed to *asprezza, bellezza*) was still the practice of a few (e.g. Marino); but the Crusca rejected it, writing *azzimo, gazza, rozzo*, like *asprezza, bellezza*, etc. The proposal made by the unknown author of *Neagrammalogia* that recourse be had to ç (as in Trissino's writings) had little chance of acceptance. In words having initial *es-* or *ess-* from *ex-*, there was still some oscillation at the beginning of the century: Galileo wrote both *esempio* and *essempio*, Marino usually wrote *essaltare, essangue, essercizio, essule*, etc. The Crusca used only *es-* in its dictionary, and Bartoli (*Ortografia*, c. IX, § 5) though quoting numerous early examples with *ess-*, declared himself in favour of spelling and pronouncing *es-*. Spadafora in his *Prosodia* referred those who looked up *essala, essarcato, essodo, essotico*, to *esala, esarcato, esodo, esotico* (but not *essagono*). The distinction between the vowel *u* and the consonant *v* was late in becoming established. In the first half of the century the spelling nearly always adopted was *v* (or *V*) at the beginning of a word, *u* inside a word, whether representing vowel or consonant. Then sporadic attempts at division of functions began to appear: Father Aprosio in an opuscule of his (G. Galistoni, *Il Buratto*, Venice 1642) distinguished between *u* and *v* as we do today. But the lead came principally from abroad: many Elzevirian editions of Italian works (*Il Nipotismo di Roma* by Leti, Amsterdam 1667; *Il Pastor fido*, 1678; *Il Goffredo*, 1678) distinguished the vowel from the consonant. While the edition of Sègneri's *Quaresimale* published at Venice in 1685 followed the old method, that of the *Cristiano istruito* published at Florence in the same year followed the new. In 1695 Mattei noted that the distinction was now observed 'nelle Stampe più corrette, nel modo anco che rigorosamente l'osservano tutte le Stampe Oltramontane'. In the third edition of the Crusca's dictionary, *u* and *v* were distinguished in the modern manner in the text, but considered as one letter in the capitals used for head-words, and so also in establishing the alphabetical order (AVARO, AVDACE, AVELLO . . .). The *j* was used mainly as a variant for *i* after another *i*: mostly at the end of words (*incendij*), but also medially (*proprijssimo, pronuntijno*). The practice gained ground of using final *j* for combined *i*+*j*, provided the *i* was atonic and the group counted as a single syllable: in the *Arte poetica* of Menzini (ed. 1688) we find *incendj*, *precipicj*, but 'ne' *Pierij* campi' (four syllables). Latin *et*, represented by &, was more and more frequently replaced by the Italian forms *e* or *ed*; but some insisted on maintaining the sign &. Accents were rarely used within a word, but some writers used them for unusual words, the acute accent being usually chosen (e.g. *lúcere, intrépido, giúe* in Stigliani's *Mondo nuovo*, Rome 1628), though some preferred the grave (*ancòra, sèguito, metròpoli* in Bargagli's *Turamino*, Siena 1602). Accenting of monosyllables was rather frequent, though Buonmattei pointed out that it was pointless and reserved it to homophonous monosyllables (*e — è, di — dì, la — là, si — sì*). In punctuation we should note that the comma was nearly always used before *e, o, che*. The century's taste for rhetorical inflation found expression in abundant use of capital letters: 'Tanto corrotta è la Historia in questo Secolo, che appresso a molti horamai di Arte Liberale, è divenuta Mecanica: & deposta la Tromba, suona dell'Arpa' (E. Tesauro, *Apologia contra la esamina del dottor Capriata*, Turin 1673, p. 1).

Phonetic variants were due to old oscillations not yet eliminated in the codification of literary Italian, to local variants and to different treatments of latinisms. The Florentine -*er*- from -*ar*- in futures and conditionals was now easily predominant, even with non-Tuscans (forms like Salvator Rosa's *soverchiarebbe* and L. Mattei's *spiegarà* being rather rare). Exceptions were more frequent outside the verb, e.g. *sonnarello*, Marino; *zàccare*, S. Rosa; *ballarina*, G. L. Sempronio, etc.; Roman chancellery usage had *Cancellaria*, *Dataria*, etc. The diphthong *uo* in free position was well maintained at Florence, while at Rome there was a tendency to monophthongize (*cori*, *camiciola*, *lenzola* as equivalents for Florentine *cuori*, *camiciuola*, *lenzuola* in the glossary published by Baldelli in *Lingua nostra*, 1952). The rule of the mobile diphthong was not well kept, as can be seen both from examples (like Lippi's *giuocando*) and from what its defenders (Pallavicino, Mattei) wrote about it. Apheresis of initial *i* (*lo 'nvocare*, etc.) was applied by the Crusca, but was not well looked upon. Politi, in the introduction to his *Dittionario*, described *l'invocare* as 'maniera non solamente più sicura, ma più naturale, e più ordinaria di questa lingua'. Apocope in connected discourse was much more subject to taste than to rules, and there was much more freedom both in prose and verse than there is now: 'uomini da bene e *buon* Cristiani' (Galileo, *Opere*, XXIVb, p. 297), 'que' *buon* Padri' (letter from Redi to Father Kircher), etc. Apocope at the end of a line (*amar*, *veder*) was a characteristic of melic poetry. Among the consonantal phenomena we note fluctuation between single and double consonants. The most difficult cases arose when Florentine usage, either living or as codified from the classics, departed from Latin, through having either reduced a double consonant or doubled a single. In these cases the grammarians were tolerant. Pallavicino remarked (*Avvertimenti gramm.*, p. 46) that in some words Florentine pronunciation differed from that of the rest of Tuscany and of Italy, as in pronouncing *abate*, *ufizio*, *roba* with single consonants; *immagine*, *innalzare*, *Ovvidio* with double. In these cases he thought nobody should be rebuked for following either of the alternatives. Pallavicino himself wrote *immitare*, *immitazione*, *scommunica*. The letters which provoked most uncertainty were *b* and palatal *g* (particularly because of the southern tendency to double them in pronunciation): *preggia* (Herrico), *palaggi*, *Pariggi*, *naufraggio* (Rosa), but, vice versa, *sogetto* (Rosa) and *esagerare*, which became generalized instead of *esaggerare*, etc. But there was oscillation, too, in the case of other consonants: *zuffolo*, but *pifero* (Marino). And in a sonnet in the *Murtoleide*

(XXXVI) Marino wrote *popponi, carcioffi, carotte, tartuffi* and *spinacci* — all words for which, it can be said, no literary tradition existed. There was argument about cases in which enclitics were added to oxytones: the Crusca censured Stigliani for having used *votti* (='ti voglio') in the line 'Roldano, con mia man punir non *votti*', but he put up a good defence (lett. 1619, in Marino, *Epistolario*, II, pp. 276-88). There was also oscillation in doubling after prefixes: *sopranaturale* (Galileo), *traffiggere* (Marino), etc. The popular Tuscan *sti-* for *schi-* and *di-* for *ghi-* appeared in words put into circulation by Tuscan writers: apart from *mastio*, already used by Cellini and now appearing in technical meanings, there were, for instance, *mustio, stidione* (Buonarroti the younger). *Diaccio, diacciare* aroused no scruples. But *diacere* was felt to be a merely popular form. Use of prosthetic *i* before *s* impure was well observed in popular usage (*non istare, per isposa*), but it sometimes went astray in writing. In unusual words the accent was not always placed where Latin quantity would lead us to expect it: *frammèa* (for 'framea', Rosa), *Pegàso* (Marino, Herrico), *Archilòco, Gorgìa* (Rosa), *Inarìme* (Marino), etc. Alongside *dissenterìa*, the pronunciation *dissentèria* existed at Florence (Menzini).

Coming to morphology, we note that, as singular article, *il* was generally used before *z*, but *gli* in the plural. There were examples of *li* before a consonant, especially outside Tuscany. Buonmattei admitted it as a variant, while Pio Rossi condemned it. After the preposition *per* the grammarians prescribed the article *lo* (*per lo*, plural *per li*), but Politi, Bartoli, Mambelli, Menagio considered *per il* to be also admissible. There was a good deal of uncertainty in the treatment of nouns in *-co* and *-go*; in many cases usage was different from that which later prevailed: *aprici, bifolci; fantastichi, reciprochi, stitichi, teologichi; dialogi*, etc. There was similar oscillation in superlatives: *cattolichissimo, laconichissimo, diabolichissimo*. Plurals in *-ei* from *-ello* (*bambinei, ruscei*) were now confined to poetic usage, which also admitted some plurals in *-a* no longer accepted in prose (*le poma*). Among the numerals *due* finally prevailed, though there were still examples of *dua*, a form not rare in Galileo, and of *duo* and *doi. Lui, lei, loro* as subject-pronouns were frequent in usage, but nearly all the grammarians condemned them; not only Buonmattei, but also Bartoli (*Torto*, c. xxxxii). *Lei* had now acquired independent existence as an allocutive, irrespective of relationship to *Signoria Vostra*. But both *Lei* and *Signoria Vostra* found difficulty in penetrating popular usage. *Cotesto* found it hard to gain acceptance outside Tuscany, and was frequently misunderstood (Buonmattei, *Della lingua toscana*, tr. XI, cap. x; P. Rossi, *Osservazioni*, p. 243). In spite of the objections of grammarians (Bartoli as well as Buonmattei), *gli* was frequently used to mean both 'a lei' and 'a loro' ('la natura . . . mai non trascendente i termini delle leggi imposte*gli*': Galileo, *Opere*, V, p. 316; 'alli padri Gesuiti . . . gli potrà dar la copia della lettera': *Opere*, V, p. 295). The form *gnene* for *gliene* appeared occasionally in writings that were not plebeian ('io *gnene* darò un tocco martedì prossimo': letter by F. Redi, Jan. 5, 1681-82). There were still some examples of the 'accusative + dative' order in sequences of atonic pronouns ('non si può dubitare, nè *se gli* può contradire': Galileo, *Nuove scienze*, in *Opere*, VIII, p. 130 and passim). There were, too, still some instances of *mia* as plural of *mio* ('*mia* affezionati padroni': Galileo, lett. 19 Nov. 1629; 'E io cheto, e vo a fare i fatti *mia*': P. Salvetti). In pairs of adverbs the *-mente* of the first was often dropped on the model of Spanish: 'favellando poetica, ed amatoriamente risponde il poeta a Laura . . .' (Tassoni), etc. In the verb we find that in the pres. indic. of the first conjug. the ending *-e* of the 2nd pers. survived only in poetry (*apprezze*, *ti vante*); the ending *-ono* in the third pers. still lived on in spite of grammarians' objections. As for forms in *-isc-* in the third conjugation, there were some of them even in the arhizotonic forms (*rapischiamo*, Neri). Buonmattei admitted without *-isc-* only the 2nd pers. plur. ind. *nutrite*; he wanted the first pers. plur. indic. and the 1st and 2nd pl. subj. of these verbs to be avoided, considering them all defective: 'non si dirà mai non solo *ambischiamo* nè *colpischiamo*, ecc. ma nè anche *ambiamo*, nè *colpiamo*, nè *ambiate* nè *colpiate*', and he suggested replacing them by synonyms (*siamo ambiziosi* and so on): 'solo *finiamo* par che alcuna volta si lasci sentire, almeno dalle bocche del popolo, e in particolare in quell'affisso *finianla*, o *finiamola* . . .' (tr. XII, c. xxxxii). We should note too, in the first pers. plural (ind. and sub.) the forms *tenghiamo*, *venghiamo*, *ponghiamo*, *salghiamo*, which were either exclusively used or overwhelmingly frequent. In the imperfect, the form in *-a* for the first pers. was usual in the most formal writing; elsewhere, alongside it, particularly in Tuscan writers, *-o* was used (e.g. in Galileo's *Saggiatore* we have *solevo*, *dicevo*, but *aveva*). Among the grammarians, Buonmattei admitted both forms, whereas the usually tolerant Bartoli considered the form in *-o* to be arbitrary. The *avea* type was admissible not only in verse, but also in prose. In the 2nd pers. plur. the type *eri*, *meritavi*, *desideravi* (Galileo) was frequent; but Buonmattei considered it vulgar. In the future, alongside the forms in *-erò* in the first conjugation, appeared some examples in *-arò* in Sienese and non-Tuscan writers; but the grammarians would have none of them. Sometimes we find the *-rr-* of spoken Florentine (*troverremo*, Galileo). *Avrò* prevailed over *arò*, although there were some examples of the latter (Galileo). In the past definite there was a certain number of strong forms used for weak and vice versa (*veddi*, Galileo; *creddi, volsi*, etc.); these forms were either unknown to grammarians or condemned by them (Bartoli discouraged the use of *persi*, recommending *perdei*). In the 1st pers. plur. northern writers, and sometimes southern writers too, continued to use the endings *-assimo, -essimo, -issimo* added to the weak stem (*vedessimo* for 'vedemmo', S. Rosa) and also *-imo* added to the strong stem (*discorsimo*, S. Rosa). In the 3rd pers. plur. the *-orno* and *-orono* endings were in process of disappearing (*pensorno, si fermoron*, Galileo). In the present subjunctive of the 2nd and 3rd conjugations, endings in *-i* for the 3rd sing. and in *-ino* for 3rd plur. were still used (*possi, debbi, vadino, eschino, intendino*, Galilei; *aggiunghino*, Politi; *ferischino*, N. Villani), but they were condemned by grammarians. There were several anomalous formations, different from those that prevailed: *vadia* 'vada' (Galileo), *vaglia* 'valga', *togga* (Galileo), *sagga, sagghiate* 'salga, saliate' (Magalotti), etc. In the imperfect subjunctive there was oscillation, especially in the 2nd pers. plur.: *se voi l'avesse, se voi mi dicesse* (Galileo); a dialectal variation was *vorrei che mi spiegassivo* (S. Rosa). In the conditional, the *-ia* type was frequent in verse, but it was used also in prose, even of a familiar kind ('mi *bisogneria* liberarmi di alcuni obblighi': lett. by Galileo, 18 June 1610; 'per farne quel capitale che si *dovrebbe*, si *richiederia*. . . .' lett. by Panciatichi, August 1674). In the future there were some examples of Florentine *-rr-* (*crederrei*, Galileo). In the 1st pers. plur. there was a form with *-ebb-* in the ending (*lauderebbamo*, Galileo), as well as the usual northern forms in *-aressimo, eressimo, -iressimo* (use of which Bartoli called 'peccato mortale di lingua').

In syntax, we note merely some salient features. The use of accusative and infinitive was in decline. Beni, after quoting examples from Boccaccio, remarked that that kind of writing was in his day less practised and 'could not fail to offend the ear' (*Anticrusca*, p. 37). Constructions with *in* (without article) plus the infinitive were frequent (*in dipigner*: Dati; '*In sentirvi* lodar le nostre donne': Rosa), as also were those with *in* plus gerund ('Siccome i fiumi *in ricevendo* i rivi': Corsini; '*in sentendole* leggere a me': Redi). As we should expect, the century's taste for exaggeration found rhetorical expression. There were superlatives of nouns: *padronissimo* (Allegri; Fagiuoli), *elefantissimo* (Galileo), 'questa mia *spadissima*' (a braggart captain in D. Cini's *Desiderio e Speranza*), *mulissima* (Marino), *bricconissimo* (Bellini); relatives and superlatives of adjectives which already had superlative force: 'le fortezze *più principali*' (Bentivoglio), '*ottimissime* sono state le tre mutazioni' (Redi), *arciscioperatonaccissimo* (Redi); and superlatives of adverbial phrases: 'Dante *a propositissimo*' (Fioretti). There entered usage, too, the word *stessissimo* which, according to Fioretti (in the introduction to *Polifemo briaco*), was formed on the model of Greek. Adjectives and nouns were commonly reinforced by repetition of the same word with a superlative ending added or by similar devices: 'vera arcinegghientissima negghienza' (Redi 1656); 'affetti casti, castissimi' (Magalotti 1679); 'chiara, evidente, evidentissima, arcievidentissima' (Redi 1683); 'è dovere arci-dovere consolarlo' (Redi 1680); 'è una frottola frottola frotto-lissima' (Redi 1682); 'una scodella scodellissima tonda' (Maga-lotti 1695); 'un vero taglio taglissimo' (Bellini, *Disc.*, XI). Frequent recourse was had, too, to the 'King of Kings' type (of Biblical origin): Marino had, apart from 'la reina de' regi' (IV, st. 15) and 'reina . . . de le reine' (XI, st. 95), 'il bel del bello in breve spazio accolto' (III, st. 196), 'quel piacer de' piacer ch'al mondo è solo' (VIII, st. 40), etc. And there was, of course, Basile's *Lo Cunto de li cunti*. The exclamative construction formed by *che* before an adjective in isolation ('Che bello!') probably came from Spain and took root first of all in northern Italy (it is still not much liked in Tuscany): we find it, for example, in Orchi's 'che beato l'orecchio . . .'

Hereditary vocabulary was expanded to supply the needs of a formalistic and hypocritical society, novelty-seeking literature, pretentious learning and the developing experimental sciences. Existing words took on new meanings, there were new creations, and words were borrowed from classical and modern languages. The search for conceits had on the whole only ephemeral linguistic effects: the effort to use a word in a new and surprising way was felt to be something momentary, leaving normal usage as it had been, while the continuing search for novelty led to new meanings being quickly abandoned.

The use of *foriero*, *foriere* to mean 'harbinger' ('l'aprile — vago *forier* d'un odorato maggio': Achillini), a metaphorical use of the word previously meaning 'forager', must have arisen in this century. From discussion of ways of speaking and writing came new words and new meanings. *Concetto* passed from its philosophical meaning to that of a literary 'conceit', and from it came not only *concettuzzo* (Rosa) and *concettino* (Magalotti), but also the verbs *concettare* (Pallavicino) and *concettizzare* (Tesauro). To him who showed skill in conceits *brillante* was applied (Redi speaks of a person 'di spiriti vivaci e *brillanti*'), while *freddura* came to mean 'a witticism that did not come off' ('le medesime voci, che col discreto uso paiono scintille, con l'abuso saran freddure': Tesauro, *Cannocchiale*, p. 170). One could be considered *manierato* or *ricercato* or *lambiccato*. *Travestire* for 'to parody' made its bow in Lalli's *Eneide travestita* (1634). In a century which attributed such importance to formality, *cerimoniale*, which previously meant 'a book listing rules of etiquette and ceremony' came to mean 'ceremonial' or 'superabundance of ceremonies', while *etichetta* was taken from Spanish. *Formalizzarsi* and *formalista* entered usage, and *omaggio* came to be merely 'a mark of respect'. Appetite for new and finer titles gave rise to some creations; Urban VIII in 1630, for example, gave the title *Eminenza* to cardinals. But their value was somewhat diminished by the readiness of people to apply them to all and sundry; T. Rinuccini, referring to Florence *c.* 1670, wrote 'è venuta a tal segno questa vanità, che s'è cominciato a chiamare qualcuno *Marchese* per adulazione, e molti se lo lasciano dire senza replicare niente'. In religious life there was an increase in *missioni* and *missionanti* (later *missionari*), but the century also witnessed the coining of *nepotismo*. *Lubrico*, which in Latin had meant only 'slippery', came to signify 'indecent', and alongside *peccato* was formed the adjective *peccaminoso*. Meditation on death led to insistence on the *punto*; Chiabrera declared in his autobiography that he never ceased to 'pensare al *punto* della mia vita', while Bartoli wrote on *L'Huomo al punto, cioè l'huomo in punto di morte* (Rome 1667). Religious men condemned *libertini* (in both the intellectual and moral sense). On the other hand, exaggerated devoutness was derided by coining *bacchettone* and *baciapile*. In the theatre *opera* triumphed. It was a combination of acting, music and scenic devices; for the man who looked after these scenic devices ('macchine') the term *macchinista* was coined. The *scenari* of the *commedia dell'arte* stated what the actors were to do and included *lazzi*. And to the old masks were added new ones, like *Meneghino* and *Pulcinella*. New means of transport brought *portantine* ('sedan-chairs', introduced at Genoa in 1645) and *calessi* or *sedie rullanti* ('gigs') which came in from France. *Poltron-*

cine also came from France in 1672, according to T. Rinuccini, but they were given an Italian name by adapting *poltrone*. There is no room to note all the terms pertaining to fashion, but we should note *moda* and *modante*, and the names of some items like *marsina* ('tail-coat, tails'), *pastrana*, later *pastrano* ('overcoat') and *ciamberga* or *giamberga* ('long coat'), all three apparently called after the persons who first wore them. Among colours *amaranto* was at one time very popular. Certain beverages, which had been known only as rare or exotic things in the preceding century, now became common, and the words for them entered everyday usage (*cioccolato, caffè, tè*). Use of tobacco led to the introduction of *pipa*. In military parlance *reggimento* began to be used, as did words for various corps (*fucilieri, granatieri*), while *partita* was used for a small section or group used for a particular purpose. Curiosity about ancient monuments and famous places led to the appearance of *ciceroni*.

Various disciplines developed longer and more precise terminologies, and some words from these entered general usage. The greater use of Italian in law led to the translation (usually merely adaptation) into it of many legal terms. Many such terms are first documented in Italian in *Il Dottor volgare* by Cardinal De Luca (1673). The literary language, however, was reluctant to accept technical terms: e.g. Politi was reproached for having used *patrocinio* in his translation of Tacitus, and Carlo de' Dottori for using two other legal terms, *competente* and *incompetente*, in his *Aristodemo*. There was similar hostility to philosophical terms, as Pallavicino noted. Whereas in law there was merely the problem of adapting and using words from ancient and medieval sources, in the physical and natural sciences new apparatus and new ideas encouraged the coining of new words. Galileo, as we have seen, preferred to make use of words of popular stamp: *momento, candore, bilancetta, pendolo*, etc. Indeed, in his correspondence with Federico Cesi this preference is clearly stated. When the Accademia dei Lincei was about to publish his observations on sunspots, in spite of Cesi's liking for *Celispicio* or *Helioscopia*, the work was entitled, certainly as Galileo himself desired, *Istoria e dimostrazioni intorno alle macchie solari e loro accidenti*. The physical sciences still bear some traces of Galileo's preference for unpedantic terms, but exchanges with other countries led to the introduction, too, of many latinisms and grecisms. At the beginning of the century, for instance, Kepler had either formed or technified: *axis* (as an optical term), *convergere, divergere, meniscus, satelles, penumbra*.

Alongside the two names that Galileo gave to his main inventions, *cannone* and *occhiale*, there arose many others: *telescopio* was coined in 1611 by G. Demisiani, a member of the Accademia dei Lincei; another member of the same academy, G. Faber, coined *microscopio* in 1624. Other such terms that were coined or given a technical meaning in the Seicento were: *spettro* as an optical term (*spectrum*, Newton), *elettrico* (*electricus* is attributed to William Gilbert, the author of the *De Magnete*, 1600, though not documented until later), *elastico* (*vis elastica* is in Pecquet, *Dissertatio anatomica de circulatione sanguinis*, 1651), *logaritmo* (coined by J. Napier, *Mirifici Logarithmorum Canonis descriptio*, 1614), *trigonometria*, *dinamica* (a study established by Galileo, developed by Huygens and Newton, but given its name only at the end of the century by Leibniz), *pantografo* and *barometro* (the original idea for which was Viviani's, though it was worked out by Torricelli, and the name is Boyle's). Not infrequently, a popular term and a learned one for the same object existed side by side: *bilancetta*, which Galileo used, or *idrostammo*, which was preferred by members of the Accademia del Cimento; *specola* or *osservatorio*, etc. Redi published (under the name of G. Cosimo Bonomo) a book entitled *Osservazioni intorno a' pellicelli del corpo umano*; but in the next century the Greek *acari* came to be used. Although Redi used much of the medical terminology of his time, he more than once protested against its recondite terms 'con quelle Iere, con quelle benedette lassative, con que' Diacattoliconi, con quei Diafiniconi, Diatriontonpipereoni, ed altri *nomi da fare spiritare i cani*' (lett. 12 June 1688: I, p. 186, ed. 1779).

The written language accepted words from spoken usage only with caution and for particular genres. But mock-heroic poems were popular. And at Florence (though not so much elsewhere) a kind of literature drawing on popular catch-phrases and witticisms enjoyed a certain vogue (Buonarroti's *Fiera*, Lippi's *Malmantile*). Through these routes a number of popular words got into the *Vocabolario della Crusca*. By the very fact of being registered in it, such words (*ammazzasette*, *lestofante*) then had a stronger chance of being accepted first into the literary language and then into general usage. There were some protests from outside Tuscany when words from Tuscan speech were used by Tuscan authors. It is notable that when Magalotti used *sollo* (in his *Saggi di naturali esperienze*, p. 111) he added an explanation of its use. But he nevertheless defended his right to employ such words, saying it would profit a man little to have been born in Tuscany, and to have learnt Italy's most perfect language, if he then had to abstain from its beauties in order to be understood by those who spoke an inferior tongue.

Several of the differences that struck people between Florentine and Sienese were noted in Politi's *Dittionario*. But the designation 'Florentine' in it frequently refers, not to living Florentine, but to fourteenth-century Florentine as registered in the *Vocabolario della Crusca*. A better idea of genuine differences can be got from the list of divergences between spoken Florentine and Roman compiled by an anonymous author and preserved in the Biblioteca Angelica at Rome (published by I. Baldelli in *Lingua Nostra*, XIII, 1952), although this is only a brief collection of everyday words. The compiler is concerned mainly with phonetic variants: (F.) *camiciuola* — (R.) *camiciola*; *cuori* — *cori*; *lenzuola* — *lenzola*; *abate* — *abbate*; *gabella* — *gabbella*; *moscadello* — *moscatello*; *cucchiaio* — *cucchiaro*; *guantaio* — *guantaro*, etc.; but he also notes the use of different words: *beccaio* — *macellaro*; *burro* — *butirro*; *ciottoli* — *selci*; *galletto* — *pollastro*; *giubba* — *giustacore*; *grembiule* — *zinale*; *guanciale* — *cuscino*; *legnaiolo* — *fallegname*; *magnano* — *chiavaro*; *oriuolo* — *orologio*; *pesche* — *perziche*; *pesciaiuolo* — *pescivendolo*; *pezzuola* — *fazzoletto*; *pizzicagnolo* — *pizzicarolo*; *popone* — *melone*; *sarto* — *sartore*, etc. In some of the above cases the two variants still survive; but generally the Florentine forms, or, more rarely, the Roman forms have prevailed. Uncertainty in nomenclature sometimes led writers (even Tuscan ones) to note geographical synonyms: 'quel male che a Firenze si chiama Vaiuolo e a Roma dicesi Morviglioni', wrote Redi, *Consulti*, in *Opere*, VI, Firenze 1726, p. 6. And the remarks of some authors inform us of the regional provenance of certain words that have now been generally accepted. From Stigliani we learn that *alzarsi* used absolutely for 'to get up from bed' was a neapolitanism, while from the testimony of Redi (*Voci aretine*) and the usage of the *Malmantile* we know that at Florence *folla* still meant 'a host, a multitude', while at Arezzo and Rome it was already limited to 'a crowd of people'. Dialectal variants (albeit in an italianizing phonetic form rather than in a crudely vernacular one) were abundantly used in practical texts: at Bologna, for example, we have the *Statuti dell'Honoranda Compagnia de' Gargiolari* (Bolognese *garzulär* 'hemp-worker') of 1667, at Rome the *Statuti dell'antica e nobile arte de' Ferrari* of 1690, etc. In the letters of Vincenzo Gonzaga *césani* and *cigni* are used with indifference. Salvator Rosa used many dialectalisms in his letters and some, too, in his *Satire*, e.g. the pejorative *faldone* in a letter of 23 Feb. 1653 ('Comedie non ne ho voluto sentir nessuna, attesoché sono troppo *faldone* . . .', p. 105 Limentani) and *Satire* III, l. 236 ('talun che col pennel trascorse — a dipinger *faldoni* e guitterie'). Marino, too, was rather free in the use he made, not only in his letters, but also in his poems, of dialectal phonetic variants (*librazzo, poemazzo, scaramuzza, seguso, trutta* 'trout') and regional words (*alare* for 'anelare'; *letturino* for 'leggio', etc.). Yet the theoreticians who permitted the use of familiar words in 'humble style' (e.g. in satire) did not allow them in the epic and the lyric. In fact, the use of regional words not sanctioned by literary usage was slighter in the Seicento than in preceding centuries. But if writers generally sought to repress dialectalisms from the 'substratum' of their own native speech, there were some who had recourse to those of other regions to give colour to their expressions, as when Salvator Rosa used the Venetian *spegazzo* ('blot; scrawl'; letter of 1663, p. 130 Limentani). A certain number of dialectalisms gained wide diffusion when the customs, foods, natural phenomena, etc., of a particular area became more generally known. When the Florentine A. Neri described glass-blowing (*L'Arte vetraria*, Florence 1612) he used some Venetian terms (*pùliga* 'little bubble', *riàvolo* 'glass-maker's rake'), which is understandable in relation to Venice's importance in the history of the glass-making industry. Boccone (*Osservazioni naturali*, Bologna 1684, p. 368) talked of 'la *Sciara*, o quella massa ferruginea prodotta dalla materia ignivoma, che vomitò il Monte Etna'. Magalotti (*Lettere*, I, p. 9) mentioned the '*Zolfatara* di Pozzuoli'. As for the dictionaries, while the Crusca's preferred to record only good Florentine words, those compiled for practical purposes abounded in non-Tuscan terms: G. Vittori (Victor) in his *Tesoro de las tres lenguas* [French, Italian and Spanish], Geneva 1609, in translating French and Spanish items, used words like *fioppa* 'poplar', *làsina* 'armpit', *regabio* 'golden oriole', and other foreign compilers made similar use of regionalisms in polyglot dictionaries. Spadafora, in listing in his *Prosodia Italiana* those words in which placing the accent might prove difficult, made great use of dialectal items (*bonìgolo, cótica, grancévola, mammana, pirone, ràgano*, etc.), sometimes adding that the words concerned were 'Lombard', or noting the authors from which they were taken.

Among archaisms, we must distinguish between those exhumed from the Duecento and Trecento and those which, though they had long since dropped out of spoken usage, had remained an integral part of the language of poetry. While the poets did not scruple to use words from the latter class, few writers (and then in verse rather than in prose) dared to have recourse to really archaic words. Some did so, however, either from admiration for the period which the Crusca considered supreme (as when Dati, in *Dell' obbligo di ben parlare*, wrote 'le *diffalte* della plebe ignorante') or as a show of linguistic virtuosity, or when in need of a rhyme (like Marino, who in the *Adone* used *feruta, maternale, visaggio* and also, through remembering wrongly, *ammiraglio* in the sense of 'mirror', VIII, st. 29). But when Fioretti in his dithyramb *Polifemo briaco* used words like *approccia, allegranza, faraggio* (and drew attention to the fact in the 'Documento' illustrating the *Polifemo, Proginn.*, III), he did so mainly because of their strangeness. Lepòreo, although professing in a sonnet that he sought 'parole nuove', really made use of revived archaisms:

> Vo a caccia, e in traccia di parole, e pescole,
> dal Rio del Cupo Oblio le purgo, e inciscole
>
> . . . .
>
> da ferrugine e rugine rinfrescole
> e da la muffa, e ruffa antica spriscole . . .

But most writers were against archaisms: Tassoni (*Pensieri diversi*, IX, qu. 15) declared that they should very rarely be used, and in the *Secchia rapita* (X, st. 7) he mocked the Count of Culagna who praised his lady thus:

> — O, diceva, bellor dell'universo
> ben meritata ho vostra beninanza.

Even supporters of the Crusca regarded many Boccaccian words as dead: O. Rucellai remarked (*Lettere*, pp. 5-6 Moreni) that in his own philosophical writings one would not find many Tuscan 'affectations in the manner of Boccaccio' 'nè *chente*, nè *neghienza*, nè *tracotanza* o somiglianti'. In fact, not many archaisms came to life again; but a few did (*malore, tracotanza, trapelare* being examples).

New formations were very numerous in this century, although those that took root in the language were much less so. There were some onomatopoeic words, like *cicisbeo*. Others changed semantic category, like the adjective *pendolo*, which Galileo turned into a noun. Immediate formation (without addition of suffix) gave some new nouns (*il gonfia, una deroga*), adjectives (*concia frangipana, tela sangalla*) and verbs (*romanzare, velocitare, accipitrare, cespugliare, mongibellare*: Tesauro). The formation of feminines was extended to new nouns, including animals (*augella, corsiera*: Marino) and things (*vocessa*, pejor., Tassoni). Great use was made of suffixes, which provided a way of transforming words without breaking with tradition: Redi's *scrupolettucciaccio* can serve as an example. In the creation of new nouns by addition of suffix there were many examples denoting agent (*missionante, fuciliere*, etc.), including many formations in *-ista* (*Ariostista*, Fioretti; *bombista, caffeista*, Redi; *casista; fattista*, De Luca; *odorista*, Megalotti; *quietista* and innumerable others). Among abstracts there were several in *-ismo* (*eroismo, nepotismo, quietismo*, etc.), in *-aggine* (*sanesaggine*, Bargagli) and in *-eria* (*franceseria; romanzeria*, Tassoni). In the adjectival field, alongside many formations of an intellectual character (*calamitico*, Galileo; *geografico*, Galileo, *algebraico*; *cicloide* — noun and adj. etc.) there were many of an affective kind (*moscareccio*, Lalli, *metaforuto*, whose creation was attributed by Stigliani to Marino, etc.). Among the prefixes, the taste for hyperbole caused an abundance of *arci-* (*arcasino*, Vannozzi; *arcimusa*, ironic, Stigliani; *arcinasarca* 'king of all noses' Marino; *arcifreddissimo, arcilunghissimo*, Redi) and of *oltra-* and *sovra-* (Stigliani criticized Marino's use of *oltrabello, oltramortale, sovramortale*). There was an abundance, too, of *anti-* (A. Guarini, *Anticupido*, Ferrara 1610; P. Beni, *Anticrusca*, Padua 1612) and *vice* (*Vicefebo*; the pope was called *Vicedio* in Testi's canzone to Innocent X, while Bartoli applied *Vicedio* to Moses). Also numerous were negative formations with *dis-* and *in-* (*disartifizio*, Fioretti; *disamabile*, Chiabrera; *disappassionato*, Redi; *impassibile, inconspicuo, indispensabile, infrangibile*, the last used by Galileo in his *Massimi sistemi* and felt to be new). Among the new verbs formed by addition of suffixes there were some in *-izzare* (*concettizzare, famigliarizzarsi, fraternizzare*) and innumerable others in *-eggiare*, some formed because terminologically opportune, like *anticheggiare*, Fioretti; *fraseggiare*, Menzini; *ritmeggiare*, G. B. Doni; but many others merely occasional formations, like *ametisteggiare, augelleggiare, asineggiare, colombeggiare, cristalleggiare, edereggiare*, etc., used for such meanings as 'to be the colour of the amethyst', 'to kiss one another like doves', etc., and of them, as L. Mattei noted in his *Teorica del verso*, p. 102, there was an endless supply. They suited the taste of a century that so loved changing appearances, but their chances of survival were slight. Parasynthetic formations were also numerous: some nominal (*correligionario*, Magalotti), many verbal (*disanellare, discifrare, disviscerare* . . .; *immedesimare*,

imporporare, inarenare, inartigliare, infielare, ingarzonire, instellare ...;
sfilosofarsi, sgemmare ...). In the creation of compounds learned
methods were in greater favour than popular ones. There were
some compounds formed from imperatives, like *scalzacane, scalza-
gatto, sputaincroce* 'atheist', *facibene, facimale, facidanno.* Chiabrera,
in his dialogue *Il Bamberini,* judged this procedure to be 'senza
leggiadria' and quoted as an example 'il reo *tagliaborse*'; but he
nonetheless used *cacciaffanni* and *spezzantenne* in his dithyramb.
Juxtaposition of two nouns was often used for concise effect:
pesciuomo (Stigliani), *donnadragone* (Tesauro) and, even more
contrived, *asinibbio* (=*asino*+*nibbio*, Peresio). Much ingenuity
went into the creation of compounds in dithyrambic poetry,
Aristotle having said that compound nouns were suitable for
dithyrambs. Chiabrera claimed in his autobiography that he
introduced into Italian dithyrambic poetry the use of compounds
like *oricrinita fenice, crocaddobbata aurora.* His 'Ditirambo all'uso dei
Greci' was probably written before Fioretti's *Polifemo briaco*
(1627). Poems in this genre by F. M. Gualterotti, C. Marucelli
(1628) and N. Villani (1634) were certainly overloaded with
compounds. Redi in his (1673, finished in 1685) was more
moderate and enjoyed greater success. The types of compounds
used in these dithyrambs displayed great variety. There were
nouns which were formed from verbs ('Bacco *cacciaffanni*', Chiabrera; una *struggicuori*, Gualterotti), others in which the first
element was co-ordinate with the second (*liricetra*, Gualterotti) or
governed by the second (*ventipreda*, Gualterotti). There were
verbs that were copulative (*cantipiange* 'canta e piange', Gualterotti) or formed with a complement, which could be direct
(*sonniprendere*, Gualterotti) or refer to the verb in a vaguer way
('*infernifoca* il mio core', Redi). But most dithyrambic compounds
were composed of adjectives: pairs of co-ordinate adjectives
(*lietofestoso, leggiadribelluccia*, Redi); pairs with reduction of
suffix (*musimagico* 'musico+magico', Gualterotti; *homicavallico*,
Marucelli); compounds in which the first element had adverbial
force as in the Latin *altitonans* type (*dolcipungente*, Gualterotti), etc.
This forced stretching of the language's ability to form compounds often led to monstrous results, and it must be considered
as a brief stylistic caprice of dithyrambic (and to a lesser extent
mock-heroic) poets, rather than a process that led to a lasting
enrichment in vocabulary. But there was a growing need for
compounds in philosophical, legal and scientific terminology, and
here words took root in cases where there was permanent need.

We shall note here some of the Latin elements that could be used to form compounds and which were adopted now to form new words in Italian. Among the nouns formed with *-cida* some (*coricida*, Fioretti; *fioricida*, Marucelli; *amanticida*, Neri) were destined to disappear, while *ussoricida* (Allegri) remained because of its connection with a legal concept. *Moschicida*, coined as a joke by Lalli, returned to service when fly-papers came on to the market. Similar observations could be made on words coined during the century having a Latin first element: the many with *semi-* (ecclesiastical terms like *semidigiuno*, *semiluterano*, *semipela-giano*, 'concistoro *semipubblico*'; or jocose words like *semidottore*, Tesauro, *semifilosofo*, Buonarroti, *semigigante*, Mascardi, *semilibro*, Galileo, etc.), those we have already quoted with *vice-*, those with *onni-* (*onnivoro*, Oudin; *onnifecondo*, Bellini) and with *uni-* (*unisillabo* or *unisillabico*, Fioretti), etc. As is well known, in Latin the forming of compounds in this way was limited to few series; Greek, on the other hand, had unlimited possibilities. And for coining scientific terminology recourse was often had to Greek — for names of sciences, names of instruments and titles of books: first of all in Latin (*ornithologia*, Aldrovandi, 1599; *giologia* 'geology', Aldro-vandi, 1603; *phytoiatria*, in the *Tabulae phytosophicae* of the Accademia dei Lincei; *kosmologia*, O. Boldoni, 1641; *telescopium*, *thermometrum*, etc.) then in Italian as well (examples being Men-zini's *Etopedia* and V. Nolfi's *Ginipedia ovvero avvertimenti civili per donna nobile*, Bologna 1662. Long, learned words coined at this period having *proto-* or *pseudo-* are very numerous. But more important was the establishment in Italian of compounds like *toscano-romano*, *melico-comico*, *heroico-satirico*, *cefalo-faringeo*, in which the copulative vowel, which is *o*, following the example of Greek compounds, usually remained invariable in flection, e.g. C. C. Scaletti's *Scuola mecanico-speculativo-pratica*, Bologna, 1611, *Ragiona-menti Tedesco-Italiani secondo la favella Toscano-Romana*, Nuremberg 1679. To consider the two adjectives to be merely juxtaposed, although joined by a hyphen (as in G. Torriano's *Della Lingua Toscana-Romana*, Londra, 1657, and the *Dimostratione Historica-Astronomica* in Tesauro's *La Vergine Trionfante*, p. 97) was less frequent. There were also examples of compounds (and not only humorous ones) with the copulative vowel *-i-* (*amante stoltisavio*, Stigliani; *traduzione prosipoetica*, Fioretti). Adjectives in *-e* were only juxtaposed (*favola morale-politica*, 1617).

Italian continued to receive contributions from Latin (and, to a lesser extent, Greek). Men of letters and men of science now

turned for new terms not only to classical, Christian and scholastic
Latin, but also to the Latin created by the sciences. Latinisms
were particularly numerous in those disciplines which had
previously been treated in Latin only, like law. But while there
was no impediment to the borrowing of technical terms for particular disciplines, there was a certain resistance to the use of
latinisms for more general purposes, and some writers showed a
tendency to excuse, as they introduced, them: Buonarotti, in the
proem to the *Aione*, wrote of the 'ore che un buon pedante
chiamerebbe *sussecive*'. *Intransitivo* was still new when Sègneri
used it in his *Manna dell'anima*: 'in senso, come dicono, *intransitivo*'.
Stigliani criticized Marino for having in noble style used Latin
words with too technical a flavour, e.g. *biblioteca, cute, disco*.
Specialists addressing non-specialists occasionally found it necessary, too, to explain their terms. Redi wrote of a young girl 'dotata
di un abito di corpo carnoso, e che da' Medici con vocabolo
greco vien chiamato *pletorico*' (*Consulti*, I, p. 6). The importance of
the Latin contribution to Italian scientific vocabulary in this
century can be gauged from this brief list of examples (though we
must bear in mind that earlier instances may be found of some of
them):

anfratto, antenna, antictoni, apogeo, bubbone, bulbo ('root of hair'),
caruncula, cellula, coerente, condensare, conoide, crostaceo (*crustaceo*,
Redi), *cuticola, deferente* (anat.), *digressione* (astron.), *estrudere*,
fecola, ignicolo, iniezione, iperbole (math.), *molecola* (from the philosophy of Gassendi), *obbiettivo* (opt.), *oculare* (opt.), *ovidutto, papilla*,
patologia, placenta (anat.; from *placenta uterina*), *pleura, pleuritide*,
podice, precessione, prisma (crystall.), *proietto, pube, rarefazione*,
scheletro, scroto, sfacelo ('gangrene'), *stratificare, vortice*, etc.

There were, too, numerous other latinisms which were used by
individual scientists who intended to make technical terms of
them, but to which other words were eventually preferred. Such
were *distrarre* in the sense of 'to dilate' and its derivative *distraibile*,
eiaculazione as an electrical term, *labefattare* ('labefattata la virtù
concottrice del medesimo stomaco' wrote Redi without irony,
Consulti I, p. 194), *lazione, stertore*, etc. Legal terms which now
came into Italian also provided a notable list of latinisms:
*aggressione, agnazione, censire, condominio, consulente, dirimere, gras-
satore, patrocinio, premorienza, prescindere, subornare, società* (commercial 'company'), *tergiversare, usucapione*, etc. Innumerable other
latinisms were brought into Italian by other disciplines:
acrostico, allidere, analfabeto, ascitizio, assurdità, convellere, cospicuo,

cromatica (mus.), *elaborare*, *elogio*, *emanazione* (theol.), *incongruo*, *incongruenza*, *incutere*, *indagare*, *indagine*, *letale*, *monotono*, *-ia*, *notula*, *onomastico*, *oriundo*, *panegirico*, *parodia*, *posticipare*, *sintassi*, *sintesi* (gramm.), *taumaturgo*, *tesi*, etc.

A host of others failed to take root: *anile*, *esardere*, *esoleto*, *espiscare*, *ferrugine*, *sinoride* are a few examples. Some latinisms which had been only sporadically used in previous centuries, now became widely used: such were *atomo*, *entusiasmo*, *escandescenza*, etc. Since borrowing latinisms was a phenomenon common to all cultured parts of Europe, it frequently happened (as also in later centuries) that latinisms came in, not directly from Latin, but from some modern language which had already taken over the word. Such words can sometimes be distinguished because we have direct testimony concerning their immediate provenance. In other cases they can be picked out because of some peculiarity in form or meaning. Stigliani (*Arte del verso*, p. 162) tells us that *assonante* (referring to rhyme) was taken from Spanish ('chiamasi da gli Spagnuoli Rima assonante, cioè di suono non medesimo ma vicino'). That another latinism, *pòcolo*, came through Spanish can be seen from the meaning ('a drink' rather than 'a cup'). The numerous scientific latinisms (and grecisms) coined in the civilized countries of Europe circulated freely: Galileo would not have spoken of *selinografia* had not Bacon already used the term (in the form *selenographia*). The form of several existing Italian words (particulary related to the sciences) was affected by Latin words: *anatomia* gained ground at the expense of *notomia* (helped by the fact that the adjective was *anatomico*), *chirurgo* ousted *cerusico* and *cirugico*, *clistere* pushed out *cristeo* and *cristero*, *emorroidi* overcame *moroide* and *morice*, etc. The form *proprio*, closer to the Latin than *propio*, was now used by most writers. Non-Tuscans tended to prefer latinizing forms: Marino, for instance, wrote *ebeno* and *Africa*; Romans preferred *orologio* to *oriuolo*, etc. It was generally the Latin forms of grecisms that were adapted to Italian; there were a few exceptions, however, in the more learned authors ('qualche ἀνέκδοτα di Prisciano': [Villani], *Considerazioni di Messer Fagiano*, p. 257; 'questa figura da' Greci è chiamata παρῳδία': Redi, *Annotazioni al Ditirambo*, p. 53).

It is not surprising that in a period of political subjugation a large number of foreign words entered Italian vocabulary. In the first part of the century, these were mostly hispanisms. They included terms connected with social life (*brio*, *etichetta*), fashion (*guardinfante*, introduced at Naples in 1631 and celebrated in

F. Frugoni's poem *La Guardinfanteide*, Perugia 1643, *marsina*, *pastrana*, *ciamberga*, *mantiglia*, *pistagna*, etc.), domestic objects (*posata* in the sense of 'cover' 'place at table', *bucchero*, *scarabattolo*, *baule*, etc.) and foods (*ogliapodrida*, *cioccolato*, *pastiglie*). The word *baccalà*, first used only in translations from Spanish, became widely known. *Scorzonera* (which looks at first sight like an Italian compound) came from the Spanish *escorzonera*, Catal. *escurçonera*, for the root of that plant was considered to be an antidote against poisonous animals. There were numerous hispanisms, too, connected with military life, like *recluta* (which Spadafora considered a paroxytone) and *borgognotta*. To the turning of horses in peace and war were applied the words *caracollo* (Sp. *caracol* 'snail, spiral staircase'), *caracollare* (*caracolear*). Naval terms included *nostromo* (Sp. *nuestramo*) and *risacca*. Games and pastimes gave *pilotta* or *pillotta* (Sp. *pelota*), *ciaccona* and *sarabanda*, as well as the game of *ombre* (Sp. *hombre*, a card-game). *Lazzarone* became established at Naples at the time of Masaniello's rising (1647) and soon became known in the rest of Italy; but *guappo* did not enjoy the same wide diffusion. Even some general terms, like *floscio*, gained a place in the language. On the other hand, many of the hispanisms of the period died out. Some denoted objects or customs that disappeared, e.g. *candiero* (a drink made of eggs, milk and sugar, Sp. *candiel*); others were words which had been used to make an impression or to amuse, like *amariglio* 'yellow' (Marino) or *corazzone* 'heart' ('Forato avea già il petto e 'l *corazzone*': Lalli, *Eneide trav.*, IV, st. 2); and there were in this category, too, some bureaucratic terms, such as *stimar preciso*, used in Milanese edicts for 'to consider necessary'. There were, too, words which referred to Spanish persons or affairs: for a long time the typical rascally beggar made famous by Mateo Alemán in his *Vida del pícaro Guzmán de Alfarache* (Ital. tr. by B. Barezzi, 1615) was known very widely — and with him the words *piccaro*, *piccaresco*, *piccariglio*. Many hispanisms penetrated the Lombard dialect and even more entered Neapolitan. Some of these survived dialectally, e.g. *ammuinare*, used by writers who wrote in Italian in the seventeenth century, and still alive in Neapolitan. The comparative adjective *masgalano*, substantivized in phrases like *combattere il masgalano*, *portare il masgalano*, etc., is still used for one of the prizes in the Sienese palio. Some German or Flemish words, too, must have entered Italy through Spanish, e.g. *bellicone*, 'a kind of glass' through the Spanish *velicomen*. And via Spanish, or, much more rarely, Portuguese, there continued to arrive a few words originally American (*chinachina, sassafrasso*, etc.) or Oriental (*mandarino*). When we examine the gallicisms of the time, we find some cases in which French and Spanish influences converged: the abstract meaning of *carriera* and the noun *bompresso* (Fr. *beaupré*, Catal. *bauprès*, Span. *bauprés*) were due to the combined pressure of those languages. *Viglietto*, which appeared alongside *biglietto* in the Seicento, was presumably due to Spanish pronunciation of the word. *Caserma* came from France halfway through the century; at Milan there existed in parallel the Italian *case herme* and the Spanish *casas yermas*, the French *caserne* having been connected with the adjective *ermo* (*yermo*). French influence, which had been slight at the beginning of the century, became predominant in the time of Louis XIV, while that of Spain declined rapidly. Some words which had previously been used only with reference to French things now became part of common usage, e.g. *lacchè, gabinetto*. In the social sphere we should record French semantic influence on *obbligante* and *suscettibile* and on the use of *libertino* and *libertinaggio* in the sense of 'freedom of thought'. In the world of fashion French contributed *moda* itself, as well as *chincaglie, coccarda, galloni, lingeria, giusta-cuore* and adjectives of colour like *dorè, gridelino* (*gridelin, gris de lin*), *ponsò*. The use of wigs came into Italy from France, changing the meaning of the word *parrucca* which in Italy in previous centuries had meant one's natural hair, but which, adopted in French, had come to mean 'wig'. Among the furniture of the time appeared *buffetto* and the *canapè*. In the cities they used *barriere*. Gallicisms in the sphere of transport were *convoio* (*convoglio*), *treno, equipaggio* (which had already entered in its naval sense during the preceding century); and, along with the objects concerned, there appeared the words *calesse* and *sedia rullante* or *rollante*. Military terms from French were *plotone, reggimento, distaccamento, blocco, bivacco, tappa, ramparo* (which Redi objected to, and which eventually died out), *decampare, bandoliera*. Units of *gendarmi* were established in Piedmont in 1676. *Piattaforma* came in as both a military and naval term; another naval term was *brulotto*. The name *parrocchetto* also penetrated, both in the sense of 'parakeet' and that of 'mizzen topsail'. In dances the *burè* enjoyed a vogue; in games *gettoni* began to be used. There were also numerous general items: *azzardo, contraccolpo, dettaglio* (Magalotti), *rango, rimarchevole, salvaguardia*. And if there were some who made objections to such words, latinisms modelled on French won their places more easily (*agire, installare, progettare*), as did figurative expressions like *fare il diavolo a quattro* (Redi), *valer la pena* (Magalotti), *mettere sul tappeto*, and phrases like *a meno che* and *presso a poco*.

Borrowers from French still preferred on the whole to adapt their borrowings to the Italian phonetic system, but some began to use French words without such adaptation: while Marino changed *parterre* to *perterra* ('vaghi perterra di grottesche erbose': *Adone*, XI, st. 21) and Neri (*Presa di Saminiato*, V, st. 8) spoke of *fare il rendevosse*, Magalotti wrote *parterre*, *rendez-vous*, *resource*, *calzoni aux bas roulés*, *pigliar le contre-pied*, *guardare de haut en bas*, etc. Many of the gallicisms that came in at this time were later eliminated: *alea* in the sense of 'avenue' (Marino), *allianza* for 'marriage' (Marino), *buona mina* (Magalotti), etc. Piedmont was more receptive to French than other regions: there the bureaucratic term *intendente* was used. Words that came into Italian from other countries were far less numerous than those from France and Spain. Such were *patrona* and *provianda* (Montecuccoli) from Germany, *renna* from Scandinavia, *musulmano* from Persia (previously *musliman*, 1623, in Pietro della Valle), etc. At this time, too, Italians came to know various oriental products (*cacciù*, *capòc*, *ginsèng*) and to know of some customs belonging to the same region (*palanchino*).

Abroad the prestige enjoyed by Italy at the height of the Renaissance had now diminished, but there was still admiration for her art, and her music grew in influence. Among the Italian words borrowed by other languages therefore there were many terms connected with art, such as *attitude* (Fr. 1653; Eng; 1668), *coupole* (Fr. 1666; English already had *cupola* from 1549), *filigrane* (Fr. 1673; Eng. 1668; Germ. 1688); *fresque* (Fr. 1669; Eng. already had *fresco* from 1548; Germ. *a fresco malen*, 1697), etc. In the theatre the most notable example was *opera* (which in France was introduced by Cardinal Mazarin about 1646; Eng. 1644; Germ. 1680); others were *comparse* and *virtuose* in French, *virtuoso* in English. German and Swedish now got *violin*, which had entered English during the preceding century, while English musical terminology accepted *adagio*, *grave*, *largo* (Purcell, 1683). An example of the names of characters from the *commedia dell'arte* which won popularity abroad was *Pulcinella* (Fr. *Polichinel*, then *Polichinelle*; English *Polichinello* and *Punchinello*, whence the abbreviation *Punch*). Molière's *Scapin*, too, was descended from *Scappino* (derived from *scappare*). Among the foods that emigrated *sedani* did so in Roman dress — *sèlleri* (Fr. *céleri*, 1680; Eng. *celery*, Germ. *Sellerie*). English also got *vermicelli* in 1669 and French *vermicelle* in 1675. These are only a few examples, of course, of the words that entered other languages. Indeed, a great deal of research remains to be done in this direction. It is notable, for example, that countries relatively far from Italy, like Sweden, received in the seventeenth century words which nations nearer to Italy had got previously: *violin, bandit, altan, gondol, lasarett, bastant.* And clearly there is much work still to do in tracing italianisms further afield.

10

The Settecento

When Croce treated the Settecento as a cultural unit he defined it as the period that extended roughly from the last quarter of the seventeenth century to the end of the third quarter of the eighteenth. A significant date, which we can regard as beginning the period for our purposes, is that of the foundation of Arcadia (1690). The outstanding dates at the end are those of the suppression of the Crusca by decree of Pietro Leopoldo (1783) and, of capital importance, the French invasion (1796). The period is divided by the Treaty of Aix-la-Chapelle (1748); the effort to build a sounder national life can be said to begin approximately at that time.

In the first half of the century Italy was involved in numerous wars, but from the Treaty of Aix-la-Chapelle until the French invasion there was a long period of comparative tranquillity. The territory of the House of Savoy was extended as far as the Ticino. The annexation of Sardinia (1718) was linguistically important; after it, the island's administrative and cultural life slowly moved from use of Spanish to use of Italian. This century saw the end of the Gonzaga, Farnese, Medici, Cybo and Este dynasties. The duchies of Milan and Mantua fell into Austrian hands, though the Valtelline still belonged to the Grisons. At Parma (1731) and Naples (1734) two Bourbon dynasties were installed. In Tuscany Francis, Duke of Lorraine, became Grand Duke, but the French linguistic influence of his courtiers was of brief duration, for Tuscany developed an Austrian political bias, due to Francis's marriage to the Hapsburg Maria Theresa. While Lombardy, Tuscany and Naples took to reform with varying degrees of readiness, the non-dynastic old states (the Papal States, Genoa, Lucca, Venice) either could not or would not. Genoa, impotent to deal with yet another insurrection in Corsica, dangerous this time because it was led by the energetic Pasquale Paoli, ceded the

island to France. But it is possible that the Corsicans would not
have turned their backs on the Italian language and culture
which had been theirs hitherto, had not Corsica been the birthplace of the man who was destined to change the face of Europe
in the name of France. A great part of Istria, parts of Dalmatia
and Albania and the Ionian islands were still held by the Venetian
Republic. At sea, England, now a mediterranean power, made
her influence felt. The American War of Independence (1774-
1781) had an important influence on Italian thinking, and the
French Revolution an even greater one. But the really shattering
political event was Napoleon's Italian campaign (1796).

The cosmopolitanism of which so many boasted was a recognition that Italy had lost the cultural primacy of Europe and
had to make an effort to catch up, making use, in order to do so,
of ideas and customs from abroad, particularly from France.
But this current directly affected only cultured persons, and then
in anything but a uniform manner: the lower strata of society
got from it only what seeped through from above. Comparison
with England and France brought home to Italians their lack of
of cohesion, and made them feel the want of a capital city.
Divisions between states hindered the circulation of both persons
and ideas. If Alfieri wished to *spiemontizzarsi*, that is, to be
italianized, there is in the Piedmontese comedy *Il conte Pioletto*, as
Croce pointed out, a strong sense of the differences between the
Piedmontese and the inhabitants of other parts of the peninsula:
'Alla larga! D' volte *sti italian* a pôrto d' stilet. . . .' Rationalism in
various forms (Cartesianism, the Enlightenment, Sensationalism)
prevailed in the thought of the time, not only among original
thinkers. The experimental method triumphed over the remaining
peripateticians, and the predominant view of the world was
naturalistic and rationalistic. Reason, Nature and Mankind were
enthroned. The distinction between *ragione* and *sentimento* was
elaborated, and passed into everyday thought and speech. Some
groups, among which that associated with the periodical *Il Caffè*
deserves special mention, sought to promote a culture based on
'things' rather than 'words' and opposed to abuses and prejudices.
Philanthropists conceived of social improvement as being mainly
greater material well-being. Catholicism was attacked from
various directions: by rationalists, Jansenists and jurisdictionalists.
The pope had to consent to the suppression of the Jesuit order.
Freemasonry came to Italy; at first its aims were mainly humanitarian, as in England, but later it developed Jacobin intentions

and pro-French activities. Some rulers lent an ear to some of the demands for reform made by the writers of the Enlightenment: antiquated institutions were abolished, and there was notable progress, particulary in Lombardy and Tuscany. While the nobles were for the most part reluctant and the lowest strata of society passive, the bourgeoisie was in the ascendant. There was a marked return to the land, with numerous land reclamation schemes (Val di Chiana, etc.) and improvements in farming. Local academies continued to enjoy influence in cultural life, but alongside them there now arose the 'colonies' of Arcadia, which first fulfilled the function of a national academy and which propagated a certain kind of stylistic teaching and a polite literary hedonism. In the second half of the century there was an increase in the number of academies that aimed at social usefulness by promoting economic, agrarian and other studies (like the Georgo-fili of Florence 1753, and the Società dei Pugni, Milan 1761). Conversazioni in the salons of the nobility provided a lively feature of social life. There were numerous works of vulgarization, some in dialogue form. And *giornali* and *gazzette* grew increasingly important: Venice produced the first daily, the *Gazzetta di Venezia*. The vogue enjoyed by *raccolte* (collections published on the occasion of marriage, taking of the veil, etc.) made the writing of poetry a sort of social obligation, while the popularity of improvizers made verse a social pastime. In the musical sphere the *melodramma* played a great role: Metastasio provided an example of simple, clear language for it. Commerce developed so rapidly that Baretti considered it 'the disease of the century'. Coal began to be used; industry was on the threshold of mechanization. The natural and experimental sciences were cultivated, sometimes with notable results (Galvani, Volta). Italian scientists were in close contact with those of other countries, a fact that had con-siderable repercussions on scientific nomenclature, which became very similar in all civilized countries. There was not yet the separation between scientists and men of letters that specializa-tion was later to impose: Manfredi and Mascheroni, for instance, were poets as well as scientists. Medicine introduced new pro-cedures, like inoculation and vaccination. Early aeronautical experiments aroused great interest. Many foreigners travelled in Italy, and many Italians made sojourns abroad. To curiosity about French and English matters (which in some cases became francomania or anglomania) was added curiosity about exotic countries (China, etc.).

Outside Tuscany, Italian was little spoken, because of the predominance of dialects, and badly spoken, on account of the speakers' dependence on a written usage that itself betrayed much uncertainty. Baretti (*Scelta delle Lettere familiari*, Part II, 26, pp. 332-8, Piccioni) wrote that in his time every part of Italy had its own dialect and that this was used daily by all the inhabitants, whatever their social rank. Those who wished to rise above it tuscanized as best they could. And since they had not mastered the language of the great writers, they spoke a tongue that was a curious and arbitrary mixture. Moreover, those who attempted to speak Tuscan in other parts of Italy than Tuscany were considered affected and mocked. Baretti also severely criticized the speech of Tuscans themselves, considering it such that a nation of eunuchs, if such existed, should be ashamed of it; but his judgement on this 'linguerella' (p. 338) is evidently based on literary and stylistic criteria, not linguistic ones. From other sources we have less evidence than we should like. Parini, in his 'Appunto per il Vespro e per la Notte', noted that to strangers Milanese ladies spoke in Milanese, while the husband of one of them still spoke with 'the pronunciation of the mountains whence he had descended' (*Poesie*, Bellorini, I, pp. 269, 271). Salvini complained of the pronunciation of *bene* and *tempo* with close *e* in Tuscany and deplored the substitution of *magnare* for *mangiare* (note to the *Tancia*, I, sc. 4). He also regretted the fact that *fazzoletto*, *uffiziolo* and *saccoccia* were tending to supplant *pezzuola*, *libriccino della Madonna* and *tasca* (note to the *Fiera*, III, IV, sc. ii). Father Onofrio Branda, however, paid handsome tribute to Tuscan pronunciation, with its sweetness and grace even in the mouths of the humble, in his *Della lingua toscana* (Milan 1759, p. 6), a work that provoked polemical replies. At Pisa Algarotti noted expressions from spoken Tuscan that seemed to him 'alive and genuine': *cima* (of a cabbage), *cesto d'insalata*, *raspìo*, *tramenìo*, *schioppettìo*, etc. (letter to A. Nicolini, Jan. 1763). And as is well known, Alfieri was a great admirer of spoken Florentine and Sienese, which he cultivated assiduously. But many of the judgements delivered in this period on the spoken language of Tuscany were connected with views on its use in the literary sphere, and are to be assessed in conjunction with attitudes to fourteenth-century Florentine and the Crusca. In northern and southern Italy, dialect was generally spoken in both town and country, and in all social strata. Only exceptionally (in the presence of strangers, for example) was the language of conversation Italian (tinged with dialect). On solemn occasions (orations, sermons, addresses) Italian in its written forms predominated. (The first University lectures given regularly in Italian, those of Genovesi at Naples in 1764, were read.) But even here there were notable exceptions: in the Venetian courts speeches by counsel were in an ennobled Venetian, halfway between their dialect and the Italian language. Examples can be seen in M. Barbaro's *Tre azioni criminali a difesa* (Venice 1786): '*Correo, Compartecipe, Provocator*; ste parole che per parte del Fisco contesta principalmente el ponto in question, ste parole che ha formà el soggetto della disputa dell'Eccell. Sior Avogador le me permetta, che le analizemo, che cerchemo cossa che le significa. . . .' (pp. 41-2). Preachers, too, when they wished to be understood by their audiences, had to seek a compromise between language and dialect.

In practice and in theory a clear distinction was made between writing in prose and writing in verse: certain grammatical, lexical and stylistic features were considered appropriate to one or the other, but not to both. This distinction was considered one of the merits of Italian, which was contrasted in this respect with French; Parini, for instance, thought that its possession of a poetic language distinguished it from other modern languages and placed it on a par with Latin and Greek (*Corso di belle lettere*, II, vi, in *Prose*, I, p. 299 Bellorini).

The early decades of the century were dominated by Arcadia. This had important effects because its principles (reaction against *secentismo* and its abuse of metaphor, return to the canon of imitation of the classics and of Petrarch, the cult of formal perfection) spread all over Italy, and because it introduced poetry into social life. If it did not produce masterpieces, it at least achieved a certain regularization, a reduction of separatist tendencies. The *canzonetta* flourished. A light composition, it proved capable, when aided by music, of becoming truly popular. Ennobled by more serious poets, it developed into an ode, in which lines ending in proparoxytones favoured latinisms. After the resounding rhythms of Frugoni and his followers, poetry tended to become more and more neo-classical, decorous and rich in allusions to the Graeco-Roman world (Savioli, Parini, Monti). When the reactions against Arcadia broke, part of its poetic armament, too, was discredited, e.g. certain recurrent platitudes (particularly of a mythological kind) like *il biondo Apollo, le caste suore* (='the Muses'), the abuse of languid diminutives (*erbetta, agnelletta, pastorella, pecorelle*) and *pastorellerie* (to use Baretti's words) in

general. Descriptive and didactic versifiers oscillated between a
certain realism and a taste for periphrasis. In the political lyric
realistic touches were tempered by classical disguises. In it foreign
names appeared, sometimes with Italian endings added, but
usually in their original form, e.g. *Rodney, Cowper* (Fantoni).
Translations were linguistically important, particularly those
from modern foreign languages; Cesarotti observed that in
translating Ossian he had to break new ground, for he was writing
in a language which, though fertile, was 'made sterile by grammatical tyranny'. The theatrical language of Maffei (*Merope,*
1714) presented a sustained poetic vocabulary that was yet simple.
This simplification in its most extreme form was seen in the
melodrammi of Metastasio: his poetic vocabulary was the traditional one, but, in order to appeal to a larger public, he avoided
its rare and archaic words. When he wrote, the words were still
important and had not yet become mere support for the music.
Metastasio's *melodrammi* enjoyed immense popularity for a long
period. Snatches of his stanzas remain in common use to this day,
e.g.

> *Passò quel tempo, Enea,*
> *che Dido a te pensò* (Didone abbandonata, II, 4).

At the opposite pole from the harmonious and sometimes vacuous
language of Metastasio is that of Alfieri's tragedies, dense, harsh
and with a character of its own.

In prose we note that in this century works inspired by formal
beauty were less important than those (historical, economic,
political, juridical) books which aimed at social usefulness. The
authors of these, too, were called *letterati.* Their activities were
carried on all over Italy, but particularly in northern Italy and
in Naples. The vacuous scintillation of seventeenth-century prose
was abandoned, but some writers (including many Neapolitans,
Vico among them) looked for models to the Trecento, while some
(like Muratori) looked to the Cinquecento. Baretti, always whimsi-
cal in his choice of word and his coinages, kept something of the
flavour of his youthful exercises in the manner of Berni. As the century advanced, French influence made itself universally felt; even
those who sought to resist gallicisms in vocabulary took to shorter
periods and more direct construction. At the end of the century
preromantic colours predominated. Historiography became a
vehicle for learning rather than rhetoric: Muratori is a worthy
example. Works of antiquarian interest (and works of erudition

generally) abounded. Legal language was usually barbarous, bristling with latinisms, technical terms and complicated subordination of clauses. Here is an example from Naples (1717): 'fare la causa pro ut de jure con processo e recognitione del carattere di detto biglietto, usque ad sententiam diffinitivam inclusive, precedenti le trine pubbliche citazioni ad comparendum' (*Critica*, XXXV, p. 472). Since Italian legal language was used for legislation in politically separate states, it displayed notable variety in terminology. Economics constituted a new field of activity; writers on this subject made an appreciable effort to leave traditional language, with its complex periods and generic vocabulary, behind them, and aimed at plain, concrete and precise means of communication. Adherence to the concrete also usually characterized the writings of those who wrote on scientific and technical subjects. Naturalists sought simplicity and intelligibility, leaving aside 'pompose descrizioni e le frasi ricercate e turgide' (G. Santi, *Viaggio per le due provincie senesi*, Pisa 1798, pp. 4-5). But scientific language did not yet have the conciseness it later achieved, nor was it so separate from literary language as to deny itself certain elegant features. Vallisnieri, Cocchi and Spallanzani wrote pages of artistic scientific prose. The three elegant dialogues of F. M. Zanotti, *Della forza dei corpi che chiamano viva* (Bologna 1752), were in the tradition of Galileo's dialogues, while Algarotti's *Newtonianismo* belongs to that of Fontenelle. The comedy lacked vigour: it suffered from Italy's want of a conversational language that was valid all over the peninsula. The comedies of Fagiuoli, Gigli and Nelli had little virtue apart from being Tuscan. Those that Goldoni wrote in Italian, unlike those he composed in dialect, lacked spontaneity. In the preface to the first collection of his comedies (1750) he declared that he had not scrupled to use 'many Lombard words and phrases' (meaning by Lombard 'north Italian'), in order that they might be understood even by the most plebeian sections of the audiences to which they were played. In style he had tried to be (he wrote) as befitted comedy, 'simple, natural, not academic, lofty' (I, p. 773 ed. Mondadori). In difficult linguistic circumstances he did, in fact, show rare feeling for what could be spoken, in spite of occasional lapses into dialect when writing Italian ('non posso vedere *a* penar nessuno', *Innam.*, I, 2) and occasional use of rare and pedantic literary forms ('la dispiacenza che in casa mia originata siasi l'infermità del vostro cuore', *Un curioso accidente*, I, 2). Translations from French far outnumbered those from other languages. They were innumerable and ranged from scientific texts to works intended merely to entertain. They did much to spread words and constructions of French origin.

The linguistic controversies of the century concerned mainly two subjects. The first was the propriety of the 'scriver toscano' (i.e. of basing one's written Italian on Trecento Tuscan, particularly in the form used by Boccaccio, and as codified in the *Vocabolario della Crusca*, the fourth edition of which appeared in 1729-38). In spite of the support that Arcadia gave to the principle of imitation, many wondered why the imitation should be applied to writers so remote and uncongenial to contemporary taste. Tuscanism affected writing at two points: vocabulary (the use of archaisms from the Duecento and Trecento) and syntax (the length and complexity of periods, as cultivated by fourteenth-century writers, with their frequent inversions). The second subject of dispute was the attitude to be adopted to gallicisms: for this century saw widespread French penetration of Italian spoken and written usage. This caused concern to certain writers. The outcome of the consequent linguistic controversy was, on the whole, unfavourable to the purist viewpoint.

In southern Italy, the school of Lionardo di Capua at Naples had in the previous century started a pro-Tuscan movement. As a consequence, as Galiani remarked, local writers embraced Tuscan idiom and turned dictionaries and grammars inside out. This current of interest was responsible for Niccolò Amenta's treatise, *Della lingua nobile toscana* (Naples 1724) and for the reprinting of some of the Trecento authors and of Salviati's *Avvertimenti* (Naples 1712). G. B. Vico, in his *Autobiografia*, praised Lionardo di Capua for his work in establishing Tuscan in prose, and he himself, feeling the need to create a language of his own (*Autobiog.*, p. 227) turned, not only to latinisms, but to Tuscan words belonging to the 'heroic' age of the language. In Vico's purism, we have, as Fubini observed, not just the purism of L. di Capua and N. Amenta, but the purism of a writer whose gaze rested on the past and who wished to preserve its voice in his pages.[1] Hence comes the use of archaic words like *appellagione, assemprare, avacciare, avolio, calogna, calognare, danaio, negghienza,* etc., and also Vico's corrections in the *Scienza nuova prima* (to forms he was subsequently to maintain): *anatomia* to *notomia, delicato* to *dilicato, magistrato* to *maestrato, proprio* to *propio,* etc. Although he was a supporter of the Crusca, A. M. Salvini did not approve of this search for Trecento trimmings, and he complained of those

---

[1] M. Fubini, *Stile e umanità di Giambattista Vico*, Bari 1946, p. 122.

Neapolitans in his time who would like Tuscan to be a dead language, in order that they should have to study 'the books of only one century'. They forgot that affectation was always a vice (L. A. Muratori, *Della perfetta poesia*, Annot. di A. M. Salvini, Venice 1730, II, p. 136). In Tuscany itself two Lucchese, D. A. Leonardi and M. Regali, in the *Dialogo dell'Arno e del Serchio* and the *Dialogo del Fosso di Lucca e del Serchio*, Lucca 1710, disputed the authority of the Crusca on some points of orthography (*pruova*, *esercizzi*, *giugnere*, etc.), while Girolamo Gigli of Siena made war on the Crusca in his *Vocabolario Cateriniano* (1717). He accused the Academy, which had adopted so many archaic Florentine words, of having neglected the works of St. Catherine of Siena, although she figured among the authors cited. In northern Italy, Cesari had a precursor in G. C. Becelli of Verona, who asked in five dialogues *Se oggidì scrivendo si debba usare la lingua italiana del buon secolo* (Verona 1737) and answered himself in the affirmative. The Tuscan vogue was satirized, however, in a dull comedy by Father F. A. Arizzi, *Il Toscanismo e la Crusca* (Venice 1739). There were some, too, who cultivated, not fourteenth-century, but sixteenth-century writers. Algarotti, in a letter (15 May 1747), observed that the devotion to Aristotle once displayed in philosophy classes seemed now to have passed to Bembo and his school in classes for the study of grammar and rhetoric. Forensic and ecclesiastical oratory also sought adornment in Trecento and Cinquecento Tuscan authors. Baretti (in a letter to C. A. Tanzi on 19 April 1758) attributed ecclesiastics' tuscanizing tendencies (with their Crusca words, Cinquecento phrases and Boccaccio-type periods) to vanity. The Milanese Father Onofrio Branda, in the dialogue *Della lingua toscana* (Milan 1759) praised living Tuscan usage and declared the need for avoiding archaisms. As models for prose he chose two sixteenth-century writers who were close to living usage: Della Casa and Caro. But the most radical opposition to the Trecento cult and the Crusca cult came from that group of Milanese writers who played so important a part in the Enlightenment in Italy: Alessandro Verri made in the *Caffè* (July 1764) his 'solenne rinunzia alla pretesa purezza della toscana favella', and further articles by him and his associates echoed this 'renunciation'.

Giuseppe Baretti was also, of course, a fierce opponent of the Crusca and of archaizers, and possibly the most colourful in language. He dealt with linguistic matters several times; of particular significance are his letter 'Al Signor Filologo Etrusco' (in the *Frusta*, n. XVIII), and his 'Diceria di Aristarco Scannabue da recitarsi nell'accademia della Crusca il dì che sarà ricevuto accademico' (in the *Frusta*, n. XXV). His taste, his reflections on the other European languages known to him and the influence of his English friends led him to desire for Italians, too, a language that would be lively, nimble, and suitable for expressing the needs of the whole nation. To attain this, Italians would have to pay attention to things and not depend on elegance of language to cover vacuity. Baretti recognized that the literary language was essentially Tuscan, and that at Florence was spoken a dialect more elegant than the others and more 'writable'. But this did not prevent him from criticizing the way in which Florentines wrote, or from attacking the Crusca as sharply as he attacked the Arcadia. According to Baretti, the *Vocabolario della Crusca* was full of disgusting items, some taken from ribald writers, others collected in Florence's brothels (*Frusta*, n. XVIII). It contained a vacuous wealth of words, which could not be used because they were archaic, mean, too specifically local, or filthy. Too many words appeared in two or three forms (like *abbadessa*, *abadessa*, *badessa*). The Crusca had been wrong to prescribe as models 'non solo ogni paroluzza che esce attualmente dalle bocche di quelle genti, ma sino ogni minimo ette trovato in que' loro tanti meschinissimi scrittorelli'. And the admiration that the early members of the academy rightly felt for Boccaccio had led to his being, through no fault of his own, the ruin of the Italian language, indeed the primary reason for Italy's not possessing a good and universal language: for the 'artificial Latin character' of the language used by Boccaccio and other early writers made it impossible that it should be read with pleasure 'by our people' (*Frusta*, n. XXV). Baretti gave various reasons for the fault he reproved in Boccaccio and other ancient writers (that they did not 'follow the natural order of ideas in their respective styles': *Frusta*, n. IV): sometimes he blamed it on the Tuscan language, sometimes, with greater justification, he attributed it to Latin influence. (Following 'the *natural* order of ideas' in the construction of the period was one of the merits that many French grammarians at this time ascribed to their own language.)

Vittorio Alfieri was from 1776 a keen student of spoken Tuscan. Indeed, reading Tuscan classics and attention to the living language alternated in his efforts to 'speak, hear, think and dream in Tuscan' (*Vita*, IV, 2). Nearly three years after Pietro Leopoldo's decree abolished the Accademia della Crusca, Alfieri composed at Colmar (on March 18, 1786) the sonnet that begins 'L'idioma gentil sonante e puro'. But what this poem expresses is regret that vandalism has destroyed a noble edifice, not acceptance of the Crusca's viewpoint.

The outstanding contribution to the debate in this century came from Melchior Cesarotti. His *Saggio sopra la lingua italiana* was published at Padua in 1785. In 1800 it re-appeared, with the addition of some notes, under the title *Saggio sulla filosofia delle lingue*. The first and second books are concerned with general linguistics; the third deals with problems of language in Italy. He wished to sweep away certain prejudices and make the language 'prudently free'. He was prepared to admit the primacy of Tuscan, but not its tyranny; he was not willing to limit the development of the language to what grew from the tradition of a single dialect. The national language could be enriched from other dialects than Tuscan, provided that words from such dialects were not adopted except when really needed, and provided they were not left in their municipal garb, but made to fit the forms of a national language (i.e. those of Tuscan). There were many excellent words apart from those recognized by the Crusca. He proposed in its place a national council, more broadly based, with headquarters in Florence, but with representation from various parts of Italy. Local committees of this body could enquire into local speech and make recommendations to the national body. Thus a great dictionary on new principles could be compiled. Of course, this suggestion was open to the objection that it would set up instead of the Crusca another authority which might become restrictive in its turn. But it could be argued that, until Italy had a common linguistic usage, it was useful to try and promote it, even by means of an academy. Moreover, this was intended to be a broader body than the Crusca. In any case, Cesarotti was most strongly criticized in his own time for his attitude to French influence rather than for his suggestion of a council. For, although he had condemned the use of needless gallicisms, he had also pointed out that, if French had terms for concepts that in Italy lacked a name, then there was no reason for not accepting a name along with each new idea. Similarly, although, in a notable examination of syntax, he showed that he was opposed to universal use of direct construction (with rigid adherence to the subject-verb-complement order), he also roundly condemned those Boccaccian imitators who tortured their sentences merely in order to prepare a place of honour for the verb at the end.

To some purists Cesarotti's moderate remarks seemed to open the door to all licence. It was with him in mind that Count Gianfrancesco Galeani-Napione (the best known of the men of letters who belonged to the academies at Turin called the Sampaolina and the Filopatria) wrote his *Dell'uso e dei pregi della lingua italiana* (Turin 1791). To him it was legitimate to take from French 'only in those very rare cases in which the Church permits stealing'. But his main concern was having Italian used in areas where Latin and French were used in his day. (As a Piedmontese he had reason to be particularly anxious about French influence.) Moreover, he condemned, not only the laxity of Cesarotti, but also the tyranny of the Crusca. Another strict purist was Carlo Gozzi, as can be seen from his *Chiacchiera intorno alla lingua litterale italiana* and his *Ragionamenti sopra una causa perduta*, which, however, remained unpublished in his own day.

To the polemics occasioned by gallicisms we shall have to return later in this chapter when dealing with the connections between Italian and other languages. But we should note that these controversies concerning linguistic standards (Tuscanism or anti-Tuscanism, sympathy for archaisms or opposition to them, purism in the face of French influence, etc.) occurred, not in isolation, but bound up with other stylistic and cultural problems (Arcadia and anti-Arcadia, Frugonianism, the expansion of the sciences and of scientific terms, etc.). They show how deep were the divisions among those who were in the best position to judge matters of language, and they reflect the gravity of the eighteenth-century linguistic crisis.

Grammarians and lexicographers were mostly bound by rigidly conservative conceptions, and their work presented little that was new. The anti-Cruscan Girolamo Gigli produced two works which were rather better than the others published in the same period: *Regole per la toscana favella*, Rome 1721, in dialogue form with exercises, and *Lezioni di lingua toscana*, Venice 1724, in the form of a treatise, but with the same exercises. The two volumes of N. Amenta, *Della lingua nobile d'Italia*, Naples 1723-24, discussed certain grammatical and lexical problems in detail, with special reference to Trecento Tuscan. D. M. Manni dealt with controversial points in grammar and rhetoric (discussing passages from writers, manuscript readings and editions) in his *Lezioni di lingua toscana*, Florence 1737 (3rd ed. rev., Lucca 1773). The descriptive grammar that enjoyed the greatest success was S. Corticelli's *Regole ed osservazioni di lingua toscana ridotte a metodo*, Bologna 1745. Then, mainly through the influence of Port-Royal and the sensationalists, came the vogue of the *grammaire raisonnée*: such were F. Soave's *Grammatica ragionata della lingua italiana*, Parma 1770, and (with still greater insistence on the connections between grammar and logic) I. Valdastri's *Corso teoretico di Logica e Lingua italiana*, Guastalla 1783.

The centre of lexicographical activity was still the Crusca, contested though its authority was by many. The fourth edition of its *Vocabolario* came out in Florence between 1729 and 1738 in six volumes. The contributors included A. M. Salvini (who drew largely on his own works for examples), Giuseppe Averani, Giovanni Bottari, D. M. Manni and many others, and use was made, too, of material collected by Redi and Cionacci. The number of authors cited was increased. They were divided into two classes: those belonging to the 'buon secolo' and those quoted for additions or confirmation. Many definitions were improved. The appearance of the new edition rekindled the fires of controversy. The tragicomedy by Father F. A. Arizzi, *Il Toscanismo e la Crusca o sia il Cruscante impazzito*, Venice 1739, was several times reprinted, though it seems hardly possible that it could have been performed. G. P. Bergantini, as if vying with the Crusca, began to collect material for an extremely full dictionary of his own. But this work, *Della volgare eloquenza*, only got as far as the first volume: A and B (Venice 1740). However, his other collections are not without their uses, though he too frequently registered the use of a word without quoting it in its context: *Voci italiane d'autori approvati dalla Crusca nel Vocabolario d'essa non registrate, con altre molte appartenenti per lo più ad arti e scienze*, Venice 1745; *Voci scoperte e difficoltà incontrate sul Vocabolario ultimo della Crusca*, Venice 1758; *Raccolta di tutte le voci scoperte sul Vocabolario ultimo della Crusca*, Venice 1760; *Scelta d'immagini o saggio d'imitazione di concetti*, Venice 1762. The Crusca itself was contemplating a new dictionary, albeit still on traditional lines: in 1741 Rossantonio Martini delivered a *Ragionamento . . . per norma di una nuova edizione del Vocabolario toscano* (printed later, Florence 1813). There were also unofficial reprintings of the *Vocabolario*, with a small number of additions, at Naples (1746-48) and Venice (1763). On 7 July 1783 Pietro Leopoldo suppressed the Crusca as an independent body, merging it with the Accademia Fiorentina and the Academy of the Apatisti under the single name of Accademia Fiorentina. Its vice-secretary, the abbé Giulio Perini, lauded its 'nuova libertà' in his inaugural address, and the following year Father Ildefonso

Fridiani presented a *Piano . . . per la nuova compilazione del Vocabolario*, in which he proposed that considerable space should be given to technical words. A table of barbarisms was to be compiled, and the equivalent 'voci buone' indicated. In 1786 those members of the academy deputed to do so chose the authors on which a future edition was to be based; but nothing came of this. However, a private individual from Nice, Francesco D'Alberti, who had already translated from the French the *Dictionnaire du citoyen* of H. Lacombe de Prezel, Paris 1761 (*Dizionario del cittadino*, Nice 1763, several times reprinted) and compiled a full French-Italian, Italian-French dictionary (1772, frequently reprinted), succeeded in completing before his death a *Dizionario universale critico-enciclopedico* (Lucca 1797-1805), though he did not live to see all of it published. He had worked through additional authors, but his quotations from them were frequently inexact or incomplete. He also included words from usage not attested in writing. His greatest innovation consisted in putting in a large number of words that were scientific or related to arts and trades. D'Alberti had, in fact, collected these directly from artisans in Tuscany, and his dictionary was the first large Italian work which attempted to fill this gap left by the Crusca. Many persons had complained of the lack of special dictionaries, and some had attempted to supply what was needed, like Vallisnieri (of the *Vocabolario filosofico-medico* that he began, there remains the *Saggio alfabetico d'istoria medica, e naturale: Opere*, III, Venice 1733, pp. 364-481) and Pasta (*Voci, maniere di dire e osservazioni di toscani scrittori . . . che possono servire d'istruzione ai giovani nell'arte del medicare . . .* Brescia 1749). Others translated encyclopaedic and technical dictionaries from French. G. A. Martignoni, in his *Nuovo metodo per la lingua italiana la più scelta*, 2 vols., Milan 1743-50, re-arranged all the words in the Crusca methodically in paragraphs (according to meaning) instead of following alphabetical order. Two other collections deserve mention: S. Pauli's *Modi di dire toscani* (Venice 1740), and C. Rabbi's *Sinonimi ed aggiunti italiani*, 2 vols. (Venice 1751). Among the bilingual dictionaries there were two which were several times reprinted during the Settecento and later: Baretti's Italian-English, English-Italian dictionary (1760) and the Italian-French, French-Italian one by D'Alberti already mentioned (1772).

Italian continued to gain ground at the expense of Latin, but the latter was still firmly entrenched in certain positions. In belletristic writing Italian predominated. But Latin was still used even for subjects which one would expect (owing to their close connection with daily life) to be treated in Italian: the satires of Cordara (who continued in the tradition of Sergardi) can serve as an example. Inscriptions were almost exclusively in Latin. And Gravina wrote the laws of Arcadia in an archaizing Latin. In works of historical scholarship Latin was widely used. Muratori used both tongues: after writing the *Antiquitates Italicae Medii Aevi* in Latin (Milan 1738-43), he himself summarized his results in Italian in the *Dissertazioni sopra le antichità italiane* (posthumously published at Milan 1751-55). Vico at first preferred to write in Latin and only later turned to Italian. Fabroni wrote biographies in Latin (*Vitae Italorum doctrina excellentium qui saec. XVII et XVIII floruerunt*, Pisa 1778). Antiquarians differed: A. F. Gori wrote in Latin, but G. Lami wrote in Italian (*Lezioni di antichità toscana*, Florence 1766), as did L. Lanzi (*Saggio di lingua etrusca*, Rome 1789). In many fields of knowledge works of fundamental importance were still written in Latin. The transactions of the Institute of Bologna were written in that language for many years by F. M. Zanotti (*De Bononiensi Scientiarum et Artium Instituto Commentarii*, Bologna 1731-91). People known in the world of Italian literature wrote scientific works in Latin: E. Manfredi, *Ephemerides motuum coelestium*, Bologna 1715-50, L. Mascheroni, *Adnotationes ad calculum integrale Euleri*, Pavia 1790-92. In botany nearly all writings were in Latin (e.g. P. A. Micheli's *Nova plantarum genera*, Florence 1720) and very few in Italian (one of the few being the *Istoria delle piante che nascono ne' lidi intorno a Venezia* by G. G. Zannichelli and his son, printed at Venice in 1735,). Some works had a bilingual text: an example was the *Istoria dell'incendio del Vesuvio accaduto nel mese di maggio dell'anno* 1737 published by the Accademia delle Scienze of Naples in 1738. Juridical works were frequently in Latin; an example was the treatise which Gravina published in Leipzig in 1708 (*Originum iuris civilis libri tres*). But the legislation of the various states was usually in the vernacular. In the Kingdom of Naples Giuseppe Pasquale Cirillo and others started work on a bilingual (Latin-Italian) codification of the laws by order of Charles III (VII), but his *Codice carolino* was never promulgated. In the states of the House of Savoy legislation was in Italian for the Cisalpine side, but some judges in the eighteenth century persisted in recording sentences in Latin. In the Church, Latin was still very widely used; indeed, in the liturgical field it alone was used, in spite of the fact that requests were made for the Mass to be celebrated in the vernacular. (The Italian Jansenists were eager

for the faithful to participate in services by responding to the
priests in Italian). A decree of Benedict XIV (1757) allowed the
reading of the Bible in approved Italian versions. In secondary
education Latin had an important place both as subject and as
medium of instruction. But many wanted Italian to have a similarly large role. Muratori wished Italian to be taught along with
Latin. And in Piedmont the Magistracy of Reform in 1729 ordered
that in schools outside the University study of Latin should proceed
pari passu with that of Italian. In Lombardy, A. Volta (1775) complained that Italian was neglected while Latin was esteemed, and
N. Onorati made a similar complaint (1783) about schools in
Naples. Carli, Gorani, Filangieri and Gozzi asked that Italian
should enjoy pre-eminence. At the universities, Latin continued
to be the usual medium of instruction; Antonio Genovesi caused a
sensation at Naples in November 1764 when he began to deliver
lectures in Italian from the Chair of Civil Economy (founded by
B. Intieri with the precise stipulation that teaching should be in
the vernacular). On the other hand Gaetana Agnesi found it
easier to use Latin than to use French when discussing mathematics and physics with a colleague from France. There was, of
course, no lack of letters, articles and dissertations on the propriety
of using Italian or Latin in various fields (particularly in
philosophy, science, etc., where the outcome of the struggle was
not yet clear): Vallisnieri and Algarotti were champions of Italian,
while G. Lagomarsini defended Latin. But these debates were
clearly much less important than the actual use of the languages
concerned.

Use of dialects in speech was extensive, but their use in writing
was not the work of popular authors, but of cultured men of
letters who consciously chose dialect with particular purposes in
view. The eminently literary nature of dialectal writing can be
seen in the influence that the Tuscan and aulic poetic language
had on dialect lyrics: this was noticeable in Venetian writers
(Gritti, Lamberti) and particularly strong in Meli. There was an
abundance — and this again confirms the deliberate choice of
dialect — of satires and mock-heroic poems, either originally
written in, or translated into, dialect. Almanacs were aimed at
popular readership; G. Pozzobon of Treviso began his *Schiesón*.
The theatre, in presenting characters from various social classes,
got nearer to dialect as spoken, particularly in the work of an
observer like Goldoni. But the alternation on the stage of characters speaking dialect with others speaking Italian (as in Goldoni,

Chiari and Carlo Gozzi) was rather artificial. Tuscan comedies, too, presented certain characters whose speech was exaggeratedly dialectal: an instance is Gigli's *Il marito più onorato del suo bisogno*, in which two characters, Ser Lapo the notary and Prizia the servant-girl, produce a superabundance of Florentine and Sienese idioms. The extremely rustic Ciapo, whom Fagiuoli put into several of his comedies, was popular in Florence, but not elsewhere in Italy. Any serious, 'noble' or 'official' use of dialect was now incompatible with the status that Italian had achieved. If such use remained at Venice, it was confined to the spoken language of the law-courts (cf. p. 303), and Galiani was thus unhistorical when he cited the 'patriotic zeal of the Venetians' in his efforts to have Neapolitans cultivate their dialect and raise its status (*Del dialetto napoletano*, repr. Nicolini, p. 7). The Accademia dei Pescatori Oretei of Palermo was guilty of similar inconsistency. It was founded in 1745 with the purpose of 'constantly refining the Sicilian tongue', but it prescribed that addresses delivered at its meetings should be in Italian. The value and functions of dialect were discussed in the polemics provoked by Onofrio Branda; Parini rightly rebuked him for deriding 'that language which, being the most natural and the purest and least corrupt in our city, is consequently to be considered the most beautiful' (*Prose*, I, p. 55 Bellorini). Several dialect dictionaries were published in the second half of the century: the *Vocabolario bresciano e toscano* attributed to the abbé Gagliardi (Brescia 1759), the anonymous *Raccolta di voci romane e marchiane* (Osimo 1768), the *Vocabolario veneziano e padovano* of Patriarchi (Padua 1775, 2nd ed. 1796), the ample *Vocabolario etimologico siciliano, italiano e latino* by Pasqualino (Palermo 1785-95) and the *Vocabolario delle parole del dialetto napoletano che più si scostano dal dialetto toscano* by F. Galiani and F. Mazzarella (Naples 1789). Apart from their practical uses, they display an attitude that is, at least embryonically, scientific. Moreover, there were authors, like Bettinelli and Cesarotti, who believed that the collection of dialectal words could be used as a basis for making additions to the national language.

In a cosmopolitan century some knowledge of foreign languages became necessary to cultured people. Many Italians realized that, if Italy was not to fall behind, they would have to pay attention to what was happening beyond Italy's frontiers. And, whereas, during the Renaissance, Italian cultural influences had flowed into France, the tide now ran the other way. For in the eighteenth century it was French language and French civilization that enjoyed hegemony in Europe and seemed to have achieved 'universality'. This was due mainly to admiration for the new rationalist philosophy (first Cartesian, then sensationalist and encyclopaedist). But there were, too, important political factors. In Italy, these were the installation of the Lorraine dynasty at Florence (1737) and that of Philip of Bourbon (husband of Louise-Elisabeth, daughter of Louis XV) as Duke of Parma (1749), and, most important, the invasion of the revolutionary armies at the end of the century. French literature enjoyed great prestige: the writers of the age of Louis XIV (as well as Voltaire, Rousseau, Diderot and innumerable minor authors, especially of fiction) were read in the original and in translations. French scientific works were consulted, and they were translated and summarized in periodicals founded for that purpose. Indeed, Algarotti complained that recourse was had to French books for all subjects; they alone were read and believed (Letter of 1752 in *Lettere filologiche*, p. 115). Matteo Borsa alleged that booksellers did not keep Italian books because there was no market for them: in the houses of Italy foreign books were everywhere, while 'i nostri buoni Italiani dormon coi Greci nelle pubbliche librerie' (*Del gusto presente in letteratura italiana*, Venice 1784, p. 18). Cesarotti, too, observed that the French language was extremely common throughout Italy. There was no person of education to whom it was not familiar, almost natural. And he added that 'la biblioteca delle donne e degli uomini di mondo non è che francese' (*Saggio sulla filosofia delle lingue*, IV, xiii). We can form an idea of the part played in Italian culture by French encyclopaedic and lexicographical compilations if we consult Carlo Battisti's *Note bibliografiche alle traduzioni italiane di vocabolari francesi enciclopedici e tecnici nella seconda metà del Settecento*, Florence 1955. They include geographical, historical (religious and profane), mathematical, physical, chemical, industrial, commercial, agricultural and maritime dictionaries (some running to several editions). And the *Encyclopédie* of D'Alembert and Diderot was twice reprinted in Italy in French (with notes calculated to reduce their anti-Christian tendencies).

French influence extended throughout Italy, but was particularly strong in two states. Piedmont was one, on account of its nearness to France and of the bilingual structure of the state (Savoy and Piedmont); as we know from the testimony of Alfieri, Galeani Napione and others, the upper classes at Turin used

French and dialect almost exclusively. The other was Parma, which became a centre of gallicization under Philip of Bourbon and his capable minister, Du Tillot. Knowledge of French in Italy was facilitated by the presence of numerous Frenchmen, particularly in some cities (like Parma) and in certain callings (cooks, hairdressers, dancing-masters, milliners), and by the visits of travellers. Moreover, many Italians travelled or settled in France, while others, moving about Europe, used French as an international language. Some wrote important works in French (Galiani, Goldoni, Denina, Lagrange). Moreover, many Italians wrote letters in French in this period, not only to Frenchmen and other foreigners, but to other Italians (e.g. Cesarotti's letters to Taruffi and Toaldo). French fashions and French cooking enjoyed a great vogue. The most eager fans of French manners (and words) were the elegant young men of the contemporary smart set. Two such are presented to us in Scipione Maffei's *Raguet* (1747). This is how Alfonso speaks (Act II, sc. 3):

> *Ed io* mi do l'onore
> *signor, di rendergli* un million di grazie.
> *E una gran* proprietà *la sua, di fare*
> *agli stranier tanta* onestà. *Ciò* marca
> *la bontà del suo cuore:* io farò in sorte
> *che mi conosca sempre* tutto a lei.

And here is Ermondo (III, ii):

> *Non le darò cibi plebei: guazzetti,*
> *manicaretti, intingoli, stufati*
>
> . . . .
>
> *Io le darò* ragù, farsì, gattò,
> cotolette, crocande; *e niente cotto*
> *sarà mai nello spiedo, ma* allo spiedo
> *anzi* alla brocca. *Non farò la mala*
> *creanza mai di far portare in tavola*
> *un cappone, se non in* fricandò
> *Non mangerà fritelle, nè presciutti,*
> *nè vil vivanda d'anitra, ma sempre*
> canàr, sambòn, bignè . . .

And in the anonymous comedy *Lo spirito forte* (Venice 1772) an irreligious and frenchified character flatters a girl with these words:

'Occhi *bleu,* capelli biondi, è un prodigio in Italia; il vostro *teint* così bianco, e vermiglio, sorpassa quello delle Moscovite; la *taille* non ne ho veduta l'uguale.'

If we allow for the exaggeration which the authors' satirical intentions have led them into in these plays (was *alla brocca* ever used for *à la broche?*), these speeches can serve to give us some idea of contemporary gallicization. It can be seen, too, in non-literary texts, in the letters and personal notes of the period. Indeed, it penetrated the dialects (as can be seen, for instance, in the *Raccolta di voci romane e marchiane*, Osimo 1768), and Florentines were themselves accused of abuse of French ('Un giardino — quale il Toscano anch'ei *Parterre* chiama — da poi che l'Arno è fatto parigino': T. Valperga di Caluso, *Il Masino*, Turin 1791, XI, 57). In fact, French influences were so pervasive that none escaped them. One could, of course, make a list of Francophiles and Francophobes, but one would then find that declared intentions did not always accord with practice. Algarotti, in a letter written in 1756 (*Lettere filologiche*, pp. 126-9), condemned Redi and Salvini for using *fare il diavolo a quattro, mettere una cosa sul tappeto* and Magalotti for borrowing *faire les yeux doux, le petit maître, la prude*. He complained, in his *Discorso sopra la ricchezza della lingua italiana ne' termini militari* of the number of gallicisms used in Italian military writings, and in another letter in 1763 (*Lettere filologiche*, p. 183) he deplored the use by Florentines of *dettaglio, regretto, debosciato*, etc. Yet he himself used *capo d'opera, colpo d'occhio, cochetta, il poema il più galante che ci sia*, etc. Bettinelli, who in his poem *Le Raccolte* (*Opere*, XVII, p. 48) protested against:

> *i franzesismi in abito italiano*
>
> . . . .
>
> fripponi *armati di stranier* ramaggio
> *a* culbuttare *tutto il buon linguaggio*

and elsewhere objected to 'i Targioni, i Grazzesi . . . e tali altri nei quali trovo or parole, or frasi franzesi', made use of dozens himself. (These facts are noted here, not in order to condemn these writers for inconsistency, but to show how the whole literary culture of the time was permeated with gallicisms).

English influence, though incomparably less than that of France, was nevertheless considerable and due to admiration (which in some assumed the proportions of a mania) for many aspects of English life: institutions, philosophy (Newton was universally admired, Locke and Hume the subjects of controversy), science, literature and industry. Knowledge of English matters (and hence words pertaining to them) came into Italy with English gentlemen on the Grand Tour and also from those quite numerous Italians who had been to England (Cocchi, Rolli, Angiolini, Rezzonico, Alfieri and many others); the strongest influence in this respect was perhaps Baretti. There was a rapid increase in Italy in the number of those who knew English; Baretti remarked in a letter to Canon Agudio in April 1754, for instance, 'che in Milano si è introdotta ora la moda per le dame di studiar la lingua inglese' (*Epistol.*, I, p. 98 Piccioni). There were translations of Pope (two versions), Addison, Defoe, Richardson, Swift, Sterne, Young. Shakespeare began somewhat tardily to be known and translated. There were many translations of English novels, though mostly not from English: Graf, in his *L'anglomania e l'influsso inglese in Italia nel sec. XVIII* (Turin 1911), estimates that in nine cases out of ten translation was from French translations. Encyclopaedic compilations were popular: Chambers' *Cyclopaedia* was translated three times. The pre-romantics at the end of the century showed the influence of themes dominant in contemporary English literature: melancholy, night, death. English had become important, too, in the commercial world, owing to the growth of English trade in the Mediterranean area.

Knowledge of Spanish declined, though there were pro-Spanish groups. The two Bourbon dynasties transplanted from Spain had little effect on this situation: that at Parma, as we saw, became a centre of French influence, while at Naples Spanish disappeared from chancellery usage after Ferdinand IV had become emancipated from his father's tutelage (1767). In Sardinia, Spanish lost ground after the island had become a possession of the House of Savoy, but this happened very slowly: only in 1764 did Italian become the official language in the courts and in teaching. A collection of *Editti, pregoni ed altri provvedimenti* ... (3 vols., Cagliari 1775) gave all the laws of the preceding half-century in Italian, including those originally promulgated in Spanish. The Spanish Jesuits who settled in Italy after the suppression of the Society of Jesus received more than they gave linguistically.

German was little known, in spite of the important political influence of Austria and the consequent circulation of persons. Only later, in the pre-romantic period, did certain German writers become known and translated.

There was still considerable knowledge of Italian among cultured people in other countries. In a musical century like the

eighteenth, it was nice to know the language in which the librettos
of nearly all operas were written. Indeed, Baretti, in a letter to
Canon Agudio (8 August 1754), reported that in England Italian
was regaining lost ground thanks to Opera. But there were
people, too, who studied Italian in order to read scientific and
learned works. And contributions to the diffusion of Italian
abroad were made by numerous adventurers as well as by outstanding writers — Baretti at London, Goldoni at Paris and
Metastasio at Vienna. In France, Voltaire judged English and
Italian to be 'les deux langues de l'Europe nécessaires à un
journaliste', and he himself had a fair knowledge of Italian, while
Goldoni in 1783 wrote: 'Cette Langue est en vogue en France plus
que jamais. Le goût de la nouvelle musique y a beaucoup con-
tribué . . .' (*Mémoires*, III, c. 35). Much the same story could be
told of Holland, Bavaria, Austria; we should not forget the
example of the Viennese court, with its living tradition of keeping
a 'poeta cesareo' who wrote *melodrammi* in Italian.

In discussing the main features of the language in the Settecento we must again stress that oscillations in written usage were
much greater than one would imagine if one limited one's reading
to modern editions of the better-known authors of the period. The
original editions, and — even more — the manuscripts of the
period, show the extent to which uniformity was lacking. In
northern and southern Italy the written language showed
peculiarities deriving from the spoken dialects. In Tuscany
standards were uncertain, not so much because of the influence of
local spoken variants, as because the *Vocabolario della Crusca* registered numerous written variants, generally without clearly
declaring a preference. In the first volume of the fourth impression,
for instance, we find *acquidotto* and *aquidoccio*; *apostolo* and *appostolo*;
circonstanza, *circostanza*, *circonstanzia*, *circostanzia*, and *circustanza*.
Sometimes, preference was indicated by reference away: those
who looked up *cirimonia* were referred to *cerimonia*. We shall note
now just a few examples of the innumerable cases of oscillation in
the linguistic usage of the time. Instances of oscillation in vowels
were   *principe — prencipe*;   *delicato — dilicato*;   *unzione — onzione*
(Vallisnieri). *Tremuoto* was much commoner than *terremoto, tuono*
more frequent than *tono*. Words offering consonantal variants
were: *sacro — sagro*; *bruciare — abbrucciare* (Vallisnieri) — *brugiare*
(Gigli, Algarotti) — *abbruggiare* (*Caffè*); *glandula — glandola* —
ghiandola; *pranzo — pranso* (e.g. Vallisnieri, Lazzarini, Chiari,
Algarotti); *gengiva — gengìa*; *chirurgia — cirurgia*; *congettura —*

conghiettura; *paralello — parallelo*, etc. Before a front vowel there was doubt about the use of *c* and *z*, especially in northern writers: *francese — franzese*; *socio — sozio*; *commercio — commerzio*; *specie — spezie* (in the meaning of 'spezie'); *speciale — speziale* (in both senses); *sufficiente — suffiziente* (Cesarotti); *Confuzio* (S. Maffei), etc. There was oscillation in the use of double consonants, particularly in series in which Tuscan usage differed from Latin: *academia — accademia*; *imagine — immagine*; *femina — femmina* (and vice-versa *grammatica — gramatica*; *commodo — comodo*); *mattematica — matematica*; *opio — oppio*; *camelo — cammello*, etc. No definitive choice had as yet been made between *procurare* and *proccurare*; *provedere* and *provvedere*; *inoltrare* and *innoltrare*; *inondare* and *innondare*. Alongside *autore* and *pratico* existed *auttore* and *prattico*, preferred by some because they more closely reflected the etymology. In writing compound particles (*sì che — sicché, tanto più — tantopiù*), Tuscans and southerners could be guided by their pronunciation in deciding whether a double consonant was needed, but northerners were often wrong. Generally it was no longer realized that *viepiù* was only *via più*; so it was written *vieppiù* (Baretti). But even in innumerable other cases — cases in which Tuscan usage was stable and registered in dictionaries — northern writers and printers doubled and reduced consonants with extreme carelessness (particularly in pretonic positions and where there were two pairs of double consonants, but also elsewhere). Examples are: *drapello* (Algarotti), *ippocondriaco* (Patriarchi), *trappellare* (for 'trapelare', C. Gozzi), *disabbitato* (Vallisnieri), *beffana, schiffo, soffà, zuffolare* (C. Gozzi), *stroffinare* (A. Verri), *Catterina* (Caffè), *barille* and *regallo* (condemned by Baretti), *guereggiare* (Beccaria), etc. Chiari in his comedies wrote *plebbe* to rhyme with *vorrebbe, vacche* with *lumacche, stuffa* with *baruffa, non calle* with *spalle* and (certain that the Venetian actors would dispose of the distinctions in their delivery) *quattro* with *teatro, brutto* with *aiuto*, etc. There were often optional endings: *lapide — lapida, addome — addomine, mestiere — mestiero, pensiere — pensiero, magistero — magisterio, alveare — alveario, cioccolata — cioccolato — cioccolate — cioccolatte*, etc. These variants were not, of course, used with complete indifference: certain authors were inclined to constant choice of one form rather than another by their cultural formation, others chose according to taste, or in conformity with a particular model. Vico wrote *iconomia* rather than *economia*, probably because of his love of archaism. Baretti used *lapida* because he found this form in Berni and Cellini. Parini preferred *mercadante* because he thought that variant more appropriate to poetry (possibly because he recalled its use in Ariosto).

From the closing decades of the Seicento there had not been much oscillation in spelling as such. The main controversies were now over. The expedient of distinguishing open tonic *e* and *o* by means of a circumflex accent, proposed by A. M. Salvini to the Accademia della Crusca on 10 February 1723-24 and used in his translation of Oppian (Florence 1728), was intended only as a didactic device designed to facilitate pronunciation for non-Tuscans. *U* was now consistently distinguished from *v*, though a strange practice was adopted by some printers of writing *v* in words like *noccivolo, givochi, vova* (but *suoi, uomo*): this can be seen in the *Opere* of Vallisnieri, Venice 1733. *J* was nearly always distinguished from *i*: *j* was used mostly in words like *jattura, gennajo, conjugale*, nearly always in the plurals of nouns and adjectives in *-io: proprj, municipj, vizj, vestigj*. Merely orthographic *i* was sometimes superfluously used, particularly by northern writers: *cappuccietto* (Goldoni), *pregievole* (Vallisnieri), *scielta* (Becelli), etc. *Y* had disappeared, save in rare examples of incompletely adapted Greek words (e.g. C. Gaudini, *Gli elementi dell'arte sfygmica*, Genoa 1769; G. Arduino, 'Saggio fisicomineralogico di Lythogonia (sic) e Orognosia', in *Atti Acc. delle scienze di Siena*, V, 1774). *H* was now used only in interjections and in *ho, hai, ha, hanno*. Etymological *h* appeared only in rare cases of very learned words, where the Latin or Graeco-Latin word was virtually kept in the Italian text: P. M. Gabrielli wrote a treatise on *L'Heliometro*, Siena 1705. Vallisnieri wrote of 'un'apoplesia parziale, detta *Hemiplexia*' (*Opere*, III, p. 522), but a little further down called it 'Emiplegia'. There were, too, some rare cases of the maintenance of *h* in Greek digraphs: Salvini (Oppian, p. 5) wrote *Parthi*, Vallisnieri (*Opere*, II, p. 215) *Lapathj* (for a plant name), while Parini, used, as a euphemism, and in order to avoid confusion with *fallo*, 'il turpe *Phallo*' (*Mattino*, l. 544). *K* remained only in *Kavaliere* (used as a title) at Venice. *C* and *q* were distributed as they are today, with a few aberrant exceptions, e.g. *risquotere* in the *Celidora* of Casotti and in the comedies of Fagiuoli. The spelling *zi* had almost entirely replaced *ti* in such words as *orazione*, etc. Some uncertainty remained in the use of double *z*, both in words like *vizi* (*vizzi* as plural of *vizio* was opposed by Leonardi) and in cases where the Latin group *ti* was preceded by a consonant (*traduzzione*, Rolli). Stress was indicated generally by grave accents on oxytonic words. Only in rare cases was stress indicated within a word, and then the accent might be acute or grave: *ironía* or *ironìa*. In certain didactic works, however, accents might be more abundantly used: an example is the *Scelta di Lettere familiari* which Baretti edited at London in 1779 for the use of young ladies in England. There was considerable oscillation in the use of accents on monosyllables (*fù, sà, quì* were mostly accented). Diæresis began to be indicated in the printing of verse. Use of the apostrophe was very similar to that of today; Corticelli gives as a rule that one should write *un uomo* (*Regole*, 1. III, c. 4), while Gigli still wrote *un'uomo* (*Lezioni di lingua toscana*). Capital letters were used with notable frequency. In Maffei's treatise *Della scienza chiamata cavalleresca* (Rome 1710, p. 39) we find: 'Quest' Onor Cavalleresco è un Idolo vano, un nome senza soggetto, ed una mera invenzione di questi Autori'. And in Algarotti's *New-tonianismo* (Naples 1737, p. 2) we have: 'La Penisoletta di Sirmione, Patria del Vezzoso Catullo, e i Monti che tante volte ripeterono i bei versi di Fracastoro, due punti dirò così tanto famosi nella Carta Poetica. . . .' Moreover, a similar abundance could still be found in works produced nearer the end of the century, e.g. Cesarotti's *Saggio sopra la lingua italiana* (Padua 1785, p. 54): 'rende sempre meno gustabili gli Autori delle Lingue Dotte', 'qualche altro Cinquecentista, adattando le frasi idolatriche dei Romani alla Liturgia del Cristianesimo', etc.

A general reform of Italian spelling was proposed by Ferdinando Caccia of Bergamo (*Opere*, Bergamo 1762-66). In his 'ortografia filosofica di soli diecinove caratteri' there would be no place for *j, v* or *z*. *H* would be kept only in *ho, hai, ha, hanno, oh, ahi,* and *deh*. He would write *otsio, gratsia, petso* and also *metso*. *U* would be omitted after *q* (*aqa*) and *g* would be banished from *palia, filio*. He would write *inprudente* and *bonba*, and he would abolish double consonants that preceded the accent (*scritore*, but *scritto*). There would be no punctuation of any kind whatsoever. And accents could be abolished if one were to write, as he proposed, *bateo* for *batté, virtute* for *virtù*, etc. It is perhaps needless to add that his proposals, which he himself followed rather inconsistently, came to nothing.

Some of the Tuscan grammarians sought to give instruction on the four letters *e, o, s, z*, which could be pronounced in more than one way: Gigli in the 'Raccolta di tutte le voci italiane di buon uso' included in his *Regole per la toscana favella* (Rome 1721) dealt with words of uncertain pronunciation, though with numerous errors. But others merely mentioned the problem, e.g. Corticelli: '*E* ... presso i Toscani ha due suoni, l'uno più aperto, come in *mensa, remo*; l'altro più chiuso, e assai frequente, come in *refe, cena*. Cotal suono però appresso i Poeti non fa noja alla rima. Petrarca, canz. 24: *Fa subito sparire ogn'altra stella, Così pare or men bella*. E pure *stella* ha il suono chiuso e *bella* aperto' (Book III, c. I; there is a similar paragraph on *o*). The conjunctions *e* and *nè* still had an open vowel, as we see from the transcription (*é, né*) in Salvini's translation of Oppian. The vogue enjoyed by French fashions caused many people to give *r* a uvular pronunciation, and, as we know from Carlo Gozzi, some adopted a French pronunciation of *u* (*Chiacchiera intorno alla lingua litterale italiana*, p. 65, Vaccalluzzo). The rule of the movable diphthong was widely broken, even by Tuscans (*risuonasse*, Cocchi; *cagnuolina*, Minzoni; *scuolare, scuolaretto*, Baretti), although grammarians continued to prescribe it (Gigli, for instance, in the stories he corrected as exercises in his *Lezioni*, changed *suonando* and *muoveva* to *sonando* and *moveva*). The reduction of the diphthong *uo* to *o* in spoken Tuscan, which was still not noticeable in the early eighteenth century (if we are to trust Gigli's representation of plebeian Florentine) must have spread later: Ildefonso Fridiani documented '*Omo* secondo il tronco pronunziare del volgo anche presente' (*Delizie degli eruditi toscani*, Florence 1770, p. cliv). In certain cases there was uncertainty as to where stress should fall. Tuscans preferred *prepàro, sepàro*, while elsewhere the latinisms *prèparo, sèparo* were frequently heard (Rosasco, *Della lingua toscana*, Torino 1777, II, p. 463). There was oscillation between *dìssipa* and *dissìpa, dìsputa* and *dispùta, proìbito* and *proibìto* (Salvini, notes to the *Fiera*, V, iii, 4). Chiari (*Il Medico viniziano al Mogol*, II, i) accented *ipocòndria* in the Latin, rather than the Greek, fashion. Since, in writing, no indication of stress was usually given, rare words were frequently learnt, and then used, with the accent on the wrong syllable: examples are Parini's *coltrìci* (*Mattino*, lines 85-6), Cerretti's *Megàra* ('Talia') and Mascheroni's *Peripàto* ('O mio Vigan . . .'). The truncation of the final vowel after a liquid or nasal and before a pause was admitted in poetry ('E la colpa e non la pena — che può farmi impallidir': Metastasio, *Temistocle*; 'Muggir di mare e rimbombar di tuon': Mazza), but sounded false in verse that was prosaic ('Per or non vado a spasso vado per un affar': Goldoni). As for truncation of the final vowel in a word connected with the following word (*volgar lingua, ragion che sopravvenga*), that was not only very frequent in verse, but often practised by many prose-writers; Foscolo inveighed against this 'vizio di troncar le parole', which he considered an 'atticismo degli ultimi gesuiti' (*Opere*, Ed. naz., VII, pp. 93-4; X, p. 357). When an enclitic was joined to a truncated word, there was no assimilation — at least, not in writing: *passiamla* (Fagiuoli, *Il cavaliere parigino*, II, vi).

Morphological examination reveals that oscillations in forms were much the same as in the previous centuries. Before *z* the article *il* was still predominant; but Bandiera, in touching up passages by Sègneri, corrected '*l zelo* to *allo zelo*. Rather more respect was shown for the rule prescribing *lo*, *gli* before *s* impure: Baretti, in commenting on a sonnet by a Frugonian poet (*Frusta lett.*, n. X) noted '*ai scritti* (doveva dire *agli scritti*)'. Cesarotti used both forms freely. *Li* as plural of the article lost ground, but was still anything but rare, particularly before a consonant: Gigli wrote that in choosing between *i* and *li* 'the ear shall be judge' (*Lezioni*, p. 42), while Mirapelli (*Delle parti del volgare parlamento*, Casale 1728, p. 26) held that *li* was more proper to a poet than a prose-writer. Only in verse was *lo* used before a consonant ('i migliori che lo ver non sanno': Gozzi, *Serm.*, XIV), except when it was used with the articulated preposition *per*, in which case grammarians continued to prescribe *per lo* (pl. *per li*) and were obeyed by many (though Genovesi wrote *pel desiderio*). *Ai, dei, nei* were nearly always replaced by *a'*, *de'*, *ne'*. In verse, some writers preferred to detach the articulated preposition from the article except when it was used with an apostrophe: Parini, for instance, wrote (in poetry, not in prose) *ne le Gallie*, but *dell'opre*. The preposition *fra* was sometimes joined to the article, too ('qualche rosa *fralle* mie spine', Fagiuoli). Uncertainties remained in the plurals of nouns and adjectives in -*co* and -*go*: *intonachi* (Targioni Tozzetti), *ittiofaghi* (Cesarotti), *filologhi* (Becelli), *paralitichi* (Fagiuoli), *astrologhi* (Gozzi), *reciprochi* (C. Gozzi, Casti), *lombrici* (Cocchi), *bruci* (Targioni Tozzetti), *catalogi* (Zannichelli), *omologi* (Galiani). Cesarotti, who had written *teologhi* in his *Saggio*, corrected this to *teologi* in the third edition. And among the superlatives we find: *cattolichissimo* (Manni), *filosofichissima dissertazione* (Baretti), *ascetichissimo e teologichissimo* (Fridiani), etc. Some plurals in -*a* were exhumed by archaizing writers (*le coltella*, G. Gozzi; *le pugna*, C. Gozzi). Among the plurals of nouns in -*ello* existed not only *capegli*, but also *campanegli* (Baretti), and in verse there was also -*ei* (*augei*, Cerretti). Some compound numbers of which *sei* or *sette* was an element still appeared in contracted form: *cinquansei* (Saccenti), *cinquanzettimo* (Cocchi), *venzett'anni*

(Baretti). Grammarians continued to argue as to whether *lui* and *lei* were admissible as subject-pronouns. For atonic object-pronouns *li* and *gli*, *lo* and *il* were still promiscuously used. Probably owing to French influence, *lo* came to be employed referring to a preceding phrase: 'l'Accademico è un personaggio distinto dal Professore, come *lo* mostrò egregiamente il mio valoroso Collega' (Cesarotti, 'Riflessioni sui doveri accademici', in *Opere scelte*, I, p. 330 Ortolani). Atonic *gli* with plural meaning was used even by a purist like C. Gozzi: 'né vergogna —*gli* prende [=agli uomini] a dare il core — alle più vili' (*Turandot*). The Tuscan *gliene* for 'glielo, gliela, etc.' was used, for instance, by Fagiuoli, and, as an archaism, by G. Gozzi ('Presemi ella la mano. Vorrei che avcste veduto con qual garbo io *gliene* baciai': *Osserv. veneto*, XXIX). Alongside the normal enclitics *mi*, *ti*, *si*, the forms *me*, *te*, *se* were admitted in verse; indeed, Parini, in correcting his printed masterpiece, changed *saettarti* to *saettarte*, and so on. In the plural *ne* for 'ci' ('us') was very frequent, even in prose. Some northern writers, misled by their dialect, confused *ci* with *si*: 'ci serviamo dello stile familiare . . . per non distaccar*si* del verisimile' (Goldoni, *Teatro comico*, II, ii). In the sequences of atonic pronouns *se gli*, *se le* for 'gli si', 'le si' still persisted: 'In questo mentre Gano *se gli* getta — ai piedi' (Forteguerri, *Ricciardetto*, XXIV, st. 69); '*se gli* facciano [al fanciullo] tirar due righe di scrittura' (Genovesi, *Lez. civ. econ.*, I, p. 203); 'gode che *se le* presenti un'occasione' (Spalletti, *Saggio sopra la bellezza*, p. 27 Natali). *Ci* and *vi* as adverbs of place (originally meaning 'here' and 'there') became confused, as Gigli testifies in his *Vocabolario cateriniano* under 'Particelle'. Bandiera recommended use of *vi* for 'here', but Parini defended the distinction in meaning. A very common construction was *il di cui libro, la di cui lettera* ('Ei si lusinga, che siate un giorno *la di lui* sposa': Goldoni, *Le smanie per la vill.*, I, xi). *Lo che* was also often used ('S'egli pur ti piacesse, *lo che* sperar non osa': Chiari, *La Veneziana in Algeri*, V, ii). *Qualche* could still be used as a plural: 'un mazzo di *qualche* belle operazioni di lingua': Salvini, *Prose toscane*, I, p. 210); '*qualche* sgrammaticature' (Alfieri, *Vita*, Year 1783), etc. The possessive adjective *suo* was sometimes used for 'their': examples in Gigli ('tante eccelse, e robuste Monarchie dalle *sue* fondamenta divelte', oration 1714 in *Lezioni*, p. 161), Becelli ('[nè il Bembo nè l'Ariosto] lasciarono di scrivere Toscanamente, perchè in altra guisa parlassero i terrazzani *suoi*': *Se oggidì scrivendo . . .*, p. 74) and Goldoni ('Le Muse, che non abbandonano i *suoi* divoti': *Il Poeta fanatico*, II, vii); here dialectal influence combined with Latin. Another dialectal feature was the reinforcement of relative pronouns and adverbs with *che*: 'Pazzi, pazzi quanti *che* siete' (Goldoni, *I malcontenti*, II, viii), 'Povera me, in che condizione miserabile *che* mi trovo!' (Goldoni, *Le smanie per la vill.*, I, vii), 'come *che* fanno i cani' (Chiari, *La bella pellegrina*, II, sc. I), etc. In verbal flection there was a great variety of variants, which the grammarians sought to reduce to order. Gigli, in his *Lezioni di lingua toscana* had, alongside the column in which he registered 'correct' forms, three others — for forms described as 'antiche', 'poetiche' and 'corrotte'. Here we should note the importance attributed to 'poetic' forms: generally he meant archaic forms still usable in verse. Naturally, some of Gigli's classification is a matter of opinion: he registered, alongside *vediamo* and *veggiamo*, classified as correct, *vedemo*, listed as archaic. It does not surprise us that the ending *-emo* is to be found in Vico, who archaized ('il di più che noi *godemo* sopra gli antichi') and in poetry ('Veder ciò che *vedem* tu solo ed io': Manfredi). Writers of verse made much of the freedom to use 'poetic' forms: we find *-e* in the 3rd pers. pres. subj. of verbs in *-are*, not only where the poet aspires to a noble tone ('E l'amo ancor che il suo destin l'*annode* — con sacro laccio a più felice amante': Zappi; 'nè perché roco ei siasi, o dolce ei *cante*': Zappi, 'Il gondolier . . .'; 'Una certa grandezza — splende, che si può dir che nulla *manche*': C. Gozzi, *Marfisa bizzarra*, VI, st. 85), but also in prosaic lines in which the form is used to facilitate rhyming ('A sé mi chiama il Duca; fa che l'udienza *aspette*': Goldoni, *T. Tasso*, II, i; 'Si cangi quanto vuole; ma trovi chi l'ascolte': Chiari, *Il poeta comico*, III, 2). Chiari even exhumed an archaic *sièno* for *siano* when he needed something to rhyme with *-eno*: 'Non dico che insoffribili gli uomini tutti *sieno*' (*Il filosofo veneziano*, I, i). Among generally admitted variants we record the two forms of the 1st pers. sing. of the imperfect. Alongside the forms *era, amava, vedeva* (which were by far the more common), there existed also *ero, amavo, vedevo* (used, for example, by Chiari and P. Verri). Another oscillating form was the 2nd pers. sing. of the pres. subj.: *che tu abbia* or *che tu abbi*. Third pers. subj. plural forms of the type *vadino, venghino* were widely used, but condemned by the grammarians. In the second pers. plural imperf. indic. Tuscans preferred the short forms *voi andavi, voi facevi* to the clumsier regular endings (*voi andavate, voi facevate*), but, Fagiuoli excepted, few dared to write them. In the conditional, third-person forms in *-ia* were frequent in verse but were used also in prose. First-person plurals in -*aressimo*, -*eressimo*, -*iressimo* appeared here and there, but the grammarians did not tolerate them: *correressimo* (Vico), *vedressimo* (C. Gozzi), *potressimo* (Alfieri). In the third pers. plural, forms in -*ebbono* were still admissible. There would be no end to our list if we were to register all the variants in the less regular verbs; we note, however, that non-Tuscans had a tendency to apply regular paradigms: *potiamo* (passim), *anderà*, *averà*, *goderà* (Goldoni), *s'opponerà* (Chiari), *veniremo* (C. Gozzi), etc. The auxiliary of improper reflexive verbs was still *avere*: 'si hanno preso la briga' Galiani), 'se *si avesse seguito* l'ampio campo' (A. Conti), 'mio fratello *se l'ha sposata* [la Bergalli]' (C. Gozzi), 'mi pare che *abbiasi fatto* più onore di quel che meritava' (Mazzuchelli), 'io penso che ... l'acqua vi *si abbia scavato* il canale più angusto' (Targioni Tozzetti), 'l'idea che codesti Signori *si hanno* di me *formato*' (Meli), etc. There would no longer have been any trace of the personal flexion of indefinite forms (*essereno*, *essendono*), formerly a feature of the southern dialects and of literary Italian based on them, had not Vico used them in his archaizing style.

In the syntactical field French influence was marked. A French type of construction can be seen in the type 'pollo *allo spiedo*' (satirized in Maffei's *Raguet*, III, ii). Partitive *di* spread beyond its traditional use in Italian: 'con più *di* energia', 'il troppo *di* varietà' (Algarotti). The vogue enjoyed by the relative superlative with repetition of the article was also due to French: 'le anime *le* più sonnacchiose' (Genovesi), 'il poema *il* più galante che ci sia', 'le verità *le* meglio dimostrate (Algarotti), 'la musica *la* più eccellente' (Goldoni), 'l'uomo *il* più grave, l'uomo *il* più plumbeo della terra' (P. Verri), 'l'uomo *il* più sensitivo della terra' (Parini), 'l'arte *la* più necessaria' (Filangieri), etc. On French, too, was modelled the construction '*È Antonio* (or *È lui*) *che* me l'ha scritto' with emphatic value: '*È* da così lungo tempo ch'io non ho nuove di lui' (Algarotti, *Opere*, XVII, p. 27), 'fors'*è* per ciò che vengono spesso a trovarmi' (Bettinelli, *Opere*, V. p. 89), etc. So was the construction '*Non* gli ho dato per elemosina *che* un quattrino'. The same thing can be said of the type *per poco che* ('per poco ch'io cambi non sono più io': Bettinelli, *Opere*, V, p. 123) and the type *troppo ... per* ('egli è troppo saggio e prudente per approvare': Fontanini). At this time, too, the periphrastic constructions *vengo di dire*, *vado a fare* (also noted by Maffei in his *Raguet*) became widely diffused. The prepositional gerund *in leggendo* (Algarotti, G. P. Zanotti) owed its increased use to the analogous French construction; but there were examples of it in the Trecento (*in aspettando*: Petrarch) and the Cinquecento, and it was therefore considered legitimate. *Malgrado* ('malgrado la lontananza', Zanotti; 'malgrado le gelosie frequenti', Bettinelli) tended, on the model of French, to replace the traditional *a malgrado di*. Recapitulation using the relative ('il dialetto particolare d'un popolo illustre dell'Italia, *il quale dialetto* . . .': Parini) also seems to have been due to analogous French constructions.

But French influence was even more obvious in choice of sentence structure than in the fortune enjoyed by particular constructions. The linear sentence tended to replace the architectonic: instead of the traditional long periods, rich in subordinate clauses ('stile periodico'), writers used short periods that were scarcely syndetic ('stile spezzato' or 'interrotto'). Moreover, whereas word-order had previously been rich in inversions, and long flowing periods had come to a close with a verb, following Latin models or the latinizing style of Boccaccio or Della Casa, many authors now preferred direct order (subject-verb-complement). The two tendencies were different, though closely connected. French grammarians were much exercized by them, influenced as they were by the ideas of Descartes and of Port-Royal, and concerned with achieving the greatest possible clarity. In Italy, innovators like Algarotti, Verri, Cesarotti praised the broken-up style and direct order (Cesarotti noting the possibilities of using both kinds in Italian in appropriate contexts), while Beccaria mocked the habit of blowing up a common idea into a hundred words arranged in a complicated and gigantic period ('Lettera sulla lingua', *Il Caffè*, tomo I, Brescia 1765, p. 70). Galeani Napione, however, defended lengthy periods, maintaining that one of the advantages of Italian was the possibility of using either direct or inverted constructions. G. Gozzi found the broken-up style intolerable. Baretti praised direct construction, but he, too, disliked periods that were split up into too many unconnected parts.

The modern sequence, in which the attribute follows the noun it limits, became ever more firmly established, particularly in the case of participles, ethnical adjectives and adjectives indicating colour, form and material. But the rule was far from absolute: it was contravened, not only in poetry, which preserved its freedom, but also in prose, owing to Latin influence. Metastasio used *l'araba fenice* in well-known lines of his *Demetrio* (II, iii); *la Veneta Marina* was part of the official usage of the Venetian Republic; Parini spoke of the *cimmeria nebbia*, the *itale voci*, the *italian Goffredo*, and so on; Baretti wrote of *alcune settentrionali isole*. And in his *Vita* Alfieri mentions a period '*di logorate grammatiche e stancati vocabolari* . . . e di *raccozzati propositi*'. Among the bold transpositions still practised in poetic language we record one used by Parini: placing a complement between the attributive adjective (or the article) and the noun: 'e le gravi per molto adipe dame' (Parini, *Notte*, line 268); 'le dal sol percosse — del suo fiotto inegual spume d'argento' (Bettinelli, 'All'abate Benaglio'); 'Su la d'olivo inghirlandata prora' (Fantoni, 'Sorgi Laware . . .'); 'la rauca di Triton buccina tace', Mascheroni, *Invito a Lesbia Cidonia*, l. 88), etc. Alfieri's brusque transpositions seemed striking to reader and listener alike; hence the line of parody composed by a wit during an evening when attendance was thin at the Teatro dei Dilettanti at Rome: 'Oh poca quanto nel teatro gente!'

Italian vocabulary reflected the Settecento's tendency to rebel against tradition when tradition seemed to conflict with Reason and Nature. Since French thinkers were the leaders in this rebellion, many of the innovations which then took their place alongside traditional elements in the Italian lexicon came from France; some were French words, others Graeco-Latin words which entered other European languages through French. We shall mention here some of the words which came to be used in this period, or which assumed new meanings or enjoyed unaccustomed vogue. *Filosofo* and *filosofico* had a very general sense, being used for all activities requiring reflection. Targioni Tozzetti, for instance, wrote: 'considerando attentamente con occhio Filosofico questa Pianura orizzontale di Pisa, si vede che l'Arno negli antichi tempi l'ha dominata in varj luoghi' (*Relazioni d'alcuni viaggi*, 2nd ed., Florence 1768, II, p. 94). Many used *filosofismo* (the Abbé Cataneo expounding *Il filosofismo delle belle*, Venice 1753), and names were given to *filosofia*'s various branches and schools (e.g. *psicologia*; *fatalismo*, *materialismo*, *monismo*, etc.). The conviction that the Age of Reason had begun led to the use of *lumi* (*secolo dei lumi*, *filosofia dei lumi*) and *illuminato*, which appeared frequently, both in the works of supporters of the new ideas, e.g. the contributors to *Il Caffè*, and, ironically, in those of their adversaries. *Letterato*, too, had a wider connotation than it has today, meaning simply 'scholarly': the *Giornale dei letterati* corresponded to the French *Journal des Sçavans*, and the gap between letters and sciences had not yet become an abyss. A concept dear to the thinkers of the period was that of *buon gusto*.

And if *ragione* was one of the great myths of the century, a very important place, too, was set aside for *sentimento*: the term *sentimentale* was coined, while *sensibile* came to mean 'easily moved, sensitive'. *Emozione* came into use, while *sublime* became fashionable. The distinction that already existed between *genio* and *ingegno* became more clearly established, *genio* being used, not only for the spontaneous impulses of the mind, but also for exceptional creative ability, and then for the man possessing ability: 'Siamo quì (sic) alla presenza, sotto gli occhi, per così dire, di . . . sì gran genio qual fu Dante' (Salvini, *Prose tosc.*, III, p. 2). The recognition of the need for tolerance led to anxiety over *fanatismo*. Unbelievers sometimes made *pregiudizio* include any manifestation of religion; hence their designation as *spregiudicati*, as well as *spiriti forti* and *liberi pensatori*. Many professed themselves *filantropi* and *cosmopoliti*. *Patria* and *nazione* were still used to denote the city or little state to which one belonged, but much more frequently they now referred to Italy. *Patriota, patriotto*, which in the Seicento meant 'compatriot', now took the meaning 'lover of one's country'; *patriot(t)ico* and *patriot(t)ismo* followed. *Democrazia* and *despotismo* came into use. And in the second half of the century *risorgimento* acquired political meaning, especially in Piedmont (the first known example in this sense being the Count of San Raffaele's 'il nostro imminente risorgimento', 1769). The linguistic disputes contributed *linguaio, parolaio, purista, neologismo*. The wide use of *abate*, employed for all manner of ecclesiastics, and the diffusion of *cicisbeo* were typical of the century. So, too, the vogue enjoyed by *improvvisatori* and *raccolte*. The double 'settenario' took the name of the poet who used it, P. I. Martelli, becoming the *martelliano*. The use of *gazzetta* and *giornale* may seem a little strange to us, for the *gazzettante* was the 'journalist' (as we today understand the term), while the *giornalista* specialized in literary journalism and was a man of letters. Some common nouns came from proper names in literary works: *vanesio* from Fagiuoli's *Ciò che pare non è* (1724), *ciana* from A. Valli's *Madama Ciana* (1738), *lillipuziano* from *Gulliver's Travels*. The words of an opera came to be consigned to a *libretto*: the term may go back to the late Seicento, but, if so, it was still not well established at the beginning of the Settecento, when Muratori in his *Della perfetta poesia* (1706) wrote: 'Mancando all'uditore il *libricciuolo* (come suol chiamarsi) dell'Opera. . . .' New literary and historical terms were *biografo, editore, diploma* (along with *diplomatico* and *diplomatica*), etc. *Secentismo* and *secentista* became pejoratives in the first half of the

Settecento. *Romanzesco*, which, at the beginning of the century simply meant 'proper to a *romanzo*', came to be used at the end of the Settecento in the sense in which *romantico* later prevailed. The pre-romantics were also fond of *patetico* and *pittoresco*. Some expressions containing *bello* became popular: *bell'ingegno, belle arti, bel mondo*. Towards the end of the century the word *barocco* became widely used with reference to the architecture and sculpture of the Seicento. Many new words referred to new fashions (often from beyond the Alps): *andrienne, falpalà* (and others to which we shall return in discussing French influence). There were some new vehicles like the *svimero*. The *pianoforte* was originally called *clavicembalo col piano e forte* by its inventor, the Paduan Bartolomeo Cristofori (and news of its invention was given by S. Maffei in the *Giornale dei letterati d'Italia* in 1711). Other new inventions were the *ventilatore*, the *scafandro* and the *aerostato*. Algarotti (letter of 1 Jan. 1763) claimed to have taken *tascabile* from spoken Tuscan. Some new games appeared (like *faraone*), while *lotto* spread to the rest of Italy from Genoa, where it was the custom to bet on the results of the *seminario* — the drawing of lots for the offices of principal magistrates from among the 120 approved names. In law, new words appeared to cover additional legal provisions (e.g. *manomorta*), but there was still much variation in terminology from state to state. The development of international trade and of the study of economics led to notable innovations in terminology: *economia politica* (with the synonyms *pubblica economia* and *economia civile*) and the derivative *economista*; *materie prime, monopolio, (libera) concorrenza, esportare* and *importare*; *milionario, aggiotatore, cambia-valute, (lettera) cambiale, tassabile, capitalista*, etc. *Manifattura* and *stabilimento* passed, on the model of French, from abstract to concrete meaning. At Milan under Maria Theresa, the first *censimento* took place in 1749 and the *catasto prediale* came into operation in 1760, while in Lombardy *camere di commercio* were created under Joseph II. These are but odd examples of new public institutions; a full survey would need to proceed state by state. Among private institutions we should note the *asilo d'infanzia* established at Genoa in 1757 by Lorenzo Garaventa.

The astounding development of the sciences in the eighteenth century brought with it corresponding increases in terminologies. Thousands of new words appeared, and scores of terms acquired a technical meaning in addition to the common one they already possessed. Moreover, many technical words became part of

common usage. This growth in scientific vocabulary was so great
that it is futile to try and illustrate it adequately in a work of this
kind. We shall simply indicate one or two of the paths followed.
In chemistry, for instance, the innumerable new terms were, for
the most part, made up by combining Greek and Latin elements,
with much ingenious use of prefixes and suffixes to indicate various
kinds of compounds. In view of its basis and structure, such
vocabulary could pass easily from French to Italian (an important point, since the new terminology owed much to the 'chemical
revolution' of Lavoisier and Guyton de Morveau). Observation of
nature, on the other hand, involved knowledge of objects and
phenomena from many parts of the word and the acceptance of
words from other languages which designated them. Some of
these, like *orango* or *urango*, were exotic. Other terms which had
previously been dialectal and limited to a particular region of
Italy now became nationally known; *lava* and *mofeta* are examples.
Sometimes, variants from different sources were noted as
synonyms, not only in scientific works of the day (e.g. Vallisnieri's *Opere fisico-mediche*), but by writers anxious to be understood in more than one region or circle, e.g. 'Calmella chiamano gli
Agricoltori quel ramicello che si adopera per innestare *a sfera*. . . .
Innesto, *nesto* lo chiamano i Fiorentini. . . . *Marza* è lo stesso, che
calmella' (Vallisnieri, III, p. 282). And when the potato became
widely used the Società Patria of Genoa published an opuscule
entitled *De' pomi di terra ossia patate*, Genoa 1793. In listing names
of animals and plants, authors who aimed at a fairly wide public
often gave first the italianized Latin forms and then the Italian,
e.g. *Relazione dell'erba detta da' Botanici Orobanche e volgarmente
Succiamele, Fiamma e Mal d'occhio*, Florence 1723. On the other
hand, B. Bartalini in his *Catalogo delle piante che nascono spontanee
intorno alla Città di Siena*, Siena 1776, employed the nomenclatures
of Tournefort and Linnaeus. L. Spallanzani added a scientific
term to give greater precision to what he had already said in
Italian: 'il lago di Orbitello, feracissimo di grosse anguille
(*Muraena anguilla*), la cui pesca si fa in ogni stagione' (*Viaggi alle
Due Sicilie*, V, p. 42), etc. Even the poet Mascheroni did this,
adding, after the lines 'Dal calice succhiato in ceppi stretta — la
mosca in seno al fior trova la tomba' (*Invito*, ll. 491-2), the note:
Muscipula Dionea. An instance of an already existing word given
a technical meaning can be seen in *saturo* 'sated', which, used by
chemists, came to mean 'saturated' in the chemical sense. New
terms, or old terms in new meanings, were not always successful.

Sometimes the theory with which they were connected collapsed under them: *flogisto* had considerable vogue in the Settecento and then faded away. It often happened, of course, that of a number of synonyms only one survived. A good instance of that is the fate of the multiplicity of words for 'volcano': *vulcano, monte vulcano, volcano, monte ignivomo* or just *ignivomo, monte fiammifero, vesuvio, mongibello.* The growth of the natural and physical sciences soon impinged on the life and culture of the time, and certain terms entered common parlance; examples from medicine alone are *oculista, ostetricia* to denote new specialisations, *pellagra, scarlattina* to designate identification of new diseases, and *innesto* and *inoculazione* (or *inserzione*) to cover new forms of treatment (*vaccina* only came in later). That technical terms should be widely used in works for specialists was to be expected. But there were didactic poets, too, who were prepared to welcome them:

> *Or gli* epicicli *de' pianeti, e il vasto*
> eccentrico *rotar laberinteo*
> *fremendo osserva* ...
> > (Rezzonico, *Il sistema de' cieli*),

though others, as we shall see presently, preferred allusive description and careful periphrasis. Pulpit orators made wide use of scientific terms for metaphors and were condemned by Mascheroni, Algarotti, Bettinelli and Gozzi for their pains. That ladies and gentlemen in polite society were also eager to affect knowledge of scientific terminology we know from some satirical passages in Parini, e.g.

> *Te con lo sguardo e con l'orecchio beva*
> *la Dama da le tue labbra rapita;*
> *con cenno approvator vezzosa il capo*
> *pieghi sovente: e il* calcolo, *la* massa
> *e l'*inversa ragion *sonino ancora*
> *su la bocca amorosa. Or più non odia*
> *de le scole il sermone Amor maestro.*
> > (*Mezzogiorno*, ll. 983-9).

In fact writers of all kinds frequently had recourse to scientific terms for metaphors: Baretti complained that Father Buonafede's thoughts 'non hanno soverchia *elasticità*', an image that did not please the latter (*Frusta*, n. XXXII: II, p. 384, Piccioni), while Brighella, in Carlo Gozzi's *Mostro turchino* (IV, 6), speaks, not without irony, of the '*inoculazion* del bon senso'. Indeed, an opuscule entitled *Italia* (1778) alleged that at Florence a *cicis-beatura matematica* was practised, with the result that one might have phrases like: *in ragion composta del vostro affetto, in ragione inversa del vostro languore, i quadrati dei tempi della mia speranza sono come i cubi della distanza del vostro consenso*, etc. Of course, some of the terms used by the scientists in the Settecento have been abandoned: *antediluviano* had a precise meaning for Vallisnieri and Targioni Tozzetti, whereas today *antidiluviano* is merely a hyperbolic synonym for 'old'.

Another series of words which entered Italian at this time referred to events, objects and customs in other countries. News of the American War of Independence brought *insurgenti*, and of the French Revolution *notabili, Stati generali*, etc., while accounts of journeys to N. America brought *sachemi* and to S. America *poncio*, etc.

Certain individuals were notably fertile in coining new words. Vico manifested his personal tastes not so much in creation of neologisms as in choice of archaic and rare words (*degnità, eroe*, etc.). But for Baretti the coining of new words, especially by the use of certain suffixes, was a frequent trick of style. We note just a few of his creations: *barbitondere, boccacceria, brunocchiuto, cinquecentesco, creanzuto, cruscheria, donnaio, eglogaio, etruscaio, fazzolettata*. Another great coiner of neologisms (this one very fond of prefixes) was Alfieri, particularly in certain works (the *Vita*, chiefly the second version; the *Satires*). Here are a few of his: *banchieresco, berlinale, disappassionarsi, disebriare, disferocire . . . microscopo, misogallo, odiosamato, omiccino, oltremontaneria, repubblichino* (pej.). Some Alfierisms entered the literary language (e.g. *misogallo, odiosamato*), and *snaturato* may owe its success to him, for it seems unlikely that the rare examples of *snaturato* and *disnaturato* in the Duecento and Trecento could have been the basis of its vogue since his time.

In word-formation the usual factors operated. There were nouns formed from verbs (*usurpo, villeggio*), and verbs from nouns (*dilazionare, parodiare, stilare*). Nouns continued to be formed, too, by the addition of the usual suffixes: *cambista, cicisbeismo, sonettaio*. Adjectives were also formed with the usual suffixes: *-ale* (*settimanale*, Casti; *nozionale*, Cesarotti), *-ico* (*centaurico*, Targioni Tozzetti; *nordico*, Cesarotti), *-esco* (*cinquecentesco*, Baretti), *-abile* and *-ibile* (*capibile*, Vallisnieri, *riflessibile*, Algarotti), while those in *-evole* were mostly formed from nouns and had an archaizing or jocose connotation. Among verbs formed with suffixes there was a large number in -*eggiare* (*inneggiare*, *tantaleggiare*) and in -*izzare*, sometimes formed independently in Italian, like *panizzare*, sometimes modelled on analogous French verbs. Prefixes were used for many formations of the type *antiscorbutico* (Vallisnieri), *co-academico* (Gozzi), *condeputato*, *incombattibile*, *innegabile*, *insalvabile* (Salvini), *protogiornale*, *sottoscala*, *vicepiè* (in the jocose phrase *un vicepiè di legno*, Gigli). There was an abundance, too, of para-synthetic formations: *antidiluviano*, *ingesuitato* (Muratori), *scocollato* (Martinelli), etc. Among compounds we note the usual impera-tival type *guardaportoni* or the humorous *parastrepito* (G. B. Vasco). Forms modelled on the classical languages included compounds like *occhi-pietoso* (Fantoni), *occhi-azzurro* (Cesarotti) and even *vini dolcepiccanti* (Rolli), etc. Arbitrary formations of a dithyrambic kind continued: '*amorarmicantante* filastrocca' (Saccenti), 'della *fiorbellaccoglitrice* Crusca' (Arisi), etc. Certain types of words formed with suffixes were used both in the poetic language and in scientific terminology: in the former *ondifero* (Varano), *racemifero* (Lamberti) and the humorous *quaglifero* (Saccenti), in the latter *bilifero*, etc. (Vallisnieri). But to these we shall return when dealing with latinisms.

The Settecento inherited from previous centuries the belief that poetry required certain differences in vocabulary. *Alma*, *augello*, *etra*, *frale*, *guardo*, *ostro*, *prence*, *pria*, *rai*, *suora* were words to be used in verse in preference to, or indeed to the exclusion of, their prose equivalents. For many normal words were not admissible in poetry (except in certain genres of an inferior kind, like satire); Maffei criticized C. M. Maggi for having used in his verse words like *appetito*, *confutare*, *congratularsi*, *dimenticarsi*, *misericordia*, *operare*, *tribolato*. Indeed, some authors felt that, merely because they were writing verse, they were entitled to use words reserved for poetic composition. Thus in verse comedies by Chiari and Goldoni we find in very pedestrian passages lines like

> *Non temete violenze; rasserenate i rai*
> (Chiari, *L'innamorato di due*, I, 4)
> *Se il suo dinar rimando, egli è perch'io nol* merto
> (Goldoni, *Il filosofo inglese*, III, 17).

And although there were some poets, as we have seen, who intro-duced realistic or technical words, an effort to avoid them by periphrasis was more frequent. In G. F. Zappi's sonnet on Michelangelo's Moses ('Chi è colui...' in *Rime*, Venice 1723), the beard is indicated not by the word *barba*, but thus:

Quest'è Mosè. Ben mel diceva il folto
onor del mento, e 'l doppio raggio in fronte;

and the periphrasis remained in circulation. Zaccaria Betti, in
his poem *Il baco da seta*, referred to dew like this:

E però quando il Sol dal verde moro
col suo calor tolse de l'Alba il pianto
(c. IV, ll. 30-31).

And Parini described coffee in his *Mattino* (ll. 141-2) as:

il legume . . . d'Aleppo
giunto e da Moca.

Chiari, in his comedy *Il poeta comico* (II, 5), called a carbine *ferrea
canna*, an expression used by many for 'gun' before its adoption
by Leopardi. Frugoni ('Sermone al conte A. Bernieri') found a
very involved way of expressing the concept 'one who served
chocolate in a cup':

abil coppier che lieto
d'indiche droghe, e d'odorata spuma
largo conforto mi recava in nappo
di cinese lavoro.

while Mascheroni made the shell *Venus literata* an excuse for:

a quelle
qual Dea del mar d'incognite parole
sparse l'eburneo dorso?

As can be seen from some of these examples, the desire to avoid a
particular word served as a point of departure for elegant playing
with words.

While archaisms were admitted or welcomed in poetic language,
they found no place in spontaneous prose. But in certain highly
contrived and ambitious prose styles they abounded still. If we
consider the difficulties writers faced in acquiring knowledge of
common vocabulary, particularly the ways in which many
of them learned Italian (by reading Boccaccio and consulting the
Crusca dictionary), we shall not be surprised to find the odd word
taken from Trecento texts. That was even more likely to happen,
naturally, in circles that approved of Trecento models anyway.
At Florence reverence for the writers consecrated by the Crusca
was at least tempered by native usage. But at Naples the Capuist

school found followers; to it G. B. Vico adhered. In Venetia we find the Veronese Giulio Cesare Becelli and Carlo Gozzi and his Granelleschi. But even Pietro Verri (*Osservazioni sulla tortura*) wrote: 'Levò, col passarvi il mantello, la *polve*'. Such archaisms can only be judged in their stylistic context (along with corresponding grammatical archaisms like *vosco*, *mel darete*, *mancheranti*). But merely in order to give some idea of the phenomenon, here is a brief list of examples: *apparare* (C. Gozzi), *avacciare* (Vico), *a bistento* (Di Gennaro), *calogna* (Vico), *continovare* (Parini), *daddovero* (Cesarotti), *danaio* (Vico, Gozzi), *diffalta* (Becelli), *durazione* (Becelli), *entragne* (Vico), *erbolaio* (Gozzi), *lunghesso* (for use of which Baretti criticized several authors), *maestrato* (Vico), *orrevole* (Gozzi), *ricadìa* 'annoyance' (Gozzi), etc. But zealous followers of the Crusca cultivating fourteenth-century words were less numerous than their adversaries. Among these Baretti frequently flayed writers for archaisms (Genovesi in no. II of the *Frusta*, Di Gennaro in no. IV, etc.). The word that perhaps incensed the anti-Cruscan most was *conciossiaché*, with its variants *conciossiacosaché*, *conciofossecosaché*, *conciossiamassimamenteché*. Poetasters who imitated Dante irritated Bettinelli, who complained (*Le Raccolte*, III, st. 41) of the

> *mille stolti*
> *ch'han repleta di bolge ogni canzone*

A little, but not a great deal, is to be learnt about the archaisms of the time from the writings of the parodists (the 'tragicomedy' *Il Toscanismo e la Crusca*, in which Ser Toscanismo and Signor Cruscanzio speak a language laden with fourteenth-century features, or some of Goldoni's comedies). That some of the archaisms won their battle (or that those who condemned them were mistaken in considering them archaic) can be seen from the fact that we today use some of those criticized: *altezzoso*, *nonpertanto*, *smagato*, *Ferragosto*, which Baretti (I, 93; II, 257, Piccioni) found intolerable; or *caparbio*, *carezzevole*, *dappoco*, *tiepido*, *istigare*, *tutti e due*, *tenere in bilico* (listed in the *Toscanismo*, I, 9). Baretti himself used archaisms for a joke: e.g. *sirocchia* ('m'accommiatai da quella angiolella e della sua formosissima *sirocchia*': *Lett. fam.*, XXXVII), *calonaco* (in the letters to Canon Agudio).

Dialectal and regional words were no longer to be expected in the lyric, or indeed in the more abstract and dignified kinds of prose. But examples were to be found in scientific language. Agricultural and maritime nomenclature, for instance, varied

considerably from region to region, and it was natural that
authors should use those employed in their own. Baretti, reviewing
L'Agricoltura by C. Trinci of Pistoia (*Frusta*, no. 24; II, pp. 239-41,
Piccioni), observed that the publisher had added to the work a
section on *morari*, without realizing it repeated what Trinci had
written on *gelsi*. Further, he had added a short dissertation by
Z. Betti *intorno la ruca de' meli*. But *ruca* turned out to be another
word for *bruco*. In cases like these, remarked Baretti, in which an
author wished to use a non-Tuscan word, he should add the
Tuscan word at some point, so that the reader could find it in the
dictionary. The importance of the silk industry in Piedmont led
Count Felice San Martino to assert: 'Quando si parla di seta, si
possono adottar senza scrupolo le voci piemontesi'. In marine
matters, Venice, Genoa, Naples did not yet feel the need to
abandon their own words. In the translation of the *Dizionario
istorico, teorico e pratico di marina* by Savérien, published at Venice
in 1769, Venetian terms abounded. Algarotti spoke of the
'angustia de' *cantieri* dell'arsenale vecchio', but also of the
'falegname di uno *scoerro* di Amsterdam' (cf. Venetian *squero*).
Parts of a town, parts of a house, articles of dress, domestic
utensils, foods bore various names in various places; Goldoni
spoke of the *calli* of Venice and its *mezà*. The different states of
Italy gave different names to their institutions: the magistracy
which in Piedmont and Nice was known as the *consolato di commercio* corresponded to the *cinque savi della mercanzia* at Venice and
to the *supremo magistrato di commercio* at Naples and Palermo. It is
not strange that Galiani should feel justified in writing (in his
Moneta, passim) *coniata, impronto, zeccare*, since these were the
terms in official use at the Neapolitan mint. Beccaria used different economic and administrative terms according to the public
he was addressing: in his *Consulte*, aimed at a Lombard public
only, he used *prestinari, sfrosi, melgone*, where, in other writings, he
employed *fornai, contrabbandi, grano turco*. In private letters and
notes, regional words naturally appeared for familiar things:
Cesarotti used *brolo* (for 'orto') and *spàresi* (for 'sparagi') in his
letters; Parini wrote *cavagnola* in his 'Appunti per il Vespro e per
la Notte', though the dialect name of this game was not used by
him in the section of the poem describing it (*Notte*, ll. 564-681).
In comedies (even in verse) non-Tuscan writers occasionally had
recourse to dialectalisms (*bìgoli*, Martelli; *buganze*, Chiari;
spazzacucina, scaffa, còttole, Gozzi). And when Gozzi in his *Memorie
inutili* wrote *muraio* instead of *muratore*, he was simply putting an

Italian suffix to the Venetian *murèr*. Sometimes it was its affective value that set a dialect word on its path to success in the national language: such was the case of *birichino* (originally *birichino di Bologna*). Sometimes writers deliberately introduced dialectalisms in the hope that they would be generally adopted. Cesarotti (*Saggio sulla filosofia delle lingue*, III, x) believed that dialects could supply words lacking in the 'principal dialect', and Vallisnieri (*Opere*, III, 396-7) defended the 'Lombard' distinction between *crine* for 'human hair' and *crena* for 'horse's mane'. Occasionally writers found authority for using dialectalisms in the fact that early authors had used them; Gasparo Gozzi, using *lacche* for 'legs', as in Venetian usage, had the example of Burchiello behind him. National words overcame local words slowly and with difficulty: Muratori, who in the 1714 edition of his treatise *Del governo della peste* had written '*le Persiche*, o sia *i Persici*' (p. 151), in the 1722 edition corrected this to '*le Pesche*, o sia le *Persiche*' (p. 128). Yet at the end of the century there appeared a *Trattato della Cultura dei Persici e degli alberi da frutto* (Venice 1792). It was the Tuscan words that generally triumphed when there were clashes, but occasionally others were victorious. We know from Salvini and Regali that at a certain moment the Roman *magnare* was preferred to *mangiare* at Florence and Lucca because it was thought to be more elegant. That fashion died out. But the Roman *cocciuto*, *pupazzo* and (the game of) *bocce* remained. And from Neapolitan dialect *malocchio* and *iettatura* entered the standard language.

We might expect that, in a century in which anti-traditionalist currents predominated, there would be relatively few new latinisms. Yet, in fact, these were not less numerous than in previous centuries. They belonged mainly to two spheres: that of the sciences and that of neo-classical poetry. Naturally, attitudes to latinisms and grecisms varied from author to author. Vico, who aimed at a majestic style, revelled in them: *edurre*, *perrompere*, *urente*, *infermo* in the sense of 'weak', etc. Salvini, in his varied activity as translator, had frequent recourse to Latin words (*hiattola*, *inspergere*, *irsuzia*, *sagena*, etc.) and coined many others on the model of Latin and Greek words. Parini used many latinisms, mostly felicitously: *accenso*, *caprìpede*, *cucùrbita*, *lituo*, *pàtera*, *pàtulo*, *ridolente* (Lat. *redolens*), *scùtica*, *solvere*, *testudo*, *venenoso*, etc. Sometimes, too, he gave back an old meaning to an ordinary word: *esaurire* 'to empty by sucking', *flagello* 'lash'. Some of his latinisms have emerged from poetic language to general usage (e.g. *àlacre*). The developing sciences needed new terminologies and made wide use both of Latin and Greek words and of new words formed from Latin and Greek elements. Here are just a few examples: *animalcolo, corolla, gluma, laciniato, monopetalo, pistillo, polipetalo, rizotomo, stalagmite, acidulo (-olo)*; *clinico, diagnosi, prognosi, patema, profilattico, rachitide* (from scientific Latin *rachitis*), *scarlattina* (from scient. Lat. *scarlatina*), *centrifugo, centripeto, ondulazione, oscillare (-atorio, -azione)*; *eliocentrico, geocentrico*; *catenaria, ellissoide*. Neologisms formed from Latin and Greek elements were particularly frequent as names for new inventions: *aeronautica, aerostato, scafandro, ventilatore*. But just as some non-scientific latinisms (*sofo*) disappeared, so did some scientific ones: *flogisto, orittogenia, orittologia*. Antiquarian disciplines also had recourse to classical languages, e.g. for *latercolo* (Gori) and *loculo* (F. Buonarrotti). But motives for using latinisms were, of course, not limited to the need for new nomenclature. They came to be used for a wide variety of reasons, not least that of producing comic effect ('ma questo in quel *protunc* non le fa pro': Casotti, *Celidora*, VI, st. 24). And the frequency of metrical schemes in which the antepenult bore the stress made Latin proparoxytones a convenience for poets ('Ha colmo il sen *tornàtile* — che neve par non tocca': A. Mazza, 'Il talamo'). Classical words did not always have in Italian the meaning they had borne in classical Latin. Sometimes they bore a medieval or Renaissance sense, or even one acquired in the seventeenth or eighteenth century. Thus *adepto* or *adetto* usually meant 'a person skilled in alchemy', and was only just beginning to assume a wider meaning: '[i libri stampati] tolsero dalle mani di pochi *adepti* le cognizioni' (Beccaria, in *Caffè*, t. II, p. 9). *Etere*, too, had acquired one new meaning in physics (due to Newton) and another in chemistry (due to Frobenius). Latinisms and grecisms were often borrowed, not directly, but through another modern language. *Immorale* could have been taken from Latin (the adverb *immoraliter* is documented), but Salvini, who praises it as an English word of great force, reveals that it was in fact an anglo-latinism. Here is a short list of latinisms and grecisms that came in through French: *analisi, aneddoto, belligerante, biografo, cariato, coalizione, concorrenza, contingente, cosmopolita, deferenza, duttile, egida* (used figuratively: *sotto l'egida di*), *emozione, epoca, esportare, importare, industria* (not in the sense of 'diligence' but in that of 'utilization of raw materials'), *irritabile, materia prima* ('raw material'), *niso, patriot(t)a* (as 'patriot'; previously the word was used for 'compatriot' in Italian); *pro-*

gresso (in the absolute sense: 'progress of civilization'), *refrattario*, *tecnico*, etc. Anglo-latinisms included *adepto*, *colonia* (in the sense 'a group of foreign residents': 'la colonia inglese che è in Livorno', Algarotti), *esibizione*, *immorale*, *imparziale*, *insignificante*, *inoculare*, *rebus*, *transazione* ('transaction' in sense of 'scientific dissertation'), and the political series: *costituzionale*, *legislatura*, *sessione*, *petizione*, etc. From the American *insurrezione* arose the new meaning *presidente* ('head of a Republic'). Germano-latinisms were less frequent. Examples are: *dicaster(i)o*, *estetica*, *etere* (in the chemical sense), *inaugurale*, etc. Some latinisms arrived by other routes: Italian botanical and zoological terminology, for instance, was influenced by the contribution made to Latin botanical terminology by the Swede Linnaeus. Latinisms and grecisms proper cannot be separated from compounds made up of Latin and Greek elements. Such words were occasionally coined for a joke (*lettericidio*, Gigli; *nasologia*, Baruffaldi) or to satisfy some momentary stylistic need (*nubiaduna*, *profondigorgo*, etc., Salvini), and did not survive. But a few general terms did: *anglomania*, *bibliofilo*, *bibliomane*. *Aeronauta* and *aerostato* also flourished. Many scientific terms of this kind became established in the language: *bilifero* (Vallisnieri) and many other compounds in *-fero*; *anguilliforme*, *proteiforme* and others in *-forme*; *xilologia* (Algarotti) and other new names of sciences in *-logia*, etc. Even more numerous than such compounds were words formed by the addition of a suffix or prefix to latinisms: formations in *-ismo*, *-ista*, *-izzare* proliferated remarkably in this period, sometimes on the analogy of words formed in other European languages, sometimes independently, e.g. *dispotismo*, *fratismo*, *moderantismo*, *neologismo*, *purismo*, etc.; *botanista*, *cambista*, *capitalista*, *deista*, etc.; *caratterizzare*, *divinizzare*, *elettrizzare*, *umanizzare*, etc. That such a word came to Italian from another modern language can occasionally be established only by examination of the earliest example of it; *purista* appeared for the first time in G. A. Costantini's translation of the *Caractères* of La Bruyère (1758), and Algarotti confirmed that it was a word that came from French into Italian. In other instances the form of a word will reveal its provenance; *fanatismo* (not *fanaticismo*) is due to the French tendency to suppress *-ic* before *-isme*. *Analizzare* and *paralizzare* owe their endings to erroneous adaptation of the French *analyser* and *paralyser*, the *-yser* in both having been treated as if it were the suffix *-iser* and equivalent to *-izzare*. Similar influence can be seen in adjectives: *energico* probably owed its success to the corresponding French forms (Fioretti had

used *energiaco* and Salvini and Genovesi *energetico*). The endings of
Latin words were adapted to the patterns of Italian as in previous
centuries: thus Mascheroni has *cacto* (*Invito*, l. 468) and Parini
Odeo. Only rarely did an author use crude latinisms (*Chelae*,
Vallisnieri). Latin vowels were also modified to fit, though
exceptionally writers used etymological *y* or *ae*, *oe* (as in the
Oenologia of Manetti, 1773). There was much oscillation, however,
in the treatment of consonantal groups: *adepto* and *adetto*, *anecdoto*
and *aneddoto* were written. On the whole, in spite of a certain
number of exceptions, it is true to say that Tuscans preferred the
forms with assimilation (*pimmeo*, Saccenti; *ennico*, Manni; *ammos-
fera*, Targioni Tozzetti), whereas non-Tuscans tended to stick to
the etymological form without assimilation.

Numerous gallicisms had come into Italian toward the end of
the Seicento. In the Settecento there was a great increase in the
influence of French, which was felt in all spheres of life, affecting
everyday language and the dialects, as well as the writings of the
more intellectual. Here we shall note just a few examples, grouped
according to meaning. Social life had *abbordo* and *abbordare*,
coc(c)hetta (Algarotti, Bettinelli, Cerretti) and *cochetteria*, *cotteria*.
Madama and *madamosella* became much more widely used.
Fashions brought *disabigliè*, *andrienne* (this female garment was
made fashionable by the actress Thérèse Dancourt playing in
Andrienne, Baron's adaptation of Terence's *Andria*, 1704), *fisciù* or
fissù, *flanella*, *frisare*, etc.; the perfume *sanspareille* and some colours:
bleu (or *blo* or *blu*), *lillà*, *sucì*. The house and its fittings gave *bidè*,
burò, *cabarè*, *etichetta*, *ghiridone* (Fr. *guéridon*, 'centre-stand of a
table'), *ridò*, *surtù*. In the sphere of food and drink Italian borrowed
bignè, *cotoletta*, *fricandò*, *ragù*; *dessert*; *framboesia* or *frambuè*, *sciam-
pagna*, etc. Means of transport were described by *cabriolè*, *cupè*,
landò, *fiàccaro*. To the sphere of roads also belonged *marciapiede*.
Military life contributed *baionetta*, *mitraglia*, *montura*, *bloccare*,
ingaggiare, *picchetto*, *ranzonare*, and that of the sailor *manovra*,
scialuppa, *andare alle deriva*. From trades and industry we take as
examples *calotta*, *cerniera*, *ghisa*, *zinco*, and from the economic
sphere *aggiotaggio*, *aggiotatore*, *beni-fondi*, *bureau* or *burò* (in the sense
of 'office'), *conto corrente*, *ferma*. French administrative terms
appeared in some states, e.g. *dipartimento* in Piedmont, but the real
flood of such terms came after 1796. In the arts we can record the
expression *belle arti*. The theatre, music and dancing borrowed
parterre, *marionetta*; *overtura*, *rondò*; *oboe* or *oboè*; *minuetto*, *rigodone*,
etc. In card-games *faraone*, *fisce* were employed. Among the many

terms that the sciences carried from France nearly all were latinisms or grecisms used in French. But there were a few others, e.g. *cretino, cretinismo, marna*. A technical term was *montare* ('to set up a piece of apparatus', etc.). The extent of French penetration can be realized from the abundance of general terms: *allarmante, cicana, debordare, invironare, papà, regrettare, rimarco, rimpiazzare, risorsa*, etc. In many cases a new gallicism took its place beside an ancient one: alongside the very old gallicism *giardino* appeared *giardinaggio*; so too *chincaglierie, congedare*, etc. Many existing Italian words took on new meanings under the influence of French. Such were: *abile* (used absolutely without complement), *adorare* (hyperbolically of a woman or thing), *affascinare* (calque of *charmer*), *alleanza* (for 'alliance in marriage'), *autorizzare* (which meant to 'give authority to' and now came to be simply 'to permit'), *caffè* ('café'), *felicitare* (the meaning 'to make happy' declined; 'to congratulate' increasingly took its place), *genio* ('man of genius'), *interessante, intraprendente, intrapresa, liquore* (previously simply 'a liquid'), *lusingarsi* (calque of *se flatter*), *materia prima, mondo* ('people'), *obbligante, obbligato* ('grateful'), *progresso* ('Progress' in absolute sense), *pubblico* (as noun: 'those for whom a book or play is intended'), *sensibile, sensibilità, sfumatura* (in the sense *nuance*), *soffrire* (absolutely: *ho sofferto molto*), *superficiale* (fig.), *toccante* ('moving'), *toccare* ('to move'), *umanità* ('mankind'), *vignetta*, etc. Similarly, expressions sprang up, which, though consisting of Italian words, were modelled on similar French phrases: *belle arti, bel mondo, buon tono, colpo d'occhio, gioco di parole, presenza di spirito, sangue freddo, spirito forte, far la corte, aver l'onore, pescar nel torbido, saltare agli occhi, a misura che, in séguito*, etc. But there were also new words that were calques: *approfondire, faniente* (from *fainéant*: Algarotti), *impagabile, passabile, riserbatoio* (*réservoir*), *sviluppamento* (from *développement*: Algarotti), etc. And we have already spoken of many formations in *-ismo, -ista, -izzare* modelled on analogous French words. In the preceding lists we have included gallicisms which later disappeared from Italian. Many more of these might have been mentioned, e.g. *degaggiato* (condemned by Carlo Gozzi), *malonesto* (used by P. Verri), *tracasseria* (A. Verri) and a host of others whose life in Italian was brief. Italian accepted gallicisms in three ways: by adapting French words to Italian phonology and spelling, by borrowing them as they were without change, and, finally, by reproducing them by means of calques. Adaptation is usually a sign that the word came through popular channels or that it penetrated to the people; the other two ways generally indicate a more cultured medium. Many writers, for instance, used French words without adaptation;' Bettinelli wrote *négligé, petit maître, badinerie, bon mot, joli, piquant, charmant, art de plaire*, etc. But in many words there was oscillation, and indeed there still is today. A typical example is *toilette*, which was written by some in French fashion, adapted by others to *tueletta, toletta, teletta*. (The forms with *-ua-* — *tualette, tualetta* — belong to the nineteenth century; in the eighteenth *oi* was still pronounced in the manner reflected in the Italian spelling *ue*.) Some gave a false translation of it: *tavoletta* (Parini, C. Gozzi). And even today the word is still written in at least five ways: *toilette, toletta, teletta, toelette, toeletta*. There were many other examples: *dettaglio/detaglio* (and, in an attempt to avoid an ill-adapted gallicism, *ritaglio*), *bureau/burò/ burrò*, etc. Sometimes italianized forms prevailed, but with many variants, e.g. *amuerro/amoerre/moerre/moerro/muerre* (Fr. *moire*). Words from other languages sometimes came to Italian through French. *Freemason* was used rarely in its English form (*Frimesson*, Miner-betti, 1740), more often in an adapted or unadapted French form (*franmassone*: L. Pascoli, quoted by Bergantini, 1745), and not infrequently in a translated form (*liberi muratori; congregazione . . . detta dei Muratori*, Diodati, 1737). *Packet-boat*, through Fr. *paquebot*, gave It. *paccheboto* (Algarotti). The Spanish *platina* probably passed through Fr. before becoming Ital. *platina*, and later *plàtino*. *Azione* in the economic sense 'share' was registered by Alberti as a 'francesismo commerciale'; but is, it seems, of Dutch origin (and, remotely, Italian, as we see from the glossary of Castellani's *Nuovi testi fiorentini*). From Nordic languages came *narvalo* through the compilations of French naturalists. *Steppa*, too, came from the Russian *step'* through the Fr. *step, steppe*. Indigenous American words, which in preceding centuries frequently arrived in Spanish dress, now presented themselves in French forms: *canoto* (Targioni Tozzetti), *piroga*. And by the same route other exotic words arrived: *kaulin* occurred in the *Dizionario del cittadino*, Nice 1763, under *porcellana*. Algarotti used *mussoni*, influenced by the French *moussons*, but this was defeated by *monsoni*, which had previously been used in Italian.

Of the other foreign words entering Italian vocabulary the main contingent came from England. They were not all easily recognizable, for some were anglo-latinisms (which we have already discussed), some were calques (*biglietto di banco, insorgere* 'to rise up against', *libero muratore, libero pensiero, senso comune*, *verso bianco*, etc.) and some were altered by passing through French. Social life contributed *Milord* (*o*) and *Miledi* (though rare examples of *milorte* or *milord* can be found earlier). In the political field, the *Giornale dei letterati d'Italia*, XVIII, 1714, explained *whig* and *tory* to its readers. Italians also learned about the *quaccheri*. *Pamphlets* came to be known (either in that form or italianized to *panfletti* or *panfleti*) and some periodicals came to be called *Magazzino*. In the field of food and drink English gave *pudding* (sometimes left thus, sometimes italianized to *pudino* or *puddingo*, later *budino* or *bodino*, after being crossed with Fr. *boudin*), *toasts* and *punch* (or *ponc*, *puncio* or *ponchio*). Anglicisms in the sphere of dress were *redengotto* (through French) and *schincherche*. The alloy invented by Christopher *Pinchbeck* was called *princisbech* (Goldoni). Through English literature came knowledge of *silfi* and *gnomi* (names coined by Paracelsus, but whose diffusion in Europe was due to Pope's *Rape of the Lock*). From Swift's *Gulliver's Travels* came *Lilliputte* (Baretti) and *lillipuziano* (Algarotti). From the well-known novel by Richardson the name *Pamela* spread to novels and plays, while from Fielding's *Joseph Andrews* the name *Fanny* (pronounced in the French fashion) became common.

In this century, few words entered Italian from Spanish-speaking countries: *flottiglia*, *fandango*, *seguidiglia* (*zighediglia* in Baretti), *platina*. From German-speaking areas came *caffeàus* (though the Germ. *Kaffeehaus* was itself modelled on English *coffee-house*), *svìmeri*, *mùfferle*, *chifel*, etc. From there, too, came a group of mineralogical terms: *cobalto* or *cobolto*, *feldspato*, *nickel* or *nìccolo*, *scorillo* or *scorlo* from *Schorl*, *spizio* (from *Spitz*). From Slav languages came news of, and the name of, the *vampiri* (whether directly from Serbo-Croat or through French or German it is difficult to say). Journeys in Slav countries also resulted in knowledge of local features: Algarotti used *czar* (with fem. *czara*) and *copicco*. Accounts of travels were probably responsible, too, for oriental words (*nabab*, Cesarotti, 1792; *tattow*, in the translations of the *Voyages* of Captain Cook: *Viaggi*, Naples-Leghorn, 1787, IV, p. 222) and American words (*maogano* and *maogani*, both in Baretti; *sachemi*, Algarotti).

Italian culture continued to hold a place in European esteem, and this was reflected in the passage of italianisms into other languages. Some referred to social life, like *cicisbeo* (Fr. in the form *sigisbé*, 1765, then *sigisbée*; Germ. 1784; Eng. 1718), *casino* (Fr. 1740, Germ. 1775, Eng. 1789), *villa* (Fr. 1743, Engl. 1755). The phrase (*dolce*) *far niente* gained wide currency in Europe.

Among artistic terms we note *pittoresco*, used to refer chiefly to landscapes of a wild kind, like those of Salvator Rosa (Fr. *pittoresque* 1721, Eng. *picturesque* 1703, Germ. *pittoresk* 1768). In the musical sphere the most notable export was clearly *pianoforte* (Fr. 1774, shortened to *piano* 1798; Eng. 1767; German oscillated between *Fortepiano* 1775 and *Pianoforte* 1786; Swedish, evidently from German, got *fortepiano* 1779). Others of this class were *mandolino, violoncello, barcarola* and the acclamation *bravo*. *Protagoniste* made its first appearance in French in Goldoni's *Mémoires*. *Improvvisatore* (or *improvvisatrice*) represented a typical aspect of Settecento literature (Fr. 1765, Germ. 1787, Eng. 1795). Two epidemics (in 1743 and 1782) contributed to wide diffusion of the Italian term *influenza* (Eng. 1743, Fr. and Germ. 1782, Swedish 1783). And we have limited ourselves to a few examples which show more or less parallel penetration of three great languages. Much longer lists could be drawn up to show penetration of single languages. Such lists would vary considerably from language to language, for there was great variety in the words which writers and travellers chose in order to give local colour to their several accounts of what they saw in Italy.

I I

From the French Invasion to
the Kingdom of Italy
(1796–1861)

With the French invasion of 1796 a new period began in Italian history, and we shall start this chapter at that point. We shall end in 1861, when the Kingdom of Italy was proclaimed and north and south had been brought together, even if Rome, Venice, Trento and Trieste were still politically not Italian. Important intermediate dates were 1815, when the reactionaries returned to power, and 1848, the year of revolutions in Europe and of Italy's first war of independence.

In the years following 1796, battles and the passage of foreign troops were succeeded by consolidation of French power throughout peninsular Italy, though by means not everywhere identical: alongside the territories directly subject to France (which included Piedmont, Genoa, Parma, Tuscany and Rome) existed the two vassal states of the 'Kingdom of Italy' (*Regno Italico*) and the Neapolitan Kingdom of Murat. In spite of their dependence on France, to whose causes blood and money had to be contributed, Italians found that they enjoyed novel benefits, such as equality before the law and the discarding of the stifling police-ridden rule of the fallen dynasties. They began to believe in the possibility of a free and independent Italy. But the fall of Napoleon led to subjection to Austria and the restoration of most of the little states that existed before his coming. Liguria was annexed to Piedmont, and Venetia came under Austrian rule. The Valtelline was joined to Lombardy. Canton Ticino was no longer the vassal of the German-speaking cantons on the other side of the St. Gotthard, but a sovereign canton in the Swiss Confederation. The movements of 1821 and 1831 demonstrated the growing force of national ideals nurtured by secret societies.

Great hopes were kindled in 1848-49. For a few months Milan, Venice, Florence, Rome, Palermo lived in freedom; parliaments met and political parties were formed. To fall again into reactionary hands was painful. But henceforth Piedmont was to be the centre of activities aimed at independence, and exiles from other states gathered there. In '59 the Franco-Piedmontese campaign against Austria led to the union of Piedmont and Lombardy, which was soon followed by plebiscites in Tuscany and Emilia. The exploits of Garibaldi and the Thousand (1860) added Sicily and Naples to Victor Emmanuel's kingdom. When the Marches and Umbria were also liberated, the nation was nearly all contained in a single state. On March 14, 1861 the Kingdom of Italy was proclaimed. A few days later Rome was acclaimed as capital in principle, though it could not yet be taken. Nice, which, though possessing a Franco-Provençal dialect, had adopted Italian as a cultural language, was lost. Malta, occupied by the English in 1800, remained in their possession. In the Ionian Islands, Dalmatia and Istria, Venetian dominion ended with the fall of the Republic.

If, as Leopardi wrote in 1823, divided Italy lacked a common 'social tone', great steps were nevertheless taken towards the acquisition of it. The vicissitudes of the period 1796-1815 had brought great changes to the lives of many who would not otherwise have left the places in which they had been born, e.g. some of the political exiles who gathered from various parts of Italy in Turin, Florence (a more liberal place than most after the movements of 1821 and 1831), Paris, London, etc. There was an increase in contacts, too, between the social classes, though the bottom stratum of society had as yet very little say in things. The Risorgimento was above all the work of the bourgeoisie, which had made great strides during Napoleon's 'Kingdom of Italy', particularly in Lombardy, but also in the duchies and legations. Rome, however, was static. And Naples suffered from the loss of some of her best sons in the repressive reaction of 1799. From the Napoleonic period administration became better and more important. The metric system was introduced on the French model and persisted (while the Republican calendar was abandoned). The influence of the *Code Napoléon*, promulgated in 1806 in Italian and French, remained after Bonaparte's fall. The periodical press enjoyed growing importance. Austria protected the *Biblioteca Italiana* and subjected the *Conciliatore* to severe censorship. Useful service to Italian culture was rendered by the

Antologia of Vieusseux, the *Politecnico* started by Cattanco in 1837 and Tenca's *Crepuscolo*. Dailies were influential mainly in the brief freedom of 1848-49. Commercial advertising began (in favour of medicinal products). The theatre flourished; Rosini rightly remarked (*Risposta ad una lettera del cav. V. Monti sulla lingua italiana*, Pisa 1818) that prose plays could be the first step towards making Italian the common spoken language of cultured people in Italy. Names and allusions were frequently taken from the more popular *melodrammi*. Education affected only the upper classes and rarely touched the people. Elementary schooling (up to the age of nine) became compulsory for all by the terms of the Casati Law of 1859 (but as yet without sanctions against the parents of non-attenders). In secondary schools the teaching of Italian was often subordinate to that of Latin. In the universities instruction was still prevalently in Latin. Its use in the University of Rome was reaffirmed by Leo XII. In the universities of Sardinia-Savoy, Latin as the medium of instruction was abolished only in 1852. The really active academies were few: the Accademia delle Scienze at Turin and the Istituto Italiano, situated at Milan during Napoleon's 'Kingdom of Italy' (later, under Austria, divided into the Istituto Lombardo and Istituto Veneto). The Accademia Fiorentina in 1808 was again divided into three classes (del Cimento, della Crusca, del Disegno): thus the name of the Crusca reappeared, and its full autonomy was renewed in 1811 by Napoleon. Much attention was paid to the literary prizes awarded by it, but its lexicographical work was rather weak. Pure and applied science advanced by leaps and bounds, while scientific congresses (beginning with that at Pisa in 1839) proved to be important meeting-places and seed-beds of unitary ideas. Life was affected by new inventions. The use of steam gave power to new industries and changed the nature of transport by land (first railways 1839) and by water (steamers). Cities were lighted by gas (Milan 1845). Matches made with phosphorus were sold (1832), and the manufacture of cigars began. Lithography had great success. Photography began. Obviously, here we cannot give anything like a complete list of the changes occasioned by new developments and inventions; we mention just a few examples in order to show the kind of changes we must bear in mind when studying the emergence of new meanings or new words in this period. In the fine arts, neo-classical taste was predominant in the Napoleonic age; it persisted for a long period later alongside manifestations of Romanticism (e.g. neo-Gothic).

Everyday language at the end of the eighteenth century was careless and gallicized. The French invasion brought more French loan-words, some administrative neologisms and a wave of rhetoric. But just as new subjugation was in the political field giving rise to a new spirit of independence, so the general linguistic slackness and the flood of French and bureaucratic terminology led to a reaction on the part of men of letters. Botta protested at the Turin Academy in a sonnet of Alfierian stamp (1803), while Monti made his protest against 'il barbaro dialetto miseramente introdotto nelle pubbliche amministrazioni' in his *Prolusione agli studj dell'Università di Pavia per l'anno 1804*. And their protests had some effect: there was a Napoleonic decree 'for the conservation of the language' in 1809, and Vaccari, Minister of the Interior in the Kingdom, recommended the avoidance of bureaucratic barbarisms (G. Bernardoni, *Elenco di alcune parole . . .*, Milan 1812, p. III). But how did writers propose that good language should be achieved? Many of them turned again to the glories of the past and the principle of imitation: the classicists looked to both the Trecento and the Cinquecento, while the more rigorous among them, known as the purists, tended to restrict their approval to the Trecento. But in 1816 the polemics on Romanticism began. The Romantics rejected imitation, proclaimed that the old mythology was dead and wanted a language and literature consonant with a young and fresh Italy. Written and spoken language should be closer together; only thus could a greater adherence to reality be achieved. A problem that caused concern in this period (and to which the Romantics particularly drew attention) was that of providing unity of language, a social instrument for a spiritually united nation. Manzoni dreamt of an Italy

> *una d'arme, di lingua, d'altare,*
> *di memorie, di sangue, di cor,*

and Poerio wanted it to be

> *fiorente — possente*
> *d'un solo linguaggio.*

But to achieve such an ideal presented even more difficulties for the Romantics than for the classicists and purists. For the latter, it was a matter of choosing the right models to imitate. But, if the Romantics wished to keep the written language close to the spoken, where were they to find the model? Some needs could be satisfied by the use of a single dialect (and Porta, who gave a brilliant example of the expressive use of his own Milanese, defended dialect against Giordani), but clearly another solution had to be found for a national language and literature. Should one then turn to spoken Tuscan, a dialect that had claims not possessed by Porta's Milanese? This was the path that Manzoni trod with increasing determination; he found many followers, but also encountered objections and reluctance. But there was another aspect to the problem of unity of language: it was not only horizontal, but vertical (i.e. going down through the social classes). Whereas those who looked forward to the territorial unity of various Italian regions were growing rapidly in number, those who envisaged the social unification of the various strata of society were very few. Nor is this so surprising if we remember that, at the period we are discussing, four out of every five Italians could neither read nor write. In fact, both the classicists' and purists' teaching and that of Manzoni had some effect on everyday prose. The purists acted as an antidote to sloveliness and gallicization, while Manzoni's example was a contribution to another task: 'a estirpar dalle lettere italiane, o dal cervello dell'Italia, l'anti-chissimo cancro della retorica' (Ascoli, *Arch. glottol. ital.*, I, p. xxviii). But even around 1860 it was still possible to perceive, in everyday utilitarian prose as well as in that of skilled writers, a classicizing current and a simpler, less cumbrous current. The reduction of the difference between the two was to be the task of the following decades. Many scientists were not indifferent to these problems; but they were more concerned about the tumultuous multiplication of terminologies, which threatened their sciences with confusion of ideas and a reduced speed of progress.

Although there was more movement from region to region than in previous centuries, Italian was still essentially a written language, little spoken outside central Italy. Manzoni has left us a description of what in the early part of the century at Milan was called *parlar finito* (*Opere inedite o rare*, V, p. 348). According to him, it involved 'using all the Italian words one knew, or those one thought were Italian, and filling in the rest as best one could, mostly, of course, with Milanese words, seeking, however, to avoid those that would have seemed excessively Milanese even to the Milanese and caused them to laugh; and giving an Italian ending to everything'. To be understood by the people, in both northern and southern Italy, one had to speak in dialect, or Italian mixed with dialect, and this was frequently done in preaching and teaching the catechism. Few felt any need to remedy this state of affairs. Foscolo, writing of himself under the name of Didimo Chierico (*Opere*, Ed. naz., V, 176) told how he went to live in the country between Florence and Pistoia in order to 'learn a better language than is taught in cities and schools'. And some Piedmontese families used to send their sons to the Collegio Tolomei at Siena. Leopardi, writing to Giordani on April 30, 1817, spoke of his idea of going to Florence to study the language. But Giordani (May 16) dissuaded him, arguing that there was no village in all Italy where they wrote worse than in Tuscany and in Florence, for there was no place where the language and its writers were less studied. Nor was there anywhere where Italian was less spoken: 'Non hanno di buona favella niente fuorché l'accento: i vocaboli, le frasi vi sono molto più barbare che altrove'. Leopardi took his word for it, and praised the accent of Recanati (letter of 30 May). Yet the accent, which seemed to Giordani the only good thing in Florentine speech, infuriated Stendhal: 'Je vole au théatre du Hhohhomero, c'est ainsi qu'on prononce le mot *cocomero*. Je suis furieusement choqué de cette langue florentine, si vantée. Au premier moment, j'ai cru entendre de l'arabe'. (*Rome, Naples et Florence*, Calmann-Lévy, p. 211). It was Manzoni, of course, who did most to exalt the importance of Florentine speech. His ideal was the spoken language of cultivated Florentines. Others stressed the virtues of popular Florentine and of the speech of the Tuscan countryside. But there was a very long way to go before any form of Italian was to become the spoken language of the nation. When the deputies in the Turin parliament strove to speak Italian, they spoke what was to them a dead language, in which they were not accustomed to converse. Many anecdotes which have come down to us preserve dialectal phrases alleged to have been spoken by famous men. Prina, advised to hide during the Milanese riots of 20 April 1814, replied: *I saria nen piemonteis*, while the enraged Cavour exclaimed, on the eve of Rattazzi's election as President of the Chamber: *A l'è na ciûla, a l'è na ciûla!* Other such stories concern Victor Emmanuel II and Ferdinand II.

Between the utilitarian prose of a newspaper article or administrative report and the contrived elegance of a Giordani there were infinite gradations. Nineteenth-century classicism aimed at a decorous language that avoided what Giordani called the 'bassezze del moderno idioma'. It turned instead to the Trecento and Cinquecento for models. It sought vocabulary in the noble

z

tradition, avoiding, wherever possible, recent borrowings from other languages and neologisms. It admitted poetic words to prose in moderation. Particular attention was given to the art of the period, which was constructed with ample clauses carefully arranged so as to produce a pleasing harmony. These general aspirations were, of course, modified by the tastes of individual writers. Botta borrowed, not only from writers in the noble tradition (particularly Guicciardini), but also from the popularizing Davanzati, from *novellieri* and comic writers, and he often used a forced and composite vocabulary. The numerous inversions in his prose, too, leave one with a sense of strain. The genres which provided the most suitable material for classical prose were history, orations and general treatises. A new field was epigraphy in Italian, practised notably by Giordani and Muzzi. The purists were even more rigorous and even more faithful to the principle of imitation than the classicists. But while they were in one sense the extreme right wing of the classicists, in another they diverged from them, for they appreciated the golden simplicity of the Trecento more than the orotundity of the Cinquecento; they looked back to a Trecento in which the language had not been corrupted, whereas the classicists' ideal was the pruning effected by Cinquecento rhetoricians. The two main representatives of purism, the Veronese Father Antonio Cesari (1760-1828) and the Neapolitan Marchese Basilio Puoti (1782-1847), won numerous followers. We remember them, not so much for their own work as writers, which was poor and arid (e.g. in the *Novelle* in which Cesari sought to treat modern matters in Trecento style), as for their activities as lexicographers, grammarians and teachers, to which we shall have occasion to return. Here is an example of the imitation of fourteenth-century features from a letter written by Father Cesari to Pederzani in 1813: 'Veramente essi ne dicono [di questo dialogo] *tanto di bene*, che non pure superò *a pezza l'espettazion mia*, ma quello *eziandio*, che il mio amor proprio avrebbe potuto desiderare'. In the letter in which he broke off relations with his faithless disciple Villardi in 1827 he began '*Fratelmo* carissimo' and ended '*A Dio, Sozio*'. The great merit of the purists lay in drawing attention to texts and encouraging study of them (publishing many of them), even though they chose only those related to their tenets (Trecento texts, with the addition of certain writers of the Cinquecento and of Daniello Bartoli, chosen because they in their turn had admired the Trecento). The purists' call for a radical change in linguistic usage provoked controversy. Many writers rejected the yoke they would have liked to impose: Berchet in 1816 described them as 'un esercito di scrutina-parole, infinito, inevitabile, sempre all'erta, e prodigo sempre di anatemi' (*Lettera semiseria*, in *Opere*, II, p. 11 Bellorini). But the classicists and purists undoubtedly had an effect on the development of Italian. They succeeded in ousting certain words and phrases that they considered barbarous, and they got others confined to non-literary usage. They promoted the use of words that they considered noble in tone and they put back into circulation certain words or phrases that had fallen into disuse or were little known. The Romantics worked on quite different principles. They thought it necessary to be natural, spontaneous, in step with their contemporaries rather than elaborate in the manner of the ancients. It should be remembered that the Romantics fought their earliest battles in the *Conciliatore*, a periodical which tried not to be merely literary but to pursue social ends. They sought expression, not in general, abstract, terms, but realistically, seizing upon concrete characteristics and calling animals, plants and things by their own names. They wished to avoid 'quello stile fraseggiato e convenzionale, che ora mai s'introduce nella prosa, come già da gran tempo si è stabilito nella poesia' (Borsieri, in the *Conciliatore*, 27 Dec. 1818); they wanted no more of *dare opera a uno studio, deporre il pugnale di Melpomene, scalzare il coturno*. Why use so many classical reminiscences, so much empty mythology? Contemporary Italian society had to be served. On the other hand, it should not be cut off from the rest of the world; the other great languages and literatures of Europe should be studied. One of the genres in which Romanticism manifested itself was the historical novel; Sir Walter Scott became the model of many Italian writers. It was a suitable genre for the distinctive and for picturesque detail; at the same time, by dealing with remote times, it freed itself from everyday life. Prose, no less than poetry, found new themes. The vogue enjoyed by the Middle Ages brought in troubadours and minstrels; castles and monasteries; fairies, witches, gnomes and sylphs; *danses macabres*, corpses, skeletons, etc. Sometimes these features brought in vocabulary that was new to the literary language. But the problem of linguistic renewal went far deeper than the diffusion of strange words; the nature of the traditional literary language, alleged to be too bookish and not popular enough, was called in question. Naturally, things did not change all at once: one can find *pria* in the *Conciliatore*, *aere* in a letter of Pellico's and *appo Lei* in a letter of Manzoni's. But, henceforth, their days were numbered (in verse as well as in prose). The Romantics tended to revivify the written language by bringing it nearer to speech. But since there was no generally used spoken tongue, that meant that Tuscan and non-Tuscan writers were in different situations. The Tuscans could use (or abuse) the idiom of their own regions; Giusti, who so pleased the Manzonians, was criticized by others for excessive tuscanism. Non-Tuscans could either have recourse to regional Italian (Nievo is an example) or turn to the study of Tuscan speech. Of those who chose the latter course, Manzoni supported Florentine forcefully both by precept (in a long series of theoretical writings) and in practice (by his revision of *I promessi sposi*). But the collective taste that Manzoni wished to see, did not yet exist. Non-Tuscans therefore had to exercise their individual tastes in turning to Tuscan speech; they did so with varying results, sometimes with exaggeration or errors. They were flayed by both non-Tuscans and Florentines. And Theophrastus was more than once paraphrased:

lo stile
troppo toscan lui non Toscano accusa (Niccolini);

dal troppo
toscaneggiar vegg'io che non sei Tosco (Giorgini).

The struggle between classicist, purist and Romantic tendencies was prolonged, and all prose, even the humblest and least literary, was affected by one or more of these currents.

A tradition stretching back over nearly five centuries lent exceptional solidity to the language of the epic and the lyric. The classicists sought to conserve its essential characteristics. Their grammar kept some traditional forms (*nui, saria, fora*); their vocabulary was rich in archaic and latinizing words (*alma, destriero, fiata, ostello; calle, delubro, ulto* 'avenged'; *luna* 'month', *sole* 'year', *polo* 'heaven'); and the poets reserved the right to make free use of latinisms. For modern geographical names, which were considered too realistic, ancient ones were substituted, e.g. 'Vidi il *tartaro* ferro e l'*alemanno* — strugger la speme dell'*ausonie* spiche' (Monti, *Mascheron.*, I). Excessively realistic words were also avoided by periphrasis: frogs became 'le rauche di stagno abitatrici' (Monti, *Mascher.*, IV); gunfire was described as 'il tuon de' cavi — fulminanti metalli' (Monti, *Bardo della Selva Nera*), 'il muggir degl'ignivomi tormenti' (G. C. Ceroni, *La presa di Tarragona*), 'un tonar di ferree canne' (Leopardi, *Il passero soli-*

tario), etc. Mythology frequently had a part in this process: 'to die' could become *scendere all'Erebo, irrompere nel Tartaro*. Constructions unknown to everyday language (e.g. the Greek accusative) abounded. There was great freedom in word-order. Use of special and technical terms was very rare, except in genres that were considered less noble (as, for instance, when Arici in the *Origine delle fonti*, IV, spoke of '*pecci* atri' or '*baccare* solinga'. Overfamiliar words, too, were usually excluded. Leopardi, after using *evviva, evviva* in *All'Italia*, felt it necessary to justify that in a note. Certainly, contemporary classicists would have thought him bold to speak of Aspasia's *bambini* (in *All'Italia* he had used *parvoli*). Schools inculcated classicist principles. Here is a description by Cantù of the instruction he received from the teacher who taught him rhetoric:

'Poesia, mi diceva esso, è favella degli iddii, e tanto miglior è, quanto più dai parlari del profano vulgo si sprolunga. E prima quanto alle parole, tu non dirai *abbrucia, affligge, cava, innalza, è lecito, spada, patria, la morte, le poesia*; ma *adugge, ange, elice, estolle, lice, brando, terra natia, fato, musa*; e così *merto, chieggio, oceàno, imago, virtude, andaro, destriero*. Dalle idee basse, che rammentano cose troppo a noi vicine abborri, figliuol mio. Ai nomi proprj sostituisci una bella circonlocuzione; non dirai *amore* ma il *bendato arciero*; non il *vino* ma *liquor di Bacco*; non il *leone*, l'*aquila*, ma la *regina de' volanti*, il *biondo imperator della foresta*, e così i *regni buj*, il *tempo edace*, la *stagione de' fiori*, il *liquido cristallo*, l'*astro d'argento*, la *cruda parca*. Vedi il Monti? non disse il *gallo*, ma il *cristato fratel di Meleagro.* . . . . '

The force of tradition was so strong that the Romantics found it difficult to put their principles into practice, especially when they wished to refer to modern life in its humbler aspects: here there was a danger of a comic clash in tone between traditional and modern elements. For archaisms and latinisms were abundantly used by Romantic poets, too. Berchet wrote: 'ei *preferse* i tetri abeti', 'dal fratello ricevi un'*aita*', 'dalle membra è svanito un *algore*', 'e co' baci una lagrima *elice*'. And in Prati's *Canti per il popolo* we find:

> *Ma chi l'ha morta? — Uno stranier soldato*
> *che il verginal suo velo*
> *tentò rapirle . . .*

One of the advantages that medieval and oriental themes offered these poets was that of using words which, though they were new in poetry and suitable for prose as well, yet had a certain distinction. Pellico wrote of Manzoni's *Carmagnola* that its subject allowed the author to avoid 'modi e vocaboli non simili alla prosa' and so to 'scostarsi di poco dal discorso comune di oggidì' (letter of Jan. 8, 1820 in Manzoni's *Carteggio*, I, 457). Like the classical poets, the Romantics considered the *cetra* to be the distinctive instrument of their calling ('infrangasi . . . — questa mia cetra': Fusinato, 'Addio a Venezia'). Moreover, in a century when there was much bellicose writing, even the Romantics tended to use the names of medieval weapons, rather than their modern equivalents: 'Su, brandisci la *lancia* di guerra', 'una selva di *lance* si scorse (Rossetti), 'dell'*elmo* di Scipio s'è cinta la testa' (Mameli), 'dove il *cimier* del barbaro — sinistramente appar' (Prati). Indeed cannons for Prati were *cavi bronzi* ('Noi e gli stranieri', 1846) and even a horse-drawn carriage an 'agil *cocchio* tratto da *palafreni*' (*Edmenegarda*). Examples could be multiplied only too easily. But when modern objects appeared under their own names, as De Lollis observed, there was apt to be a clash in tone between traditional and recent elements (as when Prati wrote of *moschetti, mitraglia, barricate* in 'Dopo la battaglia di Goito'). The strident contrast between the solemnity of the opening line and the familiar tone of the last in the following quatrain from Prati's *Canto d'Igea*

> *Né men chi* si periglia
> *coi flutti e le tempeste*
> *del nostro fior si veste*
> *se il mar* non se lo piglia

is not simply a stylistic defect in a particular line or in a particular poet, but also a symptom of the crisis in poetic language in this period. Nevertheless, with the passage of time, poetry of elevated tone tended increasingly to abandon archaizing (as in *aita*) and, to a lesser degree, latinizing. If Tommaseo has less archaisms and latinisms than Berchet and Carrer, that may be partly due to the individual poets concerned, but it is certainly partly due to the evolution of poetic language in the period between them. In poetry of a humbler tone, like satirical and jocose verse, the conflict between traditional and modern was less felt; there archaisms had been traditionally less favoured and popular elements more welcome. Since those who wrote this kind of poetry at Milan, Venice and Rome preferred dialect, Tuscans like Pananti, Guadagnoli and Giusti were dominant in the national language. In their verse they made use of many elements taken from Tuscan speech; sometimes these were peculiar to the poet's own district in Tuscany.

Many writers took part in linguistic controversies in this period. There is no space to record the opinions of all of them. We shall merely discuss the main developments in the *questione della lingua*: the puristic movement led by Father Antonio Cesari of Verona, the Montian polemics and the Manzonian theory.

Father Cesari, in his editions of the texts of Trecento ascetic writers, his translations from Latin, his religious and literary works, and above all in his new edition of the Crusca dictionary (1806-09) and in *Le Grazie* (1813), made it clear that in his view only a return to fourteenth-century language could save Italian from the corruption into which it had fallen. That was a golden age in which all wrote well: 'tutti in quel benedetto tempo del 1300 parlavano e scrivevano bene. I libri delle ragioni de' mercanti, i maestri delle dogane, gli stratti delle gabelle e d'ogni bottega menavano il medesimo oro. Senza che tutti erano aggiustati e corretti, ci rilucea per entro un certo natural candore, una grazia di schiette maniere e dolci, che nulla più'. He was not, however, prepared to define the qualities he found in fourteenth-century language: 'Che è questa bellezza di lingua? Ella è cosa che ben può essere sentita non diffinita, se non così largamente: ché nella fine questa bellezza non torna ad altro, che a un Non so che' (*Opuscoli letterari e linguistici*, ed. Guidetti, 1907, pp. 145-6). Moreover, he did not say why he considered certain 'barbarisms' in the modern language were to be condemned; he thought it enough to list examples. He was convinced that everything could be expressed in Trecento language: 'Ogni cosa potersi dire che uom voglia, e per avventura meglio'. He was ready to renounce what four centuries of Italian life had contributed to the language. Marchese Basilio Puoti was not strictly limited to the Trecento by his preferences, but he too was determined to 'côrre il più bel fiore dalle opere degli antichi'. His work as a teacher was more important than his writings. Among them less importance attaches to his editions of texts, which show that his philology was rather weak, than to those works in which he provided guides to writing Italian: his *Regole elementari della lingua italiana* (Naples 1833, many times reprinted), his *Vocabolario domestico napoletano-toscano* (Naples 1841, 2nd ed. 1852), written, not in order to document Neapolitan dialect forms, but in order that his fellow-Neapolitans should become acquainted with the equivalent words in literary Tuscan, and his *Vocabolario de' francesismi e di modi nuovi e guasti*, etc. (Naples 1845, A-E). Although in his readings with his pupils he included authors as late as Alfieri and Monti, he would have liked the Crusca to be more severe: in a letter to L. Ciampolini (1844) he maintained that it should not go beyond the seventeenth century, since he held that Magalotti 'è da allogare tra' primi corruttori della lingua'. But if moderns were to be included, Leopardi would have to be considered. Cesari and Puoti had numerous friends in various parts of Italy: M. Parenti, L. Fornaciari, G. Manuzzi, T. Azzocchi deserve mention among those who concerned themselves with language from a puristic angle. It could be argued that the purists had a beneficial influence in strengthening opposition to the unlimited acceptance of what they styled barbarisms, but it is impossible to approve of the manner in which they based their judgements on an exclusive archaizing taste.

Cesari's views were ridiculed by the poet Vincenzo Monti. In the Milanese *Poligrafo* he began in 1813 to publish anonymous satirical articles. An example was the dialogue 'Il Capro, il Frullone della Crusca e Giambattista Gelli,' in which the goat (*capro*) complains that his name has been omitted from the dictionary, in spite of having been used by Ariosto, Guarini, Menzini and others, while the much less noble *becco* has been included. In 'Il 31, il 36 e il 46' he attacked Cesari for the old rubbish he had collected (*quaranzei* and so on) and the incomplete exemplification in his dictionary. Towards the end of the Napoleonic regime and at the beginning of the Austrian, the Istituto Lombardo took the initiative in preparing for the compilation of a better dictionary, which was to be the work of scholars from all over Italy. Monti prepared an elaborate report which he presented to the Institute in 1816. The government desired that an arrangement should be sought with the Accademia della Crusca, and the directors of the Institute's two branches wrote proposing this on 6 July 1816. The Crusca replied on 10 September that it had already started work on its own account, and that it was no longer therefore a suitable time for discussing preliminaries and methods with the Institute. Between 1817 and 1824 Monti published his *Proposta di alcune aggiunte e correzioni al Vocabolario della Crusca*, four volumes divided into seven tomes, consisting of a series of notes criticizing the Crusca dictionary (arranged in the alphabetical order of words), two dissertations by Giulio Perticari (Monti's son-in-law), *Degli scrittori del Trecento e de' loro imitatori* and *Dell'amor patrio di Dante*, and contributions by various

scholars (G. Grassi, G. Gherardini and others). In the prefaces
to the various volumes of the *Proposta* Monti made his own attitude
clear; he was in favour of an 'illustrious' Italian and wanted a
dictionary 'ordinato coi metodi della filosofia, purgato d'ogni
lordura, suggellato dall'universale consenso della nazione'
(Part II: dedication to Barnaba Oriani). He objected to the
Crusca's attempt to bring Italian under the tyranny of the
Tuscan dialect and was severe on its provincialism and archaism.
He, too, conceived of the language as something literary and apart
from everyday speech. But he believed that archaic words should
be taken out of the dictionary and dealt with in a separate glossary,
that the lexicographers should work through texts wrongly
neglected or inadequately investigated (Ariosto, Rucellai, Alamanni) and that quotations from works whose admission was ill-
considered (the *Pataffio*, Burchiello, slang scenes from Salviati's
Granchio) should be excluded, as should the excessive number of
indecent words. Monti several times insisted that the 'depra-
vazioni degli ignoranti' should be eliminated. Not only did he
think that *fistiare* ('fischiare'), *frebotomia, paralello, rema* (for 'reuma'),
ritropico ('idropico'), *sanatore* ('senatore') should be cut out; he
was also clear about his preference for *arena* and *arenare* rather than
rena and *arrenare*. A part of the vocabulary that the Crusca had
unjustly omitted was the scientific ('la lingua scientifica, per la
quale uscendo dai fioriti campi dell'amena letteratura convien
mettersi nei rigorosi sentieri della filosofia e al tutto dividersi dal
parlare della moltitudine'). The *Proposta* gave rise to a good deal
of discussion and found widespread acceptance. When Monti
died (1828), Mazzini wrote that there was mourning for the
author of the *Proposta*, which had dealt the last blow to linguistic
tyranny. Francesco Torti, in his *Il purismo nemico del gusto* (Perugia
1818) welcomed the first part of Monti's *Proposta*. But, when he
reprinted this work along with other articles in his *Antipurismo*
(Foligno 1829), he complained that Monti, though destroying
'Veronese purism' based on fourteenth-century texts, had substituted for it a purism based on sixteenth-century writers, and that
he had neglected many words consecrated by usage and by the
example of illustrious authors. Indeed, he was able to find quite
a few gaps in Monti's work (*anima, genio, sensibilità, sentimento,
interesse, immoralità, società*, etc.). And he put his finger on Monti's
weakness when he emphasized the necessity for examining living
usage: 'nessuna autorità nè viva nè morta può esser la padrona di
una favella, perché l'uso è il vero sovrano delle lingue . . .' Some

of Monti's ideas lived on in Milanese writers who in the following decades kept up opposition to the Crusca and to Florentinism in general: Gherardini, Cattaneo, who several times expressed his opposition to Tuscanism and particularly to certain plebeian forms accepted by the Crusca, and Tenca, who corrected the language of the contributors to his *Crepuscolo*. It was against this background that Alessandro Manzoni's lengthy concern with the *questione della lingua* began. If Monti had represented the tendencies of classicism, Manzoni represented those of Romanticism. But he did not see the *questione* as a merely literary problem: his achievement was to transform it from being a dispute among men of letters into being a social problem concerning the whole of the Italian nation. Manzoni first showed his interest in the question in a letter to Fauriel (9 Feb. 1806), when he was barely twenty-one; in 1868 at the age of 83 he was to accept a government invitation to preside over a linguistic commission. The 1806 letter to Fauriel tells us how Manzoni then saw the problem. The division of Italy into fragments and almost general ignorance and laziness have placed so great a distance between the written and the spoken languages that the former can almost be considered a dead language. That makes it impossible to educate the people. In 1821, the year in which he expressed his vision of Italy as

> *una d'arme, di lingua, d'altare,*
> *di memorie, di sangue e di cor,*

he again wrote to Fauriel on the matter. He had for six months been working at his historical novel *Fermo e Lucia* (in later versions to become *I promessi sposi*) and was concerned with the position of the writer in a country whose citizens in various regions did not really have a language in common. A French writer would know what kind of effect a certain expression would have on his public. Not so the Italian author: 'il manque complètement à ce pauvre écrivain ce sentiment, pour ainsi dire, de communion avec son lecteur, cette certitude de manier un instrument également connu de tous les deux'. How is he to judge whether he is writing in 'Italian', if this term is capable of so many interpretations? Yet the only solution that he can think of at this stage is one that is extremely eclectic (and far removed from the out-and-out Florentinism of later years): 'il faut penser beaucoup à ce qu'on va dire; avoir beaucoup lu les italiens dits classiques, et les écrivains des autres langues, les français surtout; avoir parlé de matières importantes avec ses concitoyens ...; avec cela on peut acquérir une certaine promptitude à trouver dans la langue, qu'on appelle bonne, ce qu'elle peut fournir à nos besoins actuels, une certaine aptitude à l'étendre par l'analogie, et un certain tact pour tirer de la langue française ce qui peut être mêlé dans la nôtre, sans choquer par une forte dissonance . . .' But while he worked at the first published text of his novel (that which we read in the 1825-27 edition), he came gradually to abandon this criterion for putting together a composite language and turned to Tuscan usage as taught to him by books. In his research he was pleasantly surprised to find that Florentine expressions were more frequently in accord than he thought with those of other dialects — of which Milanese was the one that he was most concerned with. The 'lingua toscano-milanese' that he spoke of in a letter to Rossari in 1825 was to be one based on those instances of agreement between Tuscan and Milanese. He discovered with joy that *impiparsi dell'Olanda* was Lombard and Tuscan. And if Milanese had *matt de ligà* and Tuscan *matto da legare*, then the latter was what one should use, even if Cherubini (*Vocabolario milanese*) gave *pazzo da catena* as the translation. But his investigations in dictionaries and Tuscan texts still left him liable to translate a Milanese expression into a Tuscan one that no longer existed. Manzoni's journey to Florence in 1827 was a revelation; the language that he had so laboriously sought in books was presented to him living, agile, real on the lips of the cultivated Florentines he met. He wanted to have his copy of Cherubini's *Vocabolario milanese* annotated by Gaetano Cioni and Canon Giuseppe Borghi and he persuaded Cioni and Niccolini to make observations on the language of his novel. But he did not have time while in Florence to work through it with them and therefore corresponded with them after his departure about this task; he wanted the revised version he intended to publish to be such that a Florentine reader would feel at home with it. In fact, he was now ready to accept contemporary Florentine usage as decisive, as we see from his remark to Borghi on the word *orda*: 'where Usage makes itself heard, the Dictionary no longer counts in my eyes' (letter of 25 February 1829). Henceforth, Manzoni was to feel increasingly certain that the norm for literary Italian should be Tuscan usage, or, more precisely (given the varieties that existed in Tuscany), the usage of cultivated Florentines. In the decade 1830-40 he worked at a treatise on the language. This occupied a good deal of his time, too, in subsequent decades, but he never completed it, though drafts representing views he held at various stages in its composition have come down to us. He also (soon after his second marriage in 1837) revised *I promessi sposi*. Apart from the comments of Cioni and Niccolini, he got a great deal of assistance with the details of Florentine usage from Emilia Luti, a Florentine he employed as companion and governess to his last two daughters. We cannot here deal in detail with the revision of *I promessi sposi*, but we shall say as much as is necessary to illustrate Manzoni's standpoint. He aimed above all at eliminating, in the 1840 edition, those expressions that he had accepted from literary tradition but which were not alive in Florentine speech; he intended to cut out the archaic and the dialectal. In many other cases he replaced words and phrases that were literary in tone with words and phrases that were familiar in tone: *accidioso — uggioso*; *adesso — ora*; *ambedue, ambo, entrambi — tutt'e due*; *confabulare — chiacchierare*, etc. Often Florentine phonetic variants were substituted for literary forms: *dimandare — domandare*; *imagine — immagine*; *lione — leone*; *obbedire — ubbidire*; *publico — pubblico*; *sofferire — soffrire*, etc. But he also replaced *angiolo* by *angelo* and *limosina* by *elemosina*. Manzoni accepted the Tuscan pronunciation *o* in many instances where literary Italian kept *uo*. He replaced *-a* in the first pers. imperf. by *-o*. The pronoun *egli* he often omitted or replaced by *lui*. Yet *egli* remains in 61 instances (in 18 of which it refers to God). But Manzoni not only intended to choose for his own stylistic purposes those variants which conformed to familiar Tuscan; he intended that his work should be linguistically paradigmatic and lead to ostracism of the staler and stuffier forms. In short, he was not satisfied to select from the language as it was: he wanted to change it, to reform it as a social institution. Fortunately, his artistic requirements were given precedence over his doctrines. He felt that *natio* was rather literary and occasionally substituted *nativo* for it; but in the famous passage beginning 'Addio, casa *natia*, dove sedendo . . .' (Ch. VIII) he introduced *natia* during the revision in place of the *natale* of the earlier version. He did not always succeed in adapting his work to Florentine usage of the period 1830-40; doubts were raised then as to the adequacy of his knowledge of Florentine and severer criticisms have been made since (e.g. by E. Bianchi in *Annali manzon.*, III, 1942, pp. 281-312). Nor was the revision artistically happy at all points. But the novel did much to achieve what Manzoni set out to do: to bring the written language nearer to the spoken and to deal a deadly blow to the rhetorical frills which for centuries had disfigured Italian literature. The treatise on the language at which Manzoni worked for so long without ever producing a finished version, was to consist of three books. The first, of a philological character, was to deal with the nature of languages. The second was to examine the various solutions proposed for the Italian *questione della lingua* (and of this part a fragment remains on 'Cesari's system', while Manzoni's own system is known to us from its precise public formulation in other writings of his to which we shall refer). The third book was to deal with means of diffusing the form of language that he was prepared to recognize as a national language (and here again his views are known to us from other works that he published). In the philosophical part Manzoni frequently returned to certain fundamental beliefs: the need to study language in general and not only language in its more beautiful forms; the idea that each language constitutes a whole; the importance of usage, the sole arbiter in linguistic matters, to which all other criteria must yield. While he continued to test, and meditate on, the general principles of a philosophy of language, his ideas on the Italian language in particular became more and more definite. In 1846 he decided to make public in the 'letter to Carena' his views on the *questione della lingua*. This work was occasioned by publication of the first part of Giacinto Carena's *Prontuario ... per saggio di un Vocabolario metodico della lingua italiana*. In this letter (the text of which was sent to Carena in February 1847) Manzoni publicly declared for the first time that he professed 'quella scomunicata, derisa, compatita opinione, che la lingua italiana è in Firenze, come la lingua latina era in Roma, come la francese è in Parigi', and he therefore held that the service that Carena had rendered to scholars by compiling his *Prontuario* would have been greater if he had left out those locutions which were not part of living Florentine usage. What constituted a language was not the fact that it covered a greater or lesser area, but the fact that it was a quantity of words suited to the uses of a society that was genuinely a society. The error into which people commonly fell was that of associating with the word 'language', not the 'universal and perpetual idea of a social instrument', but an indeterminate and confused concept of something literary. The fact that controversies had gone on for so long proved that Italians did not really have a common language. In order to get one, some people counselled having recourse in the first instance to the dialect of Florence and then to those of other cities. But when the matter was one of substituting unity for multiplicity, when one said:

'let this one be the first', logic added: 'and the last'. And since Tuscany had languages that differed little from one another, but not a single language, one had to draw a line after Florence. Moreover, it was necessary that the agreed language should become the real possession of all Italy, and not only in writing, for the formula 'written language' propagated a concept that was not metaphorical but false. Only the language spoken in a real and continuous society had the character of universality, for the written language was only a 'fortuitous and various mixture'. A language was rich if it possessed many different words for many different concepts, not if it possessed many words for the same concept. When Carena added to the word *panna* four others meaning the same thing, Manzoni asked: what is the use of having an expert guide if he leads us to the crossroads and tells us to take whichever road we like? What Italy needed was a dictionary made by Florentines of the language that they actually used, like that of the French Academy. Manzoni was well aware of the differences between the Italian situation and the French. But this was the only way of getting a similar result. Manzoni had now reached the definitive formulation of his theory. His philosophical meditations and study of previous theories had led, not to historical analysis, but to a politico-civil programme; he was seeking to achieve linguistic unity by the means that seemed to him most logical. The letter aroused interest, but not the wide support that Manzoni was possibly hoping for. In the following years he went on working on his book on the language ('la mia opera eterna, intendi bene, *a parte ante*': letter to G. B. Giorgini, 10 December 1856). In 1855 he discussed linguistic problems fully with Tommaseo, who left an account of their conversations (*Colloquii col Manzoni*, ed. T. Lodi, Firenze 1929). In 1856 he took advantage of two brief meetings with his friend Gino Capponi to draw up with his help a sample of the kind of dictionary of usage that he wished to see (*Saggio di vocabolario italiano secondo l'uso di Firenze*, ed. G. Macchia, Florence 1957). But only during the years that were decisive for the achievement of national unity did he enter the lists to defend his theories in public. To that we shall come in the next chapter.

In the grammatical field the dispute between supporters of logical grammar (who at least in theory postulated the priority of reason over usage) and its opponents (led by De Sanctis) raged more furiously than ever. Among the numerous grammars that appeared some were described as 'filosofica' or 'ragionata'. Others more or less openly adopted the standards of purism, like Puoti's concise *Regole elementari della lingua italiana*, Naples 1833. Most grammars were based on passages from the classics and only secondarily on usage. Moreover, grammars written in the previous century continued to be used: L. Lamberti saw to the republication, with additions, of Cinonio's *Particelle* (Milan 1809-13), while P. Del Rio republished, also with additions, Corticelli's grammar (Florence 1845). A new work, containing material based on fresh exploration of authors in various countries and anything but conformist (as the author's anti-Tuscan orthographical theories, for instance, show), was Gherardini's *Appendice alle grammatiche italiane* (Milan 1847). There was still no grammar that deliberately set out to describe modern Tuscan usage. Several grammarians were concerned to illustrate verb forms. Apart from Compagnoni's collection, there was the fuller one by M. Mastrofini, *Teoria e prospetto o sia Dizionario critico de' verbi italiani conjugati*, Rome 1814, 2nd ed., Milan 1830. Very wide reading of texts, but very questionable philological premises, lie behind V. Nannucci's volumes, *Analisi critica dei verbi italiani*, Florence 1843; *Teorica dei nomi della lingua italiana*, Florence 1847; *Saggio del prospetto generale di tutti i verbi anomali e difettivi*, Florence 1853.

The lexicographers were more active than the grammarians. Father Cesari in 1806 brought out a new, unofficial edition of the Crusca dictionary (the 'Veronese Crusca'), adding to the fourth edition some 30,000 items, collected by him and his friends from Trecento texts. Unfortunately, some of his material had not been passed through a fine enough philological sieve. Re-established with full autonomy in 1811, the Crusca itself began work on a fifth edition in 1813. (Of its quarrel with Monti, whose *Proposta* dealt severely both with the Academy's work and that of its Veronese continuator, we have already spoken.) Between 1820 and 1840 lexicography attracted many scholars: those were the years of the Bologna dictionary (edited by F. Cardinali and P. Costa, Bologna 1819-28), that of Leghorn (C. A. Vanzon, Leghorn 1827), that of Padua (referred to, also, as 'della Minerva', ed. L. Carrer and F. Federici, Padua 1827-30) and most important of all, that of Naples (*Vocabolario universale italiano*, published by the *Società tipografica Tramater e C.*, Naples 1829-40), subsequently republished with additions at Mantua (Mantua 1845-56). Although it indicated clearly which words were approved by the Crusca, the Tramater dictionary recorded many new ones;

many of these came from literary sources, many from scientific and technical works. The *Vocabolario della lingua italiana* of G. Manuzzi, for which Leopardi supplied a number of entries, was based on traditional principles, though it corrected the Crusca's work in details; the 2nd edition (1859-67) was a notable improvement on the first (Florence 1833-42). The official fifth edition of the Crusca dictionary began to appear in 1843, and by 1852 seven fascicules had come out, giving rise to severe criticism: Puoti condemned it for broadening the canon unduly, Gherardini complained of plagiarism of his *Voci e maniere di dire*, and so on. Finally, the Academy decided to suspend publication until there had been further preparation. The diligent Gherardini, whose work as a grammarian we have already mentioned, began his lexicographical activity in 1812, publishing at Milan an anonymous collection, *Voci italiane ammissibili benché proscritte dall'Elenco del sig. Bernardoni*. He worked carefully through a large number of authors and presented his results in two collections: *Voci e maniere di dire additate ai futuri vocabolaristi*, Milan 1838-40, and *Supplimento ai vocabolari italiani*, Milan 1852-57. In his *Lessigrafia italiana*, on the other hand, his concern was with propounding orthographical theories (Milan 1843; 2nd ed. Milan 1849). A kind of lexicography that flourished at this time was the listing of 'barbarisms'. G. Bernardoni, urged to do so by Vaccari, the Minister of the Interior of the 'Kingdom of Italy', collected an *Elenco di alcune parole oggidì frequentemente in uso*, Milan 1812. It was concerned mainly with legal and administrative coinages, and suggested improvements or replacements. Bernardoni realized (and Gherardini stressed the point in the work he published in 1812, mentioned above), that, however much of a purist one might be, one could not proscribe words already in use in a legal code. Of other collections of this kind we mention only a few examples. A. Lissoni's *Ajuto allo scrivere purgato*, Milan 1831, provoked many replies, including an anonymous *Aiuto contro l'aiuto del signor Lissoni*, Como 1831, which was probably by Gherardini. M. Parenti put out his collections in this field in a series of instalments extending over a number of years and entitled *Catalogo di spropositi*, Modena 1839-43, and *Esercitazioni filologiche*, Modena 1844-58. Basilio Puoti's *Dizionario de' francesismi e degli altri vocaboli e modi nuovi e guasti*, Naples 1845, remained incomplete (A-E being published). G. Valeriani's *Voci e modi erronei*, Naples 1846, became, in its 2nd ed., *Vocabolario di voci e frasi erronee*, Turin 1854. Many of the words condemned in such works were defended in the well-documented *Dizionario di pretesi francesismi* of P. Viani, Florence 1858-60. Other collections were intended to furnish 'beautiful' or little known words: such were the *Frasologia* of Lissoni, of which there were two editions (Milan 1826, 1835), Puoti's *Vocabolario domestico* for Neapolitans (Naples 1841) and Azzocchi's for Romans (Rome 1839; 2nd ed. 1846). There were also some methodical dictionaries: by G. Barbaglia, Venice 1845, incomplete; G. Rambelli, Bologna 1850; F. Zanotto, Venice 1852-55. An especially important one was that by G. Carena (*Vocabolario domestico*, Turin 1846; 2nd ed. 1851; *Vocabolario metodico d'arti e mestieri*, Turin 1853; and an additional part posthumously published at Turin in 1860), which drew the criticism of Manzoni, to which we have earlier referred. Tommaseo first published at Florence in 1830-32 his deservedly famous *Dizionario dei sinonimi*; it reappeared in 1838-40 more than trebled by his labours and those of his friends; and it was several times subsequently revised by its author. Several specialist dictionaries were still being produced by translation from French or, occasionally, from English. But a fair number were compiled by Italians. Of these we list some of the most important: G. B. Gagliardi, *Vocabolario agronomico*, Milan 1804, 3rd ed. 1822; S. Stratico, *Vocabolario di marina*, Milan 1813; G. Grassi, *Dizionario militare italiano*, Turin 1817, 2nd ed. Milan 1833; L. Bossi, *Spiegazione di alcuni vocaboli geologici, litologici e mineralogici*, Milan 1817; O. Targioni Tozzetti, *Dizionario botanico italiano*, Florence 1809, 2nd ed. Florence 1825. Dictionaries of grecisms (Bonavilla, Milan 1819-21; Marchi, Milan 1828-41) were substantially vocabularies of scientific terms. The numerous dialect dictionaries then published (some of them still among the best that we have, like Cherubini's for Milanese, Milan 1814, 2nd ed. Milan 1839-56, Boerio's for Venetian, Venice 1829, 2nd ed. Venice 1856, Monti's for the dialect of Como, Milan 1845) were prepared with a double purpose in view: documenting dialect words and supplying those who needed them with the equivalent words in Italian.

The influence of French on Italian, which had been so great in the Settecento, became even greater in the age of Napoleon. Then, to cultural influence was added the effects of military occupation, of the annexation to France of a good third of Italy (divided into departments), and of the supremacy exercised by France through the 'Kingdom of Italy' and the Kingdom of Naples. So it was, for instance, that Verdi's birth was recorded in French at 'Busseto, département du Taro'. In 1809 decrees in

Rome and Tuscany placed Italian on an equal footing with French. The territory where French was most used was Piedmont — not only during the French occupation, when Denina actually proposed the use of French as a cultural language (*Dell'uso della lingua francese*, Berlin 1803), but also later, when the restoration of the bilingual state astride the Alps allowed the full weight of Savoy to be felt once again until 1860. De Laugier was astonished to find, on the gateway by which he entered Turin, and on the succeeding street: *Porta d'Italia, Via per l'Italia.* When he asked for an explanation at his inn, he was told: 'Est-ce que vous ignorez, être en Piémont, et non plus en Italie?' In the cafés and about the city he heard only French and dialect spoken. When he went to see Pomba the bookseller about some copies of *Fasti e vicende degli Italiani* that he (De Laugier) had sent to him, Pomba showed them to him, all unsold, and suggested he should take them back: 'Qui, egli dice, non si legge né si scrive che in francese, cominciando dal re e dai ministri. Anche la truppa è comandata in francese . . .' (*Concisi ricordi di un soldato napoleonico*, repr. Ciampini, Turin 1942, p. 113). The fact that they had resided in France for varying periods, or the desire for wider international circulation, induced some Italian scholars to write in French rather than in their own language, especially when publishing the results of scientific, historical or antiquarian research. Leopardi, in a letter written on 8 August 1817, criticized E. Q. Visconti for having forgotten Italy, 'avendone abbandonato non solo la terra ma la lingua'. Of many writers it was said that they knew French better than Italian. Sometimes 'knowing better' simply meant that they were able to write French with assurance because of the stability of French usage, whereas the uncertainties of Italian caused them hesitation. The knowledge of French possessed by all cultured Italians explains the abundance of gallicisms in their language: these were numerous in translations, repressed for puristic reasons in the more disciplined forms of literature, but abundant in confidential writing (personal notes, diaries, etc.). We have already mentioned the linguistic consequences of the annexation of Nice to France (1860). After 1860, moreover, even the slight Italian influence that Turin as capital had exerted on Savoy ceased. In Corsica, Italian was losing ground as a cultural language from generation to generation; but, even in the first half of the nineteenth century, books published in Italian were in a slight majority in Corsica, and preaching was still usually in that language.

Knowledge of German was incomparably less than that of French, in spite of Austrian dominion in Italy. There were, however, some translations, literary and non-literary, from German, as there were from English. A current of anglophilia (and some knowledge of English) stemmed from admiration of British institutions. Knowledge of Latin continued to be extensive among cultured people. That of Greek was less so, but still considerable. There were, too, numerous important translations from the classics at this period.

Knowledge of Italian language and culture outside Italy was not widespread. Few felt the need to go deeply into Italian literature and life, though many wished to acquire as much Italian as was necessary to singing. There were cultural contacts, however, due to the many travellers who came to Italy from various European countries and to the activities of Italian exiles in Switzerland, France, Belgium and Great Britain. On the eastern shores of the Adriatic, Italian still maintained a footing: Dalmatia gave Tommaseo and Paravia to Italian culture and the Ionian islands Foscolo and Mustoxidi. But the emergence of Illyrian (i.e. Serbo-Croat) culture and the resurgence of Greece reduced the role of Italian as a language of culture. In Malta, under English occupation from 1800, use of Italian as a cultural language continued. On the shores of the Mediterranean (particularly the eastern shores) spoken Italian was known in the simplified form of a *lingua franca*: 'Tuo console nuovo star buono, non cercare me né buono né male, inscialla tutti li consoli star come isso', said the Pasha of Tripoli, Yusuf Caramanli, in 1825 to a Sard subject (E. Rossi, in *Rivista delle colonie italiane*, 1928, special number, p. 150). In its written form it served as a diplomatic language; the trade agreement between Austria and the Bey of Tunis in 1859 was drawn up in Italian (E. Rossi, *op. cit.*, p. 151). Since Roumanian was at this time in a stage of growth and westernization, several Roumanian writers looked to Italian for suggestions. Petru Maior, a member of the Transylvanian school, in translating Fénelon (*Intîmplările lui Telemah*, Buda 1818) made use of an Italian version, which offered him more assimilable words than did the French: *faretra, isola, incuda* (=Ital. *incudine*, 'anvil'), *spesele*, etc. And Ion Heliade Rădulescu, who initiated the so-called 'Italianist' current in Roumania, started from the premise that Italian and Roumanian were two dialects of the same language; he favoured abandoning the Cyrillic alphabet, followed Italian closely in its spelling, and made abundant use of italianisms in his writings (*ciarlatanie, contagiu, în darn, scheletru,* etc.).

The spontaneous process of selection which, in an age of linguistic exchanges, leads to the reduction of groups or pairs of equivalent words or forms, did not, at this period, operate as effectively as one might expect. The great difference that persisted between the language of prose and that of poetry (and the love of rare variants evinced by many poets and a few prose writers) contributed to the preservation of numerous doublets. Moreover, while the supporters of early Italian were giving new life to words and forms that would otherwise have disappeared, the supporters of modern usage were introducing regiona elements into circulation. In addition, neologisms and recent borrowings from foreign languages frequently appeared in divergent forms, and it took time for particular forms to triumph over rivals. In the following paragraphs, therefore, we shall have occasion to observe the lack of uniformity that obtained in usage; this affected grammatical as well as lexical phenomena.

In spelling, there was uncertainty about the use of *j* initially and medially for semi-consonantal *i*, and also finally as a compendium of *ii*; those who used it, particularly in final position, were probably in a slight majority. Leopardi, who used *j* in works written in his youth, later resolutely abandoned it. In his instructions to Brighenti (letter of 5 December 1823) concerning the printing of his poems he prescribed: 'Non si usino *j* lunghi né minuscoli né maiuscoli, in nessun luogo né dell'italiano né de' passi latini'. Yet, when Stella invited him to write an article aimed at banishing it, he replied that, although he condemned it, *j* did not lack either authority or antiquity (letter of 9 Feb. 1827). Manzoni oscillated a great deal in his use of *j*: in printed versions of his early works it appears, though not in those of later works. But in his autograph manuscripts it persists until quite late. Puoti, Gioberti and Carena declared themselves to be against *j*, while Peyron and Lambruschini were for it. There were frequent oscillations, too, in the use of double consonants. Apart from spellings due to puristic respect for the Crusca (*appostolo, paralello, proccurare*) and to those which reflected etymology (*Academia, catolico, publico,* etc., and vice versa *commune, millione,* etc.)— a tendency that Gherardini encouraged — there were many cases in which northern writers, whose pronunciation did not permit them to distinguish single consonants from double, got them mixed, particularly in confidential writings: in Foscolo's letters we find *cattarro, creppare, diriggere, piacciuto, tacciuto* and *soqquadro* corrected to *soquadro*, in Berchet *cerrettani, schiffoso, piacciuto, griggi*, in Prati *tranguggiare* and *fantasticagini*, in Rajberti *zuffolare*, etc. But Leopardi, who wrote *carcioffo*, probably also pronounced it thus; and Puoti, who wrote *faggiolata* and *leggittimo* in his letters, certainly pronounced them with -*gg*-. Northern writers were also apt to introduce initial doubling wrongly in the second element of compounds: *anzicché, sempreppiù (Conciliatore), dippiù* (Borsieri). Even Foscolo and Manzoni wrote *stassera*. On the other hand, Gherardini and his followers wrote *adirittura, dacapo*, etc. Muzzi in his inscriptions wrote *aqqua, naqqui*. Another area of oscillation was the spelling of palatals: *spregievole* (Borsieri), *sciegliete* (Rosmini), *camice* (as pl. of *camicia*, Cantù), *villaggietto* (Nievo), etc. Foscolo, in a letter, wrote *oglio* for *olio*. In foreign words that had not undergone phonetic adaptation the foreign pronunciation was variously represented; presumably when *guigliottina* and *daguerrotipo* were thus spelt, they were pronounced in the same way as they were later pronounced when the spelling was italianized to *ghigliottina* and *dagherrotipo*. There was no hard and fast rule for the assimilation of enclitics after shortened verb forms: Monti and Leopardi wrote *sovviemmi*, Guerrazzi *gittarommi*, while others preferred *tienmi*, etc. *Palco scenico* was still written as two words (Pellico, *Concil.*, 25 July 1819). So, too, *Terra Santa* or *Terra-Santa* (Grossi). Guadagnoli and Giusti wrote *pian-forte*. In the same passage of the translation of Malte-Brun's *Geografia universale* (1815) occurred *alti piani* and *altipiani*. In 1851 the Kingdom of Sardinia issued the first *franco bollo*, while Tuscany put out a *francobollo*. The hyphen in words of the *italo-greco* type became fashionable on the model of the French. The traditional scarcity of accents to indicate stress persisted. A new function was attributed to the circumflex, that of indicating contractions (*tôrre*) or forms thought to be contracted (*andâr* for *andarono*), the purpose being to distinguish such words from others spelt in the same way. In verse, dieresis was marked with growing frequency: some used two dots over the vowel, as in French, while others preferred an accent (usually acute): 'La cascata parer di Níagara' (Pananti, *Il poeta di teatro*, XXXIX, st. 27 in the 1824 edition). As for the use of capitals, there was hesitation in the case of titles: Manzoni as a young man wrote *re, imperatore* and *papa* with small letters, thus provoking the wrath of Father Soave, while Cesari remarked: 'io fo sempre *Re*, e non *re*; e credo meglio fatto' (letter of 15 Feb. 1815). As for punctuation, some paid little attention to it, whereas others paid a great deal. Leopardi was most meticulous, as he himself stated in a letter to Brighenti (5 Dec. 1823) and intended to write a *Trattatello della punteggiatura*. Often authors' punctuation was regularized by publishers; in a letter to Le Monnier (3 August 1846) Giusti complained of excessive punctuation added to his study of Parini. Nothing came of proposals for spelling reform, like that of a certain N.N., *Proposta per la rettificazione dell'alfabeto ad uso della lingua italiana*, Milan 1830, who proposed introducing *k* and *y*, indicating when *i* and *u* were semi-consonantal by use of a little hook underneath them, marking voiced *z* with a grave accent, indicating palatal *sc* by use of a little line over the *c*, palatal *gl* by two dots over the *g*. Lambruschini would have been glad to see *k* added to the alphabet. Gherardini, though not advocating systematic reform of the orthographic system, wanted to change the spelling of numerous words following criteria of etymology and analogy. He was developing a line of thought that had been visible through the centuries (*anatomia* prevailing over *notomia*, *Africa* over *Affrica*, etc.) and carrying it to its extreme, logical conclusion; he not only wanted the spellings *academia*, *alume*, *amazone*, *bubone*, *catolico*, etc., and *abbate*, *commodo*, *sabbato* (with consonants single or double according to Latin usage), but also *adomine* (for *addome*), *asente* (for *assente*), *altretale*, etc. He was not without some followers. Cattaneo applied and advocated a similar reform; he also sensibly suggested that when the accent fell on the third or fourth syllable from the end of a word, it should be indicated. Gherardini's methods were applied by writers of varying importance (Giuseppe Ferrari, Rajberti, Dossi, and even, in some details, Ascoli); but they did not win general approval.

Northerners and sometimes southerners became aware at this period of peculiarities in Tuscan pronunciation which the alphabet did not convey (see p. 353). The reduction of *uo* to *o* in Florentine speech (*bono*, *novo*, etc.) took place at the end of the eighteenth and the beginning of the nineteenth centuries. In literary usage *uo* held its ground, in spite of Manzoni's attitude. Oscillation in certain words was due to tradition, not to this innovation in Tuscan: thus Leopardi used *cuopre* and *scuopre* in prose, *scopre* in verse. As for the mobile diphthong, the rule (advocating its use in stressed position, not elsewhere) was frequently not observed, even by Tuscan writers (*scuolare* in Giusti, *Lettere*, passim; *tuonare*, *suonata* in Montanelli's *Memorie*). And some even considered it an unjustified imposition of the purists; 'Manfredini scrive da Vienna esser *buonissima*, o *bonissima* come vogliono i puristi' (I. Pindemonte, letter 15 Jan. 1803). The rule that required words beginning with impure *s* to be preceded by *i* if they followed a consonant began to weaken: Guadagnoli wrote *non isviluppi*, *per isgravio*, but also *in scuola*; and two grammarians of such diverse opinions as Fornaciari (*Alcuni discorsi*, pp. 109-18) and Gherardini (*Appendice alle grammatiche*, p. 556) were agreed in reducing its rigour. The assimilation of the *r* of the infinitive to the *l* of the enclitic pronoun occurred now only in plebeian Tuscan. Generally the examples found in verse were only literary reminiscences: *pagalli* rhyming with *cavalli* in Pananti's *Poeta di Teatro* (c. L, st. 4) and, worse, *vedelli* rhyming with *chiovelli* in a translation of a Spanish *romance* by Berchet (I, p. 261 Bellorini). Giusti in 'Delenda Carthago', l. 56 uses the device to echo plebeian Tuscan: 'E non vogliam Tedeschi: *arrivedello*'. Syntactic truncation was used on a much smaller scale. Reading in Ugoni the words *una version di quest'opera* Foscolo felt it should be corrected to *versione* (*Epist.*, IV, p. 45) and considered this usage an affectation of Settecento Jesuits and 'un prettissimo barbarismo' (2nd Pavian lecture). And Tommaseo (*Memorie poetiche*, p. 18 Salvadori) said that the 'mal vezzo di troncare le parole' pursued him until his twenty-fifth year. Manzoni intended in this matter to follow Florentine usage, but, as Bianchi showed (*Annali manzoniani*, III, 1942, pp. 288-91), his knowledge of Florentine proved inadequate here and he overdid the truncating.

Coming to morphology, we note that in the plurals of nouns the principal oscillations were in those in -*co* and -*go* (*traffichi*, preferred by Manzoni and Gioberti; *parrochi*, *asparaghi*). Among nouns in -*a* we should note *i camerata* (Foscolo). Among nouns in -*ello* the plural *capegli* occurred not only in verse, but also in prose (D'Azeglio): following that model, Torelli wrote *zampigli* as plural of *zampillo*. Among the plurals of compounds it should be recorded that, whereas *sordi-muti* prevailed at the beginning of the century (*Conciliatore*, passim), it was later ousted by *sordomuti* (Ricci, *Prose letterarie*, etc.). The main oscillation in adjectives (in plurals and superlatives) was again in words in -*co* and -*go*: *aprici* (Clasio), *reciprochi* (Foscolo), *pratichi* (Puoti, Tommaseo), *poetichissimo*, *sofistichissimo* (Leopardi), *laconichissimo* (Manzoni). To form the intensive, purists exhumed the prefix *tra*- (*trasuperbo*, Cesari; *tragrande*, Gioberti, Giordani, Mamiani, Farini), and the *Amici Pedanti* (the young Carducci and his friends) still defended it. The relative superlative with repetition of the article was anything but rare: 'lo stato *il più rozzo* dell'uomo' (Pecchio); 'l'uomo *il più certo* della malizia degli uomini' (Leopardi, *Zibaldone*), 'l'uomo *il più disperato*' (Giusti). To some *acerrimo* no longer seemed a superlative: '*più acerrimo* che mai' (Giusti, *Cron. fatti Toscana*, p. 110). Shortened numerals of the *venzei, quaranzette* type had not entirely disappeared — at least, not in Tuscany ('Son ventisette lire; ma per lei — Si ha da fare all'agevole, *venzei*': Pananti, *Il poeta di teatro*, c. LVI; 'più di vensette anni fa': Tommaseo, *Colloquii col Manzoni*, p. 31 Lodi), although Monti, when he found them in Cesari's version of the Crusca dictionary, made fun of them. Of the pronoun it should be noted that *egli* was frequently used, as also *ei* (found even in prose). Manzoni found *egli* stilted, and in a large number of cases substituted *lui* for it in his revision of *I promessi sposi*. *Eglino, elle, elleno* were still occasionally used ('O che novità son elleno queste?': Guerrazzi, *Il buco nel muro*). *Gli, la, le* were quite widely used as subject pronouns, even by non-Tuscan writers ('Un re che *gli* era, fin dalla balia — pazzo pel gioco dell'altalena': Carbone, *Re Tentenna*; '*gli* è un castello di carta': Farini; '*la* è carriera di delitto e di sangue': Mazzini; 'Vaga e quasi mistica formola come *le* son tutte quelle del Mazzini': Farini). The same could be said of *e*' as an impersonal subject ('*e*' v'è': Mazzini; 'queste ferocie non sono credibili, ma *e*' sono avvenute tali e quali': Giusti). *Li* and *gli* as third person object pronouns were frequently considered interchangeable. Some writers used them promiscuously, leaving the decision as to which was to be used in any particular case to the ear ('al giudizio dell'orecchio', Parenti, *Esercitazioni filologiche*, n. 2). Others (Gioberti, Manzoni) regularly used *gli* before a vowel, *li* before a consonant ('laddove l'ingegno *li* trae fuori, *li* fonde, *li* cola, *li* purga, *gli* opera, *gli* aggiusta': Gioberti, *Rinnovamento*). *Gli* for *le* (dative sing.) was not rare (Leopardi used it), while *le* for *gli* was a dialectalism (e.g. in the letters of Quirina Mocenni). *Gli* for *loro* (dative plural) was used by Leopardi, Tommaseo and Manzoni. In Venetian writers there was sometimes confusion between *ci* and *si*: 'io e la Pisana facevamo gazzarra, contenti e beati di *vedersi* dimenticati' (Nievo, *Confessioni*). *Ne* was still frequently used for *ci* meaning 'us, to us'. In enclitic position poetic language permitted, not only *mi, ti, si, ci*, but also *me, te*, etc.: this possibility was exploited, not only by classicists (*deporse*, Monti), but also by Romantics ('Del monte ove Gesù *trasfigurosse*': Grossi, *I Lombardi*). Pairs of particles of which the second element was *lo* or *ne* were often contracted even in prose: *mel, cel, tel, vel* (and so also *nol*). In accordance with Tuscan usage, ancient and modern, *gliene* was sometimes used for *glielo* too (*rimandargliene* for 'rimandarglielo' in a letter by Leopardi, 5 March 1836). There were still very numerous cases of pairs of particles in which the dative followed the object complement: not only in poetry ('*lo si* raccolse all'odoroso seno': Monti), but also in prose ('che *se gli* possa fare una camicia': Leopardi, Note to canz. III; 'facendo*segli* il freddo sentir sempre più': Manzoni, *Prom. sp.*, XVII; 'il cuore *se gli* serrava': Cantù, *Margh. Pusterla*; 'alle domande che *se le* facevano': Carrer, *Racconti*; 'chi *lo si* mise pazientemente in tasca fu lo Sgricciolo': Nievo, *Il Varmo*; etc.). Some plurals like *qualche professori* (Berchet), *qualche decine* (Tommaseo), *qualche speranze* (Cantù), *qualche anni* (Carrer) were falling into disuse: Manzoni, who had some examples of them in the 1825-27 version of the *Prom. sp.*, abolished them in his revision for the 1840 edition. Compare, too, *nessune trattative* (Nievo). *Che* and *cui* sometimes exchanged functions ('la nube di maledizioni, di *che* lo aggravano i secoli': Mazzini), and also *che* and *chi* ('la Francia *a chi* si attribuisce . . . ': Amari). There were some instances of plural *chi* ('*chi* proseguettero i ladri'='quelli che perseguirono': Giusti). *Cosa?* in the sense of *che cosa?* found some defenders (L. Fornaciari, Gherardini). In the field of the definite article, two features in particular should be noted: the plural *li* still existed, though its use was fast diminishing; and before impure *s* and *z* there was still almost a free choice of the forms to be used. *Li* persisted, particularly in office language, but it was still occasionally used, in prose and verse, by both classicist and Romantic writers ('*li* suoi pseudo-liberali': Breme 1818; 'se a forza di sproni *li* fianchi t'ho aperti': Prati). Gherardini and Cattaneo almost regularly used *li* before a vowel and *s* impure (*li articoli*, *li uomini*, etc.). *Li* was particularly persistent before impure *s* (*li strilli*, Bresciani; *Alli spettri del 4 settembre 1847*, Giusti; *su li stinchi*, Carducci) and after *per* (see below). Before impure *s* there was great oscillation, both in prose and in verse and in both Tuscans and non-Tuscans: at the most one can note an abundance in northern writers of the type with *i*: 'ha sepoltura — già vivo, e *i* stemmi unica laude' (Foscolo); *i* stenti (Berchet); *i stupendi marmi* (Carrer). *Il* in the singular was a little less frequent: 'più azzurro *il scintillante* Eupiliondeggia' (Foscolo), *un spergiuro* (Berchet). Even freer was the alternation in the type *il zio, i zii, lo zio, gli zii*: to choose but one example from a thousand, Rosini wrote on the same page *un zelante* and *degli*

zelanti (*Riposta al cav. Monti*, p. 33). There was also great freedom
in the forms ending in vowels or the substitution of an apostrophe
for the vowel, and this in both prose and verse: thus we find *uno
anello* (Leopardi), *della istoria* (Colletta), *la idea, tutta la Italia*
(Guerrazzi) and, vice versa, *l'amicizie* (Foscolo), *le lettere e l'arti*
(Mazzini), *l'ore* (Mazzini), *nell'idee* (Niccolini), etc. As for the
articulated prepositions, we should note above all the frequency
of the forms *a', de', ne', co'*: the choice between full forms and
those with apostrophe depended frequently on euphony (Mazzini,
for instance, wrote *de' bisogni e dei desideri*, in order not to repeat the
same syllable twice). Poets oscillated between joining articulated
prepositions (*dello, allo*) and writing them separately (*da lo, a lo*):
Leopardi moved from the first method to the second between the
1815 and 1821 editions of the *Batracomiomachia*. After *per* (and also
after the rare *ver* for 'verso') many used *lo, li*, in accordance with
the rule prescribed by the old grammarians: Leopardi observed
this rule in prose and verse and stigmatized *per il suo reo delitto* as
'a linguistic error' in a review written in his youth (*Scritti letter.*,
II, p. 168). The rule was frequently adhered to, not only by
Cesari, Monti, Perticari, Gioberti, but also by Amari (*per lo
momento* in a letter of 1849) and Prati (*per lo deserto, per lo mondo*).
Carducci, while one of the 'Amici pedanti', wrote in a letter to
Chiarini (1857) 'rispondimi *per lo* procaccia'; but in the lyric on
the death of his brother, written in the same year, he used both
forms: *per li verdi oliveti* and *per i lieti campi*. This prescription
was least respected by the Tuscans (*pel cheto camposanto*, Guerrazzi; *per il suo valore intrinseco, per il malgarbo*, Giusti); and Fornaciari, appealing to the authority of Bartoli, declared that there
was no absolute rule (*Alcuni discorsi*, pp. 103-4). Manzoni, who
had used *pel* (and *pello*, according to position) in the *Promessi
sposi* of 1825-27, adopted *per il* (*per lo*) in the 1840 edition. There
was a wide range of variants in verbs. In poetic language endings
and forms which had fallen into desuetude were still usable:
avemo (Manzoni, 'Nome di Maria'), *avièno* (Monti, *Mascher.*,
III), *ghirlandorno* (Monti, *Mascher.*, III), etc. But, even in prose,
variants frequently occurred which grammarians catalogued as
old or poetic: *dee* or *debbe*; *dicea, parea*; *fia* ('quando ella fia gio-
condata dai figli', again in a letter by Guerrazzi in 1865); *saria*,
etc., *corre, sciorre, torre* for *cogliere, sciogliere, togliere*. Nor was it rare
for Tuscans to use peculiar forms: 'quando me ne *parlavi*' (2nd
pers. plur.): Fanny Targioni Tozzetti, letter 1838; 'Voi *eri* amico e
compatriotta dell'eroico Giovannetti': De Laugier, *Concisi ricordi*,

p. 200; 'in velluto e scarponi com'*eramo*': Giusti, letter of 1841 to P. Thouar, in *Epistol.*, I, p. 388 Martini. Curious forms were used in the past definite and conditional by the Elban general De Laugier, a writer not much versed in literature: *raccolsamo, sparsemo, avrebbemo, traverserebbemo* (*Gli Italiani in Russia*, Italia 1826-27, quoted by R. Ciampini in the preface to his edition of the *Concisi ricordi di un soldato napoleonico*, Torino 1942, p. 14). The construction *noi si va*, though not immune from criticism, enjoyed better fortune than others: '*Si par* di carne, e siamo — costole e stinchi ritti' (Giusti, 'La terra dei morti'); 'tutti *si può* mancare' (Manzoni, *Prom. sp.*, ch. XIX), etc. Non-Tuscans occasionally had recourse to regional forms, like the usual *-assimo, -essimo, -issimo*, a northern and Roman ending for the first pers. conditional ('*vedressimo* tanto volentieri': Giulia Manzoni Beccaria, letter 1826; 'quello che noi *vorressimo*': Costanza Arconati, letter 1832). In the first pers. plur. pres. indic. a velarization of the stem before the ending was frequent: *tenghiamo, ponghiamo, distrugghiamo* and also *conoschiamo*. The same forms existed in the subjunctive, which in addition had analogous forms in the 2nd pers. plural: *accolghiate, dirighiate*. In the imperfect the first pers. in *-a* was still very much alive, but equally frequent by this time was the form in *-o* (which, as Mastrofini put it when discussing the paradigm of *temere*, 'si vede al presente scorrere in belle scritture'). Even Tuscans writing in familiar style used forms in *-a* (*era, aspettava, sapeva*: Giusti), occasionally alternating with forms in *-o* in the space of a few pages or a few lines (*conchiudeva, doveva* but *amavo* in Guerrazzi's *Apologia*). Manzoni, in the *Prom. sposi* of 1825-27, and in the letters written before those dates and for some years after them used the forms in *-a* nearly always (there is one *bramavo* in 1829 as compared with many examples of *-a*); in the 1840 edition he corrected *faceva, non pensava* to *facevo, non pensavo*, and he kept to the *-o* form subsequently in his letters (*sapevo*, 1850). In the past definite, 1st pers. plural forms of the *ebbimo* type appeared in Tuscans (we have already mentioned De Laugier) and non-Tuscans (*vidimo*: Gargallo; *ebbimo*: Rajberti; *seppimo*: Nievo). In the subjunctive the ending *-i* in the second person was still frequent: *abbi, facci, vadi, vogli*. In the conditional, forms in *-ia* still turned up here and there in prose, and the phenomenon needs to be studied author by author: Leopardi, for instance, in the *Operette morali* preferred the *saria, dovria* type before a consonant, but *sarebbe, dovrebbe* before a vowel. In the case of verbs normally conjugated with *avere* as auxiliary, *avere* was very frequently employed even when such verbs were used in the reflexive: 'quand'anche non *si avesse conseguita* l'indipendenza, *si avrebbe giovato* all'onore italiano': Foscolo, letter 1815; 'pare che il poeta *si abbia proposto*': Leopardi, in *Nuovo Ricogl.*, 1825; 'un frate *si avea tolto* il carico di farmi venire i vostri volumetti': Puoti, letter 1845; 'tutto il vino che *si hanno bevuto*': Guerrazzi, *Apologia*; 'quel giorno *avrebbesi dovuto* installare solennemente la Signoria nuova': Capponi, *Storia Repubbl. di Fir.*, II, p. 439. In the field of invariable words we should note that there were occasionally used, even in prose, certain adverbs, conjunctions and prepositions which were later to fall entirely into disuse: *eziandio* (Gioberti), *mo* (Manzoni, *Prom. sposi* 1827), *oggimai* (Mazzini), *avvegnadio* (Guerrazzi), *appo* (Manzoni, letter 1826; *tenere appo Renzo* in the *Prom. sposi* of 1827 was replaced by *tenere presso di Renzo* in 1840), *contra* (Breme), *fuora* (Manzoni, lett.; a couple of times, too, in the *Prom. sposi* of 1827. It was used in verse by Mercantini: 'Va' *fuora* d'Italia . . .').

In syntax, conflicting stylistic ambitions were more obvious than in phonology and morphology. The classicists abounded in constructions modelled on Latin and Greek and on classical Italian writers: accusative and infinitive (extremely common, e.g. in Gioberti), Greek accusative, ablative absolute, historical infinitive, etc. The purists, in addition, revived archaic constructions: Puoti, for instance, liked ellipsis of *che* ('tutto quello fate per me': letter to L. Fornaciari, 1846). On the other hand, there was strong French influence, and tuscanisms and dialectalisms also showed from time to time. The article with surnames was often omitted, especially with the most illustrious (and also with those of foreigners): here we can refer to the discussion between Leopardi and Giordani (*Epistol.*, I, pp. 99 and 106) and D'Ovidio's analysis of Manzoni's usage (*Correzioni*, pp. 79-80). The partitive after adverbs of quantity was not rare: *più di fedeltà*: Leopardi, 1816; *con più di precisione*: Berchet; *assai di regolarità*: Torelli, *Ettore Santo*, p. 310; cf. also *un dieci di volumi*: Giusti, letter 22 Dec. 1846. The present participle with verbal force was quite rare and sounded either literary ('a me giovane annunziante che il Rosmini verrebbe . . .': Tommaseo, *Colloquii col Manzoni*, p. 181) or bureaucratic ('i Rappresentanti il Municipio': in a manifesto, Cesena 1828; 'Firmato in calce dell'originale: — Minosse presidente il Tribunale': Guadagnoli, *Poesie*, p. 521 De Rubertis). The gerund with *in* construction was also rare and merely literary: 'ma il cor mi rode acerba — doglia *in pensando*': Monti, *Iliade*, XVI; 'O sopiti *in aspettando*': Manzoni, *Resurrezione*; but it occurred in prose as well: '*in leggendo* quel tenero vostro Sonetto,' Monti to Rosini, 1818. Even rarer was the infinitive with *in*: 'molto mi dolse *in leggere* che eravate. . . .': Puoti, letter 1844. Much could be written on the subject of verbs governing prepositions; constructions here were sometimes influenced by dialectal usage ('lo intesi *a* russare': Torelli; 'pensate che turbamento mi produsse il sentire il Manzoni *a* proporre . . .': Bonghi) and on the use of tenses and moods (to express a future dependent on a verb in a past tense the simple conditional was often employed: 'mi pareva che quell'architettura, trasportata sotto il sole d'Oriente e tra le nebbie britanniche, *armonizzerebbe* del pari': Tommaseo, in *Bellezza e civiltà*, 1832). Classicists still placed the verb at the end when they wished to create a noble tone ('la vita mia che ormai verso l'occaso inchina': Botta, letter 20 Dec. 1831). With the same intention, in groups of noun +adjective, adjectives with limiting force and ethnical adjectives were occasionally put before rather than after the noun ('in questa occidentale Europa': Farini, *Lo stato Romano*, I; 'le tracce delle napoleoniche fortune': ibid.; 'nel vedersi molto appianata la via nel parlamentare arringo': Cavour, speech 5 Feb. 1852). In verse, poets (including Romantic poets) still made very wide use of transposition in their word-order ('Ma il periglio d'Ulrico ogni malnata — mitigando pur venne ira scortese': Grossi, *Ulrico e Lida*, I; 'Sento un soave di patir desio': Tommaseo). Pronominal enclisis was very frequent, even in unpretentious prose. We may suspect archaizing intention when we read in a letter of Botta's (20 Dec. 1831): '*Tienmi* Parigi e ancora *terrammi*'; but there was certainly no such intention when Borsieri (*Concil.*, n. 70) wrote: 'Il padre *avevalo* destinato allo stato ecclesiastico; però *recossi* a Gottinga', or when Rosmini wrote to Tommaseo (22 Sept. 1831): 'il Manzoni *scrissemi* una bella lettera', or in the very numerous examples of *puossi, diessi, trasportossi, lasciommi* of Pellico's *Le mie prigioni*. On the other hand, the abundance of enclitics in Carducci's letters to Chiarini in the years when they were of the company of *Amici pedanti* ('*Mandoti* subito il sonetto', 1856; 'Sceglierai questi, *metteraili* da parte', 1857) is probably not unintentional. As for the structure of prose, the attempts made by classicists to restore the art of ample, harmoniously balanced periods failed to dislodge from common usage the brief periods which had become prevalent in the Settecento. Indeed, in some reprints of classics, editors permitted themselves the introduction of a few stops to break up very long sentences: Moreni, in his preface to the *Ricordi* of the sixteenth-century Domenico Mellini (Florence 1820, p. 17) lamented that this had been done in the Pisan edition of Guicciardini in order not to strain the readers' lungs with their allegedly excessive length. And Mamiani remarked that while, in the Cinquecento, the masters of the art adapted various forms of period to various styles, people in his own time were intolerant of long periods and wanted all the members broken up. Indeed, he claimed that he could name one author famed for his eloquence and wisdom who never varied the order of nominative, verb, accusative. It is likely that further research in this field would substantially confirm Mamiani's observations.

Of the great innovations in vocabulary at this period we can only hope to give a few representative examples from various fields. First, we should mention those which were consequences of the French invasion and of the changes in Italian life that followed in its wake. The Modenese Bartolomeo Benincasa, in the *Monitore Cisalpino* of May 1798, gave a list of words 'nuovamente arrivati in Italia o di una nuova significazione, o d'un antica, ma cambiata e travisata': *aggiornare, allarmista, aristocrazia, arrestare, attivare, avvocazione, cittadino, civismo, clisciano, corporazione, correzionale, correzione, costituente, costituito, democrazia, eguaglianza, emigrato, emigrazione, ex* (prefixed particle), *federalismo, federalista, federativo, federazione, filantropia, libertà, liberticida, massa, menzione, onorevole, moderantista, monarchia, mozione, nazione, oligarchia, organizzare, patriota, patriotismo, popolo, provvisorio, rapportare, risolvere, rivoluzionare, rivoluzionario, sanculotto, scioano, teocrazia, teofilantropia, tirannia, vandeista.* A more tendentious author published anonymously at Venice a *Nuovo vocabolario filosofico-democratico indispensabile per ognuno che brama intendere la nuova lingua rivoluzionaria* (1799). If we had a complete account of the neologisms that appeared before 1814 as a result of the organization of the departments annexed to France and to the new satellites, we should find that it contained important innovations. Some idea of their extent can be got from the already mentioned *Elenco di alcune parole oggidì frequentemente in uso, le quali non sono ne' vocabolarj italiani* by G. Bernardoni (Milan 1812). Some words entered Italian usage for a brief period but then disappeared (like the names of the month according to the Republican calendar), others took firm root (like terms of measurement: *grammo, metro*, etc.). Numerous words were introduced by the *Code Napoléon* (e.g. *immobiliare, licitazione, regime della comunione dei beni*, etc.) and many of them survived. The same can be said of words connected with legal, administrative and military institutions (*Corte di Cassazione, funzionario, regìa, sotto-ufficiale*, etc.) and of a large number of bureaucratic words (*caseggiato, controllo, processo verbale, suini* used collectively; *mensile* in place of *mensuale, doganale, postale, retroattivo; centralizzare, monopolizzare,* etc.). The noun *tricolore*, which when the French came stood for the French tricolour (blue, white and red), came to indicate that of Italy (green, white and red); at first the flag of the *Republica Cispadana*, then of the Cisalpine Republic, it was recognized after 1848 as the symbol of constitutional Italy. The restoration partially re-established earlier terminologies; but new terminological changes took place in various states after the events of 1848 and those of 1859-60. Political vicissitudes, in fact, explain the developments of many words. *Risorgimento*, which had already in the Settecento in Piedmont and Lombardy designated a more or less vague idea of improvement in Italy's fortunes, took a decidedly political turn in 1847-48. (Here we should recall that *Il Risorgimento* was founded by Cesare Balbo on Dec. 15, 1847). Various sects bore various names: both that of the *Carbonari* and that of the *Calderari* followed the semantic scheme of (*Liberi*) *Muratori*; others were learned coinages: *Adelfi, Apofasimeni,* etc. While one can only speak of parties, in the modern sense, after 1848, people of various groups and sympathies obviously got labelled before that date. While some of the names applied to them were exclusively Italian (like *sanfedista, olonista, albertista, muratista*), most were connected with analogous French or English words: *destra, sinistra, assolutista, legittimista, conservatore, moderato, radicale, costituzionale, progressista oscurantista, comunista, socialista,* and so on. *Liberale,* for instance, had a long incubation before moving from the Latin meaning of 'generous, open-minded' to that denoting a political party. As far back as 1766 Baretti spoke of Italians being united under one government 'non importa se liberale o dispotico'. Two episodes stressed the political meaning of the word: Mme de Staël in 1790 declared 'je défends les idées libérales'; Napoleon, on the 19 Brumaire 1799, the day after the *coup d'état*, proclaimed that 'les idées conservatrices, tutélaires, libérales sont rentrées dans leurs droits'. Finally, in the Cortes at Cadiz, the group that was *liberal* (whose members renounced their own emoluments and defended public liberties) became clearly separate from the group that was *servil* (backward and favouring the continuance of economic abuses). Henceforth the word stood for a political party. *Fusionista* came into circulation in 1848, when there was argument as to whether Lombardy and other regions which gained their freedom should join with Piedmont; *separatista* sprang up at Nice in 1859, where some planned to become separate from Piedmont and join France. Numerous historical phrases became widely used in Italian (some of them also in other languages) at this time: such were *carne da cannone* (attributed to Napoleon), *concerto europeo* (agreement of Chaumont, 1814), *fatti compiuti* (O. Barrot, 1831), *espressione geografica* (from Metternich's statement that Italy was merely a geographical expression, 1847), *lotta di classe* (Marx, 1848), *l'Italia farà da sè* (motto of the secret society of the Raggi, taken over by Carlo Alberto, 1848), *governo negazione di Dio* (from Gladstone's description of Bourbon misrule in Naples, 1851), *grido di dolore* (from the speech of Victor Emmanuel II, 10 January 1859), etc. Jacobin, and later Mazzinian mystique brought religious words into the patriotic field (*i martiri della libertà*; 'i morti della nostra *Religione nazionale*': Mazzini, letter of 29 August 1855; etc.).

Literary developments (neo-classicism, purism, Romanticism) also had great influence on everyday language. Monti used the latinism *reduce* in his version of the *Iliad* (and Manzoni in a slightly different sense in *Ermengarda*): then in 1848 at Rome a battalion of *reduci* was formed. Classicizing forms were found, too, for new inventions (*velocifero*, *celerifero*, *fiammifero*). The Romantic movement came to Italy and with it the word *romantico*. This term had had a long Anglo-French incubation (seventeenth and eighteenth centuries). It acquired a clearly literary meaning in the circle of Mme. de Staël, where the *romantic-classical* antithesis was fixed. Romanticism affected vocabulary greatly, through the importance it lent to the sentimental (*idee color di rosa*), through the realism which led to descriptions of what would previously have been passed over (popular scenes, etc.) and through its love for the fantastic, the exotic and the medieval. Romantic attacks on mythology made periphrastic expressions like *il santuario di Temi*, *il regno di Nettuno*, so dear to classicists, seem ridiculous. With Romanticism the adjective *primaverile* (at first in competition with *primaveresco*) was born, while *autunnale*, previously rare, became widely used. *Medievale* was coined (alongside *medievitico*, which later disappeared). *Pomeriggio* entered usage. New poetic forms were the *ballata* (different from what was so called in the Middle Ages) and the *romanza*. *Mal sottile* was a Romantic euphemism for 'tuberculosis'. Among writers some were more inclined than others to neologisms. Giusti, for instance, wrote *arfasatteria*, *arlecchineggiare*, *arruffapopoli*, *articolaio*, *birrocratico*, *castrapensieri*, *grinzume, innaiolo, insugherire, meritometro, nipotame, puerperio, scal-essare, sonniloquio, vanume,* etc. Gioberti, apart from reviving numerous Graeco-Latin and early Italian words, coined *contra-scossa, cronotopo, fogliettista, scattedrare, scriviarticoli, torcilegge,* etc. Mamiani coined *bronzeo* (which took root) and *quercioso* (which did not). Numerous words and phrases used by individual writers gained wide currency: Foscolo's *ombra dei cipressi* and *lombardo Sardanapalo,* Leopardi's *procombere* and *sudate carte,* Manzoni's *disonor del Golgota* and *pareri di Perpetua* (the name *Perpetua* itself we shall mention again later). Opera affected language by the vogue it gave to certain words (*palpito*) and by the widespread use of phrases which were reminiscences of great operatic moments, like *il suon dell'arpe angeliche* (from Donizetti's *Poliuto,* libretto by Cammarano), *una furtiva lacrima* (from Donizetti's *Elisir d'amore,* libretto by Romani), *ultimo avanzo — d'una stirpe infelice* (from Donizetti's *Lucia di Lammermoor,* libretto by Cammarano), *invenzione prelibata* (from Rossini's *Barbiere di Siviglia*), etc. Pro-fessor Praz has shown that Byron's letters to Countess Guiccioli, written in rather shaky Italian, owe much to operatic locutions: 'con quei soavi palpiti', 'tutto dipende da te, la mia vita, il mio amor, il mio onor'. Although *palpito* had existed at least since the Quattrocento and had been used by some writers (Leo-pardi, Guadagnoli) of the early nineteenth century, it was not in the dictionaries; but the famous cavatina *Di tanti palpiti — di tante pene* (from Rossini's *Tancredi,* libretto by G. Rossi) 'impressed its sound and meaning', as L. Molossi put it, 'on all Italian hearts' (*Nuovo elenco di voci e maniere di dire,* Parma 1839-1841). Verdi's opera gave wide diffusion to *traviata.* And operatic characters gave examples of antonomasia like *Dulcamara* (used for 'quack pharmacist', from Donizetti's *Elisir d'amore,* 1832) and *Figaro* (whom we owe, of course, to Beaumarchais's play, but whose fame is due to Rossini's opera). The journalism of the period also reflected, mainly in rather unoriginal fashion, its literary tendencies, and oscillated between classicism and Romanticism. Journalists and authors of little merit tended to abuse abstracts, and Tommaseo complained of this. Certain Italians, he alleged, followed the French in referring to a famous man as *una sommità, un'illustrazione, una celebrità*; soon they would be calling Ariosto an *ariostizzazione* and Petrarch a *petrarchità* ('Nuova proposta', p. 19).

There was widespread use of bureaucratic terms and of foreign words. The purists who objected to these often disagreed with each other. Nevertheless, their objections had some effect. If they did not succeed in banishing most of the words of which they disapproved (*controllo*, *deperire*, *distintivo*, *funzionare*, *ispettore*, *licitazione*, *massacro*, *privativa*, *proclama*, *protocollare*, *provvisorio*, *trasferta*, *traslocare* and a thousand others which became generally accepted) some did fall by the wayside (*cadò*, *mantò*, *mere*, *merìa*, *tirabussòn*, etc.; *degrado*, *estremare*, *reatizzare*, *renuenza*, *speranzare*, etc.). Others lived on in a sort of limbo: accepted by most people, they were by others considered illegitimate or confined to office use (*bigiotteria*, *dettaglio*, *rimarco*; *miglioria*, *dilazionare*, etc.). Less resistance of a puristic nature was offered to words denoting new objects in everyday life. Such were terms that referred to dress: i *pantaloni*, la *cravatta*, il *paltò*, il *raglan*, il (*cappello a*) *cilindro* or (*cappello a*) *staio*, la *tuba*, il *gibus*, il *corsè*, il *figaro*, la *crinolina*, la *pellegrina*, il *boa*, etc. Along with them we should mention *plaid* and *percalle*, and the colours *magenta* and *solferino*, coined on the occasion of the two battles. Dances which became fashionable at this time were the *mazurka*, *polka* and *walzer*. The use of *sigari* spread, and, after the Crimean war, that of *sigarette*. Shortly after 1830 appeared phosphorus-tipped *fiammiferi*, a marked improvement on the *solfanelli* that preceded them. (The neo-classical name *fiammiferi* triumphed over the others that then appeared: *accensibili*, *lumiferi* (cf. Eng. *lucifer*, 1831). *Fulminante* still survives in northern Italy and *pròspero*, a para-etymological alteration of *fosforo*, in Rome. And in some areas the old names, *solfino*, *z-*, *solfanello*, *z-*, survive.) The field of transport provided *celeriferi* and *omnibus*; *velociferi*, *draisiennes* and *bicicli*; and a wide range of words relating to horse-carriages: *tilbury*, *padovanelli*, etc. The introduction of the railways (*strade ferrate*) to Italy (1839) brought in a new terminology: *locomotiva*, *vaporiera* (also used for 'steam-boat'), *vagone*, *tender*, *raile* (later replaced by *rotaia*), *tunnel*, *viadotto*, etc. *Ferrovia* made a rather late appearance (1852). A *tramway* (i.e. a railway with horse-drawn trams) was planned in 1856.

The great progress of sciences at this period led to more or less parallel growth in their terminologies in most of the languages of western Europe. Moreover, through the application of sciences to practical purposes, many items of the new terminologies became widely known. Chemistry was an example of a science in which a host of new terms sprang up: *boro*, *cloro*, *alluminio*, *calcio*, *iodio*, *sodio*, *destrina*, *glicerina*, *paraffina*, *stearina*, *morfina*, *acido fenico*, *cloroformio*, etc. Medicine identified *difterite*, *encefalite*, *flebite*, studied *tifo*, *cirrosi*, *vibrioni*, *batteri*, etc. It made use of auscultation

(*auscultazione*). There were developments in the field of *igiene*.
Homeopathy (*omeopatia*) and phrenology (*frenologia*) won new
adherents; and from the latter came the locution *avere il ber-*
noccolo for 'to have a marked capacity for'. Many new terms were
formed by zoologists (e.g. *plantigrado*) and botanists. Others,
which had previously been used only in scientific treatises, became
part of common usage. *Libellula*, for instance, passed from Latin
into Italian at this time, as did *medusa*. Similarly *gas*, from being
a word used in physics, became generally known after the spread
of gas lighting (from the second decade of the century, that is).
Physical geography began to speak of *alti piani* or *altipiani*;
mineralogists coined words like *dolomite*; geologists studied the
stratigrafia of rocks, coining numerous new terms (*alluvionale*,
trias, *lias*, *eocene*, *pliocene*, *devoniano*, *permiano*, etc.); and *paleontologia*
was born. Indeed, numerous new sciences or branches of sciences
appeared: *linguistica* or *glottologia*, *antropometria*, as well as new
techniques like *litografia* and *fotografia* (at first *daguerrotipia* or
dagherrotipia). Grown-ups and children found amusement in the
caleidoscopio. Early attempts at making a type-writer were
reflected in the words *tachigrafo*, *tachitipo*, *cembalo scrivano*. These
few remarks will suffice to hint at the great store of material which
awaits systematic investigation in this sphere.

The procedures of derivation were the usual ones; we shall
mention only the methods most frequently employed. Among
prefixes, the negative *in-* enjoyed considerable vogue. Sometimes
the new words reproduced a Latin or modern model; sometimes
they were direct formations. Examples are *illacrimato* (Foscolo),
illodato (Perticari), *impoetico* (Leopardi), *imponderabile* (Gioberti,
etc.), *impremiato* (*Conciliatore*), *inaffettato* (Leopardi), *indelibato*
(Leopardi), *inesatto* (Foscolo, etc.), *infilosofico* (Pellico), *inobbedito*
(Foscolo), *inoffensivo* (Pananti), *insalutare* (Colletta), etc. Among
the intensive prefixes, the purists, as we have seen, tried to
restore *tra-*, but *stra-* still prevailed (gli *Straultra*, Giusti, 1848),
and there were examples of *supra-* (*supra-romantico*, E. Visconti).
Among suffixes we should note the fortune enjoyed by *-aio* in
jocose formations: 'vo' siete — *minestraio*, *lessaio*, *fritturaio* —
pasticciaio, *arrostaio*, *polpettaio*' (Pananti, *Poeta di teatro*, c. 37),
catalogaio (Di Breme), *articolaio* (Giusti), *gesuitaio* (Cattaneo), etc.
The suffix *-ista* enjoyed a vogue in the political field, but it was
also productive of professional names: *pianista*, for example,
appeared at this time. The international fortune of some suffixes
in scientific language deserves study, e.g. *-oide* in *asteroide*, *metalloide*,

antropoide, alcaloide. The suffix *-izzare* was much used, as in French models, in bureaucratic language (*centralizzare, economizzare, mobilizzare, monopolizzare, numerizzare, popolarizzare, quotizzare, utilizzare,* etc.) and also in philosophical language (Rosmini used *individualizzare* and *universalizzazione*). The purists were strongly opposed to it. That is why some verbs in *-izzare*, which enjoyed popularity at the time, later disappeared (e.g. *mobilizzare,* which was replaced by *mobilitare*). Immediate derivation gave rise to a number of nouns formed from verbs in bureaucratic language: *accompagno, allargo, ammanco, sodisfo, spreco; compensa, consegna,* etc. From the noun *agricola* was derived the adjective *agricolo* (through *agricola* used adjectivally), under the influence of *regnicolo* and the Fr. *agricole* (adj.). Substantivization of adjectives was frequent, both in scientific language (*calorico, elettrico*) and in bureaucratic jargon (*consuntivo, preventivo*). Among compounds the imperatival type was still in favour for indicating persons, e.g. *arruffapopoli* (Giusti), *sciupateste* (id.), *vendilettere* (Foscolo), and things, e.g. *paracadute, paragrandine, paralume, tornaconto,* etc. Compounds with Greek and Latin elements abounded, particularly in scientific language, among them many hybrids (e.g. *neonato*). Compounds of other kinds, however, like *cormentale* (Maroncelli), *codafestante* (Nievo) were very rare. There were even a few compounds formed from initials: Lampredi, to satirize the initials U.F. (Ugo Foscolo) coined the verb *ufeggiare.*

Numerous semantic changes took place as a result of changes in things or concepts. Examples are the new political meanings attached to *rosso, destra* and *sinistra.* The Mazzinian gospel transferred certain religious terms to the patriotic sphere. *Esposizione* acquired a concrete meaning. *Panificio,* which in the eighteenth century had denoted the process of baking bread, came to indicate the place in which the baking took place. *Carrozza,* which had stood for a horse-drawn carriage, came to denote a railway carriage, while *treno,* which previously signified a number of persons attending a person of rank, or a military train, now came to mean a railway train. *Vettura* passed from abstract to concrete meaning. Scientific terminology also produced examples of semantic change due to the use of existing words in new conceptual systems: *fossile,* which at first indicated any body that formed part of the earth's crust, became restricted to cover only parts of animals or plants of preceding geological ages found in the strata of the earth. The names of well-known characters often assumed metaphorical value, e.g. *un Figaro, Dulcamara, Mefistofele,*

Azzeccagarbugli, una Perpetua, un Carneade (unknown to Don Abbondio, thus an unknown person), or metonymic value — like *un napoleone d'oro*. Not less numerous were words derived from place-names (*un marengo*). Naturally, the evolution of many words can be better understood if they are studied as part of the appropriate semantic field: the decline of *servo* and *servitore*, for instance, must be considered in connection with the more extensive use of *domestico*. And this very example serves to emphasize that we must never forget the powerful influence of other languages, and especially French, on Italian semantics.

When a new object was introduced, there was sometimes hesitation in choice of a word to denote it. Such was the case when envelopes came to be used for enclosing letters: the French *enveloppe* was used, an adaptation from it *inviluppo, sopraccarta, sopraccoperta* — and *busta*, which finally triumphed. Similarly for 'address' Italians employed, not only the eventual victor, *indirizzo*, but also *soprascritta, soprascritto, direzione* and occasionally *mansione, missione*. In fact, Italian often offered more than one word for a concept: there was no difference between *Costituzione* and *Statuto* (in the sense in which Charles Albert used the latter in 1848). There was long hesitation, too, in the following cases: *patata* and *pomo di terra*; *grappolo, pigna* and *ciocca* (for 'bunch'); *crestaia* and *modista* ('milliner'); *balocco* and *giocattolo* ('toy'); *pedignone, gelone* and *buganza* ('chilblain'); *fazzoletto, pezzuola, moccichino* ('hand-kerchief'), etc. Both lexical variants of this kind and variants in the form of a word were very common. And lexicographers varied in their advice according to their origin and theories. The Crusca's fourth edition (and Cesari's revision of it) registered many archaic forms. We have already mentioned the objections to it made by Monti and others. Leopardi, in annotating a *canzone* of his (IX, l. 43) excused himself for using *fratricida* when the *Vocabolario della Crusca* had only *fraticida*: he did so because, having established that Abel never was a friar (*frate*), he thought *fratricida* more appropriate a description for Cain! But other writers showed more deference to its authority: Manno, in his *Della fortuna delle parole* (Turin 1831, reprinted on several occasions), wrote *cucuzzolo, sustanza, fenestrella, nimico, nissuno, nudrimento, instruzione, sagro, denaio*, etc. Manzoni, on the other hand, preferred the forms offered by spoken Florentine (especially in the 1840 version of *I promessi sposi*: *lazzeretto, maraviglia, suggezione*, etc.). An able anti-Tuscan, Gherardini, sought to win favour for variants remodelled on Latin (*vulgo, dubio, febre, atimo, catolico*, *legitimo, academia, esaggerare,* etc.) and to generalize the distinction between negative *in-* and immissive *inn-* (*innalveare,* etc.). Often the form of the word most used then is not the one which has survived to our time. *Fisonomia* was commoner than *fisionomia, tremuoto* was still frequent in comparison with *terremoto,* and *tuono* was frequently used for 'tone'. (The distinction between *tuono* 'thunder' and *tono* 'tone', though urged by Grassi, in his *Saggio intorno ai sinonimi,* was not finally established until the twentieth century). *Nodrire* (employed by Pindemonte, Borsieri, Pellico, Perticari and others) and *nudrire* (Guerrazzi, Farini, A. Maffei and Manzoni's *Promessi sposi*) were more widely used than *nutrire.* Some words showed the struggle between the Florentine *-er-* and the *-ar-* prevalent in the rest of Italy: *lazzeretto* alternated with *lazzaretto,* which prevailed; Pecchio wrote in the same article in the *Conciliatore* (30 Sept. 1819) both *Ungheria* and *ungarese*; Giusti used *-arello* and *-erello* with almost equal frequency; and Manzoni replaced the *santarella* of 1827 by *santerella* in 1840. Among the variations caused by differing degrees of adaptation of latinisms, we should note the oscillation between *-olo* and *-ulo* in atonic suffixes, which was even more marked than it is today: alongside *cumulo* there was *cumolo,* and *immaculato* beside *immacolato,* while *formola* was more frequent than *formula.* The adaptation of consonant groups also gave rise to oscillation, both in cases in which the unassimilated form later prevailed (Leopardi wrote *Calisso* for *Calipso,* Manzoni *annegazione* for *abnegazione,* and Mussafia preferred *circollocuzione*) and in the opposite (Rosini, 1808, wrote *scepticismo*). The suffixes *-iere* and *-iero* were widely regarded as interchangeable, not only in verse (*cavaliero,* Foscolo; *mestiero,* Pananti; *pensiere, forestiere,* Guadagnoli), but also in prose: Leopardi wrote *passeggere,* Borsieri *bicchiero,* Carrer *battelliero. Pulmonia* and *polmonèa* existed alongside *pneumonia* and *pneumonite. Ossigene* and *idrogene* yielded slowly to *ossigeno* and *idrogeno.* Sometimes the maintenance of particular forms was due to the official (administrative or judicial) custom of individual states: thus there was oscillation in the cases of *officio, ufficio* and *uffizio; officiale* and *ufficiale; processura* and *procedura; fidecommisso, fideicommisso* and *fedecommesso; garantia, guarentia* and *guarentigia* (*garanzia* did not appear until very late: in 1865, according to the *Dizionario etimologico italiano*). The acceptance of foreign words also gave rise to variants. This could be caused by the problem of maintaining or adapting the original spelling: *burò* or *bureau; valz, valtz, walser, walzer.* The names of the months in the French republican calendar were variously treated (e.g. *fiorile*, *floreale*). The adoption of the decimal system gave rise to oscillation between *gramma* and *grammo*, *ara* and *aro*. When the cigar was introduced, it was called *sìgaro*, *cìgaro*, *zìgaro* and even *sigarro*. Alongside *giaguaro* existed *giagaro* (Tramater) and *sciaguaro* (Leopardi). Some wrote *feticcio*, others *fetisce*, while Gioberti preferred *fetisso*. And the list of examples of oscillation could easily be lengthened.

The literary language (with the exception of the diction used for the most illustrious kind of poetry) was more inclined, after the spread of Romantic ideas, to accept words of popular coinage, taken from the spoken tongue. Pananti, who hailed from the Sieve valley, wrote, not only *scagnozzo* ('impoverished priest seeking employment', hence 'a mediocrity'), but also *mascagnotta* ('cunning lass') and *far la stummia* ('to give oneself airs'). With Tuscan writers like him the process was often unintentional. With Giusti, however, it was deliberate; he was very fond of popular expressions, using *altogatto* ('poplar'), *balenare* (in the sense 'to vacillate'), *chiòvina* ('sewer'), *garga* (*femmina garga*, 'cunning woman'), *meggiona* ('fat woman') and idioms like *trovarsi di balla* ('to be in agreement'), *montare i fùteri* ('to get angry'), *aver più debiti della lepre*, etc. Sometimes, indeed, he verged on affectation in his accumulation of such expressions, e.g. 'scegliere una città così piccola [Lucca] per una adunanza tanto solenne [il congresso dei dotti] è un voler *mettere l'asino a cavallo*; pure quei Lucchesi si arrabattarono tanto da *levarne le gambe* meglio che non si sarebbe immaginato'. The Aretine Guadagnoli used *fitta* for 'a lot of', *gazzerare* for 'to deceive', etc. And Guerrazzi employed expressions proper to Leghorn: *brameggio* ('bait'), *mettere a picca* ('to urge, incite'), etc. For Tuscans like these, the process, whether intentional or unintentional, involved nothing more than borrowing from their own speech. Non-Tuscans who wished to exploit Tuscan idiom were in a more difficult position; they often imagined that the phrases they took from their dictionaries were part of living Tuscan when they were, in fact, locutions that had fallen into desuetude. When Manzoni wished to correct the 1825-27 edition of *I promessi sposi* in order to bring it into line with modern Florentine usage, he asked Cioni, Niccolini and Borghi for suggestions and information. Later he got much help from his children's Florentine governess, Emilia Luti. With their help he substituted *chicche* for *dolci*, *filastrocca* for *lunga enumerazione*, *impiparsene* for *ridersene*, *pezzo d'asino* for *matto minchione*, *pigionale* for *inquilino*. He did not always avoid exaggeration or misunderstanding, as when he used *tafferia* improperly in Chapter VI or *accozzare il pentolino* instead of *accozzare i pentolini* for 'to pool the food, mess together' in Chapter XXIX. He continued to take every opportunity of learning living Florentine expressions. In his wake, non-Tuscan writers like Grossi, Cantù, Tommaseo and D'Azeglio (to mention only a few) used, to varying degrees, expressions taken from spoken Tuscan. As a result of this attitude on the part of a number of Tuscan and non-Tuscan writers, many words which had previously been unknown or very rare became part of common usage: examples are *bècero* ('blackguard'), *canèa* ('barking'; (fig.) 'uproar'), *figuro* ('cast'), *sbraitare* ('to shout'). Gelmetti ascribed to Giusti the diffusion of '*birba*' ('rascal, scamp'), *musoneria* ('sulking'), *vattelappesca* (excl. 'who knows?'), *ciurlare nel manico* ('to be shifty') and other expressions, while Nieri attributed to him the vogue later enjoyed by *spadroneggiare* ('to swagger'; 'domineer').

But many non-Tuscan regional and dialectal words emerged at this time, especially in use of language for practical purposes The administrative usage of the Regno Italico, for instance, included numerous lombardisms of which we can learn from Bernardoni and Gherardini: *finca* ('column for figures', probably a hispanism buried in a dialect until this point), *ragionateria* alongside *ragioneria* ('accountancy'), *accaparrare* ('to secure by paying a deposit'; hence 'to corner'), *anta* ('shutter, windowpane'), *caseggiato* ('group of houses, block of flats'), *locale* (as noun, 'room'; 'headquarters'), *prestinaio* ('baker'), *roccolo* ('artificial arbour with nets for catching birds'), *tavolo* ('little table'), etc. If objects peculiar to one region spread to others, then the name naturally went with them: examples were the Piedmontese *grissini* ('thin sticks of bread'), the Lombard cheese *stracchino* and Emilian *cotichini* (*cotechini, coteghini,* 'a sort of boiling-sausage'). The literary use of dialectalisms depended largely, of course, not only on the authors concerned, but on the genre, tone (confidential or not) and subject. They abounded in the letters of those who were used to dialect in communicating with family and friends. Foscolo, in letters to members of his family, for instance, used venetisms: 'temo bensì che la *vera* ('wedding ring') non sia troppo stretta per la mamma' (letter 26 Sept. 1814). Manzoni in confidential letters frequently employed italianized lombardisms: 'mi vien voglia di *giavanare*' ('waste time in levity'; letter of 1822), 'vite *uccellina*' ('wild'; letter of 9 Nov. 1830), etc. In literary works proper, we should distinguish between unintentional dialectalisms and dialectalisms deliberately used for documentary or stylistic reasons (local colour, etc.). Leopardi, who had written *pesciarello* in the first edition of the *Dialogo della moda*, preferred *pesciolino* for the 1835 edition. The *Promessi sposi* of 1825-27 had numerous (mostly involuntary) lombardisms. In spite of Manzoni's intention of eliminating them, some remained in the 1840 edition. Nievo's *Confessioni di un Italiano* abounded in (voluntary and involuntary) venetisms: *bagiggi* 'peanut, ground-nut', *coppa* 'nape of neck', *guantiera* 'tray', *sfregolare* 'to rub', etc. Many dialectalisms were used with technical value in docu-mentary works, like geographical and ethnographic descriptions: Cattaneo, in the *Notizie naturali e civili su la Lombardia*, 1844, spoke of the custom of cultivating 'a *ronchi* le pendici dei monti,' and Father Bresciani, in *Dei costumi dell'isola di Sardegna*, 1850, de-scribed 'una lor danza a suono della *lionedda*', etc. In poetic language, on the other hand, dialectalisms were extremely rare; here they appeared only in poems of familiar tone. Monti, in his translation of Persius, spoke of the 'raschiatura — del rigustato *salarin*,' making use of a Ferrarese (or Venetian) word. Pananti, in the unambitious *Poeta del teatro*, spoke of 'De' buoni maccheroni col *sughillo*' (c. XXXVII), a pseudo-neapolitanism used for local colour. Mamiani used *roccolo* (see p. 392) in his idyll *Rispetti d'un Trasteverino* and defended it in his preface as a word used in the Marche and Latium. Prati's *sferlato* ('weakened') was badly received by the critics.

Poetic language continued to use its traditional vocabulary, which included words no longer alive either in speech or in every-day prose. (It continued, too, to have recourse to latinisms, with which we shall deal presently). Leopardi's *Appressamento della morte* can serve as an example of the deliberate use of archaisms in verse (*atare* for 'aiutare'; *roggio* for 'rosso', etc.). This tradition was strong enough to affect, not only classicists, but also Romantic poets, for all their efforts at renewal through greater realism. But even in prose there were tendencies to archaism, especially in certain writers. First we should note that hundreds of traditional words which later disappeared were still in use, and that these were employed by Romantics as well as classicists, e.g. *estimazione, eziandio, guiderdone, laudare, nomare, o(b)blivione, permissione,* and many others. But apart from these, there were words which classicists and purists exhumed from the ancient writers they studied: Cesari wrote *auspizio, capitanio, carminare* ('to examine rigorously'), *orrevole, poffare, sempremai, soprano,* and *sottano, sozio, tornagusto,* etc. and phrases like *andare in cappa.* Yet he professed to avoid archaisms like *diffalta, dottanza,* etc., and when his adversaries accused him of having written *carogna* for 'dead body' challenged them to say where. Leopardi used many archaic words in his prose, but claimed to be distinguishing between real archaisms (which he disapproved of) and those words which were capable of being given new life (*Zibaldone,* 28 May 1821, 1098, I, p. 738, Flora). Gioberti archaized eclectically: *animastico, bugiare, celabro, chieresia, miluogo, norte, saporetto* ('tit-bit'), *soprano, sozzopra,* etc. And he frequently used *in barbagrazia* ('for example'), a phrase taken from the burlesque poets. A genre in which archaisms abounded was epigraphy: 'Qui dorme — Nunziata di Luigi Fossati — *Fancellina* soavissima e dolcissima' (Giordani). Even Romantic writers used many rare, archaic words (apart from words used to describe institutions and customs of past ages). The presence of these archaisms was due, not to intention usually, but to the fact that their literary Italian was acquired from books. Thus we find *cocchio, compungimento, doppiere, forese, garzoncello, rangolo, sanie* in the 1825-27 version of Manzoni's *I promessi sposi; aere, egro, esponimento, garrire, martirare, nomare, trabocchello* in Pellico's *Le mie prigioni; catollo, forbottare, gavazza* in Cantù's *Margherita Pusterla,* etc. Jocose or ironic use of archaisms was, of course, a totally different matter. An example of this is the *unquanco* used by Berchet in the conclusion of his *Lettera semiseria di Grisostomo*: 'E tu, allorché uscirai di collegio, preparati a dichiararti nemico d'ogni novità, o il mio viso non lo vedrai sereno unquanco. *Unquanco,* dico, e questo solo avverbio ti faccia fede che il Vocabolario della Crusca io lo rispetto. . . .' And a satire of archaisms, abounding in such examples, was composed by J. Landoni under the pseudonym 'Maestro Ircone' (Lo Maestro Ircone Ravignano, *Dello pulcro vulgare eloquio della prisca simplicitate, naturalezza e grazia rinnovellato,* Ravenna 1823). It is difficult to say which (or how many) words were successfully revived in this period. But we can form some idea if we run through the list of words and locutions used by Botta and condemned by Borsieri as useless exhumations (P. Borsieri, *Avventure letterarie di un giorno,* Milan 1816, p. 42). Among those he lists (*mai sì, mai no, all'avvenante* 'in proportion', *popoleschi,* etc.) there are some which today we should not think twice about using in normal prose (*aver alle costole, rinfocolare*). Moreover, we should note that when De Sanctis (in 'L'ultimo dei puristi') made a list of the phrases dear to his old teacher Puoti, he included some, like *andar per la maggiore* and *tener per fermo*, at which we should hardly raise our eyebrows today.

When we come to consider the period's latinisms we must take into account, not only latinisms now used for the first time, but also those which, though occasionally used in the past, were felt to belong to Latin, rather than Italian, vocabulary. Such were *clade* and *procombere*, used by Leopardi (previously employed by Ariosto and Baretti), *munùsculo* and *trùtina*, which we find in Monti (Lorenzo de' Medici having previously used *munusculo*, and Biringuccio and Galileo *trutina*) and Foscolo's *precingere* (which was in Cavalca). To students of style it would doubtless be interesting to know whether such examples were taken directly from Latin or from previous Italian authors; but what is important to note here is that the vocabulary of Latin was considered complementary to that of Italian. Leopardi, commenting on the *incombe* which occurred in the first stanza of his canzone *Ad Angelo Mai* (*Annotazioni filol.*, canzone III), remarked that he took many words, not from the *Vocabolario della Crusca*, but from that vocabulary (i.e. the Latin language) from which classical Italian writers had ceaselessly and freely derived what seemed to them suitable, without being concerned as to whether particular (Latin) words had previously been used by their predecessors. The poetry of the classicists, indeed, abounded in latinisms. Here are some of the many found in Monti: *acervato, cassitèro* ('tin'), *cicada, cipero* ('sedge'), *combùrere, crime, èpate* ('liver'), *larario* (a word borrowed from the archaeologists of Monti's time), *nitente, oberato, transire* (to which he gave exceptional treatment, adapting a past definite *transe* from *transiit* and using it to rhyme with *franse* and *pianse*), *versuto*, etc. But Romantic poets also had recourse to latinisms: *callido* (Poerio), *cincinno* (Cantù), *lebete* (*il sospeso lebete* being no more than 'a cooking pot' in Sestini's romantic story *Pia de' Tolomei*), *uliginoso* (Grossi, Prati), and innumerable others were used in suitable or unsuitable contexts. Latinisms in prose were found most frequently in the works of those who aimed at a noble style: e.g. Foscolo in his Pavian lectures, Botta (who wrote, for instance, *eruscatore, impellersi*). Leopardi used them, not only in his most polished works, in which semantic latinisms, in particular, abounded (*ferocia* 'pride', *imbecillità* 'weakness', *sentenza* 'opinion', etc.), but also not infrequently in the *Zibaldone* (*illecebre, obruto, oppidano, tentame*). Epigraphic style was very favourable to them: *innubo, sospite, vivituro*; Muzzi even used the comparatives *celebriore* and *salubriore*. Gioberti was very fond both of latinisms and of grecisms: *circuminessione, perennare, pistrino, satellizio, succedituro,* etc.; *acroamatico, antagonia, cosmopolitia, steresi, zoolatrico,* etc. There was a flood of latinisms in the fields of law, politics and administration. Such were *cassazione, collaudare, coscritto, deportare, dilapidare, eccepire, effrazione, evadere, lasso* (referring to a period of time), *plebiscito, redigere, refurtiva, ripristinare, sovventore, tramite, utente, velite, vigile* (as noun), etc. Only a minority of these words came directly from Latin; most of them came through French or English. *Prefetti* were instituted in 1802, and the ancient name was adopted with modern, French meaning. *Cassazione* was a Napoleonic institution. The *veliti* were battalions added by Napoleon to the infantry of his guard; they were to be found again in Piedmont after the restoration. The voluntary papal militia founded by Cardinal Bernetti came to be called *centurioni.* In 1847 Roman firemen were called *vigili.* The Roman Republic brought *triumviri* into use once again. Political and parliamentary terminology (*iniziativa, preventivo, consuntivo, commissione, mozione,* etc., *conservatore, liberale, radicale,* etc.) consisted almost entirely of Latin words (or derivatives thereof: *costituzionale, assolutismo, comunismo, socialismo, cesarismo,* etc.) used with the meanings they had in contemporary England and France. The most frequent way of designating a new institution or an invention was to apply to it a Latin or Greek name or one made up of Latin or Greek elements. We have already mentioned *fiammiferi. Ambulanze* (in the sense of 'mobile hospitals') appeared in the wake of the Napoleonic armies. *Brefotrofi, orfanotrofi, manicomi* were founded. We have already spoken of the remarkable increase in scientific terminology that took place at this time. In some sciences (e.g. medicine) most new terms were formed by borrowing Latin or Greek words or elements, and were largely the same for all European languages. Of these thousands of new items, some penetrated the vocabulary of everyday life. Naturally, the meanings they bore were often not those of original Latin or Greek words. The *tifo* described by nineteenth-century clinicians was different from the τῦφος of Hippocrates. Scientists who talked of *animali parassiti* and *vegetali parassiti* technified the word, producing a new meaning. *Auscultare* had a medical technical connotation which separated it from *ascoltare.* Occasionally, classical terms were treated in free and easy or arbitrary fashion. Gay Lussac (1812) took from the Greek ἰώδης 'violet-coloured' the French *iode* to describe the violet colour of his vapours, and Italian chemists accepted the word *iodo* or *iodio. Paraffina* was a very arbitrary composition from *parum* and *affinis*. In *miocene* the union of μείων 'lesser' and καινός 'new' was barbarous. *Telegramma*, if composed by persons who had greater respect for Greek, would have been *telegrafema*. While a word formed from Greek and Latin elements by an individual writer might remain limited to his own use, it would obviously have much greater chance of permanence if it could find a place in legal, administrative or scientific terminology or was applied to some object of practical value. Lalli had vainly introduced *moschicida* in the seventeenth century; it took root with the diffusion of *carta moschida* 'fly paper'. Gioberti's use of *tellurico* ('l'infermità *tellurica* [i.e. of men on earth] non è incurabile': *Primato*, Brussels 1843, II, p. 8) won no following, but scientific use of the term (*movimenti tellurici*) was successful in establishing it. Before leaving the subject of latinisms and grecisms, we should mention the formal influence exercised on certain words by a Latin model. Here what was a sporadic phenomenon in some writers (e.g. *destruttore, nepote* in Monti) became a consistent programme with Gherardini, who wanted to detuscanize the language by bringing its orthography closer to that of Latin.

As we said earlier, the great political and cultural influence of France in this period added even more gallicisms to the host already borrowed in the eighteenth century. If purism succeeded in excluding some of them from the more elevated kinds of literary prose, they abounded in the less ambitious sorts. Thus, in Leopardi's *Zibaldone*, a work originally meant for his own eyes, we find frequent examples: 'il piacere che noi proviamo... della *raillerie*' (27 July 1822); 'sarebbero *bien fachés* di trovarsi soli' (6 July 1826); 'una donna di venti, venticinque o trenta anni ha forse più d'*attraits*, più d'illecebre' (30 June 1828), etc. In letters, too, they were widely used: 'or che gli amori della patria mi hanno *desenchanté* così infamemente' (Berchet, letter of 3 August 1848); 'mia moglie che esce da una *grippe*' (Manzoni, letter of January 11, 1858); 'sa di dover morire, glielo leggo in quegli occhi *égarés*' (De Sanctis, letter of 10 June 1858), etc. Gallicisms were particularly abundant in the military field: *affusto, ambulanza, appello, avamposto, buffetteria, casermaggio, marmitta* (which then was extended to use outside the military sphere), *pioniere*, etc. Many political terms were used first with reference to French affairs (*club, comitato, giacobino, assegnato*, etc.) only to be applied later, in increasing numbers, to Italian matters (*budget, consuntivo, preventivo*, names of parties, etc.). Administration imported a great many: *bureau* or *burò* (in Piedmont the derivative *buralista* as well), *borderò*, *controllare* (*controllo*, *controllore*), *maire* or *mere* (and *meria* 'mairie'), *paraf(f)are*, *regìa*, *timbro* ('stamp'), etc. One must remember, too, not only terms used in the administration of justice (*cassazione*, *giudice di pace*, *giurì*, etc.), but also those due to French influence in Napoleonic times in the vocabulary of the actual codes of law (*vagabondaggio*, etc.). The metric system brought *metro*, *litro*, *gramma*, etc.; the abbreviation *chilo* was sometimes pronounced *chilò* (as it still is at Leghorn and Siena) and for a long time could be used as invariable. Some items entered naval vocabulary: *pompa* (whence *pompiere*) was first documented as a naval term; *rullìo*, etc. Domestic terminology acquired words indicating rooms (*boudoir*) and furniture (*cislonga*, *comò*, *psychè*, *secrétaire*, etc.), and terms related to cooking (*griglia*, *casseruola*, etc.; *entremets*, *tartina*, cf. also *trattore*, *trattoria*) and gardening (*pepiniera*, *serra*, etc.). Many gallicisms referred to dress (*bretelle*, *calosce*, *corsè*, *paltò*, *percalle*, etc.); some, which at first designated military dress (*pompon*), later had their meaning extended. Among vehicles we should mention the *faeton*, *fiacre* and *furgone*. The theatre gave *debutto* and *messa in scena*, the fine arts *rococò* and knowledge of *danze macabre*, while games gave *sciarade*. Scientific terminology brought in, not only innumerable latinisms and grecisms suggested by analogous French terms, but also French words of a more or less popular type, e.g. in medicine *crampo*, *grippe*, etc., in ethnology *meticcio* (whereas preceding centuries had preferred *mestizzo*, following the Spanish model), in geology *morena*, *picco*, etc. The French range of penetration can, perhaps, best be measured in the domain of abstracts: the examples quoted at the beginning of this paragraph from confidential writings (Leopardi, etc.) can serve as illustrations here, as can the frequent complaints of Italian writers that their language was incapable of rendering nuances which French could manage. D'Azeglio, for instance, wrote: 'Neppur essa è stata capace di farmi rimpiangere (benedetto *regretter* che non ha equivalente esatto fra noi) Napoleone ed il dominio francese. . . .': *I miei ricordi*, c. VIII. Since Italian lacked a word for the generic notion of *exploiter*, *exploitation*, the French words were used, either in their original form or adapted (*esploatare*) until *sfruttare* was extended to cover the whole semantic field of *exploiter*. Faced with a word like *entrevoir*, for which no Italian word provided an exact equivalent, and which had to be paraphrased ('vedere un poco, cominciare a vedere'), Italians felt a desire to form a similar word in their own language. Leopardi's employed *travedere* (letter to Giordani, 30 April 1817), a word previously used, but condemned by Cesari. But it was *intravedere* (Gioberti, Capponi, Mazzini) that prevailed. *Saputa* had been used since the Cinquecento. Now, in order to translate *à l'insu*, the phrase *all'insaputa* appeared. By similar processes, in spite of purists' protests, Italian acquired words like *sedicente*, *controsenso*, *frattempo*, *malinteso*, *rendiconto*, *sorvegliare*, etc. and locutions like *essere al corrente*, etc. In the case of abstracts it was much rarer for adaptation, rather than calque, of the French word to take place: *scamotaggio*, *trantran* are examples of the few instances in which it did. On the other hand, new words without number were formed by using elements (or words) already existing in Italian or Latin, but now adapted to form a word directly modelled on French: *bonomìa*, *contabile*, *floreale*, *responsabile*, *mentalità*, *spessore*, *tasso* ('rate of interest'), *versante*, *vetrina*, *basare*, *rivoluzionare*, etc. The existence of an Italian prefix *de-*, coming from Latin *de-*, made it easier for words like *debordare* to enter the language, even if the *de-* in them had a different origin (in *déborder* it is from *dis-*). Words in *-aggio* proliferated (*cordaggio*, *drenaggio*, *lavaggio*, *vagabondaggio*, etc.). Nouns ending in *-ista*, too, gained easy acceptance (e.g. *modista*). Furthermore, since in French that suffix had acquired the force of an adjectival ending, particularly in political language, it came to be similarly used in Italian, e.g. *la chiesa Sansimonista* (Romagnosi, 1832), *l'analisi materialista* (Mazzini, 1850), *la scuola socialista* (Minghetti, 1858), alongside *gli ordini comunistici* (Giusti, 1849), etc. Indeed, passage of words to another grammatical category often happened on the model of French: it was thus that *commerciante*, *industriale*, *domestico* and *uniforme* became nouns. French also influenced the meaning of many Italian words: *domestico* became a 'servant'; *bruma* 'mist'; *giurato*, which had borne various administrative and legal meanings, came to be 'a member of a jury'; *direzione* now covered, not only the act of direction, but also the persons directing; *farmacia*, previously the 'art of pharmacy', now became the 'chemist's shop'; *fase* ceased to be a merely astronomical word and meant 'phase' in general; *tara* 'tare' acquired the meaning 'defect, blemish' and *attualità* that of 'something very modern'. Italian also began to speak of *scuola secondaria* on the model of French. This list of examples of French influence could be much extended if we were to add words which did not take root, but which made isolated appearances at this time. We shall limit ourselves to a couple of instances: *appuntamenti* in the sense of 'stipend' and *in* *sul campo* for 'immediately' (*sur le champ*). There were numerous instances, too, of French words used, either transiently or more permanently, in particular regions: *barège* at Lucca and elsewhere, *boetta, boatta, buetta, buatta* (from *boîte*) in various places, *sciarabbà* (from *char-à-bancs*) in southern dialects, etc. Whether a word maintained its French spelling or was adapted to Italian phonology depended on whether it remained restricted to cultured speech or whether it gained wide currency. In many instances there were two forms: *brochure, brossura; bureau, burò; début, debutto; rendez-vous* or *randevù* (Guadagnoli), etc. Many wrote *bleu*, but some used *blo*. Most people, however, preferred *blu*. Alongside *débauche* and *deboscia* we get the popular Florentine *bisboccia*. There was occasionally oscillation, too, between adaptation and calque: while some wrote *porte-monnaie* as in French (Fusinato, 1847), some dialects adapted it (Mil. *pormonè*); but the written language preferred the calque *portamonete*. *Coupon* was adapted to *cupone* or *copone* or translated by *tagliando* or *cedola*. We should also remember that, apart from the French words that entered Italian and the latinisms that came in through French, Italian acquired a number of words from modern foreign languages via France. The most important were anglicisms (*frac, rosbif, macadam, tender*). *Waggon* acquired in France the spelling *wagon* and came to mean 'railway carriage'. *Revue* was a French calque of *review*; of it Italian made *rivista*. *Honeymoon* was translated *lune de miel*; hence *luna di miele*. From German came thus *Thalweg*, a geographical term taken up by diplomats and found in a decree of Napoleon's in 1811. And a number of the oriental words that entered Italian at this period came through the works of French travellers and geographers: writers on Eastern customs, from the Quattrocento to the Seicento, had known the word *bazarro* or *bazzarro* in the sense of 'market' (Persia, India); in the second decade of the Ottocento it re-entered Italy in French dress (*bazar*) and with the modern meaning of 'emporium, store' (E. Visconti, *Conciliatore*, 1819). *Massaggio* was also originally used with reference to oriental habits; from the beginning it had the French suffix.

Anglicisms, though a good deal less frequent than gallicisms, were nevertheless numerous. Some came in directly, some through French. It was easier, of course, for anglo-latinisms to win acceptance than it was for English words whose form was strange to the Italian phonetic system. Politics provided the largest single group. Some of these political terms had been used in the eighteenth century with reference to English life (*costituzione, comitato, maggioranza, opposizione, petizione*): now these and others entered Italian from various directions (often, as we have said, through French political vocabulary). The Sicilian constitution of 1812, conceded under English pressure and drawn up with English precedents in mind, mentioned *bills*. From other sources came *budget, leader, meeting, self-government, speech, conservatore, radicale, assenteismo,* etc. The word *premio*, with reference to insurance, also followed English use of *premium*. English taste was influential, too, in the sphere of carriages, horses and racing: hence *poney* (with French spelling of *pony*), *brougham, tilbury, steeplechase, jockey, turf,* etc. *Bulldog* was another English contribution. Railway terminology also came largely from Britain: *rail* (which was adapted to *raile, raili,* then replaced by *guida, verga, rotaia,* of which the last triumphed), *vagone* (cfr. p. 400), *tender, tunnel, locomotiva, viadotto. Railway* or *railroad* was soon replaced by *strada ferrata, via ferrata,* later *ferrovia. Tramway* lasted longer in its original form. *Osteriggio* was a nautical adaptation of *steerage*. The world of dress gave *scialle* or *sciallo, spencer, raglan* (which dated from Lord Raglan's period as commander in the Crimean War), etc. Also connected with the sphere of fashion were *dandy, lion, fashion, fashionable* and *high life. Comfort* was used in its English form, but also in the French (*confort*) and italianized to *conforto*. Food and drink gave *roastbeef* (*rosbif, rosbiffe*) and *punch* (*ponce*). The practice of *drenaggio* also penetrated Italy through France. *Humour* and *spleen* came to be considered as typically English qualities. Many other terms came to be used in Italian to describe English life; some of these later gained wider diffusion (e.g. *plaid*, which first appeared in translations of Sir Walter Scott; *dock*, etc.). Germanisms were, in spite of Austrian political influence, less numerous. They included some military terms (*feld-maresciallo*), names of coins (*svànzica*), and of social amusements (*walzer*, variously adapted). Feeling against the occupying Austrians gave rise to *caiserlicchi* (for 'Austrians', based on *kaiser*) and *radeschi* 'a kick' (after Marshal Radetzky, who once gave his son a kick for insulting a Milanese priest). Words of Greek or Latin stamp formed in Germanic-speaking countries were also introduced into Italian, e.g. *morfologia, stilistica*. Abstract language used certain calques: *il divenire, il non-essere, il non-io*; and Rosmini's *meismo* was modelled on *Ichheit*. Some words came from Scandinavian languages (mostly by indirect route): *scaldo, Valhalla, geyser*. Spanish contributed terms connected with politics (*camarilla* and the political meaning of *liberale*) and bull-fighting (*corrida*, *torero*, *matador*).

Meanwhile, Italian influence on other languages was comparatively slight. Nevertheless, in the field of opera France adopted a considerable number of terms, many of them introduced by Stendhal: *maestro* (Stendhal 1824; already in English in 1797), *libretto* (Fr. 1827; already in Eng. in 1742; Germ. 1837), *impresario* (Stendhal 1824; already in Germ. in 1771), *diva* (Gautier 1832; Germ. 1867; Swed. 1850), *brio* (Stendhal 1824; Eng. 1855); *fioriture* (Stendhal 1824); *fiasco* (Fr. 1841; Germ. 1837) and others. *Dilettante*, which had been sporadically used in the eighteenth century, now took root in France with the meaning 'fan of Italian opera', and *dilettantisme* was derived from it. *Piccolo* (as musical instrument) entered German in about 1801, English in 1856 and French in 1923. France also acquired some words orally: *flemme* (1821), possibly *frisquet* (1827), etc. Travellers who had visited Italy took back some words relating to its peculiarities: *fata morgana* appeared in German in 1796, in English in 1818 (just when Italian was accepting the French *miraggio* as a scientific term); *fumarola* gave the English *fumarole* in 1811 and the French *fumerolle* in 1829; *bora* was used by Stendhal in a letter in 1830 and entered English in 1864; *pellagra* entered English in 1811 and French (as *pellagre*) in 1834, etc. Carnival *confetti* were long considered characteristics of Rome (Goethe 1789; Fr. 1852; in French the word later entered usage with reference to the carnival of Nice, 1873). *Vendetta* spread from Corsica (Fr. 1803; Eng. 1861). The *pila* of Volta's invention entered the electrical terminology of France (*pile*, 1800) and England (1800), but German preferred the calque *Säule*. Some Italian words which had previously entered the major European languages now reached those of other countries (often through German), e.g. Swedish now got *soprano*, first spelt thus, then *sopran*) and Hungarian *opera*, *casino*, *cupola*, *influenza* (*opera*, *kaszinó*, *kupola*, *influenza*), etc. In Rumania many italianisms were used by Ion Heliade Rădulescu, but failed to win general acceptance.

12

From Unification to
First World War
(1861–1915)

Here we shall deal with the period extending from the proclamation of the Kingdom of Italy to Italy's entry into the First World War.

The first decade of this period was dominated by the ambition to add Venice and Rome to the new state: this was satisfied by the events of 1866 and 1870. An important stage, linguistically and otherwise, was represented by the years during which Florence was the capital (1865-70). But when the temporal power of the popes was ended and the capital could be moved to Rome, the step was decisive. The creation of uniform military and civil systems for the whole country, which had begun in 1859 and received an impetus from the events of 1861, was now to proceed with greater rapidity, while Rome was to be henceforth the permanent seat of that administrative system which was originally the construction of the honest bureaucrats of Piedmont. The government was at first (until 1876) in the hands of the Right, but then passed to the Left. However, particularly from the time of Depretis's inauguration of the kind of political manœuvring that came to be called *trasformismo*, changes in government represented a switching of combinations in coalition rather than clear changes in policy. Successive enlargements of the suffrage, especially those promoted by Giolitti, gave the less privileged sections of the population a growing voice in public affairs. As elsewhere in Europe, there were aspirations to make nationality coincide with state boundaries. Irredentism was born. Later, nationalism became expansionist. The European tendency to colonial enterprise found expression in Italy in expeditions to Abyssinia and Libya. Emigration, which was very considerable in economically difficult years, was of two kinds: temporary (as in the case of the Italians who worked on the St. Gotthard tunnel) and permanent (leading to the foundation of 'little Italies' in the United States, Argentina and Brazil). Italian was in use as an official language in Canton Ticino and the Italian valleys in the Grisons. There were forces working for denationalization in Italian territories subject to Austria (Trentino, Trieste and Italian centres in Istria and Dalmatia). In Corsica, French influence on the dialects increased, while literary Italian was now known only to comparatively few. In Malta, Italian had difficulty in maintaining parity with English as a cultural language.

Political unity brought greater circulation of ideas, objects and words. After 1870, Rome (where the population increased from 220,000 inhabitants in 1871 to 542,000 in 1911) assumed ever-increasing importance in national life. But the other great cities, particularly Milan (the 'moral capital'), Turin, Bologna, Florence, Naples and Palermo, not only continued to influence the regions traditionally connected with them, but, with communications by road and rail improving, extended the spheres in which they were dominant. Northern industries developed steadily; southern industries languished. Uniform laws came into force for the whole country (civil code 1865, penal code 1889). Public administration exercised a growing influence on Italian life; after bearing a Piedmontese stamp in its early years, it gradually became predominantly southern in personnel. In the army, too, the strong influence exercised by the Piedmontese in its early years lessened. Recruiting on a national basis contributed to a certain amount of levelling in language and ideas. Differences between the social classes, which had been very great, remained great. Only very slowly did the masses, guided by a socialism that was in origin romantic and humanitarian, begin to feel that they had a place in the social order. The lower classes used dialect in their daily lives, and had little knowledge of the national language. Social and cultural differences between northern and southern Italy were still enormous. Considerable, if inadequate, progress was made in elementary education: the Coppino act of 1877 made attendance at school obligatory for children over six. This had the result of reducing the percentage of illiterates from 78% in 1861 to under 50% in 1910. Secondary schools (state and private) became the principal vehicles of literary and scientific culture, while much advanced scientific, philosophical and philological work was centred on the universities. Traditional culture underwent a remarkable transformation; De Sanctis in 1869 thought he saw new worlds being born in philosophy, criticism, art, history and philology. Positivism forced itself upon the attention of thinkers. The physical and natural sciences played an increasingly important role. Indeed, their influence became felt in other fields; in 1883 De Sanctis lectured on 'Darwinism in art'. As a reaction against positivism, there was at the turn of the century a renewal of idealistic philosophy with a resurgence of connected attitudes. The daily and periodical press grew steadily in importance. Daily papers gave space, not only to political and foreign affairs, but to news items of various kinds; often they printed novels by instalments in feuilletons. In 1901 the 'third page' made its appearance (i.e. the page now traditionally given over to literature and culture). There was still considerable affection for the theatre. Actors from Luigi Rasi's school from 1881 onwards carried cultivated Florentine pronunciation to other parts of Italy. Opera enjoyed even greater popularity; locutions from librettos continued to pass into common parlance. Various sports came to Italy. Some were destined to achieve great popularity like *ciclismo* (at first called *velocipedismo*) and soccer (*calcio*, at first called *football*). Others were limited to restricted circles (*alpinismo*, *automobilismo*). Tourism, originally a pursuit for rich foreigners, gradually acquired Italian devotees as well.

The achievement of national unity and the influence of the new capital (for a few years Florence, then permanently Rome) contributed to linguistic levelling, while the participation in public life of social classes previously excluded led to wider use of both written and spoken Italian. Already by 1860-70 purism had lost its grip. Writers who had served their apprenticeship in its schools (De Sanctis, Carducci, D'Ancona, Adolfo Bartoli and many others) escaped from its clutches. The publisher Gaspero Barbèra, discussing in his *Memorie* the state of the market in 1863, noted that by that time love for those books whose main virtue was their 'pure' language was beginning to fade. Men of letters who wished to develop an effective style followed various paths; but none now thought it sufficient to imitate some past (fourteenth-century or sixteenth-century) writers. Those users of the language who were of less literary bent frequently came to believe that language was a social instrument that one could learn to handle without reference to prescribed models in previous literature. In practice, this meant that, instead of following the example of Italy's classical writers, they formed their language from newspapers, manuals, legal usage and, occasionally, novels (including those translated from foreign languages). Tabarrini, in an address delivered in 1869 (*Relazioni sui lavori della R. Accademia della Crusca (1869-70)*, Florence 1870, pp. 28-29) noted some of the effects that national unity was likely to have on the language: less use of dialect, wider use of the national language, but with the national language undergoing considerable modifications in the process of acquiring new speakers. He expressed anxiety concerning the effects of barbarism and indiscriminate imitation of bureaucratic jargon; but he also felt confident that a free people would eventually find means of expression 'not repugnant to its genius and its traditions'. Ascoli's famous Proem to the first volume of the *Archivio glottologico italiano* (1873) was also characterized by confidence — in the 'operosa attività' of the nation and in the effects of natural selection on the use of words used by people from different regions joining in common activities. In universities the teaching of 'Eloquence' was replaced by critical study of literature. In secondary education the canons of the classicists still persisted; but some teachers substituted Manzonian theories. And, gradually, pupils were presented with literary readings closer to the living language (as in the anthologies of Martini and Pascoli) and with more modern exercises. A common written language cannot be achieved in a short period, still less a common spoken language. But in various regions of northern and southern Italy there were now growing groups of people who were capable of using the national language as well as their own dialect. They did not all use it in the same way; in varying degrees they maintained local peculiarities both in their written language and, more markedly, in their speech. But they were moving towards a common language. In some families, too, children were brought up to speak Italian only: this was variously due to the constitution of the family (as when it was based on an inter-regional marriage), to its circumstances (e.g. its moving to a region where the parents' dialect was not spoken) or simply to the parents' belief that it was better for the children to achieve fluency in Italian as their first language. Moreover, the dialects themselves, particularly in the towns, underwent italianization, not only in vocabulary, but also in phonology and morphology.

When we come to discuss the condition of the spoken language, we must once again distinguish between Tuscany and neighbouring zones (where the differences between the spoken tongue and the written language were slight) and the northern and southern regions of the peninsula (where the dialects, very different from written Italian, were still very much alive). In these territories a growing number of persons turned to spoken Italian, particularly among civil servants, who were often transferred from region to region, and among soldiers and traders. This extension of the use of the national language was greatest in cities, and especially notable at Rome, where politicians, businessmen, state employees, etc., from all over Italy had to communicate with one another. If they had brought their families with them, they sometimes continued to speak dialect at home; but the younger generations acquired Italian with Roman characteristics. Yet, the process of unification in most of Italy was slow. Outside Tuscany and Rome the situation was largely that described by Finamore as obtaining in the Abruzzi in 1880. According to him, even for the most cultured, using dialect was like using one's right hand, while following the rules of good Italian was like using one's left hand, however well trained it might be. So, throughout the Abruzzi, one would hear, not just from a mayor, a lawyer or a deputy, but even from a professor of Italian or Latin literature (provided he had not been put on his guard): *aldo* (for 'alto'), *calge* (for 'calce'), *penzjìero* (for 'pensiero'). Of the pronunciation of certain individuals we have precise descriptions (like D'Ovidio's accounts of that of De Sanctis and that of Bonghi: the first an example of semi-dialectal pronunciation, with occasional hypercorrection, the second an instance of the confusion due to a desire to tuscanize without acquiring sufficient knowledge of Tuscan phonology). As for the vocabulary, in its higher reaches, in discussion of ideas, political activities, etc., there were not notable discrepancies. But it was very different in the sphere of common objects in use at home or on the farm: here there were great differences from region to region and even from place to place. Most people were not worried by this problem. But there were many who maintained that the problem could only be solved by spreading knowledge of Tuscan nomenclature: hence the dialogues of E. L. Franceschi (*In città e in campagna: dialoghi di lingua parlata*, Turin 1868) and P. Petrocchi (*In casa e fuori: racconto dialogico illustrato*, Milan 1893) and the chapters on the 'unknown language' and the emphasis on the need for studying vocabulary in the *Idioma gentile* of E. De Amicis. A large number of dialect dictionaries appeared: their purpose was not only to record dialectal forms, but to provide the Italian equivalents for those who did not know them. Collections were published, too, of regional

Italian words to be avoided: piedmontesisms, venetisms, sardisms, etc. In fine, over the half-century we are dealing with in this chapter, Italian certainly made considerable progress at the expense of the dialects, even if we are unable to plot its expansion precisely.

The same period also saw considerable changes in Italian prose: progress was made towards unity of vocabulary (i.e. the use of the same words to express the same ideas), and at the same time the gap between the spoken and written languages was narrowed. Let us take an example. In 1877 appeared Émile Zola's *Assommoir*. Let us compare extracts from the translation published by the Neapolitan Emmanuele Rocco, a writer with traditionalist tendencies, in 1879, and from that published by the Pistoian Policarpo Petrocchi, who was a scholar with Manzonian sympathies, in 1880:

Gervasia, sempre rispondendo con compiacenza, guardava attraverso i vetri, fra i boccali di frutte in acquavite, il movimento ch'era nella strada, ove l'ora della colazione radunava una calca straordinaria. Sui due marciapiedi, nel breve spazio che le case chiudevano in mezzo, vedevansi passi frettolosi, braccia ballonzolanti, un continuo urtar di gomiti. Quelli ch'erano in ritardo, operai trattenuti dal lavoro, col viso stravolto dalla fame, attraversavano la via a gran passi, entravano di rimpetto da un panattiere; e quando riapparivano, con una libbra di pane sotto l'ascella, andavano tre porte più su, al *Vitello a due teste*, a mangiare un pasto di sei soldi. V'era pure, accanto al panattiere, una trecca che vendeva patate fritte e telline al prezzemolo; una fila continua di operaie, in lunghi grembiali, portavan via dei cartocci di patate e delle telline nelle tazze; altre fanciulle graziose in capelli, d'un' aria delicata, compravano mazzi di ravanelli.

Quando Gervasia s'inchinava da un lato, scorgeva altresì una bottega di pizzicagnolo, piena di gente, d'onde uscivano fanciulli che tenevano in mano, involta in carta ingrassata, una

La Gervasa nel tempo che rispondeva con compiacenza, guardava attraverso i vetri, tra i vasi di frutte in guazzo, il movimento della strada, dove l'ora della colazione tirava una gran calca di gente. Sopra i due marciapiedi, nella stretta gola delle case, c'era un affrettar di passi, un dondolar di braccia, un darsi delle gomitate senza fine. Gli operai tardivi, stati trattenuti al lavoro, colla cèra annoiata per la fame, attraversavano il lastricato a lanci, entravano di rimpetto da un fornaio, e quando riapparivano, con una libbra di pane sotto il braccio, andavano tre usci più avanti, al *Vitello dalle due teste*, a mangiare una solita da trenta centesimi. C'era anche, accanto al fornaio, una fruttaiola che vendeva delle patate fritte e delle telline col prezzemolo; una sfilata continua d'operaie con grembialoni, portavan via dei cartocci di patate e telline nelle tazze; dell'altre, graziose ragazze in capelli, con aria delicata, compravano dei mazzi di radici.

Quando la Gervasa si chinava, vedeva pure una bottega di norcino piena di gente, di dov'uscivan dei ragazzi con una braciola panata in mano, avvolta in una carta unta, una

costoletta crostata, un rocchio di salsiccia o un pezzo di sanguinaccio
caldo caldo. Intanto, lungo la strada
impegolata di una melma nera, anche
quand'era bel tempo, in mezzo allo
scalpiccio della folla che camminava,
alcuni operai abbandonavano già le
taverne, scendevano a frotte, andando
a zonzo, battendosi le cosce con le
mani aperte, rimpinzati di cibo, tranquilli e lenti in mezzo agli spintoni
della tumultuosa calca.

Si era formato un gruppo dinanzi
alla porta dello Scannatoio.

— Di' su, Bibi la Grillade, domandò una voce rauca, ci paghi una
bevuta in giro di vitriolo?

E. Zola, *L'Assommoir* (*Lo Scanna-
tojo*). Trad. di E. Rocco, Milan 1879,
p. 40 et seq.

salsiccia o un biroldo caldo fumante.
Intanto, lungo la strada impeciata
d'un fango nero, anche col bel tempo,
per lo scalpiccio della folla in movimento, alcuni operai lasciavan di già
le bettole, scendevano in crocchi, bi-
ghellonando colle mani aperte e cion-
doloni che gli battevano nelle cosce,
inghebbiati di mangime, tranquilli e
lenti in mezz'agli urtoni della folla.

Un crocchio s'era formato all'uscio
dell'Assommuàr.

— Dimmi dunque, Bibì-braciola,
domandò una voce fioca, lo paghi tu
un giro di zozza?

E. Zola, *L'Assommuàr*. Trad. in
lingua italiana parlata dei prof.
Petrocchi e Standaert, Milan 1880,
p. 34 et seq.

Making allowances for all differences of personality in the two
translators, we can still find here discrepancies due to two kinds
of writing, which, with innumerable nuances, continued to be
practised for some decades after unification. By 1910 two translations so profoundly different would have been inconceivable.
The gap was closed largely by what Carducci disdainfully called
'bourgeois prose' (De Amicis, etc.). Pancrazi recognized its merits
when he wrote that the bourgeois prose that was formed in those
years on Manzonian tradition, on regional models and on the
example of French naturalism, filled a vital need: it was the prose
of ordinary life, and was to be the prose of the novel and the
novella. Levelling was due, of course, above all to the demands that
life made on prose at this period. But in the process of forming the
new prose an important part was played by literary reviews (the
first example and the most important of them all was the *Fanfulla
della Domenica*, founded by F. Martini in 1879; later, around 1910,
La Voce was the most influential) and by the better newspapers.
But even the written language of everyday life was influenced by
literary models. Here we shall merely indicate the main currents
of the period. While the traditionalist stream ran on more feebly
(as in the 'Roman school'), Carducci was providing a model of a
new kind of highly wrought prose, forged by one who was familiar
with the classics of Italian and Latin, but who also found place
for fresh and lively turns of phrase from his native Tuscan. To
him turned those who were concerned with maintaining the

dignity of literary language of the 'illustrious' kind: 'a learned and aristocratic literary language' wrote E. Scarfoglio in the new preface (1911) to his *Libro di Don Chisciotte*, 'cannot nourish itself on the hundred impetuous torrents of the spoken tongue, but on the reservoir of the written language, the language of orators, historians and Latin poets'. When we discuss Manzonian influence, we must make a distinction: whereas the author of *I promessi sposi* was widely recognized to have provided in it an example for those who wished to 'write naturally', there was much opposition to his linguistic theories and to those who applied them: many attacked Broglio's well-known attempt, the *Vita di Federico il Grande*, in which familiar Tuscan words, forms and phrases often seemed false because they were too popular to be appropriate to the subject-matter. The native Tuscan flavour of Collodi, Martini or Fucini (and later of Papini and Palazzeschi) made quite a different impression from Broglio's deliberate tuscanizing in response to Manzonian precepts. After the brief interlude in which the anti-rhetorical *scapigliati* (a group of northern writers associated mainly with Milan) portrayed the macabre and the diabolical, realism in various forms became dominant for some decades. Realist authors attempted to depict popular life in city and country. This had its importance in the history of the language; whereas most of these writers, in attempting to achieve local colour, were content with occasional dialectal expressions, Verga in his best novels succeeded in making his narrative texture itself absorb dialectal constructions. It is true, however, that his style seemed too bold at the time and had little immediate influence. The original styles of Dossi, Faldella or Imbriani had even less. An outstandingly ambitious, and sometimes pretentious, verbal craftsman was Gabriele D'Annunzio. In order to express the most varied sensations — human, super-human and feral — he pushed Italian vocabulary beyond its usual limits, having recourse to archaic and technical words (taken, for instance, from Pokorny's *Storia naturale* or Gugliel-motti's *Vocabolario marino e militare*) and borrowing from Latin and Greek (directly or even through the French symbolists). 'Life,' wrote Bellonci, 'from lovers' letters to political proclamations assumed D'Annunzian forms; women became *elette* and men *despoti*.' This influence was felt, above all, in journalism, which made use of many D'Annunzian words and phrases: *teoria* in the sense of 'procession, line', *velivolo, irreale, malioso, aromale, liliale, sinfonia di odori, la declinazione del giorno, una fascinazione di con-*

tinenti sconosciuti, i dolori di nostra gente, quel volto di giovane iddio, temeva non forse egli avesse, etc. The futurist movement created a great deal of fuss and made radical noises: 'the rush of emotion-steam will burst the pipe of the period, the valves of punctuation and the bolts of adjectivization' (Marinetti, *Zang tumb tumb,* Milan 1914, p. 10); but its actual influence on the language was negligible. Writers of plays had an even harder struggle than writers of narrative to achieve a polished natural tone, for spoken usage lacked fluency and uniformity. The fact that most of the plays performed in Italy were poor adaptations of French works contributed to the fluency, but hardly to the purity, of their language. Those who wish to have a view of the whole field of Italian prose in this period need to consider, not only writers on the moral sciences (philosophy, history, etc.), but also those described by Ascoli as 'useful but not artistic'. To give but one example, the terminology of C. Lombroso and his school is interesting, not only in itself, but also because terms from it filtered through into ordinary language (e.g. *mattoide*). Scientific and technical terminology also had great importance: very many words and phrases (from medicine, electricity or law, for instance) became part of everyday usage. The jargon of administrators became more influential than ever before, and was more strongly criticized by purists. Apart from coining words like *realizzo* and *periziare* and new locutions (*donna attendente a casa*), bureaucratic language was characterized by abuse of formulas: whereas it would not seem so strange to use *prelodato* in some contexts, its use in 'i *prelodati* lupi' would hardly commend itself, and while 'un libello *a base* di calunnie' is comprehensible, 'una rissa *a base* di zoccolate' is not. Journalism also contributed to the use of clichés in everyday language (*il fior fiore dei cittadini, sotto l'egida del sindaco, i lieti concenti,* etc.). Those interested in the art of writing may admire the classical yet vigorous Carducci, the luxuriant D'Annunzio, the meditatively composed Croce. But we must recognize that on the written language in general use (e.g. in an ordinary person's letters) bureaucratic and journalistic jargon had more influence than any Carducci, D'Annunzio or Croce.

In poetry, the last decades of the century saw a continuation of that movement away from traditional aulic language which had begun with Romanticism. Realism tended to introduce everyday domestic, bourgeois subjects, and with them words from contemporary usage: 'Suoni l'ode alla calce e al rettifilo' (Boito, *Case nuove,* 1866); 'Si stava assai benino — un tempo a la Regina:

— buona cucina, — ottimo vino' (V. Betteloni, 'Per una crestaia').
Sometimes the dissonance was strident when familiar words were
used alongside the 'illustrious' words that still persisted: 'col
falerno — diamo la baia al verno' (Prati, 'Iside'); 'gli umidi
campi redolenti — di nepitella' (Rapisardi, 'Ottobre'), 'le
iperboree sizze' (Rapisardi, *Giobbe*), etc. Indeed, the poets were so
used to the aulic tradition that even those who wished to be read
by the people wrote lines that would be unintelligible to many.
In a lyric by Eliodoro Lombardi, 'Scienza e lavoro', the manual
workers say: 'Ci escluser dal santo comune *retaggio* — ci han *colmi*
e pasciuti di fiele e di oltraggio. . . .' In Giovanni Raffaelli's
lyric 'Ospizi marini' (1868) we find the exhortation: 'Ed or la
salma frale — *d'inopia* e di fatica, — perché, scarno mortale —
non *credi* all'onda amica?' Vittorio Betteloni, who was praised
by some and condemned by others for having written in the
spoken language, used *funesti augelli*; *spirto, omero mio*; Death tells
the maiden that he is '*la suprema aita*', and so on. And Felice
Cavallotti, who was called the 'bard of democracy' had: 'E
l'oste egizia *fu*' ('Marcia di Leonida'); '*prischi evi*', 'il caro *fral*'
('Lucerna di Parini'). The periphrases dear to the aulic tradition
were now rarer, but they still existed: Zanella, when he meant a
train, spoke of 'sulle compresse ali del foco — i trasvolanti carri'
('Alla Madonna di Monte Berico'), and in the same lyric
telegraphy inspired 'l'accento — come guizzo di fólgore tras-
messo'. In his youth Carducci still made considerable use of
traditional poetic vocabulary, but in his maturity he strove to
renew it, particularly by use of latinisms which, if not always
new, had at least not been worn out by use in previous centuries:
adamante, buccina, cortice, delubro, ilice, vulture; *cerulo, flavo, fumido,
occiduo, virente*, etc. Gabriele D'Annunzio began from this Carduccian position before finding his own way. Soon he was seeking
out rare and beautiful words, which he enjoyed for their own
sake, for their music or their flavour; his poetry marks an important stage in the development of *decadentismo* in Italy. He borrowed
widely, not only from Latin and Greek, but also from dialectal and
technical vocabulary. Indeed, in his verse he made Italian poetic
vocabulary wider perhaps than it had ever been before. But words
from the aulic tradition were now reduced to very few. For
Pascoli that tradition had already had its day. He avoided not
only words that were alien to popular usage, but also words that
he considered excessively generic (words that had been dear to
poetic tradition from Petrarch downwards). Instead he favoured

the concreteness of rustic words which he found in Romagna and the country around Lucca, sometimes making his verse almost unintelligible:

> *Vogliono dire ch'han la* tiglia *soda*
> *più che* nimo *altri che di mattinata*
> *porti in monte il* cavestro *o la* bardella
> ('Il ciocco', I, in *Canti di Castelvecchio*).

This tendency of Pascoli's was a form of preciosity, as we can see from the frequency of technical words (*meteci, mirmilloni, mistofori, pezeteri, pulte, teda,* etc., in the *Poemi conviviali*). On the other hand, Pascoli also had a decadentistic liking for vague, indeterminate words whose musicality suggested unknown worlds to the reader. Traditional poetic vocabulary was dead, too, so far as the anti-Carduccian, anti-Dannunzian crepuscular poets were concerned; Gozzano made use of it only when he wished to evoke his own little world (in the 'Viale delle Statue' an ancestress of his walks 'lungh'essi — i bussi e i cipressi'). The futurists' attempt to throw off previous usage led to a straining after originality in their metaphors reminiscent of Seicento poets ('O vento crocifisso dai chiodi delle Stelle!': Marinetti, *Distruzione,* 1911). To sum up, verse and prose were much closer together than they had been. Now that the traditional vocabulary of poetry had, with a few survivals, died out, the only linguistic expedients poets had at their disposal when they wished to use the traditional verse forms (and many chose not to) were greater freedom in the use of truncation and dieresis and greater freedom in word-order ('E ancor ne odora la *campestre via*': Bertacchi). Nor did the language of verse plays (Cossa, Giacosa, Cavallotti) diverge greatly from that of prose. On the other hand, the *melodramma* usually kept 'that ambiguous linguistic taste, half-way between the Romantic and the classical, in the name of which Francesco Maria Piave, with abuse of rhetoric, made Alfredo Germont ascend (*ascendere*) to Violetta's *egre soglie* and declare to her that he had *di lacrime d'uopo,* meaning that he wanted to cry' (Baldacci).

In the decades that followed unification linguistic controversy was rekindled by Manzoni. It is true that privately he had felt some doubt, when it seemed certain that Rome was eventually to be capital, about his thesis that Italians should linguistically follow Florence; but this doubt was expressed only in the confidential postscript of a letter to Giorgini. In fact, during the brief period when Florence was capital, he was presented with an

opportunity to give effective expression to his pro-Florentine
theories. On 27 October 1867 the Milanese Emilio Broglio became
Minister of Public Instruction. An admirer and linguistic follower
of Manzoni's, he appointed (in January 1868) a commission to
enquire into the most effective means of making 'good language
and good pronunciation' more widely known to Italian people of
all classes. The commission was divided into two sections: the
Milanese headed by Manzoni, who was president of the whole
commission, and the Florentine, headed by Lambruschini, the
vice-president. Manzoni, now in his eighties, drew up the report
of his section with an alacrity which Broglio himself was to
describe as prodigious; on February 19 he sent a copy to the
Minister. In this work (entitled *Dell'unità della lingua e dei mezzi di
diffonderla*) he again argued that a common language for the whole
nation was a necessity, and that the acceptance and acquisition
of Florentine were the means by which Italy could acquire a
common language. He was therefore in favour of the compilation
of a dictionary of living Florentine usage. Later, comparative
dictionaries of Florentine and of various dialects could be made,
so that people in other regions of Italy could learn Florentine.
While Manzoni's letter to Carena (p. 365) had had a limited effect,
this report (which was published in the Florentine *Nuova Antologia*
and the Milanese *Perseveranza*) provoked widespread debate.
Twenty years had passed, and the process of unification was now a
reality. Moreover, Manzoni was no longer simply a distinguished
writer criticizing a dictionary (Carena's) which had seemed to
him excessively eclectic; with official support and at the invitation
of the government, he was making a concrete proposal aimed at
giving the Italian people an adequate linguistic instrument for
their social and national requirements. His suggestions immediately won him supporters and opponents in considerable numbers.
He showed that he was ready for the fray. In a letter in the
Perseveranza (21 March 1868) he maintained that Dante's *De
Vulgari Eloquentia* was 'not about a language, Italian or any other'.
And when the Pistoiese Tigri wrote that he had no doubt that
Manzoni, in saying that the national tongue should be Florentine,
really meant 'good Tuscan', Manzoni immediately intervened to
make it clear that, since there was considerable variety in Tuscany,
he really meant *Florentine*, stating that the idea of unity, which was
'the life of languages', was also a necessary condition of their
diffusion, since 'before one can walk, one must be.' Finally, at the
end of 1868 and the beginning of 1869 he replied to the report

which had been produced by the Florentine sub-commission under Lambruschini, which had failed to share his views. His reply to them was entitled *Appendice alla Relazione intorno all'unità della lingua e ai mezzi per diffonderla* (Milan 1869). In it, he was particularly concerned to clear up points on which he had been misunderstood. Lambruschini, for instance, had assumed that Manzoni's recommendations involved making, not a complete dictionary for the use of lettered persons, but a collection, large enough to be subsequently amplified, of words and idioms from the living language useful for the everyday use of civilized people. Manzoni, in reply, denied that there was such a thing as a series of words reserved for the special use of lettered persons, and objected to the idea that a dictionary of usage could be compiled by a process of elimination. Broglio decided to accept Manzoni's suggestions. On 24 October 1868 he set up a body (having four ordinary members and some extraordinary members, with himself as president) charged with compiling a dictionary of Florentine usage. When this work began to appear, under the title *Novo Vocabolario della lingua italiana secondo l'uso di Firenze*, G. I. Ascoli took the opportunity to give his views on Manzoni's theories. He did so in the now celebrated preface to the first number of the *Archivio glottologico italiano*. (This preface, dated 10 September 1872, appeared at the beginning of 1873.) Ascoli admitted the evil: the lack of linguistic unity among Italians. This was due, of course, to historical and political factors. He contrasted conditions in Italy with those in France and Germany. Languages were in a constant state of development. It was futile to try and exclude neologisms or impose models. When a certain activity spread throughout a nation, then the process of natural selection got rid of unnecessary equivalent locutions concerning that activity. But what were Italians being asked to do? To suspend their own industry, not in order to refurnish their minds by turning to a series of books relevant to their concerns, but in order to imitate (some said ape) a municipal language, in the form in which it would be offered to them by a dictionary or a nurse or by the elementary schoolmaster who would be sent (from a region so rich in illiterates) to civilize their province. (Manzoni's *Relazione* had recommended giving preference to Tuscan teachers.) The real reasons why Italy had no firm and certain language were to be found in the scarcity of general mental activity (which was both the cause and effect of concentration of knowledge in a few) and in the fussy demands of a delicate, unstable and restless sense

of form. Ascoli paid eloquent tribute to Manzoni's contribution
as a writer: his war against rhetoric. But he could not accept the
menacing enthusiams of the new Florentinism. (He had illustrated what he meant by examining the concrete example of the
word *Novo*. When Italians in the rest of Italy had accepted a
literary language based in its essentials on Florentine phonology
and morphology, of which *nuovo* was an example, they were now
being asked to change because a modification had taken place
in Florentine pronunciation.) But, if the Italian language owed
its base to Florentine, it was over and above that base the construction of culture and literature. To attempt to destroy the work
of history in order to impose contemporary popular Florentine
was to attempt to impose artificial, extrinsic unity. The real
remedy was to renew and enlarge the mental activity of the
nation, not to create a new preoccupation of form. What was
wrong was that there was a terrible gap (defeating communication and unity of language) between the cultured few and the
ignorant masses. In other words, Ascoli fully realized that a solution to the linguistic problem could not be merely horizontal
(i.e. pushing Florentine outwards over the surface of Italy) but
had to be vertical (working down through the social classes).
Manzoni and Ascoli, of course, approached the problem from
widely different viewpoints. Manzoni had first turned to the
problem in the course of his work as a writer. But soon the citizen
took the place of the artist, and he became concerned with
remedying a social evil. He was, in fact, seeing the problem
politically. He wanted Italians of all classes to possess in the near
future a truly common language, and he no longer cared if his
works of poetry and his tragedies did not fit into the plans he
evolved for it. While it was undoubtedly to Manzoni's credit that
he saw that the problem had social importance, and was not
merely literary, it must be said that in his solution he did not set
sufficient store by the fact that the unification that had already
taken place (albeit incompletely and inadequately in places) had
been achieved in Italy by means of the written language. Nor did
he attribute enough importance to those instances in which
nearly all the rest of Italy was in agreement, through having
accepted a Florentine form or word, while Florence itself had
substituted for it some recent innovation (as in the case of *anello*
for *ditale*, or *bono, novo* for *buono, nuovo*). Ascoli, on the other hand,
was a very rigorous historian of the language who could not look
with favour upon normative interference with the language and

with what he considered a process to be left to natural selection. Francesco D'Ovidio, who devoted much effort to elucidating Manzoni's theory and practice, tried, too, to bridge the gap between him and Ascoli and to suggest a compromise solution. If Manzoni, argued D'Ovidio, deduced his theories too exclusively from the history of the first three centuries of Italian literature, when Florence and Tuscany enjoyed a sort of dictatorship, Ascoli looked with excessive favour on the following three, during which linguistic and literary activity were spread all over Italy. If in the last three centuries the situation in Italy had resembled that of Germany, in the first three it had resembled that of France. One could not skip the last three centuries and confer a dictatorship on Florence. But one could not forget either that she was once the Paris or the Athens of Italy. If it was true of Germany that one could not point to any single place and say that that was the cradle of the language of Luther, Klopstock and Kant, in Italy things were different, for one *did* know that the cradle of the Italian language was the birthplace of Dante and Machiavelli. His solution thus was, not to take Florentine as the standard when Florentine departed from well-established literary usage, but to regard it as a valuable guide, not as an absolute authority, wherever literary usage oscillated or failed to provide guidance. But it was by no means clear that Florence still had a central enough position in the activity of the nation for D'Ovidio's solution to be accepted, and the controversy continued. In this account we have, of course, mentioned only the main protagonists. On the Manzonian side, the supporters, besides Giorgini and Broglio, included Buscaino Campo, Morandi, Petrocchi and De Amicis. On the other side (against Manzoni or against abuses of his theory) stood Fanfani, Gelmetti, Settembrini, Imbriani, Scarabelli, Caix, Scarfoglio, Dossi and, with greater authority than the others, Carducci. By the turn of the century, however, the disputes were dying down. In fact, differences were already diminishing, and it was increasingly realized that abstract argument had little effect on the issue.

We have already remarked that the purism of Cesari and Puoti had little appeal in the new, united Italy. There were, however, persons who protested vigorously against the use of unnecessary gallicisms, the new bureaucratic vocabulary and the syntactic and stylistic carelessness that characterized utilitarian prose. Among them were Fanfani, Brunone Bianchi and Mamiani. And Tommaseo complained that the new jargon was to be found,

not only in public offices, schools, shops, workrooms, newspapers
and meetings, but also in more carefully composed writing and in
domestic life (N. Tommaseo, *Aiuto all'unità della lingua. Saggio di
modi . . .*, Florence 1874, p. 1). In the following decades such
laments came, not only from those who could be regarded as
successors to the purists of the preceding generation (Arlìa, R.
Fornaciari), but also from writers of very different formation (De
Amicis, Martini, D'Annunzio, Panzini . . .). This was a consequence, of course, of the crisis of growth that Italian underwent
as it spread to new users; but it was also a sign of an ever-
renascent cult of elegance. As will be evident, linguistic controversies are often inextricably linked with criticisms of individual
writers. When the Crusca in 1883 included *I promessi sposi* among
the texts to be cited in its dictionary, Tribolati objected. Several
critics (Fornaciari among them) complained of De Sanctis and
his 'worlds' (*il mondo intellettuale, il mondo morale*, etc.). Verga's
language was attacked by Petrocchi, Scarfoglio and others.
D'Annunzio, too, provoked criticism and parody, while men of
letters and members of the public revolted against the futurists.

The Manzonian controversies were echoed in the works of the
grammarians. While the fullest manuals (R. Fornaciari, *Grammatica italiana dell'uso moderno* and *Sintassi italiana dell'uso moderno*,
Florence 1881) gave some examples from classical authors and
some from more recent ones (Manzoni, Giusti, Tommaseo), the
grammars of the Manzonians (Petrocchi, 1887; Morandi-
Cappuccini, 1894) gave examples unaccompanied by authors'
names. That of Morandi and Cappuccini professed to keep to
Florentine usage, but without concealing — indeed drawing
attention to — features wherein it diverged from general living
Italian usage. Italian lexicography produced in this period,
alongside a new version of Tramater revised by L. Scarabelli
(Milan 1878), the richer and more original *Dizionario* of N.
Tommaseo and B. Bellini, published at Turin (Pomba) between
1861 and 1879. The better part is that compiled under Tommaseo's direct supervision (from the beginning to *Se*). Although the
material was not always adequately checked and the etymologies
were frequently wrong, the work is still valuable because of its
wealth of examples. In 1863 there appeared the first volume of the
fifth impression of the *Vocabolario degli Accademici della Crusca*, with
an important preface by Brunone Bianchi. The other volumes
followed slowly: the tenth came out in 1910, while the eleventh,
partly owing to the First World War, was not published until

1923, when the work was discontinued. The canons for inclusion of examples were stated. Tuscan spoken usage was taken into account as a secondary source (i.e. after the approved authors). A *Glossario*, which was to give words no longer in use, got no further than the first fascicule (*A-B*, Florence 1867). Pietro Fanfani, who had published the first edition of the widely-used *Vocabolario della lingua italiana* in 1855, made a new edition in 1865. (Another posthumous edition revised by Bruschi came out in 1890 and was frequently reprinted.) In 1875 was published the *Vocabolario della lingua parlata* by G. Rigutini. (Fanfani, whose name also appeared on the title-page, probably contributed little to it.) A new edition, again the work of Rigutini, appeared in 1893. Its insistence on the spoken language was doubtless an effect of Manzoni's programme. A direct result of that programme was, as we have indicated, the *Novo vocabolario della lingua italiana secondo l'uso di Firenze*, edited by G. B. Giorgini and E. Broglio (Florence 1870-97, 4 vols.); its importance lay in its examples of the spoken usage of cultured Florentines. No less notable was P. Petrocchi's *Novo dizionario italiano* (Milan 1887-91, 2 vols.), which was rich in examples and attempted to distinguish between vocabulary in actual use and archaic, rare and plebeian words. An unfortunate feature, due to the compilers' pro-Florentine theories, was the complete abolition of the diphthong: he wrote not only *bòno*, *nòvo*, but also, *cèco* for *cieco*, *còco* for *cuoco*. Among the works which set out to tell people which words (particularly foreign and bureaucratic ones) they should avoid, with suggestions for replacing them, we should note the *Lessico della corrotta italianità* by P. Fanfani and C. Arlìa (Milan 1877), entitled in later editions and reprints *Lessico dell'infima e corrotta italianità* (Milan 1881, 1890, 1897, 1907) and *I neologismi buoni e cattivi* by G. Rigutini (Rome 1886). A. Panzini's *Dizionario moderno* not only condemned words considered abusive, but from its first edition (Milan 1905) registered numerous dialectal, technical and slang words missing from other dictionaries. In later editions, Panzini became less severe in linguistic censure and used the dictionary as a means of making an ironic commentary on aspects of modern life. Among the numerous specialist vocabularies published at this time we should record, as being among the best, those by Canevazzi and Marconi (*Vocabolario di agricoltura*, Rocca S. Casciano, 1871-92), Rezasco (*Dizionario del linguaggio italiano storico e amministrativo*, Florence 1881), and Father Guglielmotti (*Vocabolario marino e militare*, Rome 1889). There were also reasonably good collections of vocabulary relating to crafts and trades (Gargiolli, Arlìa, Fanfani).

Although French had become less dominant as an international language, while English had grown in importance, Italian culture still looked mainly to France. French was the first foreign language to be obligatory in Italian secondary schools, Italian newspapers and journals took a great deal from those of France, and the most important French writers were read in the original language. Moreover, the most popular French novels were translated, some several times, and there were also translations of many scientific and technical works. Menus at important dinners and in ambitious restaurants were in French. In comparison, knowledge of English and German was much more limited. Naval officers knew English, as did the members of the aristocracy who frequented the houses of the large English colony at Florence. Professors of philosophy, philology, history, economics and medicine read German publications. Workers who were engaged in laying new railways in Germany, Switzerland and Austria acquired a little German. And Austrian and German tourism in northern Italy was such that it led to complaints about the violated 'italianità del *Gardasee*' (1909). Those who knew other languages, like the Slavonic or Scandinavian, were a mere handful. The multiplication of international contacts in practical affairs and in the applied sciences led to the adoption of common terms (an example being the field of electricity, with its *ampere, coulomb, farad, ohm, volt,* fixed by international congresses at Paris in 1881 and Chicago in 1893) or to precise parallels. To the situation of Italian outside Italy we can refer only briefly. Despite the alliance between Italy and Austria-Hungary, the position of Italian was threatened by German in the Trentino and by German and Slav languages at Trieste and other Italian centres in Istria and Dalmatia. The situation in Canton Ticino was less unfavourable to Italian, though there too the pressure of German made itself felt in some fields. Abroad, knowledge of Italian declined; it kept its prestige better in the Levant than in Europe. There were Italian schools in Tunisia, Egypt and Turkey. Colonial settlement in Eritrea and later in Somaliland and Libya resulted in a 'colonial Italian' being learnt by some natives. Massive Italian emigration to the United States led to the formation of hybrid forms of speech. Many of the emigrants knew only their own dialect; on to it they grafted English words altered to fit their dialectal phonetic habits. Because of their ignorance of

Italian (i.e. because they spoke only different dialects), Italian immigrants often came to prefer communicating with each other in English. Much the same story could be told of Italian emigrants who settled on the shores of the Plate river, in Brazil and elsewhere. The Dante Alighieri Society (founded in 1889) promoted Italian activities and encouraged use of the language outside Italy, as it still does.

We have often had occasion to note the lack of uniformity in Italian usage. This was still obvious. In this paragraph we shall record, not the variants in vocabulary (like *scopa/granata, lesina/ subbia, attaccapanni/cappellinaio*), but doublets showing slight differences in spelling and morphology which have since disappeared or become less common. There was oscillation between single and double consonants in words in which the Latin and Tuscan forms were divergent: hence *cammino* for *camino* (Collodi), *catedra* (Ascoli), *febrile* (D'Annunzio), *obedire* (Dossi), *femina* (Carducci, Praga, Martini, D'Annunzio), *publico, republicano* (Panzini), etc. There was a good deal of argument over the forms *Africa/ Affrica*: Bianco Bianchi intended to publish a work entitled *Africa per Affrica, ossia le più recenti deturpazioni della lingua italiana.* Martini, a supporter of *Affrica*, wrote to Carducci about it in September 1891, and got the reply: 'Affrica sempre, almeno in prosa. Altrimenti, francesismo'. It would, of course, have been more strictly accurate to describe *Africa* as a latinism common to the cultured languages of Europe. The latinizing *esaggerare* instead of *esagerare* was defended by Vittorio Imbriani only. Other variants, too, were due to Latin influence: *decembre* (Carducci, Martini), *infirmità* (Carducci), and the series *conscienza, conspetto, inspirazione, instituzione* (Carducci, D'Annunzio, Scarfoglio). There was hesitation in the use of *palimpsesto*, which sometimes yielded to *palinsesto* or *palimsesto* (Panzini). Minghetti preferred *ozione, ottare* to *opzione, optare*, which later prevailed. *Eucalitto* was ousted by *eucalipto*. Carducci preferred *Apocalipsi* to *Apocalissi. Dattilografia* triumphed over *dactilografia* (Panzini, 1st ed.). *Sdruscire* existed alongside the commoner *sdrucire*. Tuscans preferred *polenda, bodola, arrenare, zittella* to *polenta, botola, arenare, zitella*. The analogical *duecento* gained ground at the expense of the Tuscan *dugento. Viglietto* sometimes appeared for *biglietto. Guarantire* (Bonghi) and *guarentire* (Carducci) were still commoner than *garantire*. Many writers (including Carducci, Martini, Fornaciari, Fogazzaro, Panzini) still used *tuono* for 'tone' (now *tono*). Both *coltura* and *cultura* were used in both meanings of the words; but

Fanfani proposed in 1879 that *coltura* be reserved for cultivation of fields, etc., and *cultura* for 'cultivation of the mind, culture' and this distinction was eventually adopted. *Ufficio* and *ufficiale*, with the aid of the bureaucracy, won the battle against the other variants (*officio, uffizio, ufizio; officiale, uffiziale, ufiziale*). There was doubt, too, about some words recently introduced: *decentramento, dicentramento, discentramento,* or *aeroplano,* which had difficulty in overcoming the plebeian *areoplano.* The same uncertainty was felt about foreign words: *tourist* (Eng.), *touriste* (Fr.), *turista, torista; tramway, tramvia, tranvia* or the Tuscan adaptation *tranvai; vermùt, vèrmut, vermùtte, vèrmutte.* The joining of juxtaposed words also raised questions: Carducci preferred *da vero, né meno, più tosto,* to *davvero, nemmeno, piuttosto,* while Martini condemned *chissà.*

In the preceding paragraph we gave examples of oscillation in the spelling of individual words. We shall add here some general observations on orthography. *J* became much less used. The Crusca, which had abolished it initially and medially (*iattura, gennaio*), used it for the plurals of nouns in *-io* (*studj*) and a number of scholars (D'Ancona, Monaci) followed suit. Others, however, had other criteria: Mestica wrote *gennajo,* but *studii.* On the whole, even those who were unconvinced by arguments for its elimination, followed the majority in making much less use of it. A great deal of uncertainty attended the use of *i* in the groups *ce-cie, ge-gie: angoscie, roccie, scarpaccie* and derivatives like *braccietto, passeggiero* were frequent; vice versa, it was not rare to find *effige, superfice,* and plurals like *camice.* Nor was it clear whether the *i* should be regarded as absorbed in verb-forms like *sogn(i)amo, consegn(i)amo.* The habit of writing *h* in *ho, hai, ha, hanno* remained, in spite of yet another attempt to abolish it, made this time by Petrocchi. Nor did Pascoli have any success in trying to restore etymological *h, ch, ph, th, y, ae, oe* in Greek and Latin proper names: *Chariti, Phalaride, Myrmidoni, Xantho, Naevio,* etc. There was oscillation in the use of capitals in a few cases (*i Torinesi* or *i torinesi*), but nearly everyone now wrote *gennaio,* etc., *primavera,* etc. In literary prose there were two opposing currents: one involved considerable use of capitals, particularly in abstract nouns, for the purpose of personification and rhetorical magnification, and was of course obvious in the work of D'Annunzio: *la lenta ascensione del Giorno* (*Il Piacere*); *l'apparizione della Bellezza consolatrice invocata dalla Preghiera unanime* (*Il Fuoco*); the other, anti-rhetorical, even introduced personal names with small letters (Guido Gozzano speaking of himself as 'quella cosa vivente

— detta *guidogozzano*'). In spite of appeals (e.g. Dossi's) that the stress in proparoxytones should be indicated by a written accent, this was not done, although a few writers tried to lead the way. In words in which written accents were used (oxytones and certain monosyllables), the general practice was to use the grave accent only. However, attempts were made by some authors to introduce acute accents in these positions when *e* and *o* were close, not open. Some extended this use of the acute accent to *i* and *u* (*finí*, *virtú*). The use of the apostrophe was a source of uncertainty, not only because of oscillation in elision of the article, but also because there was doubt as to whether elision or truncation should take place in certain other instances, e.g. *tal è, qual era*. There was no lack of suggestions for spelling reform. A certain G.B., in an essay entitled *Di alcune riforme dell'ortografia italiana*, Milan 1878, proposed the adoption of two kinds of *e* and *o*, a special symbol for *sc*, etc. L. Gelmetti suggested a *Riforma ortografica con tre nuòvi segni alfabètici per la buona pronunzia italiana*, Milan 1886: the signs were a *j* with a little tail added to indicate plurals of nouns in *-io*, and crossed *s* and *z* to mark the occasions when they represented voiced consonants. He also wanted to use the grave accent for marking open *e* and *o*, while reserving the acute for indicating stress in proparoxytones which gave rise to doubt (*émbrice*). More interest was aroused by proposals for spelling reform made by various scholars in 1909 and following years which led to the foundation of the 'Società ortografica italiana' and which were much discussed in periodicals. But the two main systems proposed, that of P. G. Goidànich (*Sul perfezionamento dell'ortografia nazionale*, Modena 1910) and that of L. Luciani ('Per la riforma ortografica', in *Atti della Soc. Ital. per il progressso delle Scienze*, IV riunione, Naples 1910; id. in *Rivista pedagogica*, 1910, pp. 893-942) were too complicated to succeed. In the field of punctuation, we should note a trick of Carducci's which was widely copied — the suppression of commas in enumerations: '[il Leopardi] abituato a contemplare un esempio di arte lucido eguale sereno', 'Dante il Cavalcanti il cronista Giachetto Malespini il padre del Petrarca e la maggior parte degli scrittori e giureconsulti toscani d'allora' (*Rime di Cino da Pistoia*, Florence 1862, p. IV and X). The use of a pair of semicolons (rather than a pair of dashes or brackets) to mark a parenthesis was rare, but not isolated. We find it in Pascoli and Novati: 'a Dante ... pervenne un giorno; correvano gli anni estremi della sua vita; un poetico carme' (*Freschi e minii del*

Dugento, Milan 1908, p. 3). There were, of course, suggestions for changing punctuation too. Dossi, for instance, wanted a double comma to be introduced; this would be intermediate in force between a semi-colon and a comma. But none of the proposals made at this period came to anything in practice.

The Manzonians' attempt to replace the diphthong *uo* by a monophthong (*novo*, not *nuovo*) encountered strong resistance, particularly, as we have seen, from Ascoli, and ended by being rejected in written usage, even by Florentines. Only after a palatal did forms with the monophthong gain ground (*orciolo*, *fagiolo*, *figliolo*, *spagnolo*, etc.), and even there they did not succeed entirely in supplanting forms with the diphthong. As for the mobile diphthong, the rule (stating that the diphthongized form should be used in stressed position, the undiphthongized in unstressed position) was frequently not observed (*ruotare*, *infuocato*, Carducci; *rinnuoverebbe*, Tabarrini; *ruotolarsi*, Dossi; *giuocherei*, *cuoprivano*, Martini; *ricuoprirti*, D'Annunzio, etc.). The situation was even more chaotic in the case of *e-ie*: instead of *presedere*, with forms like *presedeva* (Imbriani), *presedette* (D'Ovidio), there was now an infinitive *presiedere*, with forms like *presiedeva* (Carducci, in a review in 1869: *Opere*, XXVII, p. 161). The rule requiring prosthetic *i* before impure *s* became less rigorous: Martini wrote *per istrozzarlo*, *non ispregevole*, but Carducci *in specie*. Truncation and elision were only partly covered by fixed rules; there were many optional cases. The Manzonians tried, but with little result, to transfer into the written language certain habits that characterized Florentine speech: *du' anni*, *essere nel su' elemento*, *lo 'ngrassava*. The vowels in the articles *lo* and *la* were nearly always dropped before another vowel, but sometimes the full form was used, giving the impression of a deliberate pronunciation: *lo antropofago*, *lo Allagherio* (Imbriani), 'il Poliziano alle storie de' due Testamenti e alle leggende ha sostituito *la egloga*' (Carducci, *Opere*, XII, p. 226); 'consentirvi con *la immaginazione*', 'lucevano *sulla umida* gradinata della villa' (Fogazzaro, *Piccolo mondo moderno*). The *i* of *gli* was frequently elided before another *i* (*gl'ingegni*) and the *e* of *le* before another *e* (*l'erbe*). Truncations in syntactic sequence declined in everyday language, but were still very much alive in more ambitious prose (*la tradizion familiare*, *quella istintiva esaltazion sessuale*, *l'azion dell'acido*: D'Annunzio, *Il Piacere*) and in verse. To place the accent in the right place was important, socially as well as linguistically: to err was considered a sign of little culture. But in many words two versions were admitted: *acònito* (D'Annunzio) and *aconìto* (Carducci), *adaman-tìno* (D'Annunzio) and *adamàntino* (Carducci), *crisòlito* and *crisolìto* (D'Annunzio), *dirùto* and *dìruto* (Carducci), *esìle* (Corradino) and *èsile* (passim), etc. *Chèrubo* (Boito, 1863; Dante had used *Cherùbi*) was due to the influence of the counter-tonic stress in *Cherubino*. *Incùbi* (Praga) was arbitrary, as was *Leonìda* (so pronounced by Garibaldi). *Macàbro*, which Malagoli recorded as prevalently paroxytonic, tended to become proparoxytonic on the analogy of *càlabro, cèlebre, fùnebre, lùgubre*. The plural *microbi*, which should have read *micròbi(i)*, was often pronounced *mìcrobi*, from which came a new singular *mìcrobo*. Fanfani, Petrocchi and Malagoli recorded as prevalent the pronunciation *scòrbuto*, for which it is difficult to find a cause. *Cinema* came in from French, and for some years there was oscillation between *cìnema, cinèma* and *cinemà* (of which the first triumphed).

Coming to morphology, we note that (as we have already seen in dealing with spelling) there was oscillation in writing the plurals of nouns in *-cia, -gia*. There were some changes in the plurals of nouns in *-co* and *-go*. These were mostly gains made by the palatal forms in proparoxytones: *traffici* appeared alongside the traditional *traffichi*, *parroci* gained ground, as did *stomaci*, while some people wrote *strascici* (Rajna). We should note, too, in paroxytones, the plurals *lombrici* (Rapisardi), *aprici, pudici* (Carducci, in verse). As a plural of *capello, capegli* continued to be used, both in the popular language (Petrocchi) and in the literary (Barrili). In spite of the protests of grammarians, the habit of regarding nouns in *-a* as invariable, spread: *i Belga, i comma*, etc. The plural forms of *bello* and *quello* now followed those of the definite article, except that *belli* and *quelli* were still frequently found even before a vowel, *s* impure or *z* (*i belli occhi parlanti*: Fogazzaro, *Piccolo mondo mod.*; *quelli uomini*: Martini, *La marchesa*). As for the article, *il* and *lo* (as also *un* and *uno*) now had a fixed distribution, except for some slight oscillation: *lo* before a consonant sounded either archaic or southern ('il fato — che lo tuo regno segna in terra e in mare': Carducci, *Rime Nuove*); use of *il* before *z* was not rare (*un zinzin, il Zanella, il Zanardelli*, Carducci; *dal Zambrini*, Carducci, *Op.*, XII, p. 42, but *lo Zambrini*, ib., p. 54, *il zenith* but *lo zibaldone*, Balossardi; *il zulu*, D'Ovidio; *un zuccherino*, Fogazzaro; *dal zeffiretto*, Corradino; *i zefiri*, Capuana, etc.); *il, un* were also used frequently before *ps* (*il psicologismo*: Carducci, *Op.*, XII, p. 138), although *lo, uno* were slightly commoner, and the few grammarians who dealt with the matter recommended *lo, uno*; there was oscillation, as indeed there still is, before *j* (semivocalic *i*) and before foreign nouns beginning with *h*. There was rather greater hesitation in the plural, for the form *li*, although rare, had not disappeared. Some used it before a vowel (*li ordini, li occhi*: Martini, *La marchesa*; *li occhiacci*: Verga; *li emuli, li alti fieni*: D'Annunzio; *li umani, de li umili*: De Bosis; *li organi*: S. Corazzini), some before *s* impure (*li spagnuoli, li spiriti, li scritti*: Carducci; *delli scrittori, dalli spogli degli scrittori*: Tabarrini; *delli sciami*: De Bosis; *li scogli*: Pascoli). Hardly any grammarians mentioned the problem, with the exception of Morandi and Cappuccini, who held that the use of *li* in prose was now a displeasing affectation. In the use of *i* and *gli*, as in that of *il* and *lo*, there were some aberrant examples (*dai sguardi*: Cossa; *a' zefiri*: Rapisardi; *i zamponi, coi zoccoli*: Panzini; *i gnocchi*: Panzini). In the field of articulated prepositions, we should note that *per lo* persisted sporadically in prose ('mi si aggirava la lezione *per lo capo*': De Sanctis, *Giovinezza*, c. XVI; *per lo passato*: Martini; *per lo contrario*) and in verse ('*Per lo nitido* ciel l'ardua montagna': Rapisardi, *Ottobre*). In the long struggle between forms in which article and preposition were joined and those in which they were separate (*dello — de lo, alla — a la*, etc.) those in which they were joined usually won, although Carducci and D'Annunzio were fond (especially in verse) of the divided forms and did not lack followers. The separate forms of *su* (*su la*) were rather more widely used, while *pello, pella, collo, colla* came to be considered archaic. *Tra* joined with an article was extremely rare (*tral*: Martini; *tra 'l*: Pratesi). The forms *a' co' de' pe' su'* were recommended, especially in front of words containing other diphthongs (*de' miei, co' suoi*), but some felt that this was a rather artificial imitation of Tuscan (e.g. Panzini). Among pronouns, *ei, eglino, elleno* had become very rare; but *ei* was dear to Verga: '*Ei* non ci pativa' (*Jeli*); '*ei* si pigliava le busse senza protestare' (*Rosso Malpelo*). When Martini wrote (*Di palo in frasca*) 'ci è noto il nome dei vostri maggiori parlamentari, ci son note le opinioni ch'*eglino* professano' or '*elleno* tutte pigliavano sul serio i romanzi di Paolo Perret o di Ettore Malot', his solemnity bordered on irony. *Ella* and *Lei* alternated as allocutive pronouns, with a wide degree of choice: Carducci once expressed annoyance at those who wrote 'manzonianamente, *Lei*' (*Op.*, XXIV, p. 394), while Martini, writing to Fanfani, used *Lei*, then added: '(dovrei dire *Ella*? non mi ci va)' (*Lettere*, p. 49). Pleonastic subject pronouns (personal and impersonal), which were frequent in Tuscan usage, were readily accepted by tuscanizing writers. Apart from the more common '*gli* è quel che avviene' (Betteloni), we find '*e*' fu in piazza di S. Caterina' (Betteloni), 'la verità ... *la* può esser crudele ad udirsi' (Martini), '*le* si vedevano spesso' (Martini), '*le* son baie' (Carducci); but even the Manzonian Morandi held that this use was only rarely praiseworthy (Morandi-Cappuccini, *Gramm. it.*, 374). *Egli* as pleonastic pronoun was rather more literary: '*Egli* è dunque inutile far indagini' (Martini), '*Egli* fu un istante che io avrei voluto risparmiarlo' (Barrili), etc. *Gli* for *le* was common in Tuscan and in the Italian of several other regions: 'oso pregare la signora Sansoni a fare ciò che *gli* sia meglio possibile. Io *le* scriverò quando vegga che sia il caso....' (Carducci, *Lett.*, XIX, p. 133). But the grammarians would have none of it. They also rejected, though less violently, *gli* for 'loro', which was also current in Tuscany. In northern Italy the type *io ci dico* for 'I tell him, her, or them' was widespread; it was rigorously proscribed by grammarians. *Ne* in the sense of 'us, to us' was now rare, both in verse ('pensate all'ombra del destino ignoto — che *ne* circonda': Pascoli, 'I due fanciulli') and in prose ('Siamo grati all'Inghilterra di ciò ch'ella *ne* diede': Graf, *Anglomania*, p. 427). Coming to verbs, we should note the vogue enjoyed by the construction *noi si dice* for *noi diciamo*, due to its being pushed by the Manzonians, though Manzoni himself never used it in revising *I promessi sposi*. The widespread use made by some authors of such forms annoyed non-Tuscans (like Ascoli) and Tuscans (like Fanfani, who likened it to going out in one's shirt-sleeves and with unwashed face). In the first person singular of the imperfect, the -*o* form gained ground, but not so much as entirely to oust that in -*a*. Indeed, many authors used both forms with complete indifference (i.e. without intending any stylistic nuance when moving from one to the other), sometimes using both within a few lines or pages of each other: 'Ebbi una volta un pendolo a cucù... — e lo *tenevo* in camera... Io, ripigliato sonno, ancora voi, — miei colli *rivedeva*' (Carducci, 'Intermezzo', 3); 'solo solo come *era*...', 'io non *aveva* ancora bevuto...', 'io *capitavo* a Superga' (Panzini, *La lanterna di Diogene*, pp. 17, 18, 19). Forms like *èramo* in the first person plural, *eri* in the second pers. plur. were used only by writers who wished to show off their knowledge of popular Tuscan (e.g. Gradi, translating comedies by Terence). In the past definite, strong forms like *conobbimo*, *rimasimo* sounded dialectal and were used by very few (e.g. Verga, *La peccatrice*). The forms in -*etti*, -*ette* in the 2nd and 3rd conjug. were less common than those in -*ei*, -*é*. Carducci, in both prose and poetry, used *stiè* for *stette*. In the sub-junctive, the forms *che tu sii, che tu abbi, che tu facci* in the present, *che voi fossi* in the imperfect were used only in familiar Tuscan or by conscious tuscanizers. In the conditional, the -*ia* forms now became rare even in verse and exceptional in prose ('le chiese stupende ove *saria* dolce, credendo, pregare': Carducci, 1888, in *Op.*, XXV, p. 300). The first person plural forms in -*assimo*, -*essimo*, -*issimo* were considered incorrect, but still survived in the semi-cultured language of northern Italy ('Senza di questo, chi sa cosa *saressimo* noi . . . cosa *avressimo* ora?': Verdi, letter of 12 February 1878). In the imperative, the forms *fa, va, da, sta* tended to be replaced, and not only in Tuscany, by the originally indica-tive *fai, vai, stai*, and the corresponding apocopated forms *fa'*, *va'*, etc. In the use of auxiliaries with modal verbs, the con-struction *ho potuto andare* gained ground at the expense of the traditional *sono potuto andare* (and was not infrequently used by D'Annunzio). With reflexive verbs (whether properly reflexive or no) *avere* was quite often used: 'la sola meraviglia fu che non *s'avesse mangiato* Salandra' (Verdinois, *Profili*); 'come non *ci avessimo mai conosciuto*' (Pirandello, *Il fu Mattia Pascal*); 'non ricordava *d'aversi mai tagliato* le unghie' (Deledda, *Colombi e sparvieri*, p. 159). In poetic language, some traditional poetic forms of the verbs survived, though in increasingly limited numbers: *dee, ponno, vedea, finia, vanio* ('svanì'), *avria*, etc. As for invariables, while the euphonic *ad, ed, od* persisted, *ned* became extremely rare ('*ned* è necessario': Ascoli, *Arch. glott. it.*, I, p. xvi).

In the syntactical sphere, we find, not only examples of certain traditional constructions dying out, but also instances of dialectal, bureaucratic and French influences coming in. Among nouns juxtaposed without preposition, there was an increase in elliptical sequences of the type *cassa pensioni, dazio consumo, banco lotto, scalo merci, massa rancio*, which had their origin in administrative language and were widely opposed by the purists. Less foreign to Italian tradition were pairs in which the second element consisted of a proper name (*piazza San Marco*): into this category fitted con-structions like *il ministero Giolitti, gli scandali Dessalle, le finanze Salvador, il mondo Scremin* (Fogazzaro). On the other hand, the type *il monumento Cavour* (Dupré, *Ricordi autobiografici*, passim), which succeeded in France, did not take root in Italy. The traditional type in which the second element was in apposition to the first (*il Conte duca, la serva padrona*) also enjoyed considerable increase (*coperchio-sedile*: Dossi, etc.). Although sixteenth-century Italian examples exist, it was probably French influence that was responsible for use of partitive *di* before an adjective followed by a noun: 'vendeva *di* piccole focacce che non potevano uccidere una donna' (Scarfoglio, *Il processo di Frine*), 'gli procuravano anche *di* solenni scapaccioni' (De Roberto, *I Vicerè*), 'Papà tuo passa *di* ben tristi giornate' (Martini, lett. 28 July 1914). Many observations could be made on the use of tenses; we limit ourselves to giving a typical example of a past definite used as in Sicilian: 'Mastro Cola cadde gridando: — Mamma mia! *m'ammazzarono*' (Verga, *Novelle rusticane*). There were instances, too, of indicatives being used for subjunctives, through dialectal influence: 'Il popolo credeva che il suo gran nemico *era* il Governo' (Settembrini, *Ricordanze*, I, p. 113), 'Aspettano che *suonate* mezzogiorno' (Verga, *Mastro don Gesualdo*, p. 144). Ascoli, on the other hand, often used the subjunctive in dependent clauses containing a limited statement, where the present or future indicative would normally have been used: 'Quanto poi sia conseguito per questa seconda via, se da un lato riconferma la normalità . . . della continuazione fonetica, è chiaro che *stremi* dall'altro . . . il campo' (*Arch glott. it.*, X, p. 83), 'lo Scaramuzza . . . tocca di certi rioni della sua Grado in cui *perduri* abbastanza nitida la vecchia parlata' (ib. XIV, p. 335); 'l'impressione che su voi *produca* questa mia cosa' (letter to Bianco Bianchi, 29 Nov. 1886). There was some oscillation in the governing of dependent infinitives, often due to dialectal influences: 'mi piaceva *a* vederlo sorridere' (Neera, *Anima sola*), 'ho visto il barone *a* confabulare' (Verga, *Mastro Don Gesualdo*, p. 87), 'De Zerbi, del quale aveva inteso tanto *a* parlare' (Verdinois, *Profili*, p. 211 Le Monnier), 'A Modena un tabaccaio si offerse *ad* incollarmi egli stesso i bolli' (Panzini, *La lanterna di Diogene*, p. 30). On rare occasions there were still examples of the infinitive followed by *con* without article: 'gli altri tre finirono *con* parlar di lei' (Fogazzaro, *Piccolo mondo antico*), 'mi aiutino essi *con* suggerirmi . . .' (Pascoli, note to 2nd ed. of *Fior da fiore*). The gerund not infrequently referred to other parts of the sentence than the subject: 'Al far del giorno io avevo davanti a me, in ginocchio, un soldato nemico di cavalleria, *chiedendomi* la vita' (Garibaldi, *Memorie*, p. 281), 'Rosaria . . . vide la padrona in uno stato spaventevole, *frugando* nei cassetti e negli armadi' (Verga, *Mastro Don Gesualdo*), 'Lodovico scorse Giovanni e Maria in piedi *ciarlando* affabilmente' (Ojetti, *Il gioco dell'amore*, p. 185). In word-order the use of enclisis declined. Pascoli con-

demned pretentious academic writing which made excessive use
of it, and thought it should be limited to the imperative, gerund,
participle and infinitive (*ditegli, dicendomi, dicentemi* and *dettogli,
dirti*). This did not mean, however, that there were not numerous
examples, not only in fixed formulas (*Appigionasi*), but in literary
prose, e.g. in Dossi 'tutti si rimbarcarono e *distaccaronsi* dalla riva'
(*Colonia felice*), '*rincamminossi* per le orme segnate il dì prima'
(*ib.*), and in Verga — 'il grosso pilastro rosso, sventrato a colpi
di zappa, *contorcevasi* e si piegava in arco' (*Rosso Malpelo*). But
that it was considered stale as a stylistic device can be seen from
the humorous use made of it by Faldella in a description of one
of the meetings of Arcadia: 'Si approssimò qualche poco al mio
concetto di Arcadia un vecchietto lindo e ben imbottito d'eleganza,
o meglio *approssimossi* la sua tosse' ('In Arcadia', in the vol.
Roma borghese, Rome 1882). An occasional tendency to put the
subject at the beginning of the sentence, even in cases where that
would not normally be expected, was probably due to French
influence ('Una dolcezza ci allacciava che non era di questo
mondo': Neera, *Anima sola*). Periods with verbs at the end had now
become very rare: 'viene quel giorno in cui [quei volumi] per-
mettono ad uno di fare una indagine che altrimenti far non
potrebbe' (Q. Sella, speech to the Chamber, March 1881).
Examination of the use of long and short periods, hypotaxis and
parataxis, and new techniques in dialogue, would involve a
technical study of individual authors.

We shall begin our discussion of the development of vocabulary
with a few examples of the fields that contributed new words.
The rise of evolutionist thought brought derivatives of *evoluzione*:
evoluzionario, evolubilità, etc. (though not yet *evolversi*). There was
oscillation between *selezione naturale* and *elezione*; Tommaseo condemned *selezione*. Darwin's translator, Canestrini, also jibbed at
the neologism and thus produced *Sulla origine delle specie per
elezione naturale*, Turin 1875. Ascoli, however, was not afraid of
it, and spoke of *selezione naturale* (*Arch. glott. it.*, I, p. xviii). Many
spoke metaphorically of *darwinismo* (or *darvinismo*) and of the
lotta per la vita. Ambiente, which had been a physical and biological
term, came, after Taine's use of *milieu*, to cover social conditions
in the same sense as the French word. *Trasformismo*, originally an
evolutionist term (coined by the French anthropologist Broca in
1867 with reference to Lamarck's theories), was used in Italian
politics (after the speech made by Depretis on 8 October 1882,
when he spoke of *trasformazione*) to indicate the abolition of clear

lines of division between the parties: '*Trasformismo*, brutta parolo a cosa più brutta', commented Carducci. Innumerable other words made their first appearance in the political field: *autoritario, intransigente, forcaiolo, libertario, blocco* and *bloccardo* (first used with reference to French, later to Italian politics) and *boicottare* (at first spelt *boycottare* and displaying its English origin, later completely naturalized). The new title of *sottosegretario* ('Undersecretary of State') also came into being. Phrases from the political sphere were: *questione meridionale, capitale morale* (Milan; attributed to R. Bonghi), *zone grigie* (used by Crispi to indicate frontier districts with a population of mixed nationalities) and the notorious *sacro egoismo* of A. Salandra. African wars brought in *negus, ras, ascari*; and *guerrafondaio* and *retrovie* were born at this period. The Libyan war was responsible for the importation of *ghirba*, an Arabic word ('a leather water-bucket'; (fig.) 'belly'). Social struggles also brought in new terms or gave new meanings to old ones: *lega operaia, Camera del lavoro, sciopero, serrata* (at first *lock out*, 1875), *sabotare*, etc. Affective words abounded, both approving (*compagno*) and pejorative (*succhioni* 'bloodsuckers', *crumiri* 'blacklegs' — from the name of a Tunisian tribe on the borders of Algeria whose smuggling activity was the cause of the French expedition of 1881). A popular motto was *Sole dell'avvenire*, first used by Garibaldi, probably in a letter of 5 August 1873, then given diffusion in F. Turati's *Canto dei lavoratori*, 1886. *Lor signori* was used as a pejorative term for the ruling classes. As women entered professions they had not previously graced, new feminine nouns were formed. Fornaciari noted (*Sintassi*, pp. 18-19) that the ending usually preferred was -*essa*: *avvocatessa, professoressa, studentessa*. But the generally pejorative connotation of -*essa* appeared in the use of many of the new formations: 'queste *deputatesse* pettorute' (*Giobbe* by M. Balossardi [O. Guerrini and C. Ricci], p. 60); 'alla *letteratessa* venne in mente di fare . . .' (Panzini, *Le fiabe della virtù*), etc. This led people to attempt other solutions: *le signorine studenti, la donna avvocato*, etc. Of the feminines of the names in -*tore* only *dottoressa* began to be used without disdain; *dottrice* was impossible and *dottora*, although defended by Arlìa who favoured nouns in -*tora*, was itself felt to be pejorative. Rebuilding in Italian cities led to talk of *sventramenti* ('demolitions, gutting') and *rettifili* ('straight roads'). Milan built its *famedio* ('Temple of Fame'). There were great innovations in transport. Some new types of horse-drawn carriage still appeared (*victoria*), but soon there were more revolutionary changes: hence

tramway, tram or *tranvai* (with a *trolley,* etc.), *velocipede, bicicletta* (with
the verb *pedalare*), *automobile* (with *chauffeur, capote, démarrage* —
later *avviamento,* etc.). Aviation developed with *aeroplani* (which
D'Annunzio preferred to call *velivoli*) and brought in some
French terms (*hangar, planare*) as well as encouraging some new
Italian ones (*fusoliera,* etc.). Submarines were at first called
sottomarini, but later *sommergibili* triumphed; these had a *periscopio,*
etc. Changes in male and female fashions brought in *tight, smoking,*
impermeabile, lobbia, pigiama (*pijama*), *sellino* (Fr. *tournure*), *bolero,*
tailleur, entrave, etc. In the early years of the new kingdom there
were developments in legal and bureaucratic vocabulary. Often
the terms previously used in the Kingdom of Sardinia prevailed
(*sindaci* replaced *gonfalonieri* and *podestà*), but some terms from
other states gained national currency (e.g. the Neapolitan *incarta-*
mento, which was originally the Spanish *encartamiento*). Economics
and finance contributed *correntista, percentuale, bancabile, conta-*
bilizzare and many more words; *assegno* began to oust *chèque.*
Statisticians spoke of *natalità, nuzialità,* etc. In literature many
terms indicating new tendencies came from France: *parnassiani,*
realisti, veristi, simbolisti. But *scapigliatura* was a very original
translation of the French *bohème* — although its first use in C.
Arrighi's *La scapigliatura e il 6 febbraio* (Milan 1861) was with
reference, not to a literary school, but to patriotic conspirators
responsible for the events of 6 February 1853. *Crepuscolare,* though
not without French and Italian precedents, became attached to a
particular group of writers in Italy as the result of an article by
Borgese. *Bozzetto* as a literary term was borrowed from painting
and sculpture. In the visual arts, too, there were numerous
European terms (*impressionisti, divisionisti,* etc.) and some of
Italian coinage (*macchiaioli*). Music provided the Wagnerian
Leitmotiv, the *ocarina* (invented at Budrio in 1867), the *pianola,*
which was of English origin, etc. Journalism gave *elzeviro, trafil-*
etto, terza pagina (begun in the *Giornale d'Italia,* 1901), *intervista,*
and the verb *cestinare* ('throw into the waste-paper basket'). New
interest in the moral sciences and conflicting trends in philosophy
(positivism, idealism, etc.) were reflected in *abulia, afasia, agnostico,*
autocoscienza, neoscolastica, pragmatismo, pseudoconcetto, psicanalisi,
psicometria, etc. Positivists spoke, not of *anima,* but of *psiche. Tele-*
patia aroused interest. In theology, controversy centred round
modernismo. Criminologia made its appearance. A new kind of
research was represented by the terms *preistoria* and *paletnologia:*
it, too, had its terminology (*terramare, palafitte, villanoviano*). The

biological sciences made several discoveries in the sphere of *bacilli* and *microbi(i)*. Medicine adopted *antisepsi* and *anestesia*, made progress in *parassitologia*, identified *difterite* and *tubercolosi*. Research into malaria produced the adjective *malarico*. Chemists coined words like *cocaina* and *ptomaina*, and industry produced *celluloide* and *dinamite*. Electricity used *accumulatore*, *trasformatore*, *dinamo*, *volt*, etc. The development of motors led to the employment of *macchinario*, *montaggio*, *turbina*. The growth of commerce gave rise to *merceologia* (or *merciologia*). Photography used *istantanea* and *viraggio*. The *fonografo* and the *cinematografo* made their appearance, each with a terminology of its own. There were great developments in sport (tennis, mountaineering, skiing, etc.). A large number of English and French terms were adopted, but there were also some of Graeco-Latin or Italian formation. *Maratona* was used as the name of a race from the time of the re-establishment of the Olympic games in 1896. The old Italian word *allenare* was now employed to convey the meaning of the English 'to train' and the French *entraîner*, etc. Among the other pursuits of the age were *grafologia* and *filatelia*. But we have, of course, merely scratched the surface; future workers in this field will need to establish full vocabularies (with dates) for each specialist field.

The new words which Italian acquired at this time can be divided into the following categories: new coinages, existing words which acquired new meaning, vocabulary from regional sources, exhumed archaic words, latinisms, grecisms and words from modern foreign languages.

Only very few of the newly coined words were onomatopoeic. Pascoli was very fond of onomatopoeia, not only taking up again examples occasionally used by previous writers (*bombire*, *chioccolare*, *zirlare*), but also adopting others from popular usage and himself coining new ones, either grammaticalized (the *gracilare* of hens, *sciusciuliare* of the sea) or not (the *tin tin* of robins, *uid uid* of larks, etc.). But very few onomatopoeic words obtained a permanent place in the language: one was *ticchettio* (Picciola, *Versi*; D'Annunzio, *Innocente*, *Trionfo della morte*). There was a good deal of substantivization of words, referring both to persons (*un sanitario*, *un intellettuale*) and to things (*un dirigibile*, *un'istantanea*, *un'automobile*). There were many instances, too, of direct derivations (particularly abundant in the language of offices): *realizzo*, *incrocio*, *rettifica*; *cestinare*, *pedalare*, *ostacolare*, *periziare*, *motivazione*, etc. Purists generally were against such forms, and particularly verbs

2E

derived from nouns in -*one*, like *lesionare*, *ustionare*, etc. The success of *super*- as an intensive prefix began with *superuomo* (in the preface to D'Annunzio's *Trionfo della morte*, 1894). In fact, much use was now made of elements of compound words functioning as affixes, which offered almost unlimited possibilities of forming more compounds: *aeroferetro* (1903), *autocommento* (Carducci, 1882), *autocoscienza*, *autogoverno* (1890), *automobile*, *elettroargentura*, *elettro-puntura*, *fotoincisione*, *fotoscultura*, *galvanoplastica*, etc. The most fertile suffixes were -*ismo* and -*ista*. *Ismo* was used mainly for words denoting new doctrines, movements, tendencies: *nullismo*, *verismo*, *futurismo*, *occultismo*, etc. They were mostly international words, some formed in Italy, some abroad, and Capuana devoted a volume to *Gli ismi contemporanei* (Catania 1898). But a small group of them, pertaining to sporting activities, was of obviously French derivation: *velocipedismo* (later *ciclismo*), *automobilismo*. Nouns in -*ista* also multiplied (*elettricista*, *pubblicista*, *specialista*, etc.). The venerable series of nouns in -*issimo* (*amicissimo*: Villani, etc.) received many additions: *banchettissimo*, *giornalissimo*, *palazzissimo* (Nieri), *sorellissima* (Rovetta), etc. Diminutives in -*erello* and -*arello* (the first originally Florentine, the second non-Florentine and favoured by Romans) were now used without consciousness of regional flavour: Dupré wrote *fatterello* or *fattarello*; Carducci used *fattarello*, *attarello*, *bruttarello*; Mazzoni *scrittarello*, etc. Scientific formations abounded (*psicosi*, *tubercolosi*, etc.), and the type sometimes overflowed into current usage: on the model of *mattoide*, coined by Lombroso, were formed *anarcoide*, *genialoide*; and, following nouns in -*ite* or -*itide*, came *spaghite* 'fear' and *briachitide* ('bollendogli la *briachitide* su due bone materasse': Petrocchi's translation of Zola's *L'Assommoir*, p. 128). Science, bureaucracy, journalism, poetry, all coined new adjectives: *malarico* (from *malaria*), *maidico* (from *mais*), *luetico* (from *lue*), *medianico* (*medium*), *velico* (from *vela*), *risorgimentale*, *decoramentale* (Carducci), *sensazionale*; *aromale*, *liliale*, *sinfoniale* (D'Annunzio), *furiale* (Boito), *gloriale* (Camerana), etc. Between 1900 and 1910 adjectives in -*esco* referring to centuries (*trecentesco*, etc.), which had previously been very rare, ousted those in -*istico* (or appositional -*ista*: *eleganza cinquecentistica*, *lirica cinquecentista*) which had been usual up to that time. Alongside the old words *lanificio*, *setificio*, *panificio*, which had passed from meaning the art of working in, or making, wool, salt, bread, to denoting the place where this took place, new words were formed with the same ending, particularly in Lombardy: *calzaturificio*, *canapificio*, *caseificio, cotonificio.* Alongside compounds of the usual kind, which continued to increase (*accalappiacani, pesalettere, schiaccianoci*, etc.), there were many belonging to other types, particularly in the sciences (*parolibero,* Marinetti; *avifauna,* etc.). Of course, not all new words won a permanent place; some had only a brief career in the language: *scimmietà, scimmiologo* (Tommaseo), *monumentare, manzonicidio* (Carducci), *capolavorare* (D'Annunzio), *massiccità* (Fogazzaro), etc. In some instances the inventors of successful words are known: *ptomaina* (F. Selmi), *bimetallismo* (E. Cernuschi), *paesanità* (Carducci), *guerrafondaio* (L. A. Vassallo = Gandolin). In other instances we at least know who introduced them: *velivolo* (for 'aeroplane': D'Annunzio), *congeniale* (Croce), etc.

There were important developments in semantics. A large number of scientific terms underwent extension of meaning and came to be used both in a restricted technical sense and in a figurative one; here one only has to think of words like *evoluzione, evoluto, svilupparsi; alluvione, permeare; condensare, cristallizzare; espansione; convergenza, divergenza; diagramma* ('il diagramma delle tese funi': Graf, *Medusa,* 1880), *apogeo, eclissi, orbita; embrione, germe, microbi(i), parassita; patologia, diagnosi, sintomo, nostalgia* (for only towards the end of the nineteenth century did this word emerge from medical treatises to take a place in common usage); *gestazione; atrofia,* and many others. Figurative use was made, too, of the names of instruments and processes: *termometro, sismografo* ('La seduta di ieri fu burrascosa: ma il *sismografo* politico fin dalla mattina prometteva di più': Collodi, *Note gaie,* 1876), *cinematografo* ('Che *cinematografo*', 'What a scene!'), etc. It sometimes happened, too, that a science accepted as a technical term a word already having a technical meaning in another of the sciences: Canello (*Arch. glott. ital.,* III, 1879) referred to words that had different forms in spite of having the same etymology as *allotropi,* thus borrowing a term already in use in chemistry and physics. Here are some examples of semantic change of other kinds. *Siluro,* originally 'catfish', came also (through synonymic irradiation of *torpedine*) to signify '(self-propelled) torpedo' (1866). *Fascio,* shortly after 1870 was used at Bologna for a group of workers; and in Sicily in 1893 the *Fasci dei lavoratori* came into being. The demolition of parts of cities for rebuilding became known as *sventramenti* after Depretis in 1884 had said: 'Bisogna *sventrare* Napoli.' The monocle worn by elegant gentlemen was ironically called *pasticca* (Fanfani-Arlìa, 1881), then *caramella* (Fanfani-Arlìa, 1890); and the second of these stuck. *Mosconi* for 'notes on social gossip' originated in Matilde

Serao's column 'Api, mosconi e vespe', (which first appeared in the *Corriere di Roma*). *Pescecane* 'shark' appeared in the second edition of Panzini's *Dizionario moderno* with the sense of 'profiteer'; the noun was given further currency by its use in Dario Nicco-demi's comedy *I pescicani* (1913). There were numerous cases of antonomasia. These included metaphorical nouns, like *un travet* 'an impoverished, unimportant clerk', from the Piedmontese comedy *Le miserie d'monsù Travet*, 1862, and metonymical nouns, like *lobbia* '(Homburg) hat', called after the deputy Cristiano Lobbia (cf. 'Anthony Eden hat'), *cavurrino*, *sigaro Sella*, etc. Some such words, as one would expect, died when the characters concerned disappeared from the limelight, e.g. *Capitan Dodero* (used in Liguria for an old sea-captain, after a character in a novel by A. G. Barrili). Sometimes there was not so much a change of meaning in a word as a change in its affective content. *Santo* became widely used in a lay meaning. *Retorica* for many acquired pejorative overtones, as did *filosofo* and *filosofia*. In the decadents' polemics against bourgeois standards, grocers, *droghieri*, were used (like French *épiciers*) as symbols of inability to understand art, of Philistine insensibility: 'frase volgare e *droghiera*' (Martini, preface to *Di palo in frasca*). In an age when there was a good deal of anti-clerical feeling certain ecclesiastical terms came to have pejorative connotations, e.g. *paolotto*, the popular name for members of two religious orders, was used for 'clerical'. And widespread diffusion of *oleografie* led to that word, too, having a pejorative tone, as also its adjective *oleografico*.

After unification, written and spoken Italian absorbed a number of Tuscan words and a number of dialectal words from other regions. The expansion of the Florentine contribution to the language was partly due to Florence's brief years as capital, partly to Manzonianism. After 1870, the concentration of political, social and cultural life in the new capital brought certain Roman words into general use. Better communications and the growth of regionalist realism in literature gave general diffusion, too, to a certain number of words from other dialects. Writers who were native speakers of Tuscan sometimes used expressions from spoken Tuscan which had not hitherto been part of the Italian written language. In the *Ricordi autobiografici* of Dupré, for instance, we find (p. 412): 'quella stupenda musica, che ricord-andola mi ha fatto *andar su pei peri*' (='filled me with enthusi-asm'). Carducci wrote to Annie Vivanti (21 August 1898; *Lett.*,

XX, p. 161): 'la paura t'ha diminuita, direi *striminzita*', adding, in explanation, that it was a Tuscan word. Non-Tuscan writers attempting to tuscanize often used popular Florentine expressions in unsuitable contexts. In Emilio Broglio's *Storia di Federico il Grande* (Milan 1874-76) there are many examples, e.g. 'La Prussia ci guadagnò un tanto, e fece un baratto *co' fiocchi*' (I, p. 105); 'l'era *doventata* una strega' (II, p. 131); 'moriva dunque . . . tra il *tocco* e le due a poco meno di *cinquantadu'anni*' (II, p. 372). Writers who tuscanized in this way beyond the limits observed by Tuscan writers themselves irritated Carducci and many others. But, apart from such persistent tuscanizers, there were authors (like Dossi or Faldella) who used the odd tuscanism in their attempt to build up their vocabulary eclectically. Others found some word they needed among tuscanisms not yet accepted by literary usage, as when Padula wrote *beruzzo* for a 'mid-day meal in the fields' or Verga used *sito* for 'stink'. Dialectal elements abounded, of course, in literary works with regional backgrounds; they can be found, in various proportions, in books by De Marchi, Fogazzaro, D'Annunzio, Serao, Verga, Deledda, Panzini and others. Much work remains to be done in this field (e.g. in tracing the contributions made by columns dealing with local items in newspapers and by the diffusion of objects produced in various regions, e.g. the *ocarina* invented at Budrio, etc.). But we can now make a provisional list of dialect words that entered the language at this time. Before we do so, however, it is important to remember that the differences between spoken Florentine and Italian had by this time grown considerably less. On the one hand, Tuscan words previously unknown in the rest of Italy had taken their place in the everyday usage of other regions; De Amicis, speaking of the consequences of unification in Piedmont, noted that many words and phrases which were very common at the time he wrote had been quite unknown there when he was a boy: 'Quarant'anni fa non le sarebbe mai occorso di sentir dire da un piemontese *schiacciare un sonno, appisolarsi, fare uno spuntino, fare ammodo, uomo di garbo, gente per bene, mi frulla per il capo, andare in visibilio, prendere in tasca*, faticare *parecchio*, e via discorrendo' (*L'Idioma gentile*, pp. 72-73.). On the other hand, certain Tuscan forms yielded to forms preferred by the rest of Italy, *bòdola, limosina, oriolo, polenda, spedale*, giving way to *botola, elemosina, orologio, polenta, ospedale*. In Florence itself *cassetta* (in the sense of 'drawer in a piece of furniture') was ousted by *cassetto*; *tavolo*, a form condemned by Tuscan purists, became established; and *crestaia* was pushed out by *modista*. Of the variants *officio*, *ufficio*, *uffizio*, it was, as we have already mentioned, the non-Florentine *ufficio* that triumphed. The Florentine *ammazzatoio* (registered by Fanfani and Petrocchi) had to make way for *mattatoio* (used at Siena, Ancona and Rome). The Florentine *mezzaiolo* and *mezzeria* lost their struggle against *mezzadro* and *mezzadria*. The Civil Code of 1865 (article 1647) noted the various regional forms thus: 'Colui che coltiva un fondo col patto di dividere i frutti col locatore, si chiama *mezzaiuolo*, *mezzadro*, *massaro* o *colono* . . .'; and from that time *mezzadro* and *mezzadria* generally gained ground. The Tuscan *albero* in the sense of 'poplar' was abandoned, since it gave rise to misunderstandings, one of which led to a lawsuit (mentioned by Tommaseo, *Adun. solenne della R. Acc. della Crusca*, Florence 1868, p. 83). Many dialectal words which entered the language at this period came from those regions which were playing a prominent part in national life. Here are some Piedmontese words mostly trans-mitted through military life: *arrangiarsi*, *cicchetto* ('glass of brandy'; later 'severe reprimand'), *grana* (in the phrase *piantare una grana*), *pelandrone*, *ramazza*. *Bocciare* also came from Piedmont, as did *gianduia*, *gianduiotto*. Lombardy's contribution was largely gastro-nomical: *risotto*, *erborinato*, *robiola*, *panettone; grappa*. The Lombard *brughiera* also became known, and *marcita* pushed out the Tuscan *marcitoia* (Canevazzi-Marconi, *Voc. d'Agricoltura*, s.v.). *Guardina* was Milanese. (From Milan, too, but from its offices, not from popular sources, came *famedio*, *enopolio*, *tecnomasio* and forms like *calzaturificio*.) Two Lombard words which might have seemed likely to succeed because they filled a gap in Italian, failed in fact to find a place: *ab(b)iatico* and *gibigianna*. *Abiatico* ('grandchild'), defended by Broglio and used by Fogazzaro, could have saved Italian from the ambiguity of *nipote* used in two senses. *Gibigianna* ('reflected ray of sunlight') likewise had no equivalent in Tuscan, but it was used only by Lombard writers: Stoppani, C. Bertolazzi (the author of a comedy entitled *La gibigianna*, 1898) and C. Rebora ('In gibigianna di diavolerie': *La Voce*, 6 Nov. 1913). *Fare un bacio* was used from time to time, but was always rejected as a lombardism. From Venetia came *vestaglia* and the greeting *ciao*, as well as the names of boats *bragozzo* and *fisolera* (the latter, adapted to *fusoliera*, later entered the vocabulary of aviation). *Felze*, the Venetian term for the cabin of a gondola, became widely known mainly through D'Annunzio's *Il fuoco*. From the Venetian Alps came *baita*, *malga* (two words for 'Alpine hut') and *cengia* ('a narrow ledge'). Geologists used the Friulan *foibe*, italianized as *foiba*, for 'a cavity of the Carso region'; but the Slav *dolina* prevailed. From Romagna came *ocarina* and little else (in spite of the use of Romagnol words by Carducci, Pascoli and Severino Ferrara). But the most numerous group of dialectalisms was that provided by Rome. Thence came *burino* or *burrino* ('rough peasant'). *Buzzurro* is Roman only semantically: in Florence the term had been used for the vendors of roast chestnuts and chestnut polenta; but when the capital moved to Rome, it was applied there pejoratively to the Piedmontese and other northerners who came to live in the capital. (It was used by Faldella, Carducci and D'Annunzio.) *Imbonitore* ('cheapjack') also came from Roman dialect. So did *pifferaro* ('piper'; a number of these came down from the mountains to play Christmas music). From the regions around Frosinone came the *ciociari*. *Pignolo* ('meticulous, pedantic') may have originated in Rome. From there came, too, a number of gastronomical terms (*abbacchio*, *saltimbocca*) and words connected with gastronomical expeditions (*maccaronata*, *spaghettata*) and country excursions (*ottobrata*). Less desirable habits gave *intrufolarsi* and *sbafo*. Horse-racing in the Roman campagna gave diffusion to *staccionate* ('hurdles'). Journalism presented the public with *fattacci* ('evil deeds, crimes of violence') and the *pupazzetti* ('caricatures') of Gandolin. From Naples spread *largo* ('a little piazza of irregular shape') and *rettifilo*, while the *basso* ('a one-roomed dwelling opening directly on to the street') became known as a local characteristic. Other words which retained a local connotation, though becoming widely known, were *paglietta*, *cafone*, *guaglione*, *scugnizzo*, *camorra* and *omertà*. *Pastetta*, on the other hand, came to be used in any part of Italy where there was fraudulent procedure at elections. Neapolitan gastronomical specialities included *mozzarella* and *vongole*. Numerous Neapolitan words were, too, generally accepted on account of their expressiveness: *mannaggia* (which overcame Tuscan *malannaggio*), *scocciare*, *fesso*. From Sicily came *zàgara*, *picciotti*, *carusi*, *mafia* and *mafiosi*, and from Sardinia *tanca*, *nuraghe* and *orbace* ('Sardinian woollen cloth').

Manzonianism and realism were both hostile to the use in prose (and indeed in verse) of traditional literary words which were no longer alive in the spoken language. In 1863 the *Rivista contemporanea*, dealing with a voting-machine, had been able to use the headline 'Di un ordigno per gli *squittinii*,' and in 1868 Mamiani had written '*Laonde* per me il quesito non *versa* sopra il conoscere....' But to later generations such words seemed unbearable, and they were dropped. Matteo Ricci recounted that Massimo d'Azeglio once threw a letter into his wastepaper basket, remarking that a man who began *È buona pezza che io desiderava scriverle* was necessarily an imbecile (*Rass. nazionale*, LIII, 1890, p. 234). One series that fell into disfavour was that of conjunctions like *imperocché*, *imperciocché*, etc. Even of the anti-Manzonian Settembrini it was said that a suitable epitaph for him would have been: 'Qui giace il nemico dei Borboni, dei Gesuiti e degli *imperciocché*.' If one of these conjunctions was used it was with irony: '*conciossiachè* secondo il marchese Puoti *oblio* sia parola da usarc solo in poesia, e di rado e con molto riserbo in prosa' (De Sanctis, 'L'ultimo dei puristi' in *Saggi critici*). Nevertheless, in verse, traditional poetic words which had been in use for centuries showed considerable resistance. Here one would need to proceed word by word if one aimed at a full account, and it would prove much more difficult to compile a list of those absent than of those present. But we can at least record some examples of those that *were* used: *calle* for 'cammino', not only by Graf and Zanella, but also by Cavallotti ('Sorella, non senti pel *calle*/Che lungo di frondi stormir?': 'Su in alto!'); *rai* in Stecchetti (*Postuma*, LIV); *vanni* (for 'wings') not only in Aleardi and Zanella, Carducci and Panzacchi, but in D'Annunzio (in verse in the *Primo vere* and in prose in *Il fuoco*). *Fiedere* was used by Zanella, Carducci and D'Annunzio. It is sometimes difficult to distinguish between the survival of traditional elements and the revival of words now felt to be archaisms, for the distinction is sometimes a matter of stylistic interpretation. Among the archaisms we can place not infrequent revivals of Dantesque words, like *piovorno*, which Carducci brought into his 'Miramar' and which afterwards was used by others (Pascoli, etc.), and *roggio* (Carducci, Pascoli, S. Ferrari, D'Annunzio and others). *Non mi tange* was used simply as a Dantesque allusion: 'Amore non mi tanse e non mi tange' (Gozzano, 'Convito' in the *Colloqui*). Some archaisms were also borrowed from Dante's predecessors and contemporaries (*alena*, *pascore*, etc.), but only *aulire* and *aulente* enjoyed much success in poetic diction. Some words that Carducci took from writers of the fourteenth or sixteenth centuries (*miluogo*, *misprendere*, *popolazzo*, *rinomo*, etc.) did not take root; but he succeeded in refloating *rinascita*, which he had found in Varchi and Vasari. The Florentine group which in 1877 founded *I nuovi goliardi* (G. Marradi, S. Ferrari, L. Gentile, A. Straccali, G. Biagi) were responsible for the word's new life, first in the meaning of 'bohemian student' ('il più *goliardo* della compagnia': Carducci, *Le risorse di San Miniato*) then of 'university student'. The verb *guatare* ('gaze at'), which had almost disappeared from literary usage ('voce oggidì rimasa in contado', according to Tramater, 1834) won favour again, both in verse ('Dal ciel *guata* la luna': Graf, 'Superstite' in *Medusa*) and in prose ('Oggi il palazzo reale *guatava* il viale': Abba, *Noterelle di uno dei Mille*, 9 November). Practical usage also revived some words that had fallen into desuetude. The *magistrato delle acque*, instituted by a law of 1907, revived the name of a Venetian institution (and the word here meant not 'magistrate', but 'magistracy', in which sense it was by that time archaic). *Serrata*, another historical term (Serrata del Maggior Consiglio, Venice 1296) was revived to cover the modern 'lock-out'. *Allenare*, a literary word now rare, was given a new lease of life as a sporting term (Fr. *entraîner*, Eng. *train*). And Isidoro Del Lungo had some success with his suggestion that the ancient *allibratore* should replace *bookmaker*.

Latinisms abounded in verse, especially in Carducci and his school and in D'Annunzio. In prose, we shall not expect to find them in the naturalist novel, but in the writing of those who looked to classical models. They were very plentiful in the terminologies of the sciences, both natural and moral. But in this field they were mostly indirect latinisms (coined, that is, not in Italy, but in other countries). In previous chapters we have dealt with latinisms and grecisms together. We shall again do this, but not before mentioning the fact that some words that Latin had not adopted were taken over directly from Greek (mostly without being latinized or being only partially latinized). This was particularly noticeable in historical and archaeological terminology (*lekythos*, *tholos*, *anghelos*, *logos*) and in scientific vocabulary (*kinesiterapia*), but it happened also in literary contexts: Carducci: *àgora*, *sofrosine*; Rapisardi: 'volge *Fisi* [Nature] la sua macchina eterna': *Giobbe* III, iii; D'Annunzio: *alalà*, *etaira*, *stephane*, *zoani*; Pascoli: *ananke*; 'E tu dà retta alla *dice* (=Justice) e dimentica al tutto la *bie* (=violence)', though he later amended the Greek words to *Dike* and *Bie*. Latinisms formed an essential element in the traditional language of poetry, and we could have dealt with them when discussing traditional literary vocabulary if we had only to deal with those latinisms already established in poetic diction ('d'*edaci* malori — traspaion l'impronte': Zanella; 'posan gli *àtavi* re dentro gli avelli': Carducci; 'quel prezioso e *pulcro* — rifiuto del *sepulcro*': Boito; 'Ed all'enorme *clipeo* fiero s'appoggia e sta': Cavallotti, etc.). But we have also to consider latinisms that were new, or which had been only rarely used before and had not taken root in the language. Carducci introduced such latinisms, often choosing proparoxytonic ones to match his innovations in metre. D'Annunzio began by following Carducci in this love of proparoxytones (mainly latinisms) and then went on to use more latinisms in prose and poetry than Carducci himself had done. Pascoli, who was a notable Latin scholar, used latinisms common to the other two poets, and added to their number. And minor poets of the period showed the influence of these three. Here is a brief list of these new latinisms culled from the verse of the period: *algido, auletride, avio, cècubo, cèrulo, cincinno, còllabo, cròtalo, efebico, èrbido, estuare, fimbria, ìlice, irremeabile, longicollo, lituo, luco, meduseo, multivolo.* With them we should group words used in their etymological [Latin or Greek] sense, instead of in that they normally had, e.g. *erroneo* for 'wandering', *epifania* for 'apparition', etc. Sometimes the author made his intentions clear for us: Carducci informed his readers that he had used *subsannare* in the *Chiesa di Polenta* with the sense it had in the Vulgate: 'Sprevit te et subsannavit te virgo Sion'. In some cases a latinism was suggested by the usage of another modern language. *Captivare* in D'Annunzio was the Latin *captivare,* but probably suggested by the French *captiver.* Indeed, a precise reminiscence of French symbolists is probably behind certain of D'Annunzio's latinisms, e.g. *flavescente, lattescente, iemale, ialino.* Most of these words never got beyond a restricted literary sphere; *etèra,* however, being valuable as a euphemism, went farther. The story of *velivolo* is instructive. D'Annunzio used it in his ode 'Ai bagni' (1879) in *Primo vere*: 'Con tenue murmure l'Adria *velivolo*'. It had previously been used by Latin writers (Ennius, Lucretius, Virgil, Ovid) and by Italians (Algarotti, Monti), and to date it had referred to sailing boats which had seemed almost to fly as they skimmed along the sea, and to the sea itself covered with sails. Then, in the *Corriere della sera* of 28 November 1909, in presenting extracts from his forthcoming *Forse che sì*, D'Annunzio defended his use of it in a new sense: 'aeroplane'. After that the word was used in the literary language as a noble synonym for 'aeroplano' and technically in a wider meaning ('any flying craft'). This example shows how words could have a double history: literary and technical. Thus *algido, nivale, siderale,* which were part of nineteenth-century poetic vocabulary, also had other roles in medicine (*febbre algida*), botany (*piante nivali*) or astronomy (*anno siderale*). In scientific and technical terminology there was an enormous increase in latinisms and grecisms and a still greater one in words derived and composed from Latin and Greek elements. Many of these words took their place in everyday usage as the objects and ideas to which they referred became widely known, e.g. *tubercolosi, bacillo, spirillo, anestetico, anofele, elio, ptomaina, fonografo, grammofono, aviazione, cinematografo, ascensore*, etc. Most of them were international words, of which a few had been coined in Italy and had passed into other languages, but most had originated abroad and been accepted into Italian. In law and administration, too, latinisms and grecisms abounded: *probiviri, alfabeti, analfabeti, teste* (which began to spread at the expense of *testimone*). Sometimes there were more or less arbitrary semantic changes: *gestire*, for instance, had meant, as in classical Latin, 'to gesticulate'; now, influenced by *gestione* and *gestore*, it took on the meaning 'to administer'. In practical affairs, already existing words took on new meanings: *edicola*, for example, formerly a rather rare word for a 'small chapel', became widely used for 'newspaper stall, kiosk'. *Agape* added to its Christian meaning that of 'Masonic banquet'. Even the vocabulary of sport had, alongside French and English contributions, some pseudo-classical terms, mostly themselves imported: *podismo, ciclismo, criterium*, etc. Journalists coined words and helped to establish them: *intellettuale* as a noun took on a pejorative sense at the time of the Dreyfus trial, while *amori ancillari* was a phrase that gained wide diffusion during the Murri case (1905) and became reinforced by the title 'Elogio degli amori ancillari' in Gozzano's *Colloqui* (1911). In the scientific field, as we have already seen, latinisms and grecisms circulated internationally much more readily than was the case in the literary field. It sometimes happened that they were simultaneously coined in several languages; Enrico Cernuschi, an Italian who became a naturalized Frenchman, set forth his ideas on bimetallism in works published in several languages (1875-6): *La monnaie bimétallique; Bimetallische Münze*, etc. Here are examples of franco-latinisms that entered Italian at this time: *acrobazia, ascensore* ('lift'), *automobile, aviazione* (La Landelle and Ponton d'Amécourt, 1863), *documentario, filatelia, mistificare, pacifista, pedicure, questionario, redazione* ('version of a written work'), *semantica, societario, teoria* (in the sense of 'line'), *torrenziale*, etc. Moreover, among the examples of extension of meaning and metaphorical use of scientific terms, many (in spite of being condemned by purists) were calques of French words:

creare, deleterio, fenomeno, formula, superfetazione, traiettoria, etc. Anglo-latinisms were also numerous: *acquario* (Eng. *aquarium* 1854, Germ. 1857, Fr. 1863: the aquarium at Naples dates from 1873), *criterium* (as a sporting term), *idrante, inflazione* (in the economic sense, which was born in the United States during the Civil War), *metropolitana* (referring to a railway, a sense which originated in London), *selezione, simbiosi,* etc. Germano-latinisms included *agrario* (as noun: 'landed proprietor'), *antisemita, banausico* (Croce), *caratteristica* (used by D'Ovidio in the German sense of 'characterization' as in e.g. 'to write a characterization of a work of literature'), *determinismo, epos, gipsoteca* (or *ghipsoteca*), *kinesiterapia, obiettivo, psicanalisi, recensione, tassametro,* etc. Sporadic latinisms were suggested by the usage of other languages: *intransigente,* which appeared in Spain in 1873 to indicate the Federalist Republicans, soon appeared in other European languages. We mentioned earlier the attempts made by one or two Italian writers to restore spellings containing *ch, ph, th, y* and the preference accorded by some to latinized forms (*imagine, conscienza*). When we find latinisms and grecisms with unassimilated endings, we can nearly always conclude that they penetrated indirectly: *aquarium, criterium, sanatorium, junior, senior,* etc. came into Italian from other modern European languages. It should also be remembered that the usual processes of adaptation were sometimes disturbed by analogy (*autodidatta, poliglotta, archiatra* for *autodidatto, poliglotto, archiatro; sillogisma* for *sillogismo,* etc.) or foreign influence (*autocrate,* etc.).

Of the modern languages that contributed vocabulary to Italian at this period the most influential was, as we have said, French. Not only did Italian retain many of the gallicisms it had accepted in the eighteenth and early nineteenth century, it adopted many new ones. They were incredibly abundant in second-grade literature, newspapers and letters; but even serious writers used very many. Here are a few examples of unadapted gallicisms: 'quel francesismo barocco e *langoureux* del regno di Luigi XVI' (Carducci, *Op.,* XV, p. 223); 'le vibrazioni delle *pierreries,* le luminosità dei tessuti *pailletés*' (D'Annunzio, *Tribuna,* 16 Jan. 1885); 'le osservazioni . . . potrebbero *blesser* il suo amor proprio' (letter of G. Verdi to G. Ricordi, Nov. 1886). They were even employed in verse. In their parody of Rapisardi's *Giobbe,* Guerrini and Ricci took the opportunity to satirize Francesco Fontana, who 'di prolisse—francescherie lardella il verso strano':

Voilato di nebbie
Parigi ho apperçuto
e la siloetta
che il domo del Pantheon
nel cielo progetta.
Promenasi il popolo
francese la notte;
nel fango pietinano
gommosi e cocotte,
guardati dai mille
col sabre nel fodero
sergenti di ville. . .

The protests of purists had little effect. We give now some examples of the gallicisms that entered the language at this time. Some referred to politics and administration: *comunardo, petroliere, sciovinismo, blocco* (in the political sense), *bloccardo. Dossier* became widely known in Italy during the Dreyfus case. *Estradare* was adapted from *extrader* (which in turn was an adaptation of the Latin *extradere*). Equivalents of the Parisian *Morgue* were instituted in Italy and the word *morgue* used to describe them. Conflicts in industry gave rise to *sabotare, sabotaggio.* The seamier side of life contributed *garçonnière, cocotte, Alphonse.* The house and its furnishings gave *pied-à-terre, rideau (ridò), capitonné,* etc. The language of fashion was particularly rich in gallicisms: *décolleté, plastron,* etc. So was that of cosmetics and hygiene: *brillantina, pedicure,* etc. With these words we should mention the colour *marron* (soon adapted to *marrone*) and the use of *seni* in the plural for 'breasts' (in place of the traditional *seno*). Food and culinary arts contributed *restaurant* (*ristorante*), *menu, couvert* (*coperto*), *glassare,* (mela) *renetta, marron glacé, bomboniera,* etc. Italian acquired, too, words pertaining to railways (*cantoniere, scartamento*), new means of transport (*bicicletta,* etc., *automobile, garage, chauffeur,* etc. *hangar, decollare,* etc.) and naval terms (*oblò, passerella, salvataggio*). Words denoting literary and artistic schools (*parnassiani, simbolisti, impressionisti,* etc.) came from France, as also *bohème, bohémien, vernissage,* etc. The language of journalism used the calque *trafiletto* (from *entrefilet*), and the term *réclame* (which referred originally to newspaper advertising). The theatre used a considerable number of French terms: *matinée, soirée, fumoir, foyer, claque, pochade, caffè concerto, divetta, chanteuse* (*sciantosa*), *soubrette, cancan,* etc. And sport was full of them: *pista* (from Fr. *piste,* itself a word of Italian sixteenth-century origin), *incollatura, bicicletta, velodromo, routier, pistard; boxe, masseur; pattinare; défaillance, guigne*, etc. The sciences made use, not only of many franco-latinisms, but also of *liana, falaise, banchisa*, etc., while gallicisms were even more numerous in technology: *béton (betoniera); alesare, biella, bullone, lingotto, putrella, trancia; cliché; ascensore, turbina, volante*, etc. Many general French terms also entered Italian: *élite, débâcle, surmenage, pioniere* (not simply in the military sense of 'sapper', already in use, but in that of 'precursor'); *banale, mirabolante, macabro* (now in a general sense, as well as in the phrase *danza macabra); rêver, rêveur, rêverie* (words frequently found in Carducci and De Sanctis), *turlupinare; vis-à-vis*, etc. Nor were French locutions any less plentiful: *tour de force, état d'âme* (and *stato d'animo); battere in breccia, battere in visiera* (also used by Carducci), *dare la dimissione* or *le dimissioni, incrociare le braccia, mettere i punti sugli i, passarsene* ('to skip doing something'), *volerne* (a qualcuno), and *non essere male* (in place of the adjective 'brutto' or some similar word: 'Dicono che non è male la vista qui': Fogazzaro, *Malombra*, p. 34), etc. To this summary list of examples should be added, of course, the numerous franco-latinisms we have already mentioned and those words that we could not put under that heading because of their hybridism (*cablogramma*, etc.). Indeed, the vogue enjoyed by French words was so powerful in certain fields (gastronomy, fashion) that it led to the creation of pseudogallicisms (*porte-enfant, zuppa santé* etc.). The treatment of French elements can be divided, as usual, into three kinds: some words were accepted in their French form (*élite, réclame, coup de tête, escamoter*, etc.), others were adapted phonetically (*pattinare, salvataggio, sciantosa*, etc.) and a number were copied by loan-translation (*focolare* acquiring the meaning 'centre of diffusion of an idea, etc., hotbed'; *posare* that of 'to pose as'). It is sometimes difficult to decide why certain words have retained their French form, while others have undergone adaptation. But in some instances, at least, the social forces responsible are easily recognised: *chic* is a form that would appeal to the seeker after elegance much more than the plebeian *scicche*, and similar considerations apply to *chanteuse* (as opposed to *sciantosa*) and *réclame* (as opposed to *reclàm). Ascensore*, on the other hand, fitted nicely into the Italian *-sore* type, while the distinction that could be acquired by the use of *ascenseur* instead was negligible. Gradually, the assimilated and adapted forms made gains at the expense of the unadapted, sometimes owing to the nature of the language, sometimes owing to the (by no means consistently sagacious or successful) intervention of purists. Certain French words disappeared after being in use for some time: *comptoir, blaga, gigotto, timbro* in the sense of 'bell', etc. while *coup de tête* was replaced by *colpo di testa* and *restaurant* generally by *ristorante*. Others continued to enjoy a place in current usage in spite of being avoided or considered undesirable by scrupulous writers (*debuttare, dettaglio, rimarcare*, etc.). It should also be remembered that words from other languages often came to Italian via French: before the forms *turismo* and *turista* triumphed, these two words were more often seen in the French forms (*tourisme, touriste*) than in the original English, while the final *-e* of *boxe* shows that it, too, came to Italy from France.

The next biggest group of foreign elements was supplied by English. It included terms from the fields of politics (*meeting*), economics (*trust, stock, cheque*), fashion (*tight, smoking*), architecture (*sky-scraper*, translated as *grattacielo*), communications (*ferry-boat, tramway, trolley, brougham*), household conveniences (*water-closet*), social customs (*five o'clock tea*), drinks (*gin*), sea-faring craft (*yacht, dreadnought, destroyer*), card-games (*bridge, poker*) and—by far the largest—sport (*raid, performance, record, criterium, derby, turf; football, goal; skating; sprinter*, etc.). It was the age in which tourism developed, and the *Touring Club Italiano* came into existence with a semi-English name. Some wealthy families had their children cared for by a *nurse*, and *miss* assumed the meaning 'governess'. Of the technical terms *film* had the greatest success; at first it was feminine, through the influence of *pellicola*. Some general terms, too, were borrowed, e.g. *bluff, snob, pick-pocket, flirt* (*flirt* being used, incidentally, in the sense of 'flirtation'). Some English words were adopted, too, for things met with in countries where English is spoken (*pitch-pine, bow-window*, etc.). The difference in the structure of the two languages, the prevalence of the written forms, and possibly a certain snobbishness, were responsible for the fact that adaptations to the Italian phonetic system were few and had little success. They had some chance of success when there was opportunity for the use of an Italian suffix, as in *turista, turismo* and in *brumista* alongside the Milanese *brum* for *brougham*; but *mitingaio* (from *meeting*), which had some success in the nineteenth century, later disappeared. Verdi wrote *spice* for *speech* ('Avevo preparato il mio spice che pareva un capo d'opera': lett. 8 Feb. 1865), but it was an isolated instance. The hybrid *selfinduzione* was used in technical language, but later replaced by *autoinduzione*. The adaptation of *folklore* to *folclore* was merely a change in spelling. It was possible, of course, in a certain number of instances, to provide Italian-sounding equivalents for Anglo-Saxon terms by means of calques or by other methods, e.g. *schiave bianche* was a translation used from the very beginning. Similarly, *interview* gave way to *intervista*, *meeting* was replaced by *comizio*, *lock out* yielded to *serrata*, *assegno* was substituted for *check* and *cheque*, *cacciatorpediniere* took the place of *destroyer*, etc. Pitré tried to get *demopsicologia* adopted in the place of *folklore*, but failed. As well as the large number of anglicisms that Italian borrowed at this period, there were, of course, very numerous anglo-latinisms, as we have already seen in treating latinisms and grecisms. Moreover, certain words from modern foreign languages found their way into Italian via English (*iceberg*, *giungla*), etc. A separate word should be said about English words borrowed by Italian emigrants in the United States. These were nearly all adaptations, not calques. They were subjected to powerful phonetic alteration to make them fit the dialectal habits of the speakers and occasionally crossed with Italian words: *giobba* from *job*, *ghella* from *girl*, *sciàbola* from *shovel*. Some such words were brought back by Italian emigrants and penetrated Italian dialects, particularly in southern Italy, but also elsewhere, e.g. in Lucchese.

Contacts with Germany, Switzerland and Austria led to the adoption of a number of germanisms. There were some borrowings in the field of philosophy (*Weltanschauung*, *Kulturgeschichte* or *storia della cultura*, *Aufklärung*, *Mehrwert* or *plusvalore*) and also calques (*autocoscienza*, *eticità*). The *Krach* of the Viennese Stock Exchange in May 1873 made quite an impression, and from that time that onomatopoeic word has had a place (*crac*) in financial and general language in Italy. Industrial struggles were echoed in calques like *datore di lavoro* and in the title of the newspaper *Avanti!* (1896), a translation of *Vorwärts!* The imitation of German beer-cellars led to the use of *chellerine* (from *Kellnerin*) for the girls who served in them. Importation of German foods gave *Würstel* and other such terms. The employment of German-speaking (frequently Swiss) governesses led to *Fräulein*, like *Miss*, coming to mean 'governess'. In literature there was the Franco-German *belletterista* ('frati e preti belletteristi', wrote Carducci in 1895, *Opere*, XVIII, p. 13) and *minnesinghero* (another Carduccian word). With Wagnerian music came *Leitmotiv*, the use of which was later extended to non-musical spheres. Linguistics made use of the terms *Ablaut*, *Umlaut* (De Lollis coining the verb *umlautizzare*: *Miscell. Ascoli*, Turin 1901, p. 283) and there were also calques in this field (*neogrammatico*, etc.). Germano-latinisms we have already mentioned. Some German words were used only with reference to

German affairs (*Reichstag, Kulturkampf; Burschenschaft, Backfisch,* etc.). The examples which we have cited will reveal that this borrowing took place almost entirely through the written language or by calques. Direct contact with spoken German contributed only a few words to dialects spoken by Italian emigrants: those who had worked in the St. Gotthard tunnel, for instance, brought back to the dialects of northern Venetia *isenpón* ('railway', from *Eisenbahn*), *sina* ('rail' from *Schiene*), etc.

Borrowings from other countries were much fewer. From Spain came *intransigente*, from Argentina *tango*, from Brazil *fazenda*. From Scandinavia came *saga* and *ski* (later *sci*). Words from Slavonic languages were used only with reference to objects and affairs of Slav countries, e.g. *konak; duma.* Translation of Russian novels made words like *mugik, isba* and *troika* known in Italy. *Dolina* came, not directly from Slovene or Croat, but through international scientific terminology. African wars and colonial adventure led to the importation of *ascari, ras, negus, amba, tucul, futa, ghirba* etc. Some of these words were used figuratively: 'i *ras* della magna letteratura contemporanea' (*Rivista,* 10 Jan. 1897, attacking Carducci). The name of an African tribe *crumiri* was used to denote 'blacklegs'. At this period Italian, like other European languages, also acquired exotic words from Asia and the East: *giungla, veranda, nirvana* (a word that became known, not so much from the writings of specialists in Indian philosophy as from Schopenhauer's vulgarization), *pigiama* (a Persian word that accompanied the object it referred to) and—a group of Japanese examples— *mikado, geisha, musmè, kimono, harakiri* (soon mutilated to *karakiri* in D'Annunzio's *Piacere*).

Meanwhile, italianisms that entered other languages were few; they give the impression of being isolated examples resulting from single events. Garibaldi's exploits led to the term *garibaldejka* being used in Bulgaria for a kind of blouse. Garibaldi jackets and Garibaldi blouses were also worn in England, where the Garibaldi biscuit is still popular. The term *irredentismo* was found useful in France (*irrédentisme*) and in England (*irredentism*). Other countries acquired knowledge of some of Italy's misfortunes, both material (*malaria,* Fr. 1867; but already in English since 1740) and moral (*maffia,* Fr. 1875). A popular gastronomical export was *risotto* (Eng. 1884; Fr. end of century). The *palafitte* discovered by ethnologists gave the French *palafitte* (1867), while Lombroso's *mattoide* penetrated both French (*mattoïde*) and English (*mattoid*). *Ferroviario* was coined in Italy: it passed first into French Switzerland, as *ferro-*

viaire, and from there into France itself. Naturally, this list of Italian words in other languages could be considerably expanded and made much more picturesque if we were to include in it the Italian words that foreign journalists and authors included in their articles and books when writing about Italy; in his novel *Le lys rouge,* for instance, Anatole France used very many Italian words (*briscola, libeccio, loggia, palazzo,* etc.) for the sake of local colour.

13

Recent Developments
(1915–1965)

In this chapter we shall deal with the period that extends from Italy's declaration of war in 1915 to the present day. Within that period the most important dates are 1922, when power passed into the hands of the Fascists, and 1940, when they led Italy into the Second World War, in which Fascism was defeated.

Italy's victorious emergence from the First World War raised hopes that there were better times ahead, but it did not substantially alter any of the grave economic and social problems that faced her. The collapse of the temporary war-time boom was inevitably accompanied by a certain amount of industrial unrest and political uncertainty. For a time it seemed that these circumstances might favour the parties of the Left: in the election held at the end of 1919 the Socialists gained 156 seats and Don Sturzo's *Partito Popolare* 101. But the electoral strength of the Left was matched by force of a different kind on the Right. Mussolini had formed his *fasci di combattimento* in 1919 (though at first their importance was slight and their eventual political direction far from clear). The aggressive type of nationalism favoured by D'Annunzio had thrown up his like-minded *arditi* (a war-time formation). Certain industrialists were quick to see the advantages to themselves of supporting such groups; bludgeoning and castor oil now became instruments of strike-breaking and political persuasion. Yet, although the Fascists profited from the atmosphere created by D'Annunzian nationalism and from the widespread feeling that Italy had been robbed of her share of the spoils of war, they were able to win only 35 seats in the 1921 election. However, organized in a military fashion and now substantially subsidized by employers who saw in them a weapon against labour troubles, they were able in 1922 to break a general strike and 'march on'

Rome (occupying the lines of communication to the capital from northern Italy). In October of that year the King called on Mussolini to form a government. Since this was a coalition, it still seemed to some that there had been little radical change. But the Fascists soon set about eliminating their partners and opponents, and the murder of the Socialist deputy Giacomo Matteotti in 1924 made it finally obvious that legality had disappeared from the relationship of government and opposition. After that date Italy moved rapidly to totalitarianism, and by 1929 Mussolini was holding a general election from a single list; but by that time the deputies had in any case little importance, since Mussolini had become a dictator. The *Carta del lavoro* of 1927 was but one step in the establishment of a corporate state in which it became impossible for the workers to protest effectively when their real standard of living was reduced (as during the economic slump of the early thirties). In 1929 Mussolini negotiated a Treaty and Concordat with the Vatican. A Vatican sovereign state was established, though the area covered by it was small. An indemnity was paid to the Pope to compensate him for losses sustained since 1870. Roman Catholicism became the official religion of the state (Cavour's formula 'a free church in a free state' being abandoned): religious instruction, which had already been made compulsory in elementary schools by Gentile's reform in 1923, now became obligatory in secondary schools as well, and the state accepted the church's teaching on marriage (thereby committing itself not to introduce divorce into Italy). Mussolini, however, insisted on the suppression of the Catholic scouts, thus opening the way to the indoctrination of all Italy's youth in the Fascist youth organizations. Older people were brought within the range of the state's prestige-propaganda by the *dopolavoro*, an organization for providing leisure-time activities. But all these measures, which served to tighten the party's hold on the country, did not eliminate its basic problems: inability to grow enough food, unemployment, and the gap in development between north and south. Indeed, such Fascist policies as the boosting of the birth-rate could only accentuate them. Moreover, it became clear that the Fascists were giving less attention to their internal solutions to these problems (public works, the draining of the Pontine marshes and other schemes for land reclamation, and development of Italian industry by protectionist policies) than to their hopes of making gains abroad by establishing an African empire and imposing Fascism on other countries. The bombardment and occupation of Corfù for purposes of prestige (1923) was followed by the colonization of Cyrenaica, the war against Abyssinia (1935-6) and intervention, in company with Hitler's Germany, on behalf of Franco's side in the Spanish Civil War (1936-9). The 'Rome-Berlin Axis' of 1936 became a triangle (Rome-Berlin-Tokyo) in the anti-Comintern pact of 1937. Next came the invasion of Albania (1939). Then, when France had virtually fallen and the defeat of the Allies seemed imminent, Italy entered the Second World War (10 June 1940). But Mussolini had miscalculated. The subsequent invasion of Italy by the allied armies provided opportunities, not only for the Italian anti-Fascists who had been forced to flee, but for those who had kept cells of resistance alive in Italy. The strength and appeal of such resistance were not fully realized until the partisans were engaged in war against the German forces in northern Italy during the period of Italy's co-belligerence with the Allies (1943-5). After the removal of Fascist repression, Italy showed remarkable powers of recovery. The feverish reconstruction of the post-war years was followed by rapid industrial expansion, aided by the discovery in the nineteen-fifties of methane in northern Italy and oil in Sicily and the Abruzzi. As the result of a referendum held in 1946, Italy became a Republic, and the House of Savoy went into exile. A new constitution was agreed upon in 1947. Since then the largest political party in the state has been that of the Christian Democrats, the second largest that of the Communists. The Christian Democrat party is composed of men holding widely differing ideas on economic and social questions, and, according to the tendencies temporarily dominant within it and the alliances open to it, it has governed Italy in association with Liberals, Republicans, Social Democrats and Socialists in varying combinations; for short periods it has also governed alone, with the support of Monarchists and neo-Fascists in the Chamber.

One of the striking features of Fascist government was increased centralization, with an attendant growth of bureaucracy. This led to an increase in the size and importance of Rome. Meanwhile, industrial development, which had been stimulated by the First World War, added to the size of other large Italian cities. Since the Second World War, such growth has acquired greater momentum and has resulted in unprecedented migrations of population. The most obvious movement has been that of workers from impoverished areas of southern Italy to the large manufacturing centres of northern Italy (particularly to the Milan-Turin-Genoa triangle) and to the capital. But these large centres have received new citizens, not only from the south, but also from rural areas and smaller towns in the north; the magnet of Turin, for instance, not only draws population from Sicily, but denudes mountain villages in Piedmont as well. Sometimes, too, southern workers have moved, not to northern cities, but to work on land left by northerners in their migration to industry. The social consequences of these developments hardly need stressing. For many, city life has come to symbolize freedom, not only from the shackles of poverty, but from oppressive traditions, like that of subjection to the father of the family or to the eldest brother. Industry, commerce and the professions have offered greater opportunities than ever before to women; this has increased their economic importance and given many of them, too, greater independence. Throughout the period under review, provisions for elementary education have been steadily extended. In recent years strenuous efforts have also been made to provide instruction for adult illiterates. The 1961 census showed that the percentage of Italians unable to read and write had by then been reduced to 8.3. The growth in literacy and the increase in population mean that the Italian reading public has vastly increased since the First World War. From the academic year 1963-4 schooling in the *scuola media* (for children aged 11-14) has been free; Italy is now within sight of the goal of eight years of compulsory free education for all mentioned in her Constitution. Newspapers and magazines, which had become dejectingly uniform during Fascism, have displayed great diversity and vigour since 1945. Literature and the other arts have also shown great vitality and a marked concern with the problems of modern Italian society. In the forties and fifties neo-realist directors won world-wide recognition for the Italian film industry, and Rome has now become an important centre for foreign, as well as Italian, film production. While the cinema was establishing its importance after the introduction of talking pictures in the twenties, radio achieved a parallel success, becoming widely popular in Italy in the mid-thirties. Television followed: in the fifties certain transmissions (e.g. *Lascia o raddoppia?*) won such a following that streets were almost deserted while the population flocked into houses and cafés to watch their favourite programmes. Transport by road and by air has become speedier and more widely used: this has led to travel abroad for an ever-growing proportion of the Italian people and to mushroom growth of tourist centres in Italy (where the annual number of foreign visitors rose to seventeen millions in the early sixties).

International diffusion of ideas and tastes has become very rapid. In the period since the Second World War one could list examples ranging from the influence of certain British and American philosophers on the growth of neo-positivism in Italy (helping to combat the Gentilean-Crocean idealism dominant in the inter-war years) to the triumph of Italian design in other European countries in fields extending from shoes to car-bodies. And popular entertainment in the era of the record-player and the juke-box has become remarkably similar in all the countries of Europe and America.

Some of the social and political developments we have mentioned have had important linguistic consequences. Let us begin with migration. While Turin drew its new citizens mainly from neighbouring zones in Piedmont, they could bring in features of their own dialects without destroying the Piedmontese of Turin. Now, when thousands of new Turinese come from southern Italy, the situation is quite different. A Sicilian and a Piedmontese who wish to converse had better use Italian. Even if the Sicilian speaks Italian imperfectly and with intrusive regional features, his Italian will still be more intelligible to the Piedmontese than his Sicilian. And vice versa. This mixture of population caused by industrial development, then, favours use of the national language at the expense of dialect. So, obviously, does the extension of education; the children of immigrants, some of them children of mixed marriages, will be acquiring at school a knowledge of Italian, even if, in a place like Turin, it is an Italian in which regional characteristics have an important role. Military service has also played some part in the spread of the national language. Not a few of the Italian prisoners released from prisoner-of-war camps in 1945 had been away from their own regions since leaving for the Abyssinian war ten years earlier. Radio and television sets, too, have brought the national language into villages where it was seldom heard before and to scattered homesteads that it had never previously penetrated. Films have had a good deal of influence: they have served to propagate, not only Italian, but also elements of Roman dialect and southernisms (for Rome is the centre of the film industry, and neo-realist producers have often portrayed dialect-speaking groups of the population, some of them southern immigrants). The cinema, radio and television have the advantage, of course, of reaching those whose reading ability is limited. But, as we have observed already, over 90% of the population *can* now read, and very great influence is therefore wielded by newspapers, illustrated weeklies, women's magazines, tabloids, etc. Millions of readers in northern and southern Italy who have dialectal speech backgrounds acquire much of their knowledge of Italian from what they read, and in the case of most of them this means from the language, not of literary works of art, but of journalism and administration. We must remember, of course, that there is no such thing as a unitary journalistic language: what is read in the literary *terza pagina* will be different in style from the material in the small ads or on the sports pages. But newspapers do present news from many parts of the world in the same words and phrases to large numbers of readers. They also operate some kind of selection when dealing with words and phrases that are technical or bureaucratic. They are therefore a strong unifying influence. In modern Italian society they are a strong factor in the dominance of the written language over the spoken tongue. If large numbers of inhabitants of northern and southern Italy remain impervious to the distinction between close and open *e* and *o* in Italian, this is partly because the written language does not indicate the distinction. If *edile* is now pronounced with the accent on the first syllable rather than on the second (as we should expect in view of its provenance from AEDĪLIS), this is because most people have acquired knowledge of it from phrases like *impresa edile* in their newspapers and have made it conform with adjectives like *àbile, àgile*, which are more numerous than the *gentile* type. Whereas Italian assimilated *ps* to *ss* in *collapsus>collasso*, the modern *capsula* keeps *ps*; and many other words which today have wide circulation keep, in the manner of learned words, combinations which do not fit in with the usual patterns of Italian phonology. *Sdràpano* for *shrapnel* acquired some circulation in the First World War, but it was the international written form that prevailed. Closely connected with the newspaper world is the language of advertising; certain trade names have become as familiar as common nouns (*borotalco, aspirina, meccano, ferodo*) and certain slogans have obtained a diffusion wider than that of many proverbs (*Chi beve birra campa cent'anni; Una donna senza calze è una donna qualunque*). Like newspaper headlines, it encourages brevity, especially in small ads; hence such forms as *militesente, correntacqua, tuttofare*. The use of telegrams encourages similar habits: in 1954 a list of permitted compounds (*copiafattura, secondaclasse*, etc.) was published. These influences may have contributed to the widespread use of a kind of juxtaposition whose origins are older than they are, i.e. the *vagone merci, ufficio stampa* type.

In discussing developments in spoken Italian, therefore, we must begin by noting the steady increase in the use of the national language (at the expense of the dialects) and the influence of the written language on the spoken. Today, there are still people who speak only dialect (more of them in southern Italy than in northern Italy), but their number is regularly decreasing. At the other end of the scale, there are northerners and southerners who habitually speak Italian, and some of them bring up their children in ignorance of dialect in the belief that it is likely to prove more of a hindrance than a help to them. In between these two groups an infinite number of variations is possible. Some people are completely bilingual in language and dialect. Others are only at home in dialect but are capable of speaking an Italian which has strong regional features and in which dialect, in varying quantities, may break through from time to time. Others have a smaller degree than that of bilingualism, and simply speak a language in which Italian elements and dialectal elements are mixed in varying proportions.[1] Since we have looked to Piedmont for examples earlier in this chapter, we can return to it for another. A young man who leaves his Piedmontese village every day to work in Turin, and who shares, not only the work, but also the other interests and activities of his contemporaries there, will speak a language having elements absent from the Italian of his parents who have always worked in their village. Here, increasingly, language varies, not just geographically from village to village, but from generation to generation and in accordance with the educational progress and social aspirations of the younger inhabitants. Indeed, as G. Folena has emphasised, traditional dialectology is at a crisis, for the dialects themselves are being italianized, and the degree of italianization can be very various within one community. Under the influence of Italian, for instance, some northern dialects in which use of the personal pronoun with the verb was constant, now use or omit the pronoun

---

[1] The situation is more complicated in some areas than in others. Usually we can expect the main elements to be three (Italian as written, regional Italian, dialect) or four (Italian as written, regional Italian, regional dialect, local dialect). Thus, at Udine we have Italian (as written), regional Italian (containing Venetian and Friulan features), Venetian (with Udinese colouring) and the Friulan of Udine. But in some communities people of different origins have been brought together. In Latina (one of Fascism's new towns) a watered-down *romanesco* is now spoken; but most of the immigrants were from Venetia, and many of them have continued to speak their native dialects at home. In the settlement at Tirso in Sardinia, the Venetian and Romagnol settlers have shown a tendency to keep apart (linguistically as well as otherwise) from the Sards.

with the same degree of freedom as Italian. When we come to deal with the main features discernible in the spoken language of those who know Italian in the various regions of Italy, we must again treat Tuscany differently from other zones, for there the vernaculars are so close to the national language as to make the problem different from that of the other regions. Tuscany has some regional characteristics not accepted by the national language (e.g. fricativization and aspiration of intervocalic /k/ and, to a lesser degree, of /p/ and /t/ in words like *fico, capo, patata*; Florentine reduction of *uo* to *o* in *buono, nuovo*, etc.). But, such features apart, one can hardly speak of dialectal characteristics. One curious feature of recent years in Florence has been a slight increase in the voicing of intervocalic -*s*-. Generally, Tuscany still clearly distinguishes between the voiceless *s* in *cosa* and the voiced *s* [z] in *rosa*. The slightly increased voicing now may be due to a greater prestige accorded to northern pronunciation; it may be a hypercorrection, calculated to distinguish the speaker from the southern immigrant. At Rome the national language and Roman dialect have operated on one another for a very long period. By this time the average Roman's peculiarities in Italian are reduced to a limited series of pronunciations (*abbito, cuggino, pajja* for '*paglia*'; differences in the distribution of close and open *e* and *o*, e.g. *giorno, posto* with open *o*, *pentola* with open *e*; some local slang; a few interjections (*a* as generic prefix *a Mario! aho*); and a wealth of winks and gestures. One of the reasons why his vocabulary is not frequently unintelligible is that a number of his words have recently become nationally known, a point to which we shall return. In northern and southern Italy, spoken Italian is, of course, likely to show stronger dialectal influence. Here are some instances. North Italians have a tendency to reduce or weaken double consonants (e.g. to pronounce *battete le doppie* as *batete le dopie*); their consciousness of this 'fault' sometimes leads to hypercorrections in their spelling (e.g. *scattole*). Southerners, on the other hand, tend to lengthen consonants in certain positions (*robba, libbro, adaggio, la bbella ggente*). Certain words are differently accented in certain areas, e.g. *concime* and *mollica* carry stress on the first syllable in Venice, and *baule* on the *a* in southern Italy. (In some instances Florentine pronunciation has given way in the face of a consensus of opinion in the rest of Italy; the Florentine *cattiverìa* has now yielded to *cattivèria* in Florence itself). Important regional differences are seen in the treatment of *e* and *o* and that of intervocalic *s*. Friuli, Trieste, Calabria and

Sicily are without the distinction that Tuscans make between close and open *e* and close and open *o*. Moreover, in other northern and southern areas where this distinction does exist, the distribution of close and open *e* and *o* does not correspond to their distribution in Tuscany. Baldelli has suggested that since the pronunciation of cultivated Romans agrees (except in a limited number of cases) with Tuscany, this may prove influential in getting the Tuscan distribution widely adopted. The other possibility is that mentioned by R. A. Hall and Tullio De Mauro that Italian may move from a seven-vowel system to a five-vowel system, as an increasing number of people from outside central Italy take to speaking Italian habitually. As for intervocalic *s*, northerners usually pronounce it voiced (except in compounds, e.g. *risorgimento*), while southerners usually pronounce it voiceless. Both northern and southern speakers may, of course, transfer constructions from their dialect into their Italian: such are Sicilians' *son venuto per vedere a mio padre* and the Lombard's *cosa l'è che?* And the spoken Italian of various regions still shows very great divergences in vocabulary; an 'oven-cloth' is called *presa* or *presina* in Tuscany; elsewhere it is still *patta, pattina, chiappo, chiappino, pugnetta, cuscinetto*, etc.[1] Speakers who have a dialect background, but who have studied Italian carefully, may occasionally be detected by some very small detail, like an agreement. A Venetian, for instance, referring to peaches, may say 'ne prendo *uno*' (since 'peach' in Venetian is, not *pesca*, but *pèrsego*), or he may say of rice 'mi sembrano poco *cotti*' (because Venetian uses *i risi*), etc. To conclude, one can state that there is still much regional variation in speech in Italy, but that the differences are much less than they were fifty years ago. Training in diction has been included in the programmes of the *scuola media* since the academic year 1963-64, and this is likely to reduce differences still further. But new speakers of Italian may well succeed in further transforming certain of those features of Italian which derive from its Florentine origins.

Literary prose between 1915 and the present has not lacked variety. Let us consider two passages: one written by D'Annunzio

---

[1] Nor is this lack of uniformity confined to domestic objects. For an interesting analysis of the words used by 124 informants, resident in 54 different provinces in Italy, for 242 concepts, see R. Rüegg, *Zur Wortgeographie der italienischen Umgangsprache*, Cologne 1956. Of the 242 concepts chosen by him, only one was expressed in the same way by all informants (*espresso*, for the appropriate type of coffee). The others were expressed by more than one word or locution; indeed the expressions ranged in number from 2 to 13 per concept.

in 1918 and the other by Moravia in 1960. D'Annunzio's reads:
'Parlo agli uomini in riga contro un muro di mattone che ha
il colore del sangue aggrumato. . . .

"Siamo un pugno d'uomini su tre piccoli scafi. Più dei motori
possono i cuori. Più dei siluri possono le volontà. E il vero treppiede
della mitragliatrice è lo spirito di sacrifizio.

Da poppa a prua, ordigni ed armi, vigilanza e silenzio; niente
altro. La nostra notte è senza luna; e noi non invochiamo le
stelle. V'è una sola costellazione per l'anima sola: la Buona
Causa. —

Per lasciare un segno al nemico, portiamo con noi tre bottiglie
suggellate e coronate di fiamme tricolori. Le lasceremo a galla,
stanotte, laggiù, nello specchio d'acqua incrinato, tra i rottami e
tra i naufraghi delle navi che avremo colpito.

In ognuna è chiuso questo cartello di scherno:

*In onta alla cautissima flotta austriaca occupata a covare senza fine
dentro i porti sicuri la gloriuzza di Lissa, sono venuti col ferro e col fuoco
a scuotere la prudenza nel suo più comodo rifugio i marinai d'Italia, che si
ridono d'ogni sorta di reti e di sbarre, pronti sempre a* OSARE L'INOSABILE.

*E un buon compagno, ben noto — il nemico capitale, fra tutti i nemici
il nemicissimo, quello di Pola e di Cattaro — è venuto con loro a beffarsi
della taglia."* ' (*Per la più grande Italia.*)

This is D'Annunzio's own account of 'la beffa di Buccari'; in
fact he was conveyed by motor torpedo-boat to the bay to the
east of Fiume, in which he deposited three bottles, and one
Austrian steamer was torpedoed. He is bent on the heroic, and
neither shame of being ridiculous (the little man standing in
front of a group of sailors solemnly declaring himself to be 'il
nemico capitale, fra tutti i nemici il nemicissimo') nor fear of the
meaningless ('OSARE L'INOSABILE') can compete with the over-
riding desire for fearsome superlatives. Now, here is a passage
in the matter-of-fact style of Alberto Moravia:

'Tornai meccanicamente allo studio e mi accinsi ad aspettare
Cecilia, perché quello era uno dei due o tre giorni della settimana
in cui ci vedevamo. Da qualche tempo soffrivo d'insonnia a causa
dell'angoscia che mi ispiravano i miei rapporti con Cecilia. Di
solito mi addormentavo subito dopo essermi coricato, ma non
era passata un'ora che mi svegliavo di soprassalto, come se qualcuno mi avesse dato uno scossone; allora, invincibilmente, comin-
ciavo a pensare a Cecilia e non riprendevo sonno che sul far
dell'alba, per risvegliarmi, poi, alla solita ora, cioè troppo presto.
Mi accadeva, però, durante il giorno, vinto dalle stanchezza, di

addormentarmi d'improvviso, là dove mi trovavo, e di dormire, di un sonno pesante, anche due o tre ore. Così avvenne quel giorno. . . .' (*La Noia*.)

In this novel, the hero's (or anti-hero's) tone is so unheroic, so unpretentious that one is not tempted to malicious speculation on the relationship between his account and reality. If we now note that literary prose today generally has greater sobriety than in 1915, it must not be thought that we are suggesting there is any direct route from D'Annunzio to Moravia. We quote them only as extremes and emphasize that various tendencies have existed side by side throughout the period and have often been inter-related. Between the two wars, for instance, another kind of prose influenced a large number of Italian writers: that of contributors to *La Ronda*. Their writing was generally of a highly literary kind (frequently placing adjective before noun, using ternary patterns in word-order and liking alliteration), but mostly direct and analytical in syntax (and less extravagant in epithet than D'Annunzio's). Their styles, like D'Annunzio's, occasionally influenced writers of a less ambitious stamp: authors of widely-read novels and short stories whose language grew out of the bourgeois prose of the second half of the nineteenth century. Among the most notable practitioners of this less contrived prose one can name B. Cicognani, M. Moretti and B. Tecchi. Luigi Pirandello deserves special mention because his writing, lively, fluent and free from intrusive literary ornaments, provided a language that sounded convincing when spoken (even when he was not writing in dialect); as a model, therefore, he was valuable, not only to the theatre, but to those writers for the cinema who wanted a language which, without being dialectal, did not seem hopelessly stilted. But, since his time, literary prose has become a good deal more popular in tone. Although the tendency to be 'unliterary' became increasingly apparent in the thirties in authors like Moravia and Vittorini (and one could find earlier precedents in Verga and Svevo), it is in the period since the Second World War that neo-realism has become dominant in narrative literature. Elio Vittorini, Cesare Pavese, Vasco Prato-lini and others have, in different ways, enriched the written language by exploiting the resources of popular idiom. Indeed, some writers (notably P. P. Pasolini and C. E. Gadda) have made much use of dialect and slang. This, however, seems a marginal tendency and unlikely to have more than limited linguistic consequences. The most widely read serious authors have been those who (like Carlo Cassola) have been deliberately popular in tendency without risking unintelligibility by the use of a large number of dialect and slang terms unknown to the average reader. (Cassola has, indeed, condemned the tendency to use them as another manifestation of the 'eternal D'Annunzian' in the Italian writer.) And it is notable that other writers (Giorgio Bassani, Italo Calvino) whose prose is more complex and literary than that of the authors we have mentioned earlier, also eschew the precious in diction and the over-pompous in structure. But, as we have already said, literary prose now affects the average person's written language less than what he reads in the newspaper and hears in the radio and television news bulletins. In these the language of bureaucracy and administration and the language of science and technology have extended their domains. Here are two typical reports from newspapers in which we can see examples of such developments. The first refers to the intentions of a newly-constituted government (December 1963):

'I provvedimenti anticongiunturali costituiranno il primo rilevante atto politico del governo. Si ritiene, tuttavia, che nella riunione odierna non si andrà al di là di una visione d'insieme di questi problemi, mentre una specifica attenzione sarà dedicata alle richieste dei dipendenti statali, le cui organizzazioni di categoria attendono dal governo entro i primi di gennaio una risposta circa i tempi di attuazione del conglobamento delle retribuzioni.' (*Stampa Sera*, 24 December 1963.)

The second describes an industrial injury:

'VERCELLI, 21 dicembre.

(*n.u.*) Il trentanovenne L— B—, di La Spezia, residente a Trino, è rimasto vittima oggi di un infortunio sul lavoro nel cantiere della Centrale elettro-nucleare Selni di Trino Vercellese. Una griglia di ferro del presumibile peso di 70 chilogrammi, si è staccata da una gru ed è precipitata da una decina di metri sul capo dell'operaio. Questi, trasportato immediatamente all'ospedale locale, ha ricevuto le prime cure dei medici, dott. R— e dottor G—.

Poiché le condizioni del B— andavano aggravandosi ed era materialmente impossibile trasportarlo ad altro nosocomio, i due medici chiedevano da Vercelli l'intervento del primario di traumatologia, prof. F—. Senza porre indugio, il chirurgo, giunto a Trino nel volgere di mezz'ora, assistito dai medici dell'ospedale locale, procedeva alla trapanazione del cranio. I sanitari, dopo aver svuotato un ematoma a sinistra, si sono trovati di fronte

all'irreparabile, in quanto il cervello dell'operaio era spappolato.'
(*La Stampa*, 22 December 1963.)
As in other languages, reporting has contributed to a style that
makes more use of nouns and less of verbs, which has little room
for subordinate clauses, and in which enumeration and elliptical
constructions play a large part:

'Folla natalizia, folla di sportivi, folla di partenti. Da ieri nelle
stazioni vi è la ressa che si verifica solo in due occasioni: per
Ferragosto e per Natale. I treni "rinforzati", quelli "straordinari"
sono presi d'assalto. Valigie, pacchi-dono, panettoni e bottiglie
di spumante. Molti ragazzi. Sono incominciate le vacanze nelle
scuole: si parte, si vanno a passare le feste al paese con i parenti,
o al mare o in montagna. Da due mesi le stazioni sciistiche hanno
il "tutto prenotato".' (*La Stampa*, 22 December 1963.)
Even more pithy are the advertisements, in which the desire to
economize eliminates prepositions and encourages compounds:

'TRENTACINQUENNE lunga esperienza segreteria direzione,
soggiorno estero, conoscenza lingue, referenziatissima, ricerca
impiego stabile, interessante, segretaria direzione o public
relations. Scrivere:...' (*Stampa Sera*, 24 December 1963.)

'A abbandonare affari affetti aspettate Aurelio Astrochiro-
manteradiestetico risolve amori, matrimoni, spiriti depressi,
sconforti morali...' (*La Nazione*, 26 September 1963.)
On the other hand, neither economy nor restraint are obvious
on the sporting pages. The drama of the football field often
brings out an almost baroque love of metaphor:

'COSENZA, lunedì mattina.

Il dramma del Cosenza ha trovato ieri un epilogo sconcertante,
se si tien conto che proprio in quello che avrebbe dovuto essere
l'incontro della riabilitazione e della riscossa i rossoblù hanno
perduto la battaglia sul piano soprattutto agonistico, facendosi
superare da un complesso che nulla di trascendentale ha pre-
sentato, se non una buona dose di coraggio ed anche, per la
verità, un pizzico di fortuna. L'Alessandria ha dato una spinta
forse decisiva al Cosenza. L'ha insomma fatto precipitare nel
baratro di una crisi morale forse ancor più paurosa di quella
tecnica.

In sostanza, l'incontro di ieri era molto temuto dal Cosenza.
Defenestrato, dopo tante polemiche, nel corso della settimana,
l'allenatore Todeschini ed assunto in via provvisoria l'allenatore in
seconda Del Morgine (in tribuna c'erano anche altri allenatori in
predicato per dirigere la squadra cosentina, che non naviga certo

in buone acque), molti si attendevano dal Cosenza una partita piena di orgoglio e di puntiglio; ma soprattutto si attendevano una vittoria che avrebbe dovuto risollevare l'ambiente, portare un po' di tranquillità in casa rossoblù. Ma anche ieri non c'è stato verso, anche ieri il Cosenza, ripetutamente beccato dal suo pubblico, è andato alla deriva, risucchiato dall'avversario, addirittura beffato in modo incredibile.' (*Stampa Sera*, 24 December 1963.)

In dealing with the language of poetry, as in discussing that of prose, we must stress that the history of the last fifty years is not that of a single current. Nevertheless, it is true to say that by far the most notable single feature is the continued deheroicization and delyricization of poetic diction. In preceding chapters we have observed the reduction of the role of words traditionally considered 'poetic', and in the last chapter we mentioned the parts played by Betteloni, Pascoli, the crepuscular poets and others in lowering the tone of Italian verse. Betteloni, who was anxious to produce poetry that had 'its feet on the ground' and which had its feet 'in slippers' at that, might have rejoiced at some of the developments in our period, for there has been further progress towards informality. Giuseppe Ungaretti has told us how he was determined to avoid emptily rhetorical or merely decorative use of words. His early collections (up to *Sentimento del tempo*, 1932) were written in a language which, while it did not contain popular vocabulary, was simple in structure and avoided archaisms. But since then his metrical patterns have been more complicated and his tone more literary, as we can see from examples of his diction (*immane mare, tornano al lustro labile d'un orcio gonfie ortensie, vibratili ciglia, pietrami memori, indomabile nequizia, buio inenarrabile, stolta iniquità*), as Baldelli has pointed out. Eugenio Montale, however, has been a consistent (and very influential) promoter of the humble and the unheroic. As far back as 1925 he was singing, not of the traditional swan on the traditional lake, but of eels in half dried-up ponds, while his vegetation, as Schiaffini has emphasized, contrasts with that usually dignified by inclusion in poems:

> *Ascoltami, i poeti laureati*
> *si muovono soltanto fra le piante*
> *dai nomi poco usati: bossi, ligustri o acanti.*
> *Io, per me, amo le strade che riescono agli erbosi*
> *fossi dove in pozzanghere*

mezzo seccate agguantano i ragazzi
qualche sparuta anguilla;
le viuzze che seguono i ciglioni,
discendono tra i ciuffi delle canne
e mettono negli orti, tra gli alberi dei limoni . . .

He has confessed his desire to take hold of 'the eloquence of our aulic language' and wring its neck. And he has maintained that 'a kind of verse that is also prose has been the dream of all modern poets from the time of Browning; it is the dream that that integrity of style that makes Shakespeare and Dante the newest and most contemporary of poets may once again become possible'. Quasimodo has shown, in his best poems, an ability to avoid traditional rhetoric and to write with utter simplicity and clarity without, however, deliberately bringing us down with a bump into the commonplace:

In me un albero oscilla
da assonnata riva,
alata aria
amare fronde esala. . . .

At other times, however, he, too, has used language which would suit a newspaper report as well as verse:

. . . freddamente
a colpi di pistola, senza alcuna
ragione uccisero due amanti giovani
su un' auto ferma al parco di Saint-Cloud
lungo il viale della Felicità,
sul calar della sera del ventun dicembre
millenovecentocinquantasei. . . .

Of course, what we have described will not surprise the reader of English poetry accustomed to the influence of Eliot. And, indeed, many features familiar to the student of other English poets could be discovered in Italian verse of the last fifty years: poems depending more on their succession of images or on the effects of their individual words than on logical statement (hardly surprising after D'Annunzio), curious punctuation (particularly in E. Sanguineti), odd typographical arrangements, etc. Some of the verse of the hermetic poets seemed extremely arbitrary or private, but proved rich in overtones. A good example is that of Piero Bigongiari, whose work has been characterized by Chiappelli as 'l'expérience la plus risquée (parmi celles qui ont été valablement faites dans la direction du langage personnalisé jusqu'à l'hermétisme)'. Here the sounds of the words and their associations are exploited to convey (by indirect statement, by creation of colour and atmosphere) something beyond the statement made in the poet's sentences:

> *Chioccano bacche in prati di rame*
> *da una stagione di fame celeste.*
> *Una veste ti tiene, rosa come*
> *il rosa ch'è sparito: intorno al viso*
> *è il tuo viso più grande che non vedi:*
> *camminando consumi quel che credi*
> *d'essere. E i cani dolcissimi*
> *piangono sulla sponda deserta*
> *tra i dumi di barche nelle cale*
> *di giunchiglia. Negli occhi un parapiglia*
> *di troppe notti: ma già là una luna*
> *tra le comete è senza luce astrale.*

Since the Second World War, however, direct statement has gained ground with the dominance of neo-realism. Love of the concrete detail (which Pascoli displayed in alliance with his attachment to 'little things' and Montale in connection with his taste for the down-to-earth and unhackneyed) is with us again in P. P. Pasolini, joined here with a readiness to mention the modern and the technical:

> *Fra cantieri di gesso e casupole tripoline*
> *. . . era un praticello*
> *sotto un'altura cosparsa di borraccine e grotte.*

But modern life in our big cities involves, not only experience of technology, but experience, too, of office-work and consequently of the languages of bureaucracy and advertising. Baldelli has drawn our attention to a recent example of this, too, in Italian verse:

> *Carla Dondi fu Ambrogio di anni*
> *diciassette primo impiego stenodattilo. . . .*

It is to be found in a poem entitled 'La ragazza Carla' by E. Pagliarani (in *Menabò*, 1960), a composition which includes a line attributed to Carla's boss in the office with the very convincing rhythm:

> *Sollecitudine e amore, amore ci vuole al lavoro.*

Benedetto Croce's *Estetica* was published in 1902. He continued to write prolifically in support of his ideas until 1952. If the period between the two World Wars was not one of the most fruitful in the history of linguistic discussions in Italy, that was partly due to the dominant position of Crocean idealism (and, to a lesser extent, of Gentilean idealism) in Italian intellectual life, particularly among writers and critics. For Croce, art was lyrical intuition. Language had the same irreducible individuality as art. Two identical words did not exist. Every word was different every time it was used, for language was perpetual creation: 'The ever-new impressions give rise to continual changes of sound and meaning, that is to ever-new expressions'. Primitive speech and the speech of the uncultured mass was a continuum, unaccompanied by any consciousness of division of this utterance into words and syllables, which Croce called 'imaginary entities fashioned by the schools. On these entities no law of true linguistics is founded'. In fact, holding that speech and aesthetic expression were a unity, he maintained the unity, too, of aesthetics and what he called 'general linguistics': '. . . of language there is no judgement, no history other than that which conforms to its nature, that is the aesthetic . . . extra-aesthetic study is no longer study of language, but of things, that is, of practical facts . . .'.[1] The confusion which Crocean ideas provoked in some Italian scholars was exemplified in Giulio Bertoni's futile attempt to reconcile his linguistic training with idealistic philosophy in his *Programma di filologia romanza come scienza idealistica* (Geneva 1922). Such a reconciliation had, of course, already been attempted in Germany by K. Vossler, whose resulting system was stigmatized as *glottosofia* by M. Bartoli, who was, however, himself far from insensitive to idealistic ideas. Clearly, many Italian students of language who could not accept Crocean ideas in this period felt that their duty was to ignore them and get on with their linguistic research; Giacomo Devoto in 1940 invited his fellow-scholars 'to separate linguistic study from the philosophy of language'. Nevertheless, in Italian intellectual circles Crocean ideas on language enjoyed wide currency and theoretically were not

[1] For a discussion of Croce's ideas, see, apart from Nencioni's book, G. N. G. Orsini's *Benedetto Croce: Philosopher of Art and Literary Critic*, Carbondale, 1961, particularly pp. 66-78 and the note on p. 331. Tullio De Mauro (*Storia linguistica dell'Italia unita*, especially p. 197) has argued that in practice Croce made an important contribution to linguistic liberalism. This is convincing: if one is concerned only that language should be expressive, one is not concerned with whether an expression is Florentine or non-Florentine, grammatical or ungrammatical, etc.

effectively challenged until the appearance of Giovanni Nencioni's
Idealismo e realismo nella scienza del linguaggio (Florence 1946).
Nencioni complained that Croce had lost sight of the institutional,
social character of language and its use as a system. By so doing
his theories deprived linguists of their proper field of study. It is
only fair to add that outside Italy R. A. Hall had already shown
implacable hostility to Crocean idealism, alleging (in reviews of
Bertoni and Bartoli) that Crocean ideas, joined to the reaction
against the Neo-grammarians, were encouraging an unscientifië
attitude and the substitution of subjective impressionism for
rigorous scientific analysis. We do not propose here to mention all
participants in the controversy, let alone summarize their arguments (for the dispute was about linguistics in general, not about
the Italian language as such); we record it simply because the
Crocean attitude to treatment of linguistic detail was shared by
many and is a consideration to be borne in mind in considering
the relative paucity of discussion of the Italian language in the
twenties and thirties. It should be stressed again, however, that
even if, theoretically, Croce's ideas were not rebutted until 1946,
in practice they were side-stepped by influential linguists. The
founding of *Lingua nostra* in 1939 indicated a determination to
deal with linguistic questions in a scientific manner; its director,
B. Migliorini, expressed his intention of discussing, not only the
literary uses of Italian in the past, but also the practical problems of its use for all purposes in the present. Before we leave the
idealistic philosophers, however, we must record two other
examples of their effects on Italian linguistic studies. Gentile's
educational reform (1923) banished the teaching of Italian
grammar from the schools. And Croce's ideas about grammar
and lexicography caused the abandonment (as we shall see
presently) of an unfinished dictionary by the Accademia della
Crusca. Thereafter, this body dedicated itself to a different
kind of philological activity. Since 1937 its main concern has been
the Centre of Studies in Italian Philology, which has done much
distinguished work. Linguistic discussion, however, was conditioned not only by idealist philosophers, but also by political
factors. With the xenophobia of Fascism we can associate the
outbreak of linguistic nationalism and the ostracizing of foreign
words, a process which was intensified after the application of
economic sanctions against Italy. Political formulas were echoed,
too, in linguistic formulas: Bertoni spoke of the 'Rome-Florence
axis' in connection with the manual *Prontuario di pronunzia e di*

ortografia by G. Bertoni and F. Ugolini (Rome 1939). This work noted a large number of cases in which Rome and Florence diverged in the treatment of open *e* and *o*, and made larger claims for Roman pronunciation than had previously been customary. This attitude happened to fit in with the aggrandizement of Rome on which the Fascist authorities were intent, but it was also based on the fact that (in the field of radio, for example) Rome was an important centre of linguistic activity. The controversy that followed its publication is still with us, though in somewhat different form, for other Italian regions also have their claims in the formation of the national language today. The Bertoni-Ugolini volume was followed by a number of manuals dealing, in varying ways, with Italian pronunciation, of which the best was A. Camilli's *Pronuncia e grafia dell'italiano* (Florence 1941). The whole question was reviewed by B. Migliorini in his *Pronunzia fiorentina o pronunzia romana?* (Florence 1945). Ornella Fracastoro Martini in *La lingua e la radio* (Florence 1951) emphasized the new importance that radio had conferred on the *questione della lingua*. But the new aspects of the *questione* are to be seen even more clearly when we consider the influence of the cinema and television on the Italian language. The language of the cinema has been studied by A. Menarini in *Il cinema nella lingua. La lingua del cinema* (Milan-Rome, 1955). One of the facts that it emphasizes is that, while Italian is rich in its upper, intellectual reaches, it is not correspondingly rich at lower levels of expression, for there recourse is often had to local words and to dialect. Therefore, in order to render plebeian phrases from foreign films, Italian translators frequently use dialectal expressions. Moreover, neo-realism in Italy itself has involved widespread use of dialect in films. The fact that Rome is the centre of the film industry is therefore important in winning wider currency for romanisms. And Menarini himself, in discussing recent additions to Italian vocabulary, has mentioned the 'insistenze romanesco-napoletane di cui si compiace l'intera cine-radio-tele-attività nazionale' (1963). The role of dialect in neo-realism is a subject that has attracted Italian writers into linguistic controversy once more, for since the Second World War considerable use has been made of dialects in novels as well as films. For C. Pavese dialect was 'sub-history'; the writer had to take the risk of writing in the Italian language, to enter history, 'choose and elaborate a taste, a style, a rhetoric, a danger. . . .' On the other hand, P. P. Pasolini and others have connected the use of dialect with populist political ideals; he has stated that 'in the language reaction is reflected'. To this C. Cassola has objected that: 'The mimesis of linguistic reality inevitably becomes word fetishism'. Behind the committed writer who indulges in it he sees the 'pure' littérateur, the aesthete, the eternal D'Annunzian. In the search for a language equally free from the normative and the arbitrary, Vasco Pratolini has elaborated a kind of prose which has been commended by G. Devoto as achieving a Tuscan which is popular without being dialectal. To Devoto it seemed that this might succeed in imposing itself as a model. But it is clear that Italian life in recent decades has found expression in ways that are not Florentine, that writers in other regions (as Ascoli foresaw) have other preoccupations than conformity with Tuscan standards, and that the extension of Italian to northern and southern Italy must mean that increasingly large non-Tuscan contributions will be made to it. That Manzoni should have looked to Florence in the circumstances of his time is understandable; but, as C. Dionisotti put it (1962), that *I Malavoglia* or *La Coscienza di Zeno* needed rinsing in the Arno is an idea that occurred to no one.

There is as yet no comprehensive grammar of modern Italian. A work of sound scholarship within the limits chosen by the author is P. G. Goidànich's *Grammatica italiana* (Bologna 1918; the fourth edition, 1963, has been enriched by the addition of notes that Goidànich left to be published posthumously). *La grammatica degl'Italiani* by C. Trabalza and E. Allodoli (Florence 1934; reprinted several times since) shows sensitivity in dealing with the stylistic nuances of grammatical variants, but is by no means uniformly sound. There is useful and new material in *La grammatica italiana* by S. Battaglia and V. Pernicone (Turin 1951). Among the historical grammars the best to date is that by G. Rohlfs, *Historische Grammatik der italienischen Sprache* (Berne 1949-52, 3 vols.).

Work on the fifth edition of the *Vocabolario della Crusca*, of which the first volume appeared in 1863, proceeded very slowly. In 1921 B. Croce, then Minister of Public Instruction, set up a commission which recommended that work on it should be broken off. It was, in fact, suspended by order of his successor, G. Gentile, in 1923, by which time eleven volumes had been published and the dictionary had got as far as O. Work was begun on the compilation of a new dictionary on a smaller scale, but based on more modern criteria, to be published by the Accademia d'Italia;

but that never got beyond Vol. I (A-C, 1941). In 1961 publication began of another dictionary of vast proportions, the *Grande dizionario della lingua italiana*, directed by S. Battaglia for UTET. The Accademia della Crusca, too, hopes eventually to provide Italy with an equivalent of the *Oxford English Dictionary*. Indeed, the Academy is already at work on this project, and an account of its preliminary arrangements has recently been published (G. Nencioni, 'Notizie sul Vocabolario della Crusca', in *Lingua nostra*, XXVI, 1965). Single-volume dictionaries which are very worthy of mention are those by Zingarelli (Bologna 1917; new ed., 1959), Palazzi (Milan 1939, new ed., 1957) and Cappuccini (Turin 1916; new editions by B. Migliorini 1945, 1965). Panzini's *Dizionario moderno*, first published in 1905, reached its tenth edition at Milan in 1963. The 1942, 1950 and 1963 editions have included appendices by B. Migliorini. In the 1963 edition the appendix contains 12,000 items; it is indispensable to the student of neologisms. The fifties saw the publication of three good etymological dictionaries: C. Battisti and G. Alessio's *Dizionario etimologico italiano* (Florence 1950-57, 5 vols.); B. Migliorini and A. Duro's *Prontuario etimologico della lingua italiana* (Turin 1950, 3rd ed., 1958) and A. Prati's *Vocabolario etimologico italiano* (Milan 1951).

A notable feature of the period under review has been the development of dialect studies, in which C. Merlo, the founder of the periodical *L'Italia dialettale* (1924), played an important part. As the most important single event in this field we must note the publication of a linguistic atlas of Italy, directed by two Swiss scholars, K. Jaberg and K. Jud (*Sprach und Sach-atlas Italiens und der Südschweiz*, Zofingen 1928-40). The material for the fuller *Atlante linguistico italiano* can be consulted in the Istituto dell'Atlante linguistico of the University of Turin. Its compilation was directed first by M. Bartoli and then, after his death, by B. Terracini, who is now preparing it for publication. This atlas sustained a grave loss in the death of U. Pellis, who did the field-work for those sections completed before the Second World War; after it, he was succeeded in the task by various persons. The time-lag between the pre-war and post-war investigations presents serious problems. G. Bottiglioni's *Atlante linguistico della Corsica* (Pisa 1922) covers Corsica, and, for comparison, parts of Tuscany and sections of northern Sardinia.

English has now replaced French as the foreign language most widely known in Italy. Between the two world wars French was the most frequently taught language in Italian secondary schools. There was much translation from French, not only of works of literature, but of news, for Geneva was the seat of the League of Nations. And French was still the language of diplomacy. The earliest Chairs of English in Italian universities were not instituted until 1918, a year that also saw the opening of the British Institute in Florence. After that date, English studies made steady, if not spectacular progress. The Second World War was a turning-point. British and American troops became a familiar sight in the period 1943-45, and in some areas (e.g. Trieste) remained so for many years. Since 1945 American political and economic influence has contributed enormously to the use of English all over the world, and Italy has been continuously associated with Britain and the USA in the projects promoted by NATO. English is now the language of diplomacy. There is now more translation from English than from any other language, while scientific and technical works in English are frequently read in the original. Reporting of international events involves frequent translation from English, New York being the seat of UNO. It is not surprising therefore, that English should now be much more widely taught in Italian schools than it was before the war. Moreover, teaching in the schools is supplemented by many courses of various kinds for adults. The British Council, for instance, has a number of teachers in Italy, while scores of private institutions with names like 'The British School' or 'The Anglo-American School' have sprung up. Many young Italians (particularly girls), preparing themselves for careers in education, industry and commerce, have lived and studied for periods in England. Italian workmen, too, have worked and still work in some British industries, but this transfer of labour has been smaller than such immigration to Germany, Switzerland and Belgium. In 1963 the first chairs of North American literature were founded in Italian universities. The films, radio, television and the juke-box have made other products of American and British culture (especially popular songs and dances) widely known. Anglo-American tourism, too, has increased greatly, though it must be remembered that tourists often have very limited linguistic contacts with their hosts (particularly when surrounded by so many of their own kind). German is a language fairly well known, being familiar to many engaged in scientific or philosophical study. Political events and the presence of German troops gave it wider diffusion in the period 1938-45. Moreover, in recent years Germans have formed the largest national contingent among tourists; over seven millions of them visited Italy in 1963. Indeed, along sections of the Adriatic coast, between Senigallia and Rimini, and in the vicinity of Lake Garda, notices in German (advertising rooms to let, restaurants, hotels where German is spoken, etc.) have become numerous in recent years. The development of modern language studies in Italy, political interests and improvement in communications have led, too, to a modest increase in knowledge of Russian, Arabic, Spanish and oriental languages. As a result of the First World War, Italy got Istria and the South Tirol. In these territories there were large numbers of Slavs and of German-speaking Tirolese. Many of the Slavs are no longer within Italy's frontiers; but a substantial German-speaking minority remains. There are, too, over 70,000 French-speaking citizens of Italy. In view of the grave political differences which have subsequently arisen between the Italian-speaking and German-speaking populations of the Alto Adige, it is interesting to read now what Elizabeth Wiskemann wrote just after the Second World War (1946): '. . . The pre-Fascist regime, especially with Count Sforza at the Foreign Office, showed no oppressive tendency, and in 1921 men like Reut-Nikolussi were freely elected to the Italian chamber to represent Italy's German-speaking Tirolese. But the Fascists, obsessed with ideas of national uniformity, proceeded to persecute the German- and Slav-speaking population, and tried to ignore the French traditionally spoken in the Val d'Aosta and the Waldensian valleys between Susa and Pinerolo. . . . The German-speaking subjects of Italy were something of a problem in Axis days, and in 1939 it was agreed between Berlin and Rome that the German-speaking population in Venezia tridentina should opt for Italian citizenship or departure to Germany on 31 December of that year. Out of 266,985 of them, 185,085 voted German (some of these already being German citizens), and according to the records of the Italian frontier authorities, 77,772 of them had left Italy by 1 September 1943. After the armistice the territory concerned was annexed to Germany and as thoroughly Germanized as the time allowed; it was prepared as part of the last 'Nazi Redoubt', and at the end of the war was the refuge of many of the ugliest Nazis, neo-Fascists, Vichy French, and the like. This was the Trentino and Alto Adige as received by post-Fascist Italy from the A.M.G. at the end of 1945; with a celerity which appeared almost rash she had already issued decrees (laws were not yet possible) to safeguard the use and teaching of the German language, and allowing persons who had opted for Germany in 1939 to apply for the restoration of their Italian citizenship.' (*Italy*, Oxford 1947, pp. 119-20.) Today Italian is used in the Italian Republic, the Vatican City and the Republic of San Marino, and is one of the official languages of Switzerland. Outside these states, Italian is studied in the schools and universities of various nations, and Italian cultural institutes and branches of the Dante Alighieri society contribute to the diffusion of Italian among foreigners and its preservation in colonies of emigrants. Many students from abroad attend courses at the Italian University for Foreigners at Perugia and at other centres of learning in Italy. In Malta the use of Italian has continued to decline during the last fifty years in relation to the use of Maltese and English, but the reception of Italian television programmes in the island has served to revive some interest in it. The colony of 6,000 Jews who preserved the use of a Venetian dialect for domestic purposes in Corfù was exterminated between 1943 and 1945.

There have been no radical changes in spelling in the last fifty years. The use of *j* has continued to decline, not only medially and finally, but also in initial position: *ieri* is now incomparably more frequent than *jeri*, while *Jonio*, *Jugoslavia* alternate with *Ionio*, *Iugoslavia*. The *Giornale della Scuola media*, in printing, 'Ohimè che noja!' (Dec. 1931), clearly felt that the *j* was to be associated with the pedantic and the out-of-date. *J* is no longer used for plurals (*studj*); here *studi* has become more frequent than other forms (*studii*, *studî*, *studj*). There is still oscillation in the plurals of nouns ending in *-cia*, *-gia*. One might expect these plurals to be spelt *-ce*, *-ge* in hereditary words, *-cie*, *-gie* in latinisms. But many writers are applying a different system (albeit one that gives the same result in a number of instances): *-cie*, *-gie* after a vowel, *-ce*, *-ge* after a consonant. There is hesitation, too, between *constatare* and *costatare*, *instaurare* and *istaurare* and in other words of the same type; while *iscrivere* is usually used for 'to enrol', *inscrivere* is used for 'to inscribe' in the geometrical sense. There is still uncertainty in the use of capitals: *un Italiano*/*un italiano*; *lo Stato*/*lo stato*; *Ministero degli Affari Esteri*/*degli Affari esteri*/*degli affari esteri*. In the Fascist period there was an increasing tendency to use capital letters when referring to official entities (*Stato*, *Chiesa*, *Corte*). Today the use of capitals is probably favoured by the widespread use of initial letters for abbreviated forms: AVIS as an abbreviation helps to incline one towards writing *Associazione Volontari Italiani del Sangue* with capitals. There is still chaos in the field of accents. Acute and grave accents are now widely used by printers to distinguish between close and open *e* and *o* in final vowels (*amò, caffè; perché, né*), but only sporadically to indicate the same distinction internally in cases of possible confusion of meaning (e.g. *pésca,* 'fishing', *pèsca,* 'peach'). Final stressed *i,* *-a, -u* are usually written with grave accents (*finì, città, virtù*). Some publishers, however, use the acute accent for close vowels in all positions, including the final (*finí, perché*), reserving the grave accent for open vowels (*città, amò*). In monosyllables, accents are generally used to distinguish homonyms having different meanings: *e/è; da/dà; di/dì.* (Sometimes, indeed, one finds accents on *qui* and *qua,* where they are unnecessary.) But there is less consistency in the use of such accents in the non-final vowels of polysyllabic words: *danno/dànno; era/èra; corso/còrso; cómpito/compìto; séguito/seguìto.* It will be seen that in the last two examples cited the placing of the stress on different syllables distinguishes the words. In such instances many writers use an accent, not on both members of the pair, but only on the less frequently used member, e.g. on *subìto,* past part. of *subire,* which is less often encountered than *sùbito* (which they write *subito*); others reserve the accent for proparoxytones (*sùbito*). The circumflex has given way steadily to a grave accent in *èra, còrso* and similar words. Some writers still use it for the plurals of nouns in *-io* (*esempî, criterî*); but, as we have already stated, plurals in *-i* are now triumphing in such cases (*esempi*). The circumflex is still sometimes used to distinguish between *principî* (plural of *principio*) and *principi* (plural of *principe*), though *princìpi* is also used for the former. The fact that written Italian generally gives no indication as to where stress is placed, except when it lies on the final syllable, makes it easy for the reader to mispronounce the words he does not already know, and for new pronunciations to spring up (e.g. *èdile* for *edìle*). There are isolated writers who consistently indicate stress in those cases where it does not fall on the penultimate (and even, in cases of doubt, when it does); but, as yet, they have acquired hardly any following. Alfredo Panzini, in the fourth edition of his *Dizionario moderno,* complained that, when he attempted systematic accentuation (in his *Viaggio d'un povero letterato*) the derision of critics and the opposition of printers caused him to give up.

There is comparatively little one can record as phonetic change in this period. One novelty, however, needs to be noted: the stress accent placed on the initial syllable of words of more than three syllables (e.g. *prìncipàle*) came to be used in broadcasts in 1943. There is still oscillation in the placing of the stress in a number of words (*elettrolisi, macabro, muliebre, denota, incita, separa*). In some instance, however, the question has been settled in recent years, e.g. in the cases of *càlibro* and *rècluta*, words widely used in military language. The use of *regìme* in a political sense seems to have settled its pronunciation, even in non-political contexts (*regìme dietetico*), though one still occasionally hears *règime delle acque*. *Rubrìca* has made progress through its frequent use in broadcasting. *Edile* and *utensile* are now frequently pronounced as proparoxytones, while *missile* is often stressed on the penultimate. *Bolscevico* is usually paroxytonic, but sometimes proparoxytonic. *Scandinavo* and *Magiaro* have not achieved consistent pronunciations. Foreign words like *camion, cognac, soviet* are generally pronounced with the stress on the first syllables. Surnames with consonantal endings (*Bemporad, Coen*) are similarly treated, and even north Italian family names previously stressed on the final syllable (*Carrer*). The use of prosthetic *i* (as in *la Spagna*, but *in Ispagna*) is weakening; there seems to be an increasing tendency to prefer one form for all contexts (in this instance *Spagna*), a tendency we shall see at work in other contexts. On the other hand, the forms *e/ed, a/ad, o/od* have survived, though the use of the form with *d* for reasons of euphony is inconsistent and modern usage cannot here be reduced to clear rules. There has been great reduction in the use of truncated forms. In final position (*il mio dolor, per non peccar*) they survive only in verse, and even there they are on the way out, except in very facile lyrics and popular songs. Medially, truncated forms have stood up better in some contexts than in others: one still says *per timor di peggio, son tutti fermi;* but one would no longer say *ragion pratica* for *ragione pratica*, and *edizion nazionale* would sound precious. The tendency to have one form for all contexts makes itself felt in the reduction in the use of the mobile diphthong. Instead of using the *uo* form for stressed syllables, and the *o* form for unstressed syllables, Italian today tends to have one form for both. This is to be seen, not only in cases like *io nuoto/noi nuotiamo, io vuoto/noi vuotiamo*, where the fear of confusion with forms of *notare* and *votare* may be an element, but also in *arruolamento, ruolino, cuoiaio, cuoricino, ruotismo, scuoletta, suonatore, ci muoveremo, tuonando*, etc. The tendency is even stronger in the case of *e/ie*: the mobile diphthong is alive here in only a few cases (*siedo/sediamo*) and dead in the overwhelming majority (*allieto/allietiamo, siero/sieroso*, etc.).

Coming to morphology, we note that there is growing uniformity in the use of the article, though some instances of oscillation persist. The use of the definite article before semivocalic *i* is still uncertain (*lo iato*, *l'iato* and sometimes *il iato*). The rule requiring *lo* and *uno* before *s* 'impure' and *z* is now usually observed, but there have been exceptions even in recent years: *coi zoccoli* (Panzini), *i zitellismi* (Da Verona), *il zanni* (Monelli), *certi lezii propri del zitellaggio* (Baldini), *il zazzeruto* (Praz), etc. In northern Italy one occasionally finds *lo suocero*; in this instance semi-vocalic *u* is felt to be consonantal and the *s* to be 'impure'. *Lo* tends to prevail before *ps* (*lo pseudonimo*), but *il* is frequently used. Foreign words have also occasioned uncertainty: *il Heine*, *lo Heine*, *l'Heine*: *il Joffre*, *lo Joffre* (but always *il Journal*, owing to the influence of *giornale*); *il week-end*, *lo week-end*, *l'week-end*. The feminine plural article is settling to the *le* form in all positions: *le anime*, *le arpe*, *le ernie*. Forms with the apostrophe are now felt to be too high-falutin (as in *l'armi*, *al suon dell'arpe angeliche*, *l'ali*) or too plebeian (as in *l'ernie*). *Gli* is taking the same path: the form with the apostrophe (*gl'ingegni*, *gl'italiani*) is now used only by men of letters, while jurists, scientists and others use *gli individui*, *gli incisori*, *gli incannatori*. Forms like *una emersione*, *la aviazione* are becoming ever more frequent: this tendency to reduce the article to one form for all contexts testifies to the tendency of the written language to prevail over pronunciation; it may owe something to the convenience of typists. Among the articulated prepositions, those with *per* are practically dead and those with *con* steadily giving way: *pella scuola* is no longer seen; *colla scuola* is yielding steadily to *con la scuola*. *De'*, *co'*, *su'* are constantly losing ground to *dei*, *coi*, *sui*. With the plurals of nouns ending in *-cia*, *-gia*, we have already dealt in dealing with sounds (p. 474). Oscillation has ceased in the case of *capelli*, *capei*, *capegli*: *capelli* is now the only plural of *capello*. Similarly, the plural of *tale* is now *tali* in all contexts (not *tali*, *tai*, *tagli* according to the following vowel or consonant). *Quello* and *bello* have started out on the same path: increasingly frequently one sees *belli occhi*, *belli anni*, *quelli artisti*, *quelli antichi nostri*. Here it seems likely that Gherardinism will eventually defeat Manzonianism, thanks to functional considerations: one plural formed 'regularly' from the singular (*quello*, *quelli*; *bello*, *belli*) is simpler than a number of plurals varying according to what follows. Similarly, the distinction between *li loda* (*li* before cons.) and *gli avverte* (*gli* before vowel) has almost disappeared, although it was dear to Manzonians.

There are hesitations in the plurals of nouns in *-a*: alongside the regular *i farmacisti*, *i problemi*, we find (particularly in northern Italy) the popular *i farmacista*, *i problema*. There is oscillation, too, in the plurals of nouns in *-ie*: alongside *le specie* (as approved in grammar books) one finds *le speci*, and *le superfici* is much more frequent than *le superficie*. The grammarians also approve of the paradigm *un'eco* (f.), *gli echi* (m.); but a plural *le eco* has appeared (following the type *le dinamo*, *le radio*). There is oscillation, too, in plurals of compounds: *gli altopiani/gli altipiani* (giving also *altipiano* in the singular); *i pomodori/ i pomidoro/ i pomidori*; *gli asciugamano/gli asciugamani*; *i Lungotevere/i Lungoteveri*; here grammarians vary in their prescriptions. Yet in some instances the problem has been solved: whereas Petrocchi registered *franchibolli* (as the less common form), it has now disappeared, at least from written Italian. *I divani-letto*, *le navi-cisterna* are more frequently found than *divani-letti*, *navi-cisterne*. Alongside the traditional *guanti marrone* one finds *guanti marroni*. The most widely used foreign words are considered invariable in the plural: *i film*, *gli sport*, *i vermut*. Frequently, however, one finds plurals in *-s* (*gli scooters*). Since the most influential foreign languages (English, French) have *-s* plurals, this *-s* tends to be applied to other exotic plurals, even where inappropriate (*führers*, *lieders*, etc.). There is oscillation, too, in gender: *barbera*, *marsala* are sometimes masculine (*vino* being understood), sometimes feminine (as a result of their *-a* ending). The geographers' habit of making all rivers masculine was discussed during the First World War with reference to *Piave*, *Brenta*, *Livenza*. That *il Piave* triumphed in common usage was probably due to the *canzone del Piave*. *Automobile* hesitated for long before finally becoming feminine. *Film* is now used only in the masculine. In the formation of feminine forms, *-trice* is triumphing over *-tora*: Tuscany itself has *cucitrice di bianco*, and it would be an affectation of popular speech tradition to write *Atena traditora*. The verbs also show some progress towards unification. In the first person singular of the imperfect the form *-o* (*io facevo*) has now finally prevailed. In the present subjunctive *siano*, *stiano* have virtually beaten *sieno*, *stieno*, helped in this task by the parallelism of forms like *lava/lavano*, *lavorava/lavoravano*, etc. The second person plurals *voi trovavi*, *voi potevi* of the imperfect can be found in some Tuscan writers (e.g. Palazzeschi), but have a vernacular flavour. The forms *vadino*, *venghino*, etc., can be heard in most parts of Italy, but are considered plebeian. The *risolvei* type is slowly gaining at the expense of the *risolvetti* type in the past definite tense. The present participle is becoming more and more detached from the verb and is assuming the role of an adjective. Symptomatic of this development are the extension of *-ante* outside verbal flection (e.g. in nouns like *bracciante*) and the oscillations *dormente/dormiente*; *venente/veniente*; *salente/saliente*. Slight irregularities like *scalfire/scalfitto* tend to disappear through the force of analogy: *scalfire/scalfito* on the model of *finire/finito*. (*Scalfiggere* is no longer used: *scalfittura* survives, but is not a word frequently used and is therefore inadequate as a protection for *scalfitto*.) There seems to be still freedom to make the participles agree or not agree in sentences like *ho visto una donna/ho vista una donna*.[1] The use of allocutive pronouns was disturbed by the Fascist decree abolishing *Lei* (February 1938). Although *Lei* returned after the fall of Fascism, the previous position has not been entirely restored, partly because some groups have continued to use *voi* (tram conductors, ushers in certain Roman offices, and, at least to some degree, Italians who have remained in Libya and Ethiopia), and partly because of certain reactions that took place in the Fascist period: a greater tendency to use *tu* (bilaterally among equals, unilaterally in the professor-student relationship), a growth in the use of *voialtri* for plural *voi*, etc. The use of the polite *Lei* in addressing prisoners was prescribed in 1951. Moreover, it should be noted that before the Fascist decree had disturbed the situation, there had been a tendency for *Lei* and *Ella* to acquire different social connotations: *Lei* was more familiar (*spero che Lei voglia accettare*), *Ella* more respectful (*spero che Ella voglia gradire*) or simply more distant (*Ella vorrà presentarsi*, etc.). But there was a grammatical difficulty inherent in the distinction: *Ella* has been traditionally felt to be exclusively nominative, but the preservation of the social distinction between *Ella* and *Lei* throughout a letter involved such forms as *da Ella*, *per Ella*, etc. An official letter from the University of Rome (1929) contained the sentence: 'Mi è grato rimetterLe il decreto ministeriale in data ... con cui *ad Ella* è confermata definitivamente

---

[1] Modern practice was investigated in 1958 by Professor Robert A. Hall. He found that, in the perfect tense, the participle is coming more and more to be regarded as invariable (e.g. *ho comprato due camicie; le camicie che ho comprato; mi ha visto*, where *mi* refers to a woman). The past participle *has* to agree only with a third person conjunctive direct-object pronoun (*le ho viste*) or when there is a reflexive conjunctive pronoun of any person, direct or indirect, present in the verbal core (e.g. *si è comprata un cappello*). For Hall's interesting statistics, see R. A. Hall, Jr: 'Statistica sintattica: L'accordo del participio passato coniugato con avere', *Lingua Nostra*, XIX (1958), pp. 98-100. See also R. A. Hall, Jr.: 'Modern Developments in Italian' in *The Modern Language Journal*, XLIV, 8 (1958), pp. 339-343.

l'abilitazione. . . .' The *voi* favoured by Fascism did not prosper. It is felt to have a class connotation: in the country the peasant may still call the landowner *Lei* and be addressed as *voi* in return. Most people now use *Lei* and *tu* in written language and also in speaking Italian in most cities. But in southern cities there is still considerable use of *voi*, which is also very widely used in the countryside throughout Italy, though members of the younger generation use it less than their elders. In the narrative prose the use of *gli* for 'to them' has continued to grow, though *loro* has kept this position in more formal and official prose. *Gli* is very widely preferred, however, when another pronoun has also to be used, i.e. *glielo ho detto* for *l'ho detto loro*.

In syntax, there has been great growth in nominal constructions during the last fifty years. Whereas we can see the beginnings of this process in the last century, it has increased rapidly since then, helped in this matter by influences like impressionism and futurism. It has fitted in, too, with other tendencies visible in Italian, as in other European languages, in recent years: the tendency to shorter periods and direct construction and increasing avoidance of subordination. (Even so, the Italian literary sentence still often seems long and cumbrous to an English reader: to achieve normality in English prose a translator from Italian has frequently to divide the Italian sentence at its colons and semi-colons and recast its clauses as separate units. But this is truer of works of scholarship, criticism, etc., than of modern novels, in which, e.g. in Moravia's, the Italian sentence has been much simplified.) In the First World War, official bulletins made use (and probably contributed to the diffusion) of the narrative imperfect (previously used only in inscriptions and in citations connected with the award of decorations): 'tre aerei nemici *venivano* abbattuti dalla nostra caccia'. Certain constructions have become widespread only since the Second World War. The *votate socialista* type, which appeared in France in 1936, gained diffusion in Italy around 1948. The similar *brindate Gancia*, which also appeared in 1936, has now become part of advertising language (and been satirized in *Suicidatevi Breda*). In 1950 there appeared the use of *iniziare* as an intransitive verb ('lo spettacolo inizia alle ore 21') and this, too, has spread in spite of the objection of purists. In word order, we should note that there has been a great increase in the emphatic use of the predicative adjective at the beginning of the sentence ('Straordinario era in tutte le cose il presentimento dell'alba'), a word-pattern dear to

D'Annunzio. Certain expressions in which the adjective precedes the noun (*Alta Italia, privato docente*) are due to the influence of Germanic languages. Foreign influence has probably contributed too, to the diffusion of the noun+noun *problema-base* type ('Il Trecento è un secolo-chiave nella storia della letteratura italiana!') Pronominal enclisis (*dicasi*) has continued to decline in general usage, but persists in specialized contexts (e.g. *affittasi* in advertisements and the mathematician's *come volevasi dimostrare*).

Italian vocabulary has grown by leaps and bounds in the last fifty years. Its growth reflects the events of two world wars, the course of international relations, different kinds of political activity and state organization in Italy, the enormous increase in scientific activity and its industrial consequences, the social turmoil that has accompanied the political and industrial changes (including inter-regional exchanges and the participation in public life of groups previously excluded) and the concern which Italian writers (and film and television directors) have shown with the new roles in Italian society of the masses (which has frequently involved representation of their dialectal or semi-dialectal speech).

New words have continued to be formed by direct derivation. Certain adjectives have been used as nouns (*il federale, la forestale, la stradale, un'utilitaria, la litoranea, il direttivo, fare una magra* [figura]); nouns have been formed from verbs without addition of suffixes (*decollo, sùpero*); and verbs have been derived directly from nouns (*polemicare, filmare, romanzare, deflazionare; fiume regimato*) and from participles (*editare*), etc. Certain prefixes (*a-, inter-, para-, pre-, super-, ultra-*) have enjoyed great favour. While in the first quarter of the century, for example, there had been a very limited number of creations with *super-*, from about 1924 it came to be increasingly prefixed to nouns in the sense of 'superior, excellent', particularly in advertising: *supermarca* (1927), *supercaffè* (1928), *superbar* (1926), *superespresso* (1927), *superalimento* (1929), *Pomodori Super-Cirio* (1928), *supersapone* (1926), *superlana* (1927), *superfilm* (1924), *supercinema* (1924), *supergiallo* (1936), *super-romanzo* (1937), *super-poliziotto, supergangster, supertransatlantico* (1935), *supercapitalismo* (1936), *superalcoolici* (a term officially applied to beverages having over 21% alcohol, 1928). *Super-* has also been prefixed to many adjectives, e.g. *bibita superdissetante* (1931), *supermoderna verniciatura* (1936), *superpopolare* (1938), etc. Indeed, *super* has been made an independent word in certain contexts, e.g. *la decadenza delle super'* (='superstelle' 1939), *Lampade Philips super* (1936), è di *marca super*, etc. And one asks simply for *super* when one wants the more expensive grade of petrol. *Inter-* is another prefix that has enjoyed considerable vogue, serving to describe matters that range from the *interfamiliare* to the *interurbano* and the *interplanetare*. *Para-*, which used to occur only in scientific terms of Greek origin or coined from Greek elements, has come to be prefixed to Italian adjectives (and, more rarely, nouns): the first example, and certainly the one destined to be most widely used) was *parastatale*, which appeared in 1923 and entered legal and bureaucratic usage in 1924. Other examples are *paraprovinciale*, *parascolastico* and the jocular *paraonesto* (1936). It should be noted that in expressions like *maschere antigas* Italian has acquired adjectives whose function is not suggested by their formal characteristics and which do not agree with the noun, e.g. *metalli antifrizione*, *patto anticomintern*, *torneo interzone*, *lavori extra-ufficio*, etc. Among the suffixes, much use has been made of *-iere* (*alpiere*, *autiere*, *aviere*, *armiere*, etc.). and even more of *-ista*, which has served to indicate occupations (*aerologista*, *alimentarista*, *amministrativista*, *arbitragista*, *ascensorista*, *asfaltista*, *autista*, etc.), political inclinations (*fascista*, *squadrista*, *nazista*, *razzista*, *iniziativista*, *aperturista*), sporting allegiances (*rugbista*, etc., *milanista*, *romanista*) and many things besides (*accademista*, *dopolavorista*, *contenutista*, *frammentarista*, *funzionalista*, etc.). New nouns in *-ismo* and new verbs in *-izzare* (*attivizzare*) pullulate, as do adjectives formed with various suffixes (*birrario*, *cerevisico*, *debitizio*, *vaccinale*, etc.). Here, in fact, we can give only very few examples; but the freedom with which prefixes and suffixes have recently been used (and are still being used) to form new words can be gauged from A. Junker's list of the derivatives of *fascismo*: *fascista*, *prefascista*, *fascistizzabilità*, *fascistico*, *fascistone*, *superfascista*, *afascista*, *antifascista*, *antifascismo*, *antifascistico*, *defascistizzare*, *defascistizzazione*, *defascistizzabile*, *rifascista*, *neofascista*, *neo-antifascista*. Junker also counted over 160 neologisms coined with *radio-* and over 50 with *tele-*. But here, of course, we have the new morphological type mentioned in the previous chapter: words in which elements of compounds like *aero-*, *auto-*, *avio-*, *moto-*, *radio-*, *tele-*, etc., have come to be treated as prefixes, i.e. have come to be treated as if they can be prefixed to any word that makes that semantically feasible; one can now say *autotrasporto* or *radiodiscorso* as naturally as one previously said *pseudodottore*. A few of the hundreds of examples are: *autostrada*, *autosleeping*, *autovettura*; *cinedramma*, *Cinecittà*; *elettromotore*, *elettrodomestico*, *elettrotreno*; *fonofilm*; *fotoapparecchio*;

fotocronaca, fotocronista, fotostudio; motofurgoncino, motofurgonista; radioappello, Radiocorriere, radiocronaca, radiodiffusione, carro radio- mobile, organizzazione radioscolastica; pornolettura; rotocalcografia (with its derivate *rotocalco*); *turbocompressore; vasomotore.* The presence of some hybrid compounds (e.g. *autosleeping*) should not blind any- one to the fact that a list of this kind demonstrates the large part that Latin and Greek elements continue to play in the growth of Italian. In the written language there has been a notable in- crease, too, in words formed from initials (FIAT, ONU, AGIP, IRI, *Ghepeù, Cigielle,* etc.), some of which have given rise to deriva- tives (*sucaino, fucino, igeizzare, irizzare,* etc.). Although there was a small number of words of this type before the First World War, the development became a large and important one only after it. Sometimes, too, words have been assembled, not from initials, but from fractions of other words arbitrarily stuck together: *Confindustria, Credimare, Genepesca,* etc. Nor is the process limited to names of organizations; we have *fantascienza* (for 'science fiction'), *metronotte, netturbino* (for a 'road sweeper'). The practice is, of course, rife in the field of industrial and trade names, e.g. *acmonital* (=*acciaio monetario italiano*); many such names seem foreign to the traditions of Italian phonology, with its liking for vowel endings (e.g. some of the textiles: *raion, cafioc, sodolin, viscofan,* etc.).

But, as we have seen in previous chapters, expansion in vocabu- lary does not always involve coining; existing words and phrases can be used metaphorically. Here are some examples of meta- phors taken from scientific usage: *organizzazione capillare di un partito, sistema capillare* (from *vasi capillari,* itself a metaphorical expression used first by anatomists, then by physicists); *emorragia d'oro; aerodinamico,* etc. Technology in recent years has given us *entusiasmo ad alta tensione, un po' sfasato, partire in quarta* ('to start off in top gear'), *mettere il proprio motore a regime,* etc. From the cinema come *quel libro è una rapida carrellata, sincronizzare i pareri, col rallentatore;* and from military life *i grossi calibri dell'industria* (cf. English 'big guns'), *mettersi in linea, il settore commerciale,* etc. By an extension of meaning *crociera* has come to mean not only a 'cruise', but a 'trip by land', e.g. *crociera a Parigi. Giallo,* owing to the use of yellow covers for a famous series of detective stories, can now be used as a noun in the sense of 'detective novel' and as an adjective referring to any kind of criminal adventure (*dramma giallo,* etc.). Albert Junker drew attention in 1955 to the large number of zoological names widely used for weapons in the Second World War (*airone, alcione, bisonte, coccodrillo, falco, giaguaro, grillo, maiale, mosquito, pantera, scorpione, sparviere, tigre, istrice*). But, as he added, many such creatures have also had their names borrowed for peace-time activities, e.g. *elefante* ('heavy lorry', 1935), *farfalla* ('bill of exchange'; 'nocturnal street-walker', etc.), *giraffa* ('crane-type microphone-stand'), *moscone* ('outboard motor', 1949), *pescecane* ('profiteer': First World War). *Pappagallo* has been used for more than one purpose, but it is now most commonly applied to males who pester ladies, and the genus can be sub-divided into *pappagallo della strada, pappagallo balneare, pappagallo motorizzato, pappagallo dallo scappamento aperto*, etc. *Lucciola* ('firefly, glow-worm') has come to be a 'cinema usherette' while *topo* ('mouse') has graduated to 'thief' (sub-divided according to sphere of action: *topo d'auto, topo balneare, topo di treno*, etc.). Here, too, we should mention a number of euphemisms: *manicomio* ('lunatic asylum') has given way to *ospedale psichiatrico* or *neuropsichiatrico*. In war-time both sides recorded their defeats as 'strategic withdrawals' (*ritirate strategiche*; *rettifiche, accorciamenti di fronte*). In the economic field America supplied *depressione economica*, which seemed less alarming than *crisi*, while in France M. Reynaud (May 1935) coined a phrase which was rendered into Italian as *allineamento del franco*. Increases in price have come to be called *ritocchi alle tariffe*. And *avvicendamento* (or, in Fascist days *cambio della guardia*) has served to indicate that someone has been sacked. Certain words which were rapidly declining in frequency of occurrence have been given a new importance by attachment to a new object: such is *candela*, now a 'sparking-plug'. Other words which had fallen into disfavour have become fashionable: *fiera, sagra, bottega, taverna* are examples; *ostello*, which was on the way out, was revived by becoming a 'youth hostel'. Certain words designating occupations have been considered ignoble and replaced. The *guardia municipale* became a *vigile urbano* in 1919. The *facchino* remains, but he is sometimes referred to as *portabagagli, portatore* or *fattorino. Carcerieri* (or *secondini*) are now *agenti di custodia, spazzini* in some cities are *addetti alla nettezza urbana* or *netturbini*, while attempts are made to lure persons to become *domestiche* by calling them *ausiliarie* or *collaboratrici*.

Such are some of the methods by which the Italian vocabulary has been enlarged. (Borrowing from foreign languages and dialects we leave until later in the chapter.) We shall now note a few examples from each of a small number of the areas in which Italian has expanded in the period we are now dealing with.

The First World War gave the language hundreds of neologisms, many of which have survived. *Fronte* existed before the war, when it was normally feminine. The masculine *fronte*, which came from French, owed its success partly to functional reasons: it now became possible to distinguish between *la fronte* and *il fronte*. The growth of the latter can be gauged from the many metaphorical uses which have been found for it: *fronte interno* (1915), *fronte diplomatico*, *fronte unico*, *fronte economico*, *fronte popolare*. *Settore* prospered similarly (*il settore del lavoro, il settore della produzione*). *Asso*, a metaphor drawn from the world of playing-cards, owed its use in Italy to the example of French, in which *as* (once used thus by Frederick the Great) has gained wide diffusion since 1916. The First World War saw the introduction, too, of *lanciafiamme, carri armati, guerra aerea, guerra chimica, bocche di lupo, cavalli di Frisia, mascheramenti* and other horrors. The old military metaphor *punta* was revived (*fare una punta, pattuglia di punta*) and has since been extended (*scrittori di punta*). When military commanders were sacked, it was said that they had been *silurati* ('torpedoed'). War-time economy made *surrogati* and *razionamenti* necessary, and created *imboscamenti di viveri, accaparratori* and *nuovi ricchi*. After the First World War people divided their history into *anteguerra, guerra* and *dopoguerra*. And post-war negotiations brought *wilsonismo, sanzioni* and *riparazioni*.

Fascismo, which was still placed in inverted commas in the *Popolo d'Italia* of July 2, 1919, brought with it a number of new words and caused a number of semantic changes. Of Mussolini's innovations a few are still in use, some employed ironically with reference to their creator, some in normal usage. Examples are: *accorciare le distanze, adorabile penisola, beghinità, beghismo, demoplutocrazie, inequivocabile, medagliettato, folla oceanica, polemicare, pressa(p)pochismo, retroguardismo, ruralizzare, stravittoria, stupidario, tireremo diritto, tubo di stufa* ('box hat'), *vernice* (to replace *vernissage*), *vivere pericolosamente*. The proper name *Balilla*, which was rare before Fascism, was used as a common noun for a member of the youth movement for those between 8 and 14 (Opera Nazionale Balilla). From this usage sprang another metaphor: *bottiglie balilla* for small bottles of beer. (Balilla was the nickname of the boy who threw a stone at Austrian soldiers in Genoa in 1746, thus starting an insurrection.) Fascism's ambition to restore Roman glory resulted in use of latinisms: *duce, littore, centurione*, etc. And the appeal that authority and hierarchy had for Fascists was reflected in the use of *fiduciario*, the exhumation of *podestà* and *governatore*, the reappearance of *consulta* and the stabilization of *regime* (with the stress on the *i*). Steps were taken to get rid of foreign words in Italian: in 1923 a tax was imposed on the use of foreign words in signs; in 1932 *autista* was recommended as a substitute for *chauffeur*. Other examples will be mentioned in our section on foreign vocabulary in Italian. *Autarchia* is an interesting example of semantic development. Adopted by the economists to indicate self-sufficiency, it (and its derivations *autarchico* and *autarchizzare*) gained wide currency from 1936, becoming eventually part of popular speech. But the continual worsening of the products offered to the consumer brought about semantic degradation, so that *autarchico* came to mean 'of poor quality'. Italians returning from Ethiopia in 1942 were surprised to find what a pejorative sense it had, for there it meant simply 'produced locally'. Moreover, the effort of the censorship (in August 1942) to suppress the use of *autarchico* in newspapers in references to new products proved vain. Not everyone was conformist under Fascism, and some expressed their scorn in coinings: local Fascist leaders were called *ras* from 1923, and from this word came the derivative *rassismo*; the Fascist badge was called *cimice* or *pasticca* (and, in Tuscany, *brigidino* as well); and the eagle on the fez was referred to as *il pollo*. Protest against the decisions taken by the authorities was expressed by *mugugno*, *mugugnare* and later *mugugnatore* (an originally Ligurian family of words). In Fascist ceremonies it was the custom to shout *Presente* after the names of each of the fallen. In popular Roman, in which *va a mmorì ammazzato* was, and is, current, this phrase found a variant: *te possino chiamà ppresente*. Military and political life during the Fascist period also brought *motorizzazione* (used with reference to military developments), *fucile mitragliatore*, *spezzoni*, *carristi*, *genieri*, etc. The Abyssinian war led to knowledge of certain African words (some known from previous colonial wars), *negus*, *ghebì*, *tanica* (='tank'), etc. The Spanish war brought *falangista*, *miliziano* and *controproducente* (a loan-translation from Spanish). Events in the Far East contributed *Kuomintang* and *portavoce* (in the sense of 'official spokesman; mouthpiece'). Communism and its development in Russia gave Italian *bolscevico*, *leninista*, *massimalista*, *minimalista*, *falce e martello*, *soviet*, *consiglio di fabbrica*, *commissari del popolo*, *cellule*, *Ghepeù*, *Kolkoz* (and the adapted form *colcòs*), *kulak*, *agit-prop*, etc. Fascism's alliance with Hitler's Germany taught Italy the meaning of *Reich*, *Putsch*, *Anschluss*, *Führer*, *Gauleiter*, *nazismo*, *hitlerismo*, etc. Political and social development in the U.S.A. contributed *proibizionismo*, *secco* (*dry*), *bootlegger*;

gangster, nemico pubblico numero 1; *prosperità, depressione, New Deal,* etc. But many such words (e.g. *New Deal*) were clearly destined to be of only peripheral importance in the history of Italian vocabulary.

Of the many words which entered Italian in connection with the Second World War, we shall note here just a few examples. The term *belligeranza* had been used alongside *belligerante* during the war in Spain, when there appeared, too, the concept of *non-belligeranza*. In 1940 appeared *prebelligeranza*. This was to be followed in 1943 by Italy's *co-belligeranza* with the Allies. At the beginning of the war there was much talk of *linea*. The First World War had produced the *linea di Hindenburg*; now the preposition was dropped on the linguistic model of *linea Maginot*: hence *linea Sigfrido, linea Mannerheim*, but *la linea di re Carol* (the preposition being retained where a common noun preceded the proper noun). At the beginning of the war there was much talk of *Blitzkrieg* or *guerra-lampo*; journalists were forbidden to make further use of the term in 1941 and in 1942. Other novelties were *paracadutisti, coventrizzare* (to describe a bombing like that of Coventry), *guerra dell'etere, guerra dei nervi* and *quinta colonna* (the phrase was used in the *Evening Standard* of 18 April 1940 to describe the German fifth column in the Balkans; it had previously been used during the Spanish war to describe Franco's supporters behind the Republican lines — a fifth column assisting the four that were making for Madrid). After the fall of Fascism the Badoglio government abolished much of its terminology. The kind of Fascism that survived in the 'Republic of Salò' was dubbed *repubblichino* by V. Calosso; it was an Alfierian word which Calosso revived in his BBC broadcasts to Italy. Those who then supported Fascism were frequently called *nazifascisti* because of their increasingly close collaboration with the Germans. On the other side were those whom the Fascists had called *ribelli, franchi tiratori* and *fuorilegge*, and who, to non-Fascists, were *patriotti* and (later) *partigiani*. The Allied invasion of Italy brought in *jeep, bazooka, radar, bulldozer, OK. Sciuscià* was an adaptation (reflecting Italian pronunciation) of *shoeshine*. The new conditions saw the birth of *segnorina* ('woman of easy virtue' from the American's pronunciation of *signorina*), *tombolina, mercato nero, codaiola, intrallazzo* ('racket, fiddle'), etc. In 1944 the C.L.N. (Comitato di liberazione nazionale) was very important; hence the adjective *ciellenistico*. With the rebirth of political parties came several new words: *apartitico, interpartitico, qualunquismo. Nostalgico* became a euphemism for *neofascista*. The post-war political situation at one stage brought in *governo monocolore*, *partitocrazia* and the idea of an *apertura a sinistra* (put into practice in December 1963). As the role of the state in modern society is large, a considerable bureaucracy exists in Italy, as elsewhere. It is sometimes alleged, however, that certain members of this bureaucracy are not equipped to play their modern role; the suggestion that some civil servants had survived, like prehistoric monsters, into the scientific age was conveyed by the title *I Burosauri* ('The Bureausaurs') given by Silvano Ambrogi to his play on the subject, and *burosauro* gained diffusion in 1964.

In Italy, as we have previously emphasized, the literary language has had a very marked influence on the spoken, and, for reasons already explained, this is still the case. A notable example occurred after the First World War in the search for a phrase for the 'unknown soldier': while *soldat inconnu* seemed right in French, *soldato sconosciuto* seemed too prosaic in Italian, and the latinism *milite ignoto* was employed.

There is no space here to mention more than a tiny selection of the host of new words used in connection with the expansion of scientific knowledge. It is notable that some of these have expanded widely in metaphor outside the specialized fields in which they were originally used. Einstein's theory of relativity, for instance, has given new life to *relatività*, and not only in physics. *Interferenza* has passed from the field of physics to that of psychology and hence to common usage. *Osmosi* is used of ideas, etc. Moreover, even in their scientific sense, many terms (*raggi cosmici*, *bombardamento degli atomi*) have become prominent in normal speech. Electricity is a phenomenon so widely known that much of its terminology has now become part of everyday life nearly everywhere (*elettrificazione*, *elettrotreno*, etc.), as figurative usage (*sfasato*: [electr.] 'dephased'; [fig.] 'unhinged, insane') testifies. Progress in the biological sciences and in medicine has made us all familiar with *vitamine*, *neoplasma*, *penicillina*, *elettro-cardiogramma*, etc. The application of science to industry has created terminologies which have contributed words even to the language of non-specialists (*produzione in serie*, *standardizzazione*, *normalizzazione*, *tipificazione*), while *taylorismo* and *fordismo* have been used to convey both technical excellence and lack of humanity. Metallurgy has created *duralluminio* (in this word the adjective *duro* is joined to part of the name of the firm that patented the invention: *Dürener Metallwerke*). The industry producing *plastica* (or *materie plastiche*) has given us *bachelite, galalite, moplen*, etc. New methods in road-building (*cilindratura, bitumare, bitulite*, etc.) have been applied to *autostrade* (which had been divided into *carreggiate* 'carriageways', which have been sub-divided into *corsie* 'lanes'). In connection with motoring a new type of hotel has appeared (*motel* or *autostello*), etc. To supply the oil for motoring and aviation *oleodotti* have been constructed (the word first appeared about 1931 as a translation of the English 'pipelines'). The substitution of *aeroporto* for *aerodromo* marked the passage of aviation from the experimental and spectacular stage (*aerodromo* belongs to the same series as *ippodromo, velodromo*, etc.) to the practical. Many terms from this sphere, too, have become widely familiar (*aviogetto, quadrimotore*, etc.) and have been used metaphorically ('la geografia *prende quota*'; 'la *picchiata* d'uno sciatore'). Terms associated with *astronautica* achieved even greater popularity in the early sixties (*sputnik, cosmonauta, orbitare*, etc.). The role of radio, television and record-players has been reflected in the diffusion of *disco, discoteca, altoparlante, valvole, rumori parassiti, radiopirati, sintonizzare*, etc.). In the cinema many English terms are used (*film, vamp, sex appeal*), as well as loan-translations (*cartone animato*, etc.). Many terms have become widely popular (*schermo* 'screen', etc.), and have been extended beyond the field of the cinema (*fotogenico*) and used figuratively (*a lungo metraggio, sincronizzare*, etc.). Some film actors have left their mark on the language: people still speak of *un Rodolfo Valentino* when describing a certain type and use *gretagarbeggiare, marlonbrandeggiare, monroismo*, etc. The literary world, too, has contributed neologisms (*espressionismo*, 'cose viste', *frammentismo*, 'pesci rossi', *biografie romanzate*, etc.), while the theatre has given us *pirandellismo, grotteschi*, etc. Ordinary language has, too, taken a great deal from the specialist terminologies of philosophy (*astrattismo, storicismo, concretezza, eticità, potenziamento, superamento, esistenziale*) and psychology (*complesso d'inferiorità, desideri repressi, eros, estroverso, introverso, libido, narcisismo, nevrosi, trauma*, and so on). And these are but a few of the many fields one could mention.

We have previously noted that in Italy the national language sometimes lacks words for common objects, which are known regionally by various dialect words. It is notable that in a number of recent cases where the national language has adopted a regional term, it has been a non-Tuscan one which has thus triumphed; Rome and northern Italy have acquired greater influence. Thus *stampella* has won its battle against the Florentine *gruccia*, *colazione* against *desinare*, *castagne arrostite* against *bruciate*. That this should have occurred in a period when Florence can boast of important and influential writers (Cecchi, Papini, Cicognani, Palazzeschi, Pratolini) shows that serious authors do not often have a decisive influence in the formation of modern Italian. An important role is played by cinema, television and radio. A favourable position is thus enjoyed by Rome, which has contributed both romanisms and southernisms to the language (for southern immigration to the city has been heavy in recent years). The increase, for instance, in neologisms in -*aro* (rather than the Florentine -*aio*) indicates the influence of Rome (*borsaro*, *benzinaro*, *cinematografaro*, *padellaro*, *pataccaro* ('one who sells worthless old money to foreigners'). *Iella* and *iellato* have come to be used as much as the Neapolitan *iettatura*, whereas the northern *menagramo* is confined to regional speech. Comic papers have spread the use of popular locutions like *fasullo* ('phoney'), *racchio* ('unattractive, past it'), *tardona* ('still attractive despite her years'), *beccaccione* ('cuckold'), *spupazzare* ('take out, amuse, entertain'), *tirar la catena*, *mi fa un baffo* ('I couldn't care less'). The cinema, probably, has contributed to the diffusion of *sfottere*, *spopolare* (in the sense of 'to draw great crowds'), *abbozzare*, *sveltone*, *finto tonto*, *pappagallo* (*della strada*, etc.), *che strazio!* *Ciriola*, a Roman word for 'eel', has come to be widely used in two metaphorical senses: 'a long narrow stick of bread' and 'a man who doesn't keep his word, a slippery customer'! Southern Italy has contributed popular expressions like *che vuoi da me? chi te lo fa fare? scassare* ('to crush'). *Intrallazzo* ('fiddle') is a sicilianism which spread after 1943; from it are derived *intrallazzare* and *intrallazzista*. The popularity of works by Neapolitans like De Filippo has given prominence to one or two words from Naples: *sfruculiare* ('tease; make fun of'), *fetentone*. The Milanese *balera*, for 'a place where dancing takes place' is now widely known. Northern terms whose exact place of origin is difficult to localize are *lavello* (which is ousting *acquaio*, *lavabo* and *lavandino*), *birra alla spina* ('draught beer'), *ruspa* ('scraper'), and *menabò*. Other popular terms (*bidonata* 'swindle; trick', *tirar la cinghia* 'tighten one's belt; go hungry', *fusto* 'handsome young man', *ganzo* 'handsome', *inghippo* 'fraud; swindle') belong more to slang than to dialect. Sometimes, a person who is seeking to avoid a word he uses in his regional speech will use a generic term in the standard language (*insipido* for *sciocco*, *sciapo*, *sciapito*, *scipito*) or a scientific one rather than a locally popular one (*parotite* for *gattoni*, *orecchioni*). Popular terms used by comedians have occasionally gained wide currency (e.g. Totò's *A prescindere* . . .); but most of these seem destined to have a very limited vogue. One could, of course, compile a long list of dialectalisms from the work of modern novelists (e.g. Pasolini); but it is not clear yet which of these will win a place in the language.

The influence of English (including American), which increased in the period between the two wars, has, since the Second World War, clearly been greater than that of any other language on Italian vocabulary. The phonetic differences between the languages are very great; English words cannot go as easily into Italian as, for instance, a Spanish word like *brio*. Sometimes, of course, the anglicism has been absorbed by loan-translation: Winston Churchill's *iron curtain* has become *cortina di ferro*. At other times the original word has been used, its pronunciation depending on the speaker's knowledge of English: *juke-box* may be heard pronounced as in English or as *giubox* or *giubò*. Occasionally, English linguistic habits can be seen to be influencing Italian, e.g. in the increased use of *pro-* (at the expense of *filo-*): *probritannico*, *prosovietico*, etc. There is no space to do justice to the number of borrowings from English which one sees in modern Italian; we shall limit ourselves to examples from one or two fields. A physicist, for instance, would use the following: *spin* (of an electron), *scanner*, *bit* (in the sense of *unità della macchina calcolatrice elettronica*), *radar*, *effetto tunnel*. This last example brings us to the question of translation: *tunnel* is translated *galleria*, but in *effetto tunnel* it is not translated. In a large number of words used by scientists, a translation exists but is only sometimes used, e.g. (to continue with physics) *flip-flop* (sometimes *multivibratore bistabile*, which is more a definition than a translation), *bias* (sometimes *livello*, *polarizzazione*), *cut-off* (sometimes *interdizione*). *Shift* is sometimes translated *spostamento*; but in the shift associated with the name of the Nobel prizeman Professor W. E. Lamb, it is never translated (*Lamb's shift*). *Beaker* is occasionally *recipiente*, *ripple* frequently *fluttuazione*, *range* rarely *intervallo* or *valore*, *scattering* often *diffusione*. *Gauge* is not translated in *invariante di gauge*. These, of course, are only a fraction of the technical terms taken from English. Let us turn now to another fruitful field for borrowing: the world of the teen-ager and his interests: here we have *juke-box*, *boogie-woogie*, *teddy-boy*, *pen-friend*, *blue jeans*, *twist*, *topless*, *guest-star*, *go-kart*, *transistor*, *drive in* (for which *cineparco* has been suggested), *suspense* (much used in advertising films) alongside the older *Luna Park, film,* etc. But no such list of words can give any idea of the frequency with which English terms are used in particular fields, like entertainment. One page of *Il Giorno* (of March 15, 1964) provides the following examples: 'Maria Callas e Renata Tebaldi. In uno stesso *longplaying* . . . due *big* della lirica' '*Good neighbor Sam* . . . è del genere che i *fans* di Lemmon mostrano di preferire'. . . . 'Non sono invenzioni di fantasiosi *press-agents*, ma cose che talvolta succedono'. . . . 'Per difendere i nostri capelli dal brutale assalto dei ripetuti *shampoo* che finiscono per spezzarne la resistenza. . . .' Indeed, the fact that anglicisms are fashionable is even more obvious from the fact that one so often sees pseudo-anglicisms, e.g. *big* used as a noun in the first example above, or *sexy-girl* used as a compound in the following advertisement for the Italian translation of the Denning Report: 'Lord Denning: *Il Rapporto*, traduzione di *Gennaro Pistilli. Lords* e *sexy-girls* spie ministri e polizie in un'inchiesta giudiziaria che si legge come un romanzo. . . .' (*L'Espresso*, 23 Feb. 1964). Some borrowings, of course, have developed in their own way in Italy: the English traveller may be surprised to find that *night* means *night-club* or that the sign *toast* may advertise a substantial snack made up of two layers of toast with fried ham, etc., in between. The *sig* which the little Italian boy reads aloud from his comic is, of course, the *sigh* of the Anglo-american characters. Just as reading about them may cause him to say *bang* rather than *bum,* so seeing Anglo-american films may cause his parents to say *Sì?* rather than *Pronto!* in picking up the telephone. Anglo-latinisms are naturally much less obvious phonetically than anglicisms. Such are *acculturazione* (as used by sociologists), *colloquiale* (used by linguists), *sofisticato, pubbliche relazioni, contattare, realizzare* (in the sense of 'to understand, grasp'). Some Latin forms used in English and American have been transferred unadapted into Italian, e.g. *auditorium, symposium.* As we saw in the examples of terms from physics, a borrowing and a calque sometimes exist side by side. This is the case in the pairs *selezione* and *digest, fine settimana* and *week-end.* In many instances, however, the loan-translation has definitely triumphed, e.g. *ragazza-squillo* for 'call-girl', *caccia alle streghe* for 'witch-hunt' (an expression which became well known in the fifties along with *maccartismo,* formed from the name of Senator MacCarthy), *guerra fredda* for 'cold war', etc. *Picchiatello* ('a bit touched, cracked') was coined in the thirties to translate *pixilated* in the Italian dubbing of the film *Mr. Deeds goes to town.* (It is sometimes difficult to distinguish between anglicisms from British English and anglicisms from American English, and no attempt to do so has been made in the above paragraph. We realize that a very large number of examples originated in the U.S.A.)

Of borrowings from other languages those from French have been the most numerous. These include several terms connected with fashion (*boutique, chemisier, moquette, gala*), as one would expect, but also a variety of other terms (*dépliant, avanspettacolo, antidetonante, finissaggio, gemellaggio*). There are some semantic gallicisms: the use of *chierico* in the sense of 'an intellectual' is based on French usage, stemming from J. Benda's *La trahison des clercs*. The terms *engagé, engagement* referring to literature have sometimes been translated *impegnato, impegno* (cf. English use of 'committed'). *Vacanze pagate* is also a phrase translated from French. In 1926 W. Toscanini (the son of the famous conductor) modelled *antiquariato* on the German *Antiquariat*. Similarly *congiuntura* ('the present state of the trade cycle'), *congiunturale* derive from German use of *Konjunktur*. *Dettato* was used to refer to the Italian peace-treaty in the sense of *Diktat*. In the Second World War Italians, like other European nations, acquired knowledge of *Stuka, Panzer, Flak*, etc., and, after the armistice of 1943, *Kaputt* and *raus* (from *heraus!* 'out of the way'). Historians follow German words beginning with *spät-* when they form compounds of the *tardoromanzo* type. Since the Russian Revolution a number of Russian terms have become familiar throughout the world: Italian has acquired *soviet* (hence *sovietico, sovietizzare*), *bolscevico* and *bolscevismo, stacanovismo, stalinismo* (and later *destalinizzare*), *agit-prop, diversionista*. *Apparato* in the sense of 'party-machine' is a borrowing from Russian; but Italian sometimes used *macchina*, a loan-translation from English, instead. Hispanisms have been fewer. *Embargo* became familiar during the period of economic sanctions against Italy (1935-36), but was not a direct import from Spain. The term *cattedratico* for the holder of a University chair has been in use since about 1937, but is infrequent. *Controproducente* dates from the Spanish Civil War. *Goleador* came much later: it was first used in connection with imported South American footballers.[1]

---

[1] In a chapter of this length one can, of course, give only a few examples of the growth of Italian vocabulary since 1915. Readers who are interested in a comprehensive list are referred to the 12,000 items in B. Migliorini's appendix to A. Panzini's *Dizionario moderno*, 10th edition, Milan, 1963.

We have already mentioned the fact that during the Fascist era attempts were made to substitute Italian words for foreign borrowings. Since that time attempts to limit the extent of borrowing have also been made by purists inspired, not by xenophobia, but by a desire to preserve the traditional phonetic pattern of Italian (words ending in vowels, etc.). In the nineteen-thirties the terminology of soccer was italianized: *calcio* completely replaced *football* as the name of the game, while *calcio d'angolo* and *rete* came to exist alongside *corner* and *goal*, etc. Some foreign words have, in fact, been ousted, e.g. *basket-ball* by *pallacanestro*; but others have lived on alongside the words suggested to replace them: *assegno/cheque*; *autorimessa/garage*; *quadrato/ring*; *autocarro/camion*, etc. In the case of *camion*, the purists do not object to its derivatives, *camioncino*, *camionabile*, etc., which fit the phonetic system of Italian as seen in hereditary words.[1]

The number of Italian words which have entered other languages since 1915 is not great, but some of them have become very well known. Such are *fascismo* and *fascista*, *antifascismo* and *antifascista*. The term *Duce* was copied in several countries (*Führer*, *Conducător*, *Poglavnik*, *Caudillo*). Enrico Fermi gave international physics the terms *antiprotone* and *antineutrone*. E. Segré coined *tecneto*. While words like *Fascism* and *Fascist* have been adapted to fit other languages, Italian foods have become very widely known in their native dress (*pizza*, with *pizzeria*; *osso buco*, etc.). The *vespa* and *lambretta* also achieved rapid popularity in many countries under their own names. Names of cars, too, have gained some currency (*Fiat Millecento*, etc.). *La dolce vita*, the title of Fellini's film, enabled those whose Italian had previously consisted of *dolce far niente* only, to add to their repertoire with a minimum of strain.

[1] It should be remembered, however, that foreign words ending in consonants (*bar*, *sport*, *tram*, etc.) may not seem repugnant to people who live in areas whose dialects also have words ending in consonants (*camp*, *gat*, *porc*, etc.). This is discussed (along with some effects of dialects on standard Italian) by Tullio De Mauro in his *Storia linguistica dell'Italia unita*, esp. p. 155 et seq. Nevertheless, we believe that, generally, unadapted pronunciations of these words were acquired from contemplation of the written form, not from contact with speakers from particular areas. They were first acquired by reading.

Bibliography

I. BALDELLI, *Varianti di prosatori contemporanei*, Florence 1965.

M. BARTOLI, *Saggi di linguistica spaziale*, Turin 1945.

C. BASCETTA, *Il linguaggio sportivo contemporaneo*, Florence 1962.

C. BATTISTI, *Sostrati e parastrati nell'Italia preistorica*, Florence 1959.

C. BATTISTI-G. ALESSIO, *Dizionario etimologico italiano*, Florence 1950-1957.

G. BERTONI, *Profilo linguistico d'Italia*, Modena 1940.

R. R. BEZZOLA, *Abbozzo di una storia dei gallicismi italiani nei primi secoli (750-1300)*, Zürich 1924.

T. BOLELLI, 'Le voci di origine gallica nel REW' in *Italia dialettale*, XVII-XVIII, 1941-42.

A. CAMILLI, *Pronuncia e grafia dell'italiano*, Florence 1941.

A. CASTELLANI, 'Fonotipi e fonemi in italiano', in *Studi di filologia italiana*, XIV, 1956.

A. CASTELLANI, *Nuovi testi fiorentini del Dugento*, Florence 1952.

F. CHIAPPELLI, *Langage traditionnel et langage personnel dans la poésie italienne contemporaine*, Neuchatel 1951.

V. CIAN, *La lingua di B. Castiglione*, Florence 1942.

V. CRESCINI, *Manuale per l'avviamento agli studi provenzali*, Milan 1926.

B. CROCE, *La lingua spagnuola in Italia*, Rome 1895.

B. CROCE, *La Spagna nella vita italiana durante la Rinascenza*, Bari 1915.

C. DE LOLLIS, *Saggi sulla forma poetica dell'Ottocento*, Bari 1929.

T. DE MAURO, *Storia linguistica dell'Italia unita*, Bari 1963.

G. DEVOTO, *Profilo di storia linguistica italiana*, Florence 1953.

G. DEVOTO, B. MIGLIORINI and A. SCHIAFFINI, *Cento anni di lingua italiana* (1861-1961), Milan 1962.

C. DIONISOTTI, 'Per una storia della lingua italiana', in *Romance Philology*, XVI, 1962.

C. DIONISOTTI and C. GRAYSON, *Early Italian texts*, 2nd ed., Oxford 1965.

F. D'OVIDIO, *Varietà filologiche*, Naples (*Opere*, vol. X), 1934.

W. D. ELCOCK, *The Romance Languages*, London 1960.

W. TH. ELWERT, 'La crisi del linguaggio poetico italiano nell'Ottocento', in *Anales del Instituto de Lingüística* (Mendoza), IV, 1950.

A. ERNOUT, *Les éléments dialectaux du vocabulaire latin*, Paris 1909.

G. FOLENA, *La crisi linguistica del Quattrocento e l'‘Arcadia' di I. Sannazzaro*, Florence 1952.

G. FOLENA (ed.), *Motti e facezie del Piovano Arlotto*, Milan-Naples 1953.

F. FORTI, 'L'eterno lavoro e la conversione linguistica di A. Manzoni' in Giornale storico della letteratura italiana, CXXXI, 1954.

O. FRACASTORO MARTINI, La lingua e la radio, Florence 1951.

E. GAMILLSCHEG, Romania Germanica, Berlin-Leipzig 1934-36.

E. GAMILLSCHEG, 'Studien zur Vorgeschichte einer romanischen Tempuslehre', in Sitzungsber. Ak. Wien, CLXXII, Vienna 1913.

C. GRAYSON, A Renaissance controversy: Latin or Italian?, Oxford 1960.

T. G. GRIFFITH, Avventure linguistiche del Cinquecento, Florence 1961.

R. A. HALL, Bibliografia della linguistica italiana, Florence 1958.

R. A. HALL, The Italian Questione della Lingua: an Interpretative Essay, Chapel Hill 1942.

C. HOPPELER, Appunti sulla lingua della 'Vita' di B. Cellini, Trent 1921.

K. JABERG and K. JUD, Sprach- und Sachatlas Italiens und der Südschweiz, Zofingen 1928-40.

A. JUNKER, Wachstum und Wandlungen im neuesten italienischen Wortschatz, Erlangen 1955.

P. O. KRISTELLER, Studies in Renaissance Thought and Letters, Rome 1956.

L. KUKENHEIM, Contributions à l'histoire de la grammaire italienne, Amsterdam 1932.

TH. LABANDE-JEANROY, La question de la langue en Italie, Strasbourg 1925.

TH. LABANDE-JEANROY, La question de la langue en Italie de Baretti à Manzoni, Paris 1925.

G. LAZZERI, Antologia dei primi secoli della letteratura italiana, Milan 1942.

K. LOKOTSCH, Etymologisches Wörterbuch der europäischen (germanischen, romanischen und slavischen) Wörter orientalischen Ursprungs, Heidelberg 1927.

A. MENARINI, Il cinema nella lingua. La lingua nel cinema. Saggi di filmologia linguistica, Milan-Rome 1955.

A. MENARINI, Ai margini della lingua, Florence 1947.

C. MERLO, Studi glottologici, Pisa 1934.

C. MERLO, Saggi linguistici, Pisa 1959.

P. MEYER, 'L'expansion de la langue française en Italie pendant le Moyen-âge' in Atti del Congresso internazionale di scienze storiche, IV, Rome 1904.

W. MEYER-LÜBKE, Einführung in das Studium der romanischen Sprachwissenschaft, 3rd ed., Heidelberg 1920.

W. MEYER-LÜBKE, Grammatik der romanischen Sprachen, Leipzig 1890-1902.

W. MEYER-LÜBKE, Romanisches etymologisches Wörterbuch, 3rd ed. Heidelberg 1935.

B. MIGLIORINI, Dal nome proprio al nome comune, Geneva 1927.

B. MIGLIORINI, Lingua contemporanea, 4th ed., Florence 1963.

B. MIGLIORINI, Lingua e cultura, Rome 1948.

B. MIGLIORINI, Saggi linguistici, Florence 1957.

B. MIGLIORINI, *Saggi sulla lingua del Novecento*, 3rd ed., Florence 1963.

B. MIGLIORINI-G. FOLENA, *Testi non toscani del Trecento*, Modena 1952.

B. MIGLIORINI-G. FOLENA, *Testi non toscani del Quattrocento*, Modena 1953.

E. MONACI, *Crestomazia italiana dei primi secoli*; nuova ed. per cura di F. Arese, Rome-Naples-Città di Castello 1955.

A. MONTEVERDI, *Saggi neolatini*, Rome 1945.

A. MONTEVERDI, *Studi e saggi sulla letteratura italiana dei primi secoli*, Milan-Naples 1954.

A. MONTEVERDI, *Testi volgari italiani dei primi tempi*, 2nd ed., Modena 1948.

C. MOHRMANN, *Études sur le latin des Chrétiens*, Rome 1958.

H. F. MULLER, *A Chronology of Vulgar Latin*, Halle 1929.

G. NENCIONI, 'Fra grammatica e retorica: un caso di polimorfia della lingua letteraria dal sec. XIII al XVI', in *Atti Acc. Tosc.*, XVIII (1953) and XIX (1954).

L. OLSCHKI, *Geschichte der neusprachlichen wissenschaftlichen Literatur*, I-III, Heidelberg 1919, Leipzig-Geneva 1922, Halle 1927.

L. R. PALMER, *The Latin Language*, London 1954.

E. G. PARODI, *Lingua e letteratura: Studi di teoria linguistica e di storia dell'italiano antico*, Venice 1957.

V. PISANI, *Le lingue dell'Italia antica oltre il latino*, Turin 1953.

R. L. POLITZER, *A Study of the Language of Eighth-century Lombardic Documents*, New York 1949.

A. PRATI, *Vocabolario etimologico italiano*, Milan 1951.

Problemi e orientamenti critici di lingua e letteratura italiana: collana diretta da A. Momigliano, 4 vols., Milan 1948-49.

B. REYNOLDS, *The linguistic writings of Alessandro Manzoni*, Cambridge 1950.

G. REZASCO, *Dizionario del linguaggio italiano storico ed amministrativo*, Florence 1881.

G. ROHLFS, *Historische Grammatik der italienischen Sprache*, Berne 1949-54.

G. ROHLFS, *La diferenciación léxica de las lenguas románicas*, Madrid 1960.

R. RÜEGG, *Zur Wortgeographie der italienischen Umgangssprache*, Cologne 1956.

A. SCHIAFFINI, *I mille anni della lingua italiana*, Milan 1961.

A. SCHIAFFINI, *Momenti di storia della lingua italiana*, 2nd ed., Rome 1953.

A. SCHIAFFINI, *Testi fiorentini del Dugento e dei primi del Trecento*, Florence 1926.

A. SCHIAFFINI, *Tradizione e poesia nella prosa d'arte italiana dalla latinità medievale a G. Boccaccio*, Rome 1943.

C. SEGRE, *Lingua, stile e società*, Milan 1963.

A. SOLMI, *Storia del diritto italiano*, 3rd ed., Milan 1930.

L. SORRENTO, *La diffusione della lingua italiana nel Cinquecento in Sicilia*, Florence 1921.

L. Sorrento, *Sintassi romanza: ricerche e prospettive*, Milan 1950.

B. T. Sozzi, *Aspetti e momenti della questione linguistica*, Padua 1955.

B. Terracini, *Pagine e appunti di linguistica storica*, Florence 1957.

C. Trabalza, *Storia della grammatica italiana*, Milan 1908.

F. A. Ugolini, *Testi antichi italiani*, Turin 1942.

V. Väänänen, *Le latin vulgaire des inscriptions pompéiennes*, Helsinki 1937.

G. Vidossi, 'L'Italia dialettale fino a Dante', in *Le Origini*, a cura di A. Viscardi, B. e T. Nardi, G. Vidossi, F. Arese, Milan-Naples 1956.

M. Vitale, *La lingua volgare della cancelleria visconteo-sforzesca nel Quattrocento*, Varese-Milan 1953.

M. Vitale, *La questione della lingua*, Palermo 1960.

V. Vivaldi, *Le controversie intorno alla nostra lingua dal 1500 ai nostri giorni*, 3 vols., Catanzaro 1894-98; 2nd ed., *Storia delle controversie linguistiche in Italia da Dante ai nostri giorni*, 1st vol., Catanzaro 1925.

M. L. Wagner, *La lingua sarda*, Berne 1951.

W. von Wartburg, *Die Entstehung der romanischen Völker*, Halle 1939.

W. von Wartburg, *La fragmentación lingüística de la Romania*, Madrid 1952.

W. von Wartburg, *Raccolta di testi antichi italiani*, Berne 1946.

B. Wiese, *Altitalienisches Elementarbuch*, 2nd ed., Heidelberg 1928.

E. Zaccaria, *L'elemento iberico nella lingua italiana*, Bologna 1927.

E. Zaccaria, *Raccolta di voci affatto sconosciute o mal note ai lessicografi ed ai filologi*, Marradi 1919.

Subject Index

a with the agent complement, 148
a with personal object, 149
a: the *pollo allo spiedo* type of construction, 317, 328
a-, 103, 144
-a in plurals, 22, 47, 146, 280, 325, 375, 425, 478
ablative absolute, 380
Acarisio, A., 227, 235
Accademia dei Lincei, 260, 286
Accademia del Cimento, 260, 286
Accademia della Crusca, 196, 228, 258, 260, 269–70, 272, 277, 278, 286, 302, 307, 311–12, 320, 360, 418–9, 470–1
Accademia d'Italia, 470
Accademia Fiorentina, 311
accent, pitch, 21
accent, shift of, 21, 475–6
accents, written, 144, 278, 322, 323, 423, 475
accusative and infinitive, 48, 149, 186, 243–4, 282, 380
Achillino, G. F., 217
AD, construction with, 23
adjective, the attributive and its position, 481
adjectives, comparison of, 184, 283
adjectives, agreement of, 479
administration, 198, 201, 404
adverbs in *-mente* used in pairs, 106
Alberti, L. B., 166–7
Alberti, F., see D'Alberti, F.
Alcamo, Cielo d', 84
Alderotti, T., 101
Alessandri, G. M., 235
Alessio, G., 471
Alexis, St., 71–2
Alfieri, V., 300, 308–9
Algarotti, F., 302
Alighieri, D., see Dante
'Alleluia', 94
allocutives, 184, 241, 280, 479–80
Allodoli, E., 420
Alto Adige, 473–4
Alunno, F., 227, 235
Amaseo, R., 207
Amenta, N., 310
americanisms, 493
amiatina, postilla, 63
anaphonesis, 70, 103
Andrea da Grosseto, 101
Angerius, 58

anglicisms, 154, 195, 345–6, 400–1, 447, 490–3
anglo-latinisms, 444
Antonines, 17, 18
antonomasia, 436
apheresis, 279
Appendix Probi, 17, 22
apocopation, 145, 237, 240, 279, 375, 424, 476
apposition with *di*, 147, 186, 243
ar > er, 70, 103, 390, 434
Arabic influences, 40, 55, 57, 113
arabisms, 55, 114–5, 154
Arabo-Persian influences, 113
Arcadia, 258, 299, 303
archaisms, 251–2, 306, 337–8, 357–8
areas, lateral, 29
'areal linguistics', 29
Aretino, P., 234
Ariosto, L., 232–3
Arizzi, F. A., 307, 311, 338
Arlìa, C., 418, 419
ars dictandi, 79, 100, 101
ars notaria, 79
articles, forms of, 104, 146, 184, 185, 233, 240, 241, 280, 323, 325, 377, 425–6, 477
articles, use of, 243, 325, 377, 380, 425, 477
articulated prepositions, 64, 233, 241, 280, 325, 378, 426, 477
Ascoli, G. I., 406, 415–17, 470
assimilation, 145, 146, 240, 373, 375
Ateneo, M. A., 226
au, 21, 91, 93, 145
au in the Siculo-Tuscan poets, 91
au replaced by *al* or *a*, 145, 182, 239
Augustus, 15, 17
avere used as auxiliary with reflexives, 147, 328, 279–80, 428

b and *bb*, 279
b and *v* alternating, 72, 73
Barberino, F. da, 132, 139
Barbieri, G. M., 87
Baretti, G., 307–8, 329
Bargagli, S., 272
Barsegapè, Pietro da, 97
Bartoli, D., 263, 273, 274, 275, 277
Bartoli, M., 20, 29, 30, 467, 468, 471
Bartolo da Sassoferrato, 131
Basile, G., 268

Word Index

2L

PRINTED IN GREAT BRITAIN BY ROBERT MACLEHOSE AND CO. LTD
THE UNIVERSITY PRESS, GLASGOW